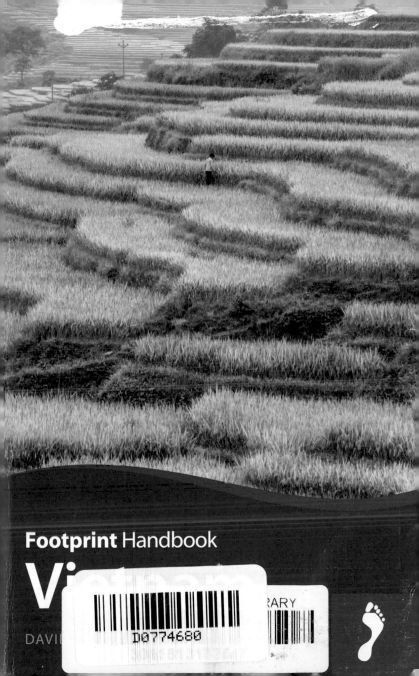

Footprint Handbook

Vi

DAVID

This is
Vietnam

Vietnam has overcome prolonged Chinese, French and American occupation to emerge strong and fiercely proud. And there is much to be proud of, from the many UNESCO-listed sites to a cuisine that is now making its mark on the world stage thanks to its emphasis on fresh ingredients and mountains of herbs. The national dish, *pho*, with its perfectly balanced blend of flavours with hints of star anise is just the tip of the iceberg. Every lunchtime the capital's streets are filled the irresistible scent of barbecuing *bun cha*, while all along the coast seafront restaurants serve up the very freshest of seafood. Meanwhile, in the former royal capital of Hué, a whole other world of food awaits with delicately prepared dishes originally created for bygone emperors now served up to us mere mortals.

While it remains a Communist state, the economic reforms of 'doi moi' in 1986 provided a springboard towards Vietnam's blistering growth. In recent years scores of gleaming high-rises have risen from paddy fields and whole new districts have grown from swampy wastelands. Among this development stand the pagodas and temples of old, the scent of incense wafting onto streets still padded by conical hat-wearing fruit sellers and pedalled by cyclos, albeit against the heavy tide of motorbikes and rising number of SUVs.

And then there are the country's utterly beautiful and diverse landscapes. The dramatic mountains of the Far North are dotted with ethnic minority villages and criss-crossed by a network of roads which serve up mountain passes that road trip dreams are made of. East of Hanoi the islands of Halong Bay compete for attention with a coastline bursting with peaceful, pristine beaches.

Elsewhere, adventure beckons in Central Vietnam with the world's largest caves now open for exploration, while further south the seas of Mui Ne are renowned for world-class kitesurfing, just minutes away from Sahara-like dunes.

David W Lloyd

Best of
Vietnam

❶ Hanoi

Vietnam's capital city is one of a kind. Chaotic it may be, but its charms far outweigh the traffic, with peaceful lakes, crumbling colonial buildings, narrow streets of the Old Quarter and one of the best street food scenes in the world. There are also plenty of great day trips to be made from your base here. Page 30.

❷ Sapa and around

This former French hill station in the northwest has become a major magnet for trekkers thanks to the wealth of ethnic minority cultures and the stunning rice terrace-clad valleys. It's also now possible to stay outside the town in a choice of excellent lodges. Page 92.

❸ Ha Giang

Bordering China, Ha Giang Province serves up the most dramatic road trip scenery in Vietnam with magnificent, rugged peaks and deep, sheer-sided gorges. Add to this a host of local minority villages and markets bustling with life and you have a rewarding destination to travel off the beaten path. Page 103.

❹ Halong Bay

A UNESCO-listed site, Halong Bay is a true wonder of nature. Thousands of limestone islands and islets punch abruptly skyward out of a pan-flat, deep-green sea. Enjoy an overnight cruise on a traditional junk boat, explore caves and hike to the top of an island for captivating vistas. Page 125.

❺ Phong Nha

Vietnam's newest hotspot for adventure travellers, Phong Nha is a tiny town on the edge of the Phong Nha-Ke Bang National Park. The surrounding limestone hills here are riddled with caves including some of the largest in the world. Take a one-, two- or even five-day trip deep into the heart of these other-worldy wonders. Page 146.

❻ Hué

Hué is a sleepy little city that was once the imperial capital of Vietnam. Emperors built lavish mausoleums all around the outskirts, many of which can be visited by taking scenic boat rides. In the heart of town the citadel complex is another major draw. It is a must-visit for history buffs. Page 152.

❾ Ho Chi Minh City

Ho Chi Minh City is an enthralling and captivating place with an infectious buzz. There is a palpable sense of dynamism here and life is fast-paced, particularly compared to Hanoi. The city's face is rapidly changing, with new urban zones taking shape and shiny new skyscrapers altering the skyline. This is a fantastic place to eat, catch a band, view art, shop and party. Page 250.

❼ Hoi An

Hoi An is an exquisitely pretty little riverside town and a former Chinese trading port. It has been remarkably well preserved and, while it is now unashamedly aimed at tourists, it retains much of its charm and character. The nearby beaches are also fantastic and the ancient Cham ruins of My Son are within striking distance. Page 189.

❽ Central Highlands

The Central Highlands are home to coffee plantations, myriad ethnic minority cultures, dramatic waterfalls and national parks where elephants can be ridden. More remote trips can be mixed with a stay in the kitsch city of Dalat. Page 215.

❿ Mekong Delta

The rice basket of Vietnam, the delta is a lush, green lowland where verdant rice paddies stretch as far as the eye can see. Head on a tour of floating markets, take in the views from the top of Sam Mountain and stay in a homestay with a local family. Page 295.

– monkeys are often spotted here. Explore the island's almost traffic-free roads and discover your own stretch of deserted beach. Page 336.

⓭ Mui Ne

The beach town of Mui Ne has developed to the south of a charming fishing village where a beautiful fleet of colourful boats still bob on the warm waters. Mui Ne has become a mecca for kitesurfers, the superb conditions and beauty of the surroundings are a huge draw. Alongside the many water sports on offer, there are two sets of magnificent, Sahara-like dunes – one with white sand, one with red – that are perfect for wandering in the late afternoon light. Page 342.

⓫ Phu Quoc

Vietnam's largest island, Phu Quoc is home to a huge range of excellent beach-side accommodation from basic backpacker bungalows to the very best five-star resorts. Explore the island's many brilliant white sand beaches and take boat tour of the outlying islands. Page 330.

⓬ Con Dao

The Con Dao archipelago is one of the most unspoilt places in Vietnam and the waters surrounding it are the best for diving. The main island is a former prison colony and the old jail building can still be visited along with a fascinating and deeply moving museum. The interior is densely forested and home to a plethora of wildlife

CHINA

Ha Giang ③
Mount Pia
Da (1980m)
② Lao Cai
Sapa
Ba Be
lake
Muong Lay
Mount
Cham Chu
(1587m)
Thac Ba
Lake
Lang
Son
Dien Bien Phu
Son La
Moc Chau
HANOI ①
Haiphong
Halong
Bay
Perfume
Pagoda
④
Mai Chau
Nam Dinh
Ninh Binh
Tam Coc
Thanh Hoa
Gulf of
Tonkin

LAOS

Vinh
Ong Mountain
(1587m)
Phong
Nha-Ke Bang
National Park
⑤
Dong Hoi

Quang Tri
Hué
Lang Co
Danang
⑦
Hoi An
My Son

THAILAND

Mekong

Ngoc Linh
(2598m)
Kontum
Kontum
Plateau
Quy Nhon
Central
Highlands
⑧
Dac Lac Plateau
Buon Ma
Thuot
Nha Trang
Bao Loc
Plateau
Dalat
Phan Rang
Tri An
Lake
⑬
⑨
Ho Chi
Minh City
Mui Ne
Phan Thiet

CAMBODIA

Gulf of
Thailand
Phu Quoc
Island
⑪
Sa Dec
My Tho
Can Tho
Rach Gia
Ben Tre
Vung Tau
Tra Vinh
Soc Trang
Mekong
Delta
⑩
Ca Mau
⑫
Con Dao
Archipelago

N

100 km
100 miles

Hanoi **1**

Sapa and around **2**

Ha Giang **3**

Halong Bay **4**

Phong Nha **5**

Hué **6**

Hoi An **7**

Central Highlands **8**

Ho Chi Minh City **9**

Mekong Delta **10**

Phu Quoc **11**

Con Dao **12**

Mui Ne **13**

*East Sea
(South China Sea)*

Route planner
Vietnam

Up to a week

the north, the centre or the south

With just a week in Vietnam it is best to concentrate on the north, centre or the south. One option would be to base yourself in beautiful and cultured **Hanoi**, and visit surrounding architectural and scenic treasures on day trips. Then you could make a two-day trip up to **Sapa** for its stunning scenery and ethnic minority villages. From Hanoi you could have a day out on **Halong Bay**.

For the centre, fly straight to **Hué**, the imperial capital, then take the wonderful coastal-edge train journey from Hué to Danang. Fans of beaches and street food may want to stop off in **Danang**, but most head straight to enchanting **Hoi An** with its fabulous nearby beaches.

A third option would be to use **Ho Chi Minh City** as your base, an energetic and exciting city. You could then explore the **Mekong Delta**, and perhaps visit **Mui Ne**, a small resort with other-worldly sand dunes.

Up to two weeks

cities, hill stations, paddy fields, UNESCO sites, beaches

With two weeks, **Hanoi** is an essential stop not only because the city itself is teeming with temples and ancient streets but also because it sits at the heart of a region similarly well endowed with monuments recording the nation's history. The scenery around Hanoi is some of the most attractive in Vietnam. Excursions to the **Perfume Pagoda** and **Tam Coc** are particularly worthwhile. The overnight train from Hanoi will get visitors to **Sapa**, the most scenic of all Vietnam's hill

Right: Statue at the Perfume Pagoda
Opposite page: My Son

Ha Giang
Sapa
Ba Be Lake
CHINA
Dien Bien Phu
Son La
Moc Chau
HANOI
Mai Chau
Perfume Pagoda
Halong Bay
Ninh Binh
Tam Coc
LAOS
Gulf of Tonkin
Hué
Lang Co
Danang
THAILAND
Mekong
Hoi An
My Son
Central Highlands
CAMBODIA
Nha Trang
Dalat
Ho Chi Minh City
Mui Ne
Gulf of Thailand
Phu Quoc Island
Sa Dec
Ben Tre
Mekong Delta
Tra Vinh
East Sea (South China Sea)
Soc Trang
Con Dao Archipelago
N
100 km
100 miles

12 •

stations. Once in Sapa there is a good selection of excellent treks ranging from a gentle Sunday stroll to trekking up the tallest mountain in Indochina. For something a little more remote, forgo Sapa and head instead, either by motorbike or with a driver, to **Ha Giang**, a relatively unexplored province with towering rice paddies, dramatic limestone peaks and ethnic minority markets. If these provinces feel too far, head out to **Moc Chau** or, even closer to Hanoi, **Mai Chau**, with its stunning paddy-field scenery. After a visit to **Halong Bay** you can then fly down to **Hué**, the old capital and home to Vietnam's last imperial dynasty. From Hué visit **Hoi An**, an old mercantile port crammed with history and absolutely full of charm. It also has excellent beaches. Following this, fly down to **Ho Chi Minh City** to experience its dynamic atmosphere.

Top: Ha Giang landscape
Above: Mui Ne dune, Panthiet

Up to one month

mountainous north, tranquil lakes, Central Highlands, ancient sites, tropical islands

In three to four weeks it is possible to take the two-week itinerary at a more leisurely pace and include some other interesting calls. From **Hanoi**, **Tam Coc**, can be added. It may be possible to fit in a circuit of the northwest, going via the delightful small settlements of **Mai Chau** and **Son La** to **Dien Bien Phu**, scene of the French defeat in 1954. A visit to tranquil **Ba Be Lake** on the way back to Hanoi is very rewarding. Once in Central Vietnam for **Hué** you could add on a stay in **Lang Co** for a tranquil beach break before heading to **Danang** for a night to enjoy its excellent food culture and the Cham museum. From Hoi An, a side trip to the ruins of My Son could be tagged on. If you can, add on trips to **Dalat** and the **Central Highlands** to encounter the area's varied ethnic cultures. Fans of beaches might like to also see **Nha Trang**, although it has become extremely touristy in recent years. The more laid-back beach resort of **Mui Ne** will appeal to many. Medium-stay visitors will have longer to get to know the people of **Ho Chi Minh City** and to get deeper into the **Mekong Delta**. Many towns such as **Soc Trang**, **Sa Dec**, **Tra Vinh** and **Ben Tre** offer a flavour of real delta life. Those looking to see Vietnam's tropical islands should make time for trips to **Phu Quoc Island** and **Con Dao**, which still remains relatively untouched by the rampant tourist development that has taken place in some of Vietnam's other top beauty spots.

The
Mekong

The Mekong River is the heart and soul of mainland Southeast Asia, a sinuous thread that binds Vietnam, Cambodia and Laos geographically, historically, culturally and economically. Indeed, the Mekong – or the Mae Nam Khong (the Mother of Waters) – is the most important geographical feature of mainland Southeast Asia.

The Mekong's origins in eastern Tibet have only been pin-pointed in the last 20 years. From here the giant river plies 4500 km through six countries, cutting through almost the entire length of Laos, dissecting Cambodia, and plunging into Vietnam's Mekong Delta before emptying into the South China Sea. The river is the 12th longest river in the world and is the world's 10th largest by volume of water dispersed into the ocean – 475 km^3.

French explorer Francis Garnier once commented: "without doubt, no other river, over such a length, has a more singular or remarkable character". The Mekong has indeed woven itself into the cultural fabric, shaping the region's history. The river is the one constant from the ancient Funan settlement in the Mekong Delta, through to the Khmer Empire who established its capital at Angkor, relying on the river for transport and agricultural production. After several European expeditions, the French took an interest in the river and the region in the mid-19th century,

developing grandiose plans to transform the Mekong into a river highway from China (the plans were thwarted upon discovering that the Mekong could not be traversed).

The river later played an integral role in shaping history during the Vietnam War when it became an important conduit for the running of Viet Cong supplies and was the scene of heavy fighting.

The river has been a major purveyor of culture, ushering in various religions, arts, customs and folklore. The enormous, colourful, boat-racing festivals of Vietnam, Cambodia and Laos are staged on the water. Similarly, the annual water festivals in Cambodia and Laos come from deep-rooted traditions stemming from the Mekong and its importance to agricultural production. The river is not free from superstition or strange phenomena. In Laos thousands of people gather each year to witness naga fireballs rising from the river's surface. Major arts have also developed from these waters including Vietnam's water puppetry. It also provided inspiration in the *Apocalypse Now* mission down the fictional Nung River, said to represent the Mekong.

Today, the Mekong is instrumental in the region's survival, with more than 60 million people in Southeast Asia dependent on the river and its tributaries for their survival.

When to go to
Vietnam

Climatically the best time to see Vietnam varies region to region. In the south December to March will be warm but not too hot with lovely cool evenings, but the north will be a bit chilly and Hanoi can be rather grey. For Hanoi, April and May are lovely as the flowers bloom and the temperature rises. The autumn time of October and November can also be delightful. Travel in the south and Mekong Delta can be difficult at the height of the monsoon (particularly September, October and November). The central regions and north sometimes suffer typhoons and tropical storms from May to November. Hué is at its wettest from September to January.

Despite its historic and cultural resonance Tet, or Vietnamese New Year, is not a good time to visit. This movable feast usually falls between late January and March and, with aftershocks, lasts for about a fortnight. It is the only holiday most people get in the year. Popular destinations are packed, roads are jammed and for a couple of days almost all restaurants are shut. All hotel prices increase, and car hire prices are increased by 50% or more.

During the school summer holidays some resorts get busy. At Cat Ba, Sapa, Phan Thiet, Long Hai and Phu Quoc, for example, prices rise, there is a severe squeeze on rooms and weekends are worse. The Central Highlands tend to fare much better with cool temperatures and a good availability of rooms.

Festivals

Vietnamese festivals are timed according to the Vietnamese lunar calendar.

Late Jan-Mar (movable, 1st-7th day of the new lunar year) **Tet**, see box, below.

Mar (movable, 6th day of 2nd lunar month) **Hai Ba Trung Day**. Celebrates the famous Trung sisters who led a revolt against the Chinese in AD 41 (see box, page 55).

Apr (5th or 6th, 3rd lunar month) **Thanh Minh** (New Year of the Dead or Feast of the Pure Light). People are supposed to walk outdoors to evoke the spirit of the dead and family shrines and tombs are traditionally cleaned and decorated.

May (15th day of the 4th lunar month) Celebration of the birth, death and enlightenment of the Buddha.

Aug (movable, 15th day of the 7th lunar month) **Trung Nguyen** (Wandering Souls Day). One of the most important festivals. During this time, prayers can absolve the sins of the dead who leave hell and return, hungry and naked, to their relatives. The Wandering Souls are those with no homes to go to. There are celebrations in Buddhist temples and homes, food is placed out on tables and money is burned.

Happy New Year

Tet is the traditional New Year. The biggest celebration of the year, the word Tet is the shortened version of *tet nguyen dan* (first morning of the new period). Tet is the time to forgive and forget and to pay off debts. It is also everyone's birthday – the Vietnamese tend not to celebrate their birthdays; instead everyone adds a year to their age at Tet. Enormous quantities of food are consumed (this is not the time to worry about money), new clothes are bought, houses painted and repaired and firecrackers lit to welcome in the New Year – at least they were until the government ban imposed in 1995. Cumquat trees are also bought and displayed. They are said to resemble coins and are a symbol of wealth and luck for the coming year. As a Vietnamese saying has it: 'Hungry all year but Tet three days full.' It is believed that before Tet, the spirit of the hearth, Ong Tao, leaves on a journey to visit the palace of the Jade Emperor where he must report on family affairs. To ensure that Ong Tao sets off in good cheer, a ceremony is held before Tet, Le Tao Quan, and during his absence a shrine is constructed (Cay Neu) to keep evil spirits at bay until his return. On the afternoon before Tet, Tat Nien, a sacrifice is offered at the family altar to dead relatives who are invited back to join in the festivities. Great attention is paid to the preparations for Tet, because it is believed that the first week of the New Year dictates the fortunes for the rest of the year. The first visitor to the house on New Year's morning should be an influential, lucky and happy person, so families take care to arrange a suitable caller.

Sep (movable, 15th day of the 8th month) **Tet Trung Thu** (Mid-Autumn Festival) This festival is particularly celebrated by children. It is based on legend and there are various stories as to its history. One of the legends is about a Chinese king who went to the moon. When he returned, the king wished to share what he had seen with the people on earth.

In the evening families prepare food including sticky rice, fruit and chicken to be placed on the ancestral altars. Moon cakes (egg, green bean and lotus seed) are baked (with some variations on these ingredients offered by some of the smarter hotels such as chocolate), lanterns made and painted, and children parade through towns with music and lanterns. It is particularly popular in Hanoi and toy shops in the Old Quarter decorate stores with lanterns and masks.

Nov (movable, 28th day of the 9th month) **Confucius' Birthday**.

Public holidays

1 Jan **New Year's Day**.

Late Jan-Mar (movable, 1st-7th day of the new lunar year) **Tet**.

3 Feb **Founding anniversary of the Communist Party of Vietnam**.

30 Apr **Liberation Day** of South Vietnam and HCMC.

1 May **International Labour Day**.

19 May **Anniversary of the Birth of Ho Chi Minh** (government holiday) The majority of state institutions will be shut on this day but businesses in the private sector remain open.

2 Sep **National Day**.

3 Sep **President Ho Chi Minh's Anniversary**.

What to do
in Vietnam

activities from caving and trekking to cookery

Many operators offer organized trips to Vietnam, ranging from a whistle-stop tour of the highlights to specialist trips that focus on a specific destination or activity. The advantage of travelling with a reputable operator is that your accommodation, transport and activities are all arranged for you in advance – particularly valuable if you only have limited time in the region. Specialist tour operators can be found on page 438.

Safety is always an issue when participating in adventurous sports: make sure you are fully covered by your travel insurance; check the credentials of operators offering adventure activities; and make sure that vehicles and safety equipment are in a good condition.

Birdwatching

Vietnam may not seem like the first choice for a birdwatching holiday (indeed, many visitors comment that there are few birds around) but for those in the know it has become one of the top birding destinations of the region in recent years. The reason is that it has no less than 10 endemic species. This is the highest number of endemic bird species of any country in mainland Southeast Asia. Around 850 species have been recorded in Vietnam but in a 3-week birding trip it should be possible to tick off around 250-300 species. The best places for birdwatching are **Bach Ma National Park**, **Cuc Phuong National Park**, **Dalat Plateau**, **Nam Cat Tien National Park**. Other areas of particular interest are **Con Dao**, **Sapa**, **Tam Dao** and **Tram Chim National Park** (Tam Nong Bird Sanctuary).

Contact
Vietnam Birding, Vietnam Birding, www.vietnambirding.com. Contact Richard Craik for more information or advice on birding, or to organize birding tours throughout Vietnam.

Cookery classes

There are increasingly more of these available with hotels and restaurants in major cities and resorts offer courses. Some operators offer tours that include half a day or one day of cooking for those who would like to see more than just the inside of a hotel kitchen. The variety is already quite broad. Check hotel flyers, the web or adverts in local magazines.

Climbing

Climbing is concentrated in Halong Bay, but it is also now on offer in other areas. A few agencies organize the activity.

Contact
Asia Outdoors, Cat Ba town, T91-376 0025, www.asiaoutdoors.com.vn. **VietClimb**, An Duong, Hanoi, T091-454 8903, www.vietclimb.vn. **X Rock**, 503a Nguyen Duy Trinh, www.xrockclimbing.com.

Cycling and mountain biking

Being flat over great distances, cycling is a popular activity in Vietnam. The main problem is the traffic. It's recommended that any tour is planned off-road or on minor roads, not Highway 1. Many cyclists prefer to bring their own all-terrain or racing bikes but it's also possible to rent from tour organizers. Those seeking more of a challenge can take on the hilly roads of the north or the **Central Highlands** where roads are relatively quiet.

Contact
Spice Roads, 14/1-B Soi Promsi 2, Sukhumvit 39, Klongtan Nua, Wattana, Bangkok, T66 2-712 5305, www.spice roads.com. A recommended biking company that operates throughout Asia. **Tien Bicycles**, 12 Nguyen Thien Ke St, Hue, T54-382 3507, www.tienbicycles. com. Organizes cross-country tours as well as those in and around Hué.

Diving and snorkelling

Snorkelling in the seas of Vietnam is a limited activity. Much of the coast has very poor visibility. Away from the deltas the water is still quite turbid. In those places where snorkelling and diving is said to be good (such as Nha Trang's **Whale Island** or **Phu Quoc**) the best time of year to dive varies with location – contact the diving operators in the relevant chapters for full details.

Ecotourism

Since the early 1990s there has been a significant growth in ecotourism, which promotes and supports the conservation of natural environments and is also fair and equitable to local communities. While the authenticity of some ecotourism operators needs to be interpreted with some care, there is both a huge demand for this type of activity and also significant opportunities to support worthwhile conservation and social development initiatives.

Contact
International Eco-Tourism Society (www.ecotourism.org) and **Tourism Concern** (www.tourismconcern.org.uk) develop and promote ecotourism projects in destinations all over the world and their websites provide details for initiatives throughout Southeast Asia.

A number of Vietnam-based operators are also now members of the **Responsible Travel Club**, www. rtcvietnam.org, which works with both WWF and SNV.

Golf

Golf in Vietnam can be traced back to the 1930s when the emperor Bao Dai laid a course in Dalat. After a period of dormancy, golf in Vietnam has mushroomed over the past few years. There are now many international standard courses all over the country and green fees are reasonable. There are very good courses around both HCMC and Hanoi as well as 3 superb options on the Central Coast. Mui Ne is also home to a good course, as is Nha Trang.

Kayaking

Kayaking in Vietnam is virtually synonymous with **Halong Bay** and **Lan Ha Bay**, but there are also now river kayaking options available around Dalat. Most beach resorts will hire out simple sit on tops for gentle paddles in the sea.

Motorbiking and Vespa tours

Touring northern Ha Giang province on a motorbike is one of the most exciting things you can do here. Other cross-country and cross-border tours are possible. Companies use a range of bikes from the temperamental Minsk to the Honda Baja. Vespa tours are available from **Ho Chi Minh City** to **Mui Ne** and **Nha Trang** and also around Hoi An.

Spas

There are a handful of devoted spa resorts in Vietnam including the **Ana Mandara** in Nha Trang, the **Evason Hideaway** in Ninh Van Bay and the all-inclusive Fusion Maia in Hoi An. There are other good hotels such as the **Sofitel**

Metropole Hanoi and the **Victoria Hotels** that offer spa facilities. In HCMC and Hanoi, central areas are full of hair salons, foot massage parlours and just about everything else. Generally good and quite good value for money. Some are sleazy but this can easily be deduced from the outside.

Trekking

Trekking is an increasingly popular activity in Vietnam. The main focus for this activity is **Sapa**, in the north of the country, but some trekking is organized around **Dalat** and other Central Highland towns. Around Sapa there are walks of varying durations demanding different fitness levels and degrees of stamina. Other popular areas for walking include **Cuc Phuong National Park**, **Nam Cat Tien National Park**, **Yok Don National Park**, **Ha Giang Province** and **Mai Chau**.

Many of the tour operators in Hanoi, listed on page 69, organize trekking tours as do those based in Sapa, see page 97. Some treks are straightforward and can be done without guides or support (ask your guesthouse for routes), whereas others need accommodation and a legal requirement to take a licensed guide. Unfortunately, there are no accurate maps for walkers in Vietnam.

Windsurfing and kitesurfing

Kite and windsurfing are found largely in Mui Ne. Here **Jibe's Beach Club** is leading the way organizing international tournaments. Mui Ne offers near-perfect conditions in season; equipment can be rented or bought at many places.

Windsurfing and surfing are popular on the beaches around Nha Trang – check out the Surf Shack and the Surf Hostel (see page 244).

Vietnam War tours

The most popular places include the **Central Highlands, Demilitarized Zone (DMZ)** and the **Cu Chi Tunnels**. Many agents in Hué offer high-quality tours see page 163.

Shopping tips

Vietnam is increasingly a good destination for shopping. A wide range of designer clothing, silk goods, high-quality handicrafts, ceramics and lacquerware are excellent value. The main shopping centres are Hanoi, Ho Chi Minh City and Hoi An. Sapa is also a good place to shop for ethnic minority wares. The majority of shops and markets in Vietnam are open daily from early in the morning to late at night and do not close for lunch.

Export of wood or antiques is banned and anything antique or antique-looking will be seized at customs. In order to avoid this happening you will need to get an export licence from the Customs Department, 162 Nguyen Van Cu St, Hanoi, T4-3872 5260. Do not buy marine turtle products.

Lacquerware is plentiful and cheap, but lacquer pictures are heavy to carry about. Small lacquer trinkets, such as boxes and trays, are more portable and make nice presents. Ethnic products, fabrics, wickerware and jewellery is best bought (and cheapest) in the uplands but plenty is available in the two main cities. Cham fabrics, for example, are available in Ho Chi Minh City while those of the Thai and Hmong minorities can be widely seen in Hanoi.

Beautiful and affordable women's clothes are now to be found in designer and boutique stores in Hanoi and Ho Chi Minh City in particular. There is a growing market in homeware accessories made of beautiful silks and woods. Junk collectors will have a field day in Ho Chi Minh City and Hanoi; many trinkets were left behind by French, Americans and Russians, including old cameras, watches, cigarette lighters (most Zippos are fake), 1960s Coca-Cola signs and 1930s Pernod ashtrays. Manufacturers of outdoor wear, rucksacks, boots and trainers have factories in Vietnam.

A considerable amount of genuine branded stock finds its way into the shops of Hanoi and Ho Chi Minh City at prices as little as 10% of European shop prices.

Where to stay
in Vietnam

colonial villas, ecolodges and homestays

Accommodation ranges from luxury suites in international five-star hotels and spa resorts to small, family hotels and homestays with local people in the Mekong Delta and with the ethnic minorities in the Central Highlands and northern Vietnam. During peak seasons – especially December to March and particularly during busy holidays such as Tet, Christmas, New Year's Eve and around Easter – booking is essential. Expect staff to speak English in all top hotels. Do not expect it in cheaper hotels or in more remote places, although most places employ someone with a smattering of a foreign language.

Private, mini hotels are worth seeking out as, being family-run, guests can expect good service. Mid-range and tourist hotels may provide a decent breakfast that is often included in the price. Many luxury and first-class hotels and some three-star hotels charge extra for breakfast and, on top of this, also charge 10% VAT and 5% service charge. When quoted a hotel price you should ask whether that includes these two taxes; it is marked as ++ (plus plus) on the bill.

There are some world-class beach resorts in Phu Quoc, Nha Trang, Mui Ne, Hoi An, Con Dao and Danang. In the northern uplands, in places such as Sapa, Ha Giang Province and Mai Chau, it is possible to stay in an ethnic minority house. Bathrooms are basic and will consist of a cold shower or warm shower and a natural or Western toilet. To stay in a homestay, you must book through a tour operator or through the local tourist office; you cannot just turn up. Homestays are also possible on farms and in orchards in the Mekong Delta.

Price codes

Where to stay	Restaurants
$$$$ over US$100	$$$ over US$12
$$$ US$46-100	$$ US$6-12
$$ US$20-45	$ under US$6
$ under US$20	

Prices refer to the cost of a double room in high season, including taxes.

Prices refer to the cost of a two-course meal for one person, excluding drinks or service charge.

National parks offer everything from air-conditioned bungalows to shared dormitory rooms to campsites where, sometimes, it is possible to hire tents. Visitors may spend a romantic night on a boat in Halong Bay or on the Mekong Delta. Boats range from the fairly luxurious to the basic. Most people book through tour operators.

You will often have to leave your passport at hotel reception desks for the duration of your hotel stay. It will be released to you temporarily for bank purposes or buying an air ticket. Credit cards are widely accepted but there is often a 2-4% fee for paying in this manner. Tipping is not expected in hotels in Vietnam.

Camping in Vietnam is limited mainly because the authorities insist on foreign visitors sleeping in registered accommodation. There are very few campsites but visitors bringing tents may be able to use them around Sapa or on Cat Ba and surrounding islands.

The age of consent in Vietnam is 18. There are rules relating to a Vietnamese person of the opposite sex being in your hotel room. It depends on the attitude of the hotel. Travellers normally get their laundry done in hotels. In cheap hotels it's inexpensive. Cheaper hotels and laundries in the hotel districts charge by weight. The smarter places charge by the item and the bill can be huge as a result.

Food & drink
in Vietnam

spicy salads, sublime stir fries, steaming soup

Food

Food is a major attraction of Vietnam; it is plentiful and almost always delicious. Outstanding Vietnamese, French and international cuisine is served in first-class restaurants and humble foodstalls alike. The quality will be, in the main, exceptional. The accent is on local, seasonal and fresh produce and the rich pickings from the sea, along Vietnam's 2000-km coastline, will always make it far inland too. While most small places will focus on one or two dishes, many larger restaurants offer a variety of cuisine from the regions. Ho Chi Minh City and Hanoi offer a wide range of cuisines besides Vietnamese. Eating out, especially at street restaurants, is very cheap.

Dishes

Pho (pronounced *fer*), a bowl of flat, white, noodle soup served with chicken or beef, is utterly delicious. The soup is made from stock flavoured with star anise, ginger and other spices and herbs but individual recipes often remain a closely guarded secret. Vietnamese usually eat *pho* in the morning, but you will be able to find it throughout the day. On each table of a *pho* restaurant in the south sits a plate of fresh green leaves: mint, cinnamon, basil and the spiky looking *ngo gai*, together with bean sprouts, chopped red chillies, barbecue sauce and sliced lemons, enabling patrons to produce their own variations on a theme.

Another local speciality found mainly further south is *com tam* or broken rice. *Com tam* stalls abound on the streets and do brisk trade at breakfast and lunch. They tend to be low-cost canteens. The steamed broken rice is eaten with fried chicken, fish, pork and vegetables and soup is normally included in the price. You will also find cheap *com* bing dan restaurants everywhere which feature rice and a wide variety of dishes which you can select, buffet style.

There are many types of Vietnamese roll: the most common are deep-fried spring rolls (confusingly, *cha gio* in the south and *nem ranh* in the north) but if

ON THE ROAD
Bird's nest soup

The tiny nests of the brown-rumped swift (*Collocalia esculenta*), also known as the edible-nest swiftlet or sea swallow, are collected for bird's nest soup, a Chinese delicacy, throughout Southeast Asia.

The semi-oval nests are made of silk-like strands of saliva secreted by the birds which, when cooked in broth, softens and becomes a little like noodles. Like so many Chinese delicacies, the nests are believed to have aphrodisiac qualities and the soup has even been suggested as a cure for HIV. The red nests are the most highly valued, and the Vietnamese Emperor Minh Mang (1820-1840) is said to have owed his extraordinary vitality to his inordinate consumption of bird's nest soup. This may explain why restaurants serving it are sometimes associated with massage parlours.

Collecting the nests is a precarious but profitable business and in some areas mafias of concessionaires vigorously guard and protect their assets. The men who collect the nests on a piecework basis risk serious injury climbing rickety ladders to cave roofs in sometimes almost total darkness, save for a candle strapped to their heads.

these appear on your table too frequently, look for the fresh or do-it-yourself types, such as *bi cuon* or *bo bia*. Essentially, these are salads with prawns or grilled meats wrapped in rice paper.

Vietnamese salads (*goi* in the south and *nom* in the north) are to die for. The best known is the green papaya salad with dried beef (*nom du du bo kho*); others include *goi xoai* (mango salad) and *goi buoi* (pomelo salad). They all involve a wonderful fusion of herbs and vegetables with sweet and spicy tastes rolled in.

Delicious seafood is a staple across the land. It would be invidious to isolate a particular seafood dish when there are so many to chose from. Prawns are prawns – the bigger and the less adulterated the better. But a marvellous dish that does deserve commendation is crab in tamarind sauce. This glorious fusion of flavours, bitter tamarind, garlic, piquant spring onion and fresh crab is quite delicious.

All Vietnamese food is dipped, whether in fish sauce, soy sauce, chilli sauce, peanut sauce or pungent prawn sauce (*mam tom* – avoid if possible) before eating. As each course is served so a new set of dips will accompany. Follow the guidance of your waiter or Vietnamese friends to get the right dip with the right dish.

Eating out

When it comes to food, Vietnamese do not stand on ceremony and (perhaps rather like the French) regard peripherals such as furniture, service and ambience as mere distractions to the task of ploughing through plates, crocks, casseroles and tureens charged with meats, vegetables and soups. Do not expect good service, courses to arrive in the right order, or to eat at the same time as your companions, but do expect the freshest and tastiest food you will find anywhere.

While it is possible to eat very cheaply in Vietnam (especially outside Hanoi and Ho Chi Minh City) the higher class of restaurant, particularly those serving foreign cuisine, can prove quite expensive, especially with wine. But with judicious shopping around it is not hard to find excellent value for money, particularly in the small, **family restaurants**. Some restaurants (mostly expensive ones) add 5% service charge and the government tax of 10% to the bill. See page 24 on restaurant classification.

For day trips, an early morning visit to the **markets** will produce a picnic fit for a king: hard-boiled quails' eggs, thinly sliced garlic sausage, pickled vegetables, beef tomatoes, cucumber, pâté, cheese, warm baguettes and fresh fruit.

The thing that separates India from China is that in the former there are prohibitions governing the consumption of just about everything. In the latter anything and everything can be – and is – eaten. Vietnam of course falls under Chinese sway. Therefore anyone who self imposes restrictions on his eating habits is regarded as a bit of a crank. There are **vegetarian restaurants** in Vietnam but these usually sell different types of tofu dressed to look like meat. The vegetable section of most 'normal' restaurants has vegetables – but cooked with pork, with beef or with prawns, rarely pure vegetables. Nevertheless there are a few Vietnamese vegetarians and twice a month a great many people eat vegetarian so restaurants are aware of the concept and the number of veggie specific places is on the up.

Given the large proportion of the population aged 16 and under no Vietnamese restaurant is put out by **children**. Indeed any restaurant frequented by Vietnamese families will have kids running around everywhere. So parents need have no fears about their children's behaviour upsetting anyone.

Note that Vietnamese get up early and so lunchtime starts at 1100 and some more local places will be shutting up shop for lunch by 1300.

Drink

Locally produced fresh beer is called *bia hoi*. It is cold and refreshing, and weak and cheap enough to drink in quite large volumes. It is usually consumed in small pavement cafés where patrons sit on small plastic stools. Most *bia hoi* places serve simple and inexpensive food. As the beer is fresh it has to be consumed within a short period of brewing hence most towns, even quite small ones, have their own brewery. Bars and restaurants do not sell *bia hoi*, hence customers usually have a choice of the regional bottled brew or Tiger, Heineken or Carlsberg. 'Beer clubs' haver become very popular in Hanoi, HCMC and Danang in the last year or two, most of which sell Czech or German beers plus a range of Belgian options by the bottle.

Rice and **fruit wines** are produced and consumed in large quantities in upland areas, particularly in the north of Vietnam. Rice wines are fairly easily found, however. There are two types of rice wine, *ruou nep* and *ruou de*. *Ruou nep* is a viscous wine made from sticky rice. *Ruou de* is a rice spirit and very strong.

The Chinese believe that **snake wines** increase their virility and are normally found in areas with a large Chinese population. It is called a wine despite being a spirit. Other wines include the body and parts of seahorses, gecko, silkworms and bees.

There is a fantastic range of different **fruit wines** but unless you make a real effort it can be quite hard to find them. Wines are made from just about all upland fruits: plum, strawberry, apple and, of course, grapes, although grape wine in Vietnam is generally disappointing. The others are fiery and warm, strong and, bought by the bottle, cheap.

Hanoi

Hanoi is a city of broad, tree-lined boulevards, lakes, parks, weathered colonial buildings, elegant squares and some of the newest office blocks and hotels in Southeast Asia. It is the capital of the world's 14th most populous country, but, in an age of urban sprawl, the city remains small and compact, historic and charming.

Much of the charm of Hanoi lies not so much in the big 'sights' but in the unofficial and informal: small shops, sidewalk coffee, an evening visit to Hoan Kiem, watching the older inhabitants exercise and practice t'ai chi around one of the city's many lakes.

Another appeal lies in the novelty of exploring a city that, until recently, has opted for a firmly socialist road to development and has been insulated from the West. Today, you'll find it enlivened by an entrepreneurial spirit manifest in new shops, bars and building developments, and an ever more cosmopolitan air reflected in the opening of new galleries and a fantastic contemporary art scene.

Best for
Architecture ▪ Coffee shops ▪ History ▪ Lakeside walks

Hoan Kiem Lake and Central
  Hanoi 33
West of Hoan Kiem Lake 40
South of Hoan Kiem Lake 40
Ho Chi Minh's Mausoleum
  complex and around. 45
Outer Hanoi 52
Around Hanoi 54

Footprint picks

★ **Hoan Kiem Lake**, page 33
A walk around the lake in the early
morning or at dusk is a must.

★ **Old Quarter**, page 35
Hectic and intoxicating – if you feel overwhelmed, jump in a cyclo.

★ **Ambassadors' Pagoda**, page 44
Not one of the conventional sights, but easily one of the most
atmospheric – arrive early or late to watch badminton.

★ **Temple of Literature**, page 48
Vietnam's first university and now its most famous temple.

★ **The Citadel**, page 52
One of the most recently opened of the official sights, the Citadel
grounds are a peaceful retreat and offer plenty of history.

★ **Tay Ho Pagoda**, page 53
The waterfront setting of this pagoda is hard to beat.

★ **Museum of Ethnology**, page 53
The country's best place to learn about the 54 ethnic groups which
inhabit it.

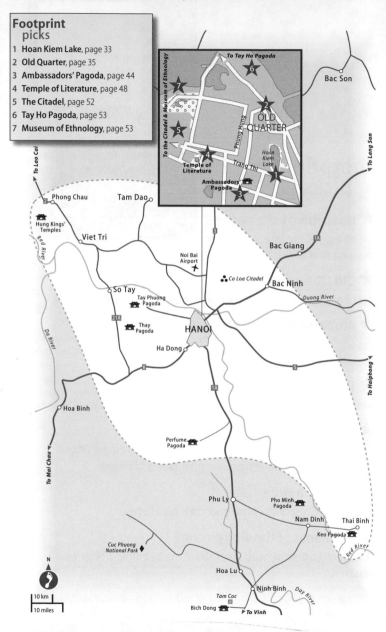

Footprint picks

1 Hoan Kiem Lake, page 33
2 Old Quarter, page 35
3 Ambassadors' Pagoda, page 44
4 Temple of Literature, page 48
5 The Citadel, page 52
6 Tay Ho Pagoda, page 53
7 Museum of Ethnology, page 53

To Tay Ho Pagoda

To the Citadel & Museum of Ethnology

Bac Son

OLD QUARTER

Phung Hung

Hoan Kiem Lake

Trang Thi

Temple of Literature

Ambassadors' Pagoda

To Lao Cai

Phong Chau

Hung Kings' Temples

Tam Dao

Viet Tri

Noi Bai Airport

Bac Giang

1A

Red River

So Tay

Tay Phuong Pagoda

21A

Thay Pagoda

Co Loa Citadel

Bac Ninh

Duong River

To Lang Son

HANOI

Ha Dong

6

1A

2

To Haiphong

Hoa Binh

Da River

To Mai Chau

Perfume Pagoda

Phu Ly

Pho Minh Pagoda

Nam Dinh

Thai Binh

Keo Pagoda

Red River

Cuc Phuong National Park

Hoa Lu

Ninh Binh

Day River

Tam Coc

Bich Dong

To Vinh

N

10 km
10 miles

Sights
Hanoi

boulevards, baguettes and bars

Hanoi has some worthy historical sights lying as it does at the heart of a region rich in history. It also has stylish shops and plentiful market stalls, and plenty of places to stop for coffee. *Colour map 1, B4.*

Hoan Kiem Lake and Central Hanoi

heart of the capital

★Hoan Kiem Lake

Hoan Kiem Lake, or Ho Guom (the Lake of the Restored Sword) as it is more commonly referred to in Hanoi, is named after an incident that occurred during the 15th century. Emperor Le Thai To (1428-1433), following a momentous victory against an army of invading Ming Chinese, was sailing on the lake when a golden turtle appeared from the depths to take back the charmed sword which had secured the victory and restore it to the lake whence it came. Like the sword in the stone of British Arthurian legend, Le Thai To's sword assures Vietnamese of divine intervention in time of national crisis and the story is graphically portrayed in water puppet theatres across the country. There is a modest and rather dilapidated tower (the **Tortoise Tower**) commemorating the event on an islet in the southern part of the lake. In fact, the lake does contain a turtle and one captured in 1968 was reputed to have weighed 250 kg. The Ho Guom tortoise has now been named *Rafetus leloii*. The wide pavement that surrounds the lake is used by the residents of the city every morning for jogging and t'ai chi. The light around the lake has a filmic quality, especially in the early morning.

Ngoc Son Temple and bridge
10,000d.

The temple was built in the early 19th century on a small island on the foundations of the old Khanh Thuy Palace. The island is linked to the shore by the Huc (Sunbeam) Bridge, constructed in 1875. The temple is dedicated to Van Xuong, the God of Literature, although the 13th-century hero Tran Hung Dao, the martial arts genius Quan Vu and the physician La To are also worshipped here. Shrouded by trees and surrounded by water, the pagoda's position is its strongest attribute.

Essential Hanoi

Finding your feet

At the heart of the city is Hoan Kiem Lake. The majority of visitors make straight for the Old Quarter (aka 36 Streets) area north of the lake. The French Quarter is south of the lake. Here you'll find the Opera House, grand hotels, shops and offices. A large block of the city west of Hoan Kiem Lake (Ba Dinh District) represents the heart of government. To the north is West Lake, Tay Ho District, fringed with the suburban homes of the new middle class and the expat quarter with bars and restaurants. Away to the southern and eastern edges are the industrial and residential zones.

Best bars

Barbetta, page 65
CAMA ATK, page 65
Madake, page 65
Tadioto, page 66

Getting around

Hanoi is getting more frenetic by the minute, and pavements are often used for parking making walking a challenge, but walking can still be pleasurable. If you like the idea of being pedalled, then a cyclo is the answer – but be prepared for some concentrated haggling. There are also *xe'om* and self-drive motorbikes for hire as well as a fleet of metered taxis. Local buses are rammed and the network is not well designed for the uninitiated.

Best museum and galleries

Vietnamese Women's Museum, page 52
Museum of Ethnology, page 53
Nha San and Art Vietnam, page 67

When to go

Hanoi benefits from glorious European-like springs and autumns when temperatures are warm and crisp. From May until September Hanoi is often fearfully hot and steamy and you cannot take a step without breaking into a sweat. From December to February it can be chilly and Hanoians wrap themselves up. Most museums are closed on Mondays.

Time required

Most sights can be seen in a weekend, but lazing in Hanoi cafés and by lakes is worth more of your time.

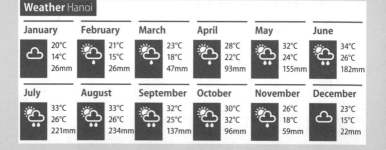

Weather Hanoi

January	February	March	April	May	June
20°C 14°C 26mm	21°C 15°C 26mm	23°C 18°C 47mm	28°C 22°C 93mm	32°C 24°C 155mm	34°C 26°C 182mm

July	August	September	October	November	December
33°C 26°C 221mm	33°C 26°C 234mm	32°C 25°C 137mm	30°C 32°C 96mm	26°C 18°C 59mm	23°C 15°C 22mm

To the side of the temple is a room containing a preserved turtle and photographs of the creatures in the lake.

★Old Quarter and 36 Streets

Stretching north from the lake is the Old Quarter (aka Pho Co or 36 Streets). Previously, it lay to the east of the citadel, where the emperor had his residence, and was squalid, dark, cramped and disease-ridden. This part of Hanoi has survived surprisingly intact, and today is one of the most beautiful areas of the city, although the old fronts of most of the buildings are now covered with unsightly advertising hordings. Narrow streets, each named after the produce that it sells or used to sell (**Basket Street**, **Paper Street**, **Silk Street**, etc), create an intricate web of activity and colour, see box, page 45.

By the 15th century there were 36 short lanes here, each specializing in a particular trade and representing one of the 36 guilds. Among them, for example, were the **Phuong Hang Dao (Dyers' Guild Street)** and the **Phuong Hang Bac (Silversmiths' Street)**. In fact, Hang Bac (*hang* means merchandise) is the oldest street in Hanoi, dating from the 13th century. The 36 streets have interested European visitors since they first started coming to Hanoi. For example, in 1685 Samuel Bacon noted how "all the diverse objects sold in this town have a specially assigned street", remarking how different this was from "companies and corporations in European cities". The streets in question not only sold different products, but were usually also populated by people from different areas of the country – even from single villages. They would live, work and worship together because each of the occupational guilds had its own temple and its own community support networks.

Some of this past is still in evidence: at the south end of Hang Dau Street, for example, is a mass of stalls selling nothing but shoes and Hang Bac is still a place for gold to be bought and sold. Generally, however, the crafts and trades of the past have given way to new activities, but it is remarkable the extent to which the streets still specialize in the production and sale of just one type of merchandise.

The dwellings in this area are known as *nha ong* (**tube houses**). The majority were built at the end of the 19th century and the beginning of the 20th; they are narrow, with shop fronts sometimes only 3 m wide, but can be up to 50 m long (such as the one at 51 Hang Dao). In the countryside the dimensions of houses were calculated on the basis of the owner's own physical dimensions; in urban areas the tube houses evolved so that each house owner could have an, albeit very small, area of shop frontage facing onto the main street; the width was determined by the social class of the owner. The houses tend to be interspersed with courtyards or 'wells' to permit light into the house and allow some space for outside activities such as washing and gardening. As geographers Brian Shaw and R Jones note in a paper on heritage conservation in Hanoi, the houses also had a natural air-conditioning system: the difference in ambient temperature between the inner courtyards and the outside street created air flow, and the longer the house the greater the velocity of the flow.

A common wall can sometimes still be seen between tube houses. Built in a step-like pattern, it not only marked land boundaries but also acted as a firebreak.

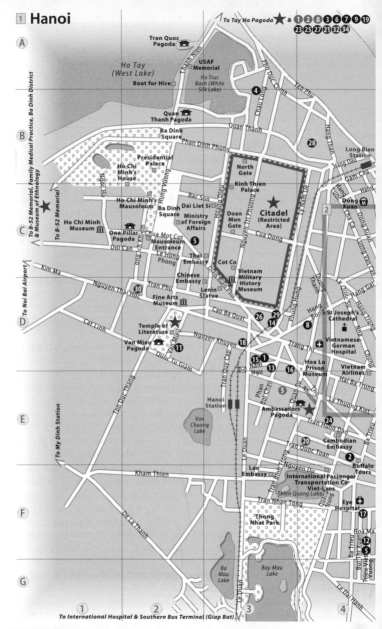

1 Hanoi

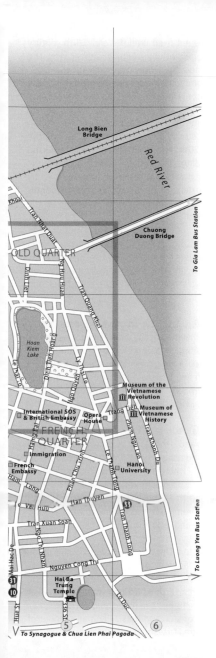

→ Hanoi maps
1 Hanoi, page 36
2 Hoan Kiem, page 41

N

400 metres
400 yards

Where to stay 🛏
InterContinental Hanoi
  Westlake **8** *A3*
Movenpick **5** *E3*
Sheraton **1** *A3*
Sofitel **2** *A3*

Restaurants & cafés 🍴
Café 129 **10** *D3*
Café Puku **14** *D3*
Chiem Beo **23** *A3*
Chim Sáo **12** *F4*
Com Chay Nang Tam **24** *E4*
Cong Café **5** *F4 and C2*
Cousins **3** *A3*
Da Paulo **6** *A3*
El Gaucho **7** *A3*
Foodshop 45 **25** *A3*
Hanoi Cooking Centre **4** *B3*
Hanoi Social Club **8** *D4*
The Kafe **26** *D3*
KOTO **11** *D2*
La Badiane **1** *D3*
La Bicicleta **9** *A3*
Luna d'Autonno **15** *D3*
Maison de Tet **27** *A3*
Manzi **28** *B4*
Namaste **16** *D3*
Net Hue **29** *D3*
Pots n Pans **17** *F4*
Quan An Ngon **13** *D3*
Ray Quan **18** *F4*
Republic **19** *A3*
Verticale **2** *E4*

Bars & clubs 🍸
84 Bar **20** *E4*
Barbetta **30** *D2*
Cama ATK **31** *G5*
Hanoi Rock City **32** *A3*
Hoan Vien **33** *F6*
Madake **34** *A3*
Summit Lounge **21** *A3*

The position of the house frontages were not fixed until the early 20th century and consequently some streets have a delightfully irregular appearance. The structures were built of bricks 'cemented' together with sugar-cane juice.

The older houses tend to be lower; commoners were not permitted to build higher than the Emperor's own residence. Other regulations prohibited attic windows looking down on the street; this was to prevent assassination and to stop people from looking down on a passing king. As far as colour and decoration were concerned, purple and gold were strictly for royal use only, as was the decorative use of the dragon. By the early 20th century inhabitants were replacing their traditional tube houses with buildings inspired by French architecture. Many fine buildings from this era remain, however, and are best appreciated by standing back and looking upwards. Shutters, cornices, columns and wrought-iron balconies and balustrades are common decorative features. An ornate façade sometimes conceals the pitched roof behind.

48 Hang Ngang Street ⓘ *At the north end of Hang Dao St, before it becomes Hang Duong St, 0800-1130, 1330-1630, 10,000d.* This is the spot where Ho Chi Minh drew up the Vietnamese Declaration of Independence in 1945, ironically modelled on the US Declaration of Independence. It now houses a museum with black and white photographs of Uncle Ho.

87 Ma May Street ⓘ *Daily 0800-1200, 1300-1700, 10,000d, guide included.* This is a wonderfully preserved example of an original shophouse, now open to the public. The house was built in the late 1800s as a home for a single family. The importance of the miniature interior courtyards providing light, fresh air and gardens can be appreciated. The wooden upstairs and pitched fish-scale-tiled roofs are typical of how most houses would have looked. From 1954 to 1999 five families shared the building as the urban population rose and living conditions declined.

The Bach Ma (White Horse) Temple ⓘ *76 Hang Buom St.* Dating from the ninth century, this temple honours Long Do and is the oldest religious building in the Old Quarter. In 1010, King Ly Thai To honoured Long Do with the title of the capital. It is said that a horse revealed to King Ly Thai To where to build the walls of the citadel.

Cua Quan Chuong Venturing further north is the last remaining of Hanoi's 16 gates. In the 18th century a system of ramparts and walls was built around Hanoi. Quan Chuong Gate was built in 1749 and rebuilt in 1817.

Dong Xuan Market Further north still, on Dong Xuan Street, is this large covered **market**. It was destroyed in a disastrous fire in 1994 and stallholders lost an estimated US$4.5 million worth of stock. They complained bitterly at the inadequacy of the fire services; one fire engine arrived with no water. The market has been rebuilt and it specializes mainly in clothes and household goods.

The streets around the market are full of street traders selling all manner of foods and spices making this a wonderful area to wander with a camera.

Hanoi's history

The original village on the site of the present city was located in a district with the local name of Long Do. The community seems to have existed as a small settlement as early as the third century AD.

The origins of Hanoi as a great city lie with a temple orphan, Ly Cong Uan. Ly rose through the ranks of the palace guards to become their commander and in 1010, four years after the death of the previous King Le Hoan, was enthroned, marking the beginning of the 200-year-long Ly Dynasty. On becoming king, Ly Cong Uan moved his capital from Hoa Lu to Dai La, which he renamed **Thang Long** (Soaring Dragon). Thang Long is present-day **Hanoi**. A number of pagodas were built at this time – most have since disappeared, although the One Pillar Pagoda and the Tran Vu Temple both date from this period

During the period of French expansion into Indochina, the Red River was proposed as an alternative trade route to the Mekong. Francis Garnier, a French naval officer, was dispatched to the area in 1873 to ascertain the possibilities of establishing such a route. Despite having only a modest force of men under arms, when negotiations with Emperor Tu Duc failed in 1882, Garnier attacked and captured the citadel of Hanoi under the dubious pretext that the Vietnamese were about to attack him. Tu Duc acceded to French demands, and from 1882 onwards, Hanoi, along with the port city of Haiphong, became the focus of French activity in the north. Hanoi was made the capital of the new colony of Annam, and the French laid out a 2-sq-km residential and business district, constructing mansions, villas and public buildings incorporating both French and Asian architectural styles. Many of these buildings still stand to the south and east of the Old City and Hoan Kiem Lake.

In the 1920s and 1930s, with conditions in the countryside deteriorating, there was an influx of landless and dispossessed labourers into the city. Before long, a poor underclass, living in squalid, pathetic conditions, had formed. At the end of the Second World War, with the French battling to keep Ho Chi Minh and his forces at bay, Hanoi became little more than a service centre of some 40,000 inhabitants.

After the French withdrew in 1954, Ho Chi Minh concentrated on building up Vietnam and in particular Hanoi's industrial base. At that time the capital had only eight small, privately owned factories. By 1965, more than 1000 enterprises had been added to this figure. However, as the US bombing of the north intensified with Operation Rolling Thunder in 1965, so the authorities began to evacuate non-essential civilians from Hanoi and to disperse industry into smaller, less vulnerable units of operation. Between 500,000 and 750,000 people were evacuated between 1965 and 1973, representing 75% of the inner-city population. Nevertheless, the cessation of hostilities led to a spontaneous migration back into the capital. By 1984 the population of the city had reached 2.7 million, and today it is in excess of three million.

religious buildings worth a peek

To the west of Hoan Kiem Lake in a little square stands the rather sombre, twin-towered neo-Gothic **Saint Joseph's Cathedral** ⓘ *open 0500-1130, 1400-1930 through a door at the back; Mass Mon-Fri 0530, 0815, Sat 0530, 1800, Sun 0500, 0700, 0900, 1100, 1600, 1800.* Built in 1886, the cathedral is important as one of the very first colonial-era buildings in Hanoi finished, as it was, soon after the Treaty of Tientsin, which gave France control over the whole of Vietnam (see page 357). It was located at the centre of the Catholic Mission. Some fine stained-glass windows remain. The area around the cathedral is hugely popular by day and night with Hanoi's youth who gather in huge numbers to drink ice lemon tea and eat sunflower seeds.

About 100 m in front of the cathedral on Nha Tho Street is a much older religious foundation, the **Stone Lady Pagoda (Chua Ba Da)**, down a narrow alley. It consists of an old pagoda and a Buddhist school. On either side of the pagoda are low buildings where the monks live. Although few of the standing buildings are of any antiquity it is an ancient site and a tranquil and timeless atmosphere prevails. Originally built in 1056 as Sung Khanh Pagoda, by the late 15th century it needed rebuilding. A stone statue of a woman was found in the foundations and was worshipped in the pagoda. By 1767 the walls needed rebuilding. Each time they were built they collapsed. The foundations were dug deeper and the stone statue was found again. Since then the walls have held fast. Although now a pagoda for the worship of Buddha it is clear that the site has had a mixed spiritual history.

North of the cathedral on Ly Quoc Su Street is the **Ly Quoc Su Pagoda**, once home to Minh Khong, a physician and the chief adviser to Ly Than Tong, the Ly dynasty emperor. He became famous in the 12th century after curing the emperor of a disease that other doctors had failed to treat. It was restored in 2010.

tree-lined boulevards and coffee shops

Opera House
www.hanoioperahouse.org.vn. Not open to the public except during public performances. See the billboards outside or visit the box office for details.

To the south and east of Hoan Kiem Lake is the proud-looking French-era Opera House. It was built between 1901-1911 by François Lagisquet and is one of the finest French colonial buildings in Hanoi. Some 35,000 bamboo piles were sunk into the mud of the Red River to provide foundations for the lofty edifice. The exterior is a delightful mass of shutters, wrought-iron work, little balconies and a tiled frieze. The top balustrade is nicely capped with griffins. Inside, there are dozens of little boxes and fine decoration evocative of the French era. Having suffered years of neglect the Opera House was eventually lavishly restored, opening in time for the Francophone Summit held in 1997. Original drawings in Hanoi and Paris were consulted and teams of foreign experts were brought in to supervise local craftsmen. Slate was carried from Sin Ho to re-tile the roof, Italians oversaw the relaying of the mosaic floor in the lobby and French artists repainted the fine ornamental details of the auditorium. The restoration cost US$14 million, a colossal sum to spend on the reappointment of a colonial edifice. A Hanoi planning department architect explained that

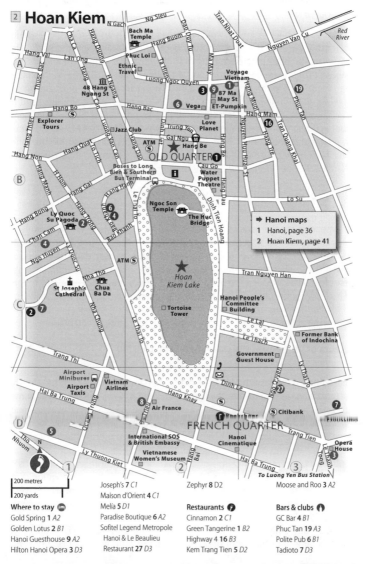

2 Hoan Kiem

➡ Hanoi maps
1 Hanoi, page 36
2 Hoan Kiem, page 41

200 metres
200 yards

Where to stay 🛏
Gold Spring 1 A2
Golden Lotus 2 B1
Hanoi Guesthouse 9 A2
Hilton Hanoi Opera 3 D3

Joseph's 7 C1
Maison d'Orient 4 C1
Melia 5 D1
Paradise Boutique 6 A2
Sofitel Legend Metropole
 Hanoi & Le Beaulieu
 Restaurant 27 D3

Zephyr 8 D2

Restaurants 🍴
Cinnamon 2 C1
Green Tangerine 1 B2
Highway 4 16 B3
Kem Trang Tien 5 D2

Moose and Roo 3 A2

Bars & clubs 🍸
GC Bar 4 B1
Phuc Tan 19 A3
Polite Pub 6 B1
Tadioto 7 D3

although the Opera House was French in style it was built by Vietnamese hands and represented an indelible part of Vietnamese history.

Sofitel Metropole
15 Ngo Quyen St.

The Metropole, built in French-colonial style in 1901, is an icon of elegance in the French quarter of the city. It quickly became the focal point of colonial life for 50 years. In 1916, it screened the first movie shown in Indochina. In 1944, Japanese POWS were temporarily housed here. In the 1950s the Vietnamese government appropriated it, named it the **Thong Nhat Hotel**, and used it as a hotel for VIPs; during the Vietnam War years the press and diplomats used it as their headquarters. Many famous celebrities and diplomats have stayed here including Graham Greene (writing *The Quiet American*), Somerset Maugham, Noel Coward, Stephen Hawking, Oliver Stone, Charlie Chaplin, Sir Roger Moore, Jane Fonda, Mick Jagger, Catherine Deneuve, George Bush Senior, Fidel Castro, Robert McNamara, Jacques Chirac and Boutros Boutros Ghali.

Museum of the Vietnamese Revolution
216 Tran Quang Khai St, T4-3825 4151, Tue-Sun 0800-1145, 1330-1615, 20,000d.

The Museum of the Vietnamese Revolution (Bao Tang Cach Mang Vietnam), housed in an old French villa, traces the struggle of the Vietnamese people to establish their independence. Following the displays, it becomes clear that the American involvement in Vietnam has been just one episode in a centuries-long struggle against foreign aggressors. The 3000 exhibits are dryly presented across 29 rooms and in chronological order. They start with the cover the struggle for independence (1858-1945); the final rooms show the peace and prosperity of reunification: bountiful harvests, the opening of large civil engineering projects, and smiling peasants.

Museum of Vietnamese History (Bao Tang Lich Su)
1 Trang Tien St, T4-325 3518, Tue-Sun 0800-1130, 1330-1630, 15,000d.

A short distance south of the Museum of the Vietnamese Revolution is the History Museum. It is housed in a splendid building, completed in 1931. It was built as the home of the École Française d'Extrême-Orient, a distinguished archaeological, historical and ethnological research institute, by Ernest Hébrard. Hébrard was responsible for many fine colonial-era buildings in Vietnam. Here he employed a distinctly Indochinese style appropriate to its original and, indeed, its current function.

The museum remains a centre of cultural and historical research. The École Française d'Extrême-Orient played an important role in the preservation and restoration of ancient Vietnamese structures and temples, many of which were destroyed or came under threat of demolition by the French to enable the growth of their colonial city.

The museum remains a centre of cultural and historical research. The collection spans Vietnamese history from the Neolithic to the 20th century of Ho Chi Minh

Urban renewal

Although Ho Chi Minh City has attracted the lion's share of Vietnam's foreign inward investment, Hanoi, as the capital, also receives a large amount. But whereas Ho Chi Minh City's investment tends to be in industry, Hanoi has received a great deal of attention from property developers, notably in the hotel and office sectors. Much of the development has been in prestigious and historical central Hanoi and has included the construction of a huge office complex on the site of the notorious 'Hanoi Hilton' prison, much to the mortification of Vietnamese war veterans, see page 44. Some commentators applauded the authorities for this attempt at putting the past behind them.

Although some architecturally insensitive schemes have dominated the cityscape, numerous old colonial villas have been tastefully restored as bars, restaurants and homes with a very positive effect on Hanoi's architectural heritage. Pollution levels in Hanoi have soared as a result of the construction boom: dust from demolition, piling, bricks and tiles and sand blown from the back of trucks add an estimated 150 cubic metres of pollutants to the urban atmosphere every day. But while asthmatics may wheeze, Hanoi's army of builders grows daily ever stronger.

and is arranged in chronological order. Galleries lead from the Neolithic (Bac Son) represented by stone tools and jewellery; the Bronze Age (Dong Son) with some fine bronze drums; Funan and the port of Oc-Eo; Champa is represented by some fine stone carvings of *apsaras*, mythical dancing girls. There are relics such as bronze temple bells and urns of successive royal dynasties from Le to Nguyen. An impressive giant turtle, symbol of longevity, supports a huge stela praising the achievements of Le Loi, founder of the Le Dynasty, who harnessed nationalist sentiment and forced the Chinese out of Vietnam. Unfortunately some of the pieces (including a number of the stelae) are reproductions.

Other French Quarter buildings

Other buildings of the 'French Concession' include the impressive former residence of the French Resident Superior of Tonkin opposite the Metropole.

The enormous **Post Office** ① *6 Dinh Le St*, facing Hoan Kiem lake, was designed by Henri Cerruti in 1942. Next door is the **Post and Telegraphic Office** ① *75 Dinh Tien Hoang St*, designed by Auguste-Henri Vildieu and completed in 1896. Further up Dinh Tieng Hoang is the **Hanoi People's Committee** building, formerly the town hall and built by Vildieu between 1897 and 1906. The main section at the front dates from the late 1980s and early 1990s demonstrating brutalist communist architecture. Vildieu also designed the **Supreme Court** ① *48 Ly Thuong Kiet*, between 1900 and 1906. It's a fine symmetrical building with a grey-tiled roof, two staircases and balustrades.

Ernest Hébrard, who worked at the Central Services of Urban Planning and Architecture, designed the **Indochina University**, now **Hanoi University** ① *19 Le*

Thanh Tong St, which was completed in 1926. It bears a remarkable resemblance to the history museum, which he also designed. Furthermore, Hébrard designed the **Ministry of Foreign Affairs** (then the **Bureau des Finances**) ① *Dien Bien Phu St*, in 1931.

Around 1000 colonial villas are still scattered around Hanoi, especially west of the Old Quarter. Many of them have been superbly restored and are used by embassies.

Hoa Lo Prison
1 Hoa Lo, T4-3824 6358, Tue-Sun 0800-1130, 1330-1630, 20,000d.

Hoa Lo Prison (Maison Centrale), better known as the **Hanoi Hilton**, is the prison where US POWs were incarcerated, some for six years, during the Vietnamese War. The final prisoners were not released until 1973, some having been held in the north since 1964.

At the end of 1992 a US mission was shown around the prison where 2000 inmates were housed in cramped and squalid conditions. Despite pleas from war veterans and party members, the site was sold to a Singapore-Vietnamese joint venture and is now a hotel and shopping complex, **Hanoi Towers**. As part of the deal the developers had to leave a portion of the prison for use as a museum, a lasting memorial to the horrors of war.

'Maison Centrale' reads the legend over the prison's main gate, which leads in to the museum. There are recreations of conditions under colonial rule when the barbarous French incarcerated patriotic Vietnamese from 1896: by 1953 they were holding 2000 prisoners in a space designed for 500. Many well-known Vietnamese were incarcerated here: Phan Boi Chau (founder of the Reformation Party; 1867-1940), Luong Van Can (Reformation Party leader and school founder; 1854-1927), Nguyen Quyen (founder along with Luong Van Can of the School for the Just Cause; 1870-1942) and five men who were later to become general secretaries of the Communist Party: Le Duan (served as general secretary 1976-1986), Nguyen Van Cu (served 1938-1940), Truong Chinh (served 1941-1956 and July-December 1986), Nguyen Van Linh (served 1986-1991) and Do Muoi (served 1991-1997). Less prominence is given to the role of the prison for holding American pilots, but Douglas 'Pete' Peterson, the first post-war American Ambassador to Vietnam (1997-2001), who was one such occupant (imprisoned 1966-1973) has his mug-shot on the wall, as does John McCain (imprisoned 1967-1973).

★Ambassadors' Pagoda
73 Quan Su St.

In the 15th century there was a guesthouse on the site of the Ambassadors' Pagoda (Quan Su Pagoda) for visiting Buddhist ambassadors. The current structure was built between 1936 and 1942. Chinese in appearance from the exterior, the temple contains some fine stone sculptures of the past, present and future Buddhas. It is very popular and crowded with scholars, pilgrims, beggars and incense sellers. The pagoda is one of the centres of Buddhist learning in Vietnam (it is the headquarters of the Vietnam Central Buddhist Congregation): at the back is a schoolroom that is in regular use; students often spill-over into the surrounding corridors to listen.

ON THE ROAD

Guild street name meanings and their current trades

Bat Dan St – clay bowls
Bat Su – ceramic bowls
Hang Bac – silver, jewellery
Hang Bo – baskets, motorbike stickers,
  barbecue squid (late night)
Hang Bong – cotton
Hang Buom – sails, coffee,
  chocolate, booze
Hang But – calligraphy brushes
Hang Can – weighing scales
Hang Dao – silk (Pho Hang Dao means
  'street where red-dyed fabrics are
  sold'), sewing things, feathers
Hang Dieu – smoking pipes,
  fake brand name handbags
Hang Duong – sugar Hang Gai – hemp,
  silk, souvenirs, galleries, tailor shops

Hang Ma – votive paper, headstones
Hang Manh – bamboo screens/mats
Hang Non – conical hats
Hang Phen St – alum sulphate
Hang Quat – paper fans,
  religious artefacts
Hang Thiec – tinsmiths, tin ovens
Hang Tre – bamboo
Hang Trong – drums, boutiques,
  galleries
Lan Ong – traditional medicine
Hang Vai – cloth street
Ngo Gach – bricks
Thuoc Bac – medicine street
To Tich – undecorated mats,
  fruit cups
Yen Thai Alley – embroidery

Nearby, on Le Duan Street just south of the railway station, stalls sell a remarkable array of US, Soviet and Vietnamese army-surplus kit.

Ho Chi Minh's Mausoleum complex and around
resting place of Vietnam's greatest hero

Ho Chi Minh's Mausoleum

Summer Tue-Thu, Sat and Sun 0730-1100. Winter Tue-Thu, Sat and Sun 0800-1100, closed 6 weeks from Sep for conservation. Before entering the mausoleum, visitors must leave cameras and possessions at the office (Ban To Chuc) on Huong Vuong, just south of and a few mins' walk from the mausoleum. Visitors must be respectful: dress neatly, walk solemnly, do not talk and do not take anything in that could be construed as a weapon, for example, a penknife.

The Vietnamese have made Ho Chi Minh's body a holy place of pilgrimage and visitors march in file to see Ho's embalmed corpse inside the mausoleum (Lang Chu Tich Ho Chi Minh).

The mausoleum, built between 1973 and 1975, is a massive square forbidding structure and must be among the best constructed, maintained and air-conditioned buildings in Vietnam. Opened in 1975, it is a fine example of the mausoleum genre and is modelled closely on Lenin's Mausoleum in Moscow. Ho Chi Minh lies in state with a guard at each corner of his bier. The embalming of his body was undertaken by the chief Soviet embalmer Dr Sergei Debrov, who also worked on such communist luminaries as Klement Gottwald (President of Czechoslovakia), Georgi Dimitrov (Prime

Minister of Bulgaria) and Forbes Burnham (President of Guyana). Debrov was flown to Hanoi from Moscow as Ho Chi Minh lay dying, bringing with him two transport planes packed with air conditioners and other equipment. To escape US bombing, the team moved Uncle Ho to a cave, taking a full year to complete the embalming process. The embalming and eternal display of Ho Chi Minh's body was however contrary to his own wishes: he wanted to be cremated and his ashes placed in three urns to be positioned atop three unmarked hills in the north, centre and south of the country.

Ba Dinh Square

In front of Ho Chi Minh's Mausoleum is Ba Dinh Square where he read out the Vietnamese Declaration of Independence on 2 September 1945. Following Ho Chi Minh's declaration, 2 September became Vietnam's National Day. Coincidentally 2 September was also the date on which he died in 1969, although his death was not officially announced until 3 September.

In front of the mausoleum on Bac Son Street is the **Dai Liet Si**, a memorial to the heroes and martyrs who died fighting for their country's independence. It appears to be modelled as a secular form of stupa and inside is a large bronze urn. The new parliament building, completed in 2014, now also stands proud directly across from the mausoleum.

Ho Chi Minh's house and the Presidential Palace

Ho Chi Minh's house, 1 Bach Thao St, T4-3804 4529; Summer Tue-Thu, Sat and Sun, 0730-1100, 1400-1600, Fri 0730-1100; winter Tue-Thu, Sat and Sun 0800-1100, 1330-1600, Fri 0800-1100, 20,000d; the Presidential Palace is not open to the public.

From the mausoleum, visitors are directed to Ho Chi Minh's house built in the compound of the former Presidential Palace. The palace, now a Party guesthouse, was the residence of the Governors-General of French Indochina and was built between 1900 and 1908 by Auguste-Henri Vildieu. In 1954, when North Vietnam's struggle for independence was finally achieved, Ho Chi Minh declined to live in the palace, saying that it belonged to the people. Instead, he stayed in what is said to have been an electrician's house in the same compound. Here he lived from 1954 to 1958, before moving to a new stilt house built on the other side of the small lake (Ho Chi Minh's 'Fish Farm', swarming with massive and well-fed carp). The house was designed by Ho Chi Minh and an architect, Nguyen Van Ninh. This modest house made of rare hardwoods is airy and personal and immaculately kept. Ho Chi Minh conducted meetings under the house, which is raised up on wooden pillars, and slept and worked above (his books, slippers and telephones are still here) from May 1958 to August 1969. Built by the army, the house mirrors the one he lived in while fighting the French from his haven near the Chinese border. Behind the house is his bomb shelter, and behind that, the hut where he actually died in 1969.

One Pillar Pagoda

Close by is the One Pillar Pagoda (Chua Mot Cot), one of the few structures remaining from the original foundation of the city. It was built in 1049 by Emperor

ON THE ROAD
Syndicated loans keep the sharks away

Throughout Vietnam, and indeed across the world wherever there are large numbers of Vietnamese, one will find *hui* in operation. *Hui* (or *ho* as it is called in the north) is a credit circle of 10 to 20 people who meet every month; the scheme lasts as many months as there are participants. In a blind auction the highest bidder takes home that month's capital. Credit is expensive in Vietnam, partly because there are few banks to make personal loans, so in time of crisis the needy have to borrow from money-lenders at crippling rates of interest. Alternatively they can join a *hui* and borrow at more modest rates.

It works like this: the *hui* is established with members agreeing to put in a fixed amount, say 100,000d, each month. Each month the members bid according to their financial needs, entering a zero bid if they need no cash. If, in month one, Mr Nam's daughter gets married he will require money for the wedding festivities and, moreover, he has to have the money so he must bid high, maybe 25,000d. Assuming this is the highest bid he will receive 75,000d from each member (ie 100,000d less 25,000d). In future months Mr Nam cannot bid again but must pay 100,000d to whoever collects that month's pot. Towards the end of the cycle several participants (those whose buffalo have not died and those whose daughters remain unmarried) will have taken nothing out but will have paid in 100,000d (minus x) dong each month; they can enter a zero bid and get the full 100,000d from all participants and with it a tidy profit. There is, needless to say, strategy involved and this is where the Vietnamese love of gambling ("the besetting sin of the Vietnamese" according to Norman Lewis) colours the picture. One day, Mr Muoi wins one million dong on the Vinh Long lottery. He lets it be known that he intends to buy a Honda Dream, but to raise the necessary purchase price he must 'win' that month's *hui* and will be bidding aggressively. In the same month Thuy, Mrs Phuoc's baby daughter, celebrates her first birthday so Mrs Phuoc needs money to throw a lavish *thoi noi* party. She has heard of old Muoi's intentions but doesn't know if he is serious. In case he is, she will have to bid high. On the day, nice Mrs Phuoc enters a knock-out bid of 30,000d but wily old Muoi was bluffing all along and he and the others make a lot of interest that month.

Ly Thai Tong, although the shrine has since been rebuilt on several occasions, most recently in 1955 after the French destroyed it before withdrawing from the country. The emperor built the pagoda in a fit of religious passion after he dreamt that he saw the goddess Quan Am (Vietnam's equivalent of the Chinese goddess Kuan-yin) sitting on a lotus and holding a young boy, whom she handed to the emperor. On the advice of counsellors who interpreted the dream, the Emperor built this little lotus-shaped temple in the centre of a water-lily pond and shortly afterwards his queen gave birth to a son. As the name suggests, it is supported on a single (concrete) pillar with a brick and stone staircase running up one side. The pagoda

The story of Quan Am

Quan Am was turned onto the streets by her husband for some unspecified wrong-doing and, dressed as a monk, took refuge in a monastery. There, a woman accused her of fathering, and then abandoning, her child. Accepting the blame (why, no one knows), she was again turned out onto the streets, only to return to the monastery much later when she was on the point of death – to confess her true identity. When the Emperor of China heard the tale, he made Quan Am the Guardian Spirit of Mother and Child, and couples without a son now pray to her.

Quan Am's husband is sometimes depicted as a parakeet, with the Goddess usually holding her adopted son in one arm and standing on a lotus leaf (the symbol of purity).

symbolizes the 'pure' lotus sprouting from the sea of sorrow. Original in design, with dragons running along the apex of the elegantly curved tiled roof, the temple is one of the most revered monuments in Vietnam. But the ungainly concrete pillar and the pond of green slime in which it is embedded detract considerably from the enchantment of the little pagoda.

Ho Chi Minh Museum
19 Ngoc Ha St, T4-3846 3752, Tue-Thu and Sat 0800-1130, 1400-1600, Fri 0800-1130, 20,000d.

Overshadowing the One Pillar Pagoda is the Ho Chi Minh Museum – opened in 1990 in celebration of the centenary of Ho Chi Minh's birth. Contained in a large and impressive modern building, likened to a white lotus, its displays trace Ho's life and work from his early wanderings around the world to his death and final victory over the south.

★ Temple of Literature
The entrance on Quoc Tu Giam St, T4-3845 2917, open daily summer 0730-1730, winter daily 0730-1700, 20,000d, 45-min tour in French or English 100,000d, 8000d for brochure.

The Temple of Literature (Van Mieu Pagoda) is the largest, and probably the most important, temple complex in Hanoi. It was founded in 1070 by Emperor Ly Thanh Tong, dedicated to Confucius who had a substantial following in Vietnam, and modelled, so it is said, on a temple in Shantung, China, the birthplace of the sage. Some researchers, while acknowledging the date of foundation, challenge the view that it was built as a Confucian institution pointing to the ascendancy of Buddhism during the Ly Dynasty. Confucian principles and teaching rapidly replaced Buddhism, however, and Van Mieu subsequently became the intellectual and spiritual centre of the kingdom as a cult of literature and education spread among the court, the mandarins and then among the common people. At one time there were said to be 20,000 schools teaching the Confucian classics in northern Vietnam alone.

The temple and its compound are arranged north–south, and visitors enter at the southern end from Quoc Tu Giam Street. On the pavement two pavilions house stelae bearing the inscription *ha ma* (climb down from your horse), a nice reminder that even the most elevated dignitaries had to proceed on foot. The main **Van Mieu Gate** (Cong Van Mieu Mon) is adorned with 15th-century dragons. Traditionally, the large central gate was opened only on ceremonial occasions. The path leads through the Cong Dai Trung to a second courtyard and the **Van Khue Gac Pavilion**, which was built in 1805 and dedicated to the Constellation of Literature. The roof is tiled according to the yin-yang principle.

Beyond lies the **Courtyard of the Stelae** at the centre of which is the rectangular pond or Cieng Thien Quang (Well of Heavenly Clarity). More important are the stelae themselves, 82 in all, on which are recorded the names of 1306 successful examination scholars (*tien si*). Of the 82 that survive (30 are missing) the oldest dates back to 1442 and the most recent to 1779. Each stela is carried on the back of a tortoise, symbol of strength and longevity but they are arranged in no order; three chronological categories, however, can be identified. Fourteen date from the 15th and 16th centuries; they are the smallest and are embellished with floral motifs and yin-yang symbols but not dragons (a royal emblem). Twenty-five stelae are from the 17th century and are ornamented with dragons (by then permitted), pairs of phoenix and other creatures mythical or real. The remaining 43 stelae are of 18th-century origin; they are the largest and are decorated with two stylized dragons, some merging with flame clouds.

Passing the examination was not easy: in 1733, out of some 3000 entrants, only eight passed the doctoral examination (*Thai Hoc Sinh*) and became Mandarins – a task that took 35 days. This tradition was begun in 1484 on the instruction of Emperor Le Thanh Tong, and continued through to 1878, during which time 116 examinations were held. The Temple of Literature was not used only for examinations, however: food was also distributed to the poor and infirm, 500 g of rice at a time. In 1880, the French Consul Monsieur de Kergaradec recorded that 22,000 impoverished people came to receive this meagre handout.

Continuing north, the **Dai Thanh Mon** (Great Success Gate) leads on to a courtyard flanked by two buildings which date from 1954, the originals having been destroyed in 1947. These buildings were reserved for 72 disciples of Confucius. Facing is the **Dai Bai Duong** (Great House of Ceremonies), which was built in the 19th century but in the earlier style of the Le Dynasty. The carved wooden friezes with their dragons, phoenix, lotus flowers, fruits, clouds and yin-yang discs are all symbolically charged, depicting the order of the universe and by implication reflecting the god-given hierarchical nature of human society, each in his place. It is not surprising that the communist government has hitherto had reservations about preserving a temple extolling such heretical doctrine. Inside is an altar on which sit statues of Confucius and his closest disciples. Adjoining is the **Dai Thanh Sanctuary** (Great Success Sanctuary), which also contains a statue of Confucius.

ON THE ROAD
The examination of 1875

The examinations held at the Temple of Literature and which enabled, in theory, even the most lowly peasant to rise to the exalted position of a Mandarin, were long and difficult and conducted with great formality.

André Masson quotes Monsieur de Kergaradec, the French Consul's, account of the examination of 1875.

"On the morning of the big day, from the third watch on, that is around one o'clock in the morning, the big drum which invites each one to present himself began to be beaten and soon students, intermingled with ordinary spectators, approached the Compound in front of the cordon formed around the outer wall by soldiers holding lances. In the middle of the fifth watch, towards four or five o'clock in the morning, the examiners in full dress came and installed themselves with their escorts at the different gates. Then began the roll call of the candidates, who were thoroughly searched at the entrance, and who carried with them a small tent of canvas, and mats, cakes, rice, prepared tea, black ink, one or two brushes and a lamp. Everyone once inside, the gates were closed, and the examiners met in the central pavilion of the candidates' enclosure in order to post the subject of the composition. During the afternoon, the candidates who had finished withdrew a few at a time through the central gate, the last ones did not leave the Compound until midnight."

Doctor Laureate on his way home. From an illustration by H Oger in 1905.

Going to the examination camp with apparatus (bamboo bed, writing box, bamboo tube for examination papers). From an illustration by H Oger in 1905.

To the north once stood the first university in Vietnam, Quoc Tu Giam, which from the 11th to 18th centuries educated first the heir to the throne and later sons of mandarins. It was replaced with a temple dedicated to Confucius' parents and followers, which was itself destroyed in 1947.

Fine Arts Museum

66 Nguyen Thai Hoc St, T4-3733 2131, Tue-Sun 0830-1700, Wed and Sat 0800-2100. Free tours in English or French, register in advance, no photography. Restaurant in museum grounds.

Not far from the northern walls of the Van Mieu Pagoda is the Fine Arts Museum (Bao Tang My Thuat), contained in a large colonial building. The oriental roof was added later when the building was converted to a museum. The ground-floor galleries display pre-20th-century art – from Dongsonian bronze drums to Nguyen Dynasty paintings and sculpture, although many works of this later period are on display in the Museum of Royal Fine Arts in Hué. There are some particularly fine stone Buddhas. The first floor is given over to folk art. There are some lovely works from the Central Highlands and engaging Dong Ho woodblock prints – one block for each colour – and Hang Trong woodblock prints, a single black ink print that is coloured in by hand. There are also some fine lacquer paintings. The top floor contains 20th-century work including some excellent watercolours and oil paintings. Contemporary Vietnamese artists are building a significant reputation for their work. There is a large collection of overtly political work, posters and propaganda (of great interest to historians and specialist collectors), and a collection of ethnic minority clothes is exhibited in the annex.

Vietnam Military History Museum and Citadel

28 Dien Bien Phu St, T4-3733 6453, www.btlsqsvn.org.vn, Tue-Thu, Sat and Sun 0800 1130, 1300-1630, 20,000d, camera use, 5000d, ATM and Highlands Coffee Café on site.

A five-minute walk east from the Fine Arts Museum is the Military History Museum (Bao Tang Quan Doi). Tanks, planes and artillery fill the courtyard. Symbolically, an untouched Mig-21 stands at the museum entrance while wreckage of B-52s, F1-11s and Q2Cs is piled up at the back. The museum illustrates battles and episodes in Vietnam's fight for independence from the struggles with China (there is a good display of the Battle of Bach Dang River of AD 938) through to the resistance to the French and the Battle of Dien Bien Phu (illustrated by a good model). Inevitably, of course, there are lots of photographs and exhibits of the American War and although much is self-evident, unfortunately a lot of the explanations are in Vietnamese only.

In the precincts of the museum is the Cot Co, a flag tower, raised up on three platforms. Built in 1812, it is the only substantial part of the original citadel still standing. There are good views over Hanoi from the top. The walls of the citadel were destroyed by the French in 1894 to 1897, presumably as they symbolized the power of the Vietnamese emperors. The French were highly conscious of the projection of might, power and authority through large structures, which helps explain their own remarkable architectural legacy. Across the road from the museum's front entrance is a **statue of Lenin**.

★ The Citadel

The UNESCO listed Citadel complex received protected status in 2010 honouring the site's importance as a military base for centuries. Work began in the 11th century on the Thang Long citadel complex by Emperor Ly Thai To. The site is home to more modern additions too, including the concrete bunker in which general Giap and his fellow officers planned their campaigns against the US invaders in the South. An exhibition space features old artefacts found when construction of the new Assembly building and also some interesting old pictures of the area. Apart from the history, this is one of the capital's most peaceful enclaves and the grounds are a lovely place to wander and enjoy some (relative) quiet. Long closed to the public, this is a relatively new tourist site in the capital and a great addition, especially for history buffs.

Vietnamese Women's Museum

36 Ly Thuong Kiet St, T4-3825 9936, www.baotangphunu.org.vn, daily 0900-1630, closed Mon, 30,000d.

A well-curated, fascinating museum containing 25,000 objects and documents that give visitors an excellent insight in to women's roles in Vietnam, past and present. Information on many of the country's 54 ethnic groups is displayed. It holds regular exhibitions and is highly recommended.

Outer Hanoi

lakes, temples and museums worth exploring

★ North of the Old City

North of the Old City is **Ho Truc Bach (White Silk Lake)**. Truc Bach Lake was created in the 17th century by building a causeway across the southeast corner of Ho Tay. At the southwest corner of the lake, on the intersection of Hung Vuong, Quan Thanh and Thanh Nien streets is the **Quan Thanh Pagoda** was originally built in the early 11th century in honour of Huyen Thien Tran Vo (a genie) but since has been much remodelled. Despite renovation, it is still very beautiful. The large bronze bell was cast in 1677.

To the east of here the Long Bien and Chuong Duong bridges cross the Red River. The former of these two bridges was built as a road and rail bridge by Daydé & Pillé of Paris and named **Paul Doumer Bridge** after the Governor General of the time. Construction was begun in 1899 and it was opened by Emperor Thanh Thai on 28 February 1902. Today it is used by trains, bicycles, motorbikes and pedestrians and is widely used for wedding photographs. Over 1.5 km in length, it was the only river crossing in existence during the Vietnam War and suffered repeated attacks from US planes, only to be quickly repaired. The Chuong Duong Bridge was completed at the beginning of the 1980s.

The much larger **Ho Tay (West Lake)** was originally a meander in the Red River. The **Tran Quoc Pagoda**, an attractive brick-red building, can be found on an islet linked to the causeway by a walkway. It was originally built on the banks of the

Red River before being transferred to its present site by way of an intermediate location. The pagoda contains a stela dated 1639 recounting its unsettled history. It is a popular place of worship and sees massive crowds around Tet (New Year). Just south, pedaloes called 'dap vit' are available for hire. Opposite, facing Truc Bach Lake, is a monument recording the shooting down of USAF's John (now US Senator) McCain on 26 October 1967. It reveals the pilot falling out of the sky, knees bent.

A few kilometres north, on the tip of a promontory, stands **Tay Ho Pagoda**, notable chiefly for its setting. It is reached along a narrow lane lined with stalls selling fruit, roses and paper votives and a dozen restaurants serving giant snails with bun oc (noodles) and fried shrimp cakes. Dominating it is an enormous bronze bell held by a giant dragon hook supported by concrete dragons and two elephants; notice the realistic glass eyes of the elephants.

A cycle around West Lake is a pleasure and there are tens of little local coffee shops lining the route as well as a healthy group of bars and restaurants along Quang An. Xuan Dieu street runs alongside the lake and signals the start of the expat enclave concentrated around To Ngoc Van Street where there are lots of cafés and eateries as well as some of the city's best late-night bars including Madake and Hanoi Rock City.

★Museum of Ethnology and B-52 memorials

Some distance west of the city centre in Cau Giay District (Nguyen Van Huyen Rd), T4-3756 2193, www.vme.org.vn, Tue-Sun 0830-1730, 25,000d, photography 50,000d, tour guide, 50,000d. Catch No 14 minibus from Dinh Tien Hoang St, north of Hoan Kiem Lake, to the Nghia Tan stop; turn right and walk down Hoang Quoc Viet St for 1 block, before turning right at the Petrolimex station down Nguyen Van Huyen; the museum is down this street, on the left. Alternatively take a taxi. Branch of Baguette & Chocolat bakery on site.

The museum opened in November 1997 in a modern, purpose-built structure. The collection here of some 25,000 artefacts, 15,000 photographs and documentaries of practices and rituals is excellent and, more to the point, is attractively and informatively presented with labels in Vietnamese, English and French. It displays the material culture (textiles, musical instruments, jewellery, tools, baskets and the like) of the majority Kinh people as well as Vietnam's 53 other designated minority peoples. The highlight is wandering the gardens at the rear where ethnic minority homes have been moved from their original homes and painstakingly re-built. There is a very good shop attached to the museum.

On the routes out to the Ethnology Museum are two B-52 memorials. The remains of downed B-52s have been hawked around Hanoi over many years but seem to have found a final resting place at the **Bao Tang Chien Tang B-52 (B-52 Museum)** ⓘ *157 Doi Can St, free.* This curious place is not really a museum but a military hardware graveyard, but this doesn't matter because what everyone wants to do is walk over the wings and tail of a shattered B-52, and the B-52 in question lies scattered around the yard. The size and strength of the B-52 is simply incredible and needs to be seen to be believed.

On Hoang Hoa Tham Street, between Nos 55 and 57, a sign points 100 m down an alley to the wreckage of a B-52 bomber sticking up out of the pond-like Huu Tiep Lake. There's a plaque on the wall stating that at 2305 on 27 December 1972, Battalion 72 of Regiment 285 shot down the plane. At the time Huu Tiep was a flower village and the lake a lot bigger.

South of Hanoi

Down Pho Hué Street is the hub of motorcycle sales, parts and repairs. Off this street, for example along Hoa Ma, Tran Nhan Tong and Thinh Yen, are numerous stalls and shops, each specializing in a single type of product – TVs, electric fans, bicycle parts and so on. It is a fascinating area to explore. At the intersection of Thinh Yen and Pho 332, people congregate to sell new and second-hand bicycles, as well as bicycle parts. Nearby Trieu Viet Vuong Street is lined with old school Hanoi coffee shops and is worth a wander.

Not far away is the venerable **Den Hai Ba Trung (Hai Ba Trung Temple)** ① *open 1st and 15th of each lunar month, 0600-1800, free,* the temple of the two Trung Sisters – overlooking a lake. The temple was built in 1142, but, like others, has been restored on a number of occasions. It contains crude statues of the Trung sisters, Trung Trac and Trung Nhi (see box, opposite), which are carried in procession once a year during February.

Around Hanoi

ancient pagodas and mountainous national parks

Compared with Ho Chi Minh City and the south, Hanoi and its surrounds are rich in places of interest. Not only is the landscape more varied and attractive, but the 1000-year-old history of Hanoi has generated dozens of sights of architectural appeal, many of which can be visited on a day trip.

Co Loa Citadel
16 km north of Hanoi. Drive north up Highway 3, Co Loa is signposted to the east.

In the third-century BC Co Loa Citadel was the region's capital, built by King An Duong with walls in three concentric rings; the outer ring is 8 km in circumference. It is an important Bronze Age site and thousands of arrow heads and three bronze ploughshares have been excavated here. Today there is little to see as electricity sub-stations and farms have obliterated much of archaeological interest.

Hung Kings' Temples
South of Yen Bai and approximately 100 km northwest of Hanoi near the industrial town of Viet Tri in Vinh Phu Province; turn off Highway 2 about 12 km north of Viet Tri; it's a morning or afternoon excursion by car from Hanoi.

The Hung Kings' Temples (Phong Chau) are popular with Vietnamese visitors especially during the **Hung Kings' Festival**. In purely topographical terms the site is striking, an almost perfectly circular hill rising unexpectedly out of the monotonous Red River

ON THE ROAD
The Trung sisters

Vietnamese history honours a number of heroines, of whom the Trung sisters are among the most revered. At the beginning of the Christian era, the Lac Lords of Vietnam began to agitate against Chinese control over their lands. Trung Trac, married to the Lac Lord Thi Sach, was apparently of a 'brave and fearless disposition' and encouraged her husband and the other lords to rise up against the Chinese in AD 40. The two sisters often fought while pregnant, apparently putting on gold-plated armour over their enlarged bellies. Although an independent kingdom was created for a short time, ultimately the uprising proved fruitless; a large Chinese army defeated the rebels in AD 43, and eventually captured Trung Trac and her sister Trung Nhi, executing them and sending their heads to the Han court at Lo-yang. An alternative story of their death has it that the sisters threw themselves into the Hat Giang River to avoid being captured, and turned into stone statues. These were washed ashore and placed in Hanoi's Hai Ba Trung Temple for worship.

floodplain with two lakes at the bottom. Given its peculiar physical setting it is easy to understand how the site acquired its mythical reputation as the birthplace of the Viet people and why the Hung Vuong kings chose it as the capital of their kingdom.

In this place, myth and historical fact have become intertwined. Legend has it that the Viet people are the product of the union of King Lac Long Quan, a dragon, and his fairy wife Au Co. Au Co gave birth to a pouch containing 100 eggs that hatched 50 boys and 50 girls. Husband and wife decided to separate in order to populate the land and propagate the race, so half the children followed their mother to the highlands and half remained with their father on the plains, giving rise to the Montagnards and lowland peoples of Vietnam. Historically easier to verify is the story of the Hung kings (Hung Vuong) who built a temple in order to commemorate the legendary progenitors of the Vietnamese people.

Hung Kings' Museum ⓘ *0800-1130, 1300-1600*. A new museum was opened in mid-2010 and displays interesting items excavated from the province. Exhibits include pottery, jewellery, fish hooks, arrow heads and axe heads (dated 1000-1300 BC), but of particular interest are the bronze drums dating from the Dongsonian period. The Dongsonian was a transitional period between the Neolithic and bronze ages and the drums are thought to originate from around the fifth to the third centuries BC. Photographs show excavation in the 1960s when these items were uncovered.

Memorial to Ho Chi Minh Ascending the hill, a track leads to a memorial to Ho Chi Minh. Nearby is the Low Temple dedicated to Au Co, mother of the country and supposedly the site where the 100 eggs were produced. At the back of the temple is a statue of the Buddha of a thousand arms and a thousand eyes. Continuing up the hill is the **Middle Temple** where Prince Lang Lieu was crowned seventh Hung king and where the kings would play chess and discuss pressing affairs of state. Prince Lang Lieu was (like the English King Alfred) something of a dab hand in the kitchen and his most enduring creation is a pair of cakes, *banh trung* and *banh day*, which to this day remain popular, eaten at Tet. This temple has three altars and attractive murals.

Oath stone Further on, towards the top of the hill, is the oath stone on which the 18th Hung king, Thuc Phan, swore to defend the country from its enemies.

Top Temple Adjacent is the Top Temple dating from the 15th century. The roof is adorned with dragons and gaudily painted mural warriors stand guard outside. A not particularly ancient drum hangs from the ceiling but smoke rising from burning incense on the three altars helps add to the antiquity of the setting. It was here that the kings would supplicate God for peace and prosperity.

Well Temple Steps lead from the back right-hand side of this temple down the hill to the mausoleum of the sixth Hung king. These steps then continue down the far side of the hill to the Well Temple built in memory of the last princess of the Hung Dynasty. Inside is a well in the reflection of which this girl used to comb her hair. Today worshippers throw money in and, it is said, they even drink the water. Turn right to get back to the car park.

Perfume Pagoda
50,000d entrance plus 40,000d/person for the boat (maximum 6 people). Taking a tour is the best way to get here.

The Perfume Pagoda (Chua Huong or Chua Huong Tich) is 60 km southwest of Hanoi. A sampan takes visitors along the Yen River, a diverting 4-km ride through a flooded landscape to the Mountain of the Perfume Traces. From here it is a 3-km hike up the mountain to the cool, dark cave wherein lies the Perfume Pagoda. Dedicated to Quan Am (see box, page 48), it is one of a number of shrines and towers built among limestone caves, and it is regarded as one of the most beautiful spots in Vietnam. The stone statue of Quan Am in the principal pagoda was carved in 1793 after Tay Son rebels had stolen and melted down its bronze predecessor to make cannon balls. Emperor Le Thanh Tong (1460-1497) described it as "Nam Thien de nhat dong" (foremost cave under the Vietnamese sky). It is a popular pilgrimage spot, particularly during the festival months of March and April.

Handicraft villages
Many tour operators arrange excursions to villages just outside of Hanoi including Van Phuc, where silk is produced, Bat Trang, where ceramics and bricks are made, and Le Mat, a snake village; here visitors can eat snake meat.

Ba Vi National Park
Ba Vi National Park is 50 km to the west of Hanoi and features a mountain up which a road climbs steeply gaining 1000 m in height. From the car park it's possible to walk

up a wooden path to a pagoda with a fine lookout. There are plenty of other tourist sites on the mountain including an old church, small waterfalls and pretty streams.

Further afield
Cuc Phuong National Park (see page 137 for details) is about 160 km south of Hanoi and can be visited as a day trip or over-nighter from Hanoi or as an excursion from Ninh Binh. Other possible day trips are excursions to **Hoa Binh** (see page 79) and **Mai Chau** (see page 79), **Haiphong** (see page 121) **Ninh Binh** (see page 133), **Hoa Lu** (see page 134), **Tam Coc** (see page 135) and **Phat Diem Cathedral** (see page 136).

Listings Hanoi *maps p36 and p41*

Tourist information

Tourist Information Center
7 Dinh Tien Hoang St, at the northern end of the lake, T4-3926 3366, www. ticvietnam.com. Daily 0800-2200.
Provides information and maps and will book hotels and transport tickets at no extra cost; also currency exchange and ATM. Good tourist information is available from the multitude of tour operators In the city, see also page 69.

Where to stay

There has been a spate of hotel building and renovation in recent years and Hanoi is now home to an excellent variety of high-quality accommodation for every budget. Cheaper hotels tend to be found in the Old Quarter.

Hoan Kiem Lake and Central Hanoi

$$$$ Sofitel Legend Metropole Hanoi
15 Ngo Quyen St, T4-3826 6919, www.sofitel.com.
The French-colonial-style cream building with green shutters is beautifully and lusciously furnished and exudes style. It boasts a diversity of bars and restaurants including the Italian **Angelina** restaurant. **Le Beaulieu** is

one of the finest restaurants in Hanoi; a pianist plays nightly at **Le Club** bar. The **Le Spa du Metropole** is seriously chic. There's also a business centre, cluster of luxury shops and smart deli, and a small pool with attractive poolside **Bamboo Bar**. The hotel has retained most of its business despite competition from newer business hotels away from the city centre and remains a hub of activity and the classiest hotel address in the country. The Graham Greene suite is sumptuous Indochine chic.

$$$ Cinnamon Hotel
26 Au Trieu St, T4-3993 8430, www.cinnamonhotel.net.
This is a stylish boutique hotel with lovely, comfortable rooms. Part of a small chain with other hotels elsewhere in Hanoi and down in Saigon. The regular bong of the cathedral bell may be disturbing so you may wish to avoid the cute balconied rooms overlooking the cathedral square and opt for a back room with a lesser view.

$$$ Golden Lotus Hotel
39 Hang Trong St, T4-3928 8583, www.goldenlotushotel.com.vn.
The **Golden Lotus** has a series of smart, attractive rooms from standard single to deluxe. Dark woods, smart white linens

and black and white photography create a smart space.

$$ Joseph's Hotel
5 Au Trieu St, T4-3938 1048, www.josephshotel.com.
Right near St Joseph's Cathedral, on Au Trieu St – a cosy street filled with good cafés, salons and souvenir shops – Joseph's Hotel is small, with just 10 smart, very clean rooms. Some rooms have a great view over the cathedral at the rear and others have tiny balconies facing the street. Recommended.

$$ Paradise Boutique Hotel
62A Hang Bac St, T4-3935 1556, www.paradiseboutiquehotel.com.
Right in the heart of the Old Quarter, this small hotel offers a range of clean rooms, each with a desk and a computer, bright white linens and good en suite bathroom. Some rooms have little balconies giving great views over the buzzing street below. Despite the central location, the rooms remain very quiet thanks to some serious double glazing. Extremely friendly staff who make a point of remembering guests' names. Highly recommended at this price.

$ Gold Spring Hotel
22 Nguyen Huu Huan St, T4-3926 3057, www.goldspringhotel.com.vn.
On the edge of the Old Quarter. 22 fine rooms that are simply decorated. Breakfast and free internet included. Good value.

$ Maison d'Orient
26 Ngo Huyen (off Hang Trong), T4-3938 2539, www.maison-orient.com.
This is a real find in the budget range. Designed by an award-winning architect, it's a unique place with one-off furniture, propaganda prints and lots of pretty touches such as red lacquer lamps and colonial-era easy chairs. There is also a beautiful breakfast room and the location is excellent. Highly recommended.

South of Hoan Kiem Lake

$$$$ Hilton Hanoi Opera
1 Le Thanh Tong St, T4-3933 0500, www1.hilton.com.
Opened in 1999 and built adjacent to, and architecturally sympathetically with, the Opera House. It is a splendid building and provides the highest levels of service and hospitality.

$$$$ Meliá Hanoi
44B Ly Thuong Kiet St, T4-3934 3343, www.meliahanoi.com.
A huge tower block in Central Hanoi. Well-appointed rooms. Popular venue for international conferences. Excellent buffets and brunches.

$$$$ Movenpick
83A Ly Thuong Kiet St, T4-3822 2800, www.movenpick-hotels.com.
Formerly the Guoman this Swiss-run hotel chain is housed in an attractive building on Ly Thuong Kiet Street, in the middle of Hanoi's business district. Rooms are smart and stylish.

$$$ Zephyr
4 Ba Trieu St, T4-3934 1256, www.zephyrhotel.com.vn.
A little business-like, but nonetheless very popular hotel, largely due to its excellent location within sight of Hoan Kiem Lake and solid service. Serves a good breakfast, including *pho* and international options.

Outer Hanoi
Hanoi's relatively small central district means that some new office complexes and hotels have tended to open a short distance out of the centre.

$$$$ InterContinental Hanoi Westlake
1A Nghi Tam, Tay Ho District, T4-6270 8888, www.ichotelsgroup.com/ intercontinental.
This is a brilliant hotel and one of Vietnam's finest with its fantastic over-water rooms and great views of the lake. Rooms are large and decorated using traditional Vietnamese elements. Fantastic buffet breakfast and impeccable service. The **Sunset Bar** here is a great place for a sundowner. Wonderful pool area too. Highly recommended.

$$$$ Sheraton Hotel
K5 Nghi Tam, 11 Xuan Dieu, Tay Ho District, T4-3719 9000, wwwsheraton.com/hanoi.
Opened in early 2004, the **Sheraton** has a scenic spot overlooking West Lake. It offers luxurious rooms and the swimming pool backs onto a lawn that leads down to the lakeshore.

$$$$ Sofitel Plaza Hanoi
1 Thanh Nien St, T4-3823 8888, www.Sofitel.com.
The 2nd Sofitel in town, it lacks the cache of the **Metropole** but is in an equally good location, by Truc Bach Lake. The rooftop bar, Summit Lounge, has the best views in town and is a must-visit for sunset cocktails.

$$$ La Maison Hai Ly
No 8, 437 Ngoc Thuy, Long Bien, T4-3976 6246.
On the far side of Long Bien Bridge, this is an extraordinarily beautiful replica of an 18th-century Hoi An house standing in a private flower garden. The property includes polished wood floors and a huge glass front with views on to a garden from a grand living area. Very elegant and very highly recommended for those seeking something truly unique.

Restaurants

Hanoi has one of the best street food cultures in the world and a growing band of excellent Western-style restaurants offering everything from great steaks to tapas and wood-fired pizzas. Korean and Japanese food is abundant and well priced.

Hoan Kiem Lake and Central Hanoi

$$$ Le Beaulieu
15 Ngo Quyen St (in the Metropole Hotel), T4-3826 6919.
A place to treat yourself in the wonderful surrounds of the classic Metropole, this is a good French and international restaurant open for breakfast, lunch and dinner. Its Sun brunch buffet is regarded as one of the best. A great selection of French seafood, oysters, prawns, cold and roast meats and cheese.

$$$ Pots n Pans
57 Bui Thi Xuan, T4-3944 0204, www.potsnpans.vn. Daily 1130-late.
An offshoot of the **KOTO** training school restaurant, this minimalist upmarket fusion restaurant serves some of the capital's most innovative cuisine. Also offers an excellent wine list and well-mixed cocktails. Best to dine on a weekend when it is busier – be sure to book ahead.

$$$ Verticale
19 Ngo Van So St, T4-3944 6317, verticale@didiercorlou.com. Open 0900-1400, 1700-2400.
Didier Corlou, former chef at the **Sofitel Metropole**, runs this restaurant. The tall multi-storey building includes a shop, restaurant, private rooms and a terrace bar. The food and presentation are an adventurous culinary journey of gustatory delight; this is certainly one of

the best dining experiences in the city for those who like high-end dining.

$$$-$$ La Badiane
10 Nam Ngu St, T4-3942 4509.
Run by a couple of Hanoi old hands, **La Badiane's** French aesthetic stops at the food. Fusion is what this restaurant is about and while its intricately decorated plates of seasonal meals won't appeal to everyone there are many who swear this is the best restaurant in town. Service is good, if over-attentive at times. The converted colonial villa is delightful. The set lunch menu is a very good deal indeed.

$$$-$ Green Tangerine
48 Hang Be St, T4-3825 1286,
greentangerine@vnn.vn.
This is a fanciful and rather touristy restaurant that is worth a visit for the courtyard seating or the indoor dining area with its lovely spiral staircase, wafting fans, tasselled curtains and abundant glassware. It's a Hanoi stalwart in a lovely 1928 house in the centre of the Old Quarter serving slightly fruit-heavy fusion and Vietnamese food. Best to come for the good value set lunch as the evening à la carte menu is a little overpriced for the quality.

$$ Luna d'Autonno
Nam Ngu St, T4-3823 7338.
Regarded as one of the city's best Italian restaurants, **Luna** has a large menu and the pizzas – particularly the *diavola* – are excellent.

$$ Moose and Roo
42 Ma May, T4-3200 1289. Daily 1000-late.
Opened in 2014, this Aussie-run joint has quickly established itself as a firm favourite with expats. The pork hash is delectable, the burgers are first-rate and the Sunday roasts are the finest in

town. Also runs the **Smoke House** at the American Club on Hai Ba Trung where massive ribs and hunks of barbecued beef are drawing accolades.

$$ Namaste
49 Tho Nhuom, T4-3935 2400, www. namastehanoi.com. Daily 1100-late.
Run by Mr Gopi this is a runner for best Indian in town. It lacks the views of **Foodshop 45**, but it serves a range of excellent curries including a great balti, and the lemon rice is second to none. Good service, but the ambience can be rather lacking.

$$-$ Chim Sáo
65 Ngo Hue St, T4-3976 0633, www. chimsao.com.
Set in an atmospheric old colonial villa, **Chim Sáo** is famous for its Northern Vietnamese food. highlights include the grilled buffalo, ethnic minority sausage, sautéed duck and the pork in a clay pot. Serves good rice wine too – try the apple variety for a milder version. Seating upstairs is on floor cushions, so book a downstairs table if needs be.

$$-$ Highway 4
3 Hang Tre St, T4-3926 4200, www. highway4.com. Open 0900-0200.
With funky decor and a variety of different cosy dining rooms, Highway 4 specializes in ethnic minority dishes from North Vietnam and also serves dishes from around the country. The popularity of the Highway 4 concept has seen it spread across Hanoi and as far afield as Hoi An. Also serves a great range of local rice wines from Son Tinh.

$$-$ Quan An Ngon
18 Phan Boi Chau St, T4-3942 8162, www. ngonhanoi.com.vn. Daily 0700-2130.
This place is insanely popular at lunch and dinner time with locals as well

Mark Lowerson has lived in Hanoi since 2002. Together with his partner, Tu, he runs Street Eats Hanoi.

What change have you seen in Hanoi's culinary scene since you arrived?
At the level that I tend to roll in – street food – there hasn't been much change at all. I'm still eating at some of the same vendors I discovered during my first year here. *Pho* is still *pho*, *bun cha* is still *bun cha* and, as far as Hanoians are concerned, you'd better not mess with it!

Hanoi is a city of seasons. What's your favourite summer dish and what do you love to eat during winter?
Dishes don't actually change that much according to season. People are just as likely to be chowing down on a steaming bowl of *pho* in 38°C heat as they are in 8°C cold. I've adapted. One dish I do love in the winter is called *banh gio*, a kind of ugly wobbling mess of tapioca and rice flour at the core of which is minced pork, wood-ear fungus and shallot all steamed in either a banana or 'dong' leaf and liberally doused in hot sauce. It's fabulous winter comfort food.

The city is best known for its beef *pho*, but where do you head for the chicken variety?
I have a few 'go-to' chicken *pho* houses in Hanoi. One is just north of the Old Quarter near the old water tower at 34 Quan Thanh.

What has been your most recent and enjoyable food discovery?
Recently, we discovered a fantastic chicken salad (*nom ga*) vendor in the Old Quarter who's been there for 20 years. We thought we just about knew the street food in that part of town like the back of our hands. Sometimes it's about being in a certain street at a certain time of day.

as tourists. In a massive and very pretty open-air courtyard setting with enormous umbrellas shading wooden tables. Diners can wander around looking at all the street food style stalls each making just 1 or 2 of the dishes from the vast menu. This is a great place for an introduction to food from all over Vietnam. There are now sister branches around town – check the website for addresses.

$$-$ Ray Quan
8A Nguyen Khuyen, T9-1357 8588.
Daily 1100-late.

It is reached by literally walking along the train tracks from Hai Ba Trung St. This quirky place offers the option to dine feet away from the trains as they thunder past. Serves a fantastic array of Vietnamese dishes from the mainstream to some very curious options. Also has one of the best rice wine menus in town including a very good cinnamon version… you've been warned!

$ Café 129
129 Mai Hac De St.
A real oddity, this is a hole-in-the wall place run by Vietnamese ladies

serving huge US, Canadian and English breakfasts alongside filling Mexican meals. Chiefly popular with the English teacher set.

$ Com Chay Nang Tam
79A Tran Hung Dao St, T4-3942 4140. Open 1100-1400, 1700-2200.
A hit with veggies, this is hidden down an alley off Tran Hung Dao St and serves excellent and inexpensive dishes in a small, family-style dining room.

$ Net Hue
36C Mai Hac De, www.nethue.com.vn, T4-3944 9769. Daily 1030-2200.
Excellent classic Hué dishes including *bun bo nam no* and a superb *bun thit nuong*. Order a few dishes to share. Rather raucous at lunch times with crowds of office workers. There are a number of **Net Hue** restaurants – see the website.

Cafés
Hanoi probably has more cafés per square foot than anywhere in the world. Almost every street has at least one simple café with tiny plastic stools on which Hanoians enjoy a *ca phd da* (iced coffee) in warmer months or a *ca phe nong* (hot) in winter. Until a few years ago there was very little other than these old school coffee houses, but recently the caffeine scene has exploded with modern local and foreign run cafés completing the more traditional options. Alongside this, the likes of **Coffee Bean** and **Tea Leaf** and **Starbucks** are attempting to muscle into the market, but the Hanoian's love of Vietnamese coffee and quirky one-off coffee shops means the individuality of the coffee culture looks set to remain strong. For a local café experience, it is best to simply wander the streets of the Old Quarter,

take a stroll along Trieu Viet Vuong or check out the road lining Truc Bach Lake – there are hundreds of places to choose from.

Café Puku
16/18 Tong Duy Tan St, T4-3928 5244.
An old favourite, **Puku** was one of the first modern, Western-style cafés to open. Alongside coffee it serves a good range of comfort food. It is also now open 24 hrs and there is a sports bar upstairs at the rear.

Cong Café
152D Trieu Viet Vuong St.
This is the original **Cong Café** but there now upwards of 12 scattered around town and as far afield as Danang. Hugely popular thanks to the great retro/military design as well as excellent coffee and smoothies. Other good Congs can be found on Dien Bien Phu, Quan Su, opposite St Joseph's Cathedral and at Truc Bach.

Hanoi Social Club
6 Hoi Vu, T4-9382117, facebook.com/ TheHanoiSocialClub.
On one of Hanoi's quieter little lanes, this Aussie-Viet partnership is a major hit. Set over 3 floors in an old town house with beautiful caustic tiled floors and comfy, funky furniture with art, music posters, and great tunes. Serves a small menu of quality international dishes and first-rate coffee. Also sells books, courtesy of **The Bookworm** store. Great roof terrace. Regular live music.

The Kafe
18 Dien Bien Phu, T4-3747 6245, www.thekafe.vn. Daily 0800-late.
Popular with Hanoi's younger crowd and hipster set, **The Kafe** has a bright, airy indoor space with whitewashed walls and light wooden tables plus a

small outdoor terrace area. Alongside the drinks is a food menu that resembles a Jamie Oliver cookbook with a range of tapas style dishes, plus burgers, fried chicken and some great salads. The freshly made fruit juices and shakes are excellent – try the carrot and apple. Also now has a sister branch, the **Kafe Village**, over at 4 Ha Hoi.

Manzi
14 Phan Huy Ich, T4-3716 3397.
Daily 0900-late.
Housed in a beautiful old colonial villa, **Manzi** is part café, part gallery and part art shop. Owned by artists and run for the artistic community, it hosts shows and talks. The coffee is good, the staff are friendly and the space is gorgeous, with whitewashed walls allowing the artwork to shine.

Ice cream

Fanny Ice Cream
Ly Thuong Khiet St, T4-3828 5656,
www.fanny.com.vn.
A huge range of ice creams and sorbet with an ice cream buffet on weekends.

Kem Trang Tien
35 Trang Tien St.
This is probably the most popular ice cream parlour in the city and it's a drive-in and park your moto affair. It's also a flirt joint for Hanoian young things. Flavours are cheap and change as to what's available.

Ho Chi Minh's Mausoleum complex and around

$$-$ KOTO
59 Van Mieu St, T4-3747 0337,
www.koto.com.au. Mon 0730-1800,
Tue-Sun 0730-2230.
A training restaurant for underprivileged young people. Next to the **Temple of Literature** so an ideal place to pop in for a good lunch after a morning's sightseeing. The food is international, filling and delicious. Upstairs is the **Temple Bar** serving good cocktails. Recommended.

Outer Hanoi
The following places are located north of the old city.

$$$ El Gaucho
99 Xuan Dieu, T4-3718 6991,
www.elgaucho.asia.
Perhaps the best steak in town – all the cuts negate the need for any of the sauces on offer and certainly merit the journey from the city centre. The chicken dishes are less inspiring, however – stick to the beef. Cool, bare-brick surroundings. Superb cocktails and a good cellar.

$$$-$$ Cousins
Quang Ba on Quang An, T12-3867 0098.
Daily 0900-late.
Tucked away at the north of West Lake, is a French-run bistro offering an interesting range of European dishes and daily specials. Slightly hipster and arty vibe, but welcoming with a lovely outdoor courtyard space. Good wine list and a decent house red. A recommended stop on your Tay Ho excursion.

$$$-$$ Republic
7A Quang An, T4-6687 1773,
www.republic.vn.
Part bar, part restaurant, **Republic** is another of the new places to take advantage of the lake front location along Quang An. Highlights of the menu include the pies with superbly light crusts and the fish and chips. The only

real downside is the starters are bizarrely expensive. Gets very busy on weekends when DJs play later on.

$$ Da Paulo
18 Lane 50 Dang Thai Mai St, T4-3718 6317. Daily 1100-late.
The location of this Italian restaurant is unrivalled looking out across the West Lake. Serves great food across the board from pizzas to pastas. On a fine day it is nicer to sit at a nearby café right on the lake and order the excellent wood fired pizzas takeaway and enjoy them with a cool lemon *sinh to* (shake) with the breeze blowing off the water. Inside, the upstairs area is cosier than downstairs.

$$ Hanoi Cooking Centre
44 Chau Long St, T4-3715 0088, www.hanoicookingcentre.com.
Lunch and breakfast only. A restaurant, café and cooking centre housed in a restored colonial villa near Truc Bach Lake. Some good Vietnamese options and also an excellent fish and chips and a solid falafel. Serves some of the best coffee in town too with a particularly good latte. Great staff. The upper floor can also be hired for functions.

$$ La Bicicleta
44 Alley 31 Xuan Dieu St, T4-3718 8246. Open 1130-late, closed Mon.
This restaurant started life as a bike shop, with the Catalan owner, Guim, converting it when his cravings for authentic Barcelona tapas became too strong. Also serves hot chocolate with churros and massive gins and tonics. Not the easiest place to find deep down an alleyway, but it is now signposted off Quang An and Xuan Dieu sts.

$$ Maison Tet Decor
36 Duong Ven Ho, T9-6661 1383, www.tet-lifestyle-collection.com. Open 0700-2300.

Bursting with character, this is a popular Tay Ho neighbourhood spot thanks to its excellent coffee, wonderful decor, home-made cakes and quiches and a solid wine list. Most of the produce is sourced from a dedicated organic farm not far from the capital.

$$ Pho Yen
66 Cua Bac St, T4-3715 0269.
This down-at-heel tables and chair joint does tasty *pho cuon*. Popular with locals.

$$-$ Chien Beo
192 Nghi Tam St, T4-3716 1461.
A Vietnamese steakhouse named after the rather portly owner who clearly enjoys his product. Serves huge platters of beef and other meats. Best to come in a group as the portions are gargantuan. Can get quite rowdy.

$ Foodshop 45
59 Truc Bach St.
A Vietnamese-run Indian restaurant with a very pretty location on Truc Bach Lake. Consistently good food for years and very welcoming, swift service. Don't miss the chicken kalmi kebab.

Bars and clubs

Hanoi's main bar street is Ta Hien, heading towards Hang Buom after it has cut across the famous Bia Hoi Corner (at Luong Ngoc Quyen). The bar scene here has exploded in recent years and now there are too many to count and the atmosphere almost every night is buzzing.

+84
23 Ngo Van So, T3-943 4540. Daily 0900-late.
Run by some of the people behind Barbetta, this bar wouldn't look out of place in East London with its bare brick

walls, dark red paint and well-stocked bar. Has live music 3 or 4 nights a week and a good vibe.

Barbetta
34C Cao Ba Quat, T4-3734 9134.
Barbetta is one of a kind. Inside it's chock full of retro knick knacks, from TV sets to type writers, while the rooftop terrace is a great spot for a well-mixed cocktail (if Cuong is behind the bar at least).

CAMA ATK
Mai Hac De. Wed-Sat 1800-2400. Happy hour 1800-2000.
Run by the boys behind Hanoi's music promotion collective – CAMA – this is a very welcome addition. Superb cocktails, regular DJ sets and film nights. No smoking.

GC
5A Bao Khanh St, T4-3825 0499.
A popular 'gay friendly' bar a few doors away from **Polite Pub**, the GC (orginally the **Golden Cock**) has been around a long time and is still crowded years on.

Hanoi Rock City
27 To Ngoc Van, T9-1351 5356, www.hanoirockcity.com.
Around the corner from Madake in the heart of expat-ville, 'HRC' is run by a Vietnamese-British partnership with a focus on live music, DJ nights and art shows. Has a great courtyard with an open fire. Depending on the night the atmosphere can be buzzing or chilled out. A great venue.

Hoa Vien
1 Tang Bat Ho St, T4-3972 5088.
Possibly the biggest and best-known of Hanoi's European-style beer halls, **Hoa Vien** is a multi-level behemoth serving beer in glasses ranging from standard to 1 litre steins. Pilsner and dark beer are both on offer as well as heart-clogging wonders such as Russian salad and pork cutlets.

Madake
81 Xuan Dieu, T4-6276 6665. Daily 0930-late.
A very welcome addition to the DJ and live music scene in the capital, **Madake** is a venue of 3 parts. The upstairs bar has a minimalist vibe, the leafy outdoor courtyard backs onto a small lake and the main music room is a brilliantly intimate space for live music with a quality sound system.

Phuc Tan Bar
Phuc Tan St, T915-9077 8551.
An out and out dive bar club. Come the weekend there are precious few places open very late at night where you can both drink and dance. Out the back **Phuc Tan** has a gorgeous view over the Red River, large outdoor seating area and a barbecue. This is where the expats end up when **Madake** and **Rock City** have kicked out and there are plenty of locals on the dance floor too.

Polite Pub
5 Bao Khanh St, T4-3825 0959.
Recently renovated, **Polite** now stocks an excellent range of single malt whisky and a good choice of bourbons. The old policy of cranking bad music has been ditched and a good cigar menu added. The most pub-like of Hanoi's drinking dens.

Summit Lounge
Sofitel Plaza, 1 Thanh Nien, T4-3823 8888. Open 1600-2400.
On the top floor of the **Sofitel Plaza**, **Summit** has the best views in town towering between Truc Bach Lake and West Lake. Aim to enjoy a cocktail here

at around 1730. Definitely warrants the price tag.

Tadioto
24 Tong Dan St, T4-2218 7200, www.tadioto.com.
Run by one of the key figures on Hanoi's creative scene, Nguyen Qui Duc, this is a sophisticated yet relaxed bar full of interesting furniture, art and people. Plays good tunes, stocks good whisky and hosts readings and talks on occasion. This is now **Tadioto's** 4th incarnation and probably the best yet. Highly recommended.

Entertainment

Cinema
CGV, *Vincom City Towers, 191 Ba Trieu St, T4-3974 3333, www.cgv.vn.* Western films with Vietnamese subtitles in this modern multiplex.
Hanoi Cinematique, *22A Hai Ba Trung St, T4-3936 2648, info2@hanoicinema.org.* This is a wonderfully atmospheric cinema-cum-film club. Membership can be bought on the spot. Film festivals, local documentaries and a nice courtyard to enjoy a drink in.

Dance and theatre
Opera House, *www.hanoioperahouse. org.vn.* Staging a variety of Vietnamese and Western concerts, operas and plays. Check *Vietnam News* or at the box office.
Water Puppet Theatre, *57b Dinh Tien Hoang St, at the northeast corner of Hoan Kiem Lake, T4-3936 4335, www. thanglongwaterpuppet.org.* This traditional Vietnamese art form is not to be missed. Very popular so advanced booking is required at the box office.

Music
The best places for live music are all bars – **Madake**, **Hanoi Rock City** and **CAMA ATK** – see the bars section for details and check the *Hanoi Grapevine* for listings.

Festivals

Jan/Feb Dong Da Hill festival (5th day of Tet). Celebrates the battle of Dong Da in which Nguyen Hue routed 200,000 Chinese troops. Processions of dancers carry a flaming dragon of straw.
Perfume Pagoda Festival, 6th day of the 1st lunar month-end of the 3rd lunar month. This focuses on the worship of Quan Am. There are dragon dances and a royal barge sails on the river.
Hai Ba Trung Festival, 3rd-6th day of the 2nd lunar month. The festival commemorates the Trung sisters, see box, page 55. On the 3rd day the temple is opened; on the 4th, a funeral ceremony begins; on the 5th the sisters' statues are bathed in a ceremony; on the 6th day a ritual ceremony is held.
Hung Kings' festival, 10th day of the 3rd lunar month. A 2-week celebration when the temple site comes alive as visitors from all over Vietnam descend on the area, as Ho Chi Minh encouraged them to. The place seethes with vendors, food stalls and fairground activities spring up. There are racing swan boats on one of the lakes.
2 Sep National Day, featuring parades in Ba Dinh Sq and boat races on Hoan Kiem Lake.

Shopping

The city is a shopper's paradise with cheap silk and good tailors, handicrafts and antiques and some good designer shops. Hang Gai St is well geared to souvenir hunters and stocks an excellent range of clothes, fabrics and lacquerware. It's rather like the small-time Silk Road of Hanoi. Hats of all descriptions abound. You will not be disappointed.

Antiques
Along **Hang Khay** and **Trang Tien** streets, south edge of Hoan Kiem Lake. Shops sell silver ornaments, porcelain, jewellery and carvings – much is not antique, not all is silver; bargain hard.

Art galleries
Hanoi has always been known as the 'artistic' city compared to Ho Chi Minh's powerhouse economy. Although many galleries do the typical conical hat and buffalo paintings, more galleries stocking the work of serious artists are popping up. Galleries abound near Hoan Kiem Lake, especially **Trang Tien St** and on **Dinh Tien Hoang St** at northeast corner.
Art Vietnam Gallery, *LACA, off Ly Quoc Su, www.artvietnamgallery.com*. Art Director Suzanne Lecht has found a new Old Quarter space here in the **Ly Quoc Su Art and Cafe Area**. It is a fine place to hang her excellently curated exhibits. Lecht represents a number of the country's top artists and has an encyclopaedic knowledge of Vietnam's contemporary art scene.
Hanoi Gallery, *17 Nha Chung St, T4-3928 7943, propaganda_175@yahoo.com*. Sells propaganda posters.
Manzi, *see Cafés*. This space showcases the work of local and international artists.
Nha San, *LACA, off Ly Quoc Su St, www. nhasanstudio.org*. Run by a group of young artists in this new small cultural quarter. Shows contemporary art and holds talks. Recommended.

Propaganda Art, *8 Nha Chung St, T4-3928 6588*. More propaganda posters and other propaganda items such as mugs and key rings.

Bicycles
Hanoi's bicycle scene has boomed in recent years and now there are scores of good quality bike shops in town. Check out THBC or **Thang Long Cycling** in Tay Ho or **Nam Anh Bikes** at 1A Tran Thanh Tong. For something cheaper, there are plenty of shops along the southern end of Ba Trieu St.

Books and maps
Private booksellers operate on Trang Tien St and have pavement stalls in the evening. On Sun book stalls appear on Dinh Le St, parallel with Trang Tien St. Many travel cafés operate book exchanges.
The Bookworm, *44 Chau Long, T4-3715 3711, www.bookwormhanoi.com*. Excellent collection of books on Vietnam and Southeast Asia, alongside the city's biggest selection of English-language novels.
Foreign Language Bookshop, *61 Trang Tien St*. A reasonable range of English-language books with plenty about Vietnam.

Camera shops
Available all around Hoan Kiem Lake. Several shops have download and printing services for digital cameras. Vu Nhat at 22 Trang Thi is a good shop for cleaning, repair and also sales.

Clothes, fashions, silk and accessories
The greatest concentration is in the Hoan Kiem Lake area particularly on Nha Tho, Nha Chung, Hang Trong and Hang Gai. **Bo Sua**, *beside skate shop Boo, 24D Ta Hien St, T4-6657 8086*. Owned by the same

people as **Boo**, **Bo Sua** is revolutionary for a Hanoian label. Day-to-day objects, such as coal briquettes, plastic sandals or foamy glasses of *bia hoi* have been turned into stylish T-shirt icons.

Chula, *Nhat Chieu, T4-3710 1102, www.chulafashion.com*. Run by long-term Spanish expat Diego, Chula has striking distinctive designs with a focus on dresses.

Co, *18 Nha Tho St, T4-3928 9925, conhatho@yahoo.com*. Clothes shop with a very narrow entrance. Some unusual prints, the craftsmanship is recommended.

Ginkgo, *44 Hang Be, T4-3936 4769, www.gingko-vietnam.com*. A great place to pick up a Hanoi or Vietnam themed T-shirt. Quality fabrics and great designs.

Ha Truong Studio, *75b Alley 56, Yen Phu, Tay Ho, T4-3715 4345, www.hatruong.com*. Stunning range of contemporary clothing from a Ha Truong, one of the leading lights on the Vietnam fashion scene.

Ipa Nima, *73 Trang Thi St, T4-3933 4000, www.ipa-nima.com*. Shiny shoes, bags, clothes and jewellery boxes. Hong Kong designer Christina Yu is the creative force behind the label.

Mosaique, *6 Ly Quoc Su St, T4-6270 0430*. Embroidered table runners, lamps and stands, silk flowers, silk curtains, metal ball lamps, and lotus flower-shaped lamps.

Things of Substance, *5 Nha Tho St, T4-3828 6965, contrabanddesign@hn.vnn.vn*. Selling swimwear, silk jewellery bags and attractive jewellery, this small shop, with excellent service in the shadow of the cathedral, offers something a bit different. An Australian designer is in charge and everything is made with the motto 'Western sizes at Asian prices' in mind.

Handicrafts and homeware

There has been a great upsurge in handicrafts on sale as the tourist industry develops. Many are also made for export. A wide range of interesting pieces is on sale all around the popular cathedral shopping cluster of Nha Tho, Ly Quoc Su and Nha Chung streets. Further shops can be found on Hang Khay St, on the southern shores of Hoan Kiem Lake, and Hai Gai St. A range of hand-woven fabrics and ethnographia from the hill tribes is also available.

Aloo Store, *37 Hang Manh St, T4-3928 9131*. An abundance of well-priced ethnic goods from the north.

Chi Vang, *63 Hang Gai St, T4-3936 0601, chivang@fpt.vn*. Sells exquisite hand-embroidered goods: baby's bed linen and clothing, cushion covers, table cloths and unusual-shaped cushions artfully arranged.

Craft Link, *43 Van Mieu St, T4-3843 7710, www.craftlink-vietnam.com*. Traditional handicrafts from a not-for-profit organization. Many are made by ethnic minorities.

Mosaique, *22 Nha Tho St, T4-3928 6181, mosaique@fpt.vn. Open 0830-2000*. An Aladdin's cave of embroidered table runners, lamps and stands, silk flowers for accessorizing, silk curtains, silk cushions, ball lamps, pillow cushions and lotus flower-shaped lamps.

Shoes

Walking boots, trainers, flip flops and sandals, many in Western sizes, are sold in the shops around the northeast corner of Hoan Kiem Lake. They are remarkably inexpensive, but bargaining is expected.

Supermarkets

Fivimart, *27a Ly Thai To St*. Large-ish supermarket stocking all the necessities.

What to do

Cookery classes

Hanoi Cooking Centre, *44 Chau Long St,
T4-3715 0088, www.hanoicookingcentre.
com*. Run by cook book author Tracey
Lister, this cooking school is the pick of
the bunch in Hanoi. A large kitchen in a
spacious building with a great courtyard
café. Lunch is eaten in the peaceful
restaurant space above the kitchen. This
is also a great location as it is just a short
walk to one of the very best markets in
town, Chau Long, where cooking students
are taken to learn about the local produce
before whipping up a feast. Classes for
children also. Highly recommended.
Highway 4, *see Restaurants, page 60*.
This popular restaurant chain also offers
fun cooking classes including a cycle trip
to a local market.

Health clubs

All the big hotels provide fitness facilities,
pool and gyms. Open usually free of
charge to residents and to non-residents
for a fee or subscription. There are now
also scores of gyms all over town, but
most require long-term memberships.
One exception to this rule is **Olympia**
at 4 Tran Hung Dao, which is extremely
cheap and offers 2 rooms with a massive
choice of weights and cardio.

Therapies

Le Spa du Metropole, *Sofitel Metropole,
15 Ngo Quyen St*. A truly luscious and
deliciously designed spa in the grounds
of the hotel. Themed rooms provide the
ambience for the ultimate spa rituals.
Expensive but worth it.

Tour operators

The most popular option for many is
the budget cafés that offer reasonably
priced tours and an opportunity to meet
fellow travellers. While an excellent way
to make friends, these tours do tend
to isolate visitors from local people.
Operators match their rivals' prices and
itineraries closely.
    Make sure to use only recommended
tour operators. Also keep in mind that you
get what you pay for and if something is
too cheap to be true, it probably is.
Asia Pacific Travel, *87 Hoang Quoc
Viet St, Cau Giay District, T4-3756 8868,
www.asiapacifictravel.vn*. Arranges tours
throughout Vietnam, including Hoi An
(biking and fishing tour) and My Son.
Branch office in Danang.
Asian Trails, *24 Hang Than St, Ba Dinh
District, T4-3716 2736, www.asiantrails.travel*.
Offers various package tours across Asia.
Buffalo Tours, *70-72 Ba Trieu,, T4-
3828 0702, www.buffalotours.com*.
Well-established and well-regarded

Footprint
Vietnam Travel

www.Footprint.Vn

organization. It has its own boat for Halong Bay trips and offers tours around the north as well as day trips around Hanoi. Cross-country and cross-border tours and tailor-made trips too. Staff are friendly and the guides are informative and knowledgeable.

Cuong's Motorbike Adventures, *46 Gia Ngu St, T09-1876 3515, www.cuongs-motorbike-adventure.com.* Tours all over Vietnam on motorbike or in military style jeeps. Specializes in trips to the northern highlands including Ha Giang which Cuong and his team know like the back of their hands.

David W Lloyd Photography Tours, *T+84-1228-403 308, www.davidwlloyd photography.com.* Professional photographer and guidebook author David Lloyd offers photography tours ranging from half-day city walks to week-long adventures into the mountains of the north or the caves of Quang Binh.

Ethnic Travel, *35 Hang Giay St, T4-3926 1951, www.ethnictravel.com.vn.* Owner, Mr Khanh, runs individual tours to Bai Tu Long Bay – next to Halong Bay – and to Ninh Binh, the Red River Delta and trekking in the Black River area around Mai Chau. Always offers homestays and always, in a non-gimicky way, tries to ensure that travellers see the 'real' Vietnam. Book exchange inside.

Exotissimo, *26 Tran Nhat Duat St, T4-3828 2150, www.exotissimo.com.* Specializes in more upmarket tours, good nationwide service.

Footprint Travel, *30 Alley 12A, Ly Nam De St, T4-3933 2844, www.footprint.vn.* This company arranges good value, custom-made cycling tours and off-the-beaten-track treks throughout Vietnam, and also in Cambodia and Laos.

Handspan Adventure Travel, *80 Ma May St, T4-3926 2828, www.handspan. com.* A reputable and well-organized business with very friendly staff. Specializes in adventure tours, trekking in the north and kayaking in Halong Bay. It has its own junk in Halong Bay and kayaks. Booking office in Sapa also.

Hanoi Street Eats, *www.sreetfoodtours hanoi.blogspot.com.* Run by long-term expat Mark (author of the excellent Sticky Rice blog) and Tu who hails from Nha Trang, these street eats tours can be tailored to guest's tastes and allow people to see the Hanoi that these two foodies love most. Tours range from a 1-hr market visit to a full-on all day eat-a-thon. Fun and highly recommended.

Luxury Travel, *5 Nguyen Truong To St, Ba Dinh Dist, T4-3927 4120, www. luxurytravelvietnam.com.* This outfit is an Asian specialist in luxury privately guided and fully bespoke holidays in Vietnam,

Laos, Cambodia, Myanmar and Thailand. They also have a new joint venture with a junk specialist in Halong Bay, **Emperor Cruises**, www.emperorcruises.com, offering 5-star cruises in Nha Trang Bay. **Topas Travel**, *52 To Ngoc Van St, Tay Ho, T4-3715 1005, www.topasvietnam.com.* Excellent, well-run tour operator offering cross-country tours as well as those in the north. Also has an office in Sapa using local guides. It organizes treks to Pu Luong Nature Reserve. A major draw card is its ecolodge in Sapa, with gorgeous villas offering peace and quiet. See page 100.

Transport

The traffic in Hanoi is becoming more frantic as each month goes by. Bicycles, cyclos, mopeds, cars, lorries and buses fight for space, but somehow it continues to function. The addition of more and more cars everyday, however, makes many wonder how much longer the city's infrastructure will be able to cope before Bangkok-style gridlock becomes a reality here.

Air
Airport information
There are an increasing number of direct international air connections with Hanoi's **Noi Bai Airport**, north of the city. The new international terminal opened in Dec 2014. Facilities include cafés, shops, restaurants, ATMs, mobile phone shops and tour desks.

It is 35 km from the city, about a 1-hr drive. The best way to get to town, other than with your own hotel's bus, is a meter taxi. These line up outside and while there is more order than in the past, it is still a slight hassle getting a taxi. The best bet is to go for a yellow **Noi Bai**

taxi – there are people with clipboards standing by the taxi rank. Look for someone in yellow and point to the fee written on the taxi board and the side of the cab. This is a fixed fare. Some taxis will offer you a meter rate, but it is best to go with one that simply states the flat fee as written on the boards. While Ho Chi Minh City has worked wonders with its taxi rank in the last year, Hanoi's has not caught up with this standard – hopefully this is something that will be addressed with the opening of the new international terminal.

Airline offices
AirAsia, 9 Hang Manh St, www.airasia. com. **Air France**, 1 Ba Trieu St, T4-3825 3484, www.airfrance.com. **Air Mekong**, 51 Xuan Dieu, T4-3718 8199, www. airmekong.com. **Cathay Pacific**, 49 Hai Ba Trung St, T4-3826 7298, www.cathay pacific.com/vn. **Lao Airlines**, 40 Quang Trung St, Hoan Kiem District, T4-3822 9951/3942 5362, www.laoairlines.com. **Malaysian Airlines**, 49 Hai Ba Trung St, T4-3826 8819, www.malaysiaairlines.com. **Singapore Airlines**, 17 Ngo Quyen St, T4-3826 8888, www.singaporeair.com. **Thai**, 44B Ly Thuong Kiet St, T4-3826 7921, www.thaiair.com. **VietJet Air**, 32 Tran Hung Dao St, T4-3728 1838. **Vietnam Airlines**, 25 Trang Thi St, T4-3832 0320, www.vietnamairlines.com.

Bicycle
Once the most common form of transport in town, it is no longer popular. However, cycling around the West Lake area is a pleasure. Bikes can be hired all over town, but good quality bikes are available at **Paradise Boutique Hotel**, see Where to stay, page 58, and at **La Bicicleta**, see Restaurants, page 64.

Bus
Local
The Hanoi city bus service is comprehensive but not easily navigable for tourists. With *xe om* and taxis so cheap and widely available, only the most fervent bus fans will hop on the crammed local variety.

Long distance
Hanoi has a number of bus stations. The **Southern bus terminal** (Giap Bat, T4-3864 1467) is out of town, but linking buses run from the northern shore of Hoan Kiem Lake. The terminal serves destinations south of Hanoi: **HCMC, Buon Ma Thuot, Vinh, Danang, Thanh Hoa, Nha Trang, Dalat, Qui Nhon, Ninh Binh, Nam Dinh** and **Nho Quan** for **Cuc Phuong National Park**. Express buses usually leave at 0500; advance booking is recommended.

Luong Yen bus station, 1 Nguyen Khoai St. The **Hoang Long** bus company, T4-3928 2828, https://hoanglongasia. com, runs deluxe buses to **HCMC** with comfortable beds, 36 hrs, 12 a day 0500-2300. **Hoang Long** also leaves for **Haiphong** from here; 7 daily from 0415-1645 and on to **Cat Ba Island** by ferry. From **Ha Dong bus station**, Tran Phu Rd, Ha Tay Province, T4-3825 209, buses leave for **Mai Chau, Hoa Binh, Son La** and **Dien Bien Phu**. Take a local bus or *xe om* to the bus station.

From **My Dinh station**, T4-3768 5549, there are buses to **Halong**, every 20 mins, 3 hrs 15 mins. Other destinations in the north are also served from here such as **Thai Nguyen, Tuyen Quang** and **Ha Giang**.

International
International buses to **Laos** are best booked via agents in the Old Quarter – many post times on notice boards in their shops.

Cyclo
Hanoi's cyclo drivers expect foreigners to pay more than locals, but have taken this to extremes; prices quoted are often radically inflated. Drivers also may forget the agreed fare and ask for more: be firm and perhaps write the price down to be clear. A good way to go about getting a hassle-free cyclo is to book via the reception at your hotel. All this said, many of the drivers are superb and friendly and this is a great way to get about town.

Motorbike
Hiring a motorbike is a good way of getting to some of the more remote places. Tourist cafés and hotels rent a variety of machines.
Cuong's Motorbike Adventures, 46 Gia Ngu St, T9-1876 3515, www.cuongs-motorbike-adventure.com. This is the place to head to rent a larger bike with lots of choice and some high quality 250cc off road machines. Also runs excellent tours around the country – see Tour operators, page 70.
Rentabike Hanoi, 27, Alley 52, To Ngoc Van St, T09-1302 6878, www.rentabikevn. com. Run by Danny and Thu, **Rentabike** has a wide range of machines on offer from automatic to 125cc rides. Everything is available for short- or long-term rents. Also sells second-hand machines. Easy to deal with and full of local advice and information on touring.

Taxi and private car
Hanoi has hundreds of good taxi drivers, but rogue cabs remain, especially around tourist sites and at the train station in the early morning. Luckily these are

easily avoided by ignoring taxi drivers who approach you and simply going for one of the reputable companies. These include **Mai Linh** and ABC. All restaurants and bars will also be happy to call you a cab.

Private cars can be chartered from most hotels and from many tour operators, see page 69.

Train

The **central station** (**Ga Hanoi**), 120 Le Duan St, at the end of Tran Hung Dao St, T4-3747 0666, is a 10-min taxi ride from the centre of town. There's an information desk at the entrance, (T4-3942 3697, open 0700-2300) but minimal English is spoken, and luggage lockers at the end of the ticket hall. The **Thong Nhat** (north–south train) booking office is on the left; northern trains office, on the right. Train times and prices can be found at www.vr.com.vn and online bookings are set to become a reality soon. The train station remains old-fashioned but fast-food joints – such as the Korean-owned **Lotteria** – have opened up near the premises if you need a last minute snack before boarding. The easiest way to book a ticket is to pay a small commission to a travel agent.

5 daily connections with **HCMC**. There are also daily trains to **Haiphong** and 3 trains daily to **Ninh Binh**. **Long Bien Station** is at the western end of Long Bien Bridge near the Red River. It is very rarely necessary to use this station, but if you are dropped there you can reach town by taxi or *xe om*.

A variety of trains ply the route to **Lao Cai** (**Sapa**) offering varying levels of comfort. **ET-Pumpkin**, www.et-pumpkin.com and **Ratraco**, www.ratraco.com.vn, run standard comfortable a/c 4-berth cabins in its carriages with complimentary water, bedside lights and space for luggage. For luxury, the **Victoria Hotel** carriages (www.victoriahotels-asia.com) rare the best choice. Places are only available to **Victoria Sapa** hotel guests.

The train is the romantic way to travel, but a new highway linking Hanoi and Lao Cai means many tour companies are now gearing up to sell high-speed bus tickets and also use the buses for their itineraries to the northwest.

Northern Vietnam

culturally interesting, breathtakingly beautiful

To many the Northwest and Far North represents the finest Vietnam has to offer. In terms of scenery, colour, human interest and the thrill of discovering the unknown, it is unrivalled. It is, in short, that myth of travellers' folklore: unspoilt Vietnam.

There are good reasons for this. The distance, rugged environment and infrastructure have all contributed to placing the area at the edge of Vietnamese space. Pockets have been discovered – Sapa for example – but for those who wish to avoid the backpacker trail and are prepared to put up with a little discomfort, the rewards are great. The region has wider significance too: the course of world history was altered at Dien Bien Phu in 1954.

No less remote are the beautiful, rugged, lime green hills that roll across the Northeast. Hilltribe minorities are much in evidence. Despite its sparse population, Northeast Vietnam features prominently in the annals of nationalist and revolutionary history.

To the east of Hanoi is Halong Bay with its thousands of jagged islands rearing dramatically from the sea. South of the city is Ninh Binh and the UNESCO-listed Trang An Landscape Complex where rivers weave among paddy fields and jungle-clad limestone peaks.

Best for
Pagodas ▪ Road trips ▪ Trekking

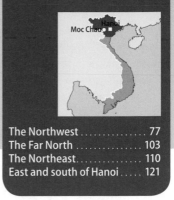

The Northwest 77
The Far North 103
The Northeast 110
East and south of Hanoi 121

Footprint picks

★ Moc Chau, page 81

The tea plantations of Moc Chau attract photographers by the bus full.

★ Sapa, page 92

Trekking, minority villages and fantastic mountain lodges.

★ Mount Fan Si Pan, page 98

The highest mountain in Indochina, adventurous tourists can summit this peak in one day or two.

★ Dong Van, page 107

Remote, high mountain town with stunning surrounds.

★ Ma Pi Leng Pass, page 107

One of the most epic roads in the country.

★ Ba Be Lake, page 111

The ideal stopover on your road trip to the north.

★ Halong Bay, page 125

One of Vietnam's most visited attractions, it lives up to the hype.

★ Tam Coc, page 135

Here rivers cut through dramatic limestone karst scenery.

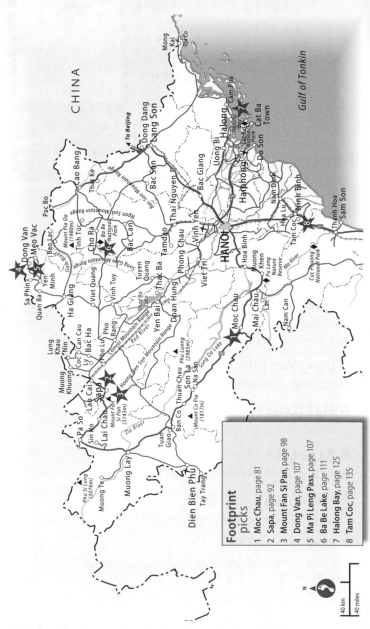

CHINA

Gulf of Tonkin

Footprint picks
1 Moc Chau, page 81
2 Sapa, page 92
3 Mount Fan Si Pan, page 98
4 Dong Van, page 107
5 Ma Pi Leng Pass, page 107
6 Ba Be Lake, page 111
7 Halong Bay, page 125
8 Tam Coc, page 135

40 km
40 miles

N

The Northwest

one of the most evocative landscapes in Vietnam

This is a mountainous region punctuated by limestone peaks and luscious valleys of terraced paddy fields, tea plantations, stilt houses and water hyacinth-quilted rivers. Large cone-shaped peaks rise dramatically, their steep sides striped with the greens and yellows of the rice crop.

Sapa is a former French hill station, home of the Hmong and set at the head of a stunning valley. Scattered around are market towns and villages populated by Vietnam's ethnic minorities. To the east, the far less visited Ha Giang Province borders China to the north, its endless mountain scenery offering up other-wordly vistas of rocky plateaus. This is extremely rewarding road trip territory with the Ma Pi Leng Pass winding vertiginously around a sheer sided gorge. The region isn't without wider significance; the course of world history was altered at Dien Bien Phu in May 1954 when the Vietnamese defeated the French. Closer to Hanoi is Hoa Binh where villages of the Muong and Dao can be seen and the beautiful Mai Chau Valley, home to the Black and White Thai whose attractive houses stand amid the verdant paddies and surrounding hills.

Essential Northwest Vietnam

Finding your feet

There are three points of entry for the Northwest circuit: the south around Hoa Binh (reached by road); the north around Lao Cai/Sapa (reached by road or by train) and in the middle Dien Bien Phu reached by plane or road. Which option you pick will depend upon how much time you have available and how much flexibility you require. Most people arrive by train or by luxury bus, the cheapest option, to Sapa.

Best motorbike journeys

Moc Chau to Sapa, page 81
Dien Bien Phu to Sapa, page 86
Ha Giang to Meo Vac, page 103

Getting around

An option, for those so inclined, is to do the whole thing by motorbike. The rugged terrain and relatively quiet roads make this quite a popular choice for many people. It has the particular advantage of enabling you to to make countless side trips and get to remote

and untouched tribal areas. Doing the whole thing by local public transport is possible, but it would require lots of time and plenty of patience.

Best mountain lodges

Topas Ecolodge, page 100
Nam Cang Riverside Lodge, page 100
Auberge Meo Vac, Ha Giang, page 109

When to go

The wettest season is from May to September, but the rice terraces look very beautiful from August to September. Owing to the altitude of much of the area winter can be quite cool, especially around Sapa, so make sure you go well prepared.

Time required

To see Sapa and around, two or three days is the minimum amount of time required, but to branch out further and include a tour of Ha Giang, five days to a week is needed.

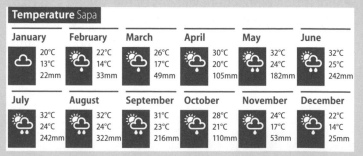

Temperature Sapa

January	February	March	April	May	June
20°C 13°C 22mm	22°C 14°C 33mm	26°C 17°C 49mm	30°C 20°C 105mm	32°C 24°C 182mm	32°C 25°C 242mm

July	August	September	October	November	December
32°C 24°C 242mm	32°C 24°C 322mm	31°C 23°C 216mm	28°C 21°C 110mm	24°C 17°C 53mm	22°C 14°C 25mm

an epic road trip on winding mountain roads

The road from Hanoi to Dien Bien Phu offers some of the most spectacular scenery anywhere in Vietnam. It winds its way for 420 km into the Annamite Mountains that mark the frontier with the Lao People's Democratic Republic; the round trip from Hanoi and back via Dien Bien Phu and Sapa is about 1200 km. There are, of course, opportunities to meet some of Vietnam's ethnic minorities and learn something about their lives and customs (see page 388).

Hanoi to Hoa Binh
Highway 6 leads southwest out of Hanoi to Hoa Binh. Setting off in the early morning, the important arterial function of this road is evident. Ducks, chickens, pigs, bamboo and charcoal (the energy and building materials of the capital) all pour in to Hanoi. Beyond the city limit the fields are highly productive, with bounteous market gardens and intensive rice production.

Hoa Binh → *Colour map 1, B4.*
Hoa Binh, on the banks of the Da (Black) River, marks the southern limit of the interior highlands. It is 75 km from Hanoi, a journey of about 2½ hours. Major excavation sites of the **Hoabinhian prehistoric civilization** (10,000 BC) were found in the province, which is its main claim to international fame. In 1979, with Russian technical and financial assistance, work began on the **Hoa Binh Dam** and hydroelectric power station; it was complete 15 years later. The reservoir has a volume of nine billion cubic metres; it provides two functions, to prevent flooding on the lower reaches of the Red River (that is Hanoi) and to generate power. Architecture buffs may want to swing by to see the Russian-influenced industrial architecture, but most people will drive straight past en route to more attractive destinations.

The road to Mai Chau
After leaving Hoa Binh, Highway 6 heads in a south-southwest direction as far as the Chu River. Thereafter it climbs through some spectacular mountain scenery before descending into the beautiful Mai Chau Valley. During the first half of this journey, the turtle-shaped roofs of the Muong houses predominate, but after passing **Man Duc** the road enters the territory of the Thai, northwest Vietnam's most prolific minority group, heralding a subtle change in the style of stilted-house architecture. While members of the Thai will be encountered frequently on this circuit, it is their Black Thai sub-ethnic group, which will be seen most often. What makes the Mai Chau area interesting is that it is one of the few places en route where travellers can encounter their White Thai cousins.

Mai Chau → *Colour map 1, B3.*
An isolated farming community until 1993, Mai Chau has undergone significant change in just a few short years. Its tranquil valley setting, engaging White Thai

inhabitants and superb rice wine make Mai Chau a very worthwhile stop and it is now extremely touristy, with large groups of Vietnamese tourists packing out the homestays every weekend and a good number of Hanoi's expats also using it as a weekend getaway. The growing number of foreign and domestic tourists visiting the area in recent years has had a significant impact on the economy of Mai Chau and the lifestyles of its inhabitants.

Lac, see below, is the main tourist village. You can stay overnight there, or alternatively, there are two up-market options in Mai Chau, with a new ecolodge offering wonderful accommodation and a swimming pool with views across the valley.

A number of interesting and picturesque **walks** and **treks** can be made in the countryside surrounding Mai Chau. These cover a wide range of itineraries and durations, from short circular walks around Mai Chau, to longer treks to minority villages in the mountains beyond. One such challenging trek covers the 20 km to the village of Xa Linh, just off Highway 6. This usually takes between two and three days, with accommodation provided in small villages along the way. Ask at the People's Committee Guesthouse or at any homestay in Lac.

Lac (White Thai village) → *Colour map 1, B3.*
Easily accessible from the main road. From the direction of Hoa Binh take the track to the right, immediately before the ostentatious, red-roofed People's Committee Guesthouse. This leads directly into the village.

This village is very popular and turning into the village one's heart may sink: minibuses are drawn up and stilt houses are full of groups gearing up for an evening karoeke session. But before you turn and flee take a stroll around the village and find a house tucked further away with a view of the paddy fields and ask if you can stay the night. Rent a bicycle from your hosts and wobble across narrow bunds to the neighbouring hamlets, enjoying the views over the rice fields as you go.

Grottoes
About 5 km south of Mai Chau on Route 15A is the Naon River on which, in the dry season, a boat can be taken to visit a number of large and impressive grottoes. Others can be reached on foot. Ask your hosts for details.

Pu Luong Nature Reserve → *Colour map 1, C4.*
Ba Thuoc Project Office, Trang Village, Lam Xa Commune, Ba Thuoc District, Thanh Hoa, T37-388 0494/671, ffiplcpbto@hn.vnn.vn.

Pu Luong Nature Reserve is a protected area of limestone forest southeast of Mai Chau that harbours the endangered Delacour's langur, clouded leopard, Owston's civet and bear. Birdwatching is best from October to March. From Ban Sai, 22 km south of Mai Chau, trekkers can visit caves and local Thai and Muong communities. From the south, near the reserve headquarters close to **Canh Nang**, there is the Le Han ferry crossing. From here visitors can see the traditional water wheels at **Ban Cong**, trek deep east to **Ban Son** and then, after overnighting, trek up

ON THE ROAD
People of the north

Ethnic groups belonging to the Sino-Tibetan language family such as the Hmong and Dao, or the Ha Nhi and Phula of the Tibeto-Burman language group are relatively recent arrivals. Migrating south from China only within the past 250-300 years, these people have lived almost exclusively on the upper mountain slopes, practising slash-and-burn agriculture and posing little threat to their more numerous lowland-dwelling neighbours, notably the Thai.

Thus was established the pattern of human and political settlement that would persist in North Vietnam right up until the colonial period – a centralized Viet state based in the Red River Delta area, with powerful Thai vassal lordships dominating the Northwest. Occupying lands located in some cases almost equidistant from Hanoi, Luang Prabang and Kunming, the Thai, Lao, Lu and Tay lords were obliged during the pre-colonial period to pay tribute to the royal courts of Nam Viet, Lang Xang (Laos) and China, though in times of upheaval they could – and frequently did – play one power off against the other for their own political gain. Considerable effort was thus required by successive Viet kings in Thang Long (Hanoi) and later in Hué to ensure that their writ and their writ alone ruled in the far north. To this end there was ultimately no substitute for the occasional display of military force, but the enormous cost of mounting a campaign into the northern mountains obliged most Viet kings simply to endorse the prevailing balance of power there by investing the most powerful local lords as their local government mandarins, resorting to arms only when separatist tendencies became too strong. Such was the political situation inherited by the French colonial government following its conquest of Indochina in the latter half of the 19th century. Its subsequent policy towards the ethnic minority chieftains of North Vietnam was to mirror that of the Vietnamese monarchy whose authority it assumed; throughout the colonial period responsibility for colonial administration at both local and provincial level was placed in the hands of seigneurial families of the dominant local ethnicity, a policy which culminated during the 1940s in the establishment of a series of ethnic minority 'autonomous zones' ruled over by the most powerful seigneurial families.

north back to Highway 6. Also from Le Han, trekkers can overnight in **Kim Giao forest** in the west of the reserve before visiting an old French airbase, **Pu Luong mountain** (1700 m) and trekking north back to the Mai Chau area. Biking and boat in and around the reserve is also possible. Contact the reserve office or Hanoi tour operators, see page 69, for details.

★Moc Chau and Chieng Yen → *Colour map 1, B3.*
North of Mai Chau, on the road to Son La, is Chieng Yen. Home to 14 villages of Thai, Dao, Muong and Kinh, there are new homestay options with trekking and

biking opportunities as well as tea farm visits at Moc Chau. These tea farms are every inch as beautiful as the rice terraces that Vietnam is more famous for, and they are starting to attract lots of visitors from Hanoi who come to photograph the stunning scenery here. Another highlight is the weekly Tuesday market.

The road to Son La

The road to Son La is characterized by wonderful scenery and superb Black Thai and Muong villages. The succession of little villages located just across the river to the left-hand side of the road between 85 km and 78 km from Son La, affords an excellent opportunity to view Black Thai stilt-house architecture. **Cuc Dua village** at the 84-km mark is photogenic.

Son La → *Colour map 1, B2.*

There is little to see in town and most people simply use Son La as a place to sleep before moving on. However, there is the **Son La Provincial Museum** ① *on Youth Hill, just off Highway 6 and near the centre of town, daily 0700-1100, 1330-1730, 10,000d.* The museum building is in fact the town's old French Penitentiary, constructed in 1908, damaged in 1909, bombed in 1952 and now partially rebuilt for tourists. The original 3-m-deep dungeon and tiny cells complete with food-serving hatches and leg-irons can be seen together with an exhibition illustrating the history of the place and the key individuals who were incarcerated here.

West to Dien Bien Phu

The scenery on leaving Son La is breathtaking. Reds and greens predominate – the red of the soil, the costumes and the newly tiled roofs, and the green of the trees, the swaying fronds of bamboo and the wet-season rice. Early morning light brings out the colours in their finest and freshest hues, and as the sun rises colours transmute from orange to pink to ochre.

Around every bend in the road is a new visual treat. Most stunning are the valley floors, blessed with water throughout the year. Here generations of ceaseless human activity have engineered a land to man's design. Using nothing more than bamboo technology and human muscle, terraces have been sculpted from the hills: little channels feed water from field to field illustrating a high level of social order and common purpose. Water powers devices of great ingenuity: water wheels for raising water from river level to field level, rice mills and huskers and mini electrical turbines.

There is a small and colourful market village 25 km from Son La and 10 km further on is **Thuan Chau**, another little market town where, in the early morning, people of different minorities in traditional dress can be seen bartering and trading. Thuan Chau is a good spot for breakfast and for buying headscarves. The settlements along this route nicely illustrate the law that describes the inverse relationship between the size of a place and the proportion of the population traditionally garbed. The road is remarkably good with crash barriers, mirrors positioned strategically on hair-pin bends and warning signs, which, considering the precipitous nature of the terrain from Thuan Chau to Tuan Giao, and that visibility is often obscured by cloud and fog, is just as well.

ON THE ROAD
Resistance in Son La

It was not until the 18th century, under the patronage of the Black Thai seigneurial family of Ha, that Son La began to develop as a town. During the late 1870s the region was invaded by renegade Chinese Yellow Flag bands taking refuge after the failed Taiping Uprising. Allying himself to Lin Yung-fu, commander of the pursuing Black Flag forces, Deo Van Tri, Black Thai chieftain, led a substantial army against the Yellow Flags in 1880, decisively defeating and expelling them from the country. Thus Tri established hegemony over all the Black and White Thai lords in the Son La area, enabling him to rely on their military support in his subsequent struggle against the French – indeed, the chieftains of Son La were to take an active role in the resistance effort between 1880 and 1888.

As the French moved their forces up the Da River valley during the campaign of 1888, the chieftains of the area were one by one obliged to surrender. A French garrison was quickly established at Son La. As elsewhere in the Northwest, the French chose to reward the chieftains of Son La district for their new-found loyalty by reconfirming their authority as local government mandarins, now on behalf of a colonial rather than a royal master.

While large-scale resistance to French rule in the Northwest effectively ceased after 1890, sporadic uprisings continued to create problems for the colonial administration. The French responded by establishing detention centres throughout the area, known to the Thai as *huon mut* (dark houses). The culmination of this policy came in 1908 with the construction of a large penitentiary designed to incarcerate resistance leaders from the Northwest and other regions of Vietnam. Just one year after the opening of the new Son La Penitentiary, prisoners staged a mass breakout, causing substantial damage to the prison itself before fleeing across the border into Laos.

During the final days of colonial rule Son La became an important French military outpost, and accordingly an air base was built at Na San, 20 km from the town. Both Na San air base and the colonial government headquarters in Son La town were abandoned to the Viet Minh in November 1953, on the eve of the Battle of Dien Bien Phu.

Tuan Giao is 75 km and approximately three hours from Son La (accommodation is available). The journey from Tuan Giao to Dien Bien Phu on Highway 279 is 80 km (about four hours) and tends to be chosen by those with a strong sense of Vietnamese history. From here you can then go on to Muong Lay. Alternatively you can go north from here to Muong Lay, see below and page 90.

North to Muong Lay
Highway 6 from Tuan Giao heads north across the Hoang Lien Son Range direct to Muong Lay. From Tuan Giao, the road climbs up through some spectacular scenery reaching altitudes of around 1800-1900 m. Red and White Hmong villages are passed en route.

Where to stay

Mai Chau

$$$$-$$$ Mai Chau Ecolodge
Signposted from the main road, T090-326 3968, www.maichau.ecolodge.asia.
This is a fantastic addition to the valley, with beautiful thatched roof bungalows, each with glorious views from balances complete with fine wooden furniture. A number of different rooms are on offer, many of which have tasteful tiled flooring. There is also a pool with superb views and a restaurant with a small outdoor balcony. Recommended.

$$$$-$$$ Mai Chau Lodge
A short walking distance southwest of Lac village, T18-386 8959, www.maichaulodge.com.
Owned and operated by **Buffalo Tours** and staffed by locals, there are 16 warmly furnished rooms with modern facilities. The attractive lodge has 2 restaurants, a bar, swimming pool, sauna and jacuzzi. Bicycling, kayaking and trekking tours are offered. Room prices include round-trip transfer from Hanoi.

Lac (White Thai village)

$ Ethnic Houses
Visitors can spend the night in a White Thai house on stilts. Mat, pillow, duvet, mosquito net, communal washing facilities (some hot showers) and sometimes fan provided. This is particularly recommended as the hospitality and easy manner of the people is a highlight of many visitors' stay in Vietnam. Food and local rice wine provided. Avoid the large houses in the centre if possible. **Mr Binh's place**,

Number 9 (T021-8386 7380) is a good option. In the adjoining, quieter, village of Ban Pom Coong, **House 3** (aka **Hung Tu**) is run by an absolutely lovely family and has good views – contact Nga at **Wide Eyed Tours** (T4-2213 2951) to request it.

Moc Chau and Chieng Yen Homestays

Homestays, with meals are possible in 2 villages. Contact Son La Province well-respected tour operator **Handspan** (www.handspan.com) in Hanoi.
There are also a number of very basic guesthouses (*nha nghi*), all of which offer simple rooms.

Son La

$ Nha Khach Cong Doan (Trade Union Guesthouse)
Xuan Thuy St, T22-385 2804.
A hulking state-run hotel with some massive rooms, a large dining hall and a good location. This is a no-frills option, but rooms have a/c and some basic English is spoken.

Restaurants

Hoa Binh

$ Thanh Toi
22a Cu Chinh Lan St, T18-385 3951.
Local specialities, wild boar and stir-fried aubergine.

Mai Chau

Most people will eat with their hosts. Mai Chau town itself has a couple of simple *com pho* places near the market. The Mai Chau Lodge, see

Where to stay, has 2 restaurants and the Mai Chau Ecolodge offers lunch and dinner to non-guests.

Son La

$ Hai Phi
189 Dien Bien St, T22-385 2394.
Goat specialities.

Entertainment

Mai Chau
Mai Chau Ethnic Minority Dance Troupe, this troupe performs most nights in Lac moving from house to house.

Shopping

Mai Chau
Villagers offer a range of woven goods and fabrics on which they are becoming dependent for a living. There are also local paintings and well-made wicker baskets, pots, traps and pouches.

What to do

Hoa Binh
Hoa Binh Tourism, *next to the Hoa Binh 1 hotel, T18-385 4374, www.hoabinhtourism. com. Daily 0730-1100, 1330-1700.* Can arrange boat hire as well as visits to minority villages, trekking and transport.

Mai Chau
Hanoi tour operators, see page 69, run overnight tours to the area.

Transport

Hoa Binh
Bus station on Tran Hung Dao St. Morning departures to **Hanoi**, 2 hrs. Buses also to **Mai Chau** and onward to **Son La**.

Mai Chau
Bus connections with **Hoa Binh**, 2 hrs, **Hanoi**, 4 hrs, and onward buses northwest to **Son La**. While it is easy and cheap to get here by bus most people visit on an organized tour.

Son La
Bus connections with **Hanoi**, 8 hrs, 5 services daily between 0400 and 0900. Onward services to **Dien Bien Phu**, 5½ hrs.

ON THE ROAD
Battle of Dien Bien Phu

On 20 November 1953, after a series of French successes, Colonel Christian de Castries and six battalions of French and French-colonial troops were parachuted into Dien Bien Phu. The location, in a narrow valley surrounded by steep, wooded peaks, was chosen specifically because it was thought by the French strategists to be impregnable. From there, they believed, their forces could begin to harry the Viet Minh close to their bases as well as protect Laos from Viet Minh incursions. At the centre of the valley was the all-important airstrip – Colonel de Castries' only link with the outside world.

In his history of Vietnam, Stanley Karnow describes de Castries thus: "Irresistible to women and ridden with gambling debts, he had been a champion horseman, dare-devil pilot and courageous commando, his body scarred by three wounds earned during the Second World War and earlier in Indochina."

In response, the famous Vietnamese General Giap moved his forces, some 55,000 men, into the surrounding area, manhandling heavy guns (with the help, it is said, of 200,000 porters) up the impossibly steep mountainsides until they had a view over the French forces. The French commander still believed, however, that his forces would have the upper hand in any set-piece confrontation and set about strengthening his position. He created a series of heavily fortified strongholds, giving them women's names (said to be those of his numerous mistresses): Anne-Marie, Françoise, Huguette, Béatrice, Gabrielle, Dominique, Claudine, Isabelle and Eliane.

As it turned out, de Castries was not luring the Viet Minh into a trap, but creating one for himself and his men. From the surrounding highlands,

Dien Bien Phu → *Colour map 1, B1.*
visited either for its historical significance or to cross into Laos

Deep in the highlands of Northwest Vietnam, close to the border with Laos and 420 km from Hanoi (although it feels much further), Dien Bien Phu is situated in a region where even today ethnic Vietnamese still represent less than one-third of the total population. The town lies in the Muong Thanh Valley, a heart-shaped basin 19 km long and 13 km wide, crossed by the Nam Yum River.

For such a remote and apparently insignificant little town to have earned itself such an important place in the history books is a considerable achievement. And yet the Battle of Dien Bien Phu in 1954 was a turning point in colonial history (see box, above). It marked the end of French involvement in Indochina and heralded the collapse of its North African empire. Had the Americans, who shunned French appeals for help, taken more careful note of what happened at Dien Bien Phu they might have avoided their own calamitous involvement just a decade later.

Giap had the French at his mercy. The shelling started in the middle of March, and the strongholds fell one by one; Béatrice first and then Gabrielle and Anne-Marie by mid-March until de Castries' forces were concentrated around the airstrip. Poor weather, which prevented the French from using their air power, and human-wave attacks gradually wore the French troops down. By this time, de Castries had withdrawn to his bunker and command had effectively been taken over by his junior officers. A furious bombardment by the heavy guns of the Viet Minh from 1 May led to the final massed assault five days later. On the final night, the Viet Minh taunted the French defenders by playing the Song of the Partisans, the theme of the French Resistance, over the garrison's radio frequencies. The colonel's HQ fell on 7 May at 1730 when 9500 French and French-colonial troops surrendered. A small force of paratroopers at the isolated southern position, Isabelle, continued to resist for a further 24 hours. The humiliation at Dien Bien Phu led the French to sue for peace at a conference in Geneva. On 20 July 1954 it was agreed that Vietnam should be divided in two along the 17th parallel: a communist north and a capitalist south. In total, 20,000 Viet Minh and over 3000 French troops were killed at Dien Bien Phu. The Geneva agreement set terms so that the dead from both sides would be honoured in a massive ossuary. But when Ngo Dinh Diem, the President of the Republic of South Vietnam, symbolically urinated over Viet Minh dead in the South rather than bury them with honour, Giap and Ho Chi Minh decided to leave the French dead to lie where they had fallen. Over the nine years of war between the Viet Minh and the French, the dead numbered between a quarter of a million and one million civilians, 200,000-300,000 Viet Minh and 95,000 French-colonial troops. Who was to guess another 20 years of warfare lay ahead.

Sights

The town of Dien Bien Phu with its neat streets is quite easy to negotiate on foot. The battlefield sites, most of which lie to the west of the Nam Yum River, are, however, a bit spread out and best visited by car or by motorbike.

On the sight of the battlefield **General de Castries' bunker** ⓘ *daily 0700-1100, 1330 1700, 5000d*, has been rebuilt and eight of the 10 French tanks (known as bisons) are scattered over the valley, along with numerous US-made artillery pieces.

On **Hill A1** (known as Eliane 2 to the French) ⓘ *daily 0700-1800*, scene of the fiercest fighting, is a bunker, a war memorial dedicated to the Vietnamese who died on the hill and around at the back is the entrance to a tunnel dug by coal miners from Hon Gai. Their tunnel ran several hundred metres to beneath French positions and was filled with 1000 kg of high explosives. It was detonated at 2300 on 6 May 1954 as a signal for the final assault. The huge crater is still there. The hill is a peaceful spot and a good place from which to watch the sun setting on the historic valley. After dark there are fireflies. Hill A1 and other sites in the area were improved in readiness for Dien Bien Phu's 60th anniversary of the French defeat in 2014.

The **Dien Bien Phu Museum** ① *daily 0700-1100, 1330-1800, 10,000d,* has a good collection of assorted Chinese, American and French weapons and artillery in its grounds. It has been renovated and there are photographs and other memorabilia together with a large illuminated model of the valley illustrating the course of the campaign and an accompanying video. The **Revolutionary Heroes' Cemetery** ① *opposite the Exhibition Museum adjacent to Hill A1, 0700-1100, 1330-1800,* contains the graves of some 15,000 Vietnamese soldiers killed during the course of the Dien Bien Phu campaign.

Located close to the sight of de Castries' command bunker is the French War Memorial (Nghia Trang Phap). It consists of a white obelisk surrounded by a grey concrete wall and black iron gates sitting on a bluff overlooking the Nam Yum River.

Dien Bien Phu's newest sight towers over the town. Erected on Hill D1 at a cost of US$2.27 million, the **Victory Monument (Tuong Dai Chien Dien Bien Phu)** ① *entrance next to the TV station on 6 Pho Muong Thanh (look for the tower and large, gated pond),* is an enormous, 120-tonne bronze sculpture. It was sculpted by former soldier Nguyen Hai and depicts three Vietnamese soldiers standing on top of de Castries' bunker. Engraved on the flag is the motto *Quyet Chien, Quyet Thang* (Determined to Fight, Determined to Win). One of the soldiers is carrying a Thai child. It was commissioned to mark the 50th anniversary of the Vietnamese defeat over the French in 1954.

Dien Bien Phu

Where to stay

Dien Bien Phu is still sorely lacking in quality accommodation, particularly at the budget end. Many of the guesthouses (*nha nghi*) go by the hour, as well as the night.

$$ Muong Thanh Hotel
25 Him Lam-TP, T0230-381 0043.
The most upmarket option, this dated but comfortable hotel has spacious, retro rooms with TV. Breakfast included with the more expensive rooms. 62 standard rooms with TV, a/c, minibar and fan. Wi-Fi, swimming pool complete with bizarre statues (10,000d for non-guests), karaoke, Thai massage and free airport transfer. Tacky souvenir shop. Very overpriced motorbike rentals – hire elsewhere.

$$-$ Nha Khach VP
7/5 Muong Thanh (behind the lake), T023-283 0338, thanhhoa.dph@gmail.com.
Hotel right in the middle of town. Absolutely massive suites complete with 70s style living areas. Doubles are clean and spacious with ac. Considering the alternatives, a very good option.

$ Hung Ha
Number 83, opposite the bus station, T023-0650 4187.
Strictly for those on a tight budget, this is the best of a bad lot, but is handy for the station. The balcony rooms aren't so bad, but interior rooms are drab and corridor-facing.

Restaurants

The main street, Nguyen Chi Thanh, has plenty of simple noodle and rice joints, but they are not places to linger. A few *bia hoi* also serve *lau* (hotpots) – Phuong Thuy at number 60 is busy in the evenings.

$$-$ Muong Thanh Hotel Restaurant
25 Him Lam-TP, T230-381 0043.
Daily 0600-2200.
Popular with tour groups. Menu includes plenty of Vietnamese choices, from familiar pork and chicken dishes to more offbeat options.

$ Lien Tuoi
6427 Street 22, behind the cemetery, Muong Thanh 8 St, next to the Vietnamese cemetery and Hill A1, T0230-382 4919. Daily 0700-2200.
Simple delicious local fare, including good fried spring rolls and grilled chicken in a family-run restaurant.

Transport

Air
The **airport** (T230-382 4416) is 2 km north of town, off Highway 12; there are daily flights to **Hanoi**.
    Airline offices Vietnam Airlines, Nguyen Huu Tho Rd, T230-382 4948.

Bus
Buses snake their way up from Hanoi via Hoa Binh and Son La. Expect overland journeys to be slow and sometimes arduous in this mountainous region but the discomfort is compensated for by the sheer majesty of the landscapes.
    The bus station is close to the centre of town, on Highway 12. It's an easy walk to the hotels. There are daily direct bus connections with **Hanoi**, 13 hrs; daily connections to **Son La**, 5½ hrs; to **Muong Lay**, 3 hrs and some buses to **Sapa**. It is also possible to reach **Mai Chau** via Thai Binh and to Hoa Binh

en route to Hanoi. There's a bus to the Laos border crossing at **Tay Trang** to Muang Khua (Laos) every day. A Laos visa is available at the border; Vietnamese visas are not available at land borders.

Car
The main roads in the Northwest have been improved in the last few years, but a 4WD is still recommended for those going off the main routes. The price of hiring a jeep has come down, and many tour operators in Hanoi (see page 69) rent them out for the 5- or 6-day round trip (1200 km via Sapa).

Dien Bien Phu to Muong Lay
remote mountain passes and minority village life

On Highway 12, it is 104 km from Dien Bien Phu to Muong Lay (formerly Lai Chau). The five-hour journey is scenically interesting and there are a few minority villages – Kho-mu and Thai on the valley floors and Hmong higher up on the way. The scenery is different from any you will have encountered so far. What is amazing around Son La is the exquisite human landscape. From Dien Bien Phu to Muong Lay what is impressive is the scenery in its natural state.

The road was originally built by an energetic French district governor, Auguste Pavie, and was used by soldiers fleeing the French garrison at Lai Chau to the supposed safety of the garrison at Dien Bien Phu in 1953. Viet Minh ambushes along the Pavie Track meant that the French were forced to hack their way through the jungle and those few who made it to Dien Bien Phu found themselves almost immediately under siege again.

Pu Ka village, 46 km from Muong Lay, is a White Hmong settlement established by the authorities to transplant the Hmong away from their opium fields.

Muong Lay and around → *Colour map 1, B1.*
little visited, there is a real sense of being off-the-beaten path

Muong Lay
Muong Lay (formerly Lai Chau) formerly occupied a majestic setting in a deep and wide valley that was cloaked in dense tiers of forest, but it has been moved up the hillside due to the construction of a dam that left this once idyllic settlement underwater. As a result, it is no longer often used as a longer stop on this northwest loop.

Sin Ho
Driving to Sin Ho is hazardous as you need to negotiate the hairpin bends and precipitous drops that characterize the road. It is best to drive slowly so you will also have the opportunity to witness the extraordinary perpendicular fields and to wonder how it is that local farmers can harvest slopes on which most people could not even stand.

The first 20 km towards Sin Ho off the main highway is one of the most spectacular drives in Vietnam. After 20 km the road levels off and meanders over the Sin Ho plateau passing hamlets of Red, White and Flower Hmong and Dao minorities. Sin Ho provides little that won't have been seen already, although the Sunday morning market is worth visiting. As with other markets in the region, the Sunday market is an important social occasion. The roads were undergoing construction at the time of writing so the journey should soon be somewhat less arduous.

Lai Chau (formerly Tam Duong)

There are some interesting walks to **Na Bo**, a Pu Na (Giay sub-group) minority village, **Giang** (Nhang minority) and **Hon** minority villages. Pu Na and Nhang people are similar in culture and clothes. Na Bo is 7 km from Lai Chau from which Giang is a further 1.5 km and Hon a further 5 km still. Alternatively a motorbike and driver can be hired.

About 35 km southeast of Lai Chau, Highway 4D swings sharply to the northeast and the altitude climbs abruptly into the **Hoang Lien Son range**. Here is harsh mountain scenery on a scale previously unencountered on this circuit of Northwest Vietnam. The geology is hard and crystalline as is the skyline, with sharp jagged peaks punching upwards into the sky. Vertical cliffs drop below and soar above; friendly rolling scenery has been replaced by 3000-m-high mountains. There are buses from Lai Chau to Sapa.

Listings Muong Lay and around

Where to stay

Sin Ho

$ People's Committee Guesthouse
On the right as you enter the town,
T23-387 0168.
The long, low building is very basic.

Lai Chau

$$ Muong Thanh Lai Chau
113 Le Duan, T0231-379 0555,
www.muongthanh.vn.
Part of Muong Thanh's growing empire, this is a sprawling hotel complex complete with a swimming pool over which a bizarre dinasaur looms. Large choice of well kitted-out and clean rooms.

Phuong Thanh
123-387 5235, phuongthanhhotel@
yahoo.com.
21 fan rooms, hot water, clean, comfortable, lovely views.

Restaurants

Sin Ho

Eat early at one of the cafés around the market. They may only have instant noodles at night and eggs for breakfast, but washed down with the local rice wine after a long journey, it tastes like a feast.

Transport

Sin Ho

Sin Ho is a 40-km detour off Highway 12. Bus connections with **Dien Bien Phu** via Muong Lay, daily from the market.

Lai Chau

From Muong Lay, Highway 12 heads almost due north following the Na river valley towards the Chinese border. At Pa So, 10 km from China (border crossing closed), take Highway 4D, southeast. Lai Chau is in fact a collection of 3 settlements, all new.

Bus services to **Hanoi** via Sapa; connections with **Lao Cai** also via Sapa, and south with **Dien Bien Phu** via Muong Lay.

Sapa → Colour map 1, A2.

former French hill station and now trekking hub of the North

★Sapa retains great charm despite the countless thousands of tourists who have poured in every year for the past decade. Its beauty derives from the impressive natural setting high on a valley side with Vietnam's tallest mountain, either clearly visible or brooding in the mist.

The huge scale of the Fan Si Pan range gives Sapa an Alpine feel and this impression is reinforced by *haute savoie* vernacular architecture with steep-pitched roofs, window shutters and chimneys. But, with an alluring blend of European and Vietnamese vegetation, the gardeners of Sapa cultivate their foxgloves and apricot trees alongside thickets of bamboo and delicate orchids, just yards above the paddy fields. In addition to trekking (see page 97), the markets of the region are popular one-day or overnight trips.

Sights

The beauty of the town is a little compromised by the new hotels sprouting up everywhere. Certainly none of the new ones can compare with the lovely old French buildings. Sapa is a great place to relax and unwind but being comparatively new it has no important historical sights though several French buildings in and around are worth visiting.

The small **church**, built in 1930, dominates the centre of Sapa. Recently rebuilt, the church was wrecked in 1952 by French artillerymen shelling the adjacent building in which Viet Minh troops were billeted. In the churchyard are the tombs of two former priests, including that of Father Jean Thinh, who was brutally murdered. In the autumn of 1948, Father Thinh confronted a monk named Giao Linh who had been discovered having an affair with a nun at the Ta Phin seminary. Giao Linh obviously took great exception to the priest's interference, for shortly after this, when Father Thinh's congregation arrived at Sapa church for mass one foggy November morning, they discovered his decapitated body lying next to the altar.

Ham Rong (Dragon's Jaw Hill) ① *0600-1800, 30,000d, free for children under 5*, on which the district's TV transmitter is stuck, is located immediately above Sapa town centre. Apart from offering excellent views of the town, the path winds its way through a number of interesting limestone outcrops and miniature grottoes as it nears the summit.

Market villages
In the region it's possible to visit **Can Cau** (Saturday market), **Muong Hum** (Sunday market), **Muong Khuong** (Sunday market), **Coc Ly** (Tuesday market), **Lung Khau Nhin** (Thursday market), **Tam Duong** (Thursday market).

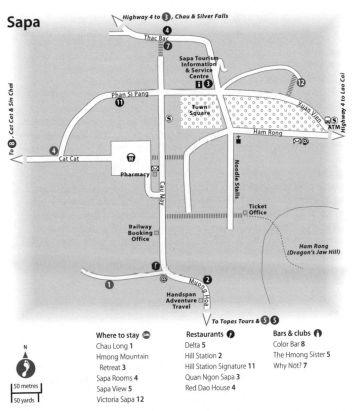

Sapa

Where to stay
Chau Long **1**
Hmong Mountain Retreat **3**
Sapa Rooms **4**
Sapa View **5**
Victoria Sapa **12**

Restaurants
Delta **5**
Hill Station **2**
Hill Station Signature **11**
Quan Ngon Sapa **3**
Red Dao House **4**

Bars & clubs
Color Bar **8**
The Hmong Sister **5**
Why Not? **7**

BACKGROUND

Sapa

Originally a Black Hmong settlement, Sapa was first discovered by Europeans when a Jesuit missionary visited the area in 1918. By 1932 news of the quasi-European climate and beautiful scenery of the Tonkinese Alps had spread throughout French Indochina. Like Dalat in the south it served as a retreat for French administrators when the heat of the plains became unbearable. By the 1940s an estimated 300 French buildings, including a sizeable prison and the summer residence of the Governor of French Indochina, had sprung up. Until 1947 there were more French than Vietnamese in the town, which became renowned for its many parks and flower gardens. However, as the security situation began to worsen during the latter days of French rule, the expatriate community steadily dwindled, and by 1953 virtually all had gone. Immediately following the French defeat at Dien Bien Phu in 1954, victorious Vietnamese forces razed a large number of Sapa's French buildings to the ground.

Sapa was also one of the places to be invaded by the Chinese in the 1979 border skirmish. Chinese soldiers found and destroyed the holiday retreat of the Vietnamese Communist Party Secretary-General, Le Duan, no doubt infuriated by such uncomradely display of bourgeois tendencies.

Distinctly oriental but un-Vietnamese in manner and appearance are the Hmong, Dao and other minorities who come to Sapa to trade. Interestingly, the Hmong have been the first to seize the commercial opportunities presented by tourism; they are engaging but very persistent vendors of hand-loomed indigo shirts, trousers and skull caps and other handicrafts. The Dao women, their hands stained purple by the dye, sell clothing on street corners, stitching while they wait for a customer. The girls roam in groups, bracelets, earrings and necklaces jingling as they walk. Saturday night is always a big occasion for Black Hmong and Red Dao teenagers in the Sapa area, as youngsters from miles around come to the so-called Love Market to find a partner. The market proved so popular with tourists that the teenagers now arrange their trysts and liaisons in private. The regular market is at its busiest and best on Sunday morning when most tourists scoot off to Bac Ha.

Listings Sapa *map p93*

Tourist information

Sapa Tourist Information Center
2 Phan Si Pang St, T20-387 1975,
www.sapa-tourism.com.
Daily 0800-1130, 1330-1730.
Free tourist information.

Where to stay

Prices tend to rise Jun-Oct to coincide with northern hemisphere university holidays and at weekends. Hoteliers are accustomed to bargaining; healthy competition ensures fair rates.

$$$$ Victoria Sapa
T020-387 1522, www.victoriahotels.asia.com.

With 77 rooms, this hotel is the best in town. Comfy, with well-appointed rooms, it is a lovely place in which to relax. In winter there are very welcome open fires in the bar and dining rooms. The food is very good and the set buffets are excellent value. The **Health Centre** offers everything from the traditional massage to reflexology. The centre, pool, tennis courts and sauna are open to non-guests. Packages available.

$$$ Sapa Rooms
18 Phan Xi Pang St, T020-650 5228, www.saparooms.com.

While the lobby and café is decorated to a very high standard, the rooms offer more of a boutique hostel experience. The owners have also opened the **Hmong Mountain Retreat**, www.hmongmountainretreat.com, outside Sapa, where guests can stay in wooden stilt houses among paddy fields with very special views. Treks can be combined with a stay here.

$$$-$$ Chau Long Hotel
T020-387 1245, www.chaulonghotel.com.

All rooms here have fantastic views down the valley and private balconies. Cosy decor. Serves an excellent buffet breakfast in the restaurant with a panoramic vista. Rates drop in low season.

$$$-$$ Sapa View Hotel
41 Muong Hoa, T020-3872388, info@sapaview-hotel.com.

With a Swiss alpine feel, many rooms have jaw-dropping views through large windows and from private balconies. Each room has its own log fire for the colder months. Good restaurant with open kitchen. Very hospitable management.

Restaurants

There are rice and noodle stalls in the market and along the path by the church.

$$$ Ta Van
In Victoria Sapa, see Where to stay, T20-387 1522.

The food served in this large restaurant is 1st class and the service is exceptional. Choose from à la carte or buffet dinners; the latter are excellent value. You'll want to eat here at least twice to savour the full range of haute cuisine. The large dining room is dominated by an open fire that is hugely warming during those chilly days and nights.

$$$-$$ The Hill Station
7 Muong Hoa St, T020-388 7111, www.thehillstation.com. Open 0800-2300.

A very sleek blend of Nordic and Hmong design from friendly Norwegian owners. Cold cuts, cheese boards, gourmet baguettes and good wine. Great Hmong staff. Recommended.

$$ Delta
Cay Mau St, T20-387 1799. Open 0730-2200.

Sapa's Italian restaurant serves good portions of pasta and pizzas as well as tasty seafood. It's great for people-watching from its big windows as it's on the main bend on the main road. There's a good wine list too.

$$ The Hill Station Signature
www.thehillstation.com.

From the same team behind the Hill Station, this restaurant has massive windows giving breathtaking views down the valley. The dishes here are inspired by the local area, with highlights including the Ta Van pork, the recipe for which comes straight out of a nearby village.

Interesting prints hang on the walls and there is a choice of floor cushion or tabled dining. A cracking spot – delicous and highly recommended.

$$ Quan Ngon Sapa
2 Phan Xi Pan, T09-34430838.
It's wrong to visit Sapa and not try the local speciality – salmon hot pot (*lau ca hoi*). It's served well here, alongside other Vietnamese dishes, in basic, sometimes raucous, surroundings.

$$ Sapa Rooms
See Where to stay, T020-387 2130, www.saparooms.com.
Aussie owner Pete and a Hanoian artist have done a great job decorating this funky establishment with hilltribe-inspired works. The KOTO-trained chefs (see page 63) whip up delicious meals. Fantastic cakes and good coffees. Try the home-made cookie and ice-cream dessert and the Sapa Rooms smoothie.

$$-$ Red Dao House
4B Thac Bac St, T020-3872927. Open 0900-2400.
Homely and warm chalet-style restaurant with very friendly waiting staff. Large range of reasonable Vietnamese food. Gets busy – reserve a table by the front windows.

Bars and clubs

Color Bar
56 Phan Si Pan, T09-7928 3398. Open 1600-2300.
A shack of a bar decorated with tens of paintings by the enthusiastic owner. Free games. Bob Marley and the like on the stereo.

The Hmong Sisters
7 Hmong Hoa St, homngsistersbar@ yahoo.com.
Atmospheric, low-ceilinged bar with ethnic fabrics covering walls and seats and funky paintings. Free American pool, tasty finger foods and quality tunes. Daily happy hours from 4–7 on drinks, including lethal daiquiris. The best bar in town.

Entertainment

Ethnic minority dancing, *Dragon's Jaw Hill. Daily at 0930 and 1500.* Also at the **Victoria Sapa**.

Shopping

The central square plays host to tens of friendly minority women selling fabrics every day, many of whom also follow tourists down the street attempting sales – if you buy from one expect more to latch on. The local authorities are trying in vain to manage this process and bring it under control. There are plenty of shops selling walking shoes, rucksacks, coats, jackets and mountaineering equipment.

May Gallery, *32 Cau May St, T020-873789.* The best place to purchase original art in town. Prices from US$10-1500. Most works are by the lovely manager's husband who exhibits internationally. Oil, lacquer and sculptures.
Wild Orchid, *29 Cau May St, T0912-135868.* A good place to pick up souvenirs and ethnic fabrics.

What to do

Therapies
Victoria Sapa, *see Where to stay, above.* Massage and other treatments are

available. The hotel also has an indoor swimming pool.

Tour operators

Handspan, *Cau May St, T20-387 1214, www.handspan.com*. Tours in the vicinity of Sapa, including treks, mountain bike excursions, homestays and jeep expeditions. This is a booking office for the **Handspan Adventure Travel** group with offices in Hanoi.

Topas, *24 Muong Hoa St, T20-387 1331, www.topastravel.vn*. A combined Danish and Vietnamese operator offering numerous treks varying from fairly leisurely 1-day walks to an arduous 4-day assault on Mount Fan Si Pan. It also organizes bicycling tours and family tours. Well-run operation employing hundreds of local people and providing equipment where necessary. It has an office in Hanoi.

Transport

You get to Sapa either by road as part of the Northwest loop, via Lao Cai on the newly built highway linking it with Hanoi, or by overnight train from Hanoi via Lao Cai. A fleet of minibuses ferries passengers from Lao Cai railway station to Sapa.

Bus

Frequent connections from the main square run to **Lao Cai** (access point) with a small extra charge payable for larger luggage. It is also possible to arrange tickets to **Hanoi** in town.

Train

Overnight trains from and to **Hanoi**, via Lao Cai. There are numerous classes of seat or berth on the trains and some hotels have their own private carriages. It is quite easy to make the travel arrangements, but booking with an operator removes the hassle. A railway office in Sapa also sells tickets for the journey back to Hanoi.

Treks around Sapa

treks through terraced rice fields to ethnic minority villages

From half-day downhill ambles with van transfers back to town to multi-day trek and the overnight climb of Indochina's highest peak, Sapa has a trek for every taste and ability. You should never just turn up in a village for homestay opportunities; book with a tour operator.

Ta Phin

The derelict French seminary is near the village of Ta Phin. The names of the bishop who consecrated it and the presiding Governor of Indochina can be seen engraved on stones at the west end. Built in 1942 under the ecclesiastical jurisdiction of the Parish of Sapa, the building was destroyed 10 years later by militant Vietnamese hostile to the intentions of the order.

To get there from Sapa, take the road 8 km east towards Lao Cai then follow a track left up towards Ta Phin; it's 3 km to the monastery and a further 4 km to Ta

Phin. Beyond the seminary, the path descends into a valley of beautifully sculpted rice terraces and past Black Hmong settlements to Ta Phin.

★ Mount Fan Si Pan

At a height of 3143 m, Vietnam's highest mountain is a two- or three-day trek from Sapa. The climb involves some steep scrambles, which are quite tough in wet conditions. Only the fit will make it to the summit. A good tour operator, either in Sapa or Hanoi, will provide camping equipment and porters.

Lau Chai (Black Hmong) village and Ta Van (Giáy) village

This is a round trip of 20 km taking in minority villages and beautiful scenery. A leisurely stroll through these villages is a chance to observe rural life led in

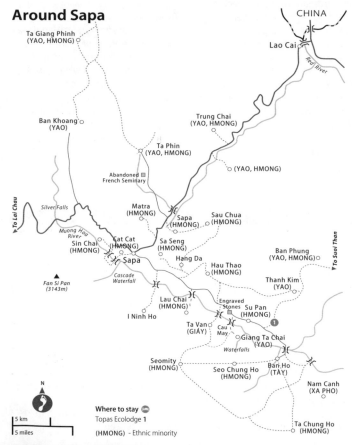

Around Sapa

CHINA

Ta Giang Phinh (YAO, HMONG)

Lao Cai

Red River

Ban Khoang (YAO)

Trung Chai (YAO, HMONG)

Ta Phin (YAO, HMONG)

(YAO, HMONG)

Abandoned French Seminary

To Lai Chau

Silver Falls

Matra (HMONG)

Sapa (HMONG)

Sau Chua (HMONG)

Muong Hoa River

Cat Cat (HMONG)

Sa Seng (HMONG)

Sin Chai (HMONG)

Sapa

Hang Da

Hau Thao (HMONG)

Ban Phung (YAO, HMONG)

To Suoi Than

Fan Si Pan (3143m)

Cascade Waterfall

Thanh Kim (YAO)

Lau Chai (HMONG)

Engraved Stones

Su Pan (HMONG)

I Ninh Ho

Ta Van (GIÁY)

Cau May

Giang Ta Chai (YAO)

Waterfalls

Seomity (HMONG)

Seo Chung Ho (HMONG)

Ban Ho (TÀY)

Nam Canh (XA PHO)

Ta Chung Ho (HMONG)

N

5 km
5 miles

Where to stay 🛏
Topas Ecolodge **1**

(HMONG) - Ethnic minority

reasonable prosperity. Wet rice forms the staple income; weaving for the tourist market puts a bit of meat on the table. Here nature is kind, there is rich soil and no shortage of water. Again it's possible to see how the landscape has been engineered to suit human needs. The terracing is on an awesome scale (in places more than 100 steps), the result of centuries of labour to convert steep slopes into level fields, which can be flooded to grow rice. Technologically, and in no sense pejoratively, the villages might be described as belonging to a bamboo age. Bamboo trunks carry water huge distances from spring to village; water flows across barriers and tracks in bamboo aqueducts; mechanical rice huskers made of bamboo are driven by water requiring no human effort; houses are held up with bamboo; bottoms are parked on bamboo chairs; and tobacco and other substances are inhaled through bamboo pipes. Any path chosen will lead to some hamlet or other; the Hmong in villages further from Sapa tend to be more reserved and suspicious; their fields and houses are often securely fenced off.

Heading southeast out of Sapa (see map, opposite), **Lao Chai** is 6 km away on the far valley side. Follow the track leading from the right-hand side of the road down to the valley floor, cross the river by the footbridge (*cau may*) and then walk up through the rice fields into Lao Chai village. You will find **Ta Van** 2 km further on.

Cross back to the north side of the river by the suspension bridge. A dip in the deep pools of the **Muong Hoa River** is refreshingly invigorating. Engraved stones are a further 2 km southeast (away from Sapa, that is) by the side of road; it is believed they are inscribed in ancient Hmong. The return walk to Sapa from the inscribed stones is a steady 10-km uphill climb. It's exhausting work but, stimulated by the views and the air and fuelled by hard-boiled eggs and warm Lao Cai beer from roadside shacks, and the prospect of cold beer at home, it is a pleasure, not an ordeal. In the late afternoon sun the rice glows with more shades of green than you would have thought possible and the lengthening shadows cast the entire landscape into vivid three-dimensional relief.

Cat Cat and Sin Chai villages
20,000d fee for taking the track.

The track heading west from Sapa through the market area offers either a short 5-km round-trip walk to Cat Cat Black Hmong village or a longer 10-km round-trip walk to Sin Chai Black Hmong village; both options take in some beautiful scenery. The path to Cat Cat leads off to the left of the Sin Chai track after about 1 km, following the line of pylons down through the rice paddies to Cat Cat village; beyond the village over the river bridge you can visit the Cascade Waterfall (from which the village takes its name) and an old French hydroelectric power station that still produces electricity. Sin Chai village is 4 km northwest of here.

The **Silver Falls** are 12 km west of Sapa on the Muong Lay road and are spectacular following rain. They are hardly worth a special visit but if passing it's quite nice to stop for a paddle in the cold pools.

Where to stay

It is possible to spend the night in one of the ethnic houses in the Sapa district. However, homestays must be organized through reputable tour operators. Villages include Ta Van (Day), Ban Ho (Tay), Nam Sai (Tay), Sin Chai (Red Dao) and Ta Phin (Red Dao).

$$$$ Topas Ecolodge
20 km southeast of Sapa, www.topasecolodge.com (Sapa office: 24 Muong Hoa St, T020-387 1331).
25 bungalows with balconies built from white granite crown a hill overlooking stunning valleys. The walk from reception to the bungalows cuts right through the area's trademark rice terraces. Bungalows are simply furnished and powered by solar energy. The food is good – evening buffets are a particular treat. Treks and mountain bike rides lead to less touristed Red Dao areas. For nature, views, peace and an eco-philosophy, the lodge is unique in Vietnam. Highly recommended.

$$$ Hmong Mountain Retreat
6 km along the Ban Ho road, T020-650 5228, www.hmongmountainretreat.com.
5 bungalows and a large, 2-bedroom Hmong House which is perfect for groups. Set on an isolated rice terrace, complete with a good restaurant. A stay can be combined with a trek to the Retreat.

$$$ Nam Cang Riverside Lodge
www.namcangriversidelodge.com.
Located deep in a remote Sapa Valley, this newcomer sits right on the bank of a fast flowing river backed by forest and next to a local minority village. The property is owned by a Red Dao minority family (headed by Mr Phu and Mrs Nhan) and operated in partnership with Topas Travel. A very special place in a very remote area, this is a great option for those looking for a true escape. Rooms are tastefully furnished and good food is served.

$ Homestays in Nam Sai and Nam Cam. Contact Sapa-based operators for homestays in this newly opened up area.

Lao Cai → *Colour map 1, A2.*

the most important border crossing with China

An important north–south transit stop for traders with caravans of pack oxen or horses since time immemorial, Lao Cai continues to have a two-way flow of people and trade passing through the city each day. Other than for border-crossers, Lao Cai holds little appeal.

There is a branch of **Sapa Tourism Center** ① *306 Khanh Yen St, T20-362 52506, www.sapa-tourism.com*, very close to the train station.

Trade with China, much of it illegal, has turned this former small town into a rich community of (dong if not dollar) millionaires and Lao Cai is experiencing something of a construction boom. Huge boulevards flanked by some enormous local government buildings are sprouting up in the main part of town, west of the Red River. In 2006 Lao Cai became a city; by 2020 it looks set to get an airport.

International border crossing

The border is open to pedestrians (0700-2200) with the correct exit and entry visas for both countries. Travellers must report to the International Border Gate Administration Center south of the bridge and near the level crossing for passport stamping and customs clearance. Visas into Vietnam must be obtained in Hong Kong or Beijing and must specify the Lao Cai crossing; they normally take a week to process and are not obtainable at the border. Visas for China must be obtained in Hanoi and must also specify the Lao Cai crossing.

Listings Lao Cai

Where to stay

$$$$ Lao Cai Swiss Belhotel
www.swiss-belhotel.com.
The best accommodation in town by a country mile, this is an international standard property from the Swiss **Belhotel** chain. Rooms on the upper floors have great views and some of the suites on offer are opulent in the extreme. Has a range of restaurant and a good bar. Popular with business travellers.

$ Lao Cai Galaxy Hotel
268 Minh Khai, 1098-812 1631,
www.khachsanlaocaigalaxy.com.
Close to both the bus and rail stations, this is one of the newer budget range hotels in town and one of the better options. Very large rooms, some with nice views so ask to see a few. Limited English spoken by the staff, but the manager is helpful.

Restaurants

$ Oishi
47 Phan Dinh Phung, 3-min walk from the station, T093-614 0581.
A popular place for travellers to wait for the train in Lao Cai, Oishi won't win any awards, but it serves up a decent range of Vietnamese and Western dishes and the staff are friendly. There are a few tables outside.

Transport

Bus
Minibuses to **Sapa** from the train station run on the hour and some hotels have their own pickup.

Town bus station on Hong Ha St. Bus to **Dien Bien Phu**, 0730, 12 hrs. To **Hanoi**, 3 a day 0300-0500, 4 hrs. To **Bac Ha**, 0530, 0730.

Train
Trains run to and from **Hanoi** daily. Tickets from Lao Cai can be booked for a small charge at the railway booking office in Sapa.

Tour operators in Hanoi (see page 69) can also book your ticket for you for a small fee. It is often less hassle than organizing it yourself and, if you are in a hurry, it's a great time saver.

Some trains will also take your motorbike – be sure to enquire ahead and book onto the correct service or your bike will end up on a different train which adds stress to the journey.

The *Victoria* carriages (www.victoria hotels-asia.com/eng/hotels-in-vietnam/sapa-resort-spa/victoria-express-train) offer the highest levels of comfort.

Bac Ha is really only notable for one thing and that is its Sunday market. That 'one thing', however, is very special. Hundreds of local minority people flock in from the surrounding districts to shop and socialize, while tourists from all corners of the earth pour in to watch them do it. Around 18 km before Bac Ha the scenery is wonderful; huge expanses of mountains, pine trees and terracing engraved by the winding road as it climbs skywards towards Bac Ha.

The **Sunday market** ⓘ *0600-1400*, draws in the Flower Hmong, Phula, Dao Tuyen, La Chi and Tay – the Tay being Vietnam's largest ethnic minority. It is a riot of colour and fun: the Flower Hmong wear pink and green headscarves; children wear hats with snail motifs and tassles. While the women trade and gossip, the men consume quantities of rice wine and cook dog and other animal innards in small cauldrons. By late morning they can no longer walk so are heaved onto donkeys by their wives and led home. The market is best experienced in the morning; arrive early if you can. If you haven't got your own transport, almost all the hotels and tour operators in Sapa organize trips.

There are a number of walks to outlying villages. **Pho village** of the Flower Hmong is around 4 km north; **Thai Giang Pho** village of the Tay is 4 km east; and **Na Hoi** and **Na Ang** villages, also of the **Tay**, are 2 km and 4 km west respectively.

Listings Bac Ha

Where to stay

$ Sao Mai
A short walk north of the centre, T20-388 0288, saomaibh@vnn.vn.
Quiet, clean and with a restaurant and free internet. The newer building has 25 rooms with a/c and TV; the old wooden building incorporates 15 rooms with fan. The hotel also offers trekking, motorbike hire, jeep tours and can book train tickets for you.

Restaurants

$ Cong Phu
On the right-hand side of the road walking towards the traditional market site, T20-388 0254.
Caters for the tourist trade with pancakes and Vietnamese dishes and a large range of drinks.

Transport

By bus, **Sapa** to Bac Ha is 3 hrs with various agents offering tours. Otherwise, catch a bus from Lao Cai, 2 hrs.

The Far North

The steep slopes of this mountainous region, which skirts the Chinese border, have been carved into curved rice terracing with paddies shimmering. Further north, where the steepness increases, patches of corn take over from rice cultivation, clinging to the rocky soil. The sparse populations that live here are predominantly indigenous groups and life goes on as it has for years. As one of the least-visited areas of the country, it offers the chance to see traditional Vietnamese life in some of the country's most spectacular scenery.

Ha Giang and around → *Colour map 1, A3.*

The road to Ha Giang
For much of its length the well-maintained Highway 2 follows the Lo River northwards from Hanoi through some delightful scenery. During the early stages of the journey as the road passes the eastern shores of the **Thac Ba Lake**, tea plantations may be seen everywhere. At **Thac Ba** it's possible to stay in White Trouser Dao communities and take boats out onto the lake.

Tuyen Quang Province has a large ethnic minority population and, not long after leaving the provincial capital, travellers will begin to see people from the two main groups of this province, the Tay and the Dao. The delightful little town of Vinh Tuy, near the banks of the Lo River, is a possible lunch stop.

Detouring to Xin Man in the far east of Ha Giang province is worth the hike. This ethnic minority town mostly draws Hmong, Nung, Tay and Dao minorities, and Sunday market time is busy and hectic.

From Xin Man, a road twists and turns towards Hoang Su Phi passing **Heaven's Gate II** and the **Hoang Su Phi Pass**.

Tan Quang is a sizeable market town located some 60 km before Ha Giang at the junction with Highway 279, the mountain road west to Bao Yen in Lao Cai Province.

Ha Giang
The provincial capital of Ha Giang lies on the banks of the Lo River just south of its confluence with the River Mien, perched picturesquely between the beautiful

Essential Far North

Getting around

Unlike Northwest Vietnam, which has so conveniently aligned its attractions along one road circuit, the far north is somewhat fragmented although through road links have improved.

When to go

There are four distinct seasons in the north (spring, summer, autumn and winter). The best times to visit are autumn and spring. From January to March the weather can be very cool, but Ha Giang remains a popular place to visit with Vietnamese due to the flowers that bloom. From August to September the rice paddies are at their most beautiful.

Time required

The loop from Ha Giang to Meo Vac and back can be done in three days on a motorbike, see Transport.

> **Best** views
> Heaven's Gate, to Yen Minh, page 103
> **Lung Cu**, page 107
> Ma Pi Leng Pass, to Meo Vac, page 107

Cam and Mo Neo mountains. Like Cao Bang and Lang Son, Ha Giang was badly damaged during the border war with China in 1979 and has since undergone extensive reconstruction. The best thing to do in Ha Giang is go motorbike touring, see Transport below for hiring options and distances.

Ha Giang Museum ① *next to Yen Bien Bridge in the centre of town, daily 0800-1130, 1330-1700, free*, contains important archaeological, historical and ethnological artefacts from in and around the region, including a very helpful display of ethnic costumes.

Located close to the east bank of the River Lo in the old quarter of the town, **Ha Giang Market** is a daily affair although it is busiest on Sunday. Tay, Nung and Red Dao people are always in evidence here, as are members of northern Ha Giang Province's prolific White Hmong.

Doi Thong (Pine Hill) lies just behind the main Ha Giang Market. The pine trees are newly planted but the hill itself is an area of ancient human settlement believed to date back some 30,000 years to the Son Vi period. Many ancient axe-heads and other primitive weapons were discovered on the hill during land clearance; these are now in the local museum and in the History Museum in Hanoi.

Listings Ha Giang

Tourist information

Ha Giang Tourist company
5 Nguyen Trai St, T219-387 5288, dulichhagiang@gmail.com. Mon-Fri 0800-1130, 1330-1700.

Where to stay

The road to Ha Giang

$$-$ Lavie Vu Linh Resort
Ngoi Tu village, Vu Linh commune, Yen Bai province, www.lavievulinh.com.

ON THE ROAD

The White Hat Revolt

The original settlement in Ha Giang lay on the east bank of the Lo River and it was here that the French established themselves following the conquest of the area in 1886. The town subsequently became an important military base, a development confirmed in 1905 when Ha Giang was formally established as one of four North Vietnamese military territories of French Indochina.

The Ha Giang area saw a number of important ethnic rebellions against the French during the early years of the colonial period, the most important being that of the Dao who rose up in 1901 under the leadership of Trieu Tien Kien and Trieu Tai Loc. The revolt was quickly put down and Trieu Tien Kien was killed during the fighting, but in 1913 Trieu Tai Loc rose up again, this time supported by another family member known as Trieu Tien Tien, marching under the slogans: "No corvées, no taxes for the French; Drive out the French to recover our country; Liberty for the Dao".

Carrying white flags embroidered with the four ideograms *To Quoc Bach Ky* (White Flag of the Fatherland) and wearing white conical hats (hence the French name 'The White Hat Revolt'), the rebels launched attacks against Tuyen Quang, Lao Cai and Yen Bai and managed to keep French troops at bay until 1915 when the revolt was savagely repressed. Hundreds of the insurgents were subsequently deported and 67 people were condemned to death by the colonial courts.

A sustainable tourism project, guests sleep in a longhouse on the floor or a private room with en suite. Trekking, rafting, fishing, boating, biking and badminton are possible. Dinner is with a local family and can be included as part of the package.

$ Ethnic minority homestay at Thac Ba Lake
T9-7284 5982.
It is possible to arrange homestays in the village of Ngoi Tu in Yen Bai province, contact **Handspan** tours (see page 70).

Ha Giang

$$ Truong Xuan Resort
430 Nguyen Van Linh, 7 km north of Ha Giang, T0219-3811 102, www.hagiangresort.com.

A riverside resort with individual bungalows, many of which have river views. There is a massage and herbal bath spa on-site and restaurant in a large traditional house. Makes a great stop at the end of a Ha Giang motorbike road trip.

$ Duc Giang Hotel
14 Nguyen Trai, T0219 387 5648.
Cheap, clean rooms with en suite bathrooms and a/c. Good value for money and located right next to the Jonny's motorbike rental place.

Restaurants

Ha Giang
There are plenty of *pho* places lining the main roads in town that open at around 0600. Simple *com* (rice) joints are also easily found on every street –

take a look at the dishes on display before taking a seat.

$ Bia hoi
On the river, 8 km north of town.
On the road to Quan Ba just beyond the Truong Xuan resort an outdoor *bia* and food place sits right next to the river. Serves great fried beef and good fries.

$ Com Pho Bo
200 m from the Huy Hoan Hotel on Nguyen Trai St.
Serves simple dishes.

$ Thit Nuong
100 m from Jonny Nam Tran's bike rental on Nguyen Trai.
Look for the barbecue outside on which skweres of beer, pork and chicken are cooked.

Shopping

In the markets it is possible to buy fabrics. Tea is the speciality produce of the region, which grows many different varieties including green, yellow, black and flower-scented. Best known is Shan Tuyet tea, a flavoursome variety which is exported but will not be to everyone's taste.

Transport

Ha Giang
Ha Giang to Dong Van via Yen Minh is 148 km; Dong Van to Meo Vac, 22 km, 1 hr and utterly spectacular. Returning from Meo Vac to Ha Giang it is possible to make a loop cutting through Cao Bang province.

Within the town, there are a few taxis and also the ubiquitous *xe om*. Local bus services are infrequent and slow. Ha Giang can be reached comfortably in a day from Sapa.

Bus
The bus station is just behind Nguyen Trai St. There are departures to **Hanoi** along Highway 2 in daylight hours, and also a night bus that departs at 0800 and arrives in Hanoi at around 0400.

Motorbike hire
'Jonny' Nam Tran, Nguyen Trai St, T0917 797 269. The best place to hire from, he has everything from 125cc semi-autos to 250cc fully manual off-road machines.

Dong Van-Meo Vac Region → *Colour map 1, A4.*
high mountain scenery like nowhere else in Vietnam

This is the northernmost tip of Vietnam, close to the Chinese border. The road between Don Van and Meo Vac, including the Ma Pi Leng Pass, is one of the most spectacular roads in all of Vietnam.

Yen Minh and Pho Bang
Yen Minh is located 98 km northwest of Ha Giang and is a convenient place to stop for lunch on the way to Dong Van and Meo Vac – a possible overnight stop for those planning to spend longer in the region. It has a Sunday market where, in addition to the groups mentioned above, you'll see Giay, Pu Peo, Co lao, Lolo and the local branch of Red Dao.

Northwest of Yen Minh right on the Chinese border lies the town of **Pho Bang**. Time seems to have stood still here with mud construction homes with a second galley floor to house firewood. This is remote but worth the hike for the ambience in the town.

Sa Phin

Crossing the old border into the former demesne of the White Hmong kings the very distinctive architecture of the White Hmong houses of the area becomes apparent; it is quite unlike the small wooden huts characteristic of Hmong settlements elsewhere in North Vietnam. These are big two-storey buildings, constructed using large bricks fashioned from the characteristic yellow earth of the region and invariably roofed in Chinese style. But it is not only the Hmong who construct their houses in this way – the dwellings of other people of the area such as the Co lao and the Pu Péo are of similar design, no doubt a result of their having lived for generations within the borders of the former Hmong kingdom.

The remote **Sa Phin Valley** is just 2 km from the Chinese border. Below the road surrounded by conical peaks lies the village of Sa Phin, a small White Hmong settlement of no more than 20 buildings from which loom the twin, white towers of the Hmong royal house, at one time the seat of government in the Dong Van-Meo Vac region, see box, page 108. A visit to the **royal house** is fascinating. The **Sa Phin market** is a treat. Duck into the food market and drink beer from bows with the locals.

Lung Cu

Lung Cu is the most northern point in Vietnam. It is marked by a hillock, flagpole and observation tower. From the top of the hill low mounds and China can be spied. There's an army post there so you'll need to register in the small town before walking up the steep steps.

★ Dong Van

This remote market town is a great place to spend a night set in an attractive valley populated mainly by Tay people. It has a street of ancient houses that is very attractive, one of which has been converted into a wondeful litte café. Dong Van has a Sunday market, but is very quiet at other times of the week.

★ Ma Pi Leng Pass to Meo Vac

Passing over the Ma Pi Leng Pass around 1500 m above the Nho Que River, the scenery is simply awesome. Like Dong Van, Meo Vac is a restricted border area and foreigners need to register with police for a permit to stay here. Mountainous peaks and chasms abound. A small **market** is held every day in the town square, frequented mainly by White Hmong, Tay and Lolo people. Meo Vac is also the site of the famous **Khau Vai 'Love Market'** held once every year on the 27th day of the third month of the lunar calendar, which sees young people from all of the main ethnic groups of the region descending on the town to look for a partner. The Lolo people, with their highly colourful clothes, make up a large proportion of the town's population. A Lolo village is nearby, up the hill from the town centre.

ON THE ROAD

Hmong Kings of Sa Phin

While it is clear that Hmong people have lived in the Dong Van-Meo Vac border region for many centuries, the ascendancy of White Hmong in the area is believed to date from the late 18th century, when the powerful Vuong family established its seat of government near Dong Van. In subsequent years the Vuong lords were endorsed as local government mandarins of Dong Van and Meo Vac by the Nguyen kings in Hué and later, following the French conquest of Indochina, by their colonial masters.

Keen to ensure the security of this key border region, the French authorities moved to further bolster the power of the Vuong family. Accordingly, in 1900 Vuong Chi Duc was recognized as king of the Hmong, and Chinese architects were brought in to design a residence befitting his newly elevated status. A site was chosen at Sa Phin, 16 km west of Dong Van; construction commenced in 1902 and was completed during the following year.

During the early years of his reign, Vuong Chi Duc remained loyal to his French patrons, participating in numerous campaigns to quell uprisings against the colonial government. In 1927 he was made a general in the French army; a photograph of him in full military uniform may be seen on the family altar in the innermost room of the house. But, as the struggle for Vietnamese independence got underway during the 1930s, Duc adopted an increasingly neutral stance. Following his death in 1944, Duc was succeeded as king of the Hmong by his son, Vuong Chi Sinh, who the following year met and pledged his support for President Ho Chi Minh.

Built between 1902 and 1903, the house of the former Hmong king faces south in accordance with the geomantic principles which traditionally govern the construction of Northeast Asian royal residences, comprising four, two-storey sections linked by three open courtyards. The building is surrounded by a moat, and various ornately carved tombs of members of the Vuong family lie outside the main gate. Both the outer and cross-sectional walls of the building are made of brick, but within that basic structure everything else is made of wood. The architecture, a development of late 19th-century Southern Chinese town-house style, features *mui luyen* or *yin-yang* roof tiles.

East from Ha Giang

Beyond Meo Vac the road used to be impassable to motorized vehicles but new bridges mean direct access to Bac Me, Bao Lac and Tinh Túc and onward to Cao Bang and Lang Son.

Bao Lac is a small town but visitors can be put up for the night at the People's Committee Guesthouse. There is a busy morning market but this is far from anywhere and food is limited. **Tinh Túc** is a tin mining town in a pretty valley. It has a simple but adequate hotel next to the post office; there's also a canteen-type diner with very cold beer. Tinh Túc to **Cho Ra** (for **Ba Be Lake**) is a scenic and rewarding trip.

Where to stay

Yen Minh and Pho Bang

$ Nha Nghi Noa Hong
T219-859557.
Rooms are spacious but bathrooms are
tiny and running cold water may not
even be available. Dinner served.

$ People's Committee Guesthouse
Yen Minh Tinh Ha Giang, T219-385 2297.
12 rooms all equipped with a/c and hot
water. The staff are friendly, most speak
no English.

Dong Van

$ Hoang Ngoc Hotel
*Main road, 10915-035141, www.
hoangngochotel2.blogspot.com.*
Right in the middle of town near the
market, Hoang Ngoc hotel has been
recently refurbished and offers good
quality, clean basic rooms right next to
a good restaurant. Popular with tour
groups so book ahead.

Meo Vac

$$-$ Auberge Meo Vac
T4-3976 6246, www.orientalbridge.com.
Very special lodgings just outside Meo
Vac in this French-run house built
overlooking the town with dried mud
walls and wooden posts and beams.
First constructed in 1930 it was originally
the fortified farm of a h'mong chief.

A lovely lounge-dining room comes
complete with beams and a fireplace.
4 double rooms, 1 twin single and a
dormitory of 8 beds. A real find and
highly recommended.

$ Hoa Cuong Hotel
T219-387 1888.
A good budget option with spacious
en suite rooms with hot water.

Restaurants

Yen Minh and Pho Bang
There are plenty of rice restaurants along
Thi Tran Yen Minh St in Yen Minh.

Dong Van

$ Pho Co Cafe
A charming café with an interior
courtyard and wooden balustrading in
an old building. Just drinks on offer.

$ Tien Nhi Restaurant
Main road, Dong Van, T219-385 6217.
Get yourself a slice of superb roasted
pig from here. Failing that, order a
coffee from this friendly restaurant.

Transport

East from Ha Giang
Buses from Ha Giang to **Bao Lam** via
Bac Me on Route 34. Direct to **Bac Me**
also. From Bao Lam to **Bao Lac**, **Tinh
Túc**, **Nguyen Binh** and **Cao Bang** daily;
7-8 hrs to Cao Bang.

The Northeast
a magical mountainous hinterland bordering China

The three provinces of Cao Bang, Bac Can and Lang Son formed the famous Cao-Bac-Lang resistance zone of the 1947-1950 Frontier Campaign. This mountainous region, heavily populated by Tay and Nung people, became the cradle of the revolution during the twilight years of the French colonial period.

Essential The Northeast

Finding your feet

For Cao Bang, Bac Can and Lang Son provinces, although it is possible to reach the larger centres by bus from Hanoi, the going is tough and detours are not possible. A 4WD vehicle is recommended or a tour.

Getting around

Getting around the provinces of Cao Bang, Bac Can and Lang Son is difficult, and taking a tour is recommended. A circuit leads north along Highway 3 from Thai Nguyen to Bac Can (with a small diversion to Ba Be National Park) continuing north to Cao Bang and Pac Bo. From here, Highway 4 leads south to Lang Son, returning to Hanoi directly Highway 1A or across the mountains along Highway 1B.

When to go

Cao Bang, Bac Can and Lang Son provinces are fairly temperate all year round.

North from Hanoi
visitors tend to go straight to Ba Be

Thai Nguyen
North from Hanoi, you'll pass through the industrial town of Thai Nguyen; the only reason to stop would be to visit the **Thai Nguyen Museum of Ethnology** ① *Tue-Sun 0800-1630, 20,000d*. This notable museum houses a collection of artefacts relating to all of Vietnam's 54 ethnic groups. It includes clothes, agricultural and handicraft tools and textiles.

Bac Can → *Colour map 1, A4.*
This market town acquired enormous strategic significance during the First Indochina War as the westernmost stronghold of the Cao-Bac-Lang battle zone. The town was captured by the Viet Minh in 1944 and its recovery was considered crucial to the success of the 1947 French offensive against the Viet Bac resistance base. Although colonial troops did retake the town, guerilla attacks on the town's garrison became so frequent that the French abandoned the town two years later.

Bac Can's daily market is frequented by all the main ethnic groups of the region, which include not only Tay but also local branches of the White Hmong and Red Dao, in addition to Coin Dao (*Dao Tien*) and Tight-Trousered Dao (*Dao Quan Chet*).

★ Ba Be National Park

44 km west of Na Phac on Highway 279, 1 hr from Cho Ra town, T281-389 4026. The park centre is located on the eastern shore of Ba Be Lake. It runs many different tours led by English-speaking guides with an expert knowledge of the area and its wildlife. These tours range from 2-hr boat trips to 2-day mountain treks staying overnight in Tay or Dao villages and visiting caves, waterfalls and other local beauty spots.

Ba Be National Park (Vuon Quoc Gia Ba Be) was established in 1992. It is Vietnam's eighth national park and comprises 23,340 ha of protected area plus an additional 8079 ha of buffer zone. It is centred on the very beautiful Ba Be Lake (ba be means 'three basins'), 200 m above sea level. The lake is surrounded by limestone hills carpeted in tropical evergreen forest.

The park itself contains a very high diversity of flora and fauna, including an estimated 417 species of plant, 100 species of butterfly, 23 species of amphibian and reptile, 110 species of bird and 50 species of mammal. Among the latter are 10 seriously endangered species, including the Tonkinese snub-nosed langur (*Rhinopitecus avunculus*) and the black gibbon (*Hylobates concolor*). Within the park there are a number of villages inhabited by people of the Tay, Red Dao, Coin Dao and White Hmong minorities.

Listings North from Hanoi

Where to stay

Ba Be National Park

$ Ba Be National Park Guesthouse
T281-389 4026.
62 nice and comfortable a/c rooms with adjoining bathrooms with hot water. Meals available in the park office.

$ Homestays
It is possible to find your own homestay in the area or they can be booked in advance from Hanoi-based agents.

Transport

Bac Can
The bus station is on Duc Xuan St. There are buses to **Ha Glang**, **Cao Bang** and **Hanoi**. Hanoi is about 288 km away, 9-10 hrs.

Cao Bang

Cao Bang is located on Highway 3 and is 270 km from Hanoi. Na Phac to Cao Bang is 83 km, 1½ hrs along a well-metalled road. The Cao Bac Pass runs between 39 km and 29 km before Cao Bang, with stunning scenery all the way and breathtaking views at its summit.

Cao Bang stands in a valley on a narrow peninsula between the Bang Giang and Hien rivers, which join just to the northwest of the town. The market here is one of the largest in the country.

From the late 1920s onwards Cao Bang became a cradle of the revolutionary movement in the north. The following years saw the establishment of many party cells through which a substantial programme of subversive activity against the colonial regime was organized. It was thus no accident that in 1940, when he returned to Vietnam after his long sojourn overseas, Ho Chi Minh chose to make remote Cao Bang Province his revolutionary headquarters during the crucial period from 1940 to 1945. Cao Bang was badly damaged during the 1979 border war with China and has since been extensively rebuilt.

There is not a lot to see in the town. A few late-19th-century French buildings have survived the ravages of war and redevelopment in the old quarter of town, which stretches down the hill from the fortress to the Hien River Bridge, makes that area worth exploring on foot.

Cao Bang Exhibition Centre ① *Hoang Nhu St, T26-385 2616, Wed and Sat 0800-1100, 1300-1700, free,* records the history of the revolutionary struggle in Cao Bang Province, with particular reference to the years leading up to the establishment of the Democratic Republic of Vietnam when Ho Chi Minh's headquarters were based at Pac Bo, 56 km north of Cao Bang. Pride of place in the exhibition hall is given to Ho's old staff car, registration number 'BAC 808'. Unfortunately all information is in Vietnamese only.

Ky Sam Temple

18 km north of Cao Bang town on Highway 203 to Pac Bo, located in the Nung village of Ngan, 200 m east of Highway 203.

This temple honours the memory of **Nung Tri Cao**, Nung lord of Quang Uyen, who led one of the most important ethnic minority revolts against the Vietnamese monarchy during the 11th century.

The story of Nung Tri Cao began in 1039 when Nung Tri Cao's father Nung Ton Phuc and his elder brother Nung Tri Thong rose in rebellion against Le Thai Tong. The Viets quickly swiftly assembled an expeditionary force and the rebels were caught and summarily executed. However, two years later Nung Tri Cao himself gathered an army, seizing neighbouring territories and declaring himself ruler of a Nung kingdom, which he called Dai Lich. He too was quickly captured by Viet troops, but having put his father and elder brother to death two years earlier, King Le Thai Tong took pity on Nung Tri Cao and let him return to Quang Uyen. For the next seven years peace returned to the area, but in 1048, Nung Tri Cao rose up in revolt yet again, this time declaring himself 'Emperor of Dai Nam' and seizing territories in southern China. For the next five years he managed to play the Viet and Chinese kings off against each other until Le Thai Tong finally captured and executed him in 1053.

There has been a temple in the village of Ngan for many centuries, but the one standing today dates from the 19th century. It comprises two buildings, the outer building housing an altar dedicated to one of Nung Tri Cao's generals, the inner sanctum originally containing statues of the king, his wife and his mother; unfortunately these statues were stolen many years ago. The poem etched onto the walls in the outer building talks of Nung Tri Cao's campaigns and declares that his spirit is ever ready to come to the aid of his country in times of need.

Ruins of Cao Binh Church
5 km north of Ky Sam Temple along Highway 203 to Pac Bo, fork left at a junction; the ruins are 500 m from the junction.

Constructed in 1906, Cao Binh Church was one of three churches administered from Cao Bang during the French period, the others being those of Cao Bang and That Khe. There used to be many French houses in the vicinity of the church, but the majority of those that survived the French war were destroyed in 1979. However, the former vicar's house still stands relatively intact, adjacent to the ruins of the church. The family that currently occupies it runs one of the Cao Bang region's most famous apiaries.

Mac Kings' Temple
1.5 km beyond Lang Den (Temple village), located on the west bank of the Dau Genh River, opposite Cao Binh. Accessible either on foot or by 4WD capable of fording the river.

Cao Binh is situated on the east bank of the Dau Genh River, a tributary of the Bang Giang River. On the opposite bank lies **Lang Den** (Temple village), which takes its name from the ruined 16th-century palace of the Mac Dynasty located on a hill just above the village.

This structure is believed to have been built during the early 1520s by Mac Dang Dung, a general of the Le army who in 1521-1522 seized control of the kingdom, forcing the 11-year-old King Le Chieu Tong into exile and setting up his younger brother Le Thung as king. Two years later Mac Dang Dung forced Le Thung to abdicate, declaring himself king of Dai Viet.

The Mac Dynasty retained control of Dai Viet for 65 years, during which period representatives of the deposed Le Dynasty mounted numerous military campaigns against the usurpers. The powerful Trinh family finally restored the Le kings to power in 1592, but in that year a nephew of Mac Mau Hop, the last Mac king, seized Cao Bang and set up a small kingdom there. Over the next 75 years three successive generations of the Mac family managed to keep the royal armies at bay, even managing to launch two successful attacks on Thang Long (Hanoi) before Cao Bang was finally recaptured by Trinh armies in 1667.

It is apparent that this building was originally constructed as a small royal residence; the original cannon placements may still be seen on the hill in front of the main entrance.

Listings Cao Bang and around

Tourist information

Cao Bang Tourist
1 Nguyen Du St, T26-385 2245.
As provincial travel agencies go, it is good and offers a selection of tours at reasonable prices. The staff are friendly and helpful.

Where to stay

$ Bang Giang Hotel
Kim Dong St, Cao Bang, T26-385 3431.
Large 70-room building that is one of the best of a rather bad lot. A choice of fan or a/c rooms. It does the job for a quick overnight stay.

Restaurants

There are plenty of places in Cao Bang to get a bowl of *pho* from 6am and a host of simple rice restaurants serving from around 1100.

$ Bac Lam
K025 Hoang Nhu St, T26-385 2697.
Open 1000-2000.
Local dishes.

$ Thanh Truc
133 Xuan Truong St, T26-385 2798.
Serves basic fare from 0800 until 2000.

Transport

The bus station is on Kim Dong St in Cao Bang. Buses to **Hanoi**, 10 hrs; to **Thai Nguyen**, 7 hrs. To **Nguyen Binh**, **Tinh Túc**, **Bao Lac**, **Bao Lam** on Route 34, 1 bus leaves between 0530-0700, another at 1400 and the last leaves at 1500.

Pac Bo → *Colour map 1, A5.*

cradle of the resistance movement

The road from Cao Bang to Pac Bo passes through 56 km of stunning scenery, taking 1½ hours. Despite its proximity to China, no special permit is needed, but walking outside the area is not permitted.

On 28 January 1941 Ho Chi Minh crossed the Sino-Vietnamese border, returning home to take charge of the resistance movement after 30 years overseas. In the days that followed, he and his colleagues set up their revolutionary headquarters in a cave in the Pac Bo valley. Of interest primarily to scholars of the fledgling Vietnamese Socialist Party, Pac Bo is the sort of pilgrimage spot that model carpet-weavers or revolutionary railwaymen might be brought to as a reward.

ON THE ROAD
From cave to Congress

Taking advantage of the surrender of the French administration to the Japanese, Ho Chi Minh returned to Vietnam setting up his headquarters at Pac Bo, an area populated mainly by the Nung people. It was from here that Ho Chi Minh – dressed in the traditional Nung costume – guided the growing revolutionary movement, organizing training programmes for cadres, translating *The History of the Communist Party in the USSR* into Vietnamese and editing the revolutionary newspaper *Independent Vietnam*.

The eighth Congress of the Communist Party Central Committee, convened by Ho Chi Minh at Pac Bo from 10-19 March 1941, was an event of great historic importance that saw the establishment of the Vietnam Independence League (*Vietnam Doc Lap Dong Minh Hoi*), better known as the Viet Minh. This Congress also assisted preparations for the future armed uprising, establishing guerilla bases throughout the Viet Bac.

The years from 1941 to 1945 were a period of severe hardship for the Vietnamese people, as the colonial government colluded with Japanese demands to exploit the country's natural resources to the full in order to support the Japanese war effort. But, by 1945, the Vichy Government in France had fallen and the French colonial administration belatedly drew up plans to resist the Japanese. However, on 9 March 1945, their plans were foiled by the Japanese who set up a new government with King Bao Dai as head of state.

At this juncture, Viet Minh guerilla activity was intensified all over the country with the result that by June 1945, almost all of the six provinces north of the Red River Delta were under Communist control. On 13 August Japan surrendered to the Allied forces; three days later Ho Chi Minh headed south from Pac Bo to Tan Trao near Tuyen Quang to preside over a People's Congress, who declared a general insurrection and established the Democratic Republic of Vietnam. The August Revolution that followed swept all in its wake; within a matter of weeks the three major cities of Hanoi, Hué and Saigon had fallen to the Viet Minh and King Bao Dai had abdicated. On 2 September 1945 President Ho Chi Minh made a historic address to the people in Hanoi's Ba Dinh Square, proclaiming the nation's independence.

Sights

The **Pac Bo Vestiges Area Exhibition Center** ⓘ *T26-385 2425, daily 0800-1700*, houses artefacts concerning the revolution and Ho Chi Minh's part in it. The centre is 2 km from the vestiges themselves and comprises two buildings: the Ho Chi Minh House of Remembrance contains an altar dedicated to Ho Chi Minh, while the museum has background information on the Pac Bo area and its historical role in the revolutionary struggle. It also contains information about Ho Chi Minh's long journey back to Vietnam between 1938 and 1941, culminating in his arrival at Pac Bo on 28 January 1941. There is a series of artefacts associated with the various periods between 1941 and 1945 during which Ho Chi Minh lived and worked at Pac Bo, including many of his private possessions. Then there are further exhibits surrounding the events leading up to Ho's journey south from Pac Bo to Tan Trao near Tuyen Quang, where a decision was taken in August 1945 to launch a general insurrection to seize power and found the Democratic Republic of Vietnam.

A further 2 km by road is a parking area located next to the Lenin Stream under the shade of Karl Marx Mountains; both names chosen by Ho Chi Minh (the place is festooned with commemorative plaques). From here, visitors can do two walks: one to **Coc Bo Cave** (500 m), where Ho lived and worked after his return from overseas, and the other to **Khuoi Nam Jungle Hut** (800 m).

Ban Doc (Ban Zop), Vietnam's most recently discovered waterfall, and apparently the highest, is about 80 km due north of Cao Bang. Views of the waterfall are incredible.

Northeast frontier → *Colour map 1, A5 and B5.*
magnificent mountain passes, magical rice paddy valleys and historical caves

From Cao Bang to Lang Son along Highway 4 is a journey of 135 km; the road is in relatively poor condition and the going can be quite hard, taking 3½ hours, but it is not without its rewards.

Cao Bang to Lang Son
About 10 km south of Dong Khe, Highway 4 climbs up to the infamous Lung Phay Pass. From here to the village of Bong Lau the wonderful mountain scenery makes it difficult to imagine the carnage that took place between 1947 and 1950, when convoy after convoy of French supply trucks ran into carefully planned Viet Minh ambushes. The War Heroes' Cemetery at Bong Lau is sited on a hill where a French military outpost once stood and marks the border between Cao Bang and Lang Son provinces.

About 30 km south of That Khe the road passes through more towering limestone outcrops before commencing its climb up through another of the Frontier Campaign's infamous battle zones.

Lang Son → *Colour map 1, B5.*
The direct route from Hanoi is along Highway 1A via Chi Lang and Bac Giang, 154 km, 3½ hrs. (Chi Lang Pass is the site of Le Loi's historic victory over 100,000 Ming invaders in 1427, effectively bringing to an end 1000 years of Chinese hegemony.) The longer, more scenic route is along Highway 1B via Bac Son and Thai Nguyen, 237 km, 7 hrs. The road passes through some delightful highland countryside settled by Tay, Nung and Dao.

The town of Lang Son lies on the Ky Lung River in a small alluvial plain surrounded by 1000-m-high mountains. Like Cao Bang, Lang Son was badly damaged during the border war of 1979 and has since been substantially rebuilt. But, the old quarter of the town, south of the Ky Cung River, still contains a number of interesting historic buildings as well as the town's markets.

The rebuilt **Dong Kinh Market** is chock-full of Chinese consumer goods brought through Dong Dang. Although rebuilt many times and finally sidelined by the gleaming new structure at Dong Kinh, **Ky Lua Market** is the oldest in Lang Son and still sees a trickle of trading activity every day. Members of the Tay and Nung are regular visitors here. **Lang Son Citadel** comprises a large section of the ancient city walls, dating back to the 18th century. The former **Lang Son monastery**, which once stood on the other side of the city walls, is south down Nguyen Thai Hoc Street from the old quarter to My Son junction.

The east- and west-facing walls of the imposing 16th-century **Mac Dynasty Citadel** are located on a limestone outcrop west of Lang Son. To get there, head out of town past the six-way junction on the Tam Thanh Road.

At the **Tam Thanh Cave** ① *on the road to the Mac Dynasty Citadel, 10,000d*, there are three chambers; the outer one functions as a pagoda with two shrines and the second one contains a fresh water pool. A poem by Ngo Thi Sy (1726-1780), military commander of the Lang Son garrison who first discovered this and other caves in the area, is carved on the wall near the entrance.

Nhi Thanh ① *south of Tam Thanh Cave, from the six-way junction take the Nhi Thanh road, 10,000d*, is perhaps the best known of Lang Son's caves. There are in fact two separate caves here – the one on the right contains the Tam Giao Pagoda, established in 1777 by Ngo Thi Sy, in which are six shrines, while the one on the left follows the Ngoc Tuyen stream deep into the mountain: the latter is particularly dramatic. More of Ngo Thi Sy's poetry adorns the walls here.

Dong Dang and the Chinese border → *Colour map 1, B5.*
Some 18 km north of Lang Son is the border with China at Dong Dang. The Chinese border town is Ping Xiang. It is possible to cross by road and by train. The road crossing is at Cua Khau Huu Nghi Dong Dang (the Friendship Pass). It is a couple of kilometres between the two international border posts. You will need to obtain a Chinese visa at the embassy in Hanoi and specify the Dong Dang crossing. For Chinese visa costs see page 439. Entering Vietnam, you will have needed to obtain a Vietnamese visa in Beijing or Hong Kong as these are not available at the border.

Bac Son → *Colour map 1, B5.*
The rural Bac Son area is mainly of interest to history buffs as a stop over on a tour of the northeast region. Settled mainly by members of the Tay and Nung ethnicity, the small market town of Bac Son has two important reasons to claim significance in the history of the Vietnamese nation. The first derives from the very large number of prehistoric artefacts unearthed here by archaeologists. The so-called **Bac Son period** (5000-3000 BC) was characterized by the development of pottery and the widespread use of refined stone implements, including distinctive axes with polished edges known as Bacsonian axes.

The second is the **Bac Son Uprising**. In September 1940, revolutionaries detained in Lang Son prison, seized the opportunity afforded by the Japanese

The Frontier Campaign of 1947-1950

The government established by Ho Chi Minh in September 1945 soon found itself in a cleft stick. The terms of the Potsdam Conference had provided for the surrender of Japanese forces to be accepted south of the 16th parallel by British-Indian forces and north of that line by the Chinese Kuomintang (Nationalist Party) troops of Chiang Kai-shek. In the south, General Gracey promptly freed thousands of French troops detained in the wake of the Japanese coup.

Unable to confront both the French and the Chinese, Ho Chi Minh decided to negotiate with the French, concluding, as we have already seen, that they were the lesser of the two evils. In February 1946 the French signed a treaty with the Chinese Nationalists that secured their withdrawal from Vietnamese territory. The following month a Franco-Vietnamese agreement confirmed the status of Vietnam as a free state within the French Union and the Indochinese Federation.

After consolidating their positions in the Red River Delta, the French resolved to launch a major offensive against the Viet Bac in October 1947 with the objective of destroying the resistance leadership. Their plan involved a pincer movement of two armed columns – one under Colonel Communal moving by water up the Red and Lo rivers to attack and occupy Tuyen Quang and Chiem Hoa, the other under Colonel Beaufre travelling to Lang Son and then north along Highway 4 to That Khe, Dong Khe and Cao Bang before heading southwards to Bac Can. The offensive was intended to take the Viet Minh by surprise but, just six days after the attack had begun, an aircraft carrying the French chief of staff was shot down near Cao Bang, allowing the plans to fall into the hands of the Viet Minh High Command.

Sailing up the Lo River, Communal's column fell into a Viet Minh ambush suffering a humiliating defeat and losing some 38 gunboats before being forced to retreat to Tuyen Quang. Meanwhile, Beaufre's forces suffered repeated ambushes at the hands of Viet Minh before finally managing to recapture the fortresses of Cao Bang and Bac Can in late October 1947. Having

attack on the town to escape, heading northwest across the mountains to Bac Son. With the support of the local Communist Party organization they fomented a general insurrection in the town, disarming the fleeing French troops and taking over the district centre to set up the first revolutionary power base in the Viet Bac. The following year French forces responded by launching a campaign of terror in the Viet Bac, forcing the leaders of the uprising to retreat into the mountains. The Bac Son uprising did, however, prove to be an important milestone in the revolutionary struggle and, in the years which followed, the tide turned steadily against the French throughout the region.

On the way into the town the road passes an unmarked white building on stilts with a Vietnamese flag fluttering on its roof – this is the **Museum of the Bac Son** failed to achieve the objective of their offensive, the French were now obliged to dig-in for a long and costly war.

The position of the French became steadily more and more precarious. Supply convoys travelling from Lang Son to Cao Bang and Bac Can were ambushed repeatedly, particularly along Highway 4. Thousands of colonial troops lost their lives en route, on what French press dubbed the 'Road of Death', the most dangerous stretches of which were the Lung Phay Pass 10 km south of Dong Khe and the Bo Cung Pass 30 km south of That Khe.

Despite massive subsidy from the United States under the emerging Truman doctrine of containing Communism, the cost of air-dropping supplies into the region was becoming an intolerable burden. The French High Command finally concluded that their position in the Viet Bac was no longer tenable and began to draw up plans for the abandonment of Cao Bang. Before these plans could be implemented, however, the Viet Minh launched a surprise attack on Dong Khe, capturing the post. Taken aback by this bold move and desperate to secure the speedy and safe retreat of its Cao Bang garrison, the French High Command ordered the post's commander, Colonel Charton, to withdraw to Lang Son.

Leaving Cao Bang on 3 October 1950, Charton's column made it no further than Nam Nang, 17 km south of the town, before running into a Viet Minh ambush. Travelling northwards from That Khe to rendezvous with Charton, Lepage's forces were also intercepted in the vicinity of Dong Khe. The subsequent battle in the hills to the west of Highway 4 resulted in a resounding Viet Minh victory, in the aftermath of which, on 8 October, some 8000 French troops had been either killed or taken prisoner. Within days the French had abandoned all their remaining posts on Highway 4.

The Viet Minh victory on Highway 4 was a major turning point in the war, which threw the colonial forces throughout the north into complete disarray. During the following two weeks the French were obliged to withdraw all their forces from Lang Son, Thai Nguyen and Tuyen Quang, while in the northwest, the French garrisons at Hoa Binh and Lao Cai were also driven out. Thus was the scene set for the final stage of the First Indochina War, which would culminate four years later in the momentous battle at Dien Bien Phu (see box, page 86).

Rebellion (① 0700–1800, free, which contains a collection of prehistoric axe-heads and other tools dating from the Bac Son period plus a large display of artefacts relating to the Bac Son Uprising. These include the weapons and personal effects of those involved in the uprising, plus letters and other documents written by Ho Chi Minh and revolutionaries such as Hoang Van Thu.

Tourist information

Lang Son Tourism and Export company
9 Tran Hung Dao St, T25-381 4848.
It arranges a good selection of tours within the vicinity. Staff have a good command of English. Friendly and helpful.

Where to stay

Lang Son

$$-$ Muong Thanh Lang Son
Ngo Quyen, T43-640 8686.
Part of the countrywide **Muong Thanh** group, this largee hotel has a broad range of rooms types, plus a restaurant and massage.

$ Dong Kinh
25 Nguyen Du St, T25-387 0166.
Near market, better rooms with own bathroom, a/c, fridge, etc, cheapest rooms shared facilities, basic but cheap.

Restaurants

Lang Son

A host of places on Le Loi and around the market street sell *pho* and rice, while at Cua Hang An Uong a variety of different *lau* (hotpot/steamboat) are on offer at good prices.

Transport

Lang Son
Bus
The bus station is at 28A Ngo Quyen St, T25-371 5975. A main highway links Lang Son with Hanoi and public buses travel along this route, 5 hrs. **Hoang Long Co** operates frequently.

Car and motorbike
It is possible to return (on a Minsk) via Halong Bay and the coast; the road to Tien Yen is a shocker and carry lunch and spare fuel with you as there are no supplies en route. From Tien Yen the road improves.

Train
1 train runs daily from **Hanoi** and back – at 1830, arriving 2240, returning 0350, arriving 0810 – to **Dong Dang** (Border Gate) and to **Lang Son** at 0540 arriving 1100.

Dong Dang and the Chinese border
Minibuses and *xe oms* travel from Lang Son to the **Friendship Pass** for the Chinese border, 30 mins. A train runs from Hanoi to the border daily.

Bac Son
Connections with **Hanoi** and **Lang Son**. The best method is to return to Lang Son and get a bus from there.

East & south
of Hanoi

where dramatic limestone crags rear from the ground

Off the coast to the east of Hanoi lies Halong Bay with its thousands of limestone islands rearing out of the sea. Cruising these waters is now firmly established as one of Vietnam's top tourist draws. Further east is the Bai Tu Long National Park; Halong Bay without the hordes has to be worth the effort.

To the south is Ninh Binh and an area know as 'Halong Bay on Land' where rivers weave among rice paddies surrounded by dramatic limestone karst formations.

Haiphong → *Colour map 1, B5.*

for most, the city is a transport hub for Halong Bay and Cat Ba

Haiphong is home to a few beautiful old French buildings, but there is little to attract the tourist other than an authentic glimpse into life without tourism. The port of Haiphong was established in 1888 on the Cua Cam River, a major distributory of the Red River. It is the largest port and the second largest city in the North.

Sights
Much of outer Haiphong is an ugly industrial sprawl that will win no environmental beauty contests. But, considering the bombing the city sustained, there is still a surprising amount of attractive colonial-style architecture in the city centre. Central Haiphong is pleasantly green with tree-lined streets.

Right in the heart of town is the **Great Theatre** ① *corner of Tran Hung Dao St and Quang Trung St*, built in 1904 using imported French materials, with a colonnaded front, and facing a wide tree-lined boulevard. In November 1946, 40 Viet Minh fighters died here in a pitched battle with the French, triggered by the French government's decision to open a customs house in Haiphong. A plaque outside commemorates the battle. The streets around the theatre support the

Essential East and south of Hanoi

Finding your feet

Haiphong is well connected, with regular flights, trains and buses. Haiphong is the departure point for Cat Ba Island; it takes an hour by hydrofoil. There are two bases from which to explore Halong Bay: Halong City or Cat Ba. Traditionally, visitors to Halong Bay went direct to Halong City from Hanoi and took a boat from there. This is still a valid option, but Cat Ba Island is becoming increasingly popular as a springboard to Halong Bay, largely because Cat Ba itself is interesting.

Getting around

Tour operators are a popular way to visit Haiphong and the Halong Bay area, especially if short of time, but equally there are plenty of frequent public transport options to this area.

When to go

It can be stormy in June, July and August; it is no fun in the bay area in the rain or fog, so get a weather forecast if you can. On Cat Ba, the busiest and most expensive time is during school summer holidays from May to September. Winters are generally cool and dry.

Best boating

Halong Bay, page 125
Tam Coc, page 135
Van Long, page 137

greatest concentration of foodstalls and shops.

Other colonial architecture includes the **People's Court** ① *31 Tran Phu St,* a fine French building with shutters; the **post office** ① *5 Nguyen Tri Phuong St,* in an attractive building, and the bank (**Vietcombank** ① *11 Hoang Dieu St*), a handsome yellow and cream building.

Haiphong Museum (Bao Tang Thanh Pho Hai Phong) ① *66 Dien Bien Phu St, Tue and Thu 0800-1030, Wed and Sun 1930-2130, 2000d,* is an impressive colonial edifice in a wash of desert-sand red, and contains records of the city's turbulent past (some labels are in English).

There are a number of street markets and flower stalls off Cau Dat Street, which runs south from the theatre, along Tran Nhat Duat and Luong Khanh Thien streets. Sat Market is to be found in the west quarter of town, at the end of Phan Boi Chau Street. A market has stood on this site since 1876. The present building is a huge six-storey concrete edifice that has never quite taken off.

Near the centre of town on Me Linh Street is the Nghe Pagoda built at the beginning of the 20th century. The pagoda is dedicated to the memory of heroine General Le Chan who fought with the Trung sisters against the Chinese. A festival is held on the eighth day of the second lunar month to commemorate her birthday and offerings of crab and noodles, her favourite foods, are made. There is also an enormous statue of her in front of a cultural building diagonally opposite the Great Theatre.

BACKGROUND

Forward thinking

Haiphong witnessed the initial arrival of the French in 1872 (they occupied Hanoi a year later) and, appropriately, their final departure from the north at 1500 in the afternoon of 15 May 1955. As the major port of the north, it was subjected to sustained bombing during the war. To prevent petrol and diesel fuel reaching the Viet Cong, nearly 80% of all above-ground tanks were obliterated by US bombing in 1966. The US did not realize that the North Vietnamese, anticipating such action, had dispersed much of their supplies to underground and concealed tanks. This did not prevent the city from receiving a battering, although Haiphong's air defence units are said to have retaliated by shooting down 317 US planes.

Around Haiphong

Du Hang Pagoda ① *1 km south of the city centre on Chua Hang St (take a* xe ôm*)*, was originally built in 1672 by wealthy mandarin-turned-monk Nguyen Dinh Sach. It has been renovated and remodelled several times since. Arranged around a courtyard, this small temple has some fine traditional woodcarving.

Dinh Hang Kenh (Hang Kenh communal house or *dinh***)** ① *51 Nguyen Cong Tru St, 2 km south of the centre*, dates back to 1856. Although built as a communal house, its chief function today is as a temple. The main building is supported by 32 columns of ironwood and the wood carvings in the window grilles are noteworthy. From the outside, the roof is the most dramatic feature, tiled in the fishscale style, and ornamented with a number of dragons. The corners of the roof turn up and it appears that the sheer weight is too much, as the roof is now propped up on bricks. There are a number of *dinh* in and around Haiphong, reflecting the traditional importance of Chinese in this area. Today Taiwanese businessmen are counted among the major investors in Haiphong.

Listings Haiphong

Tourist information

Vietnamtourism
*18 Minh Khai St, T031-382 2616,
www.haiphongtourism.gov.vn.
Mon-Sat 0800-1100, 1400-1700.*

Where to stay

Haiphong offers plenty of accommodation to meet the demands of industrialists and expats rather than travellers; standards tend to be fairly good but prices are a little high.

$$$ Avani Harbour View
*12 Tran Phu St, T31-382 7827,
www.avanihotels.com.*
Near the river, this 127-room hotel has 2 restaurants and a bar. It is well managed and comfortable but certainly not 5 star.

$$$-$$ Huu Nghi
*60 Dien Bien Phu St, T31-382 3244,
www.huunghihotel.vn.*

Central and, with 11 storeys and 162 rooms, one of Haiphong's largest. Rooms are fully equipped and quiet if dated. Staff are helpful. Gym, pool and tennis court on site. Popular with Chinese tour groups; breakfast included. From the top storey the view of the port and French colonial buildings is great.

Restaurants

Foreign-business influence is reflected in the form of Japanese, Chinese and Taiwanese restaurants.

$$$-$ Chie
18 Tran Quang Khai St, T31-382 1018.
Small Japanese restaurant with good sushi and sashimi.

$ Hoa Bien
24 Tran Hung Dao St, T31-374 5633.
Excellent Vietnamese fare with Chinese influence in a street-side setting. All dishes served fresh and piping hot.

Shopping

The large Minh Khai supermarket, Minh Khai St, will supply all your needs.

Transport

Air
Cat Bi, Haiphong's airport, lies 7 km southeast of town; the only air connections are with **HCMC**.
Airline offices Vietnam Airlines, 166 Haong Van Thu St, T31-381 0890.

Boat
Haiphong is the departure point for **Cat Ba Island** and from there with **Halong Bay**. Check all ferry information before setting out as timetables are liable to change.

Connections with Cat Ba (1-hr journey time) from the wharf on Ben Binh St where there are a number of ticket offices. Services may take motorbikes depending on ferry size. **Transtour Co** runs the Haiphong–Cat Ba ferry, T31-384 1099, www.transtourco.com.vn.

Hoang Long Co, 5 Pham Ngu Lao St, T31-392 0920, www.hoanglongasia.com, runs buses from Hanoi (Luong Yen bus station, T4-3987 7225) and Haiphong to the **Dinh Vu ferry terminal** (30 mins) and a boat from here to **Cat Ba** (1 hr 30 mins). It's worth weighing up the pros and cons of taking a tour or making your own way to Cat Ba. While the do-it-yourself method is easy and cheap, by the time you add in all the little incidental costs and the cost of a boat excursion from Cat Ba it may be just as cheap to take a tour.

Bus
Highway 5 is 100 km of fast motorway connecting capital with coast. It is one of the country's most hectic and there are frequent bus and minibus connections. Departures to **Hanoi** leave from Tam Bac bus station in front of Sat Market. **Hoang Long** bus company leaves Tam Bac station 42 times a day from 0455-1925.

Buses to Halong leave from the Lac Long bus station every 15 mins. Buses to **Ninh Binh**, **Thanh Hoa** and **Hué** leave from the Niem Nghia bus station.

Taxi
Mai Linh Taxi, T31-383 3833.

Train
5 departures daily in either direction between **Hanoi** and **Haiphong**, T31-392 0026. Trains depart from Long Bien station on Gam Cau St, Hanoi, or from the Central Station.

★Halong means 'descending dragon', and an enormous beast is said to have careered into the sea at this point, cutting the fantastic bay from the rocks as it thrashed its way into the depths. Vietnamese poets (including the 'Poet King' Le Thanh Tong) have traditionally extolled the beauty of this romantic area with its rugged islands that protrude from a sea dotted with sailing junks. The bay is now a UNESCO World Heritage Site and one of Vietnam's key tourist draws with thousands sailing on overnight cruises here every year.

Most people book their tour in Hanoi, but boat tours of the bay can be booked at the Bai Chay Tourist Wharf in Halong City and Cat Ba Town. To see the bay properly allow four to five hours but an overnight trip is enjoyable and preferable.

Karsts and caves in Halong Bay
Grotto of Wonders, Customs House Cave and Surprise Grotto are generally included in tour and the entrance fee will be included in your package price.

Geologically the tower-karst scenery of Halong Bay is the product of millions of years of chemical action and river erosion working on the limestone to produce a pitted landscape. At the end of the last ice age, when glaciers melted, the sea level rose and inundated the area turning hills into islands. The islands of the bay are divided by a broad channel: to the east are the smaller outcrops of Bai Tu Long, see page 132, while to the west are the larger islands with caves and secluded beaches.

   Among the more spectacular caves are **Hang Hanh**, which extends for 2 km. Tour guides will point out fantastic stalagmites and stalactites that, with imagination, become heroes, demons and animals. **Hang Dau Go** is the cave wherein Tran Hung Dao stored his wooden stakes prior to studding them in the bed of the Bach Dang River in 1288 to destroy the boats of invading Mongol hordes. **Hang Thien Cung (Heavenly Palace)** is a hanging cave, a short 50-m haul above sea level, with dripping stalactites, stumpy stalagmites and solid rock pillars. A truly enormous cave and one of those most visited is **Sung Sot Cave (Surprise Cave)**.

Halong City and around
Following the admission of Halong Bay to UNESCO's hallowed roll of World Heritage Sites, the two small towns of **Bai Chay** and **Hon Gai** were, in 1994, collectively elevated in status by the government and dubbed Halong City. It doesn't have much appeal to visitors; people tend to stay one night at most in order to visit Halong Bay.

   It was at Halong, arguably, that Vietnam's fate under the French was sealed. In late 1882 Captain Henri Rivière led two companies of troops to Hon Gai to seize the coal mines for France. Shortly afterwards he was ambushed and killed and his head paraded on a stake from village to village. His death persuaded the French parliament to fund a full-scale expedition to make all of Vietnam a protectorate of France. As the politician Jules Delafosse remarked at the time: "Let us, gentlemen, call things by their name. It is not a protectorate you want, but a possession."

Yen Tu Mountains

The Yen Tu Mountains are 14 km northwest of Uong Bi and climb to a maximum elevation of 1068 m. Peppered with pagodas from the 13th to 16th centuries, much has been lost to the ravages of war and climate but stupas and temples of more recent foundation survive. The site has attracted pilgrims since the 13th century when King Tran Nhan Tong abandoned the throne in favour of a spiritual life. He washed the secular dust from his body in the Tam stream and entered the Cam Thuc (Abstinence) Pagoda. His 100 concubines traced him here and tried to persuade him of the folly of his ways but despite their undoubted allure he resisted all appeals and clung to his ascetic existence. Distraught by their failure, the poor women drowned themselves. Tran Nhan Tong later built a temple to their memory. Climbing the hills, visiting the temples and admiring the views can take a full day.

Listings Halong Bay and around

Tourist information

Quang Ninh Tourism Information Promotion Centre
C29 Royal Park Area opposite the Halong 1 Hotel and near the Novotel, T33-362 8862, www.halongtourism.com.vn. Mon-Fri 0730-1630.
Provide advice about boats and hotels.

Where to stay

The past few years have seen an explosion in the number of hotels and guesthouses in Bai Chay and Hon Gai. Many of the newer hotels are badly built and, apart from the fact that some of the taller ones look structurally unsound, are quite frequently damp and musty; check the room first.

There are few hotels in Hon Gai but they tend to be more competitively priced than those in Bai Chay. In Bai Chay there are 2 main groups of hotels, 2 km apart. Most are to be found at the west end on the way in to town, set back a little from the seafront, and include Vuon Dao St composed entirely of 5- to 8-room mini hotels. A couple of kilometres further on, nearer the bridge, is a smaller group, some of which have good views.

$$$$-$$$ Halong Plaza
8 Halong Rd, Bai Chay, T33-384 5810, www.halongplaza.com.
200 rooms and suites and fantastic views over the sea, especially from upper floors. Pool, restaurants and friendly staff – a lovely seafront hotel.

$$ Viethouse Lodge
Tuan Chau Island, T33-384 2233, www.viethouselodge.com.
With rooms scattered around a hillside this can be a more pleasant alternative to staying in the city. There's a restaurant, bar, games and transport to hire. The island is now connected to the mainland by a bridge.

Restaurants

Seafood is fresh and abundant and fairly priced. Le Qui Don St in Hon Gai has good seafood restaurants. Other than the hotels (see Halong Plaza especially), Halong Rd, near the junction with Vuon Dao St, Bai Chay, is lined for several hundred metres with restaurants – the best policy here is simply to pick a busy place.

$$ Emeraude Café
Co/Royal Park, T33-384 9266.
Open 0900-2100.
An oasis of comfort food close to the main hotels and restaurants. Free Wi-Fi.

What to do

Boat tours
Boat tours can be booked from hotels in Halong and in Hanoi, see below.

Buffalo Tours, Ba Trieu St, Hanoi, T4-3828 0702, www.buffalotours.com. A top-class operator and a recommended agent with which to book. They can also arrange scenic flights to the bay from Hanoi with **Hai Vu Aviation**.

Emeraude Classic Cruises, 46 Le Thai To St, Hanoi, T4-3935 1888, www.emeraude-cruises.com. The best way to see Halong Bay in style is on the reconstructed French paddle steamer, the *Emeraude*. There are 39 cabins with extremely comfortable beds and nice touches (gift-wrapped biscuits) and old-style fans although the bathrooms are on the tiny side. There's a sumptuous buffet lunch and more delicious food than you can eat for dinner. Entertainment includes a Vietnamese spring roll demo, swimming off the boat, squid fishing, t'ai chi exercise on the sun deck at dawn and a massage service. There is also a bar.

Transport

Boat
To Cat Ba Jump on a tourist boat for a 1-way (4-hr) ride from the Bai Chay Tourist Wharf (Halong Rd, T33-384 6592).

From Hon Gai (Halong City) boat station (98 Ben Tau Rd near Long Tien pagoda) to **Quan Lan Island** and **Mong Cai**, daily.

Bus
Halong City bus station is now 5 km west of Halong city, near Halong train station. There is a bus stop right outside the Bai Chay Tourist Wharf. There are regular connections from Bai Chay bus station to **Hanoi** from 0700, taking 4-5 hrs. Buses are slow, crowded, uncomfortable and full of pickpockets. Regular connections with Haiphong's Lac Long bus station. There are also buses to **Mong Cai** and to **Bai Dai** (for ferries to Quan Lan).

Cat Ba Island → *Colour map 1, B5.*
attractive springboard into the waters of Halong Bay

Home to rare langur monkeys in the forested interior, Cat Ba Island is many Hanoians' number one weekend getaway. The island occupies a stunning setting in the south of Halong Bay. Much of the island and the seas around are designated a national park.

Cat Ba's remoteness has been steadily eroded (it only plugged into mains electricity in 1999), but despite the growth in numbers of karaoke-loving weekenders, it remains an attractive place (minus a few of the uglier buildings). Best of all it is a great springboard into the surrounding waters of Halong Bay and an increasingly popular alternative to Halong City as there is a lot to see including the stunning scenery of the interior.

Exploring the island

Cat Ba is the largest island in a coastal archipelago that includes more than 350 limestone outcrops. It is adjacent to and geologically similar to the islands and peaks of Halong Bay but separated by a broad channel as the map illustrates. The islands around Cat Ba are larger than the outcrops of Halong Bay and generally more dramatic. Cat Ba is the ideal place from which to explore the whole coastal area: besides the quality of its scenery it is a more agreeable town in which to stay, although the countless new hotels springing up are slowly eroding the difference. The island is rugged and sparsely inhabited. Outside Cat Ba town there are only a few small villages. Perhaps the greatest pleasure is to hire a motorbike and explore, a simple enough process given the island's limited road network. Half of the island forms part of a national park, see below.

For an island of its size Cat Ba has remarkably few **beaches** – only three within easy access, creatively named **Cat Co 1**, **Cat Co 2** and **Cat Co 3**. These lie just to the east of town behind a steep hill in the southern fringes of the national park. They are popular with locals and visitors, especially in the late afternoon. It's a 1-km walk to the first and a further 1-km to the second which is quieter, cleaner and more secluded; Cat Co 2 is accessible by a walkway from Cat Co 1 or by boat. Cat Co 1 and 2 feature the Cat Tien Tourism Complex: there's food, sun loungers for hire, showers, toilets, lockers, campground and bungalows for hire on Cat Co 2, see

Cat Ba Island & Halong Bay

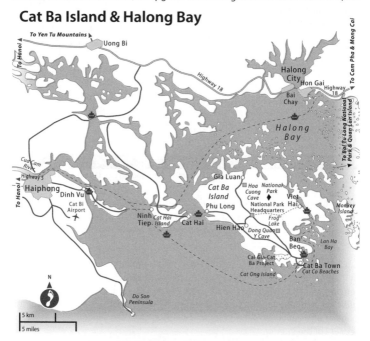

Where to stay. The Catba Island Resort & Spa on Cat Co 1 is also open to non-guests to use the pool and water slides; see Where to stay. There's also a restaurant and drinks here on the beach. Cat Co 3 (home of the Sunrise Resort) is also accessible by walkway from Cat Co 1 and by road and then stairs also.

On the way to the national park is the **Dong Quan Y Cave** ① *20,000d, 13 km from Cat Ba, 30 mins*. Built between 1960 and 1965 and used by the Americans as a hospital, it has 17 rooms and three floors. Near Gia Luan village is **Hoa Cuong Cave**, 100 m from the road.

From the park headquarters to Gia Luan the scenery is increasingly dramatic with soaring peaks rising out of the flat valley floor. **Gia Luan harbour** is used by Halong boats; there's plenty of mangrove, karst scenery, and a fishing village (black oysters and snails). Heading west, passing pine trees, you will arrive at **Hien Hao**, a village of 400 people. There's a small temple on the village outskirts; homestay is possible, see Where to stay.

Behind the town winds a road, right, up to a peak from where the views of Cat Co 2 and Lan Ha Bay are utterly spectacular. You could walk but the heat may see you on the back of a motorbike.

Offshore **Monkey Island** can be visited. It is close to Cat Ba and can be combined within a day-long cruise of Halong Bay or shorter four-hour excursion in a small boat. Accommodation is available here.

Cat Ba National Park → *Colour map 1, B5.*
Park office, T31-388 8741, open 0700-1700. Town to park gate, 15 km, is 30 mins on a motorbike.

The national park (Vuon Quoc Gia Cat Ba), established in 1986, covers roughly half the island and is some 252 km sq. Of this area, a third consists of coast and inland waters. Home to 109 bird and animal species, and of particular importance is the world's last remaining troupe of white-headed langur (around 59 animals). Their numbers dropped from around 2500 in the 1960s to 53 in 2000; the primate is critically endangered and on the World Conservation Union Red List (www.catbalangur.org). These elusive creatures (*Trachypithecus poliocephalus poliocephalus*) are rarely spotted as they Inhabit wild and remote cliff habitats. There are also several types of rare macaque (rhesus, pig-tailed and red-faced) and moose deer. Vegetation ranges from mangrove swamps in sheltered bays and densely wooded hollows, to high, rugged limestone crags sprouting caps of hardy willows. The marine section of the park is no less bounteous: perhaps less fortunate is the high economic value of its fish and crustacea populations, which keeps the local fishing fleet hard at work and prosperous. In common with other coastal areas in the region the potential for snorkelling here is zero.

Visitors are free to roam through the forest but advised not to wander too far from the path. Many hotels arrange treks from the park gate through the forest to Ao Ech (Frog Lake) on to the village of Viet Hai for a light lunch then down to the coast for a boat ride home. This takes the best part of a day (six to 10 hours). It is a good way to see the park but those preferring solitude can go their own way or go with a park guide. A short trek leads to the Ngu Lam Peak behind the park headquarters. July to October is the wet season when leeches are a problem and mosquitoes are at their worst. Bring leech socks if you have them and plenty of insect repellent. Collar, long sleeves and long trousers advisable.

Listings Cat Ba Island *map p128*

Tourist information

The Cat Hai District People's Committee Tourism Information Centre
Along the seafront, T31-368 8215, www.catba.com.vn.
Offers free travel information as well as tours. Most of the hotels also offer information and tours.

Where to stay

While in summer prices may be slightly higher than those listed, as far as possible the price ranges below give a fair indication of seasonal variations. It may still be possible to negotiate discounts in quieter periods. There are no addresses, and to confuse matters further, many hotels claim the same name.

$$$$ Cat Ba Island Resort & Spa
Cat Co 1, T31-368 8686, www.catba islandresort-spa.com.
There are 109 pleasant rooms decorated with white rattan furniture across 3 buildings facing the bay with a lovely outlook and fronting right on to the beach. The obtrusive water slides cannot be seen from the 2nd and 3rd building. 3 restaurants provide Western and Asian food and there are 2 pools, water slides, jacuzzi, massage, billiards and a tennis court. Trekking and Halong Bay tours are offered.

$$$$ Sunrise Resort
Cat Co 3, T31-388 7360, www.catba sunriseresort.com.
Low-key resort on a beach linked by road to the town and by footpath to Cat Co 1. It has beach loungers and thatched umbrellas, a pool, jacuzzi, massage, 3 restaurants and travel services.

$$-$ Cat Ba Homestay
10 mins' drive from the town, T091-664 5858, www.catba-homestay.com.
A restored century-old house in pretty grounds offers both dorm and private accommodation. With its yellow walls, wooden pillars and tiled roof, this is a quaint spot with traditional architecture. Popular with groups.

$ Cat Ba Sea View
220 Harbourfront, T031-388 8210.
The pick of the budget options along the seafront, about half of the rooms have good views in this clean and friendly hotel. Also has a decent inexpensive restaurant on the ground floor.

Cat Ba National Park

$ Park guesthouse
Viet Hai Village, Viet Hai Community Based Tourism Association, T31-388 8836.
Homestays have beds with mosquito nets. A mattress and bed sheets can also be provided.

Restaurants

After dark the front fills up with Vietnamese tourists on bicycles and tandem bikes and those out for an evening stroll. Cat Ba is not a great place for those seeking a culinary experience, but some good seafood can be found. There are tens of seafood restaurants on the island all serving the same menu of grilled and steamed varieties along with the hugely popular *lau* (hotpot), which often comes with packet instant noodles which swiftly kills the flavour of any seafood you add to the broth. None of the restaurants are particularly inspiring, so it is best to wander along and choose one with the atmosphere that suits; being a tourist town with a high turnover, a seafood restaurant can be family friendly one night and full of rowdy, beer swilling weekenders the next. There are also plenty of fried rice and *pho* places along the main road selling both beef and prawn noodle soups.

$$ Green Mango
T31-388 7151.
If the local seafood spots aren't for you, this is the island's best Western-style restaurant. It serves a variety of reasonable burgers and pastas and also offers fresh fish.

$ Oasis Bar
Near the main pier, T098-270 4659.
During the day and in the early evening this is an okay choice for a quick, budget meal, while later in the night it becomes one of the town's most popular bars.

What to do

Boat tours
Halong Bay is the most famous excursion from Cat Ba. Almost all hotels in Cat Ba offer tours as do the touts along the seafront. It is better to use a service provided by a reputable hotel (as listed in Where to stay, above).

Kayaking
Kayaking in Halong Bay and Lan Ha Bay are now regular features, especially in the summer months. It is best to go via one of the established tour operators in Hanoi, such as **Handspan** and **Buffalo Tours** or to book with **Asia Outdoors**.

Rock climbing
Climbing the rock karst limestone faces and towers on Cat Ba and Halong Bay is now possible with experienced, licensed and enthusiastic climbers, see Tour operators below. They offer roped climbs on dry land in the extremely beautiful Buffalo Valley as well as deep water solo climbing on the bay itself for which no ropes are needed – you simply jump straight into the ocean when you finish (or fall…).

Tour operators
Asia Outdoors, *222 1/4 St, Group 19, Ward 4, T31-368 8450, www.asiaoutdoors.com. vn.* Rock climbing, kayaking, trekking, boat cruises, islands stays and other adventures. Works directly with the local community on Cat Ba Island, employs both domestic and international staff and promotes the efforts to protect the endangered langur and the park's other conservation efforts. A highly recommended outfit.

Transport

There are direct hydrofoils from Haiphong or via the Dinh Vu ferry from Haiphong. Boats also leave Bai Chay and Tuan Chau 'Island' in Halong City for **Gia Luan** in the north of Cat Ba Island where a bus transports you to Cat Ba Town in the south. It is also possible to get a one-way ride with a tour leaving from the tourist wharf at Bai Chay (Halong City) direct to **Cat Ba Town** where tourist boats dock. Alternatively, organize a tour from Hanoi. The easiest way to reach Cat Ba from Hanoi is by the combined bus and ferry service (see page 72).

To get around the island go by *xe om*, hire a motorbike or get on a tour organized by a local hotel or tour operator in Hanoi.

Boat
From Haiphong, **Transtour Co** runs the Cat Ba–**Haiphong** ferry twice daily, T31-388 8314, office on the seafront. Express boats also run in the morning and afternoon. Tourist boats use the new Cat Ba pier in the middle of town.

Bus
There is a bus service between Cat Ba town and **Phu Long** where the Haiphong ferry docks along the new road and to **Gia Luan** where the Bai Chay and Tuan Chau 'Island' boats dock.

Bai Tu Long and the Chinese border → *Colour map 1, B6.*
as captivating as Halong Bay, but without the tourist hordes

Bai Tu Long is east of Halong Bay in the Gulf of Tonkin stretching towards the Chinese border. The group of islands makes up the Bai Tu Long National Park, covering 15,783 ha. It takes a longer to get here than the waters of Halong Bay, but the journey is well worth it.

Quan Lan Island
Quan Lan Island, a remote island just south of Bai Tu Long, is home to a very small community, some guesthouse accommodation, small restaurants, beaches and wild, untamed land. Bicycles can be hired at guesthouses as well as small boats.

Mong Cai
Mong Cai is located on the Gulf of Tonkin and is next to Dong Xing, China. The main point of interest in Mong Cai is the plethora of cheaply made Chinese goods available. It would also be the sensible place to cross if you are planning to go to Hainan Island. Apart from that there is not a lot to do or see. The Chinese entry visa must be issued by the embassy in Hanoi and specify the Mong Cai crossing.

The only tourist attraction is **Tra Co Beach**, 7 km from Mong Cai itself. It is a delightful sandy peninsula and, as it is 17 km long, you are bound to find a quiet spot. Avoid the Vietnamese holidays if possible as it will be crowded.

Where to stay

There are a couple of hotels and guesthouses on Quan Lan Island. Go direct from Hon Gai or arrange through My Ngoc hotel.

$ Quan Lan Resort
Son Hao Beach, T33-387 7316.
Wooden huts with en suite showers. A restaurant is available.

Transport

Boat
Daily boat service from Mong Cai to **Hon Gai** (Halong City), early afternoon 3 hrs. From Quan Lan Island to **Hon Gai** (Halong City), mid-afternoon, 2½ hrs.

Bus
Mong Cai is 360 km from Hanoi. There are 5 departures between 0530-0730, 10 hrs. There are many buses between Mong Cai and **Halong City** from 0500-1700, 6 hrs. There is also a 5-hr journey to **Lang Son**.

Ninh Binh and around → *Colour map 1, C4.*

Halong Bay on land

Ninh Binh city is capital of the densely populated province of Ninh Binh. It marks the most southerly point of the northern region. The town itself has little to commend to the tourist but it is a useful and accessible hub from which to visit some of the most interesting and attractive sights in the north.

Within a short drive lies the recently UNESCO-listed Trang An Landscape Complex including ancient capital of Hoa Lu with its temples dedicated to two of Vietnam's great kings; and the exquisite watery landscape of Tam Coc, an 'inland Halong Bay', where sampans carry visitors up a meandering river, through inundated grottoes and past verdant fields of rice. Also nearby are the Roman Catholic Phat Diem Cathedral and the wonderful Cuc Phuong National Park, with its glorious butterflies, flowers and ancient trees.

Travellers can get to the places around Ninh Binh as a day trip from Hanoi through tour agencies or by taking tours or hiring transport from the hotels in Ninh Binh. With your own transport, Hoa Lu, Tam Coc and Phat Diem can all be comfortably covered in a day.

Leaving Hanoi

From Hanoi, the route south runs through rather unattractive and expanding industrial towns. Communities that for centuries were divided by nothing more than a dirt track, now find themselves divided by four-lane highways. Beyond Phu Ly the limestone karsts start to rise dramatically out of the flat plain – a sight made more majestic by the urban sprawl driven through to reach it.

Nam Dinh → *Colour map 1, C5.*

Nam Dinh is a large and diverse industrial centre, with a reputation for its textiles. Thien Truong and Pho Minh pagodas – both highly regarded – are to be found in the village of **Tuc Mac** (My Loc district), 3 km north of Nam Dinh. Also here are the few remains of the Tran Dynasty. **Thien Truong** was built in 1238 and dedicated to the kings of the Tran family; **Pho Minh** was built rather later, in 1305, and contains an impressive 13-storey tower. You can get to the pagodas either by *xe om* from Nam Dinh or as part of a day trip by car from Hanoi or Ninh Binh.

Doi Son and **Doi Diep pagodas** are situated on two neighbouring mountains (Nui Doi Son and Nui Doi Diep). The former was originally built at some point during the early Ly Dynasty (AD 544-602). When the Emperor Le Dai Hanh (AD 980-1005) planted rice at the foot of the mountain, legend has it that he uncovered two vessels, one filled with gold and the other with silver. From that season on, the harvests were always bountiful.

North of the main channel of the Red River, 10 km southwest of Thai Binh, is the site of the 11th-century **Keo Pagoda**, which was destroyed in a flood. The present building dates back to the 17th century but has been remodelled several times. Its chief architectural attraction is a wooden, three-storey campanile containing two bronze bells.

Hoa Lu → *Colour map 1, C4.*

Hoa Lu lies about 13 km from Ninh Binh near the village of Truong Yen. It was the capital of Vietnam from AD 968 to AD 1010, during the Dinh and Early Le dynasties. Prior to the establishment of Hoa Lu as the centre of the new kingdom, there was nothing here. But the location was a good one in the valley of the Hong River – on the 'dragon's belly', as the Vietnamese say. The passes leading to the citadel could be defended with a small force, and defenders could keep watch over the plains to the north and guard against the Chinese. The kings of Hoa Lu were, in essence, rustics. This is reflected in the art and architecture of the temples of the ancient city: primitive in form, massive in conception. Animals were the dominant motifs, carved in stone.

A large part of this former capital, which covered over 200 ha, has been destroyed, although archaeological excavations have revealed much of historical and artistic interest. The two principal temples are those of Dinh Bo Linh, who assumed the title King Dinh Tien Hoang on ascending the throne (reigned AD968-980), and Le Hoan, who assumed the title King Le Dai Hanh on ascending the throne (reigned AD 980-1009).

The Temple of Dinh Tien Hoang Temple of Dinh Tien Hoang was originally constructed in the 11th century but was reconstructed in 1696. It is arranged as a series of courtyards, gates and buildings. The inscription on a pillar in the temple, in ancient Vietnamese, reads 'Dai Co Viet', from which the name 'Vietnam' is derived. The back room of the temple is dedicated to Dinh Tien Hoang, whose statue occupies the central position, surrounded by those of his sons, Dinh Lien (to the left), Dinh Hang Lang and Dinh Toan (to the right). In the 960s, Dinh Tien Hoang managed to pacify much of the Red River plain, undermining the position of a competing ruling family, the Ngos, who accepted Dinh Tien Hoang's supremacy. However, this was not done willingly, and banditry and insubordination continued to afflict Hoang's kingdom. He responded by placing a kettle and a tiger in a cage in the courtyard of his palace and decreed: "those who violate the law will be boiled and gnawed". An uneasy calm descended on Dinh Tien Hoang's kingdom, and he could concern himself with promoting Buddhism and geomancy, arranging marriages, and implementing reforms. But, by making his infant son Hang Lang heir apparent, rather than Lien (his only adult son), he sealed his fate. History records that the announcement was followed by earthquakes and hailstorms, a sign of dissension in the court, and in AD 979 Lien sent an assassin to kill his younger brother Hang Lang. A few months later in the same year, an official named Do Thich killed both Dinh Tien Hoang and Lien as they lay drunk and asleep in the palace courtyard. When Do Thich was apprehended, it is said that he was executed and his flesh fed to the people of the city.

Temple of King Le Dai Hanh The Temple of King Le Dai Hanh is dedicated to the founder of the Le Dynasty who seized power after the regicide of Dinh Tien Hoang. In fact Le Dai Hanh took not only Hoang's throne but also his wife, Duong Van Nga. Representations of her, Le Dai Hanh and Le Ngoa Trieu (also known as Le Long Dinh), his fifth son, each sit on their own altar in the rear temple. Near this temple the foundations of King Dinh's (10th century) royal palaces were found by Vietnamese archaeologists in 1998.

Nhat Tru Pagoda and Nui Ma Yen A short walk beyond Le Dai Hanh's temple is Nhat Tru Pagoda, a 'working' temple. In front of it stands a pillar engraved with excerpts from the Buddhist bible (*Kinh Phat*). Opposite Dinh Tien Hoang's temple is a hill, Nui Ma Yen, at the top of which is Dinh Tien Hoang's tomb. Locals will tell you it is 260 steps to the top. There are boat trips on the river to Xuyen Thuy cave (see below).

★**Tam Coc** → *Colour map 1, C4.*
Boats depart daily from 0700-1700.

Tam Coc means literally 'three caves'. The highlight of this excursion is an enchanting boat ride up the little Ngo Dong River through the eponymous three caves. Those who have seen the film *Indochine*, some of which was shot here, will be familiar with the nature of the beehive-type scenery created by limestone towers, similar to those of Halong Bay. The exact form varies from wet to dry season; when flooded the channel disappears and one or two of the caves may be under water. In the dry season the shallow river meanders between fields of golden rice. You can spot mountain goat precariously clinging to the rocks and locals collecting snails in the water. Women row – with both their hands and feet – through the caves at a leisurely pace. On a busy day the boats are nose to tail – to enjoy Tam Coc at its best make it your first port of call in the morning.

Bich Dong
A short drive to the south is Bich Dong. This is much harder work, so not surprisingly it is a lot quieter than Tam Coc. Bich Dong consists of a series of temples and caves built

into, and carved out of, a limestone mountain. The temples date from the reign of Le Thai To in the early 15th century. It is typical of many Vietnamese cave temples but with more than the average number of legends attached to it, while the number of interpretations of its rock formations defies belief. The lower temple is built into the cliff face. Next to the temple is a pivoted and carved rock that resonates beautifully when tapped with a stone. Next see Buddha's footprints embedded in the rock (size 12, for the curious) and the tombs of the two founding monks.

Leading upwards is the middle temple, an 18th-century bell, a memorial stone into which are carved the names of benefactors and a cave festooned with rock forms. Here, clear as can be, are the likenesses of a turtle and an elephant. More resonant rock pillars follow and a rock that enables pregnant women to choose the sex of their baby: touch the top for a boy and the middle for a girl. Best of all: scramble right to the pinnacle of the peak for a glorious view over the whole area.

Phat Diem Cathedral → *Colour map 1, B5.*
24 km southeast of Ninh Binh in the village of Kim Son, daily 0800-1700, services daily. The journey takes in a number of more conventional churches, waterways and paddy fields. Take a motorbike from Ninh Binh or hire a car from Hanoi.

Phat Diem Cathedral is the most spectacular of the church buildings in the area, partly for its scale but also for its remarkable Oriental style with European stylistic influences. Completed in 1899, it boasts a bell tower in the form of a pagoda behind which stretches for 74 m the nave of the cathedral held up by 52 ironwood pillars. The cathedral was built under the leadership of parish priest Father Tran Luc between 1875 and 1899. He is buried in a tomb between the bell tower and the cathedral proper. Surrounding the cathedral are several chapels: St Joseph's, St Peter's, the Immaculate Heart's, the Sacred Heart's and St Roch's.

In 1953 French action in the area saw artillery shells damage the eastern wing of the cathedral causing part of the roof to collapse.

The cathedral was bombed in 1972 by Americans who despatched eight missiles. St Peter's Church was flattened, St Joseph's blown to an angle, the cathedral forced to a tilt, the roof tiles hurled to the floor, and 52 of the 54 cathedral doors were damaged. Restoration of different parts of the complex is ongoing.

The approach to the cathedral is impressive: you drive down a narrow valley to be confronted with a statue of Christ the King in the middle of a huge square pond; behind are the cathedral buildings.

The Red River Delta was the first part of the country to be influenced by Western missionaries: Portuguese priests were proselytizing here as early as 1627. Christian influence is still strong despite the mass exodus of Roman Catholics to the south in 1954 and decades of Communist rule. Villages (which are built of red brick, often walled and densely populated) in these coastal provinces may have more than half-a-dozen churches, all with packed congregations, not only on Sundays. The churches, the shrines, the holy grottoes, the photographs of the parish priest on bedroom walls and the holy relics clearly assume huge significance in people's lives.

Cuc Phuong National Park → *Colour map 1, C4*

T30-384 8006, www.cucphuongtourism.com, daily 0500-2100. 1- to 6-day treks can be arranged with a guide; short treks of a couple of hours are also available; bicycle tours can also be arranged. A visit to the park can be done as a day trip from Ninh Binh or from Hanoi. Direct access by car only. An organized tour from Hanoi may be a sensible option for lone travellers or pairs, otherwise charter a car or hire a motorbike.

The park, which is around 120 km south of Hanoi and 45 km west of Ninh Binh, is probably the second most accessible of Vietnam's national parks, and for nature lovers not intending to visit Cat Ba Island, it is worthy of consideration. It is also Vietnam's oldest park, established in 1962. Located in an area of deeply cut limestone and reaching elevations of up to 800 m, the park is covered by 22,000 ha of humid tropical montane forest. It is home to an estimated 2000 species of flora including the giant parashorea, cinamomum and sandoricum trees. Wildlife has been much depleted by hunting; only 117 mammal and 307 bird species and 110 reptile and amphibian species are thought to remain. The government has resettled a number of the park's 30,000 Muong minority people, although Muong villages do remain and can be visited. April and May see fat grubs and pupae metamorphosing into swarms of butterflies that mantle the forest in fantastic shades of greens and yellows.

Endangered Primate Rescue Center ① *www.primatecenter.org, 0900-1100, 1330-1600, limited entrance every 30 mins, 20,000d*, is a big draw in the park. There are more than 30 cages, four houses and two semi-wild enclosures for the 130 animals in breeding programmes; there are some 15 different species and sub-species. The centre is responsible for discovering a new species in Vietnam, the grey-shanked douc langur (*Pygathrix cinereus*), in 1997. The centre's work is extremely interesting and it is well worth a visit. There's also the **Turtle Conservation Center**. Visitors can arrange tours to visit the 16 species kept there. Cuc Phuong also has a botanical garden that is excellent for birdwatching in the early morning as well as listening to the nearby primates' dawn chorus.

Visitors can take a number of **trekking tours** in the park and also spend the night at **homestays** with the Muong. Night spotting could enable you to see black giant squirrel, Indian flying squirrel, samba deer and Loris. Birdwatchers could see the rare feathers of the silver pheasant, red-collared woodpecker, brown hornbill and bar-bellied pitta. Two lucky tourists and their guide saw an Asiatic black bear in early 2007.

Facilities at the park headquarters include accommodation, a restaurant, visitor centre and guides' headquarters. From headquarters to the park centre is 20 km. The drive will take you past **Mac Lake**, the path for the walk to the 45-m-high **Ancient Tree** (*Tetrameles nudiflora*), and **Cave of Prehistoric man**. At the park centre you can walk the 7-km paved hike through forest to the 1000-year-old tree (45 m high and 5 m wide) and a 1000-m-long liana (*Entada tonkinensis*) and palace cave.

Van Long Nature Reserve and around → *Colour map 1, C4.*

Van Long-Ninh Binh Tourist Ecological Area ticket office, T30-386 8798, is just beyond the Van Long hotel; boat and entrance ticket, 70,000d; daily 0700-1700.

The 3000-ha Reserve is 17 km north of Ninh Binh and 8 km from Highway 1 towards Cuc Phuong (take a right down the road on the corner of which is a restaurant). It is the home to the endangered Delacour's langur (*Trachypithecus delacouri*), one of the 25 most endangered primates in the world. The species is endemic to Vietnam. The best time to spot the primates, known as Vooc Mong Trang in Vietnamese, is early morning or just before sunset. Several caves can be visited. Boat tours last two hours.

Kenh Ga → *Colour map 1, C4.*
Kenh Ga floating village is 21 km north of Ninh Binh on the Hoang Long River and 3 km from the main road. Visitors can paddle 3 km to Kenh Ga past the yellow Roman Catholic Church and watch village life go by amid limestone towers.

Listings Ninh Binh and around

Tourist information

Ninh Binh Tourism
www.ninhbinhtourism.com.vn.
The hotels all have good information.

Where to stay

Ninh Binh

$ Hoang Hai Hotel
36 Truong Han Sieu St, T30-3871 5177, www.ninhbinhhotel.com.vn.
The 11 rooms are divided into 3 types; the bigger rooms are more expensive. Runs a good tour desk and is a good source of information.

$ Thanh Thuy's Guesthouse
128 Le Hong Phong St, T30-387 1811, www.hotelthanhthuy.com.
A clean budget choice with a variety of room options, most have bathtubs.

$ Thuy Anh
55A Truong Han Sieu St, T30-387 1602, www.thuyanhhotel.com.
37 rooms in this spotless hotel in the town centre; the deluxe rooms come with a view. Breakfast included. Will arrange tours. Rooftop garden.

Tam Coc

$$$$ Tam Coc Garden Bungalows
Near the Tam Coc boat station, www.tamcocgarden.com.
An absolute gem of a resort in extremely pretty surrounds. 16 wonderful bare-stone bungalows with very tasteful furnishing are set in a garden with unbeatable views of the karsts and paddy fields. Highly recommended.

Cuc Phuong National Park
4 different areas with accommodation: at the park HQ; 1 km from the main gate; at Mac Lake; 2 km from the park HQ; at the park centre (20 km from the main gate); and at the Muong village, 15 km from the park HQ.

$ Headquarters concrete bungalows
With en suite facilities, TV, a/c and fan. These are lined up across the road from the restaurant and are clean and basic.

$ Headquarters detached bungalow
1 bungalow with en suite facilities, hot water and a/c and fan.

$ Homestay
With ethnic minorities in the park. Price per person.

$ Mac Lake Bungalow
4 bungalows with a/c and
private bathroom.

$ Park centre concrete bungalows
With en suite and a/c but more
expensive than at HQ. The 4 bungalows,
are set around a lawn.

$ Park centre stilt houses
These are near the start of the 1000-year-
old walk. They have shared bathroom
facilities and no hot water.

Van Long Nature Reserve

$$$$ Emeralda Ninh Binh
*Van Long Resort, Gia Van, Gia Vien, Ninh
Binh (coming from Hanoi, turn right off
Highway 1 at the Gian Khau crossroads
towards Cuc Phuong. After 5 km turn
right to Van Long and drive for 2 km),
T30-364 1290, www.emeraldaresort.com.*
A stunning collection of bungalows
with high vaulted wood beam ceilings,
massive beds and iron bath tubs, each
set in clusters around small pools. Great
location right by the boats for the Van
Long Reserve. The restaurant is rather
average, but there are some local spots
just a short cycle ride away selling the
local speciality   grilled goat meat.

Restaurants

Ninh Binh

$ Hoang Hai Hotel
*36 Truong Han Sieu St, T30-387 1 5177.
Open 0800-2200.*
This centrally located restaurant has
zero atmosphere but service is prompt.
Breakfast, lunch and dinner served.

$ Thanh Thuy's Guesthouse
See Where to stay, above.
The portions are plentiful.

$ Thuy Anh
See Where to stay, above.
A choice of Vietnamese fare.

Cuc Phuong National Park
$ There are 2 restaurants in the national
park, one at the main gate, the other
1 km further in. Both serve a limited, and
sometimes unavailable, range of food.
Drinks available.

Transport

Ninh Binh
Bus
From Ninh Binh's bus station at 207 Le
Dai Hanh St to Hanoi's southern terminal,
Giap Bat, hourly, 3 hrs and also to
Haiphong, 4 a day; minibuses to **Hanoi**,
2 hrs. To **Phat Diem**, 1 hr; to **Kenh Ga**
30 mins. Take the same bus for **Van Long**
and take a moto at the turn-off to the
reserve. Some **Open Tour Buses** stop
here on their way to Hanoi and Hué.

Car, motorbike and bicycle
Hoang Hai Hotel (see Where to stay,
above) rents cars, motorbikes and
bicycles. **Thanh Thuy's Guesthouse** also
rents bikes and motorbikes. To get to Cuc
Phuong National Park independently of a
tour, take a *xe om* or hire a car for the day.

Cuc Phuong National Park
Bus
For independent travel: buses depart
Giap Bat terminal in Hanoi for **Nho Quan**
throughout the day. From Nho Quan take
a *xe om*. There's also 1 daily return bus
direct from **Hanoi** to Cuc Phuong.

Nam Dinh
Regular buses connect with **Hanoi**'s
Southern terminal, 3 hrs, and with
Haiphong on Highway 10, 4 hrs.

Central Vietnam

endless beaches, gigantic caves and ancient ruins

The Central Region includes the mountains of the Annamite chain which form a natural frontier with Laos to the west and in places extend almost all the way to the sea in the east. Many of Vietnam's ethnic minorities are concentrated in these mountains.

The narrow, coastal strip, sometimes only a few kilometres wide, supported the former artistically accomplished Kingdom of Champa.

The region is traversed by Highway 1, which runs all the way from Hanoi to Ho Chi Minh City. Along much of its route, the road runs close to the coast. The northern provinces are among the poorest in the country but their inhabitants are among the friendliest.

The middle part of the Central Region is home to World Heritage Sites of the Phong Nha-Ke Bang National Park with its amazing caves; the old Imperial City at Hué, a former capital of Vietnam; My Son, one-time capital of the Cham Kingdom; and Hoi An, an old mercantile port town which retains traditional architecture. This region is richly rewarding and would easily fill a two-week holiday in its own right.

The southern part of this diverse region has stunning coast and beaches, many of which are now home to high-class resorts, while many others remain blissfully untouched.

Best for
Adventure ▪ Beaches ▪ History

Thanh Hoa to Hué 143
Hué and around 152
Danang and around 179
Hoi An and around 189
Dalat 204
Central Highlands 215
Nha Trang and around 231

Footprint picks

★ **Phong Nha**, page 146

Peaceful riverside town
surrounded by caving adventures,
jungle treks and more.

★ **Hué**, page 152

The former Imperial capital is filled with history and
magnificent mausoleums.

★ **Bach Ma National Park**, page 176

A former French Hill station with crumbling buildings,
cascading falls and jungle treks.

★ **Danang**, page 179

Fast developing, beach-side city with superb cuisine,
the Son Tra Peninsula and the Hai Van Pass.

★ **Hoi An**, page 189

An enchanting 17th-century mercantile town with stunning
nearby beaches.

★ **My Son**, page 201

Vietnam's answer to Angkor Wat.

Thanh Hoa
Sam Son
Truong Son Mountain Range
Ca River
Vinh
Cua Lo
Ong Mountain (1587m)
Ha Tinh
Cau Treo

CHINA

East Sea

Phong Nha-Ke Bang National Park
Dong Hoi
Da Mao Mountain (665m)
Len Mu Mountain (918m)
Con Cao Island
Voi Mep Mountain (1701m)
Dong Ha
Quang Tri
Lao Bao
Khe Sanh (Huong Hoa)
Hué
Cau Hai Lagoon
Lang Co
Bach Ma National Park
Danang
Bana
Hoi An
My Son
Tam Ky
Chu Lai

LAOS

THAILAND

Ngoc Linh (2598m)
Dak Glei
Dak Nay
Bo-Y
Dak To
Quang Ngai

Hoai Nhon

Footprint picks

1 **Phong Nha**, page 146
2 **Hué**, page 152
3 **Bach Ma National Park**, page 176
4 **Danang**, page 179
5 **Hoi An**, page 189
6 **My Son**, page 201

Kontum Plateau
Bien Ho Lake
Kontum
Kien My
Ba Mountain (892m)
Cha Ban
Play Ku
Dekop
Quy Nhon
Le Thanh
Central Highlands
Ba River
Song Cau
Tuy Hoa
Da Rang River
Dam Mon

CAMBODIA

Ban Don
Buon Ma Thuot
Dac Lac Plateau
Lak Lake
Ninh Hoa
Nha Trang

PHNOM PENH

Ta Dung (1971m)
Nam Cat Tien National Park
Dalat
Cam Ranh
Khanh Hai Phan Rang
Bao
Ca Na
Bac Binh
Ham Thuan Bac
Phan Thiet
Mui Ne

Tay Ninh
Dau Tieng Lake
Cu Chi
Bien Hoa
Xuan Loc
Chau Doc
Cao Lanh
Tan An
Ho Chi Minh City
Ben Tre
Ho Coc
Long Xuyen
My Tho
Ha Tien
Sa Dec
Vinh Long
Vung Tau
Duong Dong
Phu Quoc Island
Hon Chong
Rach Gia
Can Tho
Tra Vinh
Rach Soi
Soc Trang
Mekong Delta
Bac Lieu
Ca Mau

To Con Dao Archipelago

N

50 km
50 miles

Thanh Hoa
to Hué

recently discovered caves have put this area on the tourist map

In the past, visitors would largely ignore this swathe of Vietnam, but the discovery of one of the world's largest caves, Hang Son Doong, has catapulted the area to fame.

Today, Phong Nha – the small town that functions as a base for exploring the caves – is one of the country's most up-and-coming spots. Alongside the caves, the ethnic minority cultures of the area are fascinating. Not far from here in Dong Ha is the former Demilitarized Zone (DMZ), which was the scene of heavy fighting in the American War.

Thanh Hoa to Vinh → *Colour map 2, A2-B2.*

little-visted towns and villages off the beaten path

Thanh Hoa

The **Citadel of Ho** was built in 1397 when Thanh Hoa was the capital of Vietnam. Much of this great city has been destroyed, although the massive city gates are preserved. Art historians believe that they rival the finest Chinese buildings, and the site is in the process of being excavated. This town and province mark the most northerly point of the central region. For tourist information, there's **Thanh Hoa Province Tourism** ① *34 Le Loi St, T37-385 4140.*

The 160-m-long **Ham Rong Bridge** or 'Dragon's Jaw' which crosses the Ma River north of Thanh Hoa was a significant spot during the Vietnam War. The bridge, a crucial transport link with the south, was heavily fortified and the US lost 70 planes in successive abortive raids from 1965. Eventually, in 1972, they succeeded by using laser-guided 'smart' bombs, at which point the Vietnamese promptly built a replacement pontoon bridge.

Sam Son

About 15 km east of Thanh Hoa lies the coastal resort of Sam Son. The place is teeming with karaoke cafés and is of little interest to the average traveller. The beach is long and crowded with deckchairs. If you walk south along the beach and over the hill you can find a deserted cove (walk past the temple).

Vinh

Vinh is a diversified industrial centre and the capital of Nghe An Province. It was damaged by the French before 1954, and then suffered sustained bombing by US and ARVN (Army of the Republic of Vietnam) aircraft from 1964 through to 1972. In the process it was virtually razed. Vinh lies at the important point where the coastal plain narrows, forcing roads and railways to squeeze down a slender coastal strip of land. The town has since been rebuilt with assistance from the former East Germany, in startlingly unimaginative style. The dirty-brown apartment blocks make Vinh one of the most uninspired cities in Vietnam. The province of Nghe An also happens to be one of the poorest, and the mini-famine of 1989 struck hard. For tourist information go to **Nghe An Tourist Office** ⓘ *13 Quang Trung St, T38-384 4298.*

There is nothing of historical interest here, unless socialist architecture can be thought of as such. The **Central Market**, at the south end of Gao Thang Street (the continuation of Quang Trung Street), is a bustle of colour and activity.

From Vinh, buses leave for Nam Can on the border with Laos (Nam Khan on the Laos side) and Cau Treo (Nam Phao in Laos), also on the Laos border. It is possible to buy Laos visas at the border. See Transport, below.

Kim Lien village

Kim Lien village, 14 km west of Vinh, is the place where Ho Chi Minh was born in 1890. There is a reconstruction of the house he was born in together with a memorial altar.

Sen

Sen, another village close to Kim Lien, is where Ho Chi Minh lived with his father from the age of six. Although the community and surrounding area were hardly wealthy, he was fortunate to be born into a family of modest means and his father was highly educated. The house where he lived (in fact a replica built in 1955) may be thatched and crude, but it was a great deal better than the squalor that most of his countrymen had to endure (see box, page 358, for an account of Ho Chi Minh's life). There is a small museum. The province of Nghe Tinh has a reputation for producing charismatic revolutionary leaders: Phan Boi Chau – another fervent anti-colonialist – was also born here (see page 357).

Cua Lo

Cua Lo, 20 km north of Vinh, boasts 8 km of white sandy beach and is a very popular (if slightly downmarket) holiday spot with the locals. There are a number of hotels but finding a room during the holiday period (June to August) can be tricky and the prices are double what they are at other times.

Ngang Pass or Porte d'Annam

Running between the Central Highlands and the coast is a small range of mountains, the Hoanh Son, which neatly divides the north from Central Vietnam. In French times the range marked the southern limit of Tonkin and northern limit of Annam. The mountains, which reach up to 1000 m, have a marked effect on climate, blocking cold northerly winds in winter and receiving up to 3000 mm of rain. During the reign of Minh Mang a gate was built, the Hoanh Son Quan. Subsequently, Emperor Thieu Tri on a visit north composed a poem which is inscribed on a nearby rock.

Listings Thanh Hoa to Vinh

Where to stay

Thanh Hoa

$$$-$$ Sao Mai Hotel
20 Phan Chu Trinh, T37-371 2888,
www.saomaihotel.com.vn.
A large, clean hotel that mainly serves Vietnamese business travellers. Some of the rooms are gigantic and even the cheaper rooms are very large. Includes a reasonable restaurant.

Vinh

$$$-$$ Saigon Kimlien
25 Quang Trung St, T38-383 8899,
www.saigonkimlien.com.vn.
One of the best in town with a/c, restaurant, bar and sauna.

$$-$ Thai Binh Duong (aka Pacific Hotel)
92 Binh Minh St, Cua Lo, T38-382 4301,
www.huunghina.com.vn.
Large hotel good range of clean rooms All with a/c and hot water. Restaurant and breakfast included.

Transport

Thanh Hoa
Bus
Station on Ba Trieu St has regular connections with **Hanoi**'s Ha Dong bus station, 4 hrs, **Ninh Binh**, **Vinh** and other towns on Highway 1.

Train
Express trains between **Hanoi** and **HCMC** stop here, 4¼ hrs to Hanoi.

Vinh
Air
Vietnam Airlines, 2 Le Hong Phong St, T31-381 0890.

Bus
The bus station is at 2 Le Loi St. Express buses leave for **Hanoi**, **HCMC** and **Danang**. For the border of Laos at **Nam Can** there are several buses a day. There are several buses a week to **Phonsavan**, Laos. For **Cau Treo** you need to catch an early morning bus to Trung Tam and a moto or minibus to the Laos border, 25 km away. Take any bus going north to **Cua Lo**. Get a *xe om* for the last 8 km. To **Dong Hoi**, 4½ hrs.

Car
Car hire available from most hotels.

Train
The station is in the west quarter of town, 3 km from the central market, T38-353 0666. Connections with **Hanoi** and all points south to **HCMC**. Express trains stop here.

Until a few years ago there was little to entice the tourist to this area, but the opening of the area's mind-blowing caves, including Hang En and Son Doong, has put province of Quang Binh firmly on the tourism map.

Between Vinh and Hué a stretch of coastal plain crosses from the province of Nghe An to Ha Tinh to Quang Binh then to Quang Tri and on to Thua Thien Hué. During the Vietnam War, the area was pounded by bombs and shells, and sprayed with defoliants. Unexploded bombs still regularly maim farmers (1,000,000 bombs have been unearthed since the end of hostilities), and it is claimed that the enduring effects of Agent Orange can be seen in the high rates of physical deformity in both animals and humans.

Dong Hoi
The town can be used as a stopping-off point on the way north or south and it is from here that Phong Nha, the caving base, is accessed. Dong Hoi itself was virtually annihilated during the war as it lies just north of the **17th parallel**, marking the border between North and South Vietnam. Just south of the town is the **Hien Luong Bridge,** which spans the Ben Hai River – the river forming the border between the two halves of former North and South Vietnam.

★Phong Nha
Phong Nha is a small riverside town that, until just a few years ago, saw almost zero tourism and remained very poor, with the population getting by on farming, fishing and hunting. Today, however, tourism is booming thanks to the caving opportunities opened up since 1990 by British Caving Association teams and now Oxalis Adventure Tours.

The star attraction is Hang Son Doong, one of the world's largest caves. Tours of this cave are limited in number and very costly (US$3000), but tours of other fantastic caves including Hang En and the Tu Lan system are much more affordable and are also unbeatable experiences. The town itself is a sleepy place where the locals are extremely friendly and the sunrises and sunsets over the river are not to be missed. Alongside visits to the caves, there are some excellent cycling routes in the area that take in parts of the original Ho Chi Minh Trail.

Hang Son Doong It's so massive that skyscrapers could stand inside and it is home to its own forest in which monkeys and flying foxes have been spotted. Photographs of this natural wonder went viral in 2013 and 2014, helping to catapult the area into the limelight. The cave can only be accessed on a tour with Oxalis – see Tour companies, below.

Phong Nha Cave ⓘ *www.phongnhakebang.vn, boats leave from the Son River landing stage in Phong Nha.* Phong Nha Cave is a true speleological wonder. Visitors

ON THE ROAD
Into the deep

Back in 1990, two British cavers, Deb and Howard Limbert, landed in Vietnam for the first time. Geologists from Hanoi University had invited the couple with the aim of exploring the country's caves. When they arrived in Hanoi, there were no taxis at the airport, just bicycles and rickshaws, and it took them three days to reach Phong Nha-Ke Bang National Park, a journey which now takes an afternoon.

Once in Phong Nha they visited Paradise Cave and Dark Cave and very quickly saw that the area had massive potential for uncovering more. They went onto visit other parts of the country and, along with their fellow British Caving Association members, have explored and mapped tens of caves, but it was to Phong Nha that they wanted to return.

The area did not disappoint; they discovered the enormous Hang En, through which a river flows. Following this river further, the Limberts hoped to find another cave on the same epic scale, but they suffered a setback when they found that the river disappeared underground through an impenetrable pile of boulders. Undeterred, they continued to search the area for a cave entrance, but, despite coming close, they could not uncover an opening – that is, until they enlisted the help of local jungle expert, Mr Ho Khanh, who remembered coming across a small cave and feeling a fiercely strong wind gusting from within.

Mr Ho Khanh led the Limberts to the small cave, a seven-hour trek from the road, and what they then discovered was much larger than they had dared hope and would go on to be named the largest cave in the world – Son Doong. The mighty cave, the exploration of which involves roped climbs and gushing river crossings, is large enough to accommodate jumbo jets and tall enough that a 40-storey skyscraper could stand inside. Giant openings in the cave roof allow light to penetrate and jungle to grow, in which hornbills, monkeys and flying squirrels have all been spotted.

The Limberts have made Phong Nha their home and now lead multi-day expeditions into Son Doong. Although places are limited in number, there are plenty of other caving options in the area to keep visitors busy for days on end. And the Limberts are certain that there are many more caves yet to discover.

are taken upstream from Phong Nha before heading into the cave itself for around 600 m and then dropped off to explore. There are stalagmites and stalactites and those with a powerful torch can pick out the form of every manner of ghoul and god in the rocks. A team of British divers explored 9 km of the main cave system in 1990 but less than 1 km is accessible to visitors.

Thien Duong (Paradise Cave) ⓘ *120,000đ*. Paradise Cave was the first cave to put this area on the map and prior to images of Son Doong going viral, this was the area's star attraction. It is a gargantuan cave, the first 1 km or so is well lit and there is a good walking trail along it. In places it reaches a width and height of 100 m and the formations it harbours are truly captivating. It is not to be missed.

Nuoc Mooc spring and eco trail ⓘ *50,000d*. A pretty trail through woodland leads down to gushing rapids that are formed by water that emerges in a large torrent from an unknown underground source. A series of wooden walkways leads across the rapids to a pleasant spot where it's possible to take a dip – you'll be forced to wear a life jacket and, given the current a few feet away from the swimming area, this is no bad thing. The road to to Nuoc Mooc is hilly, but it makes a great bike ride which can be combined with a trip to Dark Cave.

Dark Cave ⓘ *50,000d*. Another of the caves first explored by British cavers in the early 1990s, Dark Cave is over 5 km in length and reaches heights of around 80 m. A new, fun way to reach the cave mouth is to zip line in from a high tower. As the name suggests, this cave lacks natural light so those who venture in should do so with headlamps.

Tu Lan Cave System This series of caves was made famous by National Geographic photographer Carsten Peter. The river caves, with majestic formations, are only accessible on organized one, two or three day tours which involve plenty of exciting cave swimming. On overnight tours guests camp out on pebble beaches on lagoons filled by waterfalls surrounded by limestones cliff faces – see Oxalis, page 150.

Dong Ha and the border with Laos
The **Demilitarized Zone** (DMZ), **Khe Sanh** and the **Ho Chi Minh Trail** lie to the south of Dong Hoi. These war-time sights are normally visited on a tour from Hué and are described in detail on page 173.

About 94 km south, at Dong Ha, Highway 9 branches off the main coastal Highway 1 and proceeds to the border with Laos at **Lao Bao** (Dansavanh in Laos). Dong Ha sits on the junction of Highways 1 and 9 and is prospering from the growth of trade with Laos. Dong Ha is a convenient overnight stop for those crossing into or coming from Laos. Buses now travel regularly to the border from Hué. Along this route is Khe Sanh (now also called Huong Hoa) – one of the most evocative names associated with American involvement in Vietnam (see page 173).

Close to Khe Sanh are parts of the famous **Ho Chi Minh Trail** (see box, page 175) along which supplies were ferried from the north to the south. Highway 9 has been extensively improved in recent years to provide land-locked Laos with an alternative access route to the sea. This **Lao Bao** crossing (2 km beyond Lao Bao village) to Savannakhet provides Laos visas on arrival.

Where to stay

Dong Hoi

$ Quang Ly Guesthouse
6 Thuan Ly, T52-383 7268,
quanglyguesthouse@yahoo.com.
Clean and basic place with very friendly and helpful owners. Free internet, tour information and motorcycle and bike hire. Located close to the station.

Phong Nha

$$ Phong Nha Lakehouse Resort
1 km outside Phong Nha, T978-266326,
www.phongnhalakehouse.com.
In a lovely location overlooking a lake, this resort was adding some lakefront bungalows at the time of writing which look set to be some of the best digs in town. Also has a restaurant with great views serving a wide range of delicious dishes. As is often the case here in Phong Nha, the owners are extremely warm and welcoming.

$$-$ Phong Nha Farmstay
8 km from Phong Nha, T53-3675 135,
www.phong-nha-cave.com.
The setting of this Aussie/Vietnamese owned place couldn't be better, right on the edge of beautiful paddy fields in the countryside outside Phong Nha. Alongside a range of rooms from dorms to family options, there is a great restaurant and bar, plus a pool, a rooftop bar and terrace. The staff are extremely helpful and can provide plenty of information on what to do. Bicycles available for hire. This is the kind of place people get stuck for way longer than planned. Highly recommended.

$ Easy Tiger
T53-3675 135, www.phong-nha-cave.com.
Owned by Bich and Ben of the Farmstay, this is the place of choice for backpackers, with clean dorms complete with animal fur pattern bed covers. Downstairs is a large bar/restaurant area that kicks off in the evenings. Also has a free pool table and an extremely good information desk. Runs tours and sells bus tickets.

$ Ho Khanh's Homestay
Beyond the Oxalis office, T9-1679 4506,
www.phong-nha-homestay.com.
This idyllic spot is owned by the family of Mr Ho Khanh, the man who led the British caving expedition to discover Son Doong cave, one of the world's largest. Right on the bank of the river, the views here are breathtaking, particularly on a calm, misty morning. Accommodation is simple, but charming and clean. Great breakfast pancakes too. Although their English is very limited, the hosts are wonderful and help to make this a very special place to stay.

$ Thanh Tam
T52-3677999, www.thanhtamhotel
phongnha.com.
A newly built *nha nghi* (guesthouse) that offers a host of extremely clean and cheap rooms, some with excellent river views. Also has a good restaurant serving noodles and rice dishes. A good choice for those on a budget.

Dong Ha and the border with Laos

$ Melody Hotel
62 Le Duan St, T53-355 4664,
www.melodyhoteldha.net.

25 rooms recently renovated rooms, all with ac. Offers tours to the DMZ, ticket booking and motorcycle hire.

Restaurants

Dong Ha and the border with Laos

$ Dong Que Restaurant
109 Le Duan St.
Typical Vietnamese fare catering for passing tourist trade.

Phong Nha

Alongside the places listed below, **Easy Tiger** and the **Farmstay** both have good kitchens. Phong Nha is seeing new places open on a regular basis to serve the growing number of visitors.

$ Bamboo Cafe
Main road, T52-367 8777.
Owned by the engaging Hai who also runs the fabulous eco tour of the area, **Bamboo Cafe** is a great spot to meet other travellers and enjoy Western or Vietnamese food, a good shake or an ice cold beer.

$ Best BBQ Pork in The World
Near the market – look for the wooden sign and the barbecue smoke.
This street-side barbecued pork joint also has a normal Vietnamese name, but it's the sign advertising the pork that draws in the crowds. And the sign does not lie – the barbecued pork here is outrageously good. The wonderful hosts also serve a range of Central Vietnamese dishes. Not to be missed.

$ Pub With Cold Beer
Just outside Phong Nha – see Easy Tiger for a map.
Perhaps the best grilled chicken in Vietnam served by a lovely family. The chicken comes with sublime peanut sauce that's made fresh on the premises. A gem.

$ Tuan Ngoc
Opposite Easy Tiger, T986-059441.
Run by the friendly Ngoc and her husband Tuan, this is a great place to sample some dishes local to Phong Nha and Hué. Recommended.

$ Vung Hué
Just off the main street, T942-071656.
This is where both locals and the expats head for the best Vietnamese food in town. The decor is as bare as can be, but the ribs are amazing and so is the fried beef.

What to do

Phong Nha

Oxalis Adventure Tours, *T52-367 7678, www.oxalis.com.vn/contact.* This highly professional outfit counts Howard and Deb Limbert of the British Cave Association among its staff. It is also the only operator to run tours to Son Doong. It offers a range of trips to the Tu Lan cave system for cave swimming and camping out on remote waterfall-filled lakes. A variety of options can be chosen, from 1-day to multi-night treks. One of the most exceptional treks on offer is to Hang En where trekkers camp on a beach inside an almighty cavern large enough to house a jumbo jet. Very highly recommended tours.

Phong Nha Adventure Cycling, *main road, T98-555 5827, www.phong nhacycling.jimdo.com.* Led by the inimitable Shi, a range of cycling tours are on offer, including trips to Dark Cave, villages, the **Pub With Cold Beer** and the original Ho Chi Minh Trail. A great way to see more of the area and learn about its past and present.

Transport

Dong Hoi
Air
Flights link Dong Hoi with **HCMC** and **Hanoi** – check **Vietnam Airlines** for the current schedule.

Bus
The bus station is on Tran Hung Dao St. Buses travelling up Highway 1 linking **HCMC** with **Hanoi** pass through Dong Hoi.

Train
Regular connections with **Hanoi** and **HCMC**.

Phong Nha
Local buses serve Phong Nha from Dong Hoi and it's also possible to take a taxi. It is also on the Boomerang bus route used by backpackers.

Dong Ha and the border with Laos
Bus
Sepon Travel, 189 Le Duan St, T53-385 5289, www.sepontour.com, runs buses to **Laos**. The bus station is at 425 Le Duan St, 1.5 km from the old one, T53-385 1488. Bus to **Vinh**, 12 hrs. Dong Ha is 74 km from **Hué**, buses every 30 mins 0630-1800 and 80 km from the Lao Bao border crossing; to **Huong Hoa** (Khe Sanh) every 30 mins, 0500-1800; to **Lao Bao** every 30 mins. To **Hanoi**, 1800.

Hué
& around

★Hué, an imperial city that housed generations of the country's most powerful emperors, was built on the banks of the Huong Giang (Perfume River), named after a scented shrub that is supposed to grow at its source.

Just south of the city are the last resting places of many Vietnamese emperors while the ancient Citadel complex offers a fascinating glimpse into its glorious past. A number of war relics in the Demilitarized Zone can be easily visited from Hué. Also in the region are the nearby Thuan An Beach, the charming Thanh Hoan Covered Bridge, the misty heights of Bach Ma National Park, the Lang Co Peninsula and the stunning Hai Van Pass.

Hué → *Colour map 3, A1.*

heaven for history buffs and architecture lovers

Imperial City

Entrance through the Ngo Mon Gate, 23 Thang 8 St, 0700-1730, 105,000d. Guides are available in languages including English, French, Russian, Mandarin and Japanese. Guiding can last until 1900 after the ticket desk closes.

The Citadel was built to a design of Vauban (France's 17th-century fortifications designer) and covers 520 sq ha. Its walls are 6.6 m high, 21 m thick and 10,000 m in circumference with 10 entrances topped by watch towers. Inside the Citadel, the Great Enclosure contains the Imperial City and Forbidden City.

The Imperial City is built on the same principles as the Forbidden Palace in Beijing. It is enclosed by 7- to 10-m-thick outer walls, the **Kinh Thanh**, along with moats, canals and towers. Emperor Gia Long commenced construction in 1804 after geomancers had decreed a suitable location and orientation for the palace. The site enclosed the land of eight villages (for which the inhabitants received compensation), and covers 6 sq km; sufficient area to house the emperor and all his family, courtiers, bodyguards

Essential Hué and around

Getting around

For the city itself, walking is an option – interspersed, perhaps, with the odd cyclo journey. Most guesthouses hire out bicycles and this is a very pleasant and slightly more flexible way of exploring Hué and some of the surrounding countryside. A motorbike provides even more flexibility: it makes it possible to fit so much more into a day.

Getting to and around the **Imperial Tombs** is easiest by motorbike or car as they are spread over a large area. Most hotels and tour operators organize tours. If cycling, set out early if you hope to see all the tombs in a day. It is also possible to go on the back of a motorcycle taxi. Boats can be chartered to sail up the river, but only a few of the tombs can be reached in this way.

Most visitors visit the sights of the DMZ, including Khe Sanh and the Ho Chi Minh Trail, on a tour. Buses do leave for the town of Huong Hoa (Khe Sanh) from the An Hoa bus station; the former site of the US base is 3 km from Huong Hoa bus station. From here it is possible to arrange transport to the Ho Chi Minh Trail and to other sights. A one-day tour of all the DMZ sights can be booked from any of Hué's tour operators.

Best restaurants

Le Jardin de la Carambole, page 161
Nina's Café, page 162
Omar Khayyam's, page 162

When to go

The rainy season runs from September to January and rainfall is particularly heavy between September and November; the best time to visit is therefore between February and August.

Time required

Two days for the temple and the main mausoleums.

Best places to stay

La Residence, page 160
Pilgrimage Village, page 160
Saigon Morin, page 160

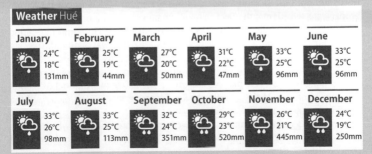

Weather Hué					
January	**February**	**March**	**April**	**May**	**June**
24°C 18°C 131mm	25°C 19°C 44mm	27°C 20°C 50mm	31°C 22°C 47mm	33°C 25°C 96mm	33°C 25°C 96mm
July	**August**	**September**	**October**	**November**	**December**
33°C 26°C 98mm	33°C 25°C 113mm	32°C 24°C 351mm	29°C 23°C 520mm	26°C 21°C 445mm	24°C 19°C 250mm

BACKGROUND
History of Hué

Hué was the capital of Vietnam during the Nguyen Dynasty and is one of the cultural cores of the country. The Nguyen Dynasty ruled Vietnam between 1802 and 1945, and for the first time in Vietnamese history a single court controlled the land from Yunnan (southern China) southwards to the Gulf of Siam. To link the north and south – more than 1500 km – the Nguyen emperors built and maintained the Mandarin Road (Quan Lo), interspersed with relay stations. Even in 1802, when it was not yet complete, it took couriers just 13 days to travel between Hué and Saigon, and five days between Hué and Hanoi. If they arrived more than two days late, the punishment was a flogging. There cannot have been a better road in Southeast Asia or a more effective incentive system. The city of Hué was equally impressive. George Finlayson, a British visitor in 1821-1822 wrote that its "style of neatness, magnitude, and perfection" made other Asian cities look "like the works of children". Although the Confucian bureaucracy and some of the dynasty's technical achievements may have been remarkable, there was continual discontent and uprisings against the Nguyen emperors. The court was packed with scheming mandarins, princesses, eunuchs (see box, page 156) and scholars writing wicked poetry. The female writer Ho Xuan Huong, wrote of the court and its eunuchs: "Why do the twelve midwives who cared for you hate each other? Where have they thrown away your youthful sexual passions? Damned be you if you should care about the twitterings of mice-like lovers, or

and servants. It took 20,000 men to construct the walls alone. Not only has the city been damaged by war and incessant conflict, but also by natural disasters such as floods which, in the mid-19th century, inundated the city to a depth of several metres.

Chinese custom decreed that the 'front' of the palace should face south (like the emperor) and this is the direction from which visitors approach the site. Over the outer moat, a pair of gates pierce the outer walls: the **Hien Nhon** and **Chuong Duc** gates. Just inside are two groups of massive cannon; four through the Hien Nhon Gate and five through the Chuong Duc Gate. These are the **Nine Holy Cannon (Cuu Vi Than Cong)**, cast in 1803 on the orders of Gia Long from bronzeware seized from the Tay Son revolutionaries. The cannon are named after the four seasons and the five elements, and on each is carved its name, rank, firing instructions and how the bronze of which they are made was acquired. They are 5 m in length, but have never been fired. Like the giant urns outside the Hien Lam Cac (see page 156), they are meant to symbolize the permanence of the empire. Between the two gates is a massive **flag tower**. The flag of the National Liberation Front flew here for 24 days during the Tet Offensive in 1968 – a picture of the event is displayed in Hué's Ho Chi Minh Museum.

Northwards from the cannon, and over one of three bridges which span a second moat, is the **Ngo Mon (Royal Gate) (1)**, built in 1833 during the reign of about a bee-like male gallant caressing his adored one … At least, a thousand years from now you will be more able to avoid the posthumous slander that you indulged in mulberry-grove intrigues."

In 1883 a French fleet assembled at the mouth of the Perfume River, not far from Hué, and opened fire. After taking heavy casualties, Emperor Hiep Hoa sued for peace, and signed a treaty making Vietnam a protectorate of France. As French influence over Vietnam increased, the power and influence of the Nguyen waned. The undermining effect of the French presence was compounded by significant schisms in Vietnamese society. In particular, the spread of Christianity was undermining traditional hierarchies. Despite the impressive imperial tombs and palace, many scholars maintain that the Nguyen Dynasty was simply too short-lived to have ever had a 'golden age'. Emperor Tu Duc may have reigned for 36 years (1847-1883), but by then the imperial family had grown so large that he had to contend with a series of damaging attempted coups d'état as family members vied for the throne. Although the French, and then the Japanese during the Second World War, found it to their advantage to maintain the framework of Vietnamese imperial rule, the system became hollow and, eventually, irrelevant. The last Nguyen Emperor, Bao Dai, abdicated on 30 August 1945.

Unfortunately for art lovers, the relative peace which descended upon Hué at the end of the Second World War was not to last. During the 1968 Tet offensive, Viet Cong soldiers holed up in the Citadel for 25 days. The bombardment that ensued, as US troops attempted to root them out, caused extensive damage to the Thai Hoa Palace and other monuments.

Emperor Minh Mang. The ticket office is just to the right. The gate, remodelled on a number of occasions since its original construction, is surmounted by a pavilion from where the emperor would view palace ceremonies. Of the five entrances, the central one – the Ngo Mon – was only opened for the emperor to pass through. The other four were for procession participants, elephants and horses. UNESCO has thrown itself into the restoration of Ngo Mon with vigour and the newly finished pavilion, supported by 100 columns, atop the gate now gleams and glints in the sun; those who consider it garish can console themselves with the thought that this is how it might have appeared in Minh Mang's time.

North from the Ngo Mon, is the **Golden Water Bridge (2)** – again reserved solely for the emperor's use – between two **tanks (3)**, lined with laterite blocks. This leads to the **Dai Trieu Nghi (Great Rites Courtyard) (4)**, on the north side of which is the **Thai Hoa Palace (Palace of Supreme Harmony) (4)**, constructed by Gia Long in 1805 and used for his coronation in 1806. From here, sitting on his golden throne raised up on a dais, the emperor would receive ministers, foreign emissaries, mandarins and military officers during formal ceremonial occasions. In front of the palace are 18 stone stelae, which stipulate the arrangement of the nine mandarinate ranks on the Great Rites Courtyard: the upper level was for ministers, mandarins and officers of the upper grade; the lower for those of

Eunuch power

Eunuchs were key members of the Nguyen Dynasty court in Hué. They were the only men allowed inside the Purple Forbidden City serving the Son of Heaven, the emperor, alongside his wives and concubines. Eunuchs became quite powerful and would play off the concubines against one another. The castrated men, who wore green and red floral gowns with flat, oval hats, arranged the emperor's night time activities and would be bribed by the concubines who wanted to be chosen for that night's sexual adventure. In 1836 Emperor Minh Mang limited their powers so they would not rise to the position of mandarin or become too powerful. He also graded their services. The premier eunuch (clerks) were paid 6 yuans and 0.8 quintals of rice (39.16 kg); the lowliest were the errand boys who earnt one yuan and 0.2 of a quintal of rice (9.8 kg). Some saw this edict as a reaction to the courtier Le Van Duyet, who was himself a eunuch. The employment of eunuchs was abolished in 1914 by Emperor Duy Tan, who reigned between 1907 and 1916.

lower grades. Civil servants would stand on the left, and the military on the right. Only royal princes were allowed to stand in the palace itself, which is perhaps the best-preserved building in the Imperial City complex. Its red and gold ironwood columns decorated with dragon motifs, symbol of the emperors' power, the tiled floor and fine ceiling have all been restored.

North of the Palace of Supreme Harmony is the **Tu Cam Thanh** (**Purple Forbidden City**) (**5**). This would have been reserved for the use of the emperor and his family, and was surrounded by 1-m-thick walls: a city within a city. Tragically, the Forbidden City was virtually destroyed during the 1968 Tet offensive. The two **Mandarin Palaces** and the **Royal Reading Pavilion** (see below) are all that survive.

At the far side of the Thai Hoa Palace, are two enormous **bronze urns** (**Vac Dong**) decorated with birds, plants and wild animals, and weighing about 1500 kg each. To either side of the urns are the **Ta** (**6**) and **Huu Vu** (**7**) pavilions – one converted into a souvenir art shop, the other a mock throne room in which tourists can pay to dress up and play the part of the emperor for five minutes. The **Royal Reading Pavilion** (**10**) has been renovated but, needless to say, has no books. On the far side of the palace are the outer northern walls of the citadel and the north gate.

Most of the surviving buildings of interest are to be found on the west side of the palace, running between the outer walls and the walls of the Forbidden City. At the southwest corner is the well-preserved and beautiful **Hien Lam Cac** (**12**), a pavilion built in 1821, in front of which stand nine massive **bronze urns** (**13**) cast between 1835 and 1837 on the orders of Emperor Minh Mang. It is estimated that they weigh between 1500 kg and 2600 kg, and each has 17 decorative figures, animals, rivers, flowers and landscapes representing between them the wealth, beauty and unity of the country. The central, largest urn is dedicated to the founder of the empire, Emperor Gia Long. Next to the urns walking northwards is **Thé Temple** (**Temple of Generations**) (**14**).

Built in 1821, it contains altars honouring 10 of the emperors of the Nguyen Dynasty behind which are meant to be kept a selection of their personal belongings. It was only in 1954, however, that the stelae depicting the three Revolutionary emperors Ham Nghi, Thanh Thai, and Duy Tan were brought into the temple. The French, perhaps fearing that they would become a focus of discontent, prevented the Vietnamese from erecting altars in their memory. North of the Thé Temple is **Hung Temple (15)** built in 1804 for the worship of Gia Long's father, Nguyen Phuc Luan, the father of the founder of the Nguyen Dynasty. The temple was renovated in 1951.

City centre

Hué Museum of Royal Fine Arts ① *3 Le Truc St, Tue-Sun 0700-1700, summer (14 Apr-14 Oct) until 1730, 35,000d.* Just east of the Imperial City is this museum

② Hué Imperial City

➡ **Hué maps**
1 Hué, page 159
2 Hué Imperial City, page 157

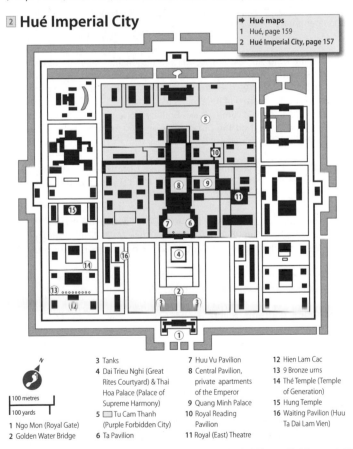

N
100 metres
100 yards

1 Ngo Mon (Royal Gate)
2 Golden Water Bridge
3 Tanks
4 Dai Trieu Nghi (Great Rites Courtyard) & Thai Hoa Palace (Palace of Supreme Harmony)
5 ☐ Tu Cam Thanh (Purple Forbidden City)
6 Ta Pavilion
7 Huu Vu Pavilion
8 Central Pavilion, private apartments of the Emperor
9 Quang Minh Palace
10 Royal Reading Pavilion
11 Royal (East) Theatre
12 Hien Lam Cac
13 9 Bronze urns
14 Thé Temple (Temple of Generation)
15 Hung Temple
16 Waiting Pavilion (Huu Ta Dai Lam Vien)

UNESCO support

UNESCO began the arduous process of renovating the complex in 1983: Vietnam at that time was a pariah state due to its invasion of Cambodia in 1978-1979 and the appeal for funds and assistance fell on deaf ears. It was, therefore, fitting testimony to Vietnam's rehabilitation in the eyes of the world when, in 1993, UNESCO declared Hué a World Heritage Site. Although it is the battle of 1968 which is normally blamed for the destruction, the city has in fact been gradually destroyed over 50 years. The French shelled it, fervent revolutionaries burnt down its buildings, typhoons and rains have battered it, thieves have ransacked its contents and termites have eaten away at its foundations. In some respects it is surprising that as many as a third of the monuments have survived relatively intact.

housed in the Long An Palace. It contains a reasonable collection of ceramics, furniture, screens and bronzeware and some stunning, embroidered imperial clothes. In the front courtyard are stone mandarins, cannon, gongs and giant bells. The building itself is worthy of note for its elegant construction with its stunning interior of 128 ironwood columns. It was built by Emperor Thieu Tri in 1845 it was dismantled and erected on the present site in 1909 as the National University Library before being renamed in 1958.

Royal College ① *2 Le Truc St, daily 0700-1700, free.* Directly opposite the Royal Fine Arts museum is the Royal College established in 1803 and moved to this site in 1908. It is lamentably short of exhibits.

Military Museum ① *23 Thang 8 St (between Dinh Tien Hoang and Doan Thi Diem Sts), T54-352 2397, Tue-Sun 0730-1100, 1330-1700, free.* Immediately in front is the Military Museum. Missiles, tanks and armoured personnel carriers fill the courtyard.

Dong Ba Market ① *Tran Hung Dao St.* Further east still, but still on the north bank of the river, next to the Dong Ba bus station, is the covered Dong Ba Market.

Huong Giang (Perfume River) Huong Giang is spanned by two bridges; downstream is the ill-fated **Trang Tien Bridge**, named after the royal mint that once stood at its northern end. It was built in 1896 and destroyed soon after by a typhoon; after having been rebuilt it was then razed once more in 1968 during the Tet Offensive. Upstream is **Phu Xuan Bridge**, built by the US Army in 1970. This carries Highway 1, in other words the main north–south highway, but a new bypass with a huge new river crossing 10 km upriver has seen traffic levels fall.

Bao Quoc Pagoda ① *Just off Dien Bien Phu St to the right, over the railway line.* Further south, the Bao Quoc Pagoda, is said to have been built in the early

18th century by a Buddhist monk named Giac Phong. Note the 'stupa' that is behind and to the left of the central pagoda and the fine doors inscribed with Chinese and Sanskrit characters.

Tu Dam Pagoda Further along Dien Bien Phu Street, at the intersection with Tu Dam Street, is the Tu Dam Pagoda. According to the Hué Buddhist Association this was originally founded in 1690-1695 but has been rebuilt many times. The present-day pagoda was built shortly before the Second World War. In August 1963, the Diem government sent its forces to suppress the monks here who were alleged to be fomenting discontent among the people. The specially selected forces – they were Catholic – clubbed and shot to death about 30 monks and their student followers, and smashed the great Buddha image here.

1 Hué

➡ Hué maps
1 Hué, page 159
2 Hué Imperial City, page 157

To Tombs of Gia Long, Minh Mang, Thieu Tri, Tu Duc, Dong Khanh & Khai Dinh

N

400 metres

400 yards

Where to stay 🛏	Restaurants 🍴	Nina's **8**
Canh Tien **1**	Lac Thien & Lac Thanh **2**	Omar Khayyam's **9**
Hung Vuong Inn **2**	Les Jardins de	
La Residence **5**	la Carambole **1**	Bars & clubs 🎵
Mimosa **12**	Gecko **5**	Brown Eye **10**
Saigon Morin **15**	Little Italy **7**	Why Not **4**
	Mandarin **6**	

Church of Mother of Perpetual Help The skyline of modern Hué is adorned by the striking pagoda-like tower of this church. This three-storey, octagonal steel tower is 53 m high and an attractive blend of Asian and European styles. The church was completed in 1962 and marble from the Marble Mountain in Danang was used for the altar. The church lies at the junction of Nguyen Hué and Nguyen Khuyen streets.

Listings Hué maps p157 and p159

Where to stay

Most hotels lie to the south of the Perfume River. Hué still suffers from a dearth of quality accommodation but this has improved in recent years and more properties are planned.

$$$$ La Residence Hotel & Spa
5 Le Loi St, T54-383 7475, www.la-residence-Hué.com.
Anyone who knew this hotel before will be stunned at its fabulous makeover. For lovers of art deco, it is an essential place to stay and to visit. Home of the French governor of Annam in the 1920s, it has been beautifully and decadently restored with 122 rooms, restaurant, lobby bar, spa and swimming pool close to the Perfume River. The citadel can be seen from the hotel. The rooms in the original governor's residence are the most stylish, with 4-poster beds and lovely dark wood furnishings; other rooms are extremely comfortable too, with all mod-cons. The breakfasts are very filling; guests also enjoy free internet. The hotel has a fascinating collection of old colonial-era photographs that are hung along the corridors. Highly recommended.

$$$$ Pilgrimage Village boutique resort and spa
130 Minh Mang Rd, T54-388 5461, www.pilgrimagevillage.com.
Tastefully designed rooms in a village setting ranging from honeymoon and pool suites to superior rooms. The rooms in small houses with private pools are gorgeous and recommended. There are 2 restaurants (see Restaurants), a number of bars, a beautiful and atmospheric spa (the Vietnamese aromatherapy massage is outstanding), open to outside guests also, and 2 inviting pools. Cooking and t'ai chi classes are available. There's a complementary shuttle service to and from town.

$$$$ Saigon Morin
30 Le Loi St, T54-382 3526, www.morinhotels.com.vn.
Recognizable as the fine hotel originally built by the Morin brothers in the 1880s. Arranged around a courtyard with a small pool, the rooms are large and comfortable. All come with a/c, satellite TV and hot water. The courtyard, lit with candles, is a delightful place to sit in the evening and enjoy a quiet drink. Service is friendly and the overall effect most agreeable. Recommended.

$ Hung Vuong Inn
20 Hung Vuong St, T54-382 1068, hung.vuong.inn@gmail.com.
There are 9 double and twin rooms above the shop that are all spotlessly clean. Rooms have a TV and mini-bar and bathtubs; some have a balcony. It is quieter on the back side of the building. The restaurant of the same name is a very popular spot.

$ Vietnam Backpackers' Hostel
*10 Pham Ngu Lao St, T54-382 6567,
www.vietnambackpackershostels.com.*
Prices include breakfast. Happy hour
2000-2100. A great travellers' hostel with a
bar downstairs and ultra clean rooms and
dorms upstairs with a lovely balcony over
the street for chilling. Tours offered too.

Guesthouses
The little *hem* (alley) opposite the
Century Riverside has some really nice
rooms in comfortable and cheerful
guesthouses in what is easily the
best value accommodation in Hué.
Particularly recommended are:

$ Canh Tien Guesthouse
9/66 Le Loi St, T54-382 2772.
12 rooms that come with fan or a/c.
Cheaper rooms have fans; the most
expensive have a balcony. Wi-Fi.

$ Mimosa
66/10 (10 Kiet 66) Le Loi St, T54-382 8068.
One of the cheapest options in town.
French is spoken when the owner is
here. 8 rooms with a/c, hot water and
bathtub that are quiet, simple and
clean but very aged. Rooms with fan
are cheaper. Wi-Fi available. A friendly
bargain basement option.

Restaurants

The influence of the royal court on
Hué cuisine is evident in a number
of ways: there are a large number of
dishes served, with each dish being
relatively light. Hué food is delicately
flavoured and requires painstaking
preparation in the kitchen: in short,
it's a veritable culinary harem in which
even the most pampered and surfeited
emperor could find something to
tickle his palate. Other Hué dishes are
more robust, notably the famed *bun
bo Hué*, round white noodles in soup
with slices of beef and laced with chilli
oil of exquisite piquancy. Restaurants
for local people usually close early; it's
best to get there before 2000. Traveller
cafés and restaurants tend to keep
serving food until about 2200.

$$$-$$ Le Jardin de la Carambole
www.lesjardinsdelacarambole.com.
A beautiful restaurant housed in an
old villa, **Les Jardins** is universally
popular and a perfect place for a
special, romantic meal. The French and
Vietnamese food are both delightful
and the waiting staff are attentive. Don't
miss the beef in banana leaf or the goat
cheese salad. A must-visit when in Hué.

$$ La Carambole
*19 Pham Ngu Lao St195, T54-381 0491,
la_carambole@hotmail.com.
Open 0700-2300.*
One of the first restaurants catering to
foreigners in town, this remains one of
the most popular and deservedly so. It
is extremely touristy being located in
the heart of the hotel area, but it retains
its charm and serves up comforting
food in a bustling atmosphere. Make a
reservation or be prepared to wait.

$$ Little Italy
*10 Nguyen Thai Hoc, T54-382 6928,
www.littleitalyHué.com.*
Owned by the people behind **DMZ
Bar**, Little Italy has shifted location
but kept the same successful formula
in place: filling pizzas and pastas and
friendly service.

$ Gecko
9 Pham Ngu Lao St, T98-668 9432.
New kid on the block, Gecko has a
well-designed open courtyard space
with bespoke furnishing and exposed

brickwork. Serves pizza, pasta and a small range of Vietnamese classics. Very friendly young staff and a good vibe.

$ Jardin de Y Thao
3 Thach Han St, T54-352 3018, ythaogarden@gmail.com.
Rather touristy, this old house in a pretty garden is nonetheless delightful.

$ Lac Thien
6 Dinh Tien Hoang St, T54-352 7348.
Lac Thien serves well prepared Hué staples at cheap prices. The owner is a gregarious chap who introduces himself to all customers when he is here. Each diner will also leave with a little gift from the staff.

$ Mandarin
24 Tran Cao Van St, T54-382 1281, www.mrcumandarin.com.
An old favourite run by Mr Cu, this café is decorated with his own black and white photos. Serves a variety of cheap, filling food. Travel services and bike rental. Mr Cu is one of the most helpful café owners in the whole of Vietnam making this a good place to book tours and get information.

$ Nina's Café
16/34 Nguyen Tri Phuong, T54-838 636, www.ninascafe.jimdo.com.
Hidden at the end the guesthouse-filled alley, this is a family-run outfit in the front garden of their home. Superb versions of many Hué specialities and great service. Ask about 'Nina's Tour' to the family village 30 km from town.

$ Omar Khayyam's
34 Nguyen Tri Phuong St, T54-382 1616.
Hué's most popular Indian restaurant for many years. Serves authentic tandoori dishes and curries.

Bars and clubs

Brown Eyes
56 Chu Van An, T54-382 7494.
On a busy night, **Brown Eyes** can get packed out and it stays open later than most. Loud music, cheap beers and plenty of backpackers. A sign states they 'open until the last person passes out'.

DMZ Bar
60 Le Loi St, T54-382 3414, www.dmzbar. com.vn. Open 0900-0200.
Hué's oldest bar, **DMZ** serves cheap cold beer and bargain cocktails making it a popular spot with budget travellers who gather to play on the free pool table. A good place to meet people and pick up tourist information.

Why Not?
46 Pham Ngu Lao, T54-3824 793, www.whynot.com.vn.
Alongside **DMZ**, this is one of the city's most busy bars. Trades on cheap drinks, music and a good atmosphere. Also serves a range of cheap food and has a pool table. Draws in a mixed crowd of travellers and locals.

Entertainment

Rent a dragon boat and sail up the Perfume River with your own private singers and musicians. Tour offices and major hotels will arrange groups.

See a Royal Court performance in the Imperial City's theatre or listen to performers during the Saigon Morin's occasional evening buffet.

Shopping

There is a much wider range of goods on sale in Hué now than was the case in the past, no longer just the *non bai tho* or poem hats. These are a form of the standard conical hat, *non lá*, which are peculiar to Hué. Made from bamboo and palm leaves, love poetry, songs, proverbs or simply a design are stencilled on to them, which are only visible if the hat is held up to the light and viewed from the inside. Shops on Le Loi and Pham Ngu Lao streets, sell ceramics, silk and clothes. There are a number of new art galleries. Perfectly decent stuff but not the range of Hoi An, where visitors are advised to shop.

No Vietnamese visitor would shake the dust of Hué off his feet without having previously stocked up on *me xung*, a sugary, peanut and toffee confection coated in sesame seeds: quite a pleasant energy booster to carry while cycling around the tombs, and with the significant advantage over Mars bars, that while it may pull your teeth out it won't melt in your pocket.

Healing the Wounded Heart Shop, *23 Vo Thi Sau St, T54-383 3694, www.spiral foundation.org*. Recycled products such as water bottles and electricity wires are fashioned into bags and homeware by disabled people. Profits fund heart surgery for poor children and support the livelihoods of Hué's disabled craftsmen.

What to do

Many hotels organize bus and boat tours to the Imperial Tombs. It is also possible to charter boats to the tombs (the most romantic way to visit them) and to Thuan An Beach. Local tour operators charge around private boat around US$15-20 return to visit Thien Mu Pagoda, Hon Chien Temple, Tu Duc, Minh Mang and Khai Dinh's Tombs, departing at 0800-0830, returning 1530-1630. Boats are available on the stretch of river bank between the Huong Giang Hotel and the Trang Tien Bridge and also from the dock behind the Dong Ba Market.

From Hué, there are also tours organized to some of the sights of the Vietnam War, taking in sights including Vinh Moc tunnels and museum, the Ho Chi Minh Trail and Khe Sanh. Those wishing to travel overland to Laos can arrange to be dropped off in Khe Sanh and pay less.

Tour operators
Almost every travellers' café acts as an agent for a tour operator and will take bookings but they do not run the tours themselves.
Café on Thu Wheels, *3/34 Nguyen Tri Phuong St, T54-383 2241, minhthuHué@ yahoo.com*. Run by Minh, Toan and Thu – 3 siblings. Motorcycle tour of Hué (US$12) and Hoi An (US$45) DMZ (US$45). The formidable Thu allows you to tailor your own tour taking in the best pagodas and sites around Hué, with well-informed English-speaking guides. DMZ bus tours are US$18.
Hue Easy Rider, *147 A/27 Ngu Binh, T9-8432 6842 www.hueeasyridertour.com*. Hugley popular motorcycle tours of Hué, the DMZ and further afield.
Mandarin Café, *24 Tran Cao Van St, T54-382 1281, www.mrcumandarin.com*. This café offers many services and its staff are also helpful. Open Tour Buses arranged. All-day trip to the tombs, Bach Ma National Park and the DMZ. Also arranges sunset boat trips.
Stop and Go Cafe, *3 Huong Vuong St, T54-382 7051, T90-512 6767 (mob), stopandgocafe@yahoo.com*. Known for its tours of the DMZ. 3 itineraries are on offer ranging from 7 to 11 hrs. Tours are led by ARVN veterans, which brings the landscape to life and an insight you won't

get on a much cheaper tour. Run by the helpful Thien and his sister. City tours and Bach Ma National Park tours also on offer. Transport ticket booking service.

Tien Bicycles, *12 Nguyen Thien Ke St, T54-382 3507, www.tienbicycles.com.* Mr Tien has been running recommended bicycling tours for 10 years. He offers long-distance rides as well as tours to the DMZ.

Transport

Phu Bai airport is a 25-min drive south of the city. The 2 bus stations and 1 railway station are more central and there are connections to Hanoi and Ho Chi Minh City – and all points between. The trains fill up, so advance booking is recommended, especially for sleepers.

Air

There is an airport bus, 30 mins, 50,000d run by **Vietnam Airlines** from 20 Ha Noi St that leaves 1 hr 40 mins before the flight. Returns also after flights. Taxi US$10-15 depending on destination – meter taxis. Use **Mai Linh** (white and green) **Taxi Vang** (yellow).

Airline offices Vietnam Airlines, 23 Nguyen Van Cu St, T54-382 4709, open 0715-1115, 1330-1630.

Bicycles

Bicycles can be hired from most hotels, guesthouses and cafés; bicycles are about 40,000d a day. **Try** Tien Bicycles (see Tour operators) for something more sturdy for longer trips.

Boat hire

Boats can be hired through tour agents and from any berth on the south bank of the river, east of Trang Tien Bridge or through travel cafés. Good for either a gentle cruise with singers in the evening,

or a more attractive way of getting to some of the temples and mausoleums. Note that if you travel by boat to the tombs you will often have to pay a driver to take you to the tomb as they are often a kilometre or so from the riverbank.

Bus and Open Tour Bus

The Ben Xe Phia Nam, 97 An Duong Vuong St, T54-382 5070, serves destinations mostly south of Hué: **Saigon** and **Dalat** and **Danang** but also services to **Savannakhet** Tue-Fri, Sun, 0830. Buses to **Vientiane** and Pakse several times per week. Book with tour operators, see above. Open Tour Buses can be booked to major destinations from hotels or tour agencies. Tourist buses to **Savannakhet**, Laos, via Lao Bao available from Sepon Travel.

The **Ben Xe Phia Bac station**, An Hoa Ward, T54-358 0562, is up at the northwest corner of the citadel and serves destinations north of Hué: **Dong Hoi** (for Phong Nha and the caves), **Dong Ha**, and many daily services to **Hanoi**. To **Khe Sanh** buses leave throughout the day. Also regular buses to **Lao Bao**, for Laos.

The **Dong Ba** station (by the central market) serves villages and **Thuan An Beach**.

Cyclos

Cyclos are available everywhere. They are pleasant for visiting the more central attractions. Cyclo drivers in Hué win the country's Oscar for persistence.

Motorbikes

Bikes can be hired from most hotels and guesthouses for around US$15-20 or more per day with a driver or US$5 without. *Xe om* are available everywhere. They are the speedier way to see the

ON THE ROAD
By train from Hué to Danang

The train journey from Hué to Danang is regarded as not just one of the most scenic in Vietnam, but in the world.

Paul Theroux in his book *The Great Railway Bazaar* recounts his impressions as the train reached the narrow coastal strip, south of Hué and approaching Danang.

"The drizzle, so interminable in the former Royal Capital, gave way to bright sunshine and warmth; 'I had no idea,' I said. Of all the places the railway had taken me since London, this was the loveliest. We were at the fringes of a bay that was green and sparkling in bright sunlight. Beyond the leaping jade plates of the sea was an overhang of cliffs and the sight of a valley so large it contained sun, smoke, rain, and cloud – all at once – independent quantities of colour. I had been unprepared for this beauty; it surprised and humbled me ... Who has mentioned the simple fact that the heights of Vietnam are places of unimaginable grandeur? Though we can hardly blame a frightened draftee for not noticing this magnificence, we should have known all along that the French would not have colonized it, nor would the Americans have fought so long, if such ripeness did not invite the eye to take it." (Penguin, London, 1977)

temples as the terrain south of town is quite hilly.

Mr Teo is a reliable and very safe driver – ask your hotel staff to arrange a booking with him on 091-447 8429 (mob).

Taxi
Mai Linh Taxi, T54-389 8989.

Train
The station is at the west end of Le Loi St, T54-382 2175, and serves all stations south to **HCMC** and north to **Hanoi**. The 4-hr journey to **Danang** is especially recommended for its scenic views. See box. Booking office open 0700-2200.

Along the Perfume River and the Imperial tombs
opulent, fanciful and grand-scale mausoleums

As the geographical and spiritual centre of the Nguyen Dynasty, Hué and the surrounding area is the site of numerous pagodas and seven imperial tombs, along with the tombs of numerous other royal personages and countless courtiers and successful mandarins.

Each of the tombs follows the same stylistic formula, although at the same time they reflect the tastes and predilections of the emperor in question. The tombs were built during the lifetime of each emperor, who took a great interest in the design and construction – after all they were meant to ensure his comfort in the next life. Each mausoleum, variously arranged, has five design elements: a courtyard with statues of elephants, horses and military and civil mandarins (originally, usually approached through a park of rare trees); a stela pavilion (with an engraved eulogy composed by the emperor's son and heir); a Temple of the

Soul's Tablets; a pleasure pavilion; and a grave. Geomancers decreed that they should also have a stream and a mountainous screen in front.

Thien Mu Pagoda
It is an easy 4-km bicycle (or cyclo) ride from the city, following the north bank of the river upstream (west).

Thien Mu Pagoda (the Elderly Goddess Pagoda), also known as the Thien Mau Tu Pagoda, and locally as the **Linh Mu Pagoda** (the name used on most local maps), is the finest in Hué. It is beautifully sited on the north bank of the Perfume River, about 4 km upstream from the city. It was built in 1601 by Nguyen Hoang, the governor of Hué, after an old woman appeared to him and said that the site had supernatural significance and should be marked by the construction of a pagoda. The monastery is the oldest in Hué, and the seven-storey **Phuoc Duyen** (Happiness and Grace Tower), built by Emperor Thieu Tri in 1844, is 21 m high, with each storey containing an altar to a different Buddha. The summit of the tower is crowned with a water pitcher to catch the rain, water representing the source of happiness.

Arranged around the tower are four smaller buildings one of which contains the **Great Bell** cast in 1710 under the orders of the Nguyen Lord, Nguyen Phuc Chu, and weighing 2200 kg. Beneath another of these surrounding pavilions is a monstrous **marble turtle** on which is a 2.6-m-high stela recounting the development of Buddhism in Hué, carved in 1715. Beyond the tower, the entrance to the pagoda is through a triple gateway patrolled by six carved and vividly painted guardians – two on each gate. The roof of the sanctuary itself is decorated with *jataka* stories. At the front of the sanctuary is a brass, laughing Buddha. Behind that are an assortment of gilded Buddhas and a crescent-shaped gong cast in 1677 by Jean de la Croix. The first monk to commit suicide through self immolation, Thich Quang Duc, came from this pagoda and the grey Austin in which he made the journey to his death in Saigon is still kept here in a garage in the temple garden.

In May 1993, a Vietnamese – this time not a monk – immolated himself at Thien Mu. Why is not clear: some maintain it was linked to the persecution of Buddhists; others that it was because of the man's frustrated love life.

Tomb of Emperor Gia Long
Daily 0630-1730, 80,000d for the upkeep of the tomb. Get there by bike or motorbike.

The Tomb of Emperor Gia Long is the most distant and the most rarely visited but is well worth the effort of getting there (see below). The tomb is overgrown with venerable mango trees, the only sound is bird call and, occasionally, the wind in the trees: otherwise a blessed silence. Devoid of tourists, touts and ticket sellers it is the most atmospheric of all the tombs, and as the political regime in Vietnam is not a fan of Gia Long it is likely to remain this way. However, given the historical changes that were to be wrought by the dynasty Gia Long founded, it is arguably the most significant tomb in Hué. It was built between 1814 and 1820 (see box, opposite, for an account of the emperor's burial). Being the first of the dynasty, Gia Long's mausoleum set the formula for the later tombs. There is a

Death and burial of Emperor Gia Long (1820)

When the Emperor Gia Long died on 3 February 1820, the thread on the ancestors' altar (representing his soul) was tied. The following day the corpse was bathed and clothed in rich garments, and precious stones and pearls were placed in his mouth. Then a ritual offering of food, drink and incense was made before the body was placed in a coffin made of catalpa wood (*Bignonia catalpa*) – a wood impervious to insect attack. At this time, the crown prince announced the period of mourning that was to be observed – a minimum of three years. Relatives of the dead emperor, mandarins and their wives each had different forms and periods of mourning to observe, depending upon their position.

Three days after Gia Long's death, a messenger was sent to the Hoang Nhon Pagoda to inform the empress, who was already dead, of the demise of her husband. Meanwhile, the new Emperor Minh Mang had the former ruler's deeds recorded and engraved on golden sheets which were bound together as a book. Then astrologers selected an auspicious date for the funeral, picking 27 May after some argument (11 May also had its supporters). On 17 May, court officials told the heaven, the earth and the dynastic ancestors, of the details for the funeral and at the same time opened the imperial tomb. On 20 May, the corpse was informed of the ceremony. Four days later the coffin left the palace for the three-day journey to its final resting place. Then, at the appointed time, the coffin was lowered into the sepulchre – its orientation correct – shrouded in silk cloth, protected by a second outer coffin, covered in resin, and finally bricked in. Next to Gia Long, a second grave was dug into which were placed an assortment of objects useful in his next life. The following morning, Emperor Minh Mang, in full mourning robes, stood outside the tomb facing east, while a mandarin facing in the opposite direction inscribed ritual titles on the tomb. The silk thread on the ancestors' altar – the symbol of the soul – was untied, animals slaughtered, and the thread then buried in the vicinity of the tomb.

(This account is adapted from James Dumarçay's *The palaces of South-East Asia*, 1991.)

surrounding lotus pond and steps lead up to a courtyard with the Minh Thanh ancestral temple, rather splendid in its red and gold. To the right of this is a double, walled and locked burial chamber where Gia Long and his wife are interred (the Emperor's tomb is fractionally taller). The tomb is perfectly lined up with the two huge obelisks on the far side of the lake. Beyond this is a courtyard with five now headless mandarins, horses and elephants on each side; steps lead up to the stela eulogizing the Emperor's reign, composed, presumably, by his eldest son, Minh Mang, as was the custom. This grey monolith engraved in ancient Chinese characters remained miraculously undisturbed during two turbulent centuries.

Gia Long's geomancers did a great job finding this site: with the mountainous screen in front it is a textbook example of a final resting place. Interestingly, despite their getting first choice of all the possible sites, it is also the furthest tomb from the palace; clearly they took their task seriously.

Nguyen Anh, or Gia Long as he was crowned in 1802, came to power with French support. Back in 1787, Gia Long's son, the young Prince Canh, had caused a sensation in French salon life when, along with soldier/missionary Georges Pigneau de Béhaine, he had sought military support against the Tay Son from Louis XVI. In return for Tourane (Danang) and Poulo Condore (Con Dao), the French offered men and weapons – an offer that was subsequently withdrawn. Pigneau then raised military support from French merchants in India and in 1799 Prince Canh's French-trained army defeated the Tay Son at Quy Nhon.

Gia Long's reign was despotic – to his European advisers who pointed out that encouragement of industry would lead to the betterment of the poor, he replied that he preferred them poor. The poor were virtual slaves – the price for one healthy young buffalo was one healthy young girl. Flogging was the norm – it has been described as the 'bamboo's golden age'. One study by a Vietnamese scholar estimated that there were 105 peasant uprisings between 1802 and 1820 alone. For this, and the fact that he gave the French a foothold in Vietnam, the Vietnamese have never forgiven Gia Long. Of him they still say *"cong ran can ga nha"* (he carried home the snake that killed the chicken).

To get to the Tomb of Emperor Gia Long take Dien Bien Phu Street out of town past the railway station. After a couple of kilometres turn right at the T-junction facing pine-shrouded Dan Nam Giao Temple (where Vietnamese emperors once prayed for good weather) and take first left onto Minh Mang. Continue on, passing the sign marking your departure from Hué and taking the right-hand branch of the fork in the road. After a short distance the road joins the river bank and heads for some 2 km towards the river crossing (the new Hué bypass – Highway 1). Follow the riverbank directly underneath this bridge and continue straight on as the road begins to deteriorate. A few metres beyond the Ben Do 1-km milestone is a red sign reading Gia Long Tomb. Down a steep path a sampan is waiting to ferry passengers across this tributary of the Perfume River (bargain); on the far side follow the track upstream for about 1 km. By a café with two billiard tables turn right and then almost immediately turn left. Keep on this path (ask for directions along the way).

Tomb of Emperor Minh Mang
Daily 0630-1730, 80,000d. Get there by bicycle or motorbike and follow the instructions for Gia Long's tomb, but cross the Perfume River using the new road bridge; on the far side of the bridge turn immediately left.

The Tomb of Emperor Minh Mang is possibly the finest of all the imperial tombs. Built between 1840 and 1843, it is sited among peaceful ponds, about 12 km from the city of Hué. In terms of architectural poise, balance and richness of decoration, it has no peer in the area. The tomb's layout, along a single central and sacred axis (*Shendao*), is unusual in its symmetry; no other tomb, with the possible exception of Khai Dinh (see page 171), achieves the same unity of constituent parts, nor draws the eye onwards so easily and pleasantly from one visual element to the next. The tomb was traditionally approached through the **Dai Hong Mon**, a gate which leads into the ceremonial courtyard containing an array of statuary; today visitors pass through a side gate. Next is the stela pavilion in which there is a carved eulogy to the dead emperor composed by his son, Thieu Tri. Continuing downwards through a series of courtyards there is, in turn, the **Sung An Temple** dedicated to Minh Mang and his empress, a small garden with flower beds that once formed the Chinese character for 'longevity', and two sets of stone bridges. The first consists of three spans, the central one of which (**Trung Dao Bridge**) was for the sole use of the emperor. The second, single bridge leads to a short flight of stairs with naga balustrades, at the end of which is a locked bronze door (no access). The door leads to the tomb itself which is surrounded by a circular wall.

Tomb of Thieu Tri
Daily 0630-1730, ticket required only for admission beyond the gatehouse, 80,000d.
7 km southwest of Hué in the village of Thuy Bang.

The Tomb of Thieu Tri was built in 1848 by his son Tu Duc, who took into account his father's wishes that it be 'economical and convenient'. Thieu Tri reigned for just seven years and unlike his forebears did not start planning his mausoleum the moment he ascended the throne. Upon his death his body was temporarily interred in Long An Temple (now the Hué Museum of Royal Fine Arts, see page 157). The tomb is in two adjacent parts, with separate tomb and temple areas; the layout of each follows the symmetrical axis arrangement of Minh Mang's tomb which has also inspired the architectural style. The memorial temple area is to the right and reached via a long flight of steps. A gatehouse incorporates Japanese triple-beamed columns (as seen in the Japanese Bridge in Hoi An) and at the back of the courtyard beyond is the temple dedicated to Thieu Tri.

The stela pavilion and tomb are a few hundred yards to the left, unmissable with the two obelisks. Just like his father, Thieu Tri is buried on a circular island reached by three bridges beyond the stela pavilion.

Tomb of Tu Duc
Daily 0630-1730, 80,000d.

The Tomb of Tu Duc is 7 km from the city and was built between 1864 and 1867 in a pine wood. It is enclosed by a wall, some 1500 m long, within which is a lake. The lake, with lotus and water hyacinth, contains a small island where the emperor built a number of replicas of famous temples – now rather difficult to discern. He often came here to relax, and from the pavilions that reach out over the lake, composed poetry and listened to music. The **Xung Khiem Pavilion**, built in 1865, has recently been restored with UNESCO help and is the most attractive building here. The tomb complex follows the formula described above: ceremonial square, mourning yard with pavilion and then the tomb itself. To the northeast of Tu Duc's tomb are the tombs of his empress, Le Thien Anh and adopted son, Kien Phuc. Many of the pavilions are crumbling and ramshackle – lending the tomb a rather tragic air. This is appropriate: although he had 104 wives, Tu Duc fathered no sons. He was

The funeral of Khai Dinh

On 6 November 1925, Dai-Hanh-Hoang-Khai-Dinh, King of Annam, 'mounted the dragon's back,' or, in other words, died. Seven diamonds were put in the mouth of the corpse, which was washed, embalmed, dressed in state robes, placed in a huge red and gold lacquer coffin and covered over with young tea leaves. Ten days later official mourning was inaugurated with the sacrifice of a bullock, a goat and a pig. A portrait of the late monarch, painted on silk, was placed on the throne. Paper invocations were burnt, massed lamentations rent the air four times daily for 60 days.

All Annam was in Hué, dressed in its best and brightest. Packed sampans swarmed about the bridge. Gay shrines lined the way, hung with flowers and paper streamers. Bunting, citron and scarlet, fluttered in the breeze. Route-keepers in green and red held the crowds in check, chasing small boys out of the way, whacking them over their mushroom hats. At the head of the column were two elephants, hung with tassels and embroidered cloths and topped with crimson *howdahs* and yellow umbrellas. Never have I seen animals so unutterably bored. They lolled against each other, eyes closed – and slumbered. But for an occasional twitch of an ear or tail they might have been dead. Their boredom was understandable when you came to think of it. An elephant is a long-lived beast. These two were full-grown; elderly, even. It is possible that they featured at the obsequies of Thieu-Tri, and there have been innumerable royal funerals since. At one period kings weren't stopping on the throne of Annam long enough to get the cushions warm. What was a very

therefore forced to write his own eulogy, a fact which he took as a bad omen. The eulogy itself recounts the sadness in Tu Duc's life. A flavour of its sentiment can be gleaned from a confession he wrote in 1867 following French seizure of territory. It was shortly after Tu Duc's reign that France gained full control of Vietnam.

Tomb of Duc Duc
11 Tan Lang St, 2 km south of the city centre, daily 0630-1730, 80,000d.

Despite ruling for just three days and then dying in prison, Emperor Duc Duc (1852-1883) has a tomb, built in 1899 by his son, Thanh Thai, on the spot where, it is said, the body had been dumped by gaolers. (Duc Duc was dethroned by the court for his pro-French sympathies). Emperors **Thanh Thai** and his son **Duy Tan** are buried in the same complex. Unlike Duc Duc, though, both were strongly anti-French and were, for a period, exiled in Réunion Island, Africa. Although Thanh Thai later returned to Vietnam and died in Vung Tau in 1953, his son Duy Tan was killed in an air crash in central Africa in 1945. It was not until 1987 that Duy Tan's body was repatriated and interred alongside his father Thanh Thai. The tomb is in three parts: the Long An Temple; Duc Duc's tomb to the south; and Thanh Thai and Duy Tan's tombs adjacent to each other.

novel and splendid exhibition to me was stale stuff to these beasts. "All very fine for you, mister", they might have said. "First time and all that. Can drop out and buy yourself a drink any time you like. All very well for you, Henry, in a featherweight gent's suiting; but what about us, tight-laced front and back with about a ton of passengers, brollies, flags and furniture up top?" An old bearded mandarin in a coat of royal blue struck with a wooden hammer on a silver gong. The procession began to shuffle forward – somebody in front had found means to rouse the elephants, apparently.

Some 160 trained porters, clad in black and white, crouched under the red lacquer poles of the giant bier – slips of bamboo had been placed between their teeth to stop them from chattering. Slowly, steadily, keeping the prescribed horizontal, the huge thing rose. Six tons it weighed and special bridges had to be built to accommodate it. Slowly, steadily it moved towards us, preceded by solemn-stepping heralds in white; flagbearers in sea-green carrying dragon banners of crimson and emerald, blue and gold. The second day was spent in getting the coffin from Nam-Gio to the mausoleum and was a mere repetition of the first. The actual interment took place on the morning of the third day. In a few minutes the mourners were out in the daylight again and the vault doors were being sealed. The spirit of Khai-Dinh was on its way to the Ten Judgement Halls of the Infernal Regions, to pass before the Mirror of the Past wherein he would see all his deeds reflected, together with their consequences; to drink the Water of Forgetfulness, and pass on through transmigration to transmigration till he attained the Pure Land and a state of blessed nothingness. And Bao-Dai – weeping bitterly, poor little chap – reigned in his stead.

(Adapted from *The Voyage from London to Indochina*, Crosbie Garstin.)

Tomb of Dong Khanh

The Tomb of Dong Khanh is 500 m from Tu Duc's tomb (walk up the path on the other side of the road from the main entrance to Tu Duc's tomb – the path is partly hidden in amongst the stalls), daily 0630-1730, 80,000d.

Dong Khanh was the nephew and foster son of Emperor Tu Duc. His tomb was built in 1889, it is the smallest of the imperial mausoleums, but nonetheless one of the most individual; it was not completed until 1923 under the authority of his son Khai Dinh. Unusually, it has two separate sections. One is a walled area containing the usual series of pavilions and courtyards and with a historically interesting collection of personal objects that belonged to the Emperor. The second, 100 m away, consists of an open series of platforms. The lower platform has the honour guard of mandarins, horses and elephants along with a stela pavilion; the third platform is a tiled area which would have had an awning; and the highest platform is the tomb itself. The tomb is enclosed within three open walls, the entrance protected by a dragon screen (to prevent spirits entering).

Tomb of Khai Dinh

Daily 0630-1730, 80,000d. Get there by motorbike or bicycle. As for Gia Long's tomb, continue under the new river crossing, but turn immediately left, through a collection of small shops and head straight on, over a small crossroads and parallel to the main road. From the riverbank a return moto trip is 30,000d.

The Tomb of Khai Dinh is 10 km from Hué. Built between 1920 and 1931, it is the last of the mausoleums of the Nguyen Dynasty and, by the time Khai Dinh was contemplating the afterlife, brick had given way in popularity to the concrete that is now beginning to deteriorate. Nevertheless, it occupies a fine position on the Chau Mountain facing southwest towards a large white statue of Quan Am, also built by Khai Dinh. The valley, used for the cultivation of cassava and sugar cane, and the pine-covered mountains, make this one of the most beautifully sited and peaceful of the tombs. Indeed, before construction could begin, Khai Dinh had to remove the tombs of Chinese nobles who had already selected the site for its beauty and auspicious orientation. A total of 127 steep steps lead up to the Honour Courtyard with statuary of mandarins, elephants and horses. An octagonal Stela Pavilion in the centre of the mourning yard contains a stone stela engraved with a eulogy to the emperor. At the top of some more stairs are the tomb and shrine of Khai Dinh, containing a bronze statue of the Emperor sitting on his throne and holding a jade sceptre. The body is interred 9 m below ground level (see box, page 170, for a description of Khai Dinh's interment). The interior is richly decorated with ornate and colourful murals (the artist incurred the wrath of the emperor and only just escaped execution), floor tiles and decorations built up with fragments of porcelain. It is the most elaborate of all the tombs and took 11 years to build. Such was the cost of construction that Khai Dinh had to levy additional taxes to fund the project. The tomb shows distinct European stylistic influences; Khai Dinh himself toured France in 1922, three years before he died.

Amphitheatre and Elephant Temple
Free. To get there, head about 3 km west of Hué railway station on Bui Thi Xuan St; turn left up a paved track opposite 203 Bui Thi Xuan St; the track for the Elephant Temple runs in front of the amphitheatre (off to the right).

Ho Quyen (Amphitheatre) lies about 4 km upstream of Hué on the south bank of the Perfume River. The amphitheatre was built in 1830 by Emperor Minh Mang as a venue for the popular duels between elephants and tigers. Elephants were symbolic of emperors and strength whereas tigers were seen as anti-imperial beasts and had their claws removed before the fight. This royal sport was in earlier centuries staged on an island in the Perfume River or on the river banks, but by 1830 it was considered desirable for the royal party to be able to observe the duels without placing themselves at risk from escaping tigers. The amphitheatre is said to have been last used in 1904 when, as was usual, the elephant emerged victorious: "The elephant rushed ahead and pressed the tiger to the wall with all the force he could gain. Then he raised his head, threw the enemy to the ground and smashed him to death," wrote Crosbie Garstin in *The Voyage from London to Indochina*. The walls of the amphitheatre are 5 m high and the arena is 44 m in diameter. At the south side, beneath the royal box, is one large gateway (for the elephant) and, to the north, five smaller entrances for the tigers. The walls are in good condition and the centre is filled either with grass or immaculately tended rows of vegetables, depending on the season.

Den Voi Re, the Temple of the Elephant Trumpet, dedicated to the call of the fighting elephant, is a few hundred metres away. It is a modest little place and fairly run down with a large pond in front and contains two small elephant statues. Presumably this is where elephants were blessed before battle or perhaps where the unsuccessful ones were mourned.

North of Hué → *Colour map 3, A1.*
the place to head for an insight into Vietnam's war with the USA

The Demilitarized Zone (DMZ)
The incongruously named Demilitarized Zone (DMZ), scene of some of the fiercest fighting of the Vietnam War, lies along the **Ben Hai River** and the better-known **17th parallel**. The DMZ was the creation of the **1954 Geneva Peace Accord**, which divided the country into two spheres of influence prior to elections that were never held. Like its counterpart in Germany the boundary evolved into a national border separating communist (the northern Democratic Republic of Vietnam) from capitalist (South Vietnam), but unlike its European equivalent it was the triumph of communism that saw its demise. As nearly all war paraphernalia has been stripped from the DMZ the visit is more of a 'pilgrimage' than anything else.

Khe Sanh Khe Sanh is the site of one of the most famous battles of the war (see box, page 174). The battleground lies along Highway 9 that runs west towards Laos, to the north of Hué, and south of Dong Hoi and is 3 km from the village of the same name. There a small **museum** at the remains of the Tacon military base, surrounded by military hardware.

Ho Chi Minh Trail The Ho Chi Minh Trail is another popular but inevitably disappointing sight, given that its whole purpose was to be as inconspicuous as possible. Anything you see was designed to be invisible – from the air at least; rather an artificial 'sight' but a worthy pilgrimage considering the sacrifice of millions of Vietnamese porters and the role it played in the American defeat (see box, page 175). The trail runs close to Khe Sanh.

Vinh Moc ① *20,000d.* These tunnels served a function similar to that of the better-known Cu Chi tunnels (see page 272). They evolved as families in the heavily bombed village dug themselves shelters beneath their houses and then joined up with their neighbours. Later the tunnels developed a more offensive role when Viet Cong soldiers fought from them. Some visitors regard these tunnels as more 'authentic' than the 'touristy' tunnels of Cu Chi. To get to the tunnels head 6 km north of Ben Hai River and turn right in Ho Xa village; Vinh Moc is 13 km off Highway 1.

Con Co Island This island was an important supply depot and anti-aircraft stronghold in the war. Life for ordinary peasants in the battlezone just north of the

ON THE ROAD

Battle at Khe Sanh (1968)

Khe Sanh (already the site of a bloody confrontation in April and May 1967) is the place where the North Vietnamese Army (NVA) tried to achieve another Dien Bien Phu (see box, page 86); in other words, an American humiliation.

One of the NVA divisions, the 304th, even had Dien Bien Phu emblazoned on its battle streamers. General Westmoreland would have nothing of it, and prepared for massive confrontation. He hoped to bury Ho Chi Minh's troops under tonnes of high explosive and achieve a Dien Bien Phu in reverse. But the American high command had some warning of the attack: a North Vietnamese regimental commander was killed while he was surveying the base on 2 January and that was interpreted as meaning the NVA were planning a major assault. Special forces long-range patrols were dropped into the area around the base and photo reconnaissance increased. It became clear that 20,000-40,000 NVA troops were converging on Khe Sanh.

With the US Marines effectively surrounded in a place which the assistant commander of the 3rd Marine Division referred to as "not really anywhere", there was a heavy exchange of fire in January 1968. The Marine artillery fired 159,000 shells, B-52s carpet-bombed the surrounding area, obliterating each 'box' with 162 tonnes of bombs. But, despite the haggard faces of the Marines, the attack on Khe Sanh was merely a cover for the Tet offensive – the commanders of the NVA realized there was no chance of repeating their success at Dien Bien Phu against the US military. The Tet offensive proved to be a remarkable psychological victory for the NVA – even if their 77-day seige of Khe Sanh cost many thousands (one estimate is 10,000-15,000) of NVA lives, while only 248 Americans were killed (43 of those in a C-123 transporter crash). Again, a problem for the US military was one of presentation. Even Walter Cronkite, the doyen of TV reporters, informed his audience that the parallels between Khe Sanh and Dien Bien Phu were "there for all to see".

DMZ was terrifying; some idea of conditions (for revolutionary peasants at least) can be gained from the 1970 North Vietnamese film *Vinh Linh Steel Ramparts*.

Rock Pile This 230-m-high limestone outcrop, just south of the DMZ, served as a US observation post. An apparently unassailable position, troops, ammunition, Budweiser and prostitutes all had to be helicoptered in. The sheer walls of the Rock Pile were eventually scaled by the Viet Cong. Jon Swain, the war correspondent, describes in his memoirs, *River of Time*, how his helicopter got lost around the Rock Pile and nearly came to disaster in this severely contested zone. The **Hien Luong Bridge** crossing the Ben Hai River on the 17th parallel which marked the boundary between north and south (see box, page 86) is included in most tours. There's a striking national monument, police post, and meeting hall equipped with mannequins in meeting pose next to the bridge.

ON THE ROAD
Ho Chi Minh Trail

The Ho Chi Minh trail was used by the North Vietnamese Army to ferry equipment from the North to the South via Laos. The road, or more accurately roads (there were between eight and 10 to reduce 'choke points') were camouflaged in places, allowing the NVA to get supplies to their comrades in the South through the heaviest bombing by US planes. Even the use of defoliants such as Agent Orange only marginally stemmed the flow.

The road was built and kept opera-tional by 300,000 full-time workers and by another 200,000 part-time North Vietnamese peasant workers. Neil Sheehan, in his book *A Bright Shining Lie*, estimates that at no time were more than one-third of trucks destroyed and by marching through the most dangerous sections, the forces themselves suffered a loss rate of only 10-20%.

Initially, supplies were transported along the trail by bicycle; later, as supplies of trucks from China and the Soviet Union became more plentiful, they were carried by motorized transport. By the end of the conflict the Ho Chi Minh trail comprised 15,360 km of all-weather and secondary roads. One Hero of the People's Army is said, during the course of the war, to have carried and pushed 55 tonnes of supplies a distance of 41,025 km – roughly the circumference of the world.

The Ho Chi Minh Trail represents perhaps the best example of how, through revolutionary fervour, ingenuity and weight of people (not of arms), the Viet Cong were able to vanquish the might of the USA.

But American pilots did exact a terrible toll through the years. Again, Sheehan writes: "Driving a truck year in year out with 20-25 to perhaps 30% odds of mortality was not a military occupation conducive to retirement on pension."

The cemetery for those who died on the trail at Truong Son, Quang Tri Province, covers 16 ha and contains 10,306 named headstones; many more died unnamed and unrecovered.

Other sights Private tours can also visit Doc Mieu Fire Base, Con Thien Fire Base and the Truong Son National Cemetery where there are more than 10,000 graves.

West of Hué → *Colour map 3, A1.*

peaceful countryside ideal for cycling

Thanh Toan Covered Bridge
Take a bicycle or motorbike as the route to the bridge, 8 km west of Hué, passes through beautiful countryside where ducks waddle along roads and paddy fields line the route. Best done in the glow of the late afternoon sun.

Thanh Toan Covered Bridge was built in the reign of King Le Hien Tong (1740-1786) by Tran Thi Dao, a childless woman as an act of charity hoping that God would bless her with a baby. The bridge, with its shelter for the tired and homeless, attracted the interest of several kings who granted the village immunity from a number of taxes. The original yin-yang tiles have been replaced with ugly green enamelled tube tiles, unfortunately, but the structure is still in good condition.

South of Hué → *Colour map 3, A2.*
stunning lagoons, wild national park land and a magnificent ocean-front mountain pass

Between Hué and Danang a finger of the Truong Son Mountains juts eastwards, extending all the way to the sea, dividing the country into two halves. This barrier to north–south communication has resulted in some spectacular engineering solutions: the railway line closely follows the coastline (fortunately it is single track and narrow gauge) sometimes almost hanging over the sea – while Highway 1 winds its way equally precariously over the Hai Van Pass. The coastline is stunning. The road used to be littered with broken-down trucks and buses for which the long haul up to the summit was just too much. Very few vehicles now use the pass following the opening of the 6-km Hai Van Tunnel.

The difficult terrain means that much remains wooded, partly because the trees are too inaccessible to cut down and partly because of government edicts preventing the clearance of steep slopes.

★Bach Ma National Park and Hill Station
www.bachmapark.com.vn, national park entry 40,000d. Buses from Hué to Cau Hai village, which is 3 km from the park gates. If you are using your own transport, simply turn off at the small town of Cau Hai.

The hilly woodlands of Bach Ma National Park stretch from the Lao border right down to the coast and although little is virgin forest quite a lot of bird and animal life flourishes within its leafy branches. It is very worthy of a day or two of exploration for anybody interested in seeing Vietnam's nature. A lovely time to visit is in March and April for the rhododendron blossom.

The French established a great many hill stations in Vietnam. Dalat was the only one to really develop as a town. Others, like Sapa, were rejuvenated a few years ago and yet others, like Bach Ma, had been forgotten about until very recently. Now the ruins of villas have been uncovered and flights of steps unearthed and old gardens and ponds cleared.

Bach Ma was established as a hill station in 1932 when the construction of a road made it accessible. By the outbreak of the Second World War there were 139 villas and a hotel. Recognizing its natural beauty and biological diversity, the French gave it protected status. In 1991 the Vietnamese government classified it as a national park with 22,031 ha at its core and a further buffer zone of 21,300 ha. The area is rugged granite overlain in places by sandstone rising to an altitude of 1448 m at the summit of Bach Ma. There are a number of trails

Tip...
Beware of the leeches during the rainy season and the crowds on summer weekends. Bear in mind also that it is at least 7°C colder than the coastal plains.

past cascades, through rhododendron woods and up the summit trail overlooking the remains of colonial villas.

The park is home to an array of mammals including the **red-shanked douc langur** and the buff-cheeked or **white-cheeked gibbon**. Birdlife here is particularly interesting. Four restricted range species are the **Annam partridge**, **crested argus**, **short-tailed scimitar babbler** and the **grey-faced tit babbler**. The most characteristic feature of Bach Ma's birdlife is the large number of pheasants. Of the 12 species of pheasant recorded in Vietnam, seven have been seen in the park. A subspecies of the silver pheasant lives here and Edwards' pheasant, believed extinct until it was rediscovered in 1996, was seen just outside the park buffer zone in 1998. There are many other species of interest including the red-collared woodpecker, Blyth's kingfisher and the coral-billed ground cuckoo.

Lang Co

The road from Hué to Lang Co passes through many pretty, red-tiled villages, compact and surrounded by clumps of bamboo and fruit trees which provide shade, shelter and sustenance. And, for colour, there's the bougainvillea – which through grafting produces pink and white leaves on the same branch. Just north of Hai Van Pass lies the once idyllic fishing village of Lang Co (about 65 km south of Hué) on a spit of land, which has a number of cheap and good seafood restaurants along the road. Shortly after crossing the Lang Co lagoon, dotted with coracles and fish traps, the road begins the long haul up to Hai Van Pass but the majority of traffic now diverts through the tunnel.

Apparently, in the first year of his reign, Emperor Khai Dinh visited Lang Co and was so impressed that he ordered the construction of a summer palace. This, it seems, was never carried out, not even by his son Bao Dai who was so fond of building palaces. There are several guesthouses and tourist resorts on Lang Co and the Banyan Tree Group's Laguna Lang Co complex with its five-star resorts, a spa, shops and a golf course on a 200-ha site.

Hai Van Pass

Hai Van Pass (Deo Hai Van, 'Pass of the Ocean Clouds' or, to the French, Col des Nuages) lies 497 m above the dancing white waves that can be seen at its foot. In historic times the pass marked the border between the kingdoms of Vietnam and Champa. The mountains also act as an important climatic barrier trapping the cooler, damper air-masses to the north and bottling it up over Hué, which accounts for Hué's shocking weather. They also mark an abrupt linguistic divide, with the Hué dialect (the language of the royal court) to the north, the source of bemusement to many southerners.

The pass is peppered with abandoned pillboxes and crowned with an old fort, originally built by the dynasty from Hué and used as a relay station for the pony express on the old Mandarin Road. Subsequently used by the French, today it is a pretty shabby affair. Looking back to the north, stretching into the haze is the lagoon of Lang Co. To the south is Danang Bay and Monkey Mountain.

Nam I and Thien Beach

Highway 1 passes through the village of **Nam O**, once famous for firework manufacture. Pages of old school books were once dyed pink, laid out in the sun to dry, rolled up and filled with gunpowder. But, alas, no more. Like other pyrotechnical villages, Nam O suffered from the government's ban on firecrackers.

Just south of Nam O is **Xuan Thieu Beach**, dubbed 'Red Beach II' by US Marines who landed here in March 1965, marking the beginning of direct intervention by the USA in the Second Indochina War. The tarmac and concrete foundations of the military base still remain.

Listings South of Hué

Where to stay

Bach Ma National Park and Hill Station
There are a variety of villas offering simple accommodation.

Lang Co

$$$$ Angsana Lang Co
T54-369 5800, www.angsana.com.
The less expensive of the 2 upscale properties on the Laguna development, the **Angsana** offers a host of different room options, many with large sea-view balconies and more decadent lodgings with private pools. Fantastic beachfront setting, massive swimming pools and a variety of wining and dining options.

$$$$ Banyan Tree Lang Co
T54-3695 888, www.banyantree.com.
Part of the massive **Laguna Lang Co** site, the **Banyan Tree** offers some of the most luxurious accommodation in the country with a small collection of seriously decadent and tasteful bungalows. The restaurant and spa are both of the highest order. Very pricey, but extremely sharp.

$$$$ Vedana Lagoon Resort and Spa
Zone 1, Phu Loc town, T54-381 9397, www.vedanaresorts.com.
A new resort of beautiful bungalows situated over the lagoon waters and run by the same folk as the **Pilgrimage Village**, 1 hr south of Hué city centre. This is a very quiet place to get away from it all for a night or 2.

$$$ Lang Co Beach Resort
T54-387 3555, www.langcobeach resort.com.
A large, full-service resort with pool, restaurant and bar. All rooms have a/c. There are some cheap budget rooms, but it is way better to go for an oceanfront villa with veranda, which is much larger with a better outlook than a garden-view villa. There are well-tended gardens here and a nice pool. The resort has certainly seen better days and can be almost eerily quiet, but it offers reasonable value and a great location.

Danang
& around

premier stretch of coast with UNESCO-listed sites

★Danang, Vietnam's third largest port and a commercial and trading centre of growing importance, has a fantastic location with excellent beaches right on its doorstep as well as the stunning Son Tra Peninsula with its heavily forested slopes and fine deserted beaches. There are also three UNESCO World Heritage Sites (Hué, Hoi An and My Son) within a short drive, plus a brilliant culinary culture.

Danang → *Colour map 3, A2.*

a friendly, forward-looking beach-side city with excellent cuisine

Danang Museum of Cham Sculpture

At the intersection of Trung Nu Vuong and Bach Dang streets, T511-357 2414, daily 0700-1730, www.chammuseum.danang.vn. Labels are in English. Guided tours are held 0800-1030 and 1400-1630.

The museum was established by academics of the École Française d'Extrême-Orient and contains the largest display of Cham art anywhere in the world. The museum buildings alone are worth the visit: constructed in 1916 in a beautiful setting, the complex is open-plan in design, providing an environment in which the pieces can be exhibited to their best advantage. There are a number of rooms each dedicated to work from a different part of Champa: **Tra Kieu, My Son** and **Dong Duong** and a new extension. Because different parts of Champa flowered artistically at different times from the fourth to the 14th centuries, the rooms show the evolution of Cham art and prevailing outside influences from Cambodia to Java. One problem with the display is the lack of any background information. The pieces are wonderful, but the visitor may leave the museum rather befuddled by the display.

Principal periods are: My Son E1 (early eighth century); Hoa Lai (early ninth century); Dong Duong (late ninth century); Late Tra Kieu (late 10th century); Thap Mam (12th to 13th century); Po Klong Garai (13th to 16th century).

Tra Kieu was the earliest Cham capital sacked by the Chinese in the fifth century. Some 40 km southwest of Danang, little remains today but the pieces on display at the museum testify to a lively and creative civilization. An altar is inscribed with scenes from the wedding story of Sita and Rama from the Ramayana, a Hindu epic.

Many pieces from My Son illustrate the Hindu trinity: Brahma the Creator, Vishnu the Preserver and Siva the Destroyer. Ganesh, the elephant-headed son of Siva, was a much-loved god and is well represented here.

At the end of the ninth century Dong Duong replaced My Son as the centre of Cham art. At this time Buddhism became the dominant religion of court although

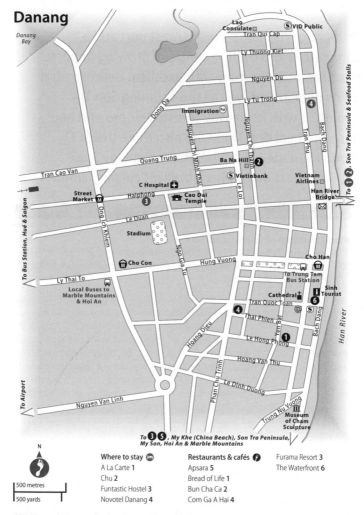

Danang

Where to stay 🛏
A La Carte **1**
Chu **2**
Funtastic Hostel **3**
Novotel Danang **4**

Restaurants & cafés 🍴
Apsara **5**
Bread of Life **1**
Bun Cha Ca **2**
Com Ga A Hai **4**

Furama Resort **3**
The Waterfront **6**

BACKGROUND
Danang – past to present

Danang lies in a region of great historical significance. Fairly close to the city lies **My Son** – the ruins of the powerful kingdom of Champa, one of the most glorious in ancient Southeast Asia. The Cham were probably of Indonesian descent, and Chinese texts give the date AD 192 as the year when a group of tribes formed a union known as Lin-Yi, later to become Champa. The polytheistic religion of Champa was a fusion of Buddhism, Sivaism and local elements – and later Islam – producing an abundance of religious (and secular) sculptures and monuments. Siva is represented as a *linga*. The kingdom reached its apogee in the 10th and 11th centuries but, unlike the Khmers, Champa never had the opportunity to create a capital city matching the magnificence of Angkor. For long periods the Cham were compelled to pay tribute to the Chinese, and after that they were dominated in turn by the Javanese, Annamese (the Vietnamese) and then the Khmers. The Cham state was finally eradicated in 1471, although there are still an estimated 90,000 Cham living in central Vietnam (mostly Brahmanists and Muslims). Given this turbulent history, it is perhaps surprising that the Cham found any opportunity for artistic endeavours. It should perhaps be added that since the demise of the kingdom, the number of Cham sculptures has grown enormously as forgers have carved more of these beautiful images.

Originally Danang was known as Cua Han (Mouth of the Han River). When the French took control they renamed it Tourane, a rough transliteration of Cua Han. Then it acquired the title Thai Phien, and finally Danang. The city is sited on a peninsula at the point where the Han River flows into the East Sea. An important port from French times, Danang gained world renown when two US Marine battalions landed here in March 1965 to secure the airfield. They were the first of a great many more who would land on the beaches and airfields of South Vietnam.

Danang Bay is a marvellous natural harbour and today the port is the third busiest in the country after Ho Chi Minh City and Haiphong. Danang represents modern Vietnam and is a pointer to the way many of Vietnam's towns will look in not so many years to come. Its transformation in the past 20 years has been quite remarkable. It has undergone a whirlwind-like period of growth and continues to expand at a phenomenal rate. The city is ringed by huge dual carriageways and new roads have been driven out into the empty spaces beyond. Within months of the new roads' arrival they are fleshed out with factories, shops and houses. A host of fantastic award-winning bridges now span the Han River and even the Son Tra Peninsula has seen some development with the InterContinental group opening a large resort. China Beach (see page 186) stretching from Danang to Hoi An is rapidly disappearing under concrete as hotel expansion advances at a very rapid rate – today almost the entire stretch is taken up with either five-star resorts or half-finished properties that have seemingly been left for the sea to claim.

it never fully replaced Hinduism. The Dong Duong room is illustrated with scenes from the life of Buddha. From this period faces become less stylistic and more human and the bodies of the figures more graceful and flowing. The subsequent period of Cham art is known as the late Tra Kieu style. In this section there are *apsaras*, celestial dancing maidens whose fluid and animated forms are exquisitely captured in stone. Thereafter Cham sculpture went into artistic decline. The Thap Mam style (late 11th to early 14th century) sees a range of mythical beasts whose range and style is unknown elsewhere in Southeast Asia. Also in this room is a pedestal surrounded by 28 breast motifs. It is believed they represent Uroha, the mythical mother of the Indrapura (My Son, Tra Kieu, Dong Duong) nation, but its significance and that of others like it is unknown.

The museum has a new collection with objects from Quang Tri, Tra Kieu, Quang Nam, Thap Mam-Binh Dinh, An My, Chien Dan, Qua Giang-KHué Trung and Phu Hung in its extension. One of its most outstanding pieces is a bronze with golden eyes, perfect breasts and stretched earlobes. It is the Avalokites Vara, an image of the Bodhisattva of compassion and dates from the ninth century.

Other sights
Danang's **Cao Dai Temple** ⓘ *63 Haiphong St*, is the second largest temple in Vietnam. **Danang Cathedral** ⓘ *156 Tran Phu St, 0500-1700, Mass is held 6 times on Sun*, built in 1923, is single-spired with a sugary-pink wash. The stained-glass windows were made in Grenoble, in 1927, by Louis Balmet who was also responsible for the windows of Dalat Cathedral (see page 206).

Listings Danang *map p180*

Tourist information

Sinh Tourist
154 Bach Dang St, T511-384 3259,
www.thesinh tourist.vn.
Helpful and can book buses as well as help with information as can other tour operators, see page 185. The website www.indanang.com is worth consulting for news and events.

Where to stay

$$$ A La Carte
Vo Nguyen Giap, T511-3959 555,
www.alacarteliving.com.
This is a fantastic addition to the Danang seafront with exceptional rooms for the

price, many of which have great sea views. The rooftop pool is a treat and affords awesome views of the Son Tra Peninsula. Highly recommended.

$$$ Novotel Danang Premier Han River
36 Bach Dang, T511-3929 999,
www.novotel.com.
Situated right on the bank of the Han River, this striking new hotel offers excellent rooms – those on the upper floors have superb views of the city and its bridges, especially by night. Polished service, a quality gym and excellent dining options and sky bar.

$$ Chu Hotel
2-4 An Thuong 1 St, T511-395 5123,
www.chuhotel.com.

In a great location by the sea, **Chu Hotel** has a choice of four rooms furnished to a very high standard, especially given the price. Exceptionally good service and good Italian coffees.

$ Funtastic Danang Hostel
115 Hai Phong, T90-356 1777, www.funtasticdanang.com.
A range of clean dorm rooms as well as a double and a twin. Great little chill out area with bean bags, a book exchange. Very friendly, welcoming staff. Motorbike and bicycle rental. The best backpacker choice in town.

Restaurants

Eating in Danang is a pleasure and makes it worth a visit in itself. There are many local specialities and the seafood is second to none. See box, page 184. Bread in Danang is particularly good, which makes *banh mi ôp la* (fried eggs and bread) a great start to the day.

$$$ Furama Resort
See Where to stay.
Sublime thin-crust pizzas and perfect pasta.

$$$ The Green House
Hyatt Regency Danang, www.danang. regency.hyatt.com.
The Green House is 1 of 3 excellent restaurants at the **Hyatt Regency** overseen by executive chef, Frederik Farina. Expect superb Italian fare. The **Beach House** restaurant is another good option, especially for special lunch with sea views.

$$-$ Apsara
222 Tran Phu St, T511-356 1409, www. apsara-danang.com. Open 1000-1400, 1700-2100.
Besides the upmarket hotel options, this is the most elegant dining in town with crisp white linens on the table and

attentive staff. There's a good spread of Vietnamese food on the menu.

$$-$ The Waterfront
150-152 Bach Dang St, T9-3507 5580, www.waterfrontdanang.com. Open 0900-2400.
Very cool 2-storey restobar serving innovative cuisine and top drawer cocktails. Great, minimalist design.

$ Bread of Life
12 Le Hong Phong St, T511-356 5185, www.breadoflifedanang.com.
Closed Sun. This is a restaurant that provides training and jobs to deaf people. It's a worthwhile cause to support and the pizzas are very tasty. Baked goods and other comfort food too. Motorbike rental also.

$ Bun Cha Ca
109 Nguyen Chi Thanh. Open 0900-1700.
Rice noodle and fish soup loaded with pineapple and tomato. Add a spritz of lime and chilli to taste and you'll be in heaven. A bargain.

$ Com Ga A Hai
96 Thai Phien.
A hugely popular spot with locals, this street side eatery dishes up delectable grilled chicken with rice. Not to be missed.

Bars and clubs

Dimples Bar and Grill
My An Beach, Vo Nguyen Giap, T120-238 9110.
Popular with expats, **Dimples** has a cooling sea breeze, a free pool table and a decent menu of comfort foods.

Sky 36
See Novotel (Where to stay).
Set at the top of the **Novotel**, **Sky 36** is more of a club than a bar, with loud

Danang specialities

Summer Le is a Danang native and author of the popular Danang Cuisine blog at www.danangcuisine.com.

What dish would you say is definitively Danang?
If I have to pick one dish to represent our cuisine, it has to be *mi quang* (a part-soup, part-salad noodle dish). *Mi Quang Hoi An* and *Mi Quang Da Nang* are quite different in terms of cooking style.

Other Danang specialities include *bun mam nem* (cold rice vermicelli with roasted pork and anchovy fish sauce), *bun cha ca* (fishcake noodle soup) and *banh trang cuon thit heo* (pork rolls).

Banh mi is excellent in your city – what are your favourite varieties?
Some of the best are *banh mi ga* (meat and pickles – only found in Danang), *banh mi bot loc* (with transparent dumplings) and *banh mi heo quay* (with roasted pork).

What are some of the newest fads to emerge in the city?
Currently milk tea with tapioca pearls and jello is very popular among youngsters. Last year it was Hanoi snacks such as *nem chua ran* (fried sour roll) and *bun dau mam tom* (fried tofu and rice vermicelli).

If people only have one day in town, what dishes should they not miss?
Definitely *mi quang* (see above), *banh xeo* (savoury fried pancakes) and noodle soup dishes such as *bun cha ca* (fishcake noodle soup).

How about dessert?
Che Xuan Trang is one of the oldest and most popular dessert shops in Danang, they serve the best *che dau do* (sweet bean dessert) and also *goi bo kho* (beef jerky salad). Other options would be *xoa xoa* (black and white jello, red tapioca pearls, sweet green mung bean paste, syrup, coconut milk and ice) or coconut jelly.

Which is your favourite place for seafood?
My personal favourite is Hoa T, 17 Huynh Thúc Kháng Street. I think their food is unbeatable. Besides the natural freshness of the seafood itself, I prefer seafood cooked with more spices and flavours (such as tamarind crab instead of steamed crab). Hoa T is the best at that. Of course they also serve great seafood cooked in the simplest ways to preserve its freshness if that's your preference. Its only downfall is the lack of beach atmosphere as it is located in the city centre.

What café would you head to after a good meal?
Cafe Long. They grow their own coffee and distribute to the whole central region. In Danang they only have one shop at 123 Le Loi Street – it is very traditional with small chairs and it is always packed with people.

music and dancers. Prices are steep and there is a smart-casual dress code. The views are outstanding.

The Waterfront
See Restaurants.

Alongside an excellent menu, **The Waterfront** does a good line in beers, wines and cocktails. The most stylish bar in town.

Shopping

Marble carvings
Available from shops in town, but particularly from the stalls around the foot of Marble Mountains (see page 187).

Markets
The city has a fair array of markets. There is a covered **general market (Cho Han)** in a building at the intersection of Tran Phu and Hung Vuong streets. Another market, **Cho Con**, is at the intersection of Hung Vuong and Ong Ich Khiem streets. The stalls close by sell basketwork and other handicrafts. On Haiphong St, running east from the railway station, there is a **street market** selling fresh produce.

What to do

Asia Pacific Travel, *79 Thanh Long St, Haichau District, T511-6286088, www. asiapacifictravel.vn.* Arranges tours to Hoi An (biking and fishing tour) and My Son.
Funtastic Danang Hostel, *115 Hai Phong, T90-356 1777, www.funtastic danang.com.* This new hostel also runs a very good tour desk with daily trips around Danang and also to Hoi An and the Tra Que vegetable village. This is also the best place to book the fantastic street tour with Summer, author of the superb local food blog, www. danangcuisine.com.

The Sinh Tourist, *154 Bach Dang St, T511-843259, www.thesinhtourist.vn.* Open Tour Buses stop at 1030 and 1530 to go to Hoi An, 1 hr, from 79,000d-89,000 in low season. To Hué at 0900 and 1400, 109,000 and 89,000 respectively. Ba Na Hill tour 850,000d including cable car and lunch.

Transport

Danang is extremely well connected. Along with the airport, it is on the north–south railway line linking Hanoi and Ho Chi Minh City, and there are also regular bus and minibus connections with all major cities in the south as far as Ho Chi Minh City, and in the north as far as Hanoi from the new bus station, 7 km north of the city. Open Tour Buses stop in the town centre.

Air
The airport, 2.5 km southwest, is on the edge of the city. Metered taxis run into town in 5-10 mins. There are connections with **Bangkok**, **Phnom Penh**, **Siem Reap**, **Singapore**, **Hong Kong** and most domestic airports.
    Airline offices Vietnam Airlines, 58 Bach Dang St, T511-381 1111.

Bicycle and motorbike
Bicycles are available from many hotels and hostels, including Funtastic (see Where to stay).
    Rent a Bike Vietnam, 80 Phan Thanh, T91-302 6878, www.rentabikevn.com. A new branch of this reliable Vietnamese/British run company which has been running in Hanoi for some years. Danny and Thu offer high quality motorbikes for rent and sale. Also a great source of local information. Good rates on longer term rentals.

Bus
Buses to **Hoi An** run from the station at the west end of Hung Vuong St, opposite Con Market. The **Ben Xe Trung Tam Danang** bus station is 7 km north of Danang and 15 km south of the Hai Van Tunnel. Buses to **Hanoi, Dong Hoi, Hué, HCMC, Buon Ma Thuot, Kontum** and **Pakse**. **Tickets** can be bought from agents in town. Sinh Tourist (see agents) also sells open tour tickets.

International connections It is possible to get a visa for Laos in Danang from the Lao consulate (see page 434) here. However, 30-day visas are available at the border on arrival, so there is no real need to do so. There are daily departures for the Lao town of **Savannakhet**, on the Mekong River from the **Hoa Minh station**. The road runs west from Dong Ha into the Annamite Mountains and crosses the border at Lao Bao, not far from the former battlefield of Khe Sanh, see page 173.

Taxi
There are many **taxi**s in town, including Mai Linh. A taxi from Hoi An along the new coastal road will cost around 500,000d.

Train
The train station is on Haiphong St, 2 km west of town, T511-375 0666, and there are express trains to and from **Hanoi**, **HCMC** and **Hué**. See also box, page 165.

---

endless white sands and a record-breaking national park cable car

Son Tra Peninsula
The Son Tra Peninsula makes an excellent day out from the city. Hire a motorbike or bicycle (but beware of the hills) and take to the road that hugs the coastline right the way around it. Climb to the top for amazing views of the city and toward Lang Co and the Hai Van Pass. There are plenty of simple seafood restaurants and also enough beaches that, with a bit of hunting, you are likely to find one all to yourself.

My Khe Beach (China Beach)
Once a fabled resort China Beach was the GI name for this US military R&R retreat during the Vietnam War, but locals never refer to it as such – here it has always been My Khe.

Until recently, My Khe was a real 'undiscovered' asset, despite being only 20 minutes from the centre of Danang. However, investors have now recognized that it has the potential to transform Danang into the Rio de Janeiro of Asia. This once-abandoned, wild stretch of beach is now nearly all taken up by resorts. Miles and miles of fine white sand, clean water and a glorious setting (the hills of Monkey Mountain to the north and the Marble Mountains clearly visible to the south) have attracted hotels such as the Nam Hai, which has garnered several major international awards, see Where to stay. Only several kilometres of a 30-km stretch between Danang and Hoi An remains public.

Marble Mountains (Nui Non Nuoc)

12 km from Danang and 20 km from Hoi An. Many visitors stop off at Marble Mountain en route to Hoi An, daily 0600-1700, 15,000d.

The Marble Mountains overlook the city of Danang and its airfield, about 12 km to the west. The name was given to these five peaks by the Nguyen Emperor Minh Mang on his visit in 1825 – although they are in fact limestone crags with marble outcrops. They are also known as the mountains of the five elements (fire, water, soil, wood and metal). An important religious spot for the Cham, the peaks became havens for communist guerrillas during the war owing to their commanding view over Danang airbase. From here, a force with sufficient firepower could control much of what went on below, and the guerrillas harried the Americans incessantly. The views from the mountain sides, overlooking Danang Bay, are impressive. On the Marble Mountains are a number of important sights, often associated with caves and grottoes formed by chemical action on the limestone rock.

At the foot of the mountains is a village with a large number of shops selling marble carvings with a bewildering array of kitsch on offer.

Of the mountains, the most visited is **Thuy Son**. There are several grottoes and cave pagodas in the mountain that are marked by steps cut into the rock. The **Tam Thai Pagoda**, reached by a staircase cut into the mountain, is on the site of a much older Cham place of worship. Constructed in 1825 by Minh Mang, and subsequently rebuilt, the central statue is of the Buddha Sakyamuni (the historic Buddha) flanked by the Bodhisattva Quan Am (a future Buddha and the Goddess of Mercy), and a statue of Van Thu (symbolizing wisdom). At the rear of the grotto is another cave, the **Huyen Khong Cave**. Originally a place of animist worship, it later became a site for Buddhist pilgrimage. The entrance is protected by four door guardians. The high ceiling of the cave is pierced by five holes through which the sun filters and, in the hour before midday, illuminates the central statue of the Buddha Sakyamuni. In the cave are various natural rock formations which, if you have picked up one of the young cave guides along the way, will be pointed out as being stork-like birds, elephants, an arm, a fish and a face.

A few hundred metres to the south on the right is a track leading to **Chua Quan The Am**, which has its own grotto complete with stalactites, stalagmites and pillars. Local children will point out formations resembling the Buddha and an elephant.

Non Nuoc Beach

A 1-km walk from Marble Mountain, this huge, white sandy beach is home to the **Sandy Beach Resort**. There's also the popular backpacker joint, Hoa's Place. Heading further south is the Montgomerie Links golf course (www.montgomerielinks.com).

Bana Hill Station

38 km west of Danang on Chua Mountain (Nui Chua). www.banahills.com.vn.

Near the top of Chua Mountain (Nui Chua, 1467 m), Bana Hills sits at 1200 m. The view in all directions is spectacular, the air is fresh and cool. Bana was founded in

1902 by the French, who came here to convalesce. Today, the site is home to the Bana Hills tourism complex which includes a fantasy theme park, an alpine coaster, a 'French village', hotels, restaurants, gardens, a funicular railway, a wine cellar-cum-bar and the jewel in the crown – the longest single-wire cable car system in the world. The cable car alone is worth the journey as it affords breathtaking views of the densely forested slopes and the steep river that dramatically cascades down the hillside.

Listings Around Danang

Where to stay

My Khe Beach (China Beach)

$$$$ Furama Resort
68 Ho Xuan Huong St, T511-384 7888, www.furamavietnam.com.
The first 5-star to open in the area, Furama is still going strong and many of its staff have been there since the beginning. Its 198 rooms and suites are beautifully designed and furnished. 2 pools, one of which is an infinity pool overlooking the beach. All facilities are first class. Water sports, diving, mountain biking, tennis and a health centre offering a number of massages and treatments. Operates a free and very useful shuttle to and from the town, Marble Mountains and Hoi An. Fantastic buffet breakfasts and good seafood barbecues in the evenings.

$$$$ Fusion Maia
T511-396 7999, www.maiadanang. fusion-resorts.com.

This innovative private pool villa resort has innovative concepts including an all inclusive spa treatments with the room rate and the chance to have your breakfast anytime and anywhere in the grounds. Very sleek design and very polished service. This is pure, unadulterated luxury. The only downside is you may not want to leave.

$$$$ Hyatt Regency Danang Resort
T511-398 1234, www.danang.regency. hyatt.com.
This massive hotel-cum-resort has been getting rave reviews since it opened for its sleek accommodation, fantastic dining and great service. A wide range of rooms on offer and frequent special offers and package deals.

$ Hoa's Place
215/214 Huyen Tran Cong Chua St, T511-396 9216, hoasplace@gmail.com.
A laid-back and very basic popular hangout that is a hit with those who want to kick back on a budget by the sand.

Hoi An
& around
enchanting town, ancient ruins, beautiful beaches

Hoi An's tranquil riverside setting, its diminutive scale (you can touch the roof of many houses), friendly and welcoming people and its wide array of shops and galleries have made it one of the most popular destinations for foreign travellers. There is plenty to see of historical interest, there is a nearby beach and, as if that were not enough, it has superb and inexpensive restaurants and a fantastic street food culture.

Hoi An → *Colour map 3, A2.*

one of the prettiest towns in Asia

★This ancient town lies on the banks of the Thu Bon River. During its heyday 200 years ago, when trade with China and Japan flourished, Hoi An became a prosperous little port. Much of the merchants' wealth was spent on family chapels and Chinese clan houses, which remain little altered today.

By the end of the 19th century the Thu Bon River had started to silt up and Hoi An was gradually eclipsed by Danang. Hoi An has, however, emerged as one of the most popular tourist destinations in Vietnam, and although Hoi An's historic character is being somewhat submerged by the rising tide of tourism, nevertheless, visitors to Hoi An are charmed by the gentleness of the people and the sedate pace of life.

Sights
Most of Hoi An's more attractive buildings and assembly halls (*hoi quan*) are found either on, or just off, Tran Phu Street. Tran Phu stretches west to east from the Japanese Covered Bridge to the market, running parallel to the river. Entrance to most historic buildings is by sightseeing ticket, 120,000d for up to five sites, on sale at the Hoi An Tourist Offices, see page 194.

Japanese Covered Bridge (Cau Nhat Ban) ⓘ *Tran Phu St, 1 token; keep your ticket to get back.* Also known as the Pagoda Bridge, the Faraway People's Bridge

Essential Hoi An and around

Getting around

Hoi An is compact and is best explored on foot. Guesthouses hire out bicycles. Motorcycles are not needed unless you want to head further afield.

When to go

The **Full Moon Festival** is held on the 14th day of the lunar month. The town converts itself into a Chinese lantern fest and locals dress in traditional costume. Candles are lit and floated in plastic lotus flowers along the river – it is an exceptionally pretty sight.

Time required

At least a full day is needed to see all the historic sites, but most people stay far longer, whether they originally intended to or not.

Best excursions
Tra Que village, page 199
An Bang Beach, page 200
My Son, page 201

and, popularly, as the Japanese Covered Bridge, this is Hoi An's most famous landmark. The bridge was built in the 16th century. On its north side there is a pagoda, Japanese in style, for the protection of sailors. At the west end of the bridge are statues of two dogs, and at the east end, of two monkeys – it is said that the bridge was begun in the year of the monkey and finished in the year of the dog. Some scholars have pointed out that this would mean a two-year period of construction, an inordinately long time for such a small bridge; they maintain that the two animals represent points of the compass, WSW (monkey) and NW (dog). Father Benigne Vachet, a missionary who lived in Hoi An between 1673 and 1683, notes in his memoirs that the bridge was the haunt of beggars and fortune tellers hoping to benefit from the stream of people crossing over it. Its popular name reflects a long-standing belief that it was built by the Japanese, although no documentary evidence exists to support this. One of its other names, the Faraway People's Bridge, is said to have been coined because vessels from far away would moor close to the bridge.

Museum of Sa Huynh Culture ⓘ *149 Tran Phu St, 1 'museum' token, daily 0700-2100*. Housed in an attractive colonial-era building east of the Covered Bridge, the museum contains a modest collection of mostly pottery unearthed at Sa Huynh, 120 km south of Hoi An. The artefacts, dating from around 200 BC, are significant because they have called into question the previous understanding that the only cultures native to Central Vietnam have been the Cham and the Viet.

Bach Dang Street Just south of the Covered Bridge, Bach Dang Street runs along the bank of the Thu Bon River. Here there are boats, activity and often a cooling breeze. The road loops round to the Hoi An Market (see below). The small but interesting **French quarter** around Phan Boi Chau Street is worth taking time over. At No 25 you can visit an 1887 building that has belonged to the same family for four generations, US$2. The French-speaking owner is happy to talk. The colonnaded fronts are particularly attractive. As everywhere in historical quarters in Vietnam visitors should raise their gaze above street level to appreciate the architectural detail of upper floors, which is more likely to have survived, and less likely to be covered up.

Museum of Trade Ceramics ⓘ *80 Tran Phu St, 1 'museum' token, daily 0700-2100.* Heading east along Tran Phu Street, the museum was opened with financial and technical support from Japan. It contains a range of ancient wares, some of them from shipwrecks in surrounding waters. There are also architectural drawings of houses in Hoi An. Upstairs, from the front balcony, there is a fascinating roofscape.

Ong Hoi An Pagoda ⓘ *1 token.* At the east end of Tran Phu Street, at No 24, close to the intersection with Nguyen Hué Street, is these two interlinked pagodas built back-to-back: **Chua Quan Cong**, and behind that **Chua Quan Am**. Their date of construction is not known, although both certainly existed in 1653. In 1824 Emperor Minh Mang made a donation of 300 luong (1 luong being equivalent to 1½ oz of silver) for the support of the pagodas. They are dedicated to Quan Cong and Quan Am, respectively.

Hoi An Museum of History and Culture ⓘ *13 Nguyen Hué St, 1 'museum' token, 0700-2100.* Adjacent to Ong Hoi An Pagoda, and housed in a former pagoda, is this museum, which sets the history of the town in its trading context with sections on all the main cultural influences.

Hoi An Market (Cho Hoi An) ⓘ *Virtually opposite the Ong Hoi An Pagoda.* The market extends down to the river and then along the river road (Bach Dang Street). At the Tran Phu Street end is a market selling mostly dry goods. Numerous cloth merchants and seamstresses will produce made-to-measure shirts in a few hours. The riverside of the market is the fish market, which comes alive at 0500-0600 as boats arrive with the night's catch.

Hoi Quan (Assembly Halls)
Chinese traders in Hoi An (like elsewhere in Southeast Asia) established self-governing dialect associations or clan houses, which owned their own schools, cemeteries, hospitals and temples. The *hoi quan* (clan houses or assembly halls) may be dedicated to a god or an illustrious individual and may contain a temple but are not themselves temples. There are five *hoi quan* in Hoi An, four for use by people of specific ethnicities: Fukien, Cantonese, Hainan, Chaozhou and the fifth for use by any visiting Chinese sailors or merchants. Strolling east from the Covered Bridge down Tran Phu Street all the assembly halls can be seen.

Quang Dong Hoi Quan (Cantonese Assembly Hall) ⓘ *176 Tran Phu St, 1 'assembly hall' token.* Merchants from Guangdong would meet at this assembly hall. It is dedicated to Quan Cong, a Han Chinese general and dates from 1786. The hall, with its fine embroidered hangings, is in a cool, tree-filled compound and is a good place to rest.

Ngu Bang Hoi Quan All (Chinese Assembly Hall) ⓘ *64 Tran Phu St, free*. Unusually for an assembly hall (sometimes referred to as Chua Ba (Goddess Temple)), it was a mutual aid society open to any Chinese trader or seaman, regardless of dialect or region of origin. Chinese vessels tended to visit Hoi An during the spring, returning to China in the summer. The assembly hall would help ship-wrecked and ill sailors and perform the burial rites of merchants with no relatives in Hoi An. Built in 1773 as a meeting place for all five groups (the four listed above plus Hakka) and also for those

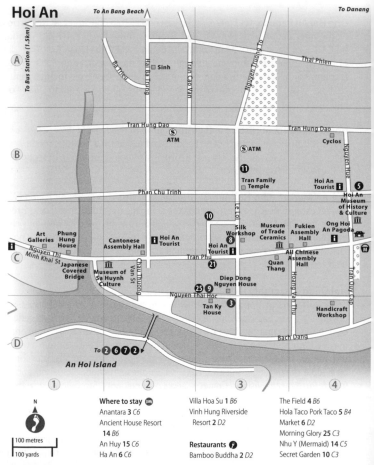

Hoi An

To An Bang Beach

To Danang

To Bus Station (1.5km)

N

100 metres
100 yards

Where to stay 🛏
Anantara **3** *C6*
Ancient House Resort **14** *B6*
An Huy **15** *C6*
Ha An **6** *C6*

Villa Hoa Su **1** *B6*
Vinh Hung Riverside Resort **2** *D2*

Restaurants 🍴
Bamboo Buddha **2** *D2*

The Field **4** *B6*
Hola Taco Pork Taco **5** *B4*
Market **6** *D2*
Morning Glory **25** *C3*
Nhu Y (Mermaid) **14** *C5*
Secret Garden **10** *C3*

with no clan house of their own, today it accommodates a Chinese School, Truong Le Nghia, where children of the diaspora learn the language of their forebears.

Phuc Kien Hoi Quan (Fukien Assembly Hall) ⓘ *46 Tran Phu St, 1 'assembly hall' token.* Founded around 1690, this served Hoi An's largest Chinese ethnic group, those from Fukien. It is an intimate building within a large compound and is dedicated to Thien Hau, goddess of the sea and protector of sailors. She is the central figure on the main altar, clothed in robes, who, together with her assistants, can hear the cries of distress of drowning sailors. Immediately on the right on entering the temple is a mural depicting Thien Hau rescuing a sinking vessel. Behind the main altar is a second sanctuary, which houses the image of Van Thien whose blessings pregnant women invoke on the lives of their unborn children.

Hai Nam Hoi Quan (Hainan Assembly Hall) ⓘ *10 Tran Phu St, 100 m east of the Fukien Assembly Hall, free.* With a rather more colourful history, this assembly hall was founded in 1883 in memory of the sailors and passengers who were killed when three ships were plundered by an admiral in Emperor Tu Duc's navy. In his defence the admiral claimed the victims were pirates and some sources maintain he had the ships painted black to strengthen his case.

Chaozhou (Trieu Chau Assembly Hall) ⓘ *362 Nguyen Duy Hieu St, 1 'assembly hall' token.* Exquisite wood carving is the highlight of this one. The altar and its panels depict images from the sea and women from the Beijing court, presumably intended to console homesick traders.

Merchants' houses
Phung Hung House ⓘ *4 Nguyen Thi Minh Khai St, 1 'old house' token.* Just west of the Japanese Bridge, this house was built over 200 years ago; it has been in the same family for eight generations. The house, which can be visited, is

Seedlings **7** *D2*
Son **1** *B6*
Streets **11** *B3*

Dive Bar **9** *C3*
White Marble
Wine Bar **3** *D3*

Bars & clubs 🎵
Before and After **8** *C3*

constructed of 80 columns of ironwood on marble pedestals. During the floods of 1964, Phung Hung House became home to 160 locals who camped upstairs for three days as the water rose to a height of 2.5 m.

Tan Ky House ⓘ *101 Nguyen Thai Hoc St, 1 'old house' token.* Built by later generations of the Tan Ky family (they originally arrived in Hoi An from China 200 years earlier), dating from the late 18th century, this house reflects not only the prosperity the family had acquired but also the architecture of their Japanese and Vietnamese neighbours, whose styles had presumably worked their influence on the aesthetic taste and appreciation of the younger family members.

Diep Dong Nguyen House ⓘ *80 Nguyen Thai Hoc St.* Two Chinese lanterns hang outside the once Chinese dispensary. The owner is friendly, hospitable and not commercially minded. He takes visitors into his house and shows everything with pride and smiles.

Quan Thang ⓘ *77 Tran Phu St, 1 'old house' token.* This is another old merchant's house, reputed to be 300 years old.

Tran Family Temple ⓘ *on the junction of Le Loi and Phan Chu Trinh streets, 1 'old house' token.* Having survived for 15 generations, the current generation has no son, which means the lineage has been broken. The building exemplifies well Hoi An's construction methods and the harmonious fusion of Chinese and Japanese styles. It is roofed with heavy *yin* and *yang* tiling, which requires strong roof beams; these are held up by a triple-beamed support in the Japanese style (seen in the roof of the covered bridge). Some beams have Chinese-inspired ornately carved dragons. The outer doors are Japanese, the inner are Chinese. On a central altar rest small wooden boxes that contain the photograph or likeness of the deceased together with biographical details; beyond, at the back of the house, is a small, raised Chinese herb, spice and flower garden with a row of bonsai trees. As with all Hoi An's family houses guests are received warmly and courteously and served lotus tea and dried coconut.

Listings Hoi An *map p192*

Tourist information

Tourist offices
At the main entrance points to the old town, see map for locations, T510-386 1327, www.hoianworldheritage.org.vn. Open 0700-1730.
The tourist kiosks provide a good map.

Where to stay

There has been a dramatic increase in the number of hotel rooms available in Hoi An but it is still advisable to book in advance as during peak times, rooms are scarce.

$$$$ Anantara Hoi An
1 Pham Hong Thai St, T510-391 4555, www.hoi-an.anantara.com.

This colonial style resort is in an excellent location right on the riverfront next to the town. The rooms are spacious and extremely comfortable. There's a restaurant, elegant café and cosy bar complete with a huge cigar collection on site. Excellent buffet breakfasts – try and grab a table with a river view. Fabulous staff. Highly recommended.

$$$$ The Nam Hai
Hamlet 1, Dien Duong Village, 11 km north of Hoi An, 30 km south of Danang on Ha My Beach, T510-394 0000, www. ghmhotels.com.
The **Nam Hai** is a stunning creation of 100 beachside villas overlooking the sea. Raised platforms inside the villas create a special sleeping and living space enveloped with white silk drapes; egg-shell lacquered baths in a black marble surround are incorporated into the platform. The restaurants serve excellent local as well as Indian food and the breakfast is excellent, with free flow bucks fizz and a cocktail that changes daily. There are 2 restaurants flanking the vast infinity pool. 3 excellent pools, a gym, tennis, badminton and basketball courts. For relaxing relaxation there's a lovely library and spa. An organic garden nextdoor provides the resort's vegetables.

$$$$ Victoria Hoi An Beach Resort & Spa
Cua Dai Beach, T510-392 7040, www.victoriahotels asia.com.
A charming, resort right on the beach with beautifully furnished rooms, many of which face the sea. There is a large pool, the **L'Annam Restaurant**, a couple of bars and live music and dancing. Charming service. A free shuttle bus runs between the hotel and the town. Also runs excellent tours, including fun days out in vintage sidecars.

$$$$-$$$ Ancient House Resort
377 Cua Dai St, T510-392 3377, www.ancienthouseresort.com.
A beautiful, small hotel set around a pretty garden complete with a pool. Rooms have plenty of character and there is a free shuttle to town and the beach as well as free bicycles. Behind the hotel is a traditional house producing rice noodles. Breakfast included.

$$$$-$$$ Hoi An Riverside Resort
175 Cua Dai Rd, Cua Dai Beach, T510-386 4800, www.hoianriverresort.com.
A short, 5-min cycle ride from the beach and a 15-min pedal from town, this hotel faces the Thu Bon River. There is a pool set in landscaped gardens with hammocks. Standard rooms have balconies; and all rooms have showers. **Song Do** restaurant is the best place to be at sunset.

$$$ Ha An Hotel
6-8 Phan Boi Chau St, T510-386 3126, www.haanhotel.com.
This is a lovely hotel with a flourishing courtyard garden. Rooms are decorated with ethnic minority accents; they are on the small side but they are bursting with character and the overall ambience is delightful. A great option in the heart of the town.

$$$ Villa Hoa Su
Hamlet 5, Cam Thanh Ward, T510-393 3933, www.villahoasu.com.
Just 5 extremely well appointed, beautiful rooms at this brilliant boutique property set around a pool and fragrant frangipani garden. Be sure to book well ahead – this place is popular with expats holidaying from Hanoi and Saigon and books up fast. A truly exceptional place.

$$$ Vinh Hung Riverside Resort
11 Ngo Quyen, T510-386 4074, www.vinhhungresort.com.

Absolutely wonderful riverfront property with beautiful rooms, impeccable service, delicious food and perhaps the best spa in town. Highly recommended.

$$ An Huy Hotel
30 Phan Boi Chau St, T510-386 2116, www.anhuyhotel.com.
Courtyards that create a breeze and shutters that keep the noise out. Spacious rooms are beautifully decorated in Japanese style.

Restaurants

A Hoi An speciality is *cao lau*, a noodle soup with slices of pork and croutons, traditionally made with water from one particular well and lots of stalls sell it along the river at night. *Mi Quang* is another local treat – it is a delicious combination of noodles, pork, shrimp, rice crackers, peanuts and plenty of herbs. Overall, the quality of food in Hoi An, especially the fish, is outstanding and the value for money is unmatched. Bach Dang St is particularly pleasant in the evening, when tables and chairs are set up almost the whole way along the river.

$$$-$$ Bamboo Buddha
13 Nguyen Hoàng, T51-0392 5000, www.bb-hoian.com.
Very sleek new French/Vietnamese-run restaurant and bar. Highlights include the Australian barbecued flap steak with *tam ky* pepper sauce and the lime leaf chicken skewers. Gourmet menu options include roast duck breast with passion fruit sauce and butter candied apple. Excellent wine list. Popular with the French expat crowd. 3rd-floor bar with some outdoor seating.

$$$-$$ Secret Garden
132/2 Tran Phu St, off Le Loi St, T510-391 1112, www.secretgardehoian.com.

An oasis amid the shopping malestrom of downtown Hoi An. Superior and attentive service in a delightful courtyard garden with delicious dishes. Try the sublime thin slices of beef with garlic and pepper, lemon juice, soya sauce, and black sesame oil or the star fruit soup. Live music is played nightly and there's a cooking school. Touristy, but recommended.

$$ The Field
Vong Nhi Hamlet, Cam Thanh Village, T510-392 3977.
Difficult to find, but worth the effort, **The Field** has a magical setting among the paddy fields outside Hoi An. Best visited at sunset. Serves a wide range of Vietnamese dishes.

$$ Nhu Y (aka Mermaid)
2 Tran Phu St, T510-386 1527, http://msvy-tastevietnam.com.
The now famous Miss Vy turns out all the local specialities as well as some of her own fantastic creations. The 5-course set dinner is particularly recommended.

$$ Seedlings
41 Nguyen Phuc Truc, T510-392 1565, www.seedlingshoian.com.
Just across the bridge on An Hoi with great views of the old town, Seedlings provides training to disadvantaged youths and excellent food to hungry tourists. Working in partnership with local youth NGO, **Reach**, the **Seedlings** model sees the restaurant graduates move on to the up-scale Laguna properties over the Hai Van Pass north of Danang. The beef rendang and banana flower salads are excellent. Also offers free bicycle rental to diners. The manager, Mai, is extremely welcoming. Soon to open rooftop bar.

$$ Streets Restaurant Café
17 Le Loi St, T510-391 1948,
www.streetsinternational.org.
A professional training restaurant for
disadvantaged youngsters (including
a Hoi An specialities tasting menu)s that
serves up very tasty Vietnamese and
Western cuisine in a lovely old property.
Trainee chefs complete an 18-month
programme here. Recommended.

$$-$ The Market
*3 Nguyen Hoang, The latest restaurant
from the inimitable Ms Vs who is now
something of a local celebrity.*
A bright open courtyard space with
beautiful floor tiling and wooden
bench style seating is surrounded by
various small cooking stations, each
filling the air with enticing aromas.
A superb place to try a wide range
of Hoi An's special dishes.

$$-$ Son Restaurant
*177 Cua Dai Rd, T98-950 1400, www.
sonhoian.com. Open 0900-2200.*
Now in a new location set back
from the river, **Son** is still serving up
excellent Vietnamese food Du. The
extremely tasty fresh fruit smoothies
are a serious contender for the best
in the land. This is a top lunch spot
and highly recommended.

$ Hola Taco Pork Taco
95000d.
Brad and Nhung came down from
Hanoi in 2014 to open this excellent
Mexican joint that serves superb tacos
and burritos.

$ Morning Glory
*106 Nguyen Thai Hoc St,
T510-324 224 1555.*
In an attractive building with a balcony
serving up Vietnamese street food such
as crispy mackerel and mango salsa,
caramel fish in clay pot and spicy prawn
curry. The restaurant is run by Miss Vy
of **Mermaid** fame.

Bars and clubs

Before and Now
51 Le Loi, T510-910599.
Often livelier than most bars, particularly
after around 2100 thanks to the
good drinks offers and classic tunes
on the stereo. A good spot to meet
fellow travellers.

Dive Bar
88 Nguyen Thai Hoc, T510-391 0782.
A popular hang out for divers and
backpackers alike, the **Dive Bar** has
a DJ, free pool table and a good
selection of cocktails.

Soul Kitchen
See Restaurants.
A great spot to lose an afternoon or
evening right on An Bang Beach. Sun
afternoons are particularly popular.

White Marble Wine Bar
*98 Le Loi St, T510-391 1862,
whitemarble@visithoian.com.
Open 1100-2300.*
Well-stocked cellar and a modern
aesthetic that somehow meshes
well with the old town setting,
White Marble is a fine place to share
a bottle. Serves good food too.

Shopping

Hoi An is a shopper's paradise – Tran
Phu and Le Loi sts being the main
shopping areas. 2 items stand out:
paintings and clothes. Hoi An is also
the place to buy handbags and purses
and attractive Chinese silk lanterns,
indeed anything that can be made
from silk. There is also a lot of quite nice

chinaware available, mostly modern, some reproduction and a few antiques. There is blue and white and celadon green, the ancient Chinese pale green glaze, here often reproduced with fine cracks. Note, however, that it is illegal to take items more than 200 years old out of the country.

Countless galleries sell original works of art. Vietnamese artists have been inspired by Hoi An's old buildings and a Hoi An school of art has developed. Hoi An buildings are instantly recognizable even distorted into a variety of shapes and colours on canvas or silk. Galleries are everywhere but in particular the more serious galleries are to be found in a cluster on Nguyen Thi Minh Khai St west of the Japanese Bridge.

Books
Randy's BookXchange, *Cam Nam Island, T93-608 9483, randy@randys bookxchange.com.* Long-standing bookstore with a wide range of genres, including travel guides. It's a welcoming place to browse.

Handicrafts and jewellery
Memory, *96A Bach Dang St and 62 Le Loi St, T510-391 1483.* Wonderful, imaginative designs, with prices for simple ear rings starting from a few dollars ranging up to around US$70 for more intricate styles.
Reaching Out Handicrafts, *103 Nguyen Thai Hoc St, T510-391 0168, www.reaching outvietnam.com.* Arts and crafts, cards and notebooks, lovely jewellery, textiles and silk sleeping bags all made by disabled artisans living in Hoi An. The shop is a fair trade one and profits support the disabled community. There is usually someone at work in the shop so you can see what they are getting up to.

Tailors and fashion
Hoi An is famed for its tailors – there are now reckoned to be more than 140 in town – who will knock up silk or cotton clothing extremely quickly. However, bear in mind that if every visitor to Hoi An wants something made in 12-24 hrs, this puts an enormous strain on staff. Quite apart from the fact that the workers having to stay up all night, the quality of the finished garment will almost certainly suffer. So, if you are in Hoi An for a few days, give yourself time to accommodate 2nd or 3rd fittings, which may be necessary. Tailors themselves recommend a minimum 36-hr period. The quality of the stitching varies from shop to shop, but many tailors will now be honest and tell you they don't make the clothing on-site, but rather send it elsewhere – this means what you are really searching for is a good measurement service. Ideally, have one thing made and check it before committing to more. The range of fabrics is limited and quality can be poor. Many stores also now sell shoes offering everything from simple heals to outrageously coloured suede boots and knock-off Nikes; again, the the quality tends to be quite poor.
Gingko, *59 Le Loi, T510-3910 796, www.ginkgo-vietnam.com.* A good choice of funky, quality cotton T-shirts with original designs as well as a more limited range of trousers and shorts. A good place to buy gifts.
Metiseko, *3 Chau Thuong Van, T510-3929 278, www.metiseko.com.* The most chic, high quality threads in town alongside interesting homewares.
O Collective, *85 Nguyen Thai Hoc, T128-327 6993.* A creative little boutique with a tempting range of fashion and homewares.

What to do

The **Hotel Hoi An** (see above) runs several activities including how to be a farmer, fisherman, make Chinese lanterns and visits to carpentry and pottery villages.

Boat rides

Boat rides are available on the Thu Bon River. You can either hire a boat and be paddles around or opt for a motorboat and head further upstream – both options are tranquil and relaxed ways of spending the early evening.

Cookery classes

The Market, *see Restaurants*. Housed in the restaurant of the same name, The Market offers a range of professionally-run courses. The Masterclass option includes breakfast as well as hands-on tuition for 675,000d, while the Countryside Bicycle Tour and cooking class is 882,000d. Pick of the bunch, however, is the Gourmet Class with charismatic owner Ms Vy, a third generation chef, for 1,155,000 per person. **Red Bridge Cooking School**, *run out of the Hai Café, 98 Nguyen Thai Hoc St, T510-386 3210*. Full-day and half-day courses on offer. Visit the market to be shown local produce, take a boat ride to the cooking school, visit a herb garden and learn to cook before enjoying a feast. This has been one of the most popular and acclaimed **cooking courses** for many years.

Diving and snorkelling

Cham Island Diving Center, *88 Nguyen Thai Hoc St, T5103-910782, www.chamislanddiving.com*. A PADI dive centre. Its Cham Island excursion is recommended for snorkellers as it gives time to explore the village on Cham Island.

Therapies

Spa & Beauty, *Victoria Hoi An Beach Resort & Spa, Cua Dai Beach, T510-927040, www.victoriahotels-asia.com. Open 0900-2100*. A lovely, friendly spa centre covering a wide range of treatments from body wraps to facials. The reflexology treatment is especially good. **The Spa at the Nam Hai**, *Hamlet 1, Dien Duong Village, Dien Ban District, 7 km from Cua Dai Beach, T510-394 0000 ext 7700, www.ghmhotels.com. Open 0900-2100*. This is one of the most gorgeous spas in Southeast Asia. Centred around a lotus pond with stilted buildings in the water, succumb to the delicious treatments on offer including massage, body polishes, facials and spa rituals. The spa's ritual treatment – 2 hrs of pampering – means submitting to an aromatherapy foot polish, aromatherapy massage, silk body scrub, honey and milk body masque and a rose and petal milk bath to complete the experience.

Tour operators

Heaven and Earth, *Hai Ba Trung St (opposite number 720), T510-386 4362, www.vietnam-bicycle.com*. A great local operator running hugely popular bicycle tours around Hoi An.
Hoi An Motorbike Adventures, *54A Phan Chau Trinh St, 191-823 0653, www.motorbiketours-hoian.com*. Highly respected and long-running outfit which runs excellent half-day to 5-day tours in the area.
Hoi An Travel, *Hotel Hoi An, 10 Tran Hung Dao St, and at Hoi An Beach Resort, T510-391 0911, www.hoiantravel.com. Open 0800-2000*. Offers a variety of tours including a visit to Tra Que vegetable village, fishing

at Thanh Nam, lantern making, visiting Kim Bong carpentry village, Thanh Ha pottery village, and visiting the Cham Islands.

Phattire Adventures, *619 Hai Ba Trung St, T510-391 7839, www.ptv-vietnam.com.* Trekking, biking, rock climbing and more from this long-running outfit which began life in Dalat. Very friendly and helpful staff.

Victoria Hoi An Beach Resort & Spa, *T510-392 7040, www.victoriahotels-asia. com.* The hotel offers a variety of services priced by the hour including boating, kayaking, fishing, windsurfing, hobie-cat sailing, tennis court use, and a trip in a restored sidecar; you can also take an adventurous 5-day sidecar trip to the Laos border.

Transport

Air

Hoi An does not have an airport. A taxi from Danang airport to Hoi An will cost about 500,000d, 40 mins. Taxi from Hoi An to Danang is around US$10. Transport to Hoi An can also be arranged through operators. **Vietnam Airlines** agent, 10 Tran Hung Dao St, T510-391 0912.

Bicycle and motorbike

Hotels and tour operators have 2WD and 4WD vehicles for hire. Bicycle hire is free at many hotels and guesthouses or around 20,000d per day. Motorcycles can be hired all over town – simply ask at your reception and one will likely be delivered to your door.

Bus and Open Tour Bus

There are direct bus connections with Ho Chi Minh City, Hanoi, Hué and Nha Trang. The bus station is about 1 km west of the centre of town on Ly Thuong Kiet St. There are also regular connections with **Danang**, 1 hr, from 0530 until 1800. Open Tour Buses go north to **Hanoi** and south to **HCMC**. Book through local tour operators.

Taxi

Mai Linh, T510-391 4914.

Around Hoi An

miles of beaches and ancient Cham-era ruins

Cua Dai Beach and An Bang Beach
You must leave your bicycle (5000d) or moto (10000d) just before Cua Dai Beach in a car park unless you are staying at one of the beach resorts.

A white-sand beach with a host of simple restaurants and sun loungers, **Cua Dai Beach** is 4 km from Hoi An, east down Tran Hung Dao Street, and is a pleasant 25-minute bicycle ride or one-hour walk from Hoi An. Alternatively, a quieter route is to set off down Nguyen Duy Hieu Street. This peters out into a footpath which can be cycled. It is a lovely path past paddy fields and ponds. Nothing is signed but those with a good sense of direction will make their way back to the main road a kilometre or so before Cua Dai. Those with a poor sense of direction can come to no harm. Four kilometres north of Hoi An, off the dual carriageway, is **An Bang Beach** where a collection of popular beach bars and some very nice accommodation has opened up. It can be more pleasantly reached by cycling 2.5 km north past paddies on Hai Ba Trung Street (15 minutes). A Cua Dai-An Bang-Hoi An loop is a pleasant couple of hours' cycle ride.

ON THE ROAD

Silk worms

Sericulture was introduced to Vietnam from China more than 1000 years ago, where the process had remained secret for years. Today Vietnam cultivates 20,000 ha of mulberry bushes which yield 1500-1800 tons of silk, around 1.8% of world output.

More recently, silk-making was developed in North Vietnam during Chinese rule and in 1975, on reunification, it was brought to Dalat. Silkworm larvae are fed mulberry leaves for about a month. They are then ready to construct their cocoons when they start rejecting food. For three days they secrete a sticky substance that binds a 750-m-long fibre into a cocoon. On completion the cocoon is plunged into boiling water to soften the thread and kill the caterpillars. Single threads are too weak and so the thread of 10 cocoons is spun into one yarn used to weave the silk. The caterpillars are then fried and eaten as a delicacy.

The **Cham Islands** are 15 km from Cua Dai Beach and clearly visible offshore. There are seven islands in the group – Lao (pear), Dai (long), La (leaf), Kho (dry), Tai (ear), Mo (tomb) and Nom (east wind). Bird's nests are collected here. You can visit the fishing villages and snorkel and camp overnight (see **Cham Island Diving Center**, page 199).

★My Son → *Colour map 3, A2.*
Daily 0630-1630, 80,000d, around 45 mins from both Hoi An and Danang. Tour operators in Hoi An and Danang also offer tours here.

Declared a World Heritage Site by UNESCO in 1999, My Son is one of Vietnam's most ancient monuments. Weather, jungle and years of strife have wrought their worst on My Son. But arguably the jungle under which My Son remained hidden to the outside world provided it with its best protection, for more has been destroyed in the past 40 years than the previous 400. Today, far from anywhere, My Son is a tranquil archaeological treasure with some beautiful buildings and details to look at. My Son is located about 60 km south of Danang, 28 km west of Tra Kieu, and consists of more than 70 monuments spread over a large area.

Not many visitors have time to make an excursion to see it which makes it all the more appealing to those that do. The thin red bricks of which the towers and temples were built have been carved and the craftsmanship of many centuries remains obvious today. The trees and creepers have been pushed back but My Son remains cloaked in green; shoots sprout up and one senses that were its custodians to turn their backs for even a short time My Son would be reclaimed by the forces of nature.

Tra Kieu, My Son and Dong Duong are the three most important centres of the former Cham Kingdom (see page 353). The characteristic Cham architectural structure is the tower, built to reflect the divinity of the king: tall and rectangular, with four porticoes, each of which is 'blind' except for that on the west face. Because Cham kings were far less wealthy and powerful than the *deva-rajas* (god kings) of Angkor, the monuments are correspondingly smaller and more personal. Originally built of wood (not surprisingly, none remains), they were later made of brick, of which the earliest (seventh century) are located at My Son. These are so-called Mi-Son E1 – the unromantic identifying sequence of letters and numbers being given, uncharacteristically, by the French archaeologists who rediscovered and initially investigated the monuments in 1898. Although little of these early examples remains, the temples seem to show similarities with post-Gupta Indian forms, while also embodying Chen-La stylistic influences. Bricks are exactly laid and held together with a form of vegetable cement probably the resin of the day tree. It is thought that on completion, each tower was surrounded by wood and fired over several days in what amounted to a vast outdoor kiln.

It is important to see My Son in the broader context of the Indianization of Southeast Asia. Not just architecture but spiritual and political influences are echoed around the region. Falling as it did so strongly under Chinese influence it is all the more remarkable to find such compelling evidence of Indian culture and iconography in Vietnam. Indeed this was one of the criteria cited by UNESCO as justification for its listing. Nevertheless one of the great joys of Cham sculpture and building is its unique feel, its graceful lines and unmistakable form. Angkor in Cambodia is the most famous example but Bagan in Burma, Borobudur in Java and Ayutthaya in Thailand, with all of which My Son is broadly contemporaneous, are temple complexes founded by Hindu or Sivaist god kings. In all these places Buddhism appeared in the seventh century and by the 11th century was in the ascendent with the result that, My Son excepted, these are all widely regarded as Buddhist holy sites. The process whereby new ideas and beliefs are absorbed into a pre-existing culture is known as syncretism. The Hindu cult of *deva-raja* was developed by the kings of Angkor and later employed by Cham kings to bolster their authority. The king was the earthly representative of the god Siva. Sivaist influence at My Son is unmissable. Siva is one of the Hindu holy trinity, destroyer of the universe. Siva's dance of destruction is the very rhythm of existence and hence also of rebirth. Siva is often represented, as at My Son and other Cham relics throughout Vietnam, by the lingam, the phallus. My Son was obviously a settled city whose population is unknown but it seems to have had a holy or spiritual function rather than being the seat of power and it was, very probably, a burial place of its god kings.

Much that is known of My Son was discovered by French archaeologists from the École Française d'Extrême-Orient. Their rediscovery and excavation of My Son revealed a site that had been settled from the early eighth to the 15th centuries, the longest uninterrupted period of development of any monument in Southeast Asia. My Son architecture is notable for its use of red brick, which has worn amazingly well. Sandstone plinths are sometimes used, as are sandstone lintels, the Cham seemingly – like the Khmer of Angkor – never having learnt the art of arch building, one of the few architectural techniques in which Europe was centuries ahead of Asia. Linga and yoni, the female receptacle into which the carved phallus was normally inserted, are also usually made of sandstone. Overwhelmingly, however, brick is the medium of construction and the raw material from which Hindu, Sivaist and Buddhist images and ornaments are so intricately carved.

Unfortunately, My Son was a Viet Cong field headquarters and therefore located within one of the US 'free fire' zones and was extensively damaged – in particular, the finest sanctuary in the complex was demolished. Of the temple groupings, Groups A, E and H were badly damaged in the war. Groups B and C have largely retained their temples but many statues, altars and linga have been removed to the Cham Museum in Danang.

Dong Duong and Tra Kieu

Dong Duong, 20 km from My Son, supplanted My Son as the centre of Cham art and culture when King Indravarman II built a large Buddhist monastery there at the end of the ninth century. Artistically, little changed – the decoration of the towers simply became more ornate and involved, and the reliefs more deeply cut. There is a room in the Cham Museum in Danang devoted to sculptures from Dong Duong, including carved Buddha images. Cham Buddhism saw its finest artistic flowering in the 10th century. In the early 10th century, the focus of Cham art returned to My Son once again under the patronage of Indravarman III (so-called Mi-Son A1 style). Here, a new and far more elegant architecture, evolved. The towers became taller and more balanced, and the decoration purer and less crude.

Tra Kieu, which today is a nondescript little place en route to My Son was, in fact, the first Cham capital in the fourth century. That it supported a flourishing artistic and religious life can be gleaned from the exhibits in the Cham Museum in Danang. Tra Kieu was sacked by the Chinese in the fifth century but appears to have flourished again in the late 10th century. Today, alas, there is little to see.

Listings Around Hoi An

Where to stay

An Bang Beach

$$$ An Bang Beach Hideaway
T91-769 8970, www.anbangbeach hideaway.com.
Just outside Hoi An in the village of An Bang, this small collection of rooms set across three buildings is truly special. Designed by the architect owner, the funky rooms are very homely, each with its own sitting area and outdoor space. An absolute gem of a place, with excellent service to boot. You won't want to check out.

Restaurants

An Bang Beach

$$ Soul Kitchen
An Bang Beach, T90-644 0320, www.soulkitchen.sitew.com.
This is a super laid-back spot with lounge seating, bean bags, day beds and more conventional tables leading from the bar area right down to the sand. The food is nothing exceptional, but the ambiance, location and music policy are all hard to beat, so this is a highly recommended spot for a chilled-out lunch that might well spill into an afternoon and evening.

Dalat

kitsch tourist town surrounded by flower gardens and orchards

Dalat is an attractive town situated on a plateau in the Central Highlands at an altitude of almost 1500 m. The town itself, a former French hill station, is centred on a lake – Xuan Huong – amid rolling countryside and is dotted with more than 2000 French villas. In the area are forests, waterfalls, and an abundance of orchids, roses and other temperate flora. *Colour map 4, A5.*

Essential Dalat

Getting around

Dalat is rather a large town and there are a number of hills. A plentiful selection of taxis is available as are the ubiquitous *xe om* drivers.

When to go

The best time to visit is from November to May when there is less rainfall and pleasant temperatures. At the weekends the centre is closed to traffic between 1900 and 2200 allowing for stalls to set up on Nguyen Thi Minh Khai Street.

Time required

A day or two is enough for most visitors to Dalat.

Sights

a wonderfully eclectic selection of sights

Dalat is the honeymoon capital of southern Vietnam and it is known as a city of romance and even, rather less explicably, the Paris of Vietnam. It also remains a hugely popular destination with Vietnamese tourists.

Xuan Huong Lake

Originally the Grand Lake, Xuan Huong Lake was renamed in 1954. It was created in 1919 after a small dam was constructed on the Cam Ly River. It is the attractive centrepiece of the town and a popular exercise area for the local inhabitants of whom many will, first thing in the morning, walk around the lake stopping every so often to perform t'ai chi exercises. Power-walking at dusk is also popular. The lake was drained in 2010 so as to remove accumulated silt and construct a new road across the center. It should be refilled by the time you read this.

BACKGROUND

Dalat

Dr Alexandre Yersin, a protégé of Louis Pasteur, founded Dalat in 1893. He stumbled across Dalat as he was trying to find somewhere cool to escape from the sweltering summer heat of the coast and lowlands. The lush alpinesque scenery of Dalat impressed the French and it soon became the secondary main city in the south after Saigon. (In the summer months the government moved lock, stock and barrel to Dalat where it was cooler.) There are plenty of original French-style villas, many of which have been converted into hotels while some remain in private ownership; others are government offices. The last emperor of Vietnam, Bao Dai, lived here and it is possible to see his former imperial residence.

Dalat soon took on the appearance of Paris in the mountains. A golf course was made and a luxurious hotel was built. In both the Second World War and the American War high-ranking officials of the opposing armies would while away a pleasant couple of days playing golf against each other before having to return to the battlefields.

Of all the highland cities Dalat was the least affected by the American War. The main reason being that at the time the only entrance into Dalat was up the Prenn Pass. There was a small heliport at Cam Ly (part of Dalat) and also a radio listening station on Langbian Mountain but nothing else of note.

Dalat Flower Garden
Vuon Hoa Dalat, 2 Phu Dong Thien Vuong St, daily 0700-1800, 10,000d.

At the northeast end of the lake is the Dalat Flower Garden. It supports a range of plants including orchids, roses, lilies and hydrangeas. Signs are not in English, only Latin and Vietnamese; the one English sign directs visitors to the orchidarium. There are kiosks selling drinks and ice creams and there's a lake with pedaloes.

Colonial villas
Many of the large colonial villas – almost universally washed in pastel yellow – are 1930s and 1940s vintage. Some have curved walls, railings and are almost nautical in inspiration; others are reminiscent of houses in Provence. Many of the larger villas can be found along **Tran Hung Dao Street** and a number of these are now being converted into villa hotels. Sadly many of the villas have fallen into a very sorry state and are looking decidedly unloved. Given their architectural significance this is a great pity. Perhaps the largest and most impressive house on Tran Hung Dao is the former residence of the Governor General at 12 Tran Hung Dao Street – now the **Hotel Dinh 2**. The villa is 1930s in style, with large airy rooms and furniture and occupies a magnificent position set among mountain pines and overlooking the town and lake. The house is a popular place for domestic tourists to have their photographs taken. It is possible to stay here although it is often booked up and is popular with members of Lam Dong People's Committee.

Dalat Cathedral

Tran Phu St. Mass is held twice a day Mon-Sat 0515 and 1715 and on Sun at 0515, 0700, 0830, 1600 and 1800. Has a good choir and attracts a large and enthusiastic congregation.

The single-tiered cathedral is visible from the lake and 100 m from the Novotel hotel. At the top of the turret is a chicken-shaped wind dial. It is referred to locally as the 'Chicken Cathedral'. Construction began in 1931, although the building was not completed until the Japanese 'occupation' in 1942. The stained-glass windows, with their vivid colours and use of pure, clean lines, were crafted in France by Louis Balmet, the same man who made the windows in Nha Trang and Danang cathedrals, between 1934 and 1940. Sadly, most have not survived the ravages of time. Lining the nave are blocks of woodcarvings of Christ and the crucifixion.

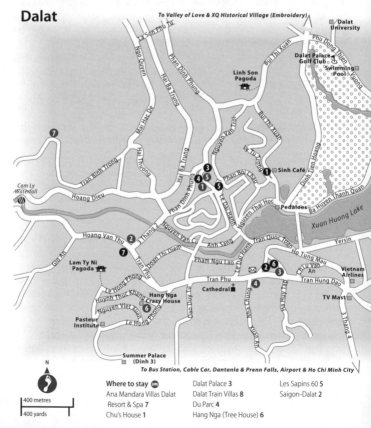

Dalat

To Valley of Love & XQ Historical Village (Embroidery)

Dalat University

Phu Dong Thien

Dalat Palace Golf Club

Swimming Pool

Linh Son Pagoda

Cam Ly Waterfall

Sinh Café

Pedaloes

Xuan Huong Lake

Lam Ty Ni Pagoda

Hang Nga Crazy House

Dalat Cathedral

Vietnam Airlines

TV Mast

Pasteur Institute

Summer Palace (Dinh 3)

To Bus Station, Cable Car, Dantanla & Prenn Falls, Airport & Ho Chi Minh City

N

400 metres
400 yards

Where to stay
Ana Mandara Villas Dalat
  Resort & Spa **7**
Chu's House **1**

Dalat Palace **3**
Dalat Train Villas **8**
Du Parc **4**
Hang Nga (Tree House) **6**

Les Sapins 60 **5**
Saigon-Dalat **2**

Summer Palace (Dinh 3) and Dinh 1

Le Hong Phong St, T63-382 6858, 0730-1100 and 1330-1600, 10000d. Café, ice creams available.

Vietnam's last emperor, Bao Dai, had a Summer Palace on Le Hong Phong Street, about 2 km from the town centre and now known as Dinh 3. Built on a hill with views on every side, it is art deco in style both inside and out, and rather modest for a palace. The palace was built between 1933 and 1938. The stark interior contains little to indicate that this was the home of an emperor – almost all of Bao Dai's personal belongings have been removed. The impressive dining room contains an etched-glass map of Vietnam, while the study has Bao Dai's desk, a few personal ornaments and photographs, noticeably of the family who, in 1954, were exiled to France where they lived. One of the family photos shows Bao Dai's son, the prince Bao Long, in full military dress uniform. He died in July 2007 in France aged 71. Emperor Bao Dai's daughters are still alive and were, in a spirit of reconciliation, invited back to visit Vietnam in the mid-1990s. They politely declined (one of the reasons given was that as they were both in their 70s it would have been too much effort), although the grandchildren may one day return. The emperor's bedroom and bathroom are open to public scrutiny as is the little terrace from his bedroom where, apparently, on a clear night he would gaze at the stars. The family drawing room is open together with a little commentary on which chair was used by whom. The palace is very popular with rowdy Vietnamese tourists who have their photographs taken wherever they can. The gardens are colourful and well maintained, though have a carnival atmosphere. From the moon balcony you can see the garden has been arranged into the shape of the Bao Dai stamp.

Pasteur Institute

Le Hong Phong, not open to the public.

The yellow-wash institute was opened in 1935 and was built to produce vaccines for keeping the colonial population healthy. Although small and modest it is quite an attractive building fashioned in a series of cubes.

Restaurants ⓕ
Bicycle Up Café 1
Da Quy 4
Hoa Binh 5
La Rabelais 6
Le Café de la Poste 2
Tau Cao 7
V Café 3

Hang Nga Crazy House
3 Huynh Thuc Khang, T63-382 2070, daily 0700-1800.

The slightly wacky theme is maintained at the nearby Tree House leading many to wonder what they put in the water for this corner of Dalat to nurture so many creative eccentrics. Doctor Dang Viet Nga has, over a period of many years, built up her hotel in organic fashion. The rooms and gardens resemble scenes taken from the pages of a fairytale book. Guests sleep inside mushrooms, trees and giraffes and sip tea under giant cobwebs. There is a honeymoon room, an ant room and plenty more. It is not a particularly comfortable place to stay and the number of visitors limits privacy. (Dr Dang Viet Nga also built the Children's Centre at 38 Tran Phu Street.)

Dalat Market
At the end of Nguyen Thi Minh Khai St.

Dalat Market (Cho Dalat) sells a dazzling array of exotic fruits and vegetables grown in the temperate climate of the area – plums, strawberries, carrots, potatoes, loganberries, artichokes, apples, onions and avocados. The forbidding appearance of the market is masked by the riot of colour of the flowers on sale, including gladioli, irises, roses, gerbera, chrysanthemums and marigolds. Sampling the immense variety of candied fruit here is the highlight of any visit to Dalat.

Linh Son Pagoda
120 Nguyen Van Troi St just up from the intersection with Phan Dinh Phung St.

The Linh Son Pagoda, built in 1942, is kept in immaculate condition. Perched on a small hillock, two dragon balustrades front the sanctuary, themselves flanked by two ponds with miniature mountain scenes. To the right is a small, Dutch-looking pagoda tower. Behind is a school of Buddhist studies attended by dozens of young, grey-clad men and women.

Lam Dong Museum
4 Hung Vuong St, T63-382239, Tue-Sat 0730-1130, 1330-1630, 4000d.

The museum contains extensive tribal artefacts from the local Lam Dong Province tribes as well as natural history exhibits and old photos from when Dalat was founded up to the modern day. Particularly interesting are the ancient Dong Son relics and artefacts from Funnan-era temples recently discovered in Cat Tien National Park.

Thien Vuong Pagoda
4 km south of the centre of town, at the end of Khe Sanh St.

Begun in the 1950s, this pagoda has been expanded and renovated and can be reached by a fun cable car ride. In the main sanctuary are three massive bronze-coloured, sandalwood standing figures with Sakyamuni, the historic Buddha, in the centre.

Waterfalls

Cam Ly Waterfall ① *2 km from the centre of town, T63-382 4145, daily 0700-1700*, is the closest waterfall to Dalat town centre. It is pleasant enough but should be avoided during the dry season. **Datanla Falls** ① *along a track, 5 km out of town on Highway 20 towards HCMC, T63-383 1804, 0700-1700*, the path leads steeply downwards into a forested ravine; it is an easy hike there, but tiring on the return journey. However, the **Alpine Coaster**, a toboggan on rails, makes the journey faster and easier. The falls – really a cascade – are hardly spectacular, but few people come here except at weekends so it is usually peaceful.

Prenn Falls ① *12 km from Dalat, on the route to HCMC, next to the road, T63-353 0785, 0700-1700*, the falls were dedicated to Queen Sirikit of Thailand when she visited them in 1959. Though it underwent renovations a few years ago, the falls began to suffer pollution and degredation because dredged silt from Xuan Huong lake in Dalat was being dumped at the source of the falls. The falls are not particularly impressive, but there is a pleasant rope bridge that can be crossed and views of the surrounding area.

Dalat cable car (Cáp Treo)

It starts south of town off 3 April Rd, T63-383 7938, 40,000d – widely popular with both locals and tourists.

The journey from top to bottom takes about 15 minutes and leads to a Thien Vien Truc Lam Pagoda and Paradise Lake.

Lake of Sighs and Valley of Love

The Lake of Sighs is 5 km northeast of Dalat and the Valley of Love is 5 km due north. Because of the cool climate, it is very pleasant to reach the lakes, forests and waterfalls around Dalat by bicycle. In fact a day spent travelling is probably more enjoyable than the sights themselves.

The lake is said by some to be named after the sighs of the girls being courted by handsome young men from the military academy in Dalat. Another unlikely theory is that the name was coined after a young Vietnamese maiden, Mai Nuong, drowned herself in the lake in the 18th century. The story is that her lover, Hoang Tung, had joined the army to fight the Chinese who were mounting one of their periodic invasions of the country, and had thoughtlessly failed to tell her. Devastated, and thinking that Hoang Tung no longer loved her; she committed suicide in the lake. Not long ago the lake was surrounded by thick forest; today it is a thin wood. The area is busy at weekends.

The Valley of Love does not refer to a Jimi Hendrix or other psychedelic-era song but to **Thung Lung Tinh Yeu**. Boats can be hired on the lake here; there is also horse riding and a few refreshment stands.

Lang Ga (Chicken Village)
Just off the Dalat–HCMC road, 18 km from Dalat, Highway 20.

This is a rather touristy village of the Coho tribe of which the most noticeable sight is a 5-m-high concrete chicken in the middle. There are numerous different stories as to why it was built with the more popular one being that it was constructed in honour of a local village wench who was tragically killed while searching for a nine-clawed chicken in the surrounding mountains to give to her fiancé for an engagement present. The local officials at the end of the war asked the inhabitants what they would like and were asked for the concrete chicken. The other version of the story of its origin is that it was built to commemorate the heroic peasant chicken farmers.

There are several weaving shops in the village that provide good-quality products at a fraction of what they would cost in Dalat or Ho Chi Minh City.

Lat village and Langbian Mountain
You pass through the Lat village to reach Langbian Mountain.

The village itself is a mixture of old and new – there are traditional wooden stilt houses that are opposite new two- to three-storey houses. It has to a large degree lost its traditional ways and succumbed to the kitsch tourism of Dalat.

Langbian Mountain itself is the highest mountain in southern Vietnam at just over 2000 m. It housed an American radar listening post during the war. Nowadays it is visited primarily for its stunning vistas of the surrounding areas and also for its abundant wildlife, in particular birds. It is a long trek to get to the top from where the views, on a clear day, are magnificent.

Listings Dalat *map p206*

Tourist information

Dalat Travel Bureau
www.dalattourist.com.vn.
The state-run travel company for Lam Dong Province.

Where to stay

$$$$ Ana Mandara Villas Dalat Resort & Spa
Le Lai St, T63-355 5888, www. anamandara-resort.com.
The previous owners, **Six Senses**, restored 17 French hillside villas built in the 1920s and 1930s. Each of the villas has a couple of bedrooms, a living room and dining room; guests have dedicated butlers. The furnishings are reminiscent of Shaker-style furniture; the beds are heavenly; the baths are on feet. **Nine Restaurant & Bar** at Villa 9 has beautiful tilework and a large central fireplace. French-style shutters open on to a small terrace. The heated pool, buried amid the secluded hillside villas, is lovely; a night swim in the cool air is invigorating and at night the air is enveloped with the smell of pine. There's a luxurious spa on site and a city excursion in a 1930s Citroen is a must.

$$$$ Dalat Palace Luxury Hotel
12 Tran Phu St, T63-382 5444.
This rambling old building, built in 1922 and restored to its former glory in 1995, is a wonderful hotel. Those that knew it before restoration will be amazed: the renovation is superb: curtains, furniture, statues, gilt mirrors and chandeliers adorn the rooms which are tastefully arranged as the French do best. The view over Xuan Huong Lake to the hills beyond is lovely and the extensive grounds of the hotel are beautifully laid out. The hotel offers guests special green fees on the nearby golf course.

$$$$-$$$ Saigon-Dalat Hotel
2 Hoang Van Thu, T63-355 6789, www.saigondalathotel.com.
Now a 4-star hotel, this is one of the largest in the city. The striking white exterior, alpine-style roof is visible throughout western Dalat. The hotel has 2 restaurants and a bar, plus the **Moulin Rouge Restaurant** across the street.

$$$ Du Parc (formerly Novotel Dalat)
7 Tran Phu St, T63-382 5777.
First opened in 1932 this was completely restored in 1995. Rooms are nicely restored and comfortably furnished, now including complementary Wi-Fi. Meals are served at the atmospheric **Café de la Poste** across the street.

$$$ Hang Nga (Tree House)
Huynh Thuc Khang St, T63-382 2070.
If you fancy a fantasy night in a mushroom, a tree or a giraffe then this is the place for you. Prices have risen and the rooms tend to be ones visited by curious tourists and the furniture is sturdily made and not too comfortable.

$$ Dalat Train Villas
1 Quang Trung, T90-334 2442, www.dalattrainvilla.com.
Housed in a beautifully restored colonial villa, this property boats the most characterful rooms in town. Just outside is a wonderful little café in a train carriage which is worth a visit in its own right.

$ Chu's House
65 Truong Cong Dinh, T63-382 5097, www.chuhouse.com.
Right in the heart of town this is a friendly and very well appointed budget option.

$ Les Sapins 60
60 Truong Cong Dinh, T63-383 0839, www.lessapins60dalathotel.com.
Family-run, this small central hotel feels brand new with sparkling clean rooms which are very quiet thanks to the thick double glazed windows. Some rooms with small balconies. Simple decor and very homely. Welcoming and knowledgable staff. Also sells its own line of coffees including robusta, Arabica and weasel varieties. Motorcycle hire available.

Restaurants

$$$ Le Rabelais
12 Tran Phu St, T63-382 5444.
A superb dining room with views down to the lake. It serves French specialities. Excellent wine list. Smart dress is required.

$$$-$ Le Cafe de la Poste
12 Tran Phu St.
Adjacent to the Sofitel and under the same management. International comfort food at near-Western prices in an airy and cool building. The 3-course lunch menu is great value. The staff look a little uncomfortable in French-style outfits. A pool table dominates the café. Upstairs is a Vietnamese restaurant.

$ Da Quy (Wild Sunflower)
49 Truong Cong Dinh St, T63-351 0883.
This sweet little family-run business is very friendly and a delightful place to eat with maroon checked tablecloths and a tidy atmosphere. The menu is varied; try the sautéed beef and snow peas.

$ Dalat Train Café
1 Quang Trung, www.dalattrainvilla.com.
Housed in a railway carriage, this place is a characterful spot for a cheap bite to eat.

$ Hoa Binh 1
67 Truong Cong Dinh St.
An all-day eatery serving standard backpacker fare – fried noodles, vegetarian dishes and pancakes at very low prices.

$ Tau Cao
217 Phung St, close to the Mimosa Hotel, T63-382 0104.
This Chinese rice noodle restaurant serves up steaming soups with or without *wan tun*. Still going strong after many years.

$ V Café
1 Bui Thi Xuan, T63-352 0215, www.vcafedalatvietnam.com.
Hugely popular spot with live music every night and a menu of comfort food – think pork chop and mash, burgers and a smattering of Mexican options. By no means fine dining, but a cosy place.

Cafés

Bicycle Up Café
82 Truong Cong Dinh.
An old bicycle and bath tub full of flowers welcome visitors to this cosy, funky little spot run by Ms Indy. With a beautiful tiled floor, mix and match furnishings and an upright piano, this is one of the finer places in town to enjoy an espresso made using La Viet speciality coffee.

Stalls
There are *pho* and *banh mi* (bread) stalls on **Tang Bat Ho St**. Noodle soup, filled baguettes and pastries available from early morning until late. The streets around the university are also good places to find a cheap local Vietnamese meal.

Bars and clubs

Beepub
74 Truong Cong Dinh, T633-825576, www.beepub.vn.
A new and very small pub with a live band most nights. A popular spot with locals and the town's expats and a good place to meet people.

Escape Bar
4 Phan Boi Chau, T63-357 8888.
This is the liveliest bar in town with a rocking house band blasting out classic covers every night of the week. Great atmosphere on busier nights.

Larry's Bar
Du Parc Hotel, see Where to stay.
Open 1600-2400.
A rustic look for this basement bar with comfortable chairs, a pool table and TV room. It was named after Larry Hillblum of DHL fame, who in 1994 spent a fortune renovating the **Sofitel**, **Mercure** and the golf course. Good selection of drinks and bar food available, but sadly it is often eerily quiet.

Festivals

Dec-Mar is when most of the festivals of the local tribes take place. For specific information contact the provincial tourist offices.

Dec or Jan Celebrates the flower capital of Vietnam in peak season.

Shopping

Dalat produces some of the best handmade silk paintings in Vietnam. During your stay in Vietnam you are bound to see shops selling them. The original place to develop this was XQ in Dalat (www.tranhtheuxq.com). It is possible to see how these works of art are produced at the XQ Historical Village on the north side of town and the XQ showroom.

Local produce is plentiful and cheap and can be purchased in Dalat market. Dalat wine is the national standard and comes in red and white. Artichoke teas, jams and dried mushrooms are also a local favourite.

What to do

Golf

Dalat Palace Golf Club, *1 Phu Dong Thien Vuong St, T63-382 3507, www. dalatpalacegolf.vn.* Originally built for Emperor Bao Dai as a 9-hole course in 1922, it was rebuilt in 1994 as an 18-hole championship golf course measuring 7009 yds. Rated by some, including Gordon Simmonds, as the finest in Vietnam and one of the best in the region,it overlooks Xuan Huong Lake. Green fees start at US$55, include caddie fee. **Sofitel** and **Mercure** guests enjoy a 30% discount. Golf lessons are available.

Pedaloes

Pedaloes on Xuan Huong Lake are available by **Thuy Ta** restaurant.

Swimming

There is an open-air swimming pool on Phu Dong Thien Vuong St (Hu Boi Nuoc Nong) next to the Dalat Flower Garden.

Therapies

L'Apothiquaire, *T63-382 5444, www. lapothiquaire.com.* In the eaves of the **Dalat Palace**.

Tour operators

Many of the hotels have tour desks, including Chu Hotel and Le Sapine 60, see Where to stay.
Original Dalat Easy Riders, *67 Truong Cong Dinh, www.dalateasyriders.vn.* Ben who now mans the office is the son of Mr Hong, one of the original easy riders from back in 1991. Hong and his team run a 1-day tour which takes in war sites as well as tea, coffee and vegetable farms, waterfalls and minority villages. Also offers trips from Dalat to Nha Trang, Hoi An on comfortable Honda Custom 250cc motorcycles. Prices from US$65 a day, including accommodation.
Phattire Adventures, *109 Nguyen Van Troi, T63-382 0331, www.ptv-vietnam. com.* Canyoning, from US$45; mountain biking, from US$37, with easy, medium and hard trails through pine forests; trekking from US$32 with options to visit Tiger Falls. Rafting on the La Ba river, where the white water can hit grade 3+ from Sep-Dec. One of the staff, Luet, is particularly helpful. High quality Giant bicycles for the cycle trips. A very professional agent.
Sinh Tourist, *22 Bui Thi Xuan St, T63-382 2663, www.thesinhtourist.vn.* Part of the nationwide **Sinh Tourist** tour operators.

Primarily provides cheap travel to HCMC and Nha Trang. It can also arrange local tours and hotel bookings.

Transport

Air
There are daily flights from Ho Chi Minh City and Hanoi. **Vietnam Airlines**, No 2 and No 40 Ho Tung Mau St, T63-383 3499. Daily 0730-1130, 1330-1630. Closes 30 mins earlier at the weekend.

Bus and Open Tour Bus
There are plenty of local buses that plough the inter provincial routes of **Buon Ma Thuot**, **Pleiku**, **Kontum**, **Nha Trang**, **HCMC**, **Gia Nghia**, **Phan Rang**, **Phan Thiet**, **Danang**. Buses to Lak Lake, 5 hrs. Open Tour Bus companies (**Phuong Trang** and **Sinh Tourist**) operate daily trips to **HCMC**, 7 hrs, **Nha Trang**, 7 hrs, and **Mui Ne**, 8 hrs.

Phuong Trang, 11A Le Quy Don St, T63-358 5858. Phuong Trang dominates southern Vietnam's bus services, and rightly so. The new Phuong Trang bus station is impressive, but more so is the top-quality service.

Car
Dalat is on Highway 20. It is possible to hire cars and taxis in Dalat. Many of the tour operators have cars for hire and there are many taxis. **Mai Linh Dalat**, 44/8 Hai Ba Trung St, T63-351 1511.

Motorbikes and bicycles
Xe oms are ubiquitous. Many places hire motorbikes including **Le Sapine 60** hotel (see Where to stay).

Train
Daily services run the 7 km between Dalat and **Trai Mat**.

Central
Highlands

coffee-growing country populated by minority groups

The Central Highlands, centred around the Truong Son Mountain Range, is commonly referred to as the backbone of Vietnam and is primarily an agrarian area; it is a huge source of flowers and vegetables with many tea and coffee plantations that supply the whole world. Tourism is an additional source of revenue for many of the inhabitants, but outside the main towns of Dalat, Buon Ma Thuot, Pleiku and Kontum the way of life remains largely unchanged.

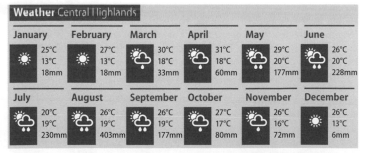

Weather Central Highlands

January	February	March	April	May	June
25°C	27°C	30°C	31°C	29°C	26°C
13°C	13°C	18°C	18°C	20°C	20°C
18mm	18mm	33mm	60mm	177mm	228mm

July	August	September	October	November	December
20°C	26°C	26°C	27°C	26°C	26°C
19°C	19°C	19°C	17°C	16°C	13°C
230mm	403mm	177mm	80mm	72mm	6mm

Essential Central Highlands

Getting around

Many buses go to Pleiku, Kontum, Nha Trang, Buon Ma Thuot, Phan Thiet, and Phan Rang. Open Tour Buses go to Nha Trang.

When to go

As different indigenous groups live in the Central Highlands, there are festivals all year round. Buffalo sacrifice ceremonies take place in Mnong, Sedang and Cotu communities after the spring harvest. Climatically the best time to visit is from November to April when there is little to no rain and the temperature is warm to hot.

Time required

To discover the national parks and minority villages around three days is required.

Dalat to Ho Chi Minh City
national parks and waterfalls

As the road descends on to the Bao Loc Plateau, the forest is replaced by tea and coffee plantations and fruit orchards. Many of the farmers on the plateau settled here after fleeing from the north following partition in 1954.

Bao and Dambri Falls

At the centre of the plateau is the town of Bao (180 km from Ho Chi Minh City, 120 km from Dalat). About 20 km north of Bao Loc are the **waterfalls** ⓘ *Jul-Nov only*, considered the most impressive in southern Vietnam and worth an excursion for those who have time. To get there take *xe om* from Bao.

Nam Cat Tien National Park

www.namcattien.vn. Getting there: 50 km south of Bao Loc, at the small town of Tan Phu, turn off Highway 20 to Nam Cat Tien, 25 km away down a rough road (not well signposted). Guides can be hired and accommodation is available.

This national park, 150 km north of Ho Chi Minh City en route for Dalat, is one of the last surviving areas of natural bamboo and dipterocarp forest in southern Vietnam. It is also one of the few places where populations of large mammals can be found in Vietnam. There are also 300 species of bird, smaller mammals, reptiles and butterflies. The Ta Lai Longhouse accommodation, set up in partnership with the WWF, has proven extremely popular here. The construction of the longhouse itself involved many people from the local area and is now run by locals too. There is much to do here, from kayaking and gibbon watching treks to to visiting a bear rescue centre, birdwatching and taking a village tour.

Tip...
Take tough, long-sleeved and long-legged clothing, jungle boots and leech socks if possible and plenty of insect repellent.

South to Ho Chi Minh City

Beyond Nam Cat Tien, Highway 20 works its way down from the plateau through scrub bamboo forest towards the rolling landscape around Ho Chi Minh City, heavily cultivated with rubber and fruit trees. About 30 km before Highway 20

BACKGROUND

Central Highlands

The Central Highlands have long been associated with Vietnam's hill tribes. French missionaries were active among the minorities of the Central Highlands (the colonial administration deterred ethnic Vietnamese from settling here) although with uneven success. Bishop Cuenot dispatched two missionaries from Quy Nhon to Buon Ma Thuot where they received a hostile reception from the Mnong, so travelled north to Kontum where among the Ba-na they found more receptive souls for their evangelizing. Today, many of the ethnic minorities in the Central Highlands are Roman Catholic, although some are Protestant (Ede around Buon Ma Thuot, for instance).

At the same time French businesses were hard at work establishing plantations to supply the home market. Rubber and coffee were the staple crops. The greatest difficulty they faced was recruiting sufficient labour. Men and women of the ethnic minorities preferred to cultivate their own small plots rather than accept the hard labour and slave wages of the plantation owners. Norman Lewis travelled in the Central Highlands and describes the situation in his book, *A Dragon Apparent*.

Since 1984 there has been a bit of a free-for-all and a scramble for land. Ethnic Vietnamese have encroached on minority land and planted it with coffee, pepper and fruit trees. From the air one sees neat rows of crops and carefully tended plots, interrupted only by large areas of scrub that are too dry to cultivate. The scene is reinforced at ground level where the occasional tall tree is the only reminder of the formerly extensive forest cover. The way of life of the minorities is at risk of disappearing with the forests.

The Mnong, Coho, Sedang and Bahnar people speak a language that stems from the Mon Khmer language. The language of the Ede, Giarai, Cham and Raglai originates from the Malayo-Polynesian language.

joins Highway 1 the road crosses **Tri An Lake**. Fishermen live in floating houses on the lake; besides fishing in conventional ways they also keep fish in cages under their houses. The road between Dalat and Ho Chi Minh City is good. At the important industrial centre of Bien Hoa, 26 km northeast of Ho Chi Minh City, a road runs south to the resort town of Vung Tau.

Listings Dalat to Ho Chi Minh City

Where to stay

Nam Cat Tien National Park

$ Park Guesthouse and Bungalows
T61-379 1228.

The **Park** offers basic accommodation with fan and or a/c, cold showers and semi-operational TV. Wi-Fi may also be available. There is a very basic restaurant on site and several small restaurants outside the entrance that provide reasonable food and snacks.

$ Ta Lai Longhouse
www.talai-adventure.vn.
Established in partnership with the WWF and the Danish International Development Agency, this project sits in the buffer zone commune of Cat Tien National Park, home to the S'tieng and Ma ethnic minority groups. Guests sleep in a communal room divided by simple curtains. A hit with kids, this is a great family option and gets consistently excellent reviews.

Transport

Nam Cat Tien National Park
Tour operators in Dalat and HCMC offer trips to Nam Cat Tien, see Dalat Tour operators, page 185, and HCMC Tour operators, page 288.

Dalat to Buon Ma Thuot

Southwest of Dalat at Nam Ban is Thac Voi (Elephant waterfall), an impressive fall that you can clamber close to; up and down rocks to an outdoor 'shower'. Driving northwest to Buon Ma Thuot you will pass acres and acres of land that has been burned for the growing of new crops, casting an enormous scar on the landscape. Although this is illegal it is out of control in this part of the southern Central Highlands. From Lak Lake, south of Buon Ma Thuot, towards the city there is not one hill or slope untouched by deforestation; the odd tree and a couple of stumps remain.

Buon Ma Thuot → *Colour map 4, A5.*

a modern city with little for the tourist

Buon Ma Thuot is the provincial capital of Daklak Province. The city has changed from being a sleepy backwater town (similar to Kontum) to a thriving modern city, but it has little to draw visitors.

Buon Ma Thuot has now surpassed its illustrious and renowned neighbour of Dalat to be the main centre for tea and coffee production, and the area has become the second largest producer of coffee in the world. The creation of the Trung Nguyen coffee empire in 1997 and the subsequent franchise of the names have meant that Trung Nguyen coffee shops are to be found everywhere in Vietnam. It is good to see that some profits have been reinvested in the community (there are new schools, roads, hospitals aplenty). There is also a sports complex to rival any to be found in Ho Chi Minh City or Hanoi.

Although it is a sprawling modern city, the heart of the city is located on the four streets that radiate out from the Victory Monument roundabout. The town is dominated by the **Victory Monument** (Tuong Dai Chien Thang) complete with a replica tank from the 10 March 1975 battle whose gun is pointing towards the door of the Roman Catholic church on the city's main roundabout.

Buon Ma Thuot Ethnographic Museum ① *182 Nguyen Du St, free*, is well worth a visit for an insight into the many ethnic minority groups that live in this part

ON THE ROAD
Buon Ma Thuot's strategic importance

Buon Ma Thuot was considered of vital strategic importance during the war, dominating a large region of the Central Highlands. The Americans had realized the importance of the city, as did the northern Vietnamese. Unfortunately the southern Vietnamese did not. In March 1975 the northern military, which had infiltrated 30,000 troops and equipment to within striking distance of Buon Ma Thuot undetected, launched an offensive against the city. Instead of a protracted two-year battle that the northern generals had anticipated, there was little resistance. The news was broadcasted on local Vietnamese radio and also on *Voice of America*. It demoralized the southern forces and within two months the war was over.

of the country. Buon Ma Thuot nowadays is much more peaceful but in recent times there has been tensions between the state and ethnic minorities. In the years following the war, the government instigated a resettlement programme primarily from Hanoi and the Red River Delta but also to a lesser degree from Ho Chi Minh City. The land that had belonged to the hill tribes was given to the new settlers. The Ede did not take kindly to having their land encroached upon by outsiders (Vietnamese). The tensions reached their peak in late 2001, early 2002 and again in 2004 when there was widespread rioting in Buon Ma Thuot. For a period of several weeks the whole area was closed to non-Vietnamese.

Listings Buon Ma Thuot

Tourist information

Daklak Tourist Office
53 Ly Thuong Khiet (underneath the Thanh Cong Hotel), T500-385 2108, www.daklaktourist.com.vn.
Some staff speak English.

Where to stay

$$$$-$$$ Saigon Ban Me
3 Phan Chu Trinh, T500-368 5666, www.saigonbanmehotel.com.vn.
Modern hotel in a prime location opposite the victory monument. The rooms are all large and come with en suite facilities. The staff are efficient and speak good English.

$$-$ Dakruco Hotel
60 Nguyen Chi Thanh, T50-397 0777, www.dakrucohotels.com.
Massive hotel on the outskirts of town with large, clean but rather business-like and slightly dated rooms. However, in this price range, this is a solid option for Buon Ma Thuot.

$$-$ Damsan Hotel
212-214 Nguyen Cong Tru St, T500-385 1234, www.damsanhotel.com.vn.
A reasonable hotel with a pool and tennis court and large restaurant. Service is good and rooms are comfortable.

$ Song Tra Hotel
42 Ly Thuong Kiet, T500-381 7897.
Ultra basic rooms, some with no windows (ask to see a few), however the price is right at just 200,000d. Very limited English spoken. Rents motorcycles for 120,000d per day. Strictly for those on a very tight budget.

Restaurants

Food stalls along Y Jut open at 1800 serving *cam tam*, *com ga* and *bun bo Hué*.

$ Bon Trieu
33 Hai Ba Trung St, T50-385 2994.
The steamed squid with ginger is very tasty but its beef in vinegar, cooked at the table, is even better.

$ Bui Saigon
11 Le Hong Phong, T50-0385-6040.
Very good value com tam rice dishes with grilled pork, beef or chicken.

$ Nem Nuong Restaurants
East side of Ly Thuong Kiet St, between Quang Truong and No Trang Long streets.
Nem nuong are roll-it-yourself fresh spring rolls with grilled meats. Inbetween the most popular budget accommodations in town are several eateries specializing in this must-try meal.

Cafés
Buon Ma Thuot is one of the coffee capitals of the world, so there are lots of nice cafés with great coffee. Many are located west of Phan Chu Trinh St in the neighborhoods around the Sports Center. Local style beer bars can also be find in these areas.

Festivals

Dec-Mar is when most of the festivals of the local tribes take place. For specific information contact the provincial tourist offices.

10 Mar Marks the fall of Buon Ma Thuot on 10 Mar 1975.

Shopping

Tea and coffee are the main items that are purchased here. This is also one of the only cities in Vietnam where authentic Central Highlands hill tribe handicrafts can be purchased in abundance.

Phuong Coffee, *20 Phan Boi Chau.* Many types of coffee on sale and you can try before you buy.
Trung Nguyen Coffee Village, *222 Le Thanh Tong St.*

What to do

Sport
Daklak Water Park, *on Highway 14, 5 km from the centre, T500-395 0403. Daily 0730-1930, 30,000d per adult and 20,000d per child.* Fun for kids, it has several water chutes and splash pools and swimming pools.
Sports Complex, *just off Nguyen Tat Thanh St about 1 km from the centre of town.* It has badminton courts and a fitness centre.
Tennis Courts, *Damsan Hotel and 3 Le Duan St (Youth Court/Cultural House).*

Tour operators
Daklak Tourist, *3 Phan Chu Trinh St, T500-385 2246, www.daklaktourist.com. vn.* Some staff speak English and French. Tours include 2-day tours to Lak Lake with elephant riding and canoe paddling;

rafting and hiking; guided cycling; and home stays at Lak Lake, from.

Vietnam Highland Travel, *1st floor, 24 Ly Thuong Kiet St, T500-385 5009, highlandco@dng.vnn.vn.* A recommended tour operator running a range of good, fun tours across the Central Highlands area. Ms Nom in the office is extremely helpful. Tours to the villages of Buon Tul A and B on the way Bon Don. Options from half day to three day tours including home stays. Also runs a popular coffee tour from November to Jan involving a farm visit to pick beans, see how coffee is processed and take part in a tasting. Elephant riding arranged in Yok Don.

Transport

Buon Ma Thuot is located on Highway 14 and can also be reached by Highway 27 from Dalat and on Highway 26 from Nha Trang. There are direct flights from Ho Chi Minh City and Danang. There are innumerable local buses that go to Pleiku, Kontum, Gia Nghia, Dalat, Ho Chi Minh City, Nha Trang and Hanoi.

Air

Vietnam Airlines, 67 Nguyen Tat Thanh St, T500-395 4442 (Inside Buon Ma Thuot Airport Hotel), 0730-1130, 1330-1630.

Bus

The bus station is 5 km from the Victory monument on Nguyen Chi Thanh St, Km 4, T500-387 6789. Regular connections to **Kontum** (241 km), **Pleiku** (197 km), **Nha Trang** (197 km), **Dalat** (217 km). There are also daily buses to **HCMC** and **Hanoi**.

Car and motorbike

Your hotel can arrange a car or you can visit **Daklak Tourist**. **Damsan Travel** also hires out cars and motorbikes.

Taxi

Mai Linh Taxi, 188 Nguyen Tat Thanh, T500-381 3813, operates in town and also from the bus station.

Around Buon Ma Thuot → *Colour map 4, A5.*

waterfalls and minority cultures

Dray Sap, Dray Nur and Gia Long waterfalls

T500-385 0123, daily 0700-1700, 30,000d for Dray Sap and Gia Long combined and another 30,000d for Dray Nur. 30 km south of Buon Ma Thuot, 2 km off Highway 14 heading in the direction of HCMC.

The waterfalls consist of several different cascades all next to each other. They form a 100-m-wide cascade and are particularly stunning in the wet season and justify the name of 'waterfall of smoke', although Dray Nur and Dray Sap are impressive even in the dry season. The best view of Gia Long is from the north side but you can't cross from the south to view it. In the wet season it may occasionally be closed, as the paths are too treacherous to use. There are two paths to take, one down by the river and the other on the high ground.

Dray Sap has been taken over by a private company. An Ede ceremonial house has been added along with a small, rather unpleasant zoo.

Lak Lake and M'nong villages

The serene **Lak Lake** is about 50 km southeast of Buon Ma Thuot. It is an attraction in its own right but all the more compelling a visit on account of the surrounding **M'nong villages**. Unfortunately, Lak Lake has been developed as a tourist attraction and Buon Jun is rather touristy now. For those going on a tour there is little choice as to where to go, but for the independent traveller on a motorbike there are plenty of villages, both ethnic Vietnamese and minority, to visit, but do not expect any English to be spoken.

Early-morning mists hang above the calm waters and mingle with the columns of woodsmoke rising from the longhouses. The M'nong Rlam at Buon Jun has been influenced by the Ede and so live in longhouses. However, most M'nong such as M'nong Chil, Noong, Gar and Bu-dang live in straw and mud- or wood-thatched homes. The lake can be explored by dugout. The canoes are painstakingly hollowed out from tree trunks by axe. The M'nong have been famed as elephant catchers for hundreds of years, although the elephants are now used for tourist rides rather than in their traditional role for dragging logs from the forest.

It is possible to stay overnight at a M'nong village, **Buon Jun** (Buon means village), indeed it is the only way to watch the elephants taking their evening wallow in the cool waters and to appreciate the tranquility of sunrise over the lake. The M'nong number about 50,000 and are matriarchal. An evening supping with your hosts, sharing rice wine and sleeping in the simplicity of a M'nong longhouse is an ideal introduction to these genial people. Between 1600 and 1730 every evening you can watch the men bring back the fish of the day to the lakeshore; the children are eager to help on the shore, buffalos are bathing and pigs are snorting around in the vegetation. Sup a beer at one of the cafés along the lakefront as the sun sets. For more information, see Where to stay, below.

Ban Don

Ban Don is the village at the centre of tourist operations in the area and is very touristy now. It is 7 km from the Yok Don National Park entrance, see below, and 43 km from Buon Ma Thuot. The locals speak Ede, Mnong and Laotian. Until 1992, when elephant catching was outlawed and the national park was set up, there used to be some 400 elephant catchers in the surrounding area. There's a restaurant at the entrance to the village, dozens of stalls selling tack and a bamboo bridge crossing to an island where an unfortunate set of animals are kept in far-too-small cages.

It is also possible to visit the tomb of Ama Cong who died in 2012 was the last surviving Mnong wild elephant catcher. He was also nephew of N'thu Knul. He learnt to catch elephants from the age of 14. In 1938 he caught two tiger cubs and sold them for two dong to Emperor Bao Dai who kept them at his villa in Buon Ma Thuot. Ama Cong is also famous for combining the leaf of the trong tree with brown sweet rice wine to create a very potent potion that is known as the Vietnamese Viagra. Ama Cong wine is, of course, heartily drunk by the local men and all visitors; it is, without doubt, absolutely lethal.

Yok Don National Park

T500-378 3049, yokdonecotourism@vnn.vn. daily 0700-2200. Tours range from elephant riding (US$40 for 2 hrs) to elephant trekking and animal spotting by night. Trekking is another option. Accommodation is available (see Where to stay, below).

A 115,545-ha wildlife reserve about 40 km northwest of Buon Ma Thuot, Yok Don National Park (Vuon Quoc Gia Yok Don) contains at least 63 species of mammals, 17 of which are on the worldwide endangered list, and 250 species of bird. There are known to be around 50 Asian elephants, Samba deer, giant muntjac, leopard, the recently discovered golden jackal and green peafowl. The park is surprisingly flat – save Yok Don Mountain in the middle at 482 m and Yok Da Mountain (482 m) further north – and is, surprisingly, a less-than-dense deciduous forest which makes it easy to trek on an elephant though few wild animals congregate where elephant treks occur. There are 120 species of tree and 854 species of flora. Within its boundaries, also, there are 25 villages of different ethnic tribes who maintain a number of domesticated elephants. Trekking deep into the park and staying in tents near Yok Don Mountain is probably the only chance of seeing wildlife of any great rarity but, alas, the rare become rarer with each passing year. The less adventurous (or those with smaller elephant-trekking budgets) will have to make do with one-hour rides or simply watching one of the village's elephants at work. Note that the rainy season is from April to October.

Listings Around Buon Ma Thuot

Where to stay

Lak Lake and M'nong villages

$$-$ Bao Dai Villa
Lak Lake, T500-358 6184,
www.daklaktourist.com.vn.
Opt for the massive King's Room with portraits on the wall for a unique stay in the area. All 6 rooms have modern comforts and bathtubs. The villa is surrounded by beautiful magnolia trees. The restaurant features old black and white photos of the emperor and his elephant team.

$ Buon Jun longhouse
Buon Jun village.
Contact **Daklak Tourist** at the entrance to the village, T500-358 6184, laklake@daklaktourist.com.vn, for arrangements.

It costs US$12 to stay in a longhouse including breakfast. Longhouses vary between traditional wooden ones to concrete ones. If you don't like creepy crawlies opt for the concrete ones which also have their own bathrooms. Those nearer the lake are noisier.

$ Lak Lake Resort
Lien Son village, near Buon Jun,
Lak Lake, T500-358 6184,
www.daklaktourist.com.vn.
There are 32 rooms with balconies in a great position overlooking the lake. Rooms have TV, a/c and bathtubs. Breakfast is included. There's a branch of **Daklak Tourist** on site.

$ Lak Lake Resort Longhouse.
2 longhouses in the grounds of the **Lak Lake Resort**, see above. The same

price as the village longhouses, but the bathrooms are better.

Ban Don

$ Ban Don Tourist
Buon N'Rech, Ea Huar commune, Buon Don district, 1 km from the main road near the entrance to Yok Don National Park, T500-385 4903/091-343 5642 (mob), www.bandontour.com.vn.
Thatched huts in gardens with en suite shower rooms with Western toilets. Mosquito nets provided. The restaurant serves good food, especially the fish and rice cooked in bamboo cane.

$ Biet Dien Hotel
In the centre of the village, T500-395 4299.
Bungalows with private bathroom and longhouses with shared bathroom.

$ Sinh Thai Tourism Facility
Krong Na Commune.
Situated on the shores of a man-made lake, this is a good option with 11 a/c rooms and 10 fan rooms plus numerous longhouses. There's a restaurant on site. It's very peaceful and lovely to watch the elephants bathing close to dusk but you'd need your own transport or ring for a pick up. Vietnamese guests receive big discounts. This is a good option if you want to get away from the tourist hordes in Ama Cong.

Yok Don National Park

$ Park Guesthouse
T500-378 3049, yokdonecotourism@vnn.vn.
Park HQ has very simple rooms with 2 beds, a/c, fan, hot showers, TV with minimal reception and Wi-Fi.

Restaurants

Lak Lake and M'nong villages

$ Lak Resort floating restaurant
Lien Son village, near Buon Jun, Lak Lake, T500-358 6184.
This restaurant juts out into the lake and is a pleasant place for a meal and a few beers in the shade with a cooling breeze.

What to do

Ban Don
Ban Don Tourist Center, *Krong Na Commune, T500-321 1200.* Situated in 1400 ha and on the shores of the man-made Dak Minh Lake. Elephant rides arranged.

Transport

Lak Lake and M'nong villages
There are hourly buses to and from Buon Ma Thuot to **Lak Lake**. Hourly buses to and from **Krong Kno** for the Dray Sap waterfall. Buses to **Dalat** from Lak Lake, 5 hrs.

Pleiku is the provincial capital of Gia Lai Province. It is located in a valley at the bottom of a local mountain, Ham Rong, clear to see from 12 km away. It is a rather forgettable place and does not attract visitors, other than those who are here for a stopover. During the monsoon the side streets turn into muddy torrents and chill damp pervades guesthouse rooms. The city itself is sprawling although there are six main streets on which you'll find all that you will need in terms of restaurants, shops, internet cafés and hotels.

The area around Pleiku is more cultivated than that of Kontum. Rubber, pepper, coffee and tea plantations abound and rice and watermelon are grown. There was fierce fighting here during the American War. Pleiku was the headquarters to two Corps, one of the four military tactical zones into which South Vietnam was divided during the war. John Vann (see Neil Sheehan's *Bright Shining Lie*) controlled massive B-52 bombing raids against the encroaching NVA from here until his death in a helicopter crash in June 1972.

According to government statistics, which are not always accurate, there are some 300,000 Gia-rai and some 150,000 Ba-na living in the province.

Listings Pleiku

Tourist information

Gia Lai Tourist
215 Hung Vuong St (on the ground floor of the Hung Vuong Hotel), T59-387 4571. Daily 0730-1100, 1330-1630.

Where to stay

$$-$ HAGL Hotel-Pleiku (Hoang Anh Gia Lai Hotel)
1 Phu Dong St, T59-371 8459.
This large hotel has 120 nicely furnished superior and deluxe rooms that are spacious with views of the entire city. There is a Vietnamese and Western restaurant, massage centre, tennis court, gym and internet.

$ Ialy Hotel
89 Hung Vuong St, T59-382 4843, ialyhotel@dng.vnn.vn.
Central location opposite the main post office. Rooms are a reasonable size with en suite facilities, coffee and chairs, a/c, satellite TV. Breakfast is included and there's an ATM in the lobby. A reasonable budget choice.

Restaurants

$ Nem
64 Nguyen Van Troi St, T59-387 4352.
This basic and very popular restaurant serves up heaps and heaps of wonderful do-it-yourself spring rolls.

$ Ngoc Huong Restaurant
76 Hung Vuong St, T59-382 2795.
Good northern Vietnamese food.

Shopping

Pleiku has a surprisingly good selection of shops and products. Coffee, tea and pepper are plentiful. It is also known for its quality of furniture (leading to rapid local deforestation). Most of the shops are along Hung Vuong St, Pham Van Dong St, Thong Nhat and also Nguyen Van Troi St.

What to do

Gia Lia Tourist, *215 Hung Vuong St (on the ground floor of the Hung Vuong Hotel), T59-387 4571.* Arranges tours to the local hill tribes, treks, elephant rides and tours of the former battle sites.

Transport

Pleiku is just off Highway 14 and is 197 km from Buon Ma Thuot. It has a modern domestic airport that is 10 mins' drive from the city centre with direct flights from Danang and Ho Chi Minh City. Plenty of local buses plough the routes to the main towns and cities, including Hanoi and Ho Chi Minh City.

Air
Vietnam Airlines, 55 Quang Trung St, T59-382 4660/382 3058.

Bus
There are regular connections by local bus to **Kontum** (44 km), **Buon Ma Thuot** (197 km), **Quy Nhon** (186 km). There are also buses to **HCMC** and **Hanoi**. **Gia Lai Tourist** runs buses to HCMC at 1830. It also runs transport to the border at **Le Thanh** where there is transport to **Ban Lung**, 70 km away. From Stung Treng, it is 210 km to a bridge crossing the border into Laos at Voen Kham; from here it is 180 km to Pakse. **Gia Lai Tourist** also plans to run buses to the Laos border, 130 km away, at **Bo-Y**.

Car
It is best to arrange car hire through your hotel

Taxi
Mai Linh Taxi, 5B Phan Dinh Phung St, T59-371 8899, www.mailinh.vn.

Kontum → *Colour map 3, B2.*

low-key, backwater town with cultural variety

The town, 49 km north of Pleiku, has a population of 36,000, many of whom are from ethnic minorities. It is a small, sleepy market town and in itself is not remarkable except that it houses the Wooden Church, Tan Huong Church and the Bishop's Seminary. These alone are worth a trip to Kontum.

Despite being one of the larger provinces within Vietnam, Kontum is the least populated and one of the poorest. It was created in 1991 when it was decided to break up Gia Lai Province.

Sights
The main sights within Kontum are the Wooden Church, Tan Huong Church, the Bishop's Seminary, the provinicial museum on the riverfront, the surrounding Bana villages, and Kontum prison.

Bishop Cuenot

The French Bishop Stephen Theodore Cuenot founded Kontum in the mid-1800s. He was a missionary priest endeavouring to convert the local tribes to Christianity. He succeeded, as many of the inhabitants are Christian. He was arrested on Emperor Tu Duc's orders (the Emperor did not like missionaries) and died in Binh Dinh prison on 14 November 1861, a day before the beheading instructions arrived. He was beatified Saint Etienne-Theodore Cuenot in 1909. His wooden church remain almost unchanged since that time.

Tan Huong Church ① *92 Nguyen Hué St (if the church is shut ask in the office adjacent and they will gladly open it).* The whitewashed façade bears an interesting depiction of St George and the dragon. It is not immediately evident that the church is built on stilts, but crouch down and look under one of the little arches that run along the side and the stilts, joists and floorboards are clear. The glass in the windows is all old, as the rippling indicates, although one of the two stained-glass windows over the altar has required a little patching up. Unfortunately the roof is a modern replacement, but the original style of fishscale tiling can still be seen in the tower. The interior of the church is exquisite, with dark wooden columns and a fine vaulted ceiling made of wattle and daub. The altar is a new, but rather fine addition, made of a jackfruit tree, as is the lectern. The original building was erected in 1853 and then rebuilt in 1860 following a fire. The current church dates from 1906.

Wooden Church Further east on the same street is the superb Wooden Church. Built by the French with Ba-na labour in 1913, it remains largely unaltered, with the original wooden frame and wooden doors. Unfortunately the windows are modern tinted-glass and the paintings on them depicting scenes from Christ's life as well as a couple of Old Testament scenes with Moses are a little crude. In the grounds stands a statue of Stephen Theodore Cuenot, the first Roman Catholic bishop of East Cochin China diocese. There is also an orphanage that is run by the church in the grounds that welcomes visitors.

Bishop's Seminary The architecturally remarkable and prominent building is set in lovely gardens with pink and white frangipani trees. It was completed in 1935; the seminary was founded by French missionary Martial Jannin Phuoc. The upstairs **exhibition room** ① *Mon-Sat 0800-1130, by donation*, displays an eclectic collection of instruments, photos and scale models; some signs are in English.

Kontum Prison ① *500 m along Truong Trong St, daily 0800-1100, 1400-1700*. Built in 1915, this was home to several prominent revolutionaries. It was abandoned by the French in 1933 and later left to collapse. There is a small museum in some new buildings and a memorial depicting malnourished prisoners. The labels are in Vietnamese only.

Ba-na villages There are scores of Ba-na villages around Kontum that can be reached by motorbike, and at least one that is easily accessible on foot. Plei To Nghia is at the westerly end of Phan Chu Trinh Street down a dusty track. Wattle and daub houses, mostly on stilts, can be seen and the long low white building on short stilts at the village entrance is the church. In the evening the elderly folk of the village go for communal prayers while the young people gather at the foot of their longhouses for a sunset chat. In and around the village are small fields heavily fortified with thorns and barbed wire, which seems a little strange considering the Ba-na do not lock their doors. In fact the defence is not against poachers but the village's large population of rooting, snuffling, pot-bellied pigs. Every family has a few pigs that roam loose. The pigs are sometimes given names and recognize the voice of their owner, coming when called.

Most houses are on stilts, with the animals living underneath. They are built from wattle and daub around a wooden frame, although brick is starting to appear as it is cheaper than declining wood resources, and modern tile is beginning to replace the lovely old fishscale tiling. Considering the tiny spaces in which most Vietnamese live, these houses are positively palatial. There is a large living room in the centre, a kitchen (with no chimney) at one end and bedroom at the other.

Kon D'Ri (Kon Jori) is a fine example of a community almost untouched by modern life (apart from Celine Dion's voice competing with the cows and cockerels!). A perfect *rong* communal house dominates the hamlet, and all other dwellings in the village are made from bamboo, or mud and reeds. The Ba-na *rong* is instantly recognizable by its tall thatched roof. The height of the roof is meant to indicate the significance of the building and make it visible to all. It is a focal point of the village for meetings of the village elders, weddings and other communal events. The stilt house close by is in fact a small Roman Catholic church.

Nearby **Kon Kotu** is similar. To get there follow Nguyen Hué Street and turn right into Tran Hung Dao Street, cross the suspension bridge (Kon Klor Bridge) over the Dakbla River (built in 1997 after a flood washed the old one away).

A lively Ba-na community can be found at **Kontum KoNam** (turn right off Nguyen Hué past the wooden church). Here the stilt houses are crowded close together and the village bustles with activity.

Around Kontum

Chu Pao Pass Twelve kilometres south of Kontum the road crosses the Chu Pao Pass. There is nothing to see in particular, but there are commanding views over the Kontum Plateau. The road descends past sugar cane plantations before crossing the Dakbla River. It is also possible to get to Kontum from Laos at the Bo-Y border crossing.

Kontum to Hoi An North of Dak To between Plei Kan and Dak Nay are **Katu villages** that speak a Mon-Khmer language. North of Dak Glei, you will pass through the most lush forests anywhere in Vietnam on the **Lo-Xo Pass**. Wild, dark green and luxuriant jungle tumbles down mountains carpeting the area in a thick, abundant forest. It is extremely beautiful and the height of the jungle-clad mountains are awe-inspiring. To the east of the road is the **Ngoc Linh Nature Reserve** and the towering **Ngoc Linh peak** at 2116 m. There is a riot of ferns, waterfalls and astoundingly beautiful scenery all around.

Other villages Twenty kilometres from Kontum it's possible to visit the Gia-rai villages of **Plei RoLay**, **Plei Bua** and **Plei Weh**. Forty kilometres from Kontum you can visit **Kon Biu**, a Xo-dang village, 7 km further on is **Kon Cheoleo**, a Jolong village (there are only 15 known Jolong villages in Vietnam; their language is similar to Ba-na). The Xo-dang build the entrance to the *rong* on the east and west in harmony with the sun, unlike the Ba-na. The Xo-dang play the drums to ask for rain. It's also possible to visit **Kon Hongor**, a Ba-na Ro Ngao community (there are only 4000 Ro Ngao in Kontum Province).

The border crossing Bo-Y is open to foreigners crossing into Laos. Lao visas should be available on arrival but it is safer to have obtained them beforehand.

Listings Kontum

Tourist information

Kontum Tourist Office
2 Phan Dinh Phung St (ground floor of the Dakbla Hotel 1), T60-386 1626. Daily 0700-1100, 1300-1700.

Where to stay

$ Indochine (Dong Duong) Hotel
30 Bach Dang St, T60-386 3335, www.indochinehotel.vn.
The views from this hotel are fantastic. You can look right up the river to the mountains beyond. Decent-sized rooms with mod-cons including hairdryer.

$ Thinh Vuong
16B Nguyen Trai St, T60-391 4729.
The more expensive bedrooms have living area, fridge, TV and bathtubs in the windowless bathrooms. Cheaper rooms are quite spacious too. Very

friendly and helpful staff make this place a very good choice.

Restaurants

There are many restaurants and cafés along Nguyen Hué St all of which are much of a muchness in terms of food, quality, choice, presentation and value. Tapioca noodles – *banh canh mi* – are excellent in Kontum.

$$ Dakbla Restaurant
Dakbla 1 Hotel, 2 Phung St, T60-386 3333.
Good selection of both Vietnamese and international cuisine. Quality and presentation are good and the service is friendly albeit a tad slow. The restaurant looks out onto the hotel courtyard.

$ Dakbla's Café
168 Nguyen Hué St, T60-386 2584, vandakbla@yahoo.com.

Filled with ethnic minority artefacts, it has the most interesting decor town. The pleasant staff are conversant in several languages (English, French and German) and there's a decent selection of reasonable food at cheap prices.

Cafés

Evacoffee
1 Phan Chu Trinh St, T60-386 2944, evacoffee@gmail.com.
A cool hideaway amid plants, sculptures and wooden furniture.

Bars and clubs

Basic beer joints are primarily found along Nguyen Hué St. For a mixed drink your best choice is one of the hotels or Evacoffee.

Festivals

Dec-Mar is when most of the festivals of the local tribes take place. For specific information contact the provincial tourist offices.

14 Nov Festival to celebrate **Bishop Cuenot**.

What to do

Kayaking and trekking
Kayaking, trekking and overnight stays with ethnic minorities can be arranged by **Kontum Tourist** (see below).

Tour operators
Highland Ecotours, *15 Ho Tung Mau T90-511 2037 (mob), www.vietnam highlands.com.* Mr Huynh speaks good English and is courteous and helpful. Formerly the manager of **Kontum Tourist**, Mr Nguyen Do Huynh now runs a private company offering river boat trips and hill tribe trecks in the surrounding province.

Kontum Tourist, *2 Phan Dinh Phung St (ground floor of the Dakbla Hotel), T60-386 1626.* The office arranges kayaking along the river, visits and overnight stays in the local Ba-na and Gia-rai villages, trekking and visits to the former battle sites and Ho Chi Minh Trail; it can also arrange tours starting and finishing from Danang, HCMC or Buon Ma Thuot.

Transport

Kontum is situated just off Highway 14 and is 44 km north of Pleiku. There are numerous local buses that plough the route from Pleiku and to a lesser degree from Buon Ma Thuot and Quy Nhon. Kontum does not have an airport but shares the airport with Pleiku, an hour's drive away.

Bus
There are daily departures from the bus station at 281 Phan Dinh Phung St, T60-386 2265, at 0700 and 0800 to **Pleiku**, **Buon Ma Thuot** and **Quy Nhon**. A bus runs from Quy Nhon via Kontum to **Laos** via the border at Bo-Y, see below.

Car and motorbike
Kontum Tourist rents cars and motorbikes. It will also organize transport to the border at Bo-Y (80 km, 1½ hrs) where you can cross to **Phu Kua** in Laos (nearest town **Attapeu**).

Nha Trang
& around

Nha Trang is a seaside city with a long golden beach, which only a few years ago was remarkably empty. However, in recent years it has been massively developed and has become a major destination for both Russians and the growing number of domestic Vietnamese tourists. Huge international hotels now line the riverfront, while a construction boom in the hotel quarter is on-going.

An important Cham settlement, the area around Nha Trang retains distinguished and well-preserved Cham towers.

Nha Trang → *Colour map 4, A6.*

beaches, museums and plenty of nearby diversions

The beach
The beach and beachside promenade have been spruced up in recent years and it is now a pleasant place to relax. Beach beds are available, the nicest being in front of the Sailing Club and La Louisiane. There are fixed thatched umbrellas in the sand and public toilets.

Cham Ponagar temple complex
Open 0600-1800, 20,000d. The best time to visit the towers is late afternoon, 1600-1700. To get to the temple complex you can either walk or catch a cyclo. Follow 2 Thang 4 St north out of town; Cham Ponagar is just over the 2nd of 2 bridges (Xom Bong bridge), a couple of kilometres from the city centre.

On a hill just outside the city is the Cham Ponagar Temple complex, known locally as Thap Ba. Originally the complex consisted of eight towers, four of which remain. Their stylistic differences indicate they were built at different times between the seventh and 12th centuries. The largest (at 23 m high) was built in AD 817 and contains a statue of Lady Thien Y-ana, also known as Ponagar (who was the beautiful wife of Prince Bac Hai), as well as a fine and very large lingam. She taught the people of the area weaving and new agricultural techniques, and they built the tower in her honour. The other towers are dedicated to gods: the central tower to Cri Cambhu (which has become a fertility temple for childless couples); the northwest tower to Sandhaka (woodcutter and foster-father to Lady Thien Y-ana); and the south tower to Ganeca (Lady Thien Y-ana's daughter).

Cai River estuary and fishing boats
En route to the towers, the road crosses the Cai River estuary where there is a diversity of craft including Nha Trang's elegant fleet of blue fishing boats, lined with red and complete with painted eyes for spotting the fish, and coracles (*cái thúng*) for getting to the boats and mechanical fish traps. The traps take the form of nets that are supported by long arms; the arms are hinged to a platform on stilts and are raised and lowered by wires connected to a capstan which is turned, sometimes by hand but more commonly by foot.

Long Son Pagoda
23 Thang 10 St.

The best-known pagoda in Nha Trang is the Long Son Pagoda, built in 1963. Inside the sanctuary is an unusual image of the Buddha, backlit with natural light. Murals depicting the *jataka* stories decorate the upper walls. To the right of the sanctuary, stairs lead up to a 9-m-high white Buddha, perched on a hill top, from where there are fine views. Before reaching the white pagoda, take a left on the stairs. Through an arch behind the pagoda you'll see a 14-m-long reclining Buddha. Commissioned in 2003, it is an impressive sight.

The pagoda commemorates the monks and nuns who died demonstrating against the Diem government – in particular those who, through self-immolation, brought the despotic nature of the Diem regime and its human rights abuses to the attention of the public.

Nha Trang Cathedral

Mass Mon-Sat 0500 and 1630, Sun 0500, 0700, and 1630.

Granite-coloured (though built of concrete) and imposing, the cathedral was built between 1928 and 1933 on a small rock outcrop. It was not until 1961, however, that the building was consecrated as a cathedral for the diocese of Nha Trang and Ninh Thuan. The cathedral has a single, crenellated tower, a fine, vaulted ceiling, with stained glass in the upper sections of its windows and pierced metal in the lower. The windows over the altar depict Jesus with Mary and Joseph, Joan of

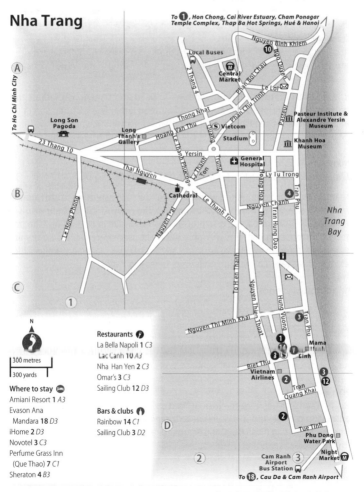

Nha Trang

To ①, Hon Chong, Cai River Estuary, Cham Ponagar Temple Complex, Thap Ba Hot Springs, Hué & Hanoi

To Ho Chi Minh City

Nguyen Binh Khiem

Local Buses

2 Thang 4

Central Market

Phan Boi Chau

Ngo Quyen

Le Loi

Thong Nhat

Phan Chu Trinh

Pasteur Institute & Alexandre Yersin Museum

Long Son Pagoda

Long Thanh's Gallery

Hoang Van Thu

Le Thanh Phuong

Yersin

Vietcom

Stadium

Khanh Hoa Museum

23 Thang 10

Thai Nguyen

General Hospital

Le Hong Phong

Le Thanh Ton

Cathedral

Nguyen Trai

Le Thanh Ton

Nguyen Chanh

Hoang Hoa Tham

Tran Hung Dao

Ly Tu Trong

Tan Phu ④

Nha Trang Bay

To H Huy Thanh

Nguyen Thai Thuat

Nguyen Thi Minh Khai

Nguyen Thien

Hung Vuong

Tran Phu ③

La Bella Napoli 1

Mama Linh ⑦

Cinh ⑦

Biet Thu

Vietnam Airlines

Tran Quang Khai

②

③ ⑫

Tue Tinh

Phu Dong Water Park

Night Market

Cam Ranh Airport Bus Station

To ⑱, Cau Da & Cam Ranh Airport

N

300 metres

300 yards

Restaurants ⊘
La Bella Napoli **1** *C3*
Lac Canh **10** *A3*
Nha Han Yen **2** *C3*
Omar's **3** *C3*
Sailing Club **12** *D3*

Bars & clubs ⊘
Rainbow **14** *C1*
Sailing Club **3** *D2*

Where to stay ⊜
Amiani Resort **1** *A3*
Evason Ana
  Mandara **18** *D3*
iHome **2** *D3*
Novotel **3** *C3*
Perfume Grass Inn
  (Que Thao) **7** *C1*
Sheraton **4** *B3*

Nha Trang

Word has spread, and Nha Trang's days as an undiscovered treasure are over. It is a firmly established favourite of Vietnamese as well as foreign visitors, particularly Russians, and Nha Trang is now set up to relieve them of their tourist dollar. Nevertheless, beyond the main tourist zones the city has some charming spots and the areas to the north and south offer fantastic coastal drives, Cham ruins and long beaches.

The name Nha Trang is thought to be derived from the Cham word *yakram*, meaning bamboo river, and the surrounding area was a focal point of the Cham Kingdom – some of the country's best-preserved Cham towers lie close by. Nha Trang was besieged for nine months during the Tay Son rebellion in the late 18th century (see page 128), before eventually falling to the rebel troops.

Arc and Sainte Thérèse. Like the windows in Dalat and Danang cathedrals they were made in Grenoble by Louis Balmet. Fourteen rather fine pictures depict the stations of the cross: they look French but there is no attribution and no one seems sure of their provenance. The path to the cathedral runs off Nguyen Trai Street.

Alexandre Yersin Museum
10 Tran Phu St, T58-382 9540, Mon-Fri 0700-1130, 1330-1700, 28,000d.

The Yersin Museum is contained within the colonnaded **Pasteur Institute** founded by the great scientist's protégé, Dr Alexandre Yersin. Swiss-born Yersin first arrived in Vietnam in 1891 and spent much of the rest of his life in Nha Trang (see box, above). The museum contains the lab equipment used by Yersin, his library and stereoscope through which visitors can see in 3-D the black-and-white slides, including shots taken by Yersin on his visits to the highlands.

Khanh Hoa Museum
16 Tran Phu St, T58-382 2277, Tue-Fri 0800-1100, 1400-1700, free. English-speaking curators will be pleased to show you around and should be tipped.

The Khanh Hoa Museum, which was renovated in 2010, contains a Dongson bronze drum and a Palaeolithic stone xylophone. There is a room of ethnographics and, of course, a Ho Chi Minh room that contains several items of interest.

Central market
The **Cho Dam** (central market) close to Nguyen Hong Son Street is a good place to wander and browse and it is quite well-stocked with useful items. In the vicinity of the market, along **Phan Boi Chau Street**, for example, are some bustling streets with old colonial-style shuttered houses.

Alexandre Yersin

Alexandre John Emille Yersin was born in 1863 in Canton Vaud, Switzerland. He enrolled at the University of Lausanne and completed his medical education in Paris where he became an assistant to Louis Pasteur. In 1888, Yersin adopted French citizenship. To the astonishment of all he became a ship's doctor; he visited the Far East and in 1891 landed in Nha Trang.

Two years later, as part of his exploration of Vietnam he 'discovered' the Dalat Plateau which he recommended for development as a hill resort owing to its beauty and temperate climate. The following year, in 1894, he was urged to visit Hong Kong to assist in an outbreak of the plague. He identified the baccilus which was named Yersinia pestis.

In 1895 he set up a laboratory in Nha Trang which, in 1902, became a Pasteur Institute, the first to be established outside France. Here he developed an anti-serum for the treatment of plague. He established a cattle farm for the production of serum and vaccines and for the improvement of breeding stock at Suoi Dau, 25 km south of Nha Trang. Yersin was responsible for the introduction to Vietnam of commercial crops such as coffee, rubber and the cinchona (quinine) tree.

In his retirement he indulged his passions – astrology, photography and observation of the hydrographic conditions of Nha Trang Bay.

Yersin died in 1943 and was buried at Suoi Dau. His tombstone, simply engraved 'Alexandre Yersin 1863-1943', can be seen today at Suoi Dau. Take Highway 1, 25 km south of Nha Trang, look for the sign 'Tombeau de Alexandre Yersin'. The key to the gate is kept with a local family. The tomb is 1.5 km from the gate.

Long Thanh's gallery
126 Hoang Van Thu St, not far from the railway station, T58-382 4875, www.longthanh art.com, open 0900-1900. Long Thanh is willing by pre-arrangement to meet photographers and organize photographic expeditions.

Long Thanh is one of Vietnam's most distinguished photographers and many of his famous pictures are taken in and around his native Nha Trang. He works only in black and white. Long Thanh has won a series of international awards and recognition for his work. He speaks English and welcomes visitors to his gallery.

Tourist information

Khanh Hoa Tours
1 Tran Hung Dao St, T58-352 6753,
www.nhatrangtourist.com.vn.
Daily 0700-1130, 1330-1700.
The official city tour office, can arrange
visa extensions, car and boat hire and
tours of the area. It's also a **Vietnam
Airlines** booking office. Not particularly
helpful, but plenty of the tour operators
in town have good information.

Where to stay

There has been a considerable increase
in the number of hotel rooms available
in Nha Trang with some huge projects
built in the last few years.

$$$$ Amiana Resort
Pham Van Dong, T58-730 5555,
www.amianaresort.com.
An absolutely stunning resort north of
the main town away from the crowds
with superb rooms, excellent service and
quality dining.

$$$$ Evason Ana Mandara Nha Trang
Tran Phu St, T58-352 2222,
www.sixsenses.com.
Nha Trang's finest beach resort.
Unashamed and exquisite luxury. Simple
but elegant designs are set against cool
woods, wafting fans and icy a/c. The
resort has sea view or garden villas that
are all beautifully furnished with special
touches and outdoor bathtubs. Every
conceivable facilitiy is available in this
enchanting retreat, including 2 pools,
a tennis court, a large gym and more.
Bicycles available. Fantastic dining. For
those wanting further pampering there

is the **Six Senses Spa**, see What to do,
page 238.

$$$$ Novotel Nha Trang
50 Tran Phu St, T58-625 6900,
www.novotel-nhatrang.com.
Super smart rooms in this new hotel
overlooking the beach.

$$$$ Sheraton Nha Trang Hotel & Spa
26-28 Tran Phu St, T58-388 0000,
www.sheratonnhatrang.com.
Excellent luxury hotel right across from
the **main** beach. Very stylish with a
wonderful pool. There are 6 restaurants
and bars. The views are outstanding
from the higher floors.

$$-$ Perfume Grass Inn (Que Thao)
4A Biet Thu St, T58-352 4286,
www.perfume-grass.com.
This long-running and and super friendly
family hotel has 21 rooms. Restaurant
and internet service downstairs. Good
value for money. Book in advance.

$ iHome Nha Trang
172/19 Bach Dang, T915-973079,
www.ihomenhatrang.com.
The pick of the budget options in town,
iHome is small but perfectly formed
with lots of unique touches, comfy beds,
a relaxing common area and excellent,
friendly staff.

Restaurants

There are a number of seafood
restaurants and cafés along the beach
road and a wide range of restaurants
elsewhere, particularly Indian and
Italian. A local speciality is *nem nuong*,
which is grilled pork wrapped in rice
paper with salad leaves and *bun*, fresh
rice noodles. The bread in Nha Trang

is excellent. All of the major hotels/resorts have good restaurants serving à la carte and huge weekend brunches. Try the Sofitel, Novotel and the Amiana (see Where to stay).

$$$-$$ Sailing Club
72-74 Tran Phu St, T58-352 4628, sailingnt@dng.vnn.vn. Open 0700-2300.
Although best known as a bar, this busy and attractive beachfront area also serves a variety of excellent cuisine and it is one of the most attractive places to eat in town.

$$ La Mancha
78 Nguyen Thien Tuat St, T58-352 7978. Open 1100-2400.
Great atmosphere, with Spanish and sangria decor, barbecued meat and plenty of tapas style dishes. Great decor.

$$ Nha Hang Yen
3/2A Tran Quang Khai, T93-376 6205.
This is a hugely popular and welcoming place that has a nice buzz in the evenings. A wide range of well executed Vietnamese dishes. The waiting staff are friendly and attentive and happy to give advice on what to order. Packs out, so it is best to book ahead. If this is full, try Lanterns at 34/6 Nguyen Thien Thuat St which does a similar line in quality Vietnamese food.

$$-$ Café des Amis
2D Biet Thu St, T58-352 1009.
Good for breakfast, vegetarian and seafood. Nice to sit outside for lunch.

$$-$ La Bella Napoli
6/0 Hung Vuong St, T58-352 7299, labellanapoli@hotmail.com.
This long-running Italian favourite serves up good wood-fired pizzas and the usual range of pastas and salads. Friendly service. Reasonable wine list.

$ Lac Canh
44 Nguyen Binh Khiem St, T58-382 1391.
Specializes in beef, squid and prawns which you barbecue at your table. Smoky atmosphere and it can be hard to get a table. A good place to dine with the locals in a lively atmosphere. Not a great place to dine alone.

$ Omar's Tandoori Cafe
89b Nguyen Thien Thuat St, T58-352 2459.
A popular Indian restaurant near the beach. Indian chef, excellent and filling food. Friendly, efficient service.

Stalls and seafood restaurants
For excellent and inexpensive beefsteak there are a couple of *Bo Ne* restaurants at the western end of Hoang Van Thu St (that is, away from the beach) that serve beef napoleon and chips. A little way from the centre but worth a visit. There are also many simple seafood restaurants lining the river road across the bridge.

Bars and clubs

Around Nguyen Thien Thuat, Biet Thu and Tran Phu there are now plenty of bars which have a distinctly seaside feel, with one of the most packed out aptly named the Booze Cruise.

Happy hours are long and the prices competitive. In many, the dress code seems to be vest and flip flops. None of these bars are particularly appealing, but there are a few better options around town.

Louisiane Brewhouse
29 Tran Phu St, T58-352 1948, www.louisianebrewhouse.com.vn.
This place has been transformed into a restaurant and brewery but has maintained its swimming pool so is popular with families for lunch and

is a polar bar in the evenings with its lovely sea breeze.

The Rainbow
90a Hung Vuong St, T58-352 4351.
Open 0600-2400.
This popular bar, run by **Rainbow Divers**, this is a popular spot. Dive information on site too. They've got draft beers and provide food in the shape of burgers and pizzas.

Sailing Club
74-76 Tran Phu St, T58-352 4628.
Open until late.
Lively bar, especially on Sat nights when well heeled locals and visitors congregate to enjoy the pool, cold beer, dancing and music.

Shopping

Nha Trang is now bursting with shops selling clothing, with everything from branded surf/beach wear to evening dresses on offer. The main hotel area is full of shops and larger malls now stand on the main beach road. There are also tens of jewellery shops in the hotel quarter.

What to do

Cookery classes
The **Ana Mandara Resort** offers a morning market tour and cookery class. Recommended.

Diving
The Evason Hideway, *Ninh Van Bay.* Has opened a PADI dive centre and are working with the Marine Protected Area Authority in Nha Trang to improve fishing practices in the area and to enlarge the protected area.
Rainbow Divers, *90A Hung Vuong St, T58-352 4351, www.divevietnam.com.*

It runs a full range of training and courses including the National Geographic dive courses. **Rainbow Divers** receives good reports regarding its equipment and focus on safety. Qualified instructors speak a variety of European languages. Top professional operation. Rainbow also operates out of Whale Island Resort, see page 245.

Theme parks, waterparks and watersports
Vinpearl Land, *Tre Island, T58-359 8123, www.vinpearlland.com.* This amusement and water park is wildly popular with Vietnamese tourists. Its Hollywood-style sign can be seen from the shore. You can take the ferry or the 4 km long cable car. A 500,000d card gets you entrance, rides and cable car ride.

Therapies
iResort, *19 Xuan Ngoc, T58-383 8838, www.i-resort.vn.* The most modern and beautiful hot spring and mud bath resort in the area.
Six Senses Spa, *Ana Mandara Resort, see Where to stay, above, www.sixsenses. com.* Offers an array of treatments – Japanese and Vichy showers, hot tubs and massages, exfoliations using fruit body smoothers in beautiful and luscious surroundings.

Tour operators
As so often happens in Vietnam, every café and guesthouse offers tours. Some tour operators can arrange trips to Buon Ma Thuot and the Central Highlands.
Khanh Hoa Tours, *1 Tran Hung Dao St, T58-352 6753, www.nhatrangtourist.com. vn. Daily 0700-1130, 1330-1700.* Official city tour office. See also page 236.
Luxury Travel, *A/9 Quang Trung St, T58-35127 9763.* With offices around Vietnam,

this agent focuses on higher end tours. Books a variety of trips including new boat tours around the bay.

Sinh Tourist, *90C Hung Vuong St, T58-352 4329, www.thesinhtouristvn.* Offers the usual **Sinh Café** formula and Open Tour tickets to Nha Trang, Hoi An, Mui Ne, HCMC, Dalat, Hué and Hanoi. **Sinh Tourist** buses arrive and depart from here. It offers the island tour, a Central Highlands tour, city tour and arranges transport nearby attractions.

Transport

Air
Connections with **HCMC**, **Hanoi** and **Danang**. Hotels can arrange bus transfers from the airport at Cam Ranh, 34 km away, 30 mins. There is an airport bus the plentiful meter taxis are far easier.

Airline offices Vietnam Airlines, 91 Nguyen Thien Thuat St, T58-352 6768.

Bicycles
Bicycles can be hired from almost every hotel and café in Nha Trang and many guesthouses now offer then for free.

Bus and Open Tour Bus
The long-distance bus station (*ben xe lien tinh*) is west out of town at 23 Thang 10 St (23 October St). *Xe oms* take passengers into town. It has connections with **HCMC**, **Phan Rang**, **Danang**, **Quy Nhon**, **Buon Ma Thuot**, **Dalat**, **Hué** and **Vinh**. Note that inter-province buses do not go into Nha Trang, they drop off at junctions on Highway 1 from where a *xe om* will deliver you to your destination. Open Tour Buses arrive at and depart from their relevant operator's café or depot (see Tour operators, above).

Motorbike
Motorbikes can be hired from almost every hotel and every café in Nha Trang.

Taxi
Mai Linh, T58-391 0910. **Nha Trang Taxi**, T58-382 6000. From Cam Ranh Airport to town, 260,000d.

Train
The station is on Thai Nguyen St, T58-382 0666. Open 0700-1130, 1330-1700, 1800-2200. The town is on the main north–south railway line and there are trains to Ho Chi Minh City and Hanoi (and stops between).

Around Nha Trang

islands and long, windswept beaches

The islands
From Cau Da pier, boats can be taken to the islands in Nha Trang Bay. Prices vary according to the number of passengers.

These islands are sometimes known as the **Salangane islands** after the sea swallows that nest here in such profusion. The sea swallow (*yen* in Vietnamese) produces the highly prized bird's nest from which the famous soup is made (see box, page 27).

On **Mieu Island** you can relax on a beach away from the hubbub of Nha Trang and visit a laid back village. Another popular nearby island is Hon Mun. The best part is anchoring offshore and jumping into the cool water to snorkel.

Hon Tre Island is now taken over by the **Vinpearl Land amusement park** ⓘ *500,000d, www.vinpearlland.com*. The island can be reached by cable car or boat and the entry fee includes access to a huge water park with around 20 slides and a massive wave pool. There are also plenty of fairground rides and other kid-friendly attractions. A fun family day out.

West of Nha Trang to Dalat
The road rises sharply out of the plain, past banana plantations and water pipes. The Ngoan Muc Pass is spectacular and you pass the Da Nhim power station. Above D'Ran the landscape gives way to pine trees. In 2007, a 54-km road from Nha Trang to Dalat opened, cutting the journey by 80 km and passing through the Bidup National Park of the Ba (Lady) Mountain. The road linked route 723 of Lam Dong Province to Provincial Route 2 of Khanh Hoa Province.

North of Nha Trang
From Cham Ponagar (see page 231) proceed a few hundred metres north then turn off to the right down to the sea; from Nha Trang take Tran Phu street north and over the new bridge, follow the new road around the coast until you see the promontory. **Hon Chong** (Husband Rocks) are perched at the end of the promontory which has a large, rather pudgy indentation in it – said to have been made by the hand of a male giant.

North of Hon Chong is the attractive **Hon Chong Bay** with beautiful rock formations. There are now a few guesthouses and restaurants here.

Thap Ba Hot Springs ⓘ *T58-383 5335, www.thapbahotspring.com.vn, charges vary for the different baths and services*, aren't far from the Cai River; go a short distance past Ponagar and turn left, then carry on for couple of kilometres. A soak in mineral water or mud bath is supposed to do you good. Twenty kilometres north up Highway 1, followed by a 2-km hike will bring you to **Ba Ho**, the name given to a sequence of three pools and rapids to be found in a remote and attractive woodland setting. Huge granite boulders have been sculpted and smoothed by the dashing torrent, but it is easy enough to find a lazy pool to soak in.

Some 40 km north of Nha Trang – turn right off Highway 1 at Ninh Hoa – is the beach area of **Doc Lech**. Take a taxi or hire a car from your hotel. The beach here is gentler and more protected than Hon Chong. The sea is quite beautiful with multicoloured boats bobbing on the small waves and the beach is dotted with fishing baskets. Doc Lech is very popular with groups of Vietnamese holiday-makers. Given that it is a long haul from Nha Trang it is probably best to go only mid-week out of the holiday season. There are resorts, guesthouses and restaurants (see below). On the way you will pass workers on the salt flats.

Ninh Van Bay is accessed from the private speedboat dock of the Evason group where they have a luxurious island hideaway. North of Doc Lech, off a long peninsula accessed by Dam Mon, is **Whale Island**, an island resort offering relaxation, diving and boat trips.

BACKGROUND

Tay Son Rebellion (1771-1788)

At the time of the Tay Son rebellion in 1771, Vietnam was in turmoil and conditions in the countryside were deteriorating to the point of famine. The three Tay Son brothers found a rich lode of dissatisfaction among the peasantry, which they successfully mined. Exploiting the latent discontent, they redistributed property from hostile mandarins to the peasants and raised a motley army of clerks, cattle-dealers, farmers, hill people, even scholars, to fight the Trinh and Nguyen lords. Brilliant strategists and demonstrating considerable leadership skills, the brothers and their supporters swept through the country extending the area under their control south as far as Saigon and north to Trinh.

The Chinese, sensing that the disorder and dissent caused by the conflict gave them an opportunity to bring the entire nation under their control, sent a 200,000-strong army southwards in 1788. In the same year, the most intelligent (by all accounts) of the brothers, Nguyen Hue, proclaimed himself emperor under the name of Quang Trung and began to prepare for battle against the cursed Chinese. On the fifth day of Tet in 1789, the brothers attacked the Chinese near Thang Long catching them unawares as they celebrated the New Year. (The Viet Cong were to do the same during the Tet Offensive nearly 200 years later.) With great military skill, they routed the enemy, who fled in panic back towards China. Rather than face capture, one of the Chinese generals committed suicide. This victory at the Battle of Dong Da is regarded as one of the greatest in the annals of Vietnamese history. Quang Trung, having saved the nation from the Chinese, had visions of recreating the great Nam Viet Empire of the second century BC, and of invading China. Among the reforms that he introduced were a degree of land reform, a wider programme of education, and a fairer system of taxation. He even tried to get all peasants to carry identity cards with the slogan 'the great trust of the empire' emblazoned on them. These greater visions were not to be, however: Quang Trung died suddenly in 1792, failing to provide the dynastic continuity that was necessary if Vietnam was to survive the impending French arrival.

As a postscript to the Tay Son Rebellion, in 1802 the new Emperor Gia Long ordered his soldiers to exhume the body of the last of the brothers and urinate upon it in front of the deceased's wife and son. They were then torn apart by four elephants. Quang Trung and the other Tay Son brothers – like many former nationalist and peasant leaders – are revered by the Vietnamese and honoured by the communists.

Quy Nhon and around → *Colour map 3, C3.*

Quy Nhon, the capital of Binh Dinh Province, has a population of nearly 250,000 and is situated on a spur just 10 km off Highway 1. The town, established by royal decree in 1898, is taking a breather after a flurry of economic growth based on the export of logs and smuggling but it is growing in popularity after a number of high-end resorts and low-key places have found their home here. A seaside town, it has reasonable swimming off the sandy **Quy Nhon Beach** and a number of sights in the vicinity. A French priest, Paul Maheu founded a leper colony here in 1929; the patients and their families were cared for by nuns. **Binh Dinh Tourism Company** ① *10 Nguyen Hué St, T56-389 2524*, offers tourist information.

Walk or bicycle northwest on Tran Hung Dao Street, past the bus station, and after 2 km turn right onto Thap Doi Street to Thap Doi Cham towers, a short distance along this street. The area around Quy Nhon was a focus of the Cham Empire, and a number of monuments (13, it is said) have survived the intervening years.

Tay Son District is famous as the place where three brothers led a peasant revolt in 1771 (see box, page 241). To get there take a bus from the station on Tay Son Street and it is about 50 km from Quy Nhon off Highway 19, running west towards Pleiku. The Vietnamese have a penchant for celebrating the exploits of the poor and the weak, and those of the Tay Son brothers are displayed in the **Quang Trung Museum** in Kien My village, Binh Thanh commune, approximately 45 km from Quy Nhon. It is dedicated to Nguyen Hué, a national hero of the 18th century who was one of the three brothers who led the Tay Son insurrection.

Hoang De Citadel (also known as **Cha Ban**) is about 27 km north of Quy Nhon. Originally a Cham capital which was repeatedly attacked by the Vietnamese, it was taken over by the Tay Son brothers in the 18th century and made the capital of their short-lived kingdom. Not much remains except some **Cham ruins**, within the citadel walls, in the vicinity of the old capital.

Quang Ngai → *Colour map 3, B3.*

Quang Ngai is a modest provincial capital on Highway 1, situated on the south bank of the Tra Khuc River and 130 km from Danang. Few people spend the night here as facilities are still pretty basic. Its greatest claim to fame is its proximity to **Son My** – the site of the **My Lai massacre** (see box, page 243). There is an extensive **market** running north from the bus station, along Ngo Quyen Street (just east of Quang Trung Street or Highway 1). Also in the city is a citadel built during the reign of Gia Long (1802-1820).

Son My (My Lai) → *Colour map 3, B3.*

13 km from Quang Ngai, 10,000d to contribute to the upkeep of the memorial. Motorbikes and taxis can take the track to Son My from the main road.

Just over 1 km north of town on Highway 1, soon after crossing the bridge over the Tra Khuc River, is a plaque indicating the way to Son My. Turn right, and continue for 12 km to the subdistrict of Son My where one of the worst, and certainly the most publicized, atrocities committed by US troops during the Vietnam War occurred (see box, page 243). The massacre of innocent Vietnamese villagers is better known as the My Lai Massacre – after one of the four hamlets of Son My. In the centre of the village of Son My is a memorial with a military cemetery 400 m beyond. There is an exhibition of contemporaneous US military photos of the massacre and a reconstruction of an underground bomb shelter; the creek where many villagers were dumped after being shot has been preserved.

BACKGROUND

Son My (My Lai) massacre

The massacre at Son My was a turning point in the American public's view of the war, and the role that the USA was playing. Were American forces defending Vietnam and the world from the evils of communism? Or were they merely shoring up a despotic government which had lost all legitimacy among the population it ostensibly served?

The massacre occurred on the morning of 16 March 1968. Units from the 23rd Infantry Division were dropped into the village of Son My. The area was regarded as an area of intense communist presence – so much so that soldiers referred to the villages as Pinkville. Only two weeks beforehand, six soldiers had been killed after stumbling into a mine field. The leader of the platoon that was charged with the job of investigating the hamlet of My Lai was 2nd Lieutenant William Calley. Under his orders, 347 people, all unarmed and many women and children, were massacred. Some of Calley's men refused to participate, but most did.

Neil Sheehan, in his book *A Bright Shining Lie*, wrote: "One soldier missed a baby lying on the ground twice with a .45 pistol as his comrades laughed at his marksmanship. He stood over the child and fired a third time. The soldiers beat women with rifle butts and raped some and sodomized others before shooting them. They shot the water buffalos, the pigs, and the chickens. They threw the dead animals into the wells to poison the water. They tossed satchel charges into the bomb shelters under the houses. A lot of the inhabitants had fled into the shelters. Those who leaped out to escape the explosives were gunned down. All of the houses were put to the torch".

In total, more than 500 people were killed at Son My; most in the hamlet of My Lai, but another 90 at another hamlet (by another platoon) in the same village.

The story of the massacre was filed by Seymour Hersh, but not until November 1969 – 20 months later. The subsequent court-martial only convicted Calley, who was by all accounts a sadist. He was sentenced to life imprisonment, but had served only three years before President Nixon intervened on his behalf (he was personally convicted of the murder of 22 of the victims). As Sheehan argues, the massacre was, in some regards, not surprising. The nature of the war had led to the killing and maiming of countless unarmed and innocent peasants; it was often done from a distance. In the minds of most generals, every Vietnamese was a potential communist; from this position it was only a small step to believing that all Vietnamese were legitimate targets.

South of Nha Trang → *Colour map 4, A6.*
Cau Da is a small fishing port 5 km south of Nha Trang along the beach road (Tran Phu). **Bao Dai's Villas**, yet another villa belonging to the last emperor of Vietnam, is attractively sited on a small promontory outside Cau Da with magnificent views on all sides. It is now a hotel (see below).

ON THE ROAD

Superior God of the Southern Sea

The whale has long been worshipped in Vietnam. Ever since the days of the early Champa the whale has been credited with saving the lives of drowning fishermen. The Cham believed that Cha-Aih-Va, a powerful god, could assume the form of a whale in order to rescue those in need.

Emperor Gia Long is said to have been rescued by a whale when his boat sank. After he ascended the throne, Gia Long awarded the whale the title Nam Hai Cu Toc Ngoc Lam Thuong Dang Than (Superior God of the Southern Sea).

Coastal inhabitants always try to help whales in difficulty and cut them free of their nets. If a whale should die a full funeral is arranged. The person who discovered its dead body is considered to be the whale's 'eldest son' and will head the funeral procession dressed in white as if it were his own father's funeral.

Bai Dai Beach
23 km south of Nha Trang.

The name of this stretch of sand literally translates as 'Long Beach' as it stretches for some 20 km. In the past, while it was popular with Vietnamese tourists it remained largely off the map for foreign visitors, but now The Surf Shack ① *www. shackvietnam.com*, has opened up bringing in both surfers and those in search of a good meal on the fine white sand. Now run by a lovely French couple, surf lessons (seasonal: October through April) are on offer and boogie boards can be hired. The food is good (try fish and chips) and the beers are ice cold. This is a fine place to spend a day away from the glitz of Nha Trang. At the north end of the beach some very basic but very welcoming accommodation has recently opened in the form of The Surf Hostel ① *www.longbeachboardriders.com*. At the time of writing things were being put in place by owner Allan Goodman for a chilled-out beachfront dorm space and camping area on a former lobster farm right on the water. He also has plans for a sailing school nearby.

Cam Ranh Bay → *Colour map 4, A6.*
Cam Ranh Bay, one of the world's largest natural harbours, lies 34 km south of Nha Trang. Highway 1 skirts around the bay – once an important US naval base and subsequently taken over by the Soviets. In fact the Soviets, or at least the Russians, were here before the Americans: they used it for re-provisioning during the Russo-Japanese war of 1904, which they emphatically lost. After re-unification in 1975, the Vietnamese allowed the Soviets to use this fine natural harbour once again as part-payment for the support (political and financial) they were receiving. However, from the late 1980s, the former Soviet fleet began to wind down its presence here as Cold War tensions in the area eased and economic pressures forced the former USSR to reduce military expenditure. Now the port is almost deserted.

Cam Ranh is also a centre for Vietnam's salt industry; for miles around the scenery is white with salt pans (looking like wintry paddy fields) producing pure, crystalline sea salt. There is a modest **Cao Dai Church** near the intersection of Highway 1 and the road leading towards the Bay (Da Bac Street). Continuing east along Da Bac Street, the road leads to a thriving fish market (down a pair of narrow alleys) and then to a busy boatyard producing small fishing vessels. At 120 Da Bac Street is **Chua Phuoc Hai**, an attractive little Buddhist temple.

Nha Trang's airport is now here and there is a new coastal road linking the city to the airport. The views are truly magnificent of white sands and perfect blue seas – and are even more staggering from the air.

Listings Around Nha Trang

Where to stay

North of Nha Trang
Thanks to the new Tran Phu bridge and extension of Tran Phu St to the north of Nha Trang it is now an easy 4-km ride to get to **Hon Chong Beach**. Consequently all sorts of new guesthouses and cafés are opening in what was previously just a fishing village.

$$$$ Evason Hideaway & Six Senses Spa at Ana Mandara
Ninh Van Bay, 30 km north of Nha Trang (it is 20 km to the boat launch at Pearl Farm and then 10 km offshore to the island), T58-372 8222, www.sixsenses.com.
Beach Villas, Rock Villas and Hilltop Villas are laid out in the full dramatic curve of Ninh Van Bay. You can't get more exceptionally luxurious than this; the Rock Villas are perched on rocks at the tip of the bay with bathrooms overlooking the sea and fronted by small infinity pools from where you can gaze out into the bay. The resort is large; from the Rock Villas to the main restaurant is almost a hike. Beach Villas are more centrally located. While your days away in the herb garden, **Six Senses Spa**, library, bar and wine cave and be attended by your personal butler. It's highly romantic, very secluded and very expensive; the food is exceptional.

$$ Whale Island Resort
T58-384 0501, www.iledelabaleine.com.
Bungalows right on this island beach, 2½ hrs north of Nha Trang. The price includes breakfasts. Transfers to Nha Trang and from Nha Trang, twice daily. Activities include diving (**Rainbow Divers**), windsurfing, canoeing and catamaran sailing.

$ Jungle Beach Resort
Ninh Phuoc, Ninh Hoa, T58-362 2384, www.junglebeachvietnam.com.
North of Nha Trang is this bay backed by mountains. Guests sleep in bamboo huts or newer accommodation and meals are eaten at communal tables. Note that the price is per person and includes meals. Ring the owners to check availability as it can often be full and it is a long way to go to find that out. If you want the basic beach hut experience right on the sands next to the sea, this may be perfect for you, but it is not for everyone.

Quy Nhon

$$$$ Avani Quy Nhon
Ghenh Rang, Bai Dai Beach, T56-384 0132, www.avanihotels.com/quynhon/.
Lovely resort inspired by Cham architecture with 63 rooms all facing the sea. Extremely tasteful rooms with fine furnishings and divine beds. It offers spa wellness activities and excellent cuisine including great breakfasts which can be taken al fresco overlooking the water. Superb spa facilities overlooking the bay.

$$-$ Haven Vietnam
Bai Xep village, T9-8211 4906, www.havenvietnam.com.
Run by Alex and Duyen, this is a hugely popular, friendly spot where traveller are known to get stuck longer than intended. Just four doubles and a family room at this simple, homely house. Home-cooked meals served in the communal dining area create a sociable vibe. Books and board games are on offer together with free snorkeling gear. Right next to Bai Xep fishing village, this is a good place to get a feel for the everyday live in coastal Vietnam.

South of Nha Trang

$$$$ Mia Nha Trang
www.mianhatrang.com.
An exceptional resort and one of Vietnam's most unique. Spilling down a steep cliff toward a private beach, it is well hidden from the road. Villas are uber stylish and finished to an extremely high standard. The pool area is wonderful and the dining, while expensive, is truly superb. A wide choice of accommodation including cliff top villas with knock out views from private plunge pools. The resort has won accolades for its architecture.

$$$ Bao Dai's Villas
Tran Phu St (just before Cau Da village), T58-359 0147.
Several villas of former Emperor Bao Dai, with magnificent views over the harbour and outlying islands, sited on a small promontory. Rooms are rather over-priced and distinctly lack the elegance of the emperor's own quarters. Overrun with sightseers during holiday periods.

Transport

Quy Nhon
Air
The airport is 35 km to the north. Connections with **HCMC** and **Danang**. Take a motorbike or taxi to the airport.

Bus
The bus station is on Tay Son St. Express buses leave for **Hanoi**, **HCMC**, **Nha Trang**, **Danang**, **Dalat**, **Hué**.

Train
The station is just over 1 km northwest of the town centre, on Hoang Hoa Tham St, which runs off Tran Hung Dao St. Express trains do not stop here. To catch the express, take the shuttle train to Dieu Tri, 10 km away.

Quang Ngai
Bus
The bus station is on Le Thanh Ton St south of the centre.

Train
The station is about 3 km west of town. There are regular connections with **Hanoi** and **HCMC** and all stops between the two.

Phan Rang was once the capital of Champa, when it was known as Panduranga, and there are a number of Cham towers (Thap Cham) nearby. The town and surrounding area are still home to a small population of Cham but few tourists stop in the small seaside town of about 150,000 people and the capital of Ninh Thuan Province.

Phan Rang

Phan Rang divides into three loosely connected areas: Phan Rang town itself the beach area – Ninh Chu; and Thap Cham, the Cham tower and railway station. The towers make an interesting visit and can be done as a comfortable side excursion on the drive from Nha Trang to Phan Thiet, see below.

Po Klong Garai
2 km beyond the village of Thap Cham.

Thap Cham is the name of a small village that boasts a railway station and the towers of Po Klong Garai, a group of three Cham towers on the road towards Dalat, 6 km from Phan Rang. Other than My Son, they are perhaps the best Cham relics in the country and are in good condition. Built during the 13th century, they are located on a cactus- and boulder-strewn hill with commanding views over the surrounding countryside. To the north you can see the remains of Thanh Son, the former US airbase. Raised up on a brick base, the towers have been extensively renovated. Apart from the renovations there is no sign of cement at all, the cohesion of the red bricks being one of the ingenious mysteries of the Cham. The central tower has a figure of dancing Siva over the main entrance. The door jambs are made of what looks like polished sandstone on which are ancient Cham engravings. Tucked inside the dimly lit main chamber full of incense smoke, is Siva's vehicle, the bull Nandi and other statues.

Nearby is the **railway station**, a very neat and orderly affair. The platform is attractively decorated with plants and there are good views of the towers.

Po Ro Me
The towers are a 1-km walk from the car park; this is the only path as the hill is strewn with cactus.

Po Ro Me is another group of more recently constructed Cham buildings – indeed the last Cham towers to be built – which can be seen in the distance from Po Klong Garai, rising up from the valley floor. To get there drive south on Highway 1 from Phan Rang towards Ho Chi Minh City; turn right by a sign to Ho Tan Giang which is 200 m past the Ninh Phuoc post office. It is a further 5-7 km from here; keep asking for directions.

There used to be three towers but only one remains; a lingam and yoni have been positioned on the site of one former tower. The towers were built during the reign of King Po Ro Me, the last king of independent Champa (1627-1651), who died a prisoner of the Vietnamese. His statue sits inside the remaining tower. With his manifold arms it is hard not to regard the statue as a depiction of Siva but the Cham custodian is adamant on this point.

Cham bricks are notable for their lightness. This is because (unlike the reproduction bricks of today which lie around) the clay was mixed with rice husks before firing. Indeed a close inspection shows the porous nature of the original bricks this produced. Roughly 10% of the tower has been rebuilt using modern brick.

An interesting feature of this (as with other Cham towers) are the curvaceous flowing lines achieved despite the use of rectangular brick. Quite whether the bricks were made to this pattern and carefully assembled as a jigsaw or whether they were carved into shape once finished it is hard to say.

King Po Ro Me had two wives. A statue of his second wife (Tha Kachanh) sits next to him in the tower. She was from the Rhade minority group. The statue of the king's first wife sits in a small hut behind the tower. Her fault of course was her inability to have children. Sadly the statues here are replacements for the originals, which were stolen in 1993 and 1994.

Finally, there is a third group of Cham towers, in poor condition, 16 km north of town right at the side of Highway 1.

Cham villages

The surrounding Cham villages are of some interest notably for the different style of houses (built of a very primitive looking wattle and daub) and for the appearance and dress of the people (women wearing sarongs, for instance). The village of **Phuoc Dan** (off Highway 1, turn to the right a short way before Ninh Phuoc post office) is notable for its Cham pottery. Rather heavy (in weight and texture) but simple in design and decoration it is moulded mostly into Etruscan-looking urns and vases. These are piled up and covered in firewood which is in turn heaped with rice husks and ignited. The husks prevent combustion and the wood converts to charcoal baking the pots slowly overnight. Pots near the charcoal are black and those in the centre emerge red, all being to some degree rather attractively mottled. These earthernware pieces make striking and unusual gifts and can be bought very cheaply.

Tuan Tu is a small Cham village, about 5 km south of Phan Rang. Like most Cham these villagers have renounced Hinduism in favour of Islam and their names reflect this, boys are called Mo Ham Mat, Su Le Man and so on.

Ninh Chu Beach

About 6-7 km northeast of Phan Rang is Ninh Chu Beach. Overall it's not a bad beach – at least it's fairly quiet. There are several cafés that rent chairs and umbrellas in addition to selling drinks. For accommodation there's a variety of odds and ends including some local guesthouses and there are inexpensive restaurants on the beach. Very popular with local tourists and can become busy and rather litter strewn on busy weekends, so it is best to visit out of peak season and mid-week.

Ca Na

About 36 km south of Phan Rang, nestled between boulder-strewn hills to the west and wild rocky surf to the east. There are a couple of small restaurants selling decent road-food and drinks and a couple of guesthouses that are as close to the highway as they are to the beach. It's worth a stop for noodles and a quick walk up the hill to see the small pagoda that is visible from the road, and a stroll on the boulder strewn beach.

Phan Rang to Dalat

The old 100-km trip between Phan Rang and Dalat is spectacular. The narrow strip of land between the highlands and the coast is an area of intensive rice, tobacco and grape cultivation. Winding upwards, the road passes under a massive pipe carrying water from the mountains down to the turbines of a hydropower plant in the valley. It then works its way through the dramatic Ngoan Muc Pass to the Dalat Plateau.

In 2007 a more direct road was opened between Dalat and Nha Trang shortening the journey time, see West of Nha Trang to Dalat, page 240.

Listings Phan Rang and around

Where to stay

Phan Rang
Little in the way of good accommodation.

$ Thong Nhat
343 Thong Nhat St, T68-382 7201,
thongnhathotel_pr@hcm.vnn.vn.
This is one of the mini-hotels with 34 rooms and all the modern conveniences but little charm or character.

Ninh Chu Beach

$$$ Bau Truc
T68-387 4047, www.bautrucresort.com.
Vast with acres of land and attractive bungalows. There's a pool, tennis court and restaurant.

Vinh Hy Bay

$$$$ Amanoi
Vinh Hy Bay, T6-8377 0777,
www.amanresorts.com.
An exceptional new resort with an idyllic, isolated location on the coast accessed via a scenic drive through the Nui Chua park.

Restaurants

Phan Rang
There are no cafés or restaurants catering to travellers. There are, however, quite a few *pho* stands and *bia hoi* joints on the west end of **Quang Trung St**, as well as some rice stalls near the bus station.

Transport

Phan Rang
Open Tour Buses stop beneath Po Klong Garai and there are plenty of *xe oms*.

Bus
The bus station is on the east side of Thong Nhat, near the post office. Local buses, however, leave from the south side of town. Regular connections with **HCMC**, **Dalat** and **Nha Trang**.

Train
The closest stop is **Thap Cham**, about 5 km west of town, T68-388 8084.

Ho Chi Minh City

skyscrapers of glass dwarf shophouses of old

Ho Chi Minh City, the largest city in Vietnam, is frenetic, exciting, riddled with traffic and enlivened by great shops, bars and restaurants. This thoroughly dynamic city, in one of the fastest-growing regions of the world, is morphing before our eyes.

Despite government restrictions, thousands of young men and women make their way here every week in search of a better life. Only 25 years ago Tan Son Nhat, the airport, was right out at the edge of the city; it has been an inner suburb for years, long ago leapfrogged by the sprawl that is pushing outwards into former paddy fields with astonishing speed.

Visitors to Ho Chi Minh City shouldn't miss the heart of the downtown, taking in the grand opera house and old post office and the art deco buildings of Dong Khoi. A sense of adventure will be richly rewarded here, especially when getting lost among the temple-filled streets of the Chinese quarter. This is also a city for the tastebuds, with a diverse street food alongside a slew of first-rate international dining options and plenty of great rooftop bars to round-off your day of exploration.

Best for
Art ▪ Bars ▪ Food ▪ Walking tours

City centre 253
Pham Ngu Lao 266
Cholon (Chinatown) 267
Outer Ho Chi Minh City 270
Around Ho Chi Minh City 272

Footprint picks

★ **Notre Dame Cathedral**, page 256

Visit this grand landmark during a service when crowds gather on motorbikes out front.

★ **War Remnants Museum**, page 260

Harrowing, but informative and the best way to get an understanding of Vietnam's recent wars from a Vietnamese perspective.

★ **Fine Arts Museum**, page 265

Art fan or not, this cool and peaceful gallery housing many of the country's finest works is a magical place to spend an hour or two.

★ **Chinatown pagodas**, page 267

Ornate, peaceful and atmospheric, the pagodas of Cholon are not to be missed.

★ **Binh Tay Market**, page 269

Less visited that the famous Ben Thanh market, Binh Tay has a distinctly local feel and a vast array of wholesale goods.

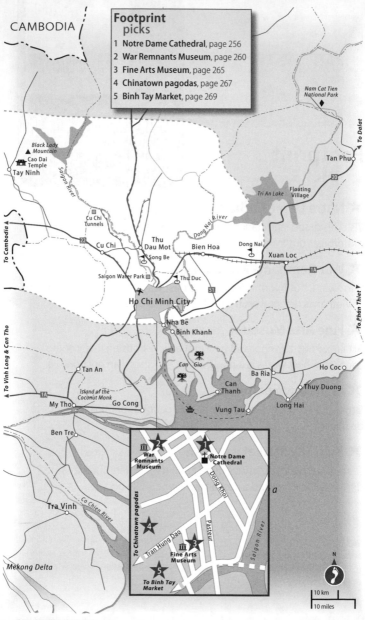

CAMBODIA

Footprint
picks

1 **Notre Dame Cathedral**, page 256
2 **War Remnants Museum**, page 260
3 **Fine Arts Museum**, page 265
4 **Chinatown pagodas**, page 267
5 **Binh Tay Market**, page 269

Nam Cat Tien
National Park

To Dalat

Black Lady
Mountain
Cao Dai
Temple
Tay Ninh

Saigon River

Tan Phu

Tri An Lake

Floating
Village

20

Cu Chi
Tunnels

Dong Nai River

To Cambodia

22

Cu Chi

Thu
Dau Mot

Bien Hoa

Dong Nai

Xuan Loc

Song Be

1A

To Phan Thiet

Saigon Water Park

Thu Duc

51

Ho Chi Minh City

Nha Be

Binh Khanh

To Vinh Long & Can Tho

Tan An

Can
Gio

Ba Ria

Ho Coc

1A

Island of the
Coconut Monk

Can
Thanh

Thuy Duong

My Tho

Go Cong

Vung Tau

Long Hai

Ben Tre

War
Remnants
Museum

Notre Dame
Cathedral

Dong Khoi

a

Co Chien River

Tra Vinh

To Chinatown pagodas

Tran Hung Dao

Pasteur

Fine Arts
Museum

Saigon River

Mekong Delta

To Binh
Tay Market

N

10 km

10 miles

Sights

palaces, pagodas, paintings aplenty

From the majestic Notre Dame Cathedral, opera house and the old post office to the art deco buildings of Donh Khoi street, there are many sights from the French colonial era. The markets of Ben Thanh and the more local Binh Tay are great places to get a sense of the city. Ho Chi Minh City has a wealth of museums and galleries, while pagoda hunters could lose days in Chinatown alone.

City centre → Colour map 4, B3.

more elegant, less frenzied

The core of Ho Chi Minh City is, in many respects, the most interesting and historical. Remember, of course, that 'historical' here has a very different meaning from that In Hanoi. In Ho Chi Minh City a 100-year-old building is ancient – and, alas, increasingly rare. Still, a saunter down Dong Khoi Street, in District 1, the old rue Catinat can still give one an impression of life in a more elegant and less frenzied era. Much remains on a small and personal scale and within a 100-m radius of just about anywhere on Dong Khoi or Thai Van Lung streets there are dozens of cafés, restaurants and increasingly upmarket boutiques. However, the character of the street has altered with the opening of luxury chain names and the Times Square development. A little bit of Graham Greene history was lost in 2010 when the Givral Café in the Eden Centre, which featured in *The Quiet American*, was closed as Vincom Towers built another tower block on Lam Son Square.

Lam Son Square and around
Opera House (Nha Hat Thanh Pho) ① *7 Lam Son Sq, T08-3832 2009, nhahat_ ghvk@hcm.fpt.vn*. The impressive, French-era Opera House dominates Lam Son Square. It was built in 1897 to the design of French architect Ferret Eugene and restored in 1998. It once housed the National Assembly; nowadays, when it is open, it provides a varied programme of events, for example, traditional theatre, contemporary dance and gymnastics.

Essential Ho Chi Minh City

Finding your feet

Virtually all of the sights visitors wish to see lie to the west of the Saigon River. To the east there are many large new developments, homes of the city's expat population and the growing Vietnamese middle class.

Most visitors head straight for hotels in Districts 1 (the historic centre) or 3. Cholon or Chinatown (District 5) is a mile west of the centre and is a fascinating place to wander. Port of Saigon is in districts 4 and 8. Few visitors venture.

All the sights of Central Ho Chi Minh City can be reached on foot in no more than 30 minutes from the major hotel areas of Nguyen Hue, Dong Khoi and Ton Duc Thang streets. Visiting all the sights described below will take several days. Quite a good first port of call, however, is the **Panorama 33 Café** on the 33rd floor of Saigon Trade Center, 37 Ton Duc Thang Street, Monday-Friday 1100-2400, Saturday-Sunday 0900-2400.

Best views
Chill Skybar, page 283
OMG bar, page 284
Saigon Saigon bar, page 284

Best pagodas and temples
Xa Loi, page 262
Phung Son Tu, page 266
Thien Hau, page 268
Quan Am, page 269

Getting around

The abundant transport is fortunate, because it is a hot, large and increasingly polluted city. Metered taxis, motorcycle taxis and a handful of cyclos vie for business in a healthy spirit of competition. Many tourists who prefer some level of independence opt to hire a bicycle or motorbike.

Tip...
Take care when carrying handbags and purses. Drive-by snatchings are on the increase.

When to go

Ho Chi Minh City is a great place to visit all year around.

Time required

The major sights can be seen in a weekend, but take a few days longer to soak up the city and explore it further.

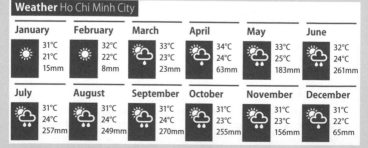

Weather Ho Chi Minh City

January	February	March	April	May	June
31°C 21°C 15mm	32°C 22°C 8mm	33°C 23°C 23mm	34°C 24°C 63mm	33°C 25°C 183mm	32°C 24°C 261mm

July	August	September	October	November	December
31°C 24°C 257mm	31°C 24°C 249mm	31°C 24°C 270mm	31°C 23°C 255mm	31°C 23°C 156mm	31°C 22°C 65mm

Continental Hotel North of the Opera House, now repainted, was built in 1880 and is an integral part of the city's history. Graham Greene stayed here and the hotel features in the novel *The Quiet American*. Old journalists' haunt Continental Shelf was, according to war journalist Jon Swain, "a famous verandah where correspondents, spies, speculators, traffickers, intellectuals and soldiers used to meet during the war to glean information and pick up secret reports, half false, half true or half disclosed. All of this is more than enough for it to be known as Radio Catinat. I sometimes went there for a late evening drink among the frangipani and hibiscus blossom ... It was the reverse of the frenzy of the war, and a good place to think".

The Continental lines **Dong Khoi Street** (formerly the bar-lined Tu Do Street, the old Rue Catinat), which stretches down to the river. Many shops specialize in, or sell a mix of, silk clothes and accessories, jewellery, lacquerware and household goods and there are now a number of swanky cafés along the stretch.

Hotel Caravelle Facing the **Continental**, also adjoining Dong Khoi Street, is the Hotel Caravelle, which houses boutique shops selling luxury goods. The **Caravelle** opened for business in 1959. The 10th floor housed a famous **Saigon** bar, a favourite spot for wartime reporters, and during the 1960s the *Associated Press*, *NBC*, *CBS*, the *New York Times* and *Washington Post* based their offices here. The press escaped casualties when, on 25 August 1964, a bomb exploded in room 514, on a floor mostly used by foreign reporters. The hotel suffered damage and there were injuries but the journalists were all out in the field. It was renamed **Doc Lap** (Independence Hotel) in 1975 but not before a Vietnamese tank trundled down the rue Catinat to Place Garnier (now Lam Son Square) and aimed its turret at the hotel; to this day nobody knows why it did not fire. During the filming of Graham Greene's *The Quiet American*, actors Michael Caine and Brendan Fraser stayed at the hotel.

Nguyen Hue Boulevard At the northwest end of Nguyen Hue Boulevard is the yellow and white **City Hall**, formerly the French Hôtel de Ville built in 1897 and now the Ho Chi Minh City People's Committee building, which overlooks a **statue of Bac Ho** (Uncle Ho) offering comfort, or perhaps advice, to a child. This is a favourite spot for Vietnamese to have their photograph taken, especially newly-weds who believe old Ho confers some sort of blessing.

South of City Hall, the **Rex Hotel**, a pre Liberation favourite with US officers, stands at the intersection of Le Loi and Nguyen Hue boulevards. This was the scene of the daily 'Five O'Clock Follies' where the military briefed an increasingly sceptical press corps during the Vietnam War. Its bar is now somewhat aged, but the view from it is still excellent so it is a worthwhile stop for an afternoon drink.

On weekend evenings thousands of young Saigon men and women and young families cruise up and down Nguyen Hue Boulevard (and Le Loi Boulevard and Dong Khoi Street) on motorbikes. There are now so many motorbikes on the streets of Ho Chi Minh City that intersections seem lethally confused. Miraculously, the riders miss each other (most of the time) while pedestrians safely make their way through waves of machines.

★Notre Dame Cathedral

Visiting times are given as 0500-1100 and 1500-1730. Communion is celebrated here 7 times on Sun (drawing congregations Western churches can only dream of) and 3 times on weekdays.

North up Dong Khoi Street, in the middle of **Cong Xa Paris** (Paris Square), is the imposing, austere red-brick, twin-spired Notre Dame Cathedral, overlooking a grassed square in which a statue of the Virgin Mary stands holding an orb. The statue was the subject of intense scrutiny in 2006 as it was said that it had shed tears. The cathedral was built between 1877 and 1880 and is said to be on the site of an ancient pagoda. A number of the homeless sleep under its walls at night;

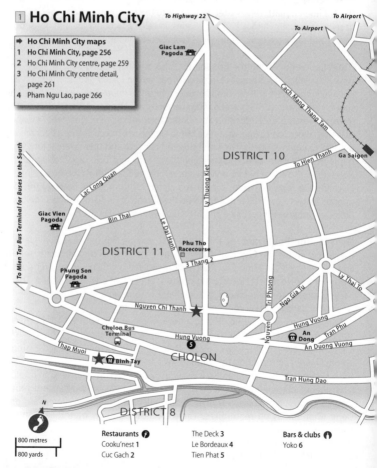

1 Ho Chi Minh City

➡ **Ho Chi Minh City maps**
1 Ho Chi Minh City, page 256
2 Ho Chi Minh City centre, page 259
3 Ho Chi Minh City centre detail, page 261
4 Pham Ngu Lao, page 266

To Highway 22
To Airport
To Airport

Giac Lam Pagoda

Cach Mang Thang Tam

DISTRICT 10   Ga Saigon

To Mien Tay Bus Terminal for Buses to the South

Lac Long Quan

To Hien Thanh

Ly Thuong Kiet

Giac Vien Pagoda

Bin Thal

Le Dai Hanh

Phu Tho Racecourse

DISTRICT 11

3 Thang 2

Ly Thai To

Phung Son Pagoda

Tri Phuong

Ngo Gia Tu

Hung Vuong

Tran Phu

Nguyen Chi Thanh ★

Cholon Bus Terminal

Hung Vuong   An Dong

❺   An Duong Vuong

Thap Muoi   Binh Tay ★   CHOLON

Tran Hung Dao

DISTRICT 8

N

| 800 metres |
| 800 yards |

Restaurants 🍴
Cooku'nest **1**
Cuc Gach **2**

The Deck **3**
Le Bordeaux **4**
Tien Phat **5**

Bars & clubs 🍸
Yoko **6**

unfortunately the signs asking Vietnamese men not to treat the walls as a public urinal do not deter this unpleasant but widespread practice. Mass times are a spectacle as crowds, unable to squeeze through the doors, listen to the service while perched on their parked motorbikes in rows eight or nine deep.

General Post Office
2 Cong Xa Paris, daily 0730-1930.

Facing onto the Paris Square is the General Post Office, built in the 1880s in French style, it is a particularly distinguished building. The front façade has attractive cornices with French and Khmer motifs and the names of notable French men of

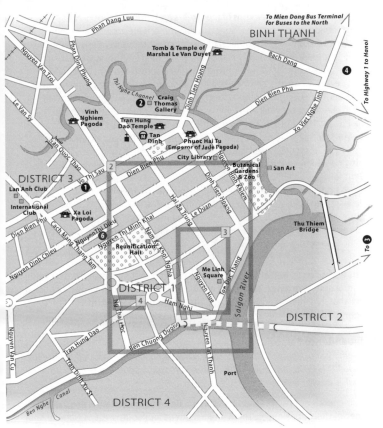

ON THE ROAD

The changing face

Vietnam's economic reforms are most in evidence in Ho Chi Minh City where the average annual income is considerably higher than outside the city. Consequently, ever larger holes are being torn in the heart of central Ho Chi Minh City. Whereas a few years ago it was common to see buildings disappear, now whole blocks fall to the wrecker's ball. From the holes left behind, concrete, steel and glass monuments emerge. There is, of course, a difference from earlier periods of remodelling of the city. Then, it was conducted on a human scale and the largest buildings, though grand, were on a scale that was in keeping with the dimensions of the streets and ordinary shophouses. French buildings in Dong Khoi Street, for example, were consistent with the Vietnamese way of life: street-level trading with a few residential floors above.

The landmark Bitexco tower stands tall in the heart of the city, a graphic symbol of its ambitions for future growth. Other plush modern office and lifestyle spaces such as Kumho Plaza are being joined by developments such as the 25-floor German House across the road and the Vietcombank Tower which stands on the river and ranks as the city's second tallest skyscraper. The Phu My Hung urban area, across the river, offers modern living for the growing Vietnamese middle class and the many expats that call the city home. The latest new urban area, Thu Thiem, has been a long time coming. This vast swathe of land was cleared of its thousands of occupants in the late 1990s, but construction has stalled and it is yet to take shape. Work has also begun on the first underground railway, which is slated to feature grand 3 level station downtown at Ben Thanh market. The much-photographed statue of General Tran Nguyen Han in front of the market was removed in 2014 to make way for this development, providing another signal of the city's intent to look forward, not back.

letters and science. Inside, the high, vaulted ceiling and fans create a deliciously cool atmosphere in which to scribble a postcard. Note the old wall-map of Cochin China that has miraculously survived. The enormous portrait of Ho Chi Minh, hanging at the end of the hall, completes the sense of grandeur.

Independence Palace
135 Nam Ky Khoi Nghia St, T08-3822 3652, www.dinhdoclap.gov.vn, daily 0730-1100, 1300-1600, 15,000d, brochure 10000d, documentary 50,000d. Tours every 10 mins. The hall is sometimes closed for state occasions.

The Independence Palace (also known as the **Reunification Hall**) is in a large park to the southeast of Nguyen Thi Minh Khai Street and southwest of Nam Ky Khoi Nghia Street. The residence of the French governor was built on this site in 1868 and was later renamed the Presidential Palace. In February 1962, a pair of planes took off to attack Viet Cong emplacements – piloted by two of the south's finest

2 Ho Chi Minh City centre

➡ **Ho Chi Minh City maps**
1 Ho Chi Minh City, page 256
2 Ho Chi Minh City centre, page 259
3 Ho Chi Minh City centre detail, page 261
4 Pham Ngu Lao, page 266

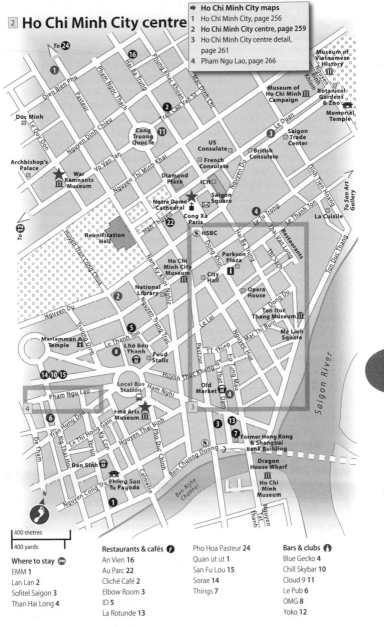

Where to stay 🛏
EMM 1
Lan Lan 2
Sofitel Saigon 3
Than Hai Long 4

Restaurants & cafés 🍴
An Vien 16
Au Parc 22
Cliché Café 2
Elbow Room 3
ID 5
La Rotunde 13

Pho Hoa Pasteur 24
Quan ut ut 1
San Fu Lou 15
Sorae 14
Things 7

Bars & clubs 🍸
Blue Gecko 4
Chill Skybar 10
Cloud 9 11
Le Pub 6
OMG 8
Yoko 12

airmen – but they turned back to bomb the Presidential Palace in a futile attempt to assassinate President Diem. The president, who held office between 1955-1963, escaped with his family to the cellar, but the palace had to be demolished and replaced with a new building. (Diem was later assassinated after a military coup.) One of the two pilots, Nguyen Thanh Trung is a Vice President of **Vietnam Airlines** and still flies government officials around every couple of months to keep his pilot's licence current. One of the most memorable photographs taken during the war was of a North Vietnamese Army (NVA) tank crashing through the gates of the Palace on 30 April 1975 – symbolizing the end of South Vietnam and its government. The President of South Vietnam, General Duong Van Minh, along with his entire cabinet, was arrested in the Palace shortly afterwards. The hall has been preserved as it was found in 1975 and visitors can take a guided tour. In the **Vice President's Guest Room**, there is a lacquered painting of the Temple of Literature in Hanoi, while the **Presenting of Credentials Room** contains a fine 40-piece lacquer work showing diplomats presenting their credentials during the Le Dynasty (15th century). In the basement there are operations rooms, military maps, radios and other paraphernalia. In essence, it is a 1960s-style building filled with 1960s-style official furnishings that now look very kitsch. Not only was the building designed according to the principles of Chinese geomancy but the colour of the carpets – lurid mustard yellow in one room – was also chosen depending on whether it was to calm or stimulate users of the rooms. Visitors are shown an interesting film about the Revolution and some fascinating photographs and memorabilia from the era. A replica of the tank that bulldozed through the gates of the compound heralding the end of South Vietnam is displayed in the forecourt.

★War Remnants Museum

28 Vo Van Tan St, Q3, T08-3930 5587, www.baotangchungtichchientranh.vn, daily 0730-1200, 1330-1700, 15,000d.

All the horrors of the Vietnam War from the nation's perspective – photographs of atrocities and action, bombs, military tanks and planes and deformed foetuses – are graphically displayed in this well laid-out museum building. In the courtyard are tanks, bombs and helicopters, while the new museum, arranged in five new sections, records man's inhumanity. The display covers the Son My (My Lai) massacre on 16 March 1968 (see box, page 243), the effects of napalm and phosphorous, and the after-effects of Agent Orange defoliation (this is particularly disturbing, with bottled malformed human foetuses). This museum has gone through some interesting name changes in recent years. It began life as the Exhibition House of American and Chinese War Crimes. In 1990, 'Chinese' was dropped from the name, and in 1994 'American' was too. Since 1996 it has simply been called the War Remnants Museum.

Archbishop's Palace

330 Nguyen Dinh Chieu St and corner of Tran Quoc Thao St.

Around this area is a number of very fine French-era buildings still standing; some have been allowed to fall into decay but others have been well maintained. In particular the Archbishop's Palace and the high schools, **Le Qui Don** ⓘ *2 Le Qui Don St*, and **Marie Curie** ⓘ *Nam Ky Khoi Nghia St*. All have had extensions built in recent years, but at least the schools have attempted to blend the new buildings in with the old. The palace is believed to be the oldest house in Ho Chi Minh City, built

③ Ho Chi Minh City centre detail

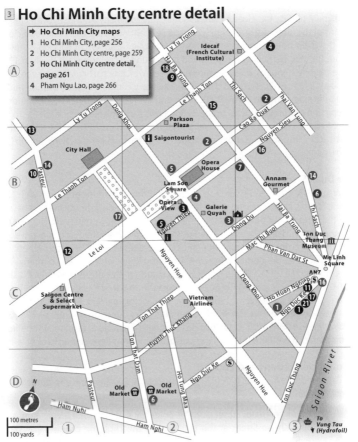

➡ Ho Chi Minh City maps
1 Ho Chi Minh City, page 256
2 Ho Chi Minh City centre, page 259
3 **Ho Chi Minh City centre detail, page 261**
4 Pham Ngu Lao, page 266

Where to stay 🛏
Caravelle **4** *B2*
Continental **5** *B2*
Grand **1** *C3*
Ho Sen **14** *B3*
Park Hyatt Saigon **2** *B2*
Renaissance
  Riverside **16** *C3*
Rex **17** *B1*
Sheraton **3** *B2*
Thai Hai Long **6** *D2*

Restaurants & cafés 🍴
13 Ngo Duc Ke **1** *C3*
Ashoka **4** *A3*
Augustin **5** *B2*
Hoang Yen **17** *C3*
Kem Bach Dang **12** *C1*
Koto **9** *A2*
La Fenêtre Soleil **13** *B1*
La Fourchette **21** *C3*
L'Usine **3** *B2*
Refinery, Hua Tuc
  & Vasco's **15** *A2*
Velo de Piste **10** *B1*
The Workshop **11** *C3*

Bars & clubs 🍸
Alibi **16** *B3*
Apocalypse Now **6** *B3*
Blanchy's Tash **7** *B3*
La Habana **2** *A3*
Pasteur Street
  Brewing Company **14** *B1*
Tous Les Jours **18** *A2*

in 1790 (although not originally on this spot) for the then French bishop of Adran, Pierre Pigneau de Behaine.

Xa Loi Pagoda
89 Ba Huyen Thanh Quan St, daily 0630-1100, 1430-1700.

Ho Chi Minh City has close to 200 pagodas – far too many for most visitors to see. Many of the finest are in Cholon (see page 267), although there is a selection closer to the main hotel area in central Ho Chi Minh City. The Xa Loi Pagoda is not far from the War Remnants Museum and is surrounded by food stalls. Built in 1956, the pagoda contains a multi-storeyed tower, which is particularly revered, as it houses a relic of the Buddha. The main sanctuary contains a large, bronze-gilded Buddha in an attitude of meditation. Around the walls are a series of silk paintings depicting the previous lives of the Buddha (with an explanation of each life to the right of the entrance into the sanctuary). The pagoda is historically, rather than artistically, important as it became a focus of dissent against the Diem regime (see box, page 265).

Le Duan Street
North of the cathedral is Le Duan Street, the former corridor of power with Ngo Dinh Diem's Palace at one end, the zoo at the other and the former embassies of the three major powers, France, the USA and the UK, in between. Nearest the Reunification Hall is the compound of the **French Consulate**. A block away is the **former US Embassy**. After diplomatic ties were resumed in 1995 the Americans lost little time in demolishing the 1960s building which held so many bad memories. The US Consulate General now stands on this site. A memorial outside, on the corner of Mac Dinh Chi Street, records the attack by Viet Cong special forces during the Tet offensive of 1968 and the final victory in 1975. At 2 Le Duan Street is the **Museum of Ho Chi Minh Campaign (Bao Tang Quan Doi)** ① *T08-3822 9387, Tue-Sun 0730-1100, 1330-1630, 15,000d*, with a tank and warplane in the front compound. It contains an indifferent display of photographs and articles of war.

Botanical Gardens and Zoo
2 Nguyen Binh Khiem St, T08-3829 3728, daily 0700-2000, entrance to gardens and zoo, 12,000d.

At the end of Le Duan Street are the Botanical Gardens which run alongside Nguyen Binh Khiem Street at the point where the Thi Nghe channel flows into the Saigon River. The gardens were established in 1864 by French botanist Jean-Batiste Louis Pierre; by the 1970s they had a collection of nearly 2000 species, and a particularly fine display of orchids. With the dislocations of the immediate postwar years, the gardens went into decline, a situation from which they are still trying to recover. In the south quarter of the gardens is a mediocre zoo with a rather moth-eaten collection of animals that form a backdrop to smartly dressed Vietnamese families posing for photographs.

BACKGROUND

History of the city

Before the 15th century, the area was a small Khmer village surrounded by a wilderness of forest and swamp. By 1623 Ho Chi Minh City had become an important commercial centre, and in the mid-17th century it became the residence of the so-called Vice-King of Cambodia. In 1698, the Viets managed to extend their control this far south and finally Ho Chi Minh City was brought under Vietnamese control.

In the middle of the 19th century, the French began to challenge Vietnamese authority in the south of the country. Between 1859 and 1862, in response to the Nguyen persecution of Catholics in Vietnam, the French attacked and captured the city. They named it Saigon (Soai-gon – 'wood of the kapok tree'), and the Treaty of Saigon in 1862 ratified the conquest and created the new French colony of Cochin China. Saigon was developed in French style: wide, tree-lined boulevards, street-side cafés, elegant French architecture, boutiques and the smell of baking baguettes.

During the 1960s and early 1970s the city boomed and flourished under the American occupation (it was the seat of the South Vietnam government) until the fall or liberation – depending upon your point of view. Officially Ho Chi Minh City (HCMC) since 1975, it remains to most the bi-syllabic, familiar, old 'Saigon'.

Museum of Vietnamese History
2 Nguyen Binh Khiem St, T08-3829 8146, www.baotanglichsuvn.com, Tue-Sun 0800-1130, 1330-1700,15,000d. Labels in English and French. Water puppet shows (see also page 285) are held here daily.

The history museum (Bao Tang Lich Su Viet Nam) is an elegant building constructed in 1928 and is pagodaesque in style. It displays a wide range of artefacts from the prehistoric (300,000 years ago) and the Dongson periods (3500 BC-AD 100), right through to the birth of the Vietnamese Communist Party in 1930. Particularly impressive are the Cham sculptures, of which the standing bronze Buddha, dating from the fourth to sixth century, is probably the finest. There is also a delicately carved Devi (Goddess) dating from the 10th century as well as pieces such as the head of Shiva, Hindu destroyer and creator, from the eighth to ninth century and Ganesh, elephant-headed son of Shiva and Parvati, also dating from the eighth to ninth century.

There are also representative pieces from the Chen-la, Funan, Khmer, Oc-eo and Han Chinese periods, and from the various Vietnamese dynasties together with some hill tribe artefacts. Labelling is in English, French and Vietnamese.

Other highlights include the wooden stakes planted in the Bach Dang riverbed for repelling the war ships of the Mongol Yuan in the 13th century, a beautiful Phoenix head from the Tran dynasty (13th to 14th century) and an Hgor (big drum) from the Jarai people, made from the skin of two elephants. It belonged to the Potauoui (King of Fire) family in Ajunpa district, Gia Lai Province. There are some fine sandstone sculptures too including an incredibly smooth linga from Long An Province (seventh to eighth century) in the Mekong Delta. The linga represents the cult of Siva and signifies gender, energy, fertility and potency.

Near the History Museum is the **Memorial Temple** ① *Tue-Sun 0800-1130, 1300-1600*, constructed in 1928 and dedicated to famous Vietnamese.

Ho Chi Minh City Museum and around
65 Ly Tu Trong St, T08-3829 9741, www.hcmc-museum.edu.vn, daily 0800-1700, 15,000d.

This museum includes a mixed bag of displays concerning the revolution, with a display of photographs, a few pieces of hardware (helicopter, anti-aircraft guns) in the back compound, and some memorabilia. Other exhibits chart the development of the city and its economy. The building itself is historically important. Dominating a prominent intersection, the grey-white classical French-designed building was built as a museum before it became the palace for the governor of Cochin China in 1890. After the 1945 revolution it was used for administrative offices before returning to the French as the High Commissioner's residence in September 1945. During the War, Ngo Dinh Diem resided here under its new name as Southern Governor's Palace; during the reign of Nguyen Van Thieu (1967-1975), it operated as the supreme court.

Southwest from the museum on the corner of Ly Tu Trong Street and Nam Ky Khoi Nghia is the National Library.

Mariamman Hindu Temple
45 Truong Dinh St.

Although clearly Hindu, with a statue of Mariamman flanked by Maduraiveeran and Pechiamman, the temple is largely frequented by Chinese worshippers, providing the strange sight of Chinese Vietnamese clasping incense sticks and prostrating themselves in front of a Hindu deity, as they would to a Buddha image. The Chinese have always been pragmatic when it comes to religions.

Ben Thanh Market (Cho Ben Thanh)
A large, covered central market, Ben Thanh Market sits on a large and chaotic roundabout which, at the time of writing, was undergoing construction as part of the city's first metro line project. Ben Thanh is well stocked with cheap clothes (think souvenir T-shirts), household goods, and a wide choice of souvenirs, lacquerware, embroidery and so on, as well as some terrific lines in food, fresh and dried fruits. Rather touristy, it is still used by locals, but to get a more authentic sense of a busy city market, head to Binh Tay Market (see page 269).

Ben Thanh is also home to a food stall corner offering a huge variety of dishes from around the south of the country.

Outside the north gate (*cua Bac*) on Le Thanh Ton Street are some particularly tempting displays of fresh fruit and beautiful cut flowers.

ON THE ROAD
Buddhist martyrs: self-immolation as protest

In August 1963 there was a demonstration of 15,000 people at the Xa Loi Pagoda, with speakers denouncing the Diem regime and telling jokes about Diem's sister-in-law, Madame Nhu (who was later to call monks "hooligans in robes"). Two nights later, ARVN special forces (from Roman Catholic families) raided the pagoda, battering down the gate, wounding 30 and killing seven people. Soon afterwards Diem declared martial law. The pagoda became a focus of discontent, with several monks committing suicide through self-immolation to protest against the Diem regime.

The first monk to immolate himself was 66-year-old Thich Quang Du, from Hué. On 11 June 1963, his companions poured petrol over him and set him alight as he sat in the lotus position. Pedestrians prostrated themselves at the sight; even a policeman threw himself to the ground in reverence. The next day, the picture of the monk in flames filled the front pages of newspapers around the world. Some 30 monks and nuns followed Thich's example in protesting against the Diem government and US involvement in South Vietnam. Two young US protesters also followed suit, one committing suicide by self-immolation outside the Pentagon and the other next to the UN, both in November 1968.

Madame Nhu, a Catholic, is reported as having said after the monks' death: "Let them burn, and we shall clap our hands." Within five months Diem had been killed in a military coup.

In May 1993, a Vietnamese man immolated himself at the Thien Mu Pagoda in Hué – the pagoda where the first monk-martyr was based (see page 166).

The Ben Thanh Night Market has flourished since 2003. Starting at dusk and open until after midnight the night market is Ho Chi Minh City's attempt to recreate Bangkok's Patpong market. As the sun sinks and the main market closes stalls spring up in the surrounding streets. Clothes and cheap jewellery and an abundance of food stalls are the key attractions.

★ Fine Arts Museum
97A Pho Duc Chinh St, T08-3829 4441, daily 0900-1700.

Housed in an atmospheric colonial building which is slightly dishevelled but rather charming for it, the Fine Arts Museum is a very pleasant place to escape the heat of the city and take a look at some 20s architecture close up. The interior is wonderfully tiled and there is a courtyard to the rear, and an ancient iron lift. The art collection dates spans works from the fourth century right up to the contemporary era. The American War features heavily in the post-1975 work and the theme can become a little tiresome, but there is plenty of other art on offer, including some interesting Cham-era pieces. This is also a good place to pick up prints, with works by Vietnamese artists as well as propaganda posters on offer.

Phung Son Tu Pagoda
338 Nguyen Cong Tru St.

This is a small temple built just after the Second World War by Fukien Chinese; its most notable features are the wonderful painted entrance doors with their fearsome armed warriors. Incense spirals hang in the open well of the pagoda, which is dedicated to Ong Bon, the Guardian of Happiness and Virtue.

The **War Surplus Market (Dan Sinh)** ⓘ *Yersin between Nguyen Thai Binh St and Nguyen Cong Tru St*, is not far from the Phung Son Tu Pagoda. Merchandise on sale includes dog tags and military clothing and equipment (not all of it authentic). The market is popular with Western visitors looking for mementoes of their visit, so bargain particularly hard.

Pham Ngu Lao

an area catering for the backpacker

Most backpackers arriving overland in Ho Chi Minh City are dropped off in this bustling district, a 10- to 15-minute walk from downtown. The countless hotels, guesthouses and rooms to rent open and close and change name or owner with remarkable speed. The area is littered with restaurants, cafés, bars, email services, laundries, tour agencies and money changers, all fiercely competitive; there are mini-supermarkets and shops selling rucksacks, footwear, DVDs, pirated software and ethnic knick-knacks.

➡ **Ho Chi Minh City maps**
1 Ho Chi Minh City, page 256
2 Ho Chi Minh City centre, page 259
3 Ho Chi Minh City centre detail, page 261
4 Pham Ngu Lao, page 266

4 **Pham Ngu Lao**

Where to stay 🛏
Beautiful Saigon 4
Chau Long Mini 1
Long Hostel 2

Restaurants & cafés 🍴
Café Zoom 9
Good Morning
Vietnam 13

Kim Café 4

Not to scale

★This is the heart of Ho Chi Minh City's Chinese community. Cholon is an area of commerce and trade; not global but nevertheless international. In typical Chinese style it is dominated by small and medium-size businesses and this shows in the buildings' shop fronts (look for the Chinese characters on signs over the door). Cholon is home to a great many temples and pagodas – some of which are described below. As one would expect from a Chinese trading district, there is plenty of fabric for sale in the markets.

Cholon or Chinatown is inhabited predominantly by Vietnamese of Chinese origin. Despite a flow of Chinese out of the country post-1975, there is still a large population of Chinese Vietnamese living here. The area encompasses District 5 to the southwest of the city centre, and to the casual visitor appears to be the most populated, noisiest and in general the most vigorous part of Ho Chi Minh City, if not of Vietnam. It is here that entrepreneurial talent and private funds are concentrated; both resources that the government are keen to mobilize in their attempts to reinvigorate the economy.

Cholon is worth visiting not only for the bustle and activity, but also because the temples and assembly halls found here are the finest in Ho Chi Minh City. As with any town in Southeast Asia boasting a sizeable Chinese population, the early settlers established meeting rooms that offered social, cultural and spiritual support to members of a dialect group. These assembly halls (hoi quan) are most common in Hoi An and Cholon. There are temples in the buildings, which attract Vietnamese as well as Chinese worshippers, and indeed today serve little of their former purpose. The elderly meet here occasionally for a natter and a cup of tea.

Nghia An Assembly Hall
678 Nguyen Trai St, not far from the Arc en Ciel Hotel.

A magnificent, carved, gold-painted wooden boat hangs over the entrance to the Nghia An Assembly Hall. To the left, on entering the temple, is a larger-than-life representation of Quan Cong's horse and groom. (Quan Cong was a loyal military man who lived in China in the third century.) At the main altar are three figures in glass cases: the central red-faced figure with a green cloak is Quan Cong himself; to the left and right are his trusty companions, General Chau Xuong (very fierce) and the mandarin Quan Binh respectively. On leaving, note the fine gold figures of guardians on the inside of the door panels.

Tam Son Assembly Hall
118 Trieu Quang Phuc St, just off Nguyen Trai St.

The temple, built in the 19th century by Fukien immigrants, is frequented by childless women as it is dedicated to Chua Thai Sanh, the Goddess of Fertility. It is an uncluttered, 'pure' example of a Chinese/Vietnamese pagoda – peaceful and quiet. Like Nghia An Hoi Quan, the temple contains figures of Quan Cong, his horse and two companions.

Thien Hau Temples
710 and 802 Nguyen Trai St.

The Thien Hau Temple at 710 Nguyen Trai Street is one of the largest in the city. Constructed in the early 19th century, it is Chinese in inspiration and is dedicated to the worship of both the Buddha and to the Goddess Thien Hau, the goddess of the sea and the protector of sailors. Thien Hau was born in China and as a girl saved her father from drowning, but not her brother. Thien Hau's festival is marked here on the 23rd day of the third lunar month. One enormous incense urn and an incinerator can be seen through the main doors. Inside, the principal altar supports the gilded form of Thien Hau, with a boat to one side. Silk paintings depicting religious scenes decorate the walls. By far the most interesting part of the pagoda is the roof, which can be best seen from the small open courtyard. It must be one of the finest and most richly ornamented in Vietnam, with the high-relief frieze depicting episodes from the Legends of the Three Kingdoms. In the post-1975 era, many would-be refugees prayed here for safe deliverance before casting themselves adrift on the East Sea. A number of those who survived the perilous voyage sent offerings to the merciful goddess and the temple has been well maintained since. On busy days it is very smoky. Look up on leaving to see over the front door a picture of a boiling sea peppered with sinking boats. A benign Thien An looks down mercifully from a cloud.

A **second temple** dedicated to Thien Hau is a couple of blocks away at 802 Nguyen Trai Street. Chinese migrants from Fukien Province built it in the 1730s, although the building on the site today is not old. The roof can be seen from the road and in addition to the normal dragons are some curious models of what appear to be miniature Chinese landscapes carried by bowed men. Inside it is less busy than the first Thien Hau temple but on good days worshippers hurry from one image of Thien Hau (depicted here with a black face) to another waving burning joss sticks in front of her. Whatever happens in these temples is not religious in the sense of worshipping a god but more a superstition, entreating the spirits for good fortune (hence the lottery ticket sellers outside) or asking them to stave off bad luck. Note that these are not pagodas in the sense that they are not a place for the worship of Buddha and you will see no Buddhist monks here and have no sense of serene or enlightened calm. This temple has some nicely carved stone pillars of entwined dragons and on the wall to the right of the altars is a frieze of a boat being swamped by a tsunami. The walls are festooned with calendars from local Chinese restaurants and gold shops.

Ming Dynasty Assembly Hall
380 Tran Hung Dao St.

The Ming Dynasty Assembly Hall (Dinh Minh Huong Gia Thanh) was built by the Cantonese community which arrived in Saigon via Hoi An in the 18th century.

The assembly hall was built in 1789 to the dedication and worship of the Ming Dynasty although the building we see today dates largely from an extensive renovation carried out in the 1960s. There is some old furniture; a heavy marble-topped table and chairs that arrived in 1850 from China. It appears that the Vietnamese Emperor Gia Long used the Chinese community for cordial relations with the Chinese royal court and one of the community, a man called Trinh Hoai Duc, was appointed Vietnamese ambassador to the Middle Dynasty. In the main hall there are three altars which, following imperial tradition, are: the central altar dedicated to the royal family (Ming Dynasty in this case), the right-hand altar dedicated to two mandarin officers (military) and the left-hand altar dedicated to two mandarin officers (civil).

The hall behind is dedicated to the memory of the Vuong family who built the hall and whose descendants have lived here ever since. There is, in addition, a small side chapel where childless women can seek divine intercession from a local deity, Ba Me Sanh.

Quan Am Pagoda
12 Lao Tu St (just off Luong Nhu Hoc St).

The Quan Am Pagoda is thought to be one of the oldest in the city. Its roof supports four sets of impressive mosaic-encrusted figures, while inside, the main building is fronted with old, gold and lacquer panels of guardian spirits. The main altar supports a seated statue of A-Pho, the Holy Mother. In front of the main altar is a white ceramic statue of Quan Am, the Goddess of Purity and Motherhood (Goddess of Mercy) – see box, page 48. The pagoda complex also contains a series of courtyards and altars dedicated to a range of deities and spirits. Outside, hawkers sell caged birds and vast quantities of incense sticks to pilgrims.

★Binh Tay Market
While most tourists visit Ben Thanh Market, it is Binh Tay Market which is the more rewarding. Sandwiched between Thap Muoi and Phan Van Khoe streets, it is one of the most colourful and exciting markets in Ho Chi Minh City, with a wonderful array of noises, smells and colours and stalls that have past from generation to generation creating a rich sense of history and belonging among the stall holders. It sprawls over a large area and is contained in what looks like a rather decayed Forbidden Palace. Every conceivable space is used with stalls festooned with everything from spices to flip flops. This is also a good place to seek out a bowl of noodles or grab a cup of strong iced coffee and watch the madness unfold in front of you. A new high-rise market – the five-storey **An Dong Market** – opened at the end of 1991 in Cholon. It was built with an investment of US$5 million from local ethnic Chinese businessmen.

Outer Ho Chi Minh City includes a clutch of scattered pagodas in several districts, namely Districts 3, 10, 11 and Binh Thanh. All are accessible by cyclo, moto or taxi. There's also a new museum of traditional medicine in District 10.

Phung Son Pagoda

A 40-min walk or 8-min motorbike ride from the Binh Tay Market, set back from the road at 1408 3 Thang 2 Blvd.

The Phung Son Pagoda, also known as **Go Pagoda**, was built at the beginning of the 19th century on the site of an earlier Cambodian structure and has been rebuilt several times. At one time, it was decided to move the pagoda, and all the temple valuables were loaded on to the back of a white elephant. The beast stumbled and the valuables tumbled out into the pond that surrounds the temple. This was taken as a sign from the gods that the pagoda was to stay where it was. In the sanctuary, there is a large, seated, gilded Buddha, surrounded by a variety of other figures from several Asian and Southeast Asian countries. This, being a pagoda, has a very different atmosphere from the temples of Chinatown. There is no frenzied scrum in front of the altars and only a few whisps of smoke. Monks sit in contemplation.

Giac Vien Pagoda

At the end of a narrow and rather seedy 400-m-long alley running off Lac Long Quan St (just after No 247). There is also a temple down here of no interest whatsoever, the pagoda is right at the end.

Giac Vien Pagoda (Buddha's Complete Enlightenment) is similar in layout, content and inspiration to Giac Lam Pagoda (see below). Visiting just one of the two pagodas would be enough for most visitors. The Giac Vien Pagoda was built in 1771 and dedicated to the worship of the Emperor Gia Long. Although restored, Giac Vien remains one of the best-preserved temples in Vietnam. It is lavishly decorated, with more than 100 carvings of various divinities and spirits, dominated by a large gilded image of the Buddha of the Past (Amitabha or *A Di Da Phat* in Vietnamese). It is everything a pagoda should be: demons and gods jump out around every corner, a confusion of fantastic characters. With the smoke and smells, the richness of colour and the darkness, it's an assault on the senses. Among the decorations, note the 'Buddha lamp', funerary tablets and urns with photographs of the deceased. Outside there is a small pavilion in which the ashes of the dead are stored in small urns.

Giac Lam Pagoda

118 Lac Long Quan St, Ward 10, Q Tan Binh, T08-865 3933, about 2 km northeast of Giac Vien Pagoda, through an arch and down a short track about 300 m from the intersection with Le Dai Hanh St. Near the intersection is a modern 7-storey tower and beyond a giant Buddha statue which is also modern. Daily 0500-1200, 1400-2100.

The Giac Lam Pagoda (Forest of Enlightenment) was built In 1744 and is the oldest pagoda in Ho Chi Minh City. There is a sacred Bodhi tree in the temple courtyard and the pagoda is set among fruit trees and vegetable plots. Inside Giac Lam it feels, initially, like a rather cluttered private house. In one section, there are rows of funerary tablets with pictures of the deceased – a rather moving display of man's mortality. The main altar is impressive, with layers of Buddhas, dominated by the gilded form of the Buddha of the Past. Note the 49-Buddha oil lamp with little scraps of paper tucked in. On these scraps are the names of the mourned. The number seven is very important in Buddhism and most towers have seven storeys. Behind the main temple in the section with the funerary tablets is a bust of Ho Chi Minh. At the very back of the pagoda is a hall with murals showing scenes of torture from hell. Each sin is punished in a very specific and appropriate way. The monks are very friendly and will probably offer tea. Some speak good English and French as well as having detailed knowledge of the history of the pagoda. It is a small haven of peace. An unusual feature is the use of blue and white porcelain plates to decorate the roof and some of the small towers in the garden facing the pagoda. These towers are the burial places of former head monks.

Phuoc Hai Tu (Emperor of Jade Pagoda) and around
73 Mai Thi Luu St off Dien Bien Phu St, 0700-1800.

The Phuoc Hai Tu can be found, nestling behind low pink walls, just before the Thi Nghe Channel. Women sell birds that are set free to gain merit, and a pond to the right contains large turtles. The Emperor of Jade is the supreme god of the Taoists, although this temple, built in 1900, contains a wide range of other deities. These Include the archangel Michael of the Buddhists, a Sakyamuni (historic) Buddha, statues of the two generals who tamed the Green Dragon (representing the east) and the White Dragon (representing the west), to the left and right of the first altar respectively, and Quan Am (see box, page 48). The Hall of Ten Hells in the left-hand sanctuary has reliefs depicting the 1000 tortures of hell.

Nearby, the architecturally interesting **city library** ⓘ *3 Nguyen Dinh Chieu*, has a cool, modern façade; there is a memorial at the front of the building.

Tran Hung Dao Temple
Near the Emperor of Jade Pagoda at 34 Vo Thi Sau St, daily 0700-1100, 1430-1700.

The small Tran Hung Dao Temple, built in 1932, was dedicated to the worship of the victorious 13th-century General Hung Dao and contains a series of bas-reliefs depicting the general's successes, along with weapons and carved dragons. In the front courtyard is a larger-than-life bronze statue of this hero of Vietnamese nationalism.

Vinh Nghiem Pagoda
To the west, on Nguyen Van Troi St, and just to the south of the Thi Nghe Channel.

Another modern pagoda, the Vinh Nghiem Pagoda, was completed in 1967 and is one of the largest in Vietnam. Built in the Japanese style, it displays a classic seven-storey pagoda in a large and airy sanctuary. On either side of the entrance are two fearsome warriors; inside is a large Japanese-style Buddha in an attitude of meditation, flanked by two goddesses. Along the walls are a series of scrolls depicting the jataka tales, with rather quaint (and difficult to interpret) explanations in English.

Tomb and Temple of Marshal Le Van Duyet
126 Dinh Tien Hoang St, a 10- to 15-min cyclo ride across the Thi Nghe Channel and almost into the suburbs, 0500-1800.

Le Van Duyet was a highly respected Vietnamese soldier who put down the Tay Son Rebellion (see page 241) and who died in 1831. The pagoda was renovated in 1937 – a plaque on the left lists those who made donations to the renovation fund. The main sanctuary contains a weird assortment of objects: a stuffed tiger, a miniature mountain, whale baleen, spears and other weapons of war. Much of the collection is made up of the Marshal's personal possessions. In front of the temple is the tomb itself, surrounded by a low wall and flanked by two guardian lions and two lotus buds. The pagoda's attractive roof is best seen from the tomb.

Museum of Vietnamese Traditional Medicine
41 Hoang Du Khuong St, District 10, T08-386 42430, www.fitomuseum.com.vn, daily 0830-1730.

A fascinating exploration into traditional medicine with 3000 exhibits including instruments, manuscripts, ceramic jars and model of a 19th-century pharmacy.

Around Ho Chi Minh City
there isn't much to see around the city

The Cu Chi Tunnels are the most popular day trip, followed closely by an excursion to the Mekong Delta, especially My Tho (see page 295). It is possible to get to the coast and back in a day by visiting Vung Tau, but this is not a particularly appealing destination for most. Ho Chi Minh City does, on the other hand, have several out-of-town sports facilities with three golf courses and the exhilarating Saigon Water Park all within less than an hour's drive (see page 288).

Cu Chi Tunnels
Most visitors reach Cu Chi on a tour or charter a car and include a visit to Tay Ninh – see below. Regular buses leave for Cu Chi town from the Mien Tay station (Cholon) and the Ham Nghi station; from Cu Chi it is necessary to take a taxi to the tunnels or the infrequent Ben Suc bus, 10 km. It is also possible to take a motorbike from Ho Chi Minh City and back but the road is becoming increasingly dangerous with fast and heavy traffic. Daily 0700-1630, 90,000d.

Cu Chi Tunnels are about 40 km northwest of Ho Chi Minh City. Cu Chi town is on the main road to Tay Ninh and the Cao Dai temple and both the tunnels and the temple can be visited in a single day trip. Dug by the Viet Minh, who began work in 1948, they were later expanded by the People's Liberation Armed Forces (PLAF, or Viet Cong, VC, see page 362) and used for storage and refuge, and contained sleeping quarters, hospitals and schools. Between 1960 and 1970, 200 km of tunnels were built. At the height of their usage, some 300,000 were living underground. The width of the tunnel entry at ground level was 22 cm by 30 cm. The tunnels are too narrow for most Westerners, but a short section of the 250 km of tunnels has been especially widened to allow tourists to share the experience. Tall or large people might still find it a claustrophobic squeeze.

Cu Chi was one of the most fervently communist of the districts around Ho Chi Minh City and the tunnels were used as the base from which the PLAF mounted the operations of the Tet Offensive in 1968. Communist cadres were active in this area of rubber plantations, even before the Second World War. Vann and Ramsey, two American soldiers, were to notice the difference between this area and other parts of the south in the early 1960s: "No children laughed and shouted for gum and candy in these hamlets. Everyone, adult and child, had a cold look" (*A Bright Shining Lie*, Sheehan 1989).

When the Americans first discovered this underground base on their doorstep (Dong Du GI base was nearby) they would simply pump CS gas down the tunnel openings and then set explosives. They also pumped river water in and used German Shepherd dogs to smell out air holes. The VC, however, smothered the holes in garlic to deter the dogs. They also used cotton from the cotton tree – kapok – to stifle the smoke from cooking; 40,000 VC were killed in the tunnels in 10 years. Later, realizing that the tunnels might also yield valuable intelligence, volunteer 'tunnel rats' were sent into the earth to capture prisoners.

Cu Chi district was a free-fire zone and was assaulted using the full battery of ecological warfare. Defoliants were sprayed and 20 tonne Rome Ploughs carved up the area in the search for tunnels. It was said that even a crow flying over Cu Chi district had to carry its own lunch. Later it was also carpet bombed with 50,000 tonnes dropped on the area in 10 years.

At **Cu Chi 1** (Ben Dinh) ① *90,000d*, visitors are shown a somewhat antique but nevertheless interesting film of the tunnels during the war before being taken into the tunnels and seeing some of the rooms and the booby traps the GIs encountered. The VC survived on just cassava for up to three months and at both places you will be invited to taste some dipped in salt, sesame, sugar and peanuts. You will also be invited to a firing range to try your hand with ancient AK47s at a buck a bang.

Cu Chi 2 (Ben Duoc), has a temple, the **Ben Duoc Temple**, in memory of the 50,000 Saigon dead; the exterior is covered in mosaic murals. It stands in front of a rather beautiful sculpture of a tear called *Symbol of the Country's Spiritual Soul*.

Near the tunnels is the Cu Chi graveyard for patriots with 8000 graves. It has a very interesting large and striking bas-relief of war images along the perimeter of the entrance to the cemetery.

Cao Dai Great Temple

Ceremonies are held each day at 0600, 1200, 1800 and 2400, visitors can watch from the cathedral's balcony. Visitors should not enter the central portion of the nave – keep to the side aisles – and also should not wander in and out during services. If you go in at the beginning of the service you should stay until the end (1 hr). Take a tour, or charter a car in Ho Chi Minh City. Regular buses leave for Tay Ninh, via Cu Chi, from Mien Tay station (2½ hrs) or motorbike.

Tay Ninh, the home of the temple, is 96 km northwest of Ho Chi Minh City and 64 km further on from Cu Chi town. It can be visited on a day trip from the city and can easily be combined with a visit to the Cu Chi tunnels. The idiosyncratic Cao Dai Great Temple, the 'cathedral' of the Cao Dai religion (see page 412 for background on Cao Daism), is the main reason to visit the town.

The Cao Dai Great Temple, built in 1880, is set within a very large complex of schools and administrative buildings, all washed in pastel yellow. The twin-towered cathedral is European in inspiration but with distinct oriental features. On the façade are figures of Cao Dai saints in high relief and at the entrance is a painting depicting Victor Hugo flanked by the Vietnamese poet Nguyen Binh Khiem and the Chinese nationalist Sun Yat Sen. The latter holds an inkstone, symbolizing, strangely, the link between Confucianism and Christianity. Novelist Graham Greene in *The Quiet American* called it "The Walt Disney Fantasia of the East". Monsieur Ferry, an acquaintance of Norman Lewis, described the cathedral in even more outlandish terms, saying it "looked like a fantasy from the brain of Disney, and all the faiths of the Orient had been ransacked to create the pompous ritual...". Lewis himself was clearly unimpressed with the structure and the religion, writing in *A Dragon Apparent* that "This cathedral must be the most outrageously vulgar building ever to have been erected with serious intent".

After removing shoes and hats, women enter the cathedral through a door to the left, men to the right, and they then proceed down their respective aisles towards the altar, usually accompanied by a Cao Dai priest dressed in white with a black turban. During services they don red, blue and yellow robes signifying Confucianism, Taoism and Buddhism respectively. The men in coloured robes sporting an embroidered divine eye on their costumes are more senior. During services, on the balcony at the back of the cathedral, a group of men play a stringed instrument called a Dan Co between their feet using a bow; women sing as they play.

Two rows of pink pillars entwined with green dragons line the nave, leading up to the main altar which supports a large globe on which is painted a single staring eye – the divine, all-seeing-eye. The roof is blue and dotted with clouds, representing the heavens, and the walls are pierced by open, lattice-work windows with the divine eye as the centrepiece to the window design. At the back of the cathedral is a sculpture of Pham Com Tac, the last pope and one of the religion's founders who died in 1957. He stands on flowers surrounded by huge brown snakes and is flanked by his two assistants; one is the leader of spirits, the other the leader of materialism.

There are nine columns and nine steps to the cathedral representing the nine steps to heaven. Above the altar is the Cao Dai pantheon: at the top in the centre is Sakyamuni Buddha. Next to him on the left is Lao Tzu, master of Taosim. Left of Lao Tzu, is Quan Am, Goddess of Mercy, sitting on a lotus blossom. On the other side of the Buddha statue is Confucius. Right of the sage is the red-faced Chinese God of War and Soldiers, Quan Cong. Below Sakyamuni Buddha is the poet and leader of the Chinese saints, Li Ti Pei. Below him is Jesus and below Christ is Jiang Zhia, master of Geniism.

About 500 m from the cathedral (turn right when facing the main façade) is the **Doan Ket**, a formal garden.

The town of Tay Ninh also has a good **market** and some **Cham temples** 1 km to the southwest of the town.

Black Lady Mountain (Nui Ba Den)

Buses go from the bus station on Cach Mang Tam Tang St by the western edge of Tan Son Nhat Airport. From Tay Ninh to Nui Ba Den go by taxi. There is now a cable car to the summit.

Also known as *Nui Ba Den*, Black Lady Mountain is 10 km to the northeast of Tay Ninh and 106 km from Ho Chi Minh City. The peak rises dramatically from the plain to a height of almost 1000 m and can be seen in the distance, to the right, on entering Tay Ninh. The Black Lady was a certain Ly Thi Huong who, while her lover was bravely fighting the occupying forces, was ordered to marry the son of a local mandarin. Rather than complying, she threw herself from the mountain. Another version of this story is that she was kidnapped by local scoundrels. A number of shrines to the Black Woman are located on the mountain, and pilgrims still visit the site. Fierce battles were also fought here between the French and Americans, and the Viet Minh. There are excellent views of the surrounding plain from the summit reached by cable car.

Border crossings to Cambodia

The province of Tay Ninh borders Cambodia and, before the 17th century, was part of the Khmer Kingdom. Between 1975 and December 1978, soldiers of Pol Pot's Khmer Rouge periodically attacked villages in this province, killing the men and raping the women. Ostensibly, it was in order to stop these incursions that the Vietnamese army invaded Cambodia on Christmas Day 1978, taking Phnom Penh by January 1979.

Travellers taking the bus to Phnom Penh from Ho Chi Minh City cross at **Moc Bai** (Bavet in Cambodia). Cambodian visas are available at the border; Vietnamese visas are not.

Tourist information

Tourist Information Center
92-96 Nguyen Hue St, T08-8322 6033,
www.ticvietnam.com. Daily 0800-2100.
Provides free information,
hotel reservations, an ATM
and currency exchange.

Where to stay

City centre

$$$$ Caravelle
19 Lam Son Sq, T08-3823 4999,
www.caravellehotel.com.
Central and one of HCMC's top hotels,
this is a true heritage option having
opened in 1959, although a new tower
was added in 1998. Very comfortable
with 335 rooms, fitted out with all the
mod cons, many with incredible views
and well-trained and friendly staff.
Breakfast is sumptuous and filling and
Restaurant Nineteen, see below, serves
a fantastic buffet lunch and dinner.
Saigon Saigon, see page 284, the rooftop bar, draws the crowds until the early
hours and offers knockout veiws. A suite
of boutique shops plus a pool and Qi Spa
complete the luxury experience.

$$$$ Continental
132-134, Dong Khoi St, T08-3829 9201,
www.continentalhotel.com.vn.
Built in 1880 and renovated in 1989, the
Continental has an air of faded colonial
splendour. There are now smarter
options in town in this price bracket,
but few can match it for history.

$$$$ Grand
8 Dong Khoi St, T08-3823 0163,
www.grandhotel.vn.
A 1930s building in the heart of the
shopping district that might look more
comfortable on Brighton's seafront than
in HCMC. It was renovated 10 years ago
but the stained glass and marble staircase
have largely survived the process. Lovely
pool (try to get a pool-side room) and a
very reasonably priced restaurant.

$$$$ Park Hyatt Saigon
2 Lam Son Sq, T08-3824 1234,
www.saigon.park.hyatt.com.
This striking hotel is in a class of its own.
It exudes elegance and style and its
location north of the Opera House is
unrivalled. Works of art are hung in the
lobby, rooms are classically furnished in
French colonial style but with modern
touches; the pool area is lovely; the
wonderful lounge area features a baby
grand piano and there are a number of
very good restaurants. **Square One**, is an
excellent restaurant with open kitchens
and displays. There's also a fitness centre
and spa.

$$$$ Renaissance Riverside
8-15 Ton Duc Thang St, T08-3822 0033,
www.marriott.com.
Overlooking the water, this upmarket
option offers some of the finest views
in the city in the riverside rooms. It also
has Vietnam's highest atrium. Several
excellent restaurants including Kabin
Chinese restaurant and attractive pool.
Executive floors provide breakfast and
all-day snacks.

$$$$ Rex
141 Nguyen Hué Blvd, T08-3829 2185,
www.rexhotelvietnam.com.
A historically important hotel in the heart
of Saigon. During the Vietnam War the
American Information Service made

its base at the hotel and it became a base for daily press briefings to foreign correspondents known as the five o'clock follies. There is now a newer fabulous side extension that has become the principal entrance complete with high-end shopping arcade. The original lobby is decorated entirely in wood and tastefully furnished with wicker chairs. New wing premium rooms are very smart, if a little business-like; cheaper 'Superior' rooms in the old wing have small bathtub and are interior facing.

$$$$ Sheraton
88 Dong Khoi St, T08-3827 2828, www.sheraton.com/saigon.
This tall glass-clad hotel has certainly proved popular since it opened in late 2003. There is very good lunch and dinner on offer at the **Saigon Café**, and Level 23, with its brilliant views across HCMC, is recommended for a night-time drink. The hotel, with modern, stylish rooms is sandwiched into a downtown street and boasts boutique shops, a gorgeous pool, a spa and tennis courts.

$$$$ Sofitel Plaza Saigon
17 Le Duan St, T08-3824 1555, www.sofitel.com.
A smart, fashionable and comfortable hotel with a fantastic roof-top pool surrounded by frangipani plants. Gets rave reviews for its excellent service.

$$$ EMM Hotel Saigon
157 Pasteur, T08-3936 2100, www.emmhotels.com.
This is the first of what promises to be a new chain of funky modern hotels in Vietnam. Set over 2 floors, the rooms are very well furnished with modern touches and prints of the city. A good buffet breakfast is served in a cool restaurant space with an outdoor area offering great views. A reasonable gym and a travel desk for tour bookings.

$$$ Lan Lan Hotel 2
46 Thu Khoa Huan, T08-3822 7926, www.lanlanhotel.com.vn.
Excellent value rooms. Those on the upper floors have expansive views of the city. Helpful staff, buffet breakfast and in-room wifi. Has a 2nd location on the same road.

$$ Ho Sen
4B-4C Thi Sach St, T08-3823 2281, www.hosenhotel.com.vn.
This rather bland-looking hotel is nonetheless very clean and in a great location, so it's a good find. Rooms are very quiet and fairly spacious. Staff are friendly and helpful.

$$ Tan Hai Long 3
65 Ho Tung Mau St, T08-3915 1888, www.thlhotelgroup.com.
A well-positioned hotel with small rooms, good-sized bathrooms and good service. Great value.

Pham Ngu Lao

$$ Beautiful Saigon
62 Bui Vien St, T08-3836 4852, www.beautifulsaigonhotel.com.
A good addition to the backpacker zone replacing an old hotel, this is more for the flashpackers and welcome it is too. Very nice smart and tidy rooms all with mod cons, Wi-Fi and breakfast at fair prices and recommended by happy guests.

$ Chau Long Mini Hotel
185/8 Pham Ngu La, T08-3836 9667.
Simple, clean rooms, some with balconies. Family-run and welcoming. Great budget option.

$ Long Hostel
373/10 Pham Ngu Lao, T08-3836 0184,
longhomestay@yahoo.com.
Run by the supremely friendly and
charming Ms Long, a retired teacher
who serves tea and fruit to guests on
arrival, this hotel has spotless rooms, all
with TV and a/c. Highly recommended.
Book ahead.

Outer Ho Chi Minh City

$$$$ Thao Dien Village
*195 Nguyen Van Huong St, Thao Dien
Ward, Q2, T08-3744 6458,
www.thaodienvillage.com.*
A stylish boutique hotel and spa resort in
the expat enclave. Lovely to escape the
hustle of downtown. Popular restaurant.
Also a great spa and pool.

Restaurants

HCMC has a rich culinary tradition
and, as home to people from most
of the world's imagined corners, its
cooking is diverse. You could quite
easily eat a different national cuisine
every night for several weeks. French
food is well represented and there are
many restaurants from neighbouring
Asian countries especially Japan, Korea,
China and Thailand. The area between
Le Thanh Ton and Hai Ba Trung streets
has become a 'Little Tokyo' and 'Little
Seoul' on account of the number of
Japanese and Korean restaurants.

Pham Ngu Lao, the backpacker area, is
chock-a-block with low-cost restaurants
many of which are just as good as the
more expensive places elsewhere. Do
not overlook street-side stalls where
staples include of *pho* (noodle soup),
bánh xeo (savoury pancakes), *cha
giò* (spring rolls) and *banh mi pate*
(baguettes stuffed with pâté and salad),
all usually fresh and very cheap. The
major hotels all have gourmet shops
selling bread and pastries. Eating out
is an informal business; suits are not
necessary anywhere, and in Pham Ngu
Lao expect shorts and sandals.

The Ben Thanh night market
(see page 264) is a major draw for
Vietnamese and overseas visitors.
Stalls are set up at dusk and traffic
suppressed. There is a good range of
inexpensive foodstall dishes and lots of
noodles; it stays open until around 2300.

City centre

$$$ An Vien
*178A Hai Ba Trung St, T08-3824 3877.
Daily 1200-2300.*
Excellent and intimate restaurant
that serves the most fragrant rice in
Vietnam. Attentive service and rich
decor. The *banh xeo* and crispy fried
squid are recommended.

$$$ Hoa Tuc
*74 Hai Ba Trung St, T08-3825 1676.
Open 1000-2230.*
Set in the buzzing Hai Ba Trung
courtyard space. Dine amid the art deco
accents on soft shell crab or a salad of
pink pomelo, squid and crab with herbs.
The desserts are tantalizing.

$$$ La Fourchette
*9 Ngo Duc Ke St, T08-3829 8143.
Daily 1200-1430, 1830-2230.*
Truly excellent and authentic French
bistro offering a warm welcome, well-
prepared dishes and generous portions

> **Tip…**
> If Japanese food is your thing, eat
> up. HCMC, it is said, has some of the
> cheapest Japanese food in the world.

of tender local steak. Booking advised. Recommended.

$$$ San Fu Lou
76A le Lai St, T08-3823 9513, www.sanfulou.com.

Opened in 2014, this is an uber-cool venue with sharp service offering excellent dim sum with some classic dumplings and some unique creations. A buzzing joint. Best to dine with a group and try as much as possible.

$$$ Sorae Sushi
AB Tower, 76A Le Lai St, T08-3827 2372, www.soraesushi.com.

Outrageously slick space on the upper floors of the AB Tower affording awesome views through massive floor-to-ceiling windows, although the sleek interior means there is plenty for the eyes inside. The food is first-rate, as is the service. Truly high end dining that would slot right in among London's finest. Expect to do some serious damage to your wallet if you arrive hungry or in the mood for a fine sake.

$$$-$$ The Refinery
74 Hai Ba Trung St, T08-3823 0509. Open 1100-2300.

This former opium factory (through the arch and on the left) is a little understated in its reincarnation. It could equally be slotted into this guide's 'bar' section thanks to the great cocktails, but it also does some quality dishes such as the herb-encrusted steak and grilled barramundi. Always busy with a good atmosphere.

$$ Augustin
10D Nguyen Thiep St, T0890-382966, 294 8081. Mon-Sat 1100, 1130-1400 and 1800-2230.

Fairly priced and some of the best, unstuffy French cooking in HCMC;

tables pretty closely packed, congenial atmosphere. Excellent onion soup, baked clams and rack of lamb.

$$ Elbow Room
52 Pasteur St, T08-3821 4327, www.elbowroom.com.vn.

Cosy, bare-brick American diner serving the best burgers in town and awesome shakes – don't miss the vanilla version.

$$ Guc Cach
10 Dang Tat, T08-4801 4410.

The 2nd restaurant run by a local architect, **Guc Cach** is known for its great atmosphere, old school Saigon decor and excellent Vietnamese fare. The soft shell crab is superb. Recommended.

$$ KOTO Saigon
151A Hai Ba Trung St, T08-3934 9151, www.koto.com.au.

KOTO stands for Know One, Teach One. It is a training restaurant for disadvantaged young people, plus it serves good food, so a visit here is a no brainer. Serves a selection of Vietnamese classics alongside other Southeast Asian options and a handful of Belgian dishes.

$$ Quan Ut Ut
168 Vo Van Kict, T9 3914 4500, www.quanutut.com.

Set over 3 floors with canal views, this ever-buzzing joint is a temple for grilled meat lovers. Tender ribs cooked to pefection, first-rate mac and cheese and a burger that's a solid contender for the best in town. Also serves a very tasty pale ale. A top spot.

$$-$ Ashoka
17A/10 Le Thanh Ton St, T08-3823 1372. Daily 1100-1400, 1700-2230.

Indian restaurant popular with expats. Highlights are the mutton shami kebab, prawn vindaloo and kadhai fish –

barbecued chunks of fresh fish cooked in *kadhai* (a traditional Indian-style wok with Peshwari ground spices and sautéd with onion and tomatoes).

$ 13 Ngo Duc Ke
15 Ngo Duc Ke St, T08-3823 9314. Daily 0600-2230.
Fresh, well cooked, honest Vietnamese fare. Chicken in lemongrass is a great favourite and *bo luc lac* melts in the mouth. Popular with locals.

$ Au Parc
23 Han Thuyen St, T08-3829 2772. Mon-Sat 0730-2230, Sun 0800-1700.
Facing on to the park in front of the old Presidential Palace, this stylish café serves a some delicious Greek and Turkish options, sandwiches, salads, juices and drinks. Also does a good Sunday brunch that's popular with the city's expats.

$ Hoang Yen
5-7 Ngo Duc Ke St, T08-3823 1101. Daily 1000-2200.
Plain setting and decor but absolutely fabulous Vietnamese dishes, as the throngs of local lunchtime customers testify. Soups and chicken dishes are ravishing.

$ Pho Hoa Pasteur
260C Pasteur St. Daily 0600-2400.
Probably the best known *pho* restaurant and packed with customers. The *pho* costs more than average, but it is good quality and there are around 10 varieties on the English menu.

Cafés

Cooku'nest Café
13 Tu Xuong St, Q3, T08-2241 2043.
This kooky venue looks like it has been hoiked off an Alpine slope. It's a pine cabin equipped with cuckoo clock. Sit upstairs on the floor next to tiny tables and mingle with the local student gang. There's live music every night. Wi-Fi available.

Kem Bach Dang
26-28 Le Loi Blvd.
On opposite corners of Pasteur St. A very popular café serving fruit juice, shakes and ice cream. Try the coconut ice cream (*kem dua*) served in a coconut.

La Fenêtre Soleil
2nd floor, 135 Le Thanh Ton St (entrance at 125 Nam Ky Khoi Nghia St), T08-3822 5209. Mon-Sat, café 0900-1900, bar 1900-2400.
Don't be put off by the slightly grimy side entrance; clamber up into the boho-Indochine world of this gorgeous café/bar, artfully cluttered with antiques, lamps, comfy sofas and home-made cakes, muffins, smoothies and other delights. The high-energy drinks of mint, passionfruit and ginger juice are lovely. Highly recommended.

Tous les Jours
180 Hai Ba Trung St, Q3, and also in several other locations including Diamond Plaza, T08-3823 8302. Open 0600-2300.
A smorgasbord of cakes and pastries awaits the hungry visitor.

Pham Ngu Lao
Nearly all these restaurants are open all day every day from early or mid-morning until 2230 or later – when the last customer leaves, as they like to say. All are geared to Westerners and their habits and tastes and in just about all of them there will be at least one person who speaks English and French. Most tend to be cheap but prices have risen in recent times; do check.

ON THE ROAD

Betel nut

Betel nut has been a stimulant for the Vietnamese for hundreds of years. The ingredients combine the egg-shaped betel palm (*Areca catechu*) nut (*cau*) with Piper betel vine leaves (*trau*) and lime. When chewed (known as *An trau*) the ingredients stain the mouth and lips and red juice can often be seen dribbling down the chins of users. It often stains teeth black due to the polyphenol in the nut and leaf, which is considered attractive. The origin of the substance lies in Vietnamese legend and its use is found at weddings where a betel quid (a combination of powdered betel nut, betel leaves, lime and other flavourings) is laid out for guests. The areca nut is also a customary wedding gift given to the bride's family by the bridegroom's family. Betel and areca nuts are also presented at Tet (Lunar New Year).

$$ Good Morning Vietnam
197 De Tham St, T08-3837 1894.
Open 0900-2400.
One of the popular chain of Italian restaurants in southern Vietnam. Italian owned and run and serving up Italian flavours. Their pizzas are delicious and salads are good.

$ Cafe Zoom
169A De Tham St, T1222 993585,
www.vietnamvespaadventure.com.
Laid-back vibe and venue serving top burgers and fries – look for the classic Vespas lined up out front.

$ Kim Café
268 De Tham St, T08-3836 8122.
Open from early till late.
Wide range of food, popular with travellers.

Cholon
In Cholon you'll find a few cavernous Chinese restaurants and also lots of tiny streetside noodle stands.

$$ Tien Phat
18 Ky Hoa St, Q9, T08-3853 6217.

Conveniently located near the temples of Cholon. Open for breakfast and lunch. Specializes in dim sum. There is a good selection all freshly prepared, nice with hot tea.

Outer Ho Chi Minh City

$$$ The Deck
38 Nguyen U Di, An Phu, Q2, T08-3744 6322, www.thedecksaigon.com.
A very popular expat spot with tables on a deck right on the Saigon River. The food is, in the main, delicious and creative.

$$$-$$ Le Bordeaux
72 D2 St, Cu Xa Van Thanh Bac, Q Binh Thanh, T08-3899 9831, www.restaurant-lebordeaux.com.vn. Mon 1830-2130, Tue-Sat 1130-1330, 1830-2130.
Rather a tragedy that it is in such an awkward location. If you can find it you are in for a treat. Lovely decor and warm atmosphere, receives high accolades for its French cuisine but it is not cheap.

Food stalls
For those staying centrally, a wander along Nguyen Thai Binh is

recommended. At number 75 you'll find **Pho Phuong Bac** which sells good *pho* in the morning and a variety of great dished throughout the day and evening. All along this road there are small eateries selling everything from spring rolls to rice buffets (*com bing dan*), most of which are packed out with office workers during lunch time. Nearby at 40 Ton That Dam St, **Hu Tieu Nam Loi** is a long-running chicken and fish *hu tieu* joint that is worth seeking out. Just north of the centre on the south side of Tan Dinh is another good area to seek out food, including excellent *banh xeo*. The stalls in Benh Thanh shouldn't be overlooked; the *banh canh cua* (40,000d) and *nuoc mia* (sugarcane juice, 10,000d) at stall 1028 are delectable. Over in District 4, Vinh Kanh St is the place to head for roadside seafood. The great scallops and crab claws at **Can An Hien** (number 12) are mouth watering. **Anh Thu**, 49 Dinh Cong Trang St, and other stalls nearby on the south side of Tan Dinh market serve *cha gio*, *banh xeo* and *bi cuon*.

Cafés

A swathe of new thoughtfully designed, original, one-off cafés have opened, invigorating the city's caffeine scene. Alongside this, Starbucks has entered the fray alongside chains including **Gloria Jean's**, **Coffee Bean** and **Tea Leaf**.

A Cafe
15 Huynh Khuong Ninh.
Run by artist, Nguyen Thanh Truc, this is real find. The intimate café offers a peaceful place to enjoy a good book, quiet conversation and superb coffee. Beans are roasted on-site and the coffee can be brewed in every way imaginable. Well worth going out of your way for.

Cliché Café
20 Tran Cav Van, T08-3822 0412.
Open 0800-1030.
Head straight upstairs to take a seat among all manner of knick knacks in this popular café. Serves excellent, strong iced coffee and good value set lunches.

ID
34D Thu Khoa Huan. Open 0800-2230.
Plenty of comfortable seating, low lighting, vinyl nailed to the walls, and, like most cafés in this vein, a collection of retro audio equipment. A good place to relax.

La Fenêtre Soleil
44 Ly Tu Trong St, T08-3824 5994.
This place has moved and reinvented itself with a cool café vibe by day but regular DJ and salsa moves by night.

La Rotunde
77B Ham Nghi, T0983-889935.
More like somebody's Indochina apartment than a public café, this is a wonderfully unique café space that also serves an excellent Vietnamese buffet lunch.

L'Usine
151 Dong Khoi, District 1, T08-6674,
www.lusinespace.com.
Part café, part lifestyle store, **L'Usine** is an uber cool venue. Legendary cupcakes, delicious freshly cut sandwiches and perfect shakes. A hipster hangout. There is also now a 2nd branch on Le Loi.

Things
14 Ton That Dam. Open 0900-2200.
Shabby chic, with such oddities as a cupboard full of Converse and a bed in the corner. Friendly owner Linh (also a TV presenter) is a good source of what's new in town. Very quirky.

Velo de Piste
10 Pasteur.
By day this café is referred to as Heritage, but later in the afternoon tables made from suitcases perched on stools appear on the pavement and the place takes on a decidedly Shoreditch-esque hipster vibe. Single speed bikes hang from the walls and a collection of old typewriters sit on shelves.

The Workshop
27 Ngo Duc Ke St.
An extremely sleek coffee shop that makes the very best of the period building that houses it, with exposed brick, huge windows and chunky wooden tables. Run by self-professed coffee nerds Dung and Duy with consultation from one of Asia's leading coffee minds, Will Frith. The first-rate coffee is roasted on the premises. Highly recommended.

Bars and clubs

Along with the influx of foreigners and the freeing up of Vietnamese society has come a rapid increase in the number of bars in HCMC and they cater to just about all tastes. Everything is on offer, from roadside plastic chair drinking to uber-chic sky bar cocktails with killer views.

Alibi
5A Nguyen Sieu St, T08-3823 0237, www.alibi.vn.
Goes on after hours and is a magnet for tourists and expats. Consistently popular and in a new location. Very smooth 2-floor venue decorated with deep reds and pictures of old Saigon. Remains under the tourist radar. Weekend DJs, a long wine list and a well-rounded menu to boot.

Apocalypse Now
2BCD Thi Sach St, T08-3825 6124.
Cover charges at weekends. Open until 0300/0400. This legendary venue remains one of the most popular and successful bars and clubs in HCMC. Draws a very wide cross section of punters of all ages and nationalities. DJs often spin a fun/cheesey selection of floor fillers. Can take on a slight meat market feel in the wee hours.

Blanchy's Tash
95 Hai Ba Trung, T09-0902 8293, www. blanchystash.com. Open 1100-late.
Upscale bar. Weekends are rammed downstairs where music blasts, while the rooftop terrace is more relaxed. Regular DJ nights, excellent cocktails, and an expensive, well-regarded restaurant.

Blue Gecko
31 Ly Tu Trong St, T08-3824 3483, www.bluegeckosaigon.com.
This bar has been adopted by HCMC's Australian community so expect cold beer and Australian flags above the pool table.

Chill Skybar
76A Le Lai, District 1, T09-3272 0730, www.chillsaigon.com. Open 1600-late.
With a view that has to be seen to be believed, a mixologist of international acclaim and the kind of crowd that means you'll want to dress your best (flip flops and shorts are not permitted), Chill Skybar is a rather pretentious, but worth a look to see Saigon's more lavish side. The cocktails are wallet-busting.

Cloud 9
2 Cong Truong Quoc Te, District 3, T08-0948-343399.
Another of the city's roof-top bars, **Cloud 9** is a chic nightspot with

contemporary design and excellent drinks. Dress sharp.

La Habana
6 Cao Ba Quat, T08-3829 5180, www.lahabana-saigon.com.
Latin beats and mojitos make for a great night out, particularly on salsa nights when the dance floor fills with local talent keen to show off their skills. Serves the finest paella in town.

Le Pub
175/22 Pham Ngu Lao, T08-3837 7679. Open 0900-2400.
The no-nonsense pub formula here makes a good place for a cold beer although an awful music policy can sometimes make it impossible to bear. Western and Vietnamese food.

OMG bar
15 Nguyen An Ninh, T09-3720 0222.
While it will be a little heavy on the neon for some tastes, the reason to drink here isn't to enjoy the decor, but to enjoy the excellent view of downtown HCMC, looking right out across Ben Thanh market and the Bitexco Tower. Also serves food and holds regular party nights.

Pasteur Street Brewing Company
144 Paster St, T9-0551 4782.
The first craft beer establishment in town, this is a very cool operation run by beer geeks who have scoured Vietnam to come up with interesting locally brewed beers with bite. Sleek decor, a small menu of food designed to complement the beer and knowledgable staff make this a must for any beer connoisseur.

Rex Hotel Bar
See Where to stay, above.
An open-air rooftop bar which has a kitsch revolving crown. There are good views, cooling breeze, snacks and meals – and a link with history (page 255).

Saigon Saigon
10th floor, Caravelle Hotel, 19 Lam Son Sq, T08-3824 3999.
Breezy and cool, with large comfortable chairs and superb views by day and night. Excellent cocktails but not cheap.

Vasco's
74/7D Hai Ba Trung St, T08-3824 2888. Open 1600-2400.
A hugely popular spot in a great courtyard setting. A great place to kick off an evening out. Good happy hour offers.

Yoko
22A Nguyen Thi Dieu, T08-3933 0577. Open 1800-2400.
Ever busy live music venue. Slightly more rock and underground than the **Acoustic Cafe** over on Ngo Thoi Nhiem. An excellent night out. Arrive early to bag a seat.

Entertainment

Cinemas
French Cultural Institute (Idecaf), *31 Thai Van Lung, T08-3829 5451, www.idecaf.gov.vn.* Shows French films.
Lotte Cinema, *Diamond Plaza, 34 Le Duan St, www.lottecinemavn.com.* The cinema on the 13th floor of this shopping centre screens English-language films.

Traditional music and opera
Conservatory of Music (Nhac Vien Thanh Pho Ho Chi Minh), *112 Nguyen Du St, T08-3824 3774, www.hcmcons.vn.* Traditional Vietnamese music and classical music concerts are performed by the young students who study music here and sometimes by local and visiting musicians.

Opera House, *Lam Son Sq, T08-3832 2009, www.hbso.org.vn.* Regular classical concerts, opera and ballet. Check the website for upcoming shows.

Water puppetry

Golden Dragon Water Puppet Theatre, *55B Nguyen Thi Minh Khai St, T08-3930 2196, www.thaiduongtheatre. com.* A 50-min performance daily at 1700, 1830 and 1945.

Museum of Vietnamese History, *2 Nguyen Binh Khiem St, T08-3829 8146, www.baotanglichsuvn.com.* There are daily 15-min water puppetry performances in the tiny theatre in an outdoor, covered part of the museum, see page 263. The advantage of this performance over the Hanoi theatre is that the audience can get closer to the puppetry and there is better light.

Shopping

Antiques

Most shops are on **Dong Khoi**, **Mac Thi Buoi** and **Ngo Duc Ke** streets. For the knowledgeable, there are bargains to be found, especially Chinese and Vietnamese ceramics – however you will need an export permit to get them out of the country (see page 433). Also available are old watches, colonial bric-a-brac, lacquerware and carvings, etc. For the less touristy stuff, visitors would be advised to spend an hour or so browsing the treasure trove shops in **Le Cong Trieu St** (aka **Antique St**). It runs between Nam Ky Khoi Nghia and Pho Duc Chinh streets just south of Ben Thanh Market. Among the bric-a-brac and tat are some interesting items of furniture, statuary, stamps, candlesticks, fans, badges and ceramics. Bargaining is the order of the day and some pretty good deals can be struck.

Art galleries

Craig Thomas Gallery, *27i Tran Nhat Duat, T09-0388 8431, www. cthomasgallery.com.* Tue-Sat 1200-1800, Sun 1200-1700. Exhibitions of young, emerging and mid-career Vietnamese contemporary artists.

Galerie Quynh, *Dong Khoi, T08-3836 8019, www.galeriequynh.com.* Tue-Sat 1000-1800. Promotes a select group of Vietnamese artists and plays host to travelling international exhibitions.

San Art, *ground floor, 48/7 Pham Viet Chanh, T08-3840 0898, www.san-art.org.* Tue-Sat 1030-1830. Artist-run exhibition space and reading room. Regular programme of events, including lectures.

Bicycles

As well as the cheap shops along Le Thanh Ton St, close to the Ben Thanh Market there are now a handful of shops selling high quality international brands including **Saigon Cycles** which stocks Surly and Trek – **Skygarden**, Phu My Hung, www.xedapcaocap.com.

Books, magazines and maps

Books and magazines All foreigners around Pham Ngu Lao and De Tham streets are game to the numerous booksellers who hawk mountains of pirate books under their arms. The latest bestsellers together with enduring classics (ie *The Quiet American*) can be picked up for a couple of dollars.

Artbook, *43 Dong Khoi St, T08-3910 3518, www.artbookvn.com.* For art, architecture and coffee table books.

Fahasa, *40 Nguyen Hue Blvd, T08-3912 5358, www.fahasasg.com.* A very large store with dozens of English titles and magazines.

Maps HCMC has the best selection of maps in Vietnam, at stalls on Le Loi Blvd between Dong Khoi St and Nguyen Hue Blvd. Bargain hard – the bookshops are probably cheaper.

Western newspapers and magazines
Sold in the main hotels. Same day *Bangkok Post* and *The Nation* newspapers (English-language Thai papers), and up-to-date *Financial Times*, *Straits Times*, *South China Morning Post*, *Newsweek* and *The Economist*, available from larger bookshops.

Ceramics
Vietnam has a ceramics tradition going back hundreds of years. There has been a renaissance of this art in the past decade. Shops selling new and antique (or antique-looking ceramics) abound on the main shopping streets of **Dong Khoi** and **Le Thanh Ton**. There is a lot of traditional Chinese-looking blue and white and also very attractive celadon green, often with a crackled glaze. There are many other styles and finishes as local craftsmen brush the dust off old ideas and come up with new ones. **Nga Shop**, see Lacquerware, below, has a good range.

Clothing, silk and *ao dai*
Dong Khoi is home to many excellent boutiques. Vietnamese silk and traditional dresses (*ao dai*) are to be found in the shops on here. A number of shops in De Tham St sell woven and embroidered goods including bags and clothes.
Devon London, *151 Dong Khoi, www.devonlondon.com*. Modern clothing from one of Vietnam's most promising young designers.
Ipa Nima, *77-79 Dong Khoi St and in the New World Hotel, T08-3822 3277,*

www.ipa-nima.com. Sister branch of the Hanoi store with sparkling bags and accessories.
Khaisilk, *107 Dong Khoi, T08-3829 1146*. **Khaisilk** belongs to Mr Khai's growing empire. He has a dozen shops around Vietnam. Beautifully made, quality silk products from dresses to scarves to ties can be found in this luxury outlet.

Department stores
Diamond Department Store, *Diamond Plaza 1st-4th floor, 34 Le Duan St, T08-3822 5500. Open 1000-1000*. HCMC's central a/c department store set over a couple of floors. It sells luxury goods, clothes with some Western brands, watches, bags and perfumes. There is also a small supermarket inside. A bowling alley complex and cinema dominate the top floor.
Parkson Plaza, *35 Bis-45 Le Thanh Ton St*. A high-end department store.

Foodstores
Shops specializing in Western staples, such as cornflakes, peanut butter and Marmite, abound on Ham Nghi St around Nos 62 and 64 (**Kim Thanh**). There are also now mini-marts, such as **Circle K**, on many of the streets downtown.
Annam Gourmet Hai Ba Trung, *16-18 Hai Ba Trung St, T08-3822 9332, www.annam-gourmet.com. Mon-Sat 0800-2100, Sun 1000-2000*. Local organic vegetables and other international delicacies at this new culinary emporium.

Gifts and handicrafts
Dogma, *43 Ton That Thiep, www.dogma.vietnam.com*. Sells propaganda posters, funky T-shirts and postcards.
Gaya, *1 Nguyen Van Trang St, corner of Le Lai St, T08-3925 2495, www.gayavietnam.com. Open 0900-2100*.

A 3-storey shop with heavenly items: exquisitely embroidered tablecloths, bamboo bowls, ceramics and large home items such as screens; also gorgeous and unusual silk designer clothes by, among others, Romyda Keth, based in Cambodia. If you like an item but it does not fit they will take your measurements but it could take a fortnight to make.

Mai Handicrafts, *298 Nguyen Trong Tuyen St, Q Tan Binh, T08-3844 0988.* A little way out of town but sells an interesting selection of goods, fabrics and handmade paper all made by disadvantaged people in small income-generating schemes.

Nagu, *132-134 Dong Khoi St (next to the Park Hyatt), www.zantoc.com.* Delicate embroidered silk products among other fashion, home and giftware.

Nguyen Freres, *2 Dong Khoi St, T08-3823 9459, www.nquyenfreres.com.* An absolute Aladdin's cave. Don't miss this even if it's just to potter among the collectable items.

Saigon Kitsch, *43 Ton That Tiep St. Open 0900-2000.* This is the place to come for communist kitsch ranging from propaganda art posters to placemats and mugs. Also retro bags and funky jewellery on sale.

Jewellery

Jewellery is another industry that has flourished in recent years and there is something to suit most tastes. At the cheaper end there is a cluster of gold and jewellery shops around **Ben Thanh Market** and and also in the **International Trade Centre** on Nam Ky Khoi Nghia St. In these stalls because skilled labour is so cheap one rarely pays more than the weight of the item in silver or gold. At the higher end **Therese**, with a shop in the **Caravelle Hotel**, has established an international reputation.

Lacquerware

Vietnamese lacquerware has a long history, and a reputation of sorts (see page 400). Visitors to the workshop can witness the production process and, of course, buy the products if they wish. Lacquerware is available from many of the handicraft shops on Nguyen Hue Blvd and Dong Khoi St. Also from the **Lamson Lacquerware Factory**, 106 Nguyen Van Troi St (opposite **Omni Hotel**). Accepts Visa and MasterCard.

Duy Tan, *41 Ton That Thiep St, T08-382 3614. Open 1100-2000.* Pretty ceramics and lacquerware.

Nga Shop, *49-57 Dong Du St, T08-3823 8356, www.huongngafinearts.vn.* **Nga** has become one of the best-known lacquer stores as a result of her high-quality designs. Other top-quality rosewood and ceramic handicrafts suitable for souvenirs are available.

Linen

Good-quality linen tablecloths and sheets are avaliable from shops on Dong Khoi and Le Thanh Ton streets.

Outdoor gear

Vietnam produces a range of equipment for camping, such as walking boots, fleeces and rucksacks. Real and fake goods can be bought, especially from around Pham Ngu Lao and De Tham streets.

War surplus

From **Dan Sinh Market**, Yersin St, between Nguyen Thai Binh St and Nguyen Cong Tru St.

What to do

Bowling
Diamond Superbowl, *4th floor of Diamond Plaza, 34 Le Duan St, right behind the cathedral, T08-3825 7778, ext 12.* 24 lanes on the top floor, which also has a fast-food outlet, video games and plenty of pool tables.

Cookery classes
Saigon Cooking Class, *held at the new Hoa Tuc (see Restaurants), 74 Hai Ba Trung St, T08-3825 8485, www.saigoncookingclass.com.*
Vietnam Cookery Center, *362/8 Ung Van Khiem St, Q Binh Thanh, T08-3512 2764, www.vietnamese-cooking-class-saigon.com.* Offers short and in-depth courses for adults and children.

Golf
Bochang Dong Nai Golf Resort, *Dong Nai Province, 50 km north of HCMC up Highway 1, T61-386 6288, http://dongnaigolf.com.vn.* A very attractive 27-hole golf course with restaurant and bar and accommodation.
Golf Vietnam and Country Club, *Long Thanh My Ward, Q9, T08-6280 0124, http://vietnamgolfcc.com.* An internationally owned 36-hole course with an east and west course, just north of the city. The complex also has tennis and badminton courts, a boating lake and children's playground. On-site accommodation is available.
Song Be Golf Resort, *77 Binh Duong Blvd, Lai Thieu, Q Thuan An, Binh Duong Province, 22 km from HCMC on Highway 13, T650-375 6660, http://songbegolf.com.* An attractive golf resort set in 100 ha of land with lakes and tree-lined fairways. For non-golfers there are tennis courts, a gym, sauna and children's playground.

Swimming
Some hotels allow non-residents to use their pool for a fee. Decent pools are at the **Sofitel Plaza**, **Grand** and **Caravelle**.
International Club, *285B Cach Mang Thang Tam St, Q10, T08-3865 7695.*
Lan Anh Club, *almost next door to the International Club at 291 Cach Mang Thang Tam St, T08-3862 7144.* Pleasant with a nice pool and tennis courts.
Saigon Water Park, *Go Dua Bridge, Kha Van Can St, Q Thu Duc, T08-3897 0456. Mon-Fri 0900-1700, Sat and Sun 0900-2000.* Admission is charged according to height. A little way out but is enormous fun. It has a variety of water slides of varying degrees of excitement and a child's pool on a 5-ha site. It is hugely popular with the Vietnamese.

Tennis
Tennis is possible at the **Rex Hotel** and **New World Hotel** and also **Lan Anh Club**, 291 Cach Mang Thang Tam St.

Therapies
L'Apothiquaire, *61-63 Le Thanh Ton St, T08-3822 1218, www.lapothiquaire.com.* Massages, chocolate therapy, spa packages and slimming treatments in this lovely spa.
Qi Salon and Spa, *Caravelle Hotel, www.qispa.com.vn.* You can indulge in everything from a 20-min Indian head massage to a blow-out 5-hr Qi Special.

Tours
Buffalo Tours, *81 Mac Thui Buoi St, T08-3827 9170, www.buffalotours.com.* Organizes trips to the Mekong Delta, city tours, the Cu Chi tunnels and Cao Dai Temple. Staff are helpful. Good countrywide operator with longstanding reputation. Also has an office in the **EMM Hotel** (see Where to stay).

Exotissimo, *64 Dong Du St, T08 3827 2911, www.exotissimo.com.* An efficient agency that can handle all travel needs of visitors to Vietnam. Its local excursions are very well guided.

Handspan Adventure Travel, *F7, TitanCentral Park Building, 10th floor, 18A Nam Quoc Cang, 208 Nguyen Trai, Q1, T08-3925 7605, www.handspan. com.* Reputable and well-organized. Specializes in adventure tours.

Kim Café, *189 De Tham St, District 1, T08-3920 5552, www.kimtravel.com.* Organizes minibuses to Nha Trang, Dalat, etc, and tours of the Mekong. A good source of information. Backpacker friendly prices.

Sinh Tourist (formerly **Sinh Café**), *246-248 De Tham St, T08-3838 9597, www.thesinhtourist.vn.* Sinh Tourist now has branches and agents all over main towns in Vietnam. Its tours are generally good value and its open ticket is excellent value. For many people, especially budget travellers, **Sinh** is the first port of call. The company also deals with visa extensions, flight, train and hotel bookings and car rentals. This one is the HQ.

Sophie's Tour, *T0121-830 3742, www. sophiesarttour.com.* Run by Sophie, a long-term Saigon expat with a passion for the city and its art. Engaging 4-hr tour looking at the works of artists who studied, fought and witnessed major events in Vietnam's recent history from colonialism to the present. Highly recommended.

XO Tours, *T09-3308 3727, www.xotours.vn.* XO tours take clients around the city on the back of motorbikes ridden by women wearing traditional ao dai. The foodie tour introduces dishes and districts tourists don't normally see. Shopping and sightseeing tours also offered. Fun, different and highly rated.

Vietnam Vespa Adventures, *Cafe Zoom, 169A De Tham St, T08-3920 3897, www.vietnamvespaadventure.com.* Half-day tours of the city, 3-day tours to Mui Ne and 8-day tours to Dalat and Nha Trang. The city tours are fun, insightful and recommended.

Transport

Air
Airport information
HCMC may not be Vietnam's capital, but it is the economic powerhouse of the country and the largest city and thus well connected with the wider world – indeed, more airlines fly into here than into Hanoi.

Tan Son Nhat Airport, 49 Truong Son, Tan Binh, T08-3844 8358, www. saigonairport.com, is 30-40 mins northwest of the city, depending on the traffic. Airport facilities include banks and ATMs and locker rooms, desks for airlines including **Vietnam Airlines** and VietJetAir, and an information desk. Lost and found, T08-3844 6665 ext 7461.

Airline offices
AirAsia, 254 De Tham St, T08-3838 9810, www.airasia.com. **Air France**, 130 Dong Khoi St, T08-3829 0981, www.airfrance. com. **Bangkok Airways**, Unit 103, Saigon Trade Center, 37 Ton Duc Thang St, T08-3910 4490, www.bangkokair.com. **Cathay Pacific**, 72-74 Nguyen Thi Minh Khai St, T08-3822 3203, www.cathaypacific.com. **Emirate Airlines**, 170-172 Nam Ky Khoi Nghia, Q3, T08-3930 2939, www.emirates. com. **Eva Air**, 2A-4A, Ton Duc Thang St, T08-3844 5211, www.evaair.com. **Gulf Air**, 18 Dang Thi Nhu St, Q1, T08-3915 7614, www.gulfair.com. **JAL**, www.jal. co.jp. **Jetstar**, 112 Hong Ha, Q Tan Binh, T08-3845 0092, www.jetstar.com.

Lao Airlines, www.laoairlines.com. Lufthansa, 19-25 Nguyen Hue Blvd, T08-3829 8529, www.lufthansa.com. Malaysia, Saigon Trade Center, 37 Ton Duc Thang St, T08-3829 2529, www.malaysiaairlines.com. Qantas, HT&T Vietnam, Level 2, Ben Thanh TSC Building, 186-188 Le Thanh Ton St, T08-3910 5373, www.quantas.com.au. Qatar, Suite 8, Petro Vietnam Tower, 1-5 Le Duan St, T08-3827 3777, www.qatarairways.com. Singapore Airlines, 29 Le Duan St, T08-3823 1588, www.singaporeair.com. Thai Airways, 29 Le Duan St, T08-3822 3365, www.thaiairways.com.vn. Tiger Airways, T1206 0114, www.tigerairways.com. Vietnam Airlines, 6th floor, Sun Wah Tower, 115 Nguyen Hue St, T08-3832 0320, www.vietnamairlines.com. Mon-Fri 0800-1830, Sat 0800-1200, 1330-1700.

Bicycle and motorbike
If staying in HCMC for any length of time it might be a good idea to buy a bicycle (see Shopping, above, and page 285). Alternatively, bikes and motorcycles can be hired for cheaply around Pham Ngu Lao.

Bikes should always be parked in designated compounds (gui xe) for a small fee (don't lose your ticket!) or with a guard in front of businesses.

Bus
Local
The bus service in HCMC has now become more reliable and frequent. They run at intervals of 10-20 mins – depending on the time of day. In rush hours they are jammed with passengers and can run late. There are bus stops every 500 m or so. Most buses start from or stop by the Ben Thanh bus station opposite Ben Thanh Market, T08-3821 4444. A free map of all bus routes can

also be obtained here in the chaotic waiting room.

Long distance
With the completion of a new ring road around HCMC, long-distance public buses, unless specifically signed HCMC or 'Ben Xe Ben Thanh' do not come into the city. Passengers are dropped off on the ring road at Binh Phuoc bridge. However, companies such as Sinh Tourist and Phuong Trang (futabuslines.com.vn) run services from Pham Ngu Lao.

From Mien Dong Terminal, north of the city, buses north to Dalat, Hué, Danang and all significant points on the road to Hanoi. The Hoang Long bus company runs deluxe buses daily to Hanoi. Has an office at 47 Pham Ngu Lao, T08-915 1818 and it is possible to book online at www.hoanglongasia.com.

From Mien Tay Terminal, some distance southwest of town, buses south to the Mekong Delta towns. There is also a bus station in Cholon which serves destinations such as Long An, My Thuan, Ben Luc and My Tho.

International bus
Many tour operators run tours and transport to Cambodia (see Tour operators) crossing the border at Moc Bai. Visas for Cambodia can be bought at the border. Sapaco Tourist, 309-327 Pham Ngu Lao St, T08-3920 3623, www.sapacotourist.com, runs buses from Pham Ngu Lao to Phnom Penh from 0600-1400, 8 daily 6 hrs; to Siem Reap, US, 12 hrs.

Cyclos
Cyclos are a peaceful way to get around the city. They can be hired by the hour or to reach a specific destination. Some drivers speak English. Each tends to

have his own patch, which is jealously guarded. Expect to pay more outside the major hotels.

Cyclos are much rarer these days but can be found waiting in tourist spots. Some visitors complain of cyclo drivers in HCMC 'forgetting' the agreed price (though Hanoi is worse). Cyclos are being banned from more and more streets in the centre of HCMC, which may involve a longer and more expensive journey. This excuse is trotted out every time (particularly if extra money is demanded) and it is invariably true. If taking a tour agree a time and price and point to watches and agree on the start time.

Taxi

HCMC has quite a large fleet of meter taxis. There are many taxi companies fighting bitterly for trade. Competition has brought down prices so they are now reasonably inexpensive and for 2 or more are cheaper than cyclos or *xe om* (motorcycle taxi).

Not all taxis are trustworthy, but it is easy to avoid scams. Simply use one of these companies, which are all over town: **Mai Linh** (T08-3822 2666, www.mailinh.vn) or **Vinasun** (T08-3827 2727).

Xe om are the quickest way to get around town and cheaper than cyclos; agree a price and hop on the back. *Xe om* drivers hang around on most street corners. Short journeys run from around 15,000d but you may end up paying more.

Train

The station is 2 km from the centre of the city at 1 Nguyen Thong St, Q3, T08-3931 2795. Facilities for the traveller are much improved and include a/c waiting room, post office and bank (no TCs). Regular daily connections with **Hanoi** and all points north. Trains take between 29½ and 42½ hrs to reach Hanoi; hard and soft berths are available. Sleepers should be booked in advance.

There is now a **Train Booking Agency** at 275c Pham Ngu Lao St, T08-3836 7640, 0730-1830, which saves an unnecessary journey out to the station. Alternatively, for a small fee, most travel agents will obtain tickets. The railway timetable can be seen online at www.vr.com.vn.

Southern Vietnam

beaches, islands and riverine delta life

The Mekong Delta, the rice basket of Vietnam, comprises a great swathe of Southern Vietnam. At its verdant best the delta is a riot of greens – pale green rice seedlings deepen in shade as they sprout ever taller, while palm trees and orchards make up an unbroken horizon of green hues.

Formal sights are thin on the ground and travel can be slow. But herein lies the first contradiction of the delta, for the journey is often more fun than the destination. Boat trips along canals, down rivers and around islands hold more appeal than many of the towns and the main roads that are straggled with mile upon mile of homes and small, and increasingly large, industry. The southern end of Vietnam is also home to Mui Ne with its Sahara-like dunes and Phu Quoc island, Vietnam's largest. Also off the southern coast lies the wonderfully unspoiled former prison colony island of Con Dao.

Best for
Diving ▪ River trips ▪ Water sports

My Tho and around 295
Can Tho and around.......... 311
Chau Doc and around 320
Phu Quoc Island............. 330
Con Dao..................... 336
Phan Thiet and Mui Ne 342

Footprint picks

★ **Sa Dec**, page 305

A charming market town with river trip options.

★ **Tram Chim National Park**, page 309

Home to 220 bird species and spectacular floating rice field scenery.

★ **Can Tho floating markets**, page 312

All manner of food produce sold from boats and barges with a buzz like no other.

★ **Nui Sam (Sam Mountain)**, page 323

Climb past pagodas to the summit for magnificent vistas of paddy fields as far as the eye can see.

★ **Phu Quoc**, page 330

Vietnam's largest island with a forested interior and a great choice of amazing beaches.

★ **Con Dao**, page 336

Unspoilt archipelago with a beguiling former prison colony island at its heart.

★ **Mui Ne**, page 342

Kitesurfing capital and home to Sahara-like red and white dunes.

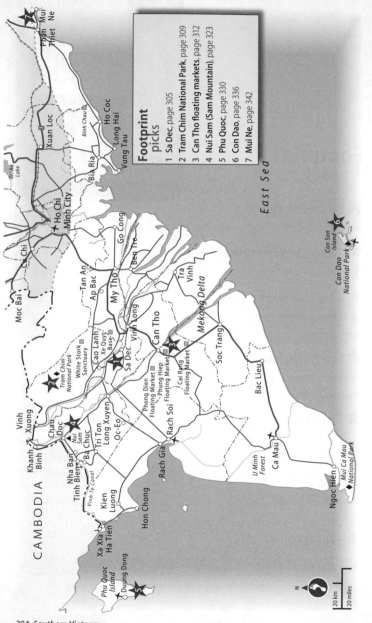

Footprint picks

1 Sa Dec, page 305
2 Tram Chim National Park, page 309
3 Can Tho floating markets, page 312
4 Nui Sam (Sam Mountain), page 323
5 Phu Quoc, page 330
6 Con Dao, page 336
7 Mui Ne, page 342

East Sea

CAMBODIA

Moc Bai
Cu Chi
Ho Chi Minh City
Xuan Loc
Phan Thiet
Mui Ne
Ho Coc
Long Hai
Vung Tau
Bia Ria
Binh Chau
Tri An Lake
Go Cong
Tan An
Ap Bac
My Tho
Ben Tre
Tra Vinh
Vinh
Khanh Binh
Chau Doc
Nui Sam
Nha Ban
Tinh Bien
Ba Chuc
Vinh Te Canal
Tri Ton
Long Xuyen
Oc-Eo
Cao Lanh
Xe Quyt Base
Sa Dec
Vinh Long
Can Tho
Phong Dien Floating Market
Phung Hiep
Rach Soi Floating Market
Cai Rang Floating Market
Soc Trang
Bac Lieu
Tram Chim National Park
White Stork Sanctuary
Mekong Delta
Rach Gia
Kien Luong
Hon Chong
Xa Xia
Ha Tien
Duong Dong
Phu Quoc Island
U Minh Forest
Ca Mau
Ngoc Hien
Mui Ca Mau National Park
Con Son Island
Con Dao National Park

20 km
20 miles
N

294 • Southern Vietnam

My Tho
& around

fruit orchards and local life

My Tho is an important riverside market town, 71 km southwest of Ho Chi Minh City and 5 km off the main highway to Vinh Long. It is the stepping-off point for boat trips to islands in the Tien River. Visitors enjoy the chance to wander among abundant fruit orchards and witness local industries at first hand. Around My Tho are the northern delta towns of Ben Tre, Vinh Long, Tra Vinh, Sa Dec and Cao Lanh.

Vinh Long at the end of the 19th century
Source: *The French in Indochina*, first published in 1884

The town has had a turbulent history: it was Khmer until the 17th century, when the advancing Vietnamese took control of the surrounding area. In the 18th century Thai forces annexed the territory, before being driven out in 1784. Finally, the French gained control in 1862. Today, it is much more peaceful destination.

Sights

On the corner of Nguyen Trai Street and Hung Vuong Street, and five minutes' walk from the central market, is My Tho church painted with a yellow wash with a newer, white campanile. The central market covers a large area from Le Loi Street down to the river. The river is the most enjoyable spot to watch My Tho life go by.

It is a long walk to **Vinh Trang Pagoda** ⓘ *60 Nguyen Trung Trac St, daily 0900-1200, 1400-1700 (best to go by bicycle or xe om)*. The entrance to the temple is through an ornate porcelain-encrusted gate. The pagoda was built in 1849 and displays a mixture of architectural styles: Chinese, Vietnamese and colonial. The façade is almost fairytale in inspiration. Two huge new statues of the Buddha now dominate the area.

Not far from My Tho is the hamlet of **Ap Bac**, the site of the communists' first major military victory against the ARVN. The battle demonstrated that without direct US involvement the communists could never be defeated. John Paul Vann was harsh in his criticism of the tactics and motivation of the South Vietnamese Army who failed to dislodge a weak VC position. As he observed from the air, almost speechless with rage, he realized how feeble his Vietnamese ally was; an opinion that few senior US officers heeded – to their cost (see *Bright Shining Lie* by Neil Sheehan).

Essential My Tho and around

Getting around

The much-improved Highway 1 is the main route from Ho Chi Minh City to My Tho, and there are regular connections with other main towns in the area. There is an efficient public bus service, taxis aplenty, a few river taxis and boats and *xe om*.

When to go

December to May is when the Mekong Delta is at its best. During the monsoon from June to November the weather is poor with constant background drizzle interrupted by bursts of torrential rain.

Time required

Ideal for a weekend.

Best sleeping and eating

A bowl of hu tieu my tho, page 298
Banh Xeo 46, page 298
A homestay on Cai Mon island, page 298

Tourist information

Tien Giang Tourist
8 30 Thang 4 St on the river, Ward 1,
T730-387 3184, www.tiengiangtourist.vn.
Boat trips, fishing tours and even nigh
firefly watching tours. Also has a ticket
office for transport. The staff are friendly
and helpful and have a good command
of several languages.

Where to stay

$$-$ Song Tien Annex
33 Trung Trac St, T0730-397 7883,
www.tiengiangtourist.com.
This is a large 20-room hotel boasting
big beds and bathtubs on legs. The large,
renovated Song Tien around the corner
is another good option if this is full.

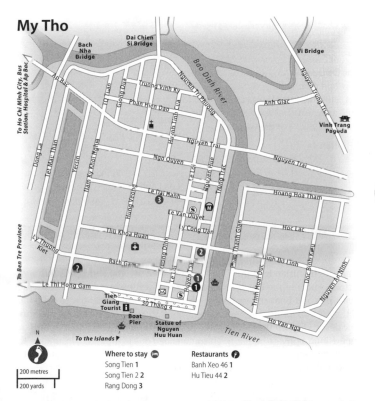

My Tho

Where to stay 🛏
Song Tien **1**
Song Tien 2 **2**
Rang Dong **3**

Restaurants 🍴
Banh Xeo 46 **1**
Hu Tieu 44 **2**

200 metres
200 yards

$ Rang Dong
No 25, 30 Thang 4 St, T730-3874400,
www.rangdonghotel.net.
Private mini hotel, near river with a/c,
TV and hot water. Friendly staff are
very helpful.

Restaurants

A speciality of the area is *hu tieu my
tho* – a spicy soup of vermicelli, sliced
pork, dried shrimps and fresh herbs.
At night, noodle stalls spring up on
the pavement on Le Loi St at the
junction with Le Dai Han St.

$ Banh Xeo 46
11 Trung Trac St.
Serves *bánh xèo*, savoury pancakes filled
with beansprouts, mushrooms and
prawns; delicious.

$ Bo De Quan
69A Nguyen Trung Truc.
Just across the street from a pretty
temple, this is a great veggie Vietnamese
restaurant set in a verdant garden.

$ Hu Tien 44
44 Nam Ky Khoi Nghia St. Daily 0500-1200.
Specializes in *hu tien my tho.*

What to do

Ben Tre Tourist, *8, 30 Thang 4 St,
T730-387 5070, www.bentretourist.vn.*
Although this company operates island
tours from My Tho, it would be best to
use its specialist knowledge of Ben Tre
province. Escape the My Tho crowds
with homestays at Cai Mon and take a
tour to the gardens and canals of this
neigbouring province.
Tien Giang Tourist, *Dockside location
is at No 8, 30 Thang 4 St, T730-387 3184,
www.tiengiangtourist.com.* Dinner with
traditional music on the Mekong, canoe
and boat hire.

Transport

Boat
As in all Mekong Delta towns, local travel
is often by boat to visit the orchards,
islands and remoter places.

Bus
The bus station (Ben Xe My Tho) is
3-4 km from town on Ap Bac St towards
HCMC with regular connections every
30 mins from 0430 to **HCMC**'s Mien Tay
station (2 hrs); **Vinh Long** (2½ hrs); and
Cao Lanh (2½ hrs). There are also buses
to **Can Tho** and **Chau Doc**.

The islands

go in the afternoon when they are quieter

There are four islands in the Tien River between My Tho and Ben Tre: Dragon,
Tortoise, Phoenix and Unicorn. The best way of getting to them is to take a tour.
A vast pier and boat service centre has been built on 30 Thang 4 Street where
all the tour operators are now concentrated. To avoid the hundreds of visitors
now descending on these islands, go in the afternoon after the tour buses have
gone. Hiring a private boat is not recommended due to the lack of insurance, the
communication difficulties and lack of explanations. Prices vary according to the
number of people and which islands you choose to visit.

Dragon Island

Immediately opposite My Tho is Dragon Island, Tan Long Island. It is pleasant to wander along its narrow paths. Tan Long is noted for its longan production but there are many other fruits to sample, as well as honey and rice whisky.

Phoenix Island

The Island of the **Coconut Monk**, also known as Con Phung (Phoenix Island), is about 3 km from My Tho. The 'Coconut Monk' established a retreat on this island shortly after the end of the Second World War where he developed a new 'religion', a fusion of Buddhism and Christianity. He is said to have meditated for three years on a stone slab, eating nothing but coconuts – hence the name. Persecuted by both the South Vietnamese government and after reunification, the monastery has fallen into disuse.

Unicorn Island

Unicorn Island is a garden of Eden – stuffed with longan, durian, roses, pomelo and a host of other fruit trees. Honey is made on this island too.

Ben Tre → *Colour map 4, B3.*

appealing backwater delta town

Ben Tre is a typical Vietnamese delta town with a charming riverfront feel. The small bridge over the river is wooden slatted but with iron supports. Bountiful fruit stalls are laid out on the waterfront and locals sell potted plants on barges by the river. Small cargo ships pass dilapidated shacks falling into the muddy waters. It doesn't attract a lot of visitors. Its main claim to fame is that it is the birthplace of Nguyen Dinh Chieu, a blind and patriotic poet. In recent years, though, it has improved its tourism facilities.

Ben Tre is no longer an island province; a bridge links it from just outside My Tho. The province is essentially a huge island of mud at one of the nine mouths of the Mekong. It depends heavily on farming, fishing and coconuts although there are some light industries engaged in processing the local farm output and refining sugar. During the wars of resistance against the French and Americans, Ben Tre earned itself a reputation as a staunch Viet Minh/Viet Cong stronghold.

Sights

Vien Minh Pagoda is located on Nguyen Dinh Chieu Street and is the centre for the association of Buddhists in Ben Tre Province. It was originally made of wood but was rebuilt using concrete in 1958.

In **Binh Phu village**, 2 km from downtown, you can see rice wine being made. **Phu Le village** also makes rice wine.

Nguyen Dinh Chieu Temple is 36 km from the town centre in An Duc village. The temple is dedicated to the poet Nguyen Dinh Chieu who is Ben Tre's most famous son. It is well kept and photogenic and worth a visit. The monks are friendly and helpful.

Tourist information

Ben Tre Tourist
*16 Hai Ba Trung St, T75-382 2392,
www.bentretourist.vn.*
Friendly and helpful.

Where to stay

$ Hung Vuong
148-166 Hung Vuong St, T75-382 2408.
Spacious a/c rooms (39 in total) with
huge bathtubs feature in this waterfront
hotel that is in a great location. Each
room has 2 beds plus TV, fridge and
balcony. Restaurant; breakfast is
included. Some English is spoken.

Restaurants

Most of the hotels have restaurants;
there is a floating restaurant on the
river but it has moved from its town
centre location to 1 km upstream. The
best option is local noodle and rice
stands. The hotel restaurants are open
all day.

$ Nha Hang Noi Ben Tre
*Hung Vuong, T75-382 2492.
Open 0700-2200.*
A large space popular with big groups.
Serves a variety of dishes plus karaoke.

Shopping

The main items to buy are coconuts
and related coconut-made products.
They might not be too versatile but
they are very pretty and make ideal
novelty presents for friends and family
at home.

What to do

Tours of the islands in the Tien River
from Ben Tre cost half the price of
those leaving from My Tho and include
taking a horse and cart. The 4-hr Ben
Tre ecological tour will take you to see
local agricultural industries.

Ben Tre Tourist, *16 Hai Ba Trung St,
T75-382 2392, www.bentretourist.vn.
Daily 0700-1100, 1300-1700.* Island tours,
bicycle rental and a motorboat for hire.

Transport

Car or bus
Hourly buses connect Ben Tre with
HCMC (150 km) via the My Thuan toll
bridge. Regular services connect Ben Tre
with **My Tho**, 16 km, 30 mins and **Can
Tho** (100 km, 2½ hrs).

Vinh Long → *Colour map 4, B3.*

a base for boat trips

Vinh Long is a rather ramshackle, but nonetheless clean, riverside town on the
banks of the Co Chien River and is the capital of Vinh Long Province. It is the
launch pad for lovely boat trips through An Binh Island via the small floating
market at Cai Be. An Binh is the centre of the Mekong homestay industry (see
box, opposite). Vinh Long makes a reasonable stopping-off point on the road to
Long Xuyen, Rach Gia and Ha Tien.

ON THE ROAD

Mekong homestays

Facing Vinh Long town in the Co Chien River, a tributary of the Mekong, is a large island known as An Binh that is further sliced into smaller islands by ribbons of canals. **Cuu Long Tourist** runs several homestays on the island – a wonderful way to immerse yourself in local life.

The accommodation is basic with camp beds, shared bathrooms and mosquito nets and a home-cooked dinner of the fruits of the delta (elephant ear fish with abundant greens including mint and spring rolls and beef cooked in coconut).

Sunset and drinks in patios or terraces or riverfront lookouts chatting with the owner completes the night. A dawn paddle in the Mekong, surrounded by floating water hyacinth and watching the sun rise is the reward for early risers.

These tranquil islands are stuffed with fruit-bearing trees and flowers. Travel is by sampan or you can walk down the winding paths that link the communities.

During your stay you will take tea and fruit at a traditional house, see rice cakes and popcorn being made, and visit a brick factory and watch terracotta pots being created close to the unusually shaped kilns that dot this area of the delta.

Sights

Vinh Long was one of the focal points in the spread of Christianity in the Mekong Delta and there is a cathedral and Roman Catholic seminary in town. The richly stocked and well-ordered **Cho Vinh Long** (central market) is on 1 Thang 5 Street down from the Cuu Long hotel and stretches back to near the local bus station. A new market building has also been built opposite the existing market. There is a **Cao Dai church** not far from the second bridge leading into town from Ho Chi Minh City and My Tho, visible on the right-hand side.

At sunset families cluster along the **river promenade** to fly colourful kites in animal shapes. In the mornings, fruits are for sale along **Hung Dao Vuong Street** and teenagers play ball and throw home-made shuttlecocks in the afternoons along **Hung Vuong Street**.

Vinh Long Museum ① *T70-382 3181, daily 0800-1100 and 1330-1630, Fri-Sun 1800-2100, free*, displays photographs of the war including the devastation of the town in 1968, some weaponry and a room dedicated to Ho Chi Minh.

Van Thieu Mieu Temple ① *0500-1100, 1300-1900*, a charming mustard yellow cluster of buildings is 2 km from town along Tran Phu Street. In the first building to the right on entering the complex is an altar dedicated to Confucius.

The **Khmer Temples** at Tra Vinh (see below) can be visited on a day trip from Vinh Long.

ON THE ROAD

Hydrology of the Mekong Delta

The Mekong River enters Vietnam in two branches known traditionally as the Mekong and the Bassac but now called the Tien and the Hau. Over the 200-km journey to the sea they divide to form nine mouths, the so-called Nine Dragons or *Cuu Long*.

In response to the rains of the Southwest monsoon, river levels begin to rise in June, usually reaching a peak in October and falling to normal in December. This seasonal pattern is ideal for rice growing, around which the whole way of life of the delta has evolved.

The Mekong has a unique natural flood regulator in the form of Cambodia's great lake, the Tonlé Sap. As river levels rise the water backs up into the vast lake which more than doubles in size, preventing more serious flooding in the Mekong Delta. Nevertheless, the Tien and Hau still burst their banks and water inundates the huge Plain of Reeds (*Dong Thap Muoi*) and the Rach Gia Depression, home to thousands of waterbirds.

The annual flood has always been regarded as a blessing bringing, as it does, fertile silt and flushing out salinity and acidity from the soil. Since the 1990s, however, frequent serious flooding has made this annual event less benign and an increasingly serious problem.

From 1705 onwards Vietnamese emperors began building canals to improve navigation in the delta. This task was taken up enthusiastically by the French in order to open up new areas of the delta to rice cultivation and export. Interestingly it is thought the canals built prior to 1975 had little effect on flooding.

Since 1975 a number of new canals have been built in Cambodia and Vietnam and old ones deepened. The purpose of some of these predominantly west–east canals is to carry irrigation water to drier parts. Their effect has been to speed up the flow of water across the delta from about 17 days to five. Peak flows across the border from Cambodia have tripled in 30 years, partly as a result of deforestation and urbanization upriver.

In addition, the road network of the delta has been developed and roads raised above the normal high-water levels. This has the effect of trapping floodwater, preventing it from reaching the Gulf of Thailand or East Sea and prolonging floods. Many canals have gates to prevent the inundation of sea water; the gates also hinder the outflow of floodwaters.

(Information taken from a paper by Quang M Nguyen)

River trips

The river trips taking in the islands and orchards around Vinh Long are as charming as any in the delta, but getting there can be expensive. See What to do, below.

There is a floating market at **Cai Be**, about 10 km from Vinh Long. This is not quite so spectacular as the floating markets around Can Tho (see page 312) but nevertheless make for a diverting morning's trip.

An Binh Island, just a 10-minute ferry ride from Phan Boi Chau Street, represents a great example of delta landscape. The island can be explored either by boat, paddling down narrow canals, or by following the dirt tracks and crossing monkey bridges on foot. Monkey bridges are those single bamboo poles with, if you are lucky, a flimsy handrail that is there for psychological reassurance rather than to stop you from falling off. But don't worry, the water is warm and usually shallow and the mud soft. On the island is the ancient **Tien Chau Pagoda** and a *nuoc mam* (fish sauce factory).

Listings Vinh Long

Tourist information

Cuu Long Tourist
No 1, 1 Thang 5 St, T70-382 3616, www.
cuulongtourist.com. Daily 0700-1700.
This is one of the friendlier and more helpful of the state-run companies and runs tours and homestays.

Where to stay

For homestays, see box, page 301.

$ Cuu Long (B)
No 1, 1 Thang 5 St (ie No 1 May St), T70
382 3616, www.cuulongtourist.com.
Set back from the river, in the centre of action. 34 comfortable a/c rooms; price includes breakfast.

$ Nam Phuong
11 Le Loi St, T70-382 2226,
khachsannamphuongvl@yahoo.com.
These are extremely basic and cheap rooms – one for those on a serious budget.

Restaurants

There are a few restaurants along 1 Thang 5 St, just beyond Cuu Long Hotel.

$ Nem Nuong
12 1 Thang 5 St. Open all day.
Sells grilled meat with noodles.

$ Phuong Thuy Restaurant
No 1, 1 Thang 5 St, T70-382 4786.
Open 0600-2100.
A restaurant on the river with Vietnamese and Western dishes and welcoming service. Cuttlefish and shrimp feature strongly.

What to do

Cuu Long Tourist, *No 1, 1 Thang 5 St,*
T70-382 3616, www.cuulongtourist.com.
Trips to An Binh Island include a visit to the floating market of Cai Be. A tour of the area including homestay, dinner and breakfast can be arranged (see box, page 301). A day trip to Cai Be passing the floating market is possible, as is the arrangement from HCMC.
Mekong Travel, *No 8, 30 Thang 5 St,*
T70-383 6252, www.mekongtravel.com.vn.
Offers the same homestay and floating market options.

Transport

The road runs direct from Ho Chi Minh City via the My Thuan bridge. There are good connections to all other Mekong towns.

Bus
The local bus station is on 3 Thang 2 St, between Hung Dao Vuong and

Hung Vuong in the centre of town with services to Sa Dec and Can Tho. The long-distance bus station is at Dinh Tien Hoang St, Ward 8 for connections with **HCMC**'s Mien Tay station. Links with **My Tho**, **Long Xuyen**, **Tra Vinh**, **Rach Gia**, and other **Mekong Delta** destinations.

Tra Vinh → *Colour map 4, C3.*

religious edifices and Khmer culture

Tra Vinh is the capital of the province of the same name and has a large Khmer population – 300,000 people (30% of the province's population) are Khmer, and at the last count there were 140 Khmer temples. The large Khmer population is a bit of an enigma, for while Khmer people can be found across the Mekong Delta the concentration is highest in this, the most distant Mekong province from Cambodia. For whatever reason, Tra Vinh established itself as a centre of population some 500 years ago; then, as Vietnamese settlers began fanning across the delta displacing the Khmer, the population of this area remained firmly rooted creating a little pocket of Cambodian ethnicity and culture far from home. The modern market building, adorned with a huge picture of Ho Chi Minh, is the pivot of the city.

Sights

For those interested in religious edifices, Tra Vinh is the place to visit. In one of the more obscure surveys undertaken to calculate the number of religious buildings per head of population it was found that with more than 140 Khmer temples, 50 Vietnamese pagodas, five Chinese pagodas, seven mosques and 14 churches serving a town of only 70,000 souls, Tra Vinh was the outright winner by miles.

So many attractive buildings coupled with the tree-lined boulevards – some trees are well over 30-m tall – make this one of the more attractive cities in the delta. It is well worth an overnight stay here to recharge the batteries.

The market is on the central square between Dien Bien Phu Street – the town's main thoroughfare – and the Tra Vinh River, which is a relatively small branch of the Mekong compared with most delta towns. A walk through the market and along the riverbank makes a pleasant late afternoon or early evening stroll.

The **Ong Met Pagoda** on Dien Bien Phu Street north of the town centre dates back to the mid-16th century. It is a gilded Chinese-style temple where the monks will be only too happy to ply you with tea and practice their English, although the building itself is fairly unremarkable.

The two best reasons to come to Tra Vinh are to see the **storks** and the **Khmer temples**. Fortunately, these can be combined at the nearby **Hang Pagoda**, also known as **Ao Ban Om**, about 5 km south of town and 300 m off the main road. It is not particularly special architecturally, but the sight of the hundreds of storks that rest in the grounds and wheel around the pointed roofs at dawn and dusk (1600-1800) is truly spectacular.

There's also the **Bao Tang Van Hoa Dan Toc Khmer** ① *0700-1100, 1300-1700*, a small collection of artefacts next to the square-shaped lotus filled pond of Ba

Om just south of town (there are plans for a hotel here). Labels are in Vietnamese and Khmer only; naga heads, Hanuman masks and musical instruments feature. Opposite is the **Chua Angkorajaborey (Ang)** or Chua Van Minh in Vietnamese dating from AD 990, which is rather peaceful.

Listings Tra Vinh

Tourist information

Tra Vinh Tourist
64-66 Le Loi St, T74-385 8556,
travinhtourist@yahoo.com.
Owner of the **Cuu Long Hotel**,
friendly and helpful. City tours offered.

Where to stay

$ Cuu Long
999 Nguyen Thi Minh Khai St,
T74-386 2615.
The rooms are equipped with a/c,
satellite TV, and en suite facilities.
The restaurant provides a good
selection of food but the service can
be very slack with a lack of English.

$ Tra Vinh Palace
3 Le Thanh To St, T74-386 4999.
A comfortable but rather gaudy hotel
with very large rooms 10 mins' walk from
the central market. The sister hotel, Tra

Vinh Palace 2 has cheaper rooms and is a
few streets away.

Restaurants

$ Cuu Long
See Where to stay.
Restaurant has a good selection of food.

$ Tuy Huong
8 Dien Bien Phu St.
Opposite the market; good, simple
Vietnamese dishes.

$ Viet Hoa
80 Tran Phu St.
Walk through the garage to sample
the squid, shrimp and crab dishes.
English menu.

Transport

The bus station is on Nguyen Dang St,
about 500 m south of town. Regular
connections with **Vinh Long**.

Sa Dec → *Colour map 4, B2.*

riverside market town

★Sa Dec's biggest claim to fame is that it was the birthplace of French novelist Marguerite Duras, and the town's three main avenues – Nguyen Hue, Tran Hung Dao and Hung Vuong garlanded with fragrant frangipani – together with some attractive colonial villas betray the French influence on this relatively young town. Sa Dec, a small and friendly town about 20 km west of Vinh Long, is also renowned for its flowers and bonsai trees.

The town was formerly the capital of Dong Thap Province, a privilege that was snatched by Cao Lanh in 1984 but a responsibility that Sa Dec is better off without.

BACKGROUND

Mekong Delta

The region has had a restless history. Conflict between Cambodians and Vietnamese for ownership of the wide plains resulted in ultimate Viet supremacy although important Khmer relics remain. But it was during the French and American wars that the Mekong Delta produced many of the most fervent fighters for independence.

The Mekong Delta or Cuu Long (Nine Dragons) is Vietnam's rice bowl and, before the partition of the country in 1954, rice was traded from the south where there was a rice surplus, to the north where there was a rice deficit, as well as internationally. Even prior to the creation of French Cochin China in the 19th century, rice was being transported from here to Hué, the imperial capital. The delta covers 67,000 sq km, of which about half is cultivated. Rice yields are in fact generally lower than in the north, but the huge area under cultivation and the larger size of farms means that both individual households and the region produce a surplus for export. In the Mekong Delta there is nearly three times as much rice land per person as there is in the north. It is this that accounts for the relative wealth of the region.

The Mekong Delta was not opened up to agriculture on an extensive scale until the late 19th and early 20th centuries. Initially it seems that this was a spontaneous process: peasants, responding to the market incentives introduced by the French, slowly began to push the frontier

The delightful journey between the two towns passes brick kilns, and bikers transporting their wares (namely tropical fish in bottles and dogs).

Sights

Sa Dec's bustling riverside market on Nguyen Hue Street is worth a visit. Many of the scenes from the film adaptation of Duras' novel *The Lover* were filmed in front of the shop terraces and merchants' houses here. Sit in one of the many riverside cafés to watch the world float by – which presumably, as a young woman, is what Duras did.

Duras' lover **Huynh Thuy Le's house** ① *Nha Co Huynh Thuy Le, 255A Nguyen Hue St, Ward 2, T67-377 3937, Mon-Sat 0730-1700, Sun 0830-1700, 10,000d*, is a lovely Sino-influenced building on the main street. There are stunning gold-leaf carved animal figures framing arches and the centrepiece is a golden shrine to Chinese warrior Quan Cong. The Ancient House was built in 1895 and restored in 1917. There are photographs of the Huynh family (he later married and had five daughters and three sons; he died in 1972), Duras and the Sa Dec school. Duras' childhood home is not across the river as some guidebooks say; it no longer exists. She lived in a house near the Ecole de Sa Dec (now Truong Vuong primary school on the corner of Hung Vuong and Ho Xuan Huong St), which is pictured inside the Nha Co Huynh Thuy Le.

of cultivation southwards into this wilderness area. The process gathered pace when the French colonial government began to construct canals and drainage projects to open more land to wet rice agriculture. By the 1930s the population of the delta had reached 4.5 million with 2,200,000 ha of land under rice cultivation. The Mekong Delta, along with the Irrawaddy (Burma) and Chao Phraya (Thailand) became one of the great rice exporting areas of Southeast Asia, shipping over 1.2 million tonnes annually.

Given their proximity to prosperous Ho Chi Minh City the inhabitants of the Mekong Delta might have expected some of the benefits of development to trickle their way: in this they have largely been disappointed. Most of the Mekong Delta provinces are trying and to a degree securing investment into their respective provinces. Be it hotels, cafés, karaoke in Ha Tien to canning and storage plants in Can Tho, they are trying to improve their collective lot. The main problem that they face is that everyone knows that each year during the monsoon season wide areas of the Mekong flood. The government is slowly but surely building up river defences against the annual floods but it is a laborious process.

Tourist services are improving year on year. A series of bridges have opened over the years drastically cutting road travel time to the delta region, but it still takes the best part of a day to get down to Chau Doc. Ho Chi Minh City tour operators run tours to Can Tho, My Tho and Chau Doc and agents within these towns run tours to surrounding sights and organize onward transport. Many local and Ho Chi Minh City operators also arrange boat and bus transport to Phnom Penh, Cambodia.

Phuoc Hung Pagoda ① *75/5 Hung Vuong St*, is a splendid Chinese-style pagoda constructed in 1838 when Sa Dec was a humble one-road village. Surrounded by ornamental gardens, lotus ponds and cypress trees, the main temple to the right is decorated with fabulous animals assembled from pieces of porcelain rice bowls. Inside are some marvellous wooden statues of Buddhist figures made in 1838 by the venerable sculptor Cam. There are also some superbly preserved gilded wooden beams and two antique prayer tocsins. The smaller one was made in 1888 and its resounding mellow tone changes with the weather. The West Hall contains a valuable copy of the 101 volume Great Buddhist Canon. There are also some very interesting and ancient photos of dead devotees and of pagoda life in the past.

A few kilometres west of Sa Dec is the **Tu Ton Rose Garden (Vuon Hong Tu Ton)** ① *28 Vuon Hong St, Khom 3, Ward 3, T67-376 1685, 0600-2000, free*. The garden is next to a lemon yellow building with yellow gates. This 6000-ha nursery borders the river and is home to more than 40 varieties of rose and 540 other types of plant, from medicinal herbs to exotic orchids. Wander amid the potted hibiscus, beds of roses and bougainvillea and enjoy the visiting butterflies.

Tourist information

Dong Thap Tourist Company
Based at the Huynh Thuy Le Old House, T67-377 3937, www.dongthaptourist.com, is a contact here; its main office is in Cao Lanh.
Trips to Xeo Quit and Cao Lanh organized.

Where to stay

$ Bong Hong
251A Nguyen Sinh Sac St, T67-386 8287, bonghonghotel@yahoo.com.vn.
Massive hotel a short distance before the bus station on Highway 80 leading into town. Some good-value a/c rooms with TV and fridge. Cheaper rooms have fan and cold water only. Breakfast not included. Tennis court on site.

$ Nha Co Huynh Thuy Le
255A Nguyen Hue St, Ward 2, T67-377 3937.
Run by **Dong Thap Tourist**, this lovely home has 4 fan rooms with 2 single beds in each and would be the most enjoyable way to spend time in Sa Dec. The 2 front rooms are much more attractive than the plain 2 back rooms with stained-glass windows and carved wooden doors. The shared bathroom is at the back with cold water. The price includes breakfast and dinner. See also Restaurants, below.

Restaurants

$ Cay Sung
2/4 Hung Vuong St. Open all day.
It serves a good selection of rice dishes. There is a menu in English available.

$ Nha Co Huynh Thuy Le
255A Nguyen Hue St, Ward 2, T67-377 3937.
Run by **Dong Thap Tourist**, reserve a day in advance for the chance to dine in the home of Marguerite Duras' lover.

Transport

The bus station is about 500 m southeast of town on the main road just before the bridge. Buses to **Vinh Long** and **Long Xuyen** leave from here. The town is 143 km from HCMC and 102 km from Chau Doc, and 20 km from Vinh Long along Highway 80.

Cao Lanh for many years was a small, underdeveloped Mekong town. However, since becoming the capital of Dong Thap Province, an honour previously bestowed on Sa Dec, it has changed and has become a thriving market town. It also benefits from being the closest main city to Xeo Quyt base (Rung Cham forest), and Tram Chim National Park and its bird sanctuary, which are main tourist attractions. In fact, the excursions are the only real reason to visit Cao Lanh.

Sights

To the northeast along Nguyen Hue Street is the war memorial, containing the graves of Vietnamese who fell in the war with the USA. The **tomb of Ho Chi Minh's father** ⓘ *Nguyen Sinh Sac (Tham Quan Khu Di Tich Nguyen Sinh Sac), next to Quan Nam restaurant at 137 Pham Huu Lau St, open 0700-1130, 1330-1700, small fee*, is set under a shell structure and sits in front of a lotus pond. A small stilt-house museum sits in the tranquil grounds.

The vast **Plain of Reeds (Dong Thap Muoi)** is a swamp that extends for miles north towards Cambodia, particularly in the late monsoon season (September to November). It is an important wildlife habitat (see below) but in the wet season, when the water levels rise, getting about on dry land can be a real problem. Extraordinarily, the Vietnamese have not adapted the stilt house solution used by the Khmer and every year become flooded. In the rural districts houses are built on the highest land available and in a good year the floor will be just inches above the lapping water. At these times all transport is by boat. When the sky is grey the scene is desolate and the isolation of the plain can truly feel like the end of the Earth has been reached. Tower Mound (Go Thap) is the best place from which to get a view of the immensity and beauty of the surrounding Plain of Reeds. There was a watchtower here although no one seems sure if it was 10-storeys high or the last in a chain of 10 towers. There are earthworks from which General Duong and Admiral Kieu conducted their resistance against the French between 1861 and 1866.

★**Tram Chim National Park (Tam Nong Bird Sanctuary)** ⓘ *T67-382 7436*, is an 8000-ha reserve 45 km northwest of Cao Lanh. It contains around 220 species of bird at various times of year, but most spectacular is the red-headed crane (sarus), rarest of the world's 15 crane species. Between August and November these spectacular creatures migrate across the nearby Cambodian border to avoid the floods (cranes feed on land), but at any other time, and particularly at dawn and dusk, they are a magnificent sight. Floating rice is grown in the area around the bird sanctuary and although the acreage planted diminishes each year this is another of nature's truly prodigious feats. The leaves float on the surface while the roots are anchored in mud as much as 4-5 m below; but as so much energy goes into growing the stalk little is left over for the ears of rice, so yields are low.

Tourist information

Dong Thap Tourist Co
2 Doc Binh Kieu St, T67-385 5637,
www.dongthaptourist.com.
Mon-Sat 0700-1130, 1330-1700.
Some staff have a reasonable command
of English and are helpful.

Where to stay

$$$-$ Song Tra
178 Nguyen Hue St, T67-385 2624,
www.dongthaptourist.com.
A rather basic hotel, but Cao Lanh is
short on better options. The rooms
come equipped with a/c, satellite TV
and en suite facilities.

$ Binh Minh Hotel
157 Hung Vuong St, T67-385 3423.
A good little hotel but note that it's
actual entrance is not on Hung Vuong,
it is just around the corner on Do
Cong Tuong St. The owner, a local
schoolteacher, is friendly and helpful.
If you are travelling solo or on a budget
then this would be a good choice. Fan
and a/c rooms.

Restaurants

The restaurants in Song Tra, Xuan Mai
and Hoa Binh hotels are all open for
breakfast, lunch and dinner. There is
not much difference in their quality,
presentation choice and value.

$ A Chau
Ly Thuong Kiet St. Open 0800-2100.
Specializes in fried pancakes.

$ Hong Nhien
143 Hung Vuong St, behind the Song
Tra Hotel.
Serves *com tam* and *hu tieu* in a simple
set up.

What to do

Birdwatching at the nearby sanctuaries
is the most common activity. It is also
possible to hire boats from **Dong Thap**
Tourist Company, 2 Doc Binh Kieu St,
T67-385 5637. Dong Thap also organizes
trips to the mausoleum of Nguyen Sinh
Sac, Xeo Quyt, Sa Dec and the Gao Giong
Eco-tourism Zone.

Transport

The bus station is located at the corner
of Ton That Tung and Doc Binh Kieu St.
Connections with all delta towns. To
HCMC from the bus station on Vo Thi
Sau St and Nguyen Van Troi St, 3 hrs.

Can Tho
& around

floating markets and river trips

Can Tho is a large and rapidly growing commercial city lying chiefly on the west bank of the Can Tho River. Capital of Can Tho Province and the region's principal transport hub, it is also one of the most welcoming of the delta towns and launch pad for trips to see some of the region's floating markets. South of Can Tho are the towns of Soc Trang, Bac Lieu and Ca Mau.

Can Tho → *Colour map 4, B2.*

the largest city in the heart of the delta

A small settlement was established at Can Tho at the end of the 18th century, although the town did not prosper until the French took control of the delta a century later and rice production for export began to take off. Despite the city's rapid recent growth there are still strong vestiges of French influence apparent in the broad boulevards flanked by flame trees, as well as many elegant buildings. Can Tho was also an important US base.

Sights
Hai Ba Trung Street, alongside the river, is the heart of the town; at dusk families stroll in the park here in their Sunday best. Opposite the park is **Chua Ong Pagoda** ① *34 Hai Ba Trung St*, dating from 1894 and built by Chinese from Guangzhou. Unusually for a Chinese temple it is not free-standing but part of a terrace of buildings. The right-hand side of the pagoda is dedicated to the Goddess of Fortune, while the left-hand side belongs to General Ma Tien, who, to judge from his unsmiling statue, is fierce and warlike and not to be trifled with. The layout is a combination of typical pagoda – with a small open courtyard for the incense smoke to escape – and typical meeting house, complete with its language school, of the overseas Chinese in Southeast Asia.

The bustling market that used to operate on Hai Ba Trung Street along the bank of the river, and gave the town a bit of character, has been moved 1 km downriver.

Essential Can Tho and around

Getting around

Some of the sites, the floating markets for instance, are best visited by boat. There are also river taxis and an efficient public bus service.

When to go

As in all the other Mekong cities the best time is from December to April when the temperatures are warm and there is no rain. May to November is the monsoon season and as such it is prone to flooding (although it does fare better than other cities).

Time required

Two days is enough.

A new riverside promenade has been created. There's also a new crafts market building with a riverside restaurant, see Restaurants, page 314.

Munirang-syaram Pagoda ① *36 Hoa Binh Blvd (southwest of post office)*, was built just after the Vietnam War and is a Khmer Hinayana Buddhist sanctuary. **Bao Tang Can Tho** ① *Hoa Binh St, Tue-Thu 0800-1100, 1400-1700, Sat-Sun 0800-1100, 1830-2100*, in an impressive building, is the local history museum.

Binh Thuy Temple ① *7 km north along the road to Long Xuyen*, dates from the mid-19th century; festivals are held here in the middle of the fourth and 12th lunar months. Nearby, 500 m down Bui Huu Nghia Road, opposite Binh Thuy temple, visit **Nha Co Binh Thuy aka the ancient house** ① *10,000d to go inside the house* (also known as Vuon Lan if you get a moto to take you there), which was used as a setting in the film The Lover.

★Floating markets
The daily markets are busiest at around 0600-0900. Women with sampans to rent will approach travellers in Hai Ba Trung St near the market waving a book of testimonials from previous satisfied customers. A trip of at least 5 hrs is recommended to see the landscape at a leisurely pace. If you take a larger boat you will not be able to manoeuvre in and out of the market.

There are boat trips to the floating markets at Phung Hiep, 33 km away (an eight-hour round trip by sampan or take a bus to Phung Hiep and rent a boat there) and Phong Dien, 15 km down the Can Tho River (a five-hour trip). Cai Rang is 7 km away and is easy to visit for those with only a couple of hours to spare.

Bustling affairs, the vendors attach a sample of their wares to a bamboo pole to attract customers. Up to seven vegetables can be seen dangling from staffs – wintermelon, pumpkin, spring onions, giant parsnips, grapefruit, garlic, mango, onions and Vietnamese plums. Housewives paddle their sampans from boat to boat and barter, haggle and gossip in the usual way. At the back of the boats, the domesticity of life on the water is in full glare – washing is hung out and motors are stranded high above the water. Orchards and gardens abound; small sampans are best as they can negotiate the narrowest canals to take the visitor into the heart of the area, a veritable Garden of Eden. Phung Hiep also features yards making traditional fishing boats and rice barges.

Where to stay

$$$$ Victoria Can Tho Resort
Cai Khe ward, T710-381 0111,
www.victoriahotels.asia.

A 92-room riverside hotel set in lovely, well-tended garden on its own little peninsula. It is Victoria Hotel 'French colonial' style at its best with a breezy open reception area and emphasis on comfort and plenty of genuine period features. It has a pool, spa pavilion, tennis court and restaurant. The staff are multilingual and helpful. The a/c rooms are well decorated and have satellite TV, Wi-Fi, en suite facilities, decent-sized bathtub, well-stocked minibar and electronic safe in the room. Even if you decide to stay in a more centrally and somewhat cheaper hotel then a visit to the grounds and one of the restaurants would be a pleasant experience. The hotel offers a complimentary boat shuttle to the town centre.

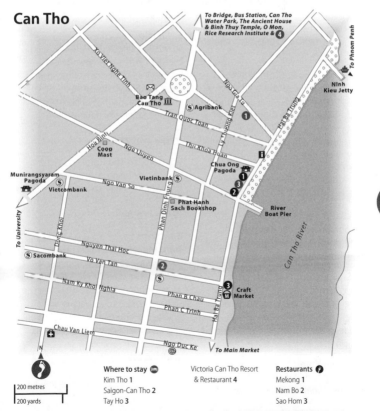

Can Tho

To Bridge, Bus Station, Can Tho Water Park, The Ancient House & Binh Thuy Temple, O Mon, Rice Research Institute & **4**

To Phnom Penh

Ninh Kieu Jetty

To Phnom Penh

Xo Viet Nghe Tinh

Ngo Gia tu

Hai Ba Trung

Bao Tang Can Tho

Ⓢ Agribank **1**

Tran Quoc Toan

Hoa Binh

Coop Mast

Ngo Uuyen

Thi Khoa Huan

Munirangsyaram Pagoda

Ⓢ Vietcombank

Ngo Van So

Vietinbank Ⓢ

Chua Ong Pagoda **1**

3
2

To University

Dong Khoi

Phan Dinh Phung

Phat Hanh Sach Bookshop

River Boat Pier

Can Tho River

Nguyen Thai Hoc

Ⓢ Sacombank

Vo Van Tan

2

Nam Ky Khoi Nghia

Ⓢ

Phan B Chau

3 Craft Market Ⓜ

Hai Ba Trung

Phan C Trinh

Chau Van Liem

Ngo Duc Ke

To Main Market

N

200 metres
200 yards

Where to stay 🛏
Kim Tho **1**
Saigon-Can Tho **2**
Tay Ho **3**

Victoria Can Tho Resort & Restaurant **4**

Restaurants 🍴
Mekong **1**
Nam Bo **2**
Sao Hom **3**

$$ Kim Tho
14 Ngo Gia Tu St, T710-322 2228,
www.kimtho.com.
A lovely if a little dated hotel with some rooms offering great river views. Very welcoming and plenty of character. The standout attraction is the roof-top café with fabulous views. Includes breakfast.

$ Saigon-Can Tho
55 Phan Dinh Phung St, T710-382 5831,
www.saigoncantho.com.vn.
A/c, comfortable, central business hotel in the competent hands of Saigontourist. The staff are friendly and helpful. The rooms are well equipped with a/c, satellite TV, en suite facilities and minibar. There's a currency exchange, free internet and Wi-Fi for guests, sauna and breakfast included.

$ Tay Ho
42 Hai Ba Trung St, T710-382 3392,
tay_ho@hotmail.com.
This lovely place has a variety of rooms and a great public balcony that can be enjoyed by those paying for back rooms. All rooms now have private bathrooms. River view rooms cost more. The staff are friendly.

Restaurants

Hai Ba Trung St by the river offers a good range of excellent and very well-priced little restaurants, and the riverside setting is an attractive one.

$$$-$$ Victoria Can Tho Spices
See Where to stay.
Excellent location on the riverbank where it's possible to dine alfresco or inside its elegant restaurant. The food is delicious and the service is excellent.

$$-$ Sao Hom
Nha Long Cho Co, T710-381 5616,
http://saohom.transmekong.com.
This new and very busy restaurant on the riverfront serves plentiful food and provides very good service. Watching the river life and the floating pleasure palaces at night is a good way to spend an evening meal here. Shame about the illuminated billboards on the opposite bank. This place is popular with large tour groups that alter the character of the restaurant when they swarm in.

$ Mekong
38 Hai Ba Trung St.
Perfectly good little place near the river in this popular restaurant strip. Serves decent Vietnamese fare at reasonable prices.

$ Nam Bo
50 Hai Ba Trung St, T710-382 3908.
Excellent little place serving tasty Vietnamese and French dishes in an attractive French house on the corner of the street; try to get a table on the balcony. Small café downstairs.

Bars and clubs

The **Golf Can Tho Hotel** and **Victoria Can Tho Hotel** have well-stocked bars (see Where to stay, above).

What to do

Boat trips
Trans Mekong, *97/10 Ngo Quyen, P An Cu, T710-382 9540, www.transmekong. com.* Operates the *Bassac*, a converted 24-m wooden rice barge that can sleep 12 passengers in 6 a/c cabins with private bathrooms. Prices include dinner and breakfast, entry tickets to visited sites, a French- or English-speaking guide on board and access to a small boat, *Bassac II*, catering for 24 guests. The Victoria Can Tho operates the

Lady Hau, an upmarket converted rice barge for trips to the floating markets.

Cookery classes
The Victoria Can Tho, *see Where to stay.* Offers a Vietnamese cooking class in the hotel, in a rice field, at the 'Ancient House' or on its boat the *Lady Hau* with a trip to the local market.

Swimming
The Victoria Can Tho (see Where to stay, above) has a pool open to the public for a fee.

Tennis
Tennis courts are available at the **Golf Hotel** and **Victoria Can Tho** (see Where to stay).

Therapies
The Victoria Can Tho boasts several massage cabins on the riverfront offering a host of treatments. Open to non-guests.

Tour operators
Can Tho Tourist, *20 Hai Ba Trung St, T710-382 1852, http://canthotourist.vn.* Organizes tours in small and larger

boats – the latter not the best way to see the delta. The staff are helpful and knowledgeable. Tours include trips to Cai Rang, Phong Dien and Phung Hiep floating markets, to Soc Trang, city tours, canal tours, bicycle tours, trekking tours, stork sanctuary tour and homestays that involve working with farmers in the fields. General boat tours also arranged. **Victoria Can Tho**, *T710-381 0111, www. victoriahotels.asia.* Expensive tours to see delta sights; city tour; floating markets and Soc Trang offered. The *Lady Hau* cruises to Cai Rang floating market (breakfast on board). Sunset cruises also possible.

Transport

Air
Vietnam Airlines 66 Chau Van Liem St. The airport is situated about 7 km from the city centre. Flights to **Hanoi**.

Bicycle
Bikes can be hired for from **Can Tho Tourist**, see Tour operators above.

Boat
A bridge has been built to Can Tho but ferries will still operate for direct

routing as the bridge is 10 km from Can Tho. There are no public boats leaving Can Tho.

Bus
The bus station is about 2 km northwest of town along Nguyen Trai St, at the intersection with Hung Vuong St. Hourly connections to **HCMC**'s Mien Tay terminal, 4-5 hrs (**Phuong Trang** bus company, T710-376 9768, provides a good service), and other towns in the Mekong Delta: **Rach Gia**, 0400-1800, 5 hrs; **Chau Doc**, 8 daily, 4 hrs; **Long Xuyen**, 6 daily; **My Tho**, hourly; **Vinh Long**, hourly, 55,000d; **Ca Mau**, hourly Soc Trang. **Can Tho Tourist**, see Tour operators, above, will book a ticket for you for a small fee and include transfer from your hotel to the bus station.

Car
Cars with drivers can be hired from larger hotels.

Taxi
Mai Linh Taxi, T710-382 8282.

Bac Lieu → *Colour map 4, C2.*

Bac Lieu is a small and pretty riverside city and the provincial capital of Bac Lieu Province. New hotels and buildings are being erected and they are trying to capture some of the lucrative Tra Vinh market (there are many Khmer living here and several temples). Bac Lieu has a bird sanctuary that has large numbers of white herons.

It is not as rich in rice production as other Mekong provinces on account of its proximity to the sea, so the enterprising locals have salt farms instead. They also make a living out of oysters and fishing. Life has always been hard in the province due to saltwater intrusion.

Sights
The **bird sanctuary**, 3 km southwest of town, is home to a large white heron population. The best times to visit are December and January. The birds nest in January and then migrate and do not return until late May. Do apply plenty of mosquito repellent as the place is inundated with biting insects.

Xiem Can Temple (Komphir Sakor Prekchru) ① *12 km west of Bac Lieu, free to enter but alms would be appreciated*, is a pretty Khmer temple complex. It was built in 1887 and a small group of monks still resides here.

Hoi Binh Moi Temple (Resay Vongsaphuth lethmay) is one of the newer temples, constructed in 1952. A recent addition (1990) is the ossuary tower. There is a small monastic school attached to the temple.

Tourist information

Bac Lieu Tourist Company
*2 Hoang Van Thu St, T781-382 4272,
www.baclieutourist.com.*
Has a reasonable selection of quite
moderately priced tours.

Where to stay

$$ Cong Tu Bac Lieu
*13 Dien Bien Phu St, T781-395 3304,
http://congtubaclieu.vn/.*
A stunning French colonial home that
has undergone a rather over the top
sprucing up. Its ochre front with duck
egg blue shutters looks out over the
river. There's fanciful stucco work and
elaborate tiling throughout.

$ Bac Lieu Hotel
*4-6 Hoang Van Thu St, T781-382 2437,
baclieuhotel@yahoo.com.*
Very basic, but very cheap lodgings.

Restaurants

Bac Lieu hotel has reasonable restaurants
for breakfast, lunch and dinner.

$ Cong Tu Bac Lieu
This compound is popular all day. Serves
up Vietnamese food in the surrounds of
a colonial mansion.

Festivals

Late Nov/early Dec The main festival in
the area is the **Ngo boat racing**, which
is held in Soc Trang, 70 km north of Bac
Lieu, at the same time as the **Soc Trang
Oc Om Boc festival**.

Tip...
If you wish to see the boat races in
a more relaxed atmosphere then
base yourself in Bac Lieu, just over
an hour's drive away.

Transport

Bac Lieu is 70 km from Soc Trang,
113 km from Can Tho, 287 km from
Ho Chi Minh City and 67 km from
Ca Mau. The roads have improved
but it is a long drive.
   Buses go to **Soc Trang**, **Can Tho**,
HCMC, **Ca Mau** and **Long Xuyen**
from the station on Hai Ba Trung St.

Ca Mau Province → *Colour map 4, C2.*

an area of interest to botanists and ornithologists

Ca Mau is the provincial capital of Ca Mau Province, Vietnam's most southerly
province, and is a huge, ugly, cluttered urban sprawl. The province consists
primarily of the U Minh cajeput forest and swamp, both of which are the largest
in Vietnam. Right at the tip of the country is the new Mui Ca Mau National Park.
Apart from a reasonable selection of churches and pagodas Ca Mau's main
attractions interest botanists and ornithologists.

Cao Mau

A **Cao Dai Temple** is located on Phan Ngoc Hien Street. Although not as large as the main one in Tay Ninh it is still an impressive structure. It houses quite a few monks and is thriving. The monks will be happy to explain Cao Daism.

U Minh Forest

U Minh Forest is the main reason most people visit Ca Mau. It was a favoured hiding place for the Viet Cong troops during the war. Despite the chemical damage and the huge postwar deforestation to make way for shrimp farms there are still trees and large numbers of birds to be seen and it is a favourite destination for ornithologists. It is also of interest to botanists. **Minh Hai Tourist** operates an all-day tour of the forest and mangrove swamps for US$52 per person including tour guide, car and ticket. Note that tours may be off limits from May to October due to forest fires. In the monsoon season flooding occurs on a regular basis. December to February should be the best months to visit.

Mui Ca Mau National Park

Mui Ca Mau National Park, at the southern edge of the country, has been named a UNESCO World Biosphere Reserve. The 41,862-ha park of mangrove and mudflats is home to hundreds of animals and birds. Some of the birds include the Far Eastern curlew, Chinese egret and black-headed ibis.

Listings Ca Mau

Tourist information

Du Lick Ca Mau
91 Phan Ngoc Hien St, T780-383 1828, www.dulichcamau.com. Mon-Fri 0730-1100, 1330-1700, Sat 0730-1100.
A well-run and professional travel agency offering the full spectrum of services.

Where to stay

$ Dong Anh
25 Tran Hung Dao.
Probably the best option in town with very clean rooms and decent beds.

$ Quoc Te
179 Phan Ngoc Hien St, T780-366 6666, www.hotelquocte.com.
Ca Mau is short on good options which makes this rather average budget hotel a reasonable option, but don't expect great things.

Restaurants

There are plenty of very cheap restaurants close to the market on Ly Bon St.

$ Hu Tieu Nam Vang
2C Tran Hung Dao St, diagonally opposite Hoang Gia hotel.
Cheap and friendly and serving *hu tieu*.

$ Trieu Phat
26 Phan Ngoc Hien St.
Serves *com* and hu *tieu*.

Transport

There are direct flights from Ho Chi Minh City, bus connections and a boat from Rach Gia. The city has plenty of taxis and river taxis and a public bus service.

Air
The airport is located at 93 Ly Thuong Kiet St heading out of town. Flights to **HCMC**.

Boat
It is possible to take a daily ferry from Ca Mau to **Rach Gia**, from Ferry Pier B (located off Cao Thang St near the floating market).

Bus
Ca Mau is almost at the end of Highway 1A. Bac Lieu, Soc Trang and onwards connection to Can Tho are along Highway 1A. Rach Gia is reached by Highway 63. Good bus connections to **Can Tho**, **Bac Lieu**, **Soc Trang** and **Rach Gia**. The bus service to **HCMC** takes 11 hrs by regular bus and 8 hrs by express, daily 0530-1030.

Chau Doc
& around

wetland bird sanctuary and a sacred, pagoda-dotted mountain

Chau Doc was once an extremely attractive riverside town on the west bank of the Hau. It still has a pretty riverfront, but the bustling market town is no longer as appealing as it once was. One of its biggest attractions is the nearby Nui Sam, which is dotted with pagodas and tombs. Across the river you can boat over to Cham villages and see the floating fish farms. South of Chau Doc the road passes the sorrowful Ba Chuc ossuary. There are also three international border crossings to Cambodia.

Chau Doc → *Colour map 4, B2.*

an important trading centre for the surrounding agricultural communities

The large market sprawls from the riverfront down and along Le Cong Thanh Doc, Phu Thu, Bach Dang and Chi Lang streets. It sells fresh produce and black-market goods smuggled across from Cambodia.

Near the market and the river, at the intersection of Tran Hung Dao Street and Nguyen Van Thoai Street, is the **Chau Phu Pagoda**. Built in 1926, it is dedicated to Thai Ngoc Hau, a former local mandarin. The pagoda is rather dilapidated, but has some fine carved pillars, which miraculously are still standing. A **Cao Dai temple**, which welcomes visitors, stands on Louise Street.

The **Vinh Te Canal**, north of town, is 90 km long and is a considerable feat of engineering, begun in 1819 and finished in 1824 using 80,000 workers. Its purpose was twofold: navigation and defence from the Cambodians. So impressed was Emperor Minh Mang in the achievement of its builder, Nguyen Van Thoai (or Thoai Ngoc Hau), that he named the canal after Thoai's wife, Chau Thi Vinh Te.

Listings Chau Doc

Where to stay

$$$$-$$$ Victoria Chau Doc
*32 1 Le Loi St, T076-386 5010,
www.victoriahotels-asia.com.*
This old, cream building with its
beautiful riverfront deck and pool
complete with loungers and view of
the river confluence is the perfect place
location in which to relax. All rooms
are attractively decorated. The hotel
group runs a daily speedboat to and
from Phnom Penh. A refined place with
superb service.

$$$$-$$$ Victoria Nui Sam Lodge
Sam Mountain, www.victoriahotels.asia.
A fantastic addition to the area, this
beautiful resort offers 36 bungalows
dotted across the mountain offering
knock-out views. The service is excellent
and the kitchen is first rate. A fantastic
hideaway in the Mekong. Also has
a wonderful swimming pool with
unobstructed views of the paddy fields
stretching as far as the eye can see.
Recommended.

$ Hai Chau hotel
63 Thuong Dang Le St.
A good budget option. The garish
exterior doesn't bode well, but the
rooms are clean and the a/c works well.

Restaurants

$$$ La Bassac
In Victoria Chau Doc.
The French and Vietnamese menus
at this suave riverside restaurant with
stunning terrace include buffalo paillard
with shallot confit, basa in banana leaf

with saffron, rack of lamb coated in
Mekong herbs, sweet potato puree and
pork wine reduction or spaghetti with
flambéed shrimps in vodka paprika
sauce. The bar is a lovely spot for a pre-
dinner drink.

$$ Thanh Thao
74 Trung Nu Vuong T073-869095.
Serves a huge selection of fresh seafood,
including crab, squid and lobster. A
no-nonsense eatery that's very popular
with locals.

$ Bay Bong
22 Thung Dang Le St, T076-386 7271.
Specializes in hot pots and soups and
also offers a good choice of fresh fish.
The staff are friendly.

A gift for Phuc Khoat

Until the mid-18th century Chau Doc was part of Cambodia: it was given to the Nguyen lord, Nguyen Phuc Khoat, after he had helped to put down a local insurrection. The area still supports a large Khmer population, as well as the largest Cham settlement in the delta. Cambodia's influence can be seen in the tendency for women to wear the *kramar*, Cambodia's famous chequered scarf, instead of the *non la* conical hat, and in the people's darker skin, indicating Khmer blood.

$ Mekong
41 Le Loi St, T076-386 7381, opposite Victoria Chau Doc. Open for lunch and dinner.
It is located right beside a in a lovingly restored French villa. Good selection of food including grilled prawns and fried rice dishes and the staff are friendly.

$ Sunrise Palace
Next to the tourist pier. Open 1100-2230.
The beef in Chau Doc is probably the best in Vietnam and here the *bo nuong* (grilled beef), served with herbs, is excellent. Good *de nuong* (goat) too. Serves delicious Russian live beer that goes perfectly with the food. The outdoor seating is best – inside is a wedding venue space.

Bars and clubs

Victoria Chau Doc
See Where to stay, above.
Has a bar and a pool table.

Festivals

On all almost every weekend there is one festival or another. The busiest festivals are centred on Tet, 4 months after Tet and the mid-autumn moon festival.

What to do

Swimming
There is a swimming pool at the **Victoria Chau Doc**.

Therapies
A massage and fitness centre can be found at the **Victoria Chau Doc**. All the services are available to the general public.

Tour operators
Mekong Tours, *Vinh Phuoc Hotel, and 14 Nguyen Huu Canh St, T076-386 8222, and at Thanh Nam 2 hotel.* Local trips include the fish farms, floating markets and Cham village. Trips to Phu Quoc and boat trips to Phnom Penh (8-10 hrs or express boat 5 hrs; Cambodian visas can be bought at the border). A/c and public buses also booked to Ha Tien. Open Tour Bus ticketing and visa applications. Private boats can be arranged, but this is now rare so prices are not set.
Victoria Chau Doc, *32 Le Loi St, T76-386 5010, www.victoriahotels-asia.com.*
Tours to Nui Sam, the city and a very interesting tour to the floating market, fish farms and Muslim village, cooking class, Tra Su forest tour, farming tour and Le Jarai cruise tour. Minimum 2 people for all tours.

Transport

It is possible (but expensive) to get to Chau Doc by boat from Can Tho (private charter only or by the Victoria Hotel group boat for guests only). Road connections with Can Tho, Vinh Long and Ho Chi Minh City are good.

Boat
There are daily departures to **Phnom Penh**. A couple of tour operators in town organize boat tickets, see Tour operators, above. **Victoria Hotel** speedboats go to Phnom Penh. Make sure you have a valid Vietnamese visa if you are entering the country as these cannot be issued at the

border crossing; Cambodian visas can be bought at all the nearby crossings.

Bus
The station is 3 km south from the town centre T76-386 7171. Minibuses stop in town on Quang Trung St. Connections with **HCMC** (6 hrs), hourly, 0600-2400; **Tra Vinh**; **Ca Mau**; **Long Xuyen**; **Can Tho**, every 30 mins; **Rach Gia**; and **Ha Tien**. There is an uncomfortable 10-hr bus ride from Chau Doc to Phnom Penh via Moc Bai, see page 275.

Mekong Tours, see Tour operators, runs a bus to **Phnom Penh** via Tinh Bien (see border crossings to Cambodia, page 275).

Around Chau Doc → *Colour map 4, B1-B2.*

a mountain, mosques and fish farms

★Nui Sam (Sam Mountain)
Take a bus (there is a stop at the foot of the mountain) or xe om.

This mountain, about 5 km southwest of town, was designated a 'Famed Beauty Spot' in 1980 by the Ministry of Culture and is one of the holiest sites in southern Vietnam. Rising from the flood plain, Nui Sam is a favourite spot for Vietnamese tourists who throng here, especially at festival time.

The mountain, really a barren, rock-strewn hill, can be seen at the end of the continuation of Nguyen Van Thoai Street. It is honeycombed with tombs, sanctuaries and temples. Most visitors come only to see Tay An Pagoda, Lady Xu Temple, and the tomb of Thoai Ngoc Hau (see below). But it is possible to walk or drive right up the hill for good views of the surrounding countryside: from the summit it is easy to appreciate that this is some of the most fertile land in Vietnam. At the top is a military base, formerly occupied by American soldiers and now by Vietnamese watching their Cambodian flank. Near the top the Victoria Hotel group has built a hotel used for conferences only.

Tay An Pagoda is at the foot of the hill, facing the road. Built originally in 1847, it has been extended twice and now represents an eclectic mixture of styles – Chinese, Islamic, perhaps even Italian. The pagoda contains a bewildering display of more than 200 statues.

A short distance on from the pagoda, to the right, past shops and stalls, is the **Chua Xu**. This temple was originally constructed in the late 19th century, and then rebuilt in 1972. It is rather a featureless building, though highly revered by the Vietnamese and honours the holy Lady Xu whose statue is enshrined in the new multi-roofed pagoda. The 23rd to the 25th of the fourth lunar month is the period when the holy Lady is commemorated, during which time, hundreds of Vietnamese flock to see her being washed and reclothed. Lady Xu is a major pilgrimage for traders and business from Ho Chi Minh City and the south, all hoping that sales will thereby soar and profits leap.

On the other side of the road is the **tomb of Thoai Ngoc Hau** (1761-1829); an enormous head of the man graces the entranceway. Thoai is a local hero having played a role in the resistance against the French but more for his engineering feats in canal building and draining swamps. He is also known as Nguyen Van Thoai and this name is given to one of Chau Doc's streets. The real reason to come here is to watch the pilgrims and to climb the hill.

Hang Pagoda, a 200-year-old temple situated halfway up Nui Sam, is worth visiting for several reasons. In the first level of the temple are some vivid cartoon drawings of the tortures of hell. The second level is built at the mouth of a cave which last century was home to a woman named Thich Gieu Thien. Her likeness and tomb can be seen in the first pagoda. Fed up with her lazy and abusive husband she left her home in Cholon and came to live in this cave, as an ascetic supposedly waited on by two snakes.

Nui Sam is the most expensive burial site in southern Vietnam. Wealthy Vietnamese and Chinese believe it is a most propitious last resting place. This is why the lower flanks are given over almost entirely to tombs.

Cham villages

There are a number of Cham villages around Chau Doc. **Phu Hiep**, **Con Tien** and **Chau Giang** are on the opposite bank of the Hau River. There are several mosques in the villages as the Cham in this part of Vietnam are Muslim. At Chau Phong visitors can enjoy homestays. To reach the villages, take a sampan from the ferry terminal near the Victoria Chau Doc Hotel.

A visit to the floating fish farm villages (some 3000 floating houses), such as **Con Tien**, is a worthwhile and informative experience. A floating farm will have some 150,000 carp contained in a 6-m-deep iron cage beneath the house. Fish are worth around 600d for a baby and up to 25,000d for 500 g for a five-month-old fish. Catfish and mullet are also raised. (Chau Doc has a catfish monument on the riverfront promenade.) When the fish are ready for sale, boats with nets under them are used to transport the fish to Long Xuyen.

Border crossings to Cambodia

It is possible to cross the border to Cambodia north of Chau Doc at the **Vinh Xuong** (Omsano in Cambodia) boat crossing; just south of Chau Doc at **Tinh Bien** near Nha Ban (Phnom Den, Takeo, on the Cambodian side), and at **Xà Xía**, near Ha Tien (Prek Chak in Cambodia). It is possible to exit at Vinh Xuong and get a Cambodian visa but it's not possible to get a Vietnamese visa to enter Vietnam. At Tinh Bien you can buy a Cambodian visa but not a Vietnamese visa on entering. At Xà Xía, you can get a Cambodian visa but not a Vietnamese visa. There is a Vietnam consulate in Sihanoukville.

Chau Doc to Ha Tien

Ha Tien can be reached either by boat or by road. The scenery as the road skirts the Cambodian border is beautiful and the local way of life little changed in hundreds of years. The road passes Ba **Chuc ossuary** where the bones of 1000 Vietnamese killed in 1978 by the Khmer Rouge are displayed in a glass-sided memorial. Skulls are also stacked up in a glass-sided memorial, and each section is categorized by gender and by age – from children to grandparents. Nearby, there is a house in a small row of shops where photographs of the massacre are displayed; they are grisly and abhorrent.

An alternative route to Ha Tien is to follow Highway 91 to **Nha Ban town**. Turn right and follow the signs to Tri Ton town, along the way you drive through the Plain of Reeds, pass Cam Mountain and also various Khmer temples that are beautiful and thankfully tourist free. Upon arrival in **Tri Ton town** (some of the shops have signs in Khmer script) turn right and head for the Vam Ray ferry. Once across the **Ha Tien-Rach Gia canal** you are on Highway 80. Turn left to **Rach Gia** and right to **Ha Tien**.

Rach Gia → *Colour map 4, B2.*

thriving port with little touristic appeal

Despite Rach Gia having undergone somewhat of a transformation in recent years, from being a rather unpleasant little town to a thriving port with a new urban development on reclaimed land, there isn't much reason for the tourist to linger. Rach Gia is the capital of Kien Giang Province. The wealth of the province is based on rice, seafood and trade. *Nuoc mam*, the renowned Vietnamese fish sauce, is produced here.

Sights

There are a number of pagodas to visit, the wharf area is interesting and the bustling fish market displays the wealth of the seas here. Some attractive colonial architecture survives. The centre of the town is in fact an island at the mouth of the Cai Lon River.

Rach Gia's pagodas include the **Phat Lon Pagoda**, which is on the mainland north of town just off Quang Trung Street, and the **Nguyen Trung Truc Temple**, which is not far away at 18 Nguyen Cong Tru Street, close to the port. The latter is dedicated to the 19th-century Vietnamese resistance leader of the same name. Nguyen Trung Truc was active in Cochin China during the 1860s, and led the raid that resulted in the attack on the French warship *Esperance*. As the French closed in, he retreated to the island of Phu Quoc. From here, the French only managed to dislodge him after threatening to kill his mother. He gave himself up and was executed at the market place in Rach Gia on 27 October 1868. His statue also dominates the main small city park at the top of Le Loi street and the riverbank.

Tam Bao Temple dates from the 18th century but was rebuilt in 1917. During the First Indochina War it was used to conceal Viet Minh nationalists who published a newspaper from here. There is the small **Rach Gia Museum** ⓘ *27 Nguyen Van Troi St, T77-386 3727, Mon-Fri 0700-1100, free*, which houses a good selection of pottery and artefacts from Oc-Eo in a lovely old building.

Listings Rach Gia

Tourist information

Du Lich Kien Giang
392 Lâm Quang Ky, T0939-759 888, www. dulichkiengiang.vn.

Where to stay

$ Hoang Gia 2
32 Le Thanh Ton St, T77-392 0980, www. hoanggiahotels.com.vn.
Located near the bus station, this is a basic budget option.

$ Kim Co
141 Nguyen Hung Son St, T77-387 9610, www.kimcohotel.com.
Good, clean rooms and well located. Wi-Fi available.

Restaurants

There is a good selection of cafés on Nguyen Trung Truc, Nguyen Thai Hoc and Tran Hung Dao. At the centre of the coastal strip is the Lac Hong Park where you'll find food stalls, cafés and the Lagoon Seafood Center as well as dozens of folk flying colourful kites.

$ Hai Au
2 Nguyen Trung Truc St, T77-386 3740.
Good choice of food, well presented in a smart building with a lovely outdoor terraced area covered in creepers overlooking the river.

Festivals

Apart from the main festival they have occasional processions to thank Ca Ong, the God of the Sea, for protecting them.

Transport

There are daily flights from Ho Chi Minh City and Phu Quoc. In the peak season it is advisable to book well in advance as the flights tend to fill up fast. There are good road connections with Ha Tien, Long Xuyen, Can Tho. There are also boats to Phu Quoc.

Air
Daily connections with **Phu Quoc Island**, 40 mins, and **HCMC**, 50 mins. The airport is at Rach Soi about 10 km south of Rach Gia. **Airline offices Vietnam Airlines**, 16 Nguyen Trung Truc St, T77-392 4320.

Boat
Daily connections to **Phu Quoc**, departing from the ferry terminal on Nguyen Cong Tru St. A variety of ferry companies including **Superdong** ferries, T77-387 7742, **Duong Dong Express**, T77-387 9765, www.duongdongexpress. com.vn, and **Savanna** leave daily at 0745-0800 arriving 1030 and 1300. From the Rach Meo ferry terminal, 2 km south of town on Ngo Quyen St close to the junction with Nguyen Van Cu St, boats go to **Vinh Thuan** and **Ca Mau**.

Bus
There are 2 stations; the city centre terminal at Nguyen Binh Kiem St and a terminal at Rach Soi, 7 km south of town near the airport. From the 1st bus station, connections to **HCMC**, 8 hrs, **Can Tho**, **Vinh Long**, **Ha Tien** and **Long Xuyen**. **Mai Linh** and **Phung Trang** companies operate express buses to **HCMC**, 5 hrs. From the 2nd bus station, services to **Chau Doc** and **HCMC**.

Taxi
Mai Linh wait at the Nguyen Truc Trac city park. **Taxi Phuong Trinh**, 26 Nguyen Van Troi St, T77-387 8787.

Oc-Eo

piles of stones is all that is left of this ancient city

The site is near the village of Tan Hoi and is only accessible by boat. Hire a small boat (the approach canal is very shallow and narrow) from the river front beyond the Vinh Tan Van Market, northeast along Bach Dang St. The trip takes several hours.

Oc-Eo is an ancient city about 10 km inland from Rach Gia. It is of great interest and significance to archaeologists, but there is not a great deal for the visitor to see bar a pile of stones on which sits a small bamboo shrine. The site is overseen by an elderly custodian who lives adjacent to it.

This port city of the ancient kingdom of Funan (see page 353) was at its height between the first and sixth centuries AD. Excavations have shown that buildings were constructed on piles and the city was interlinked by a complex network of irrigation and transport canals. Like many of the ancient empires of the region, Oc-Eo built its wealth on controlling trade between the East (China) and the West (India and the Mediterranean). Vessels from Malaya, Indonesia and Persia docked here. No sculpture has yet been found, but a gold medallion with the profile of the Roman emperor Antonius Pius (AD 152) has been unearthed.

Ha Tien → *Colour map 4, B1.*

one-time attractive town now spoiled by development

Ha Tien used to be a quaint small town with a tranquil pace of life and an attractive US-built pontoon bridge that carried bikers and pedestrians across to the opposite bank of the river. However, today hotels clutter the riverbank and there is lots of construction. The boom has no doubt been helped by the opening of the border with Cambodia at Xa Xia. Step back off the main thoroughfare and you will find vestiges of its quaint appeal.

Sights
Despite its colourful history, modern Ha Tien does not contain a great deal of interest to the visitor and apart from a handful of buildings there is little of architectural merit.

Ha Tien's history is strongly coloured by its proximity to Cambodia, to which the area belonged until the 18th century. The numerical and agricultural superiority of the Vietnamese allowed them to gradually displace the Khmer occupants and eventually military might, under Mac Cuu, prevailed. But it is not an argument the Khmer are prepared to walk away from, as their incursions into the area in the late 1970s showed, and bitter resentments remain on both sides of the border.

There are a number of pagodas in town. The **Tam Bao Temple**, at 328 Phuong Thanh Street, was founded in the 18th century, as too was **Chua Phu Dung** (Phu Dung Pagoda), which can be found a short distance along a path to the northwest just off Phuong Thanh Street. A lengthy story is attached to this temple, the 'Cotton Rose Hibiscus Pagoda'. In 1730, newly widowed Nguyen Nghi fled invaders from Laos and landed in Ha Tien with his son and 10-year-old daughter, Phu Cu (the ancient form of Phu Dung with the same floral meaning). Nguyen Nghi was soon appointed Professor of Literature and Poetry to Duke Mac Cuu's son, Mac Tu (see Den Mac Cuu below) and privately tutored his own little daughter, who had taken to dressing as a boy in order to be able to attend school. After Duke Mac Cuu's untimely death in 1735 his son was granted the name Mac Thien Tich and the title Great Admiral Commander-in-Chief, Plenipotentiary Minister of Ha Tien Province. Later he inaugurated a poetry club at which young Phu Cu, still in the guise of a boy, declaimed exquisitely, setting passions ablaze. Surreptitious investigations put the Great Admiral's mind at rest: 'he' was in fact a girl. A long poetic romance and royal wedding followed. After years of happy marriage the angelic Phu Cu one day begged her husband to let her break with their poetic love of the past and become a nun. The Great Admiral realized he could not but comply. He built the Phu Cu, Cotton Rose Hibiscus Pagoda, wherein his beloved wife spent the rest of her life in prayer and contemplation. The towering pagoda was built so high that it served as a constant reminder and could, in due course, be seen from his own tomb.

Den Mac Cuu, the temple dedicated to the worship of the Mac Cuu and his clan, was built in 1898-1902. Mac Cuu was provincial governor under the waning Khmer rule and in 1708 established a Vietnamese protectorate. The temple lies a short way from the town and sits at the foot of Nui Lang (Tomb Mountain). To the left of the altar house is a map showing the location of the tombs of members of the clan. Mac Cuu's own tomb lies a short distance up the hill along a path leading from the right of the temple, from where there are good views of the sea.

Around the back of Nui Lang (a short drive, or longish trek) is **Lang Mo Ba Co Nam** (tomb of Great Aunt Number Five), an honorary title given to the three-year-old daughter of Mac Cuu who was buried alive. It has become an important shrine to Vietnamese seeking her divine intercession in time of family crisis and is more visited than Mac Cuu's tomb.

Tourist information

Ha Tien Tourism Coop Ltd
1 Phuong Thanh St, T77-395 9598,
hatientourism@gmail.com.
Organizes boat tickets to Phu Quoc and
buses to Cambodia and destinations in
the south of Vietnam including Ho Chi
Minh City.

Where to stay

$$$ River Hotel Ha Tien
Tran Hau Business Centre, T077-3955 888,
www.riverhotelvn.com.
Very smart, new riverfront hotels with
high quality rooms, many of which have
excellent views. The best place in town.

$ Du Hung
27A Tran Hau St, T77-395 1555.
A recommended budget hotel with
spacious rooms and all facilities close
to the ferry port.

$ Kim Co 1
141 Nguyen Hun Son.
A good central option with clean rooms
and pleasant staff.

Restaurants

There are numerous food stalls along
the river and Ben Tran Hau and Dong
Ho streets.

$ Ha Tien Floating Restaurant
T77-395 9939.
Quite a nice surprise for Ha Tien
with Australian beef on the menu.

There's a huge menu of chicken, frog
and eel as well as fish. Popular with
local businesspeople.

Cafés

Thuy Tien Café
Nguyen Van Hai St.
This is the pick of the bunch. A small,
stilted affair overlooking the river and
the pontoon bridge. It's a wooden café
from where you can sit and watch the
world go by.

Transport

Ha Tien can be reached by road from
Chau Doc, Rach Gia and also by ferry
from Phu Quoc Island.

Bicycle
Ha Tien Tourism Coop Ltd rents bikes
and motorbikes.

Boat
The ferry wharf is opposite the Ha Tien
hotel. Ferries to **Phu Quoc** leave at 0800-
0830 and at 1000.

Bus
The bus station is on the way to the
Cambodia border on Highyway 80
north of town. There are buses to
HCMC, at 0700, 0800 and 0900, 10-
12 hrs; and connections with **Rach Gia**,
4 hrs; **Chau Doc**; **Can Tho**; as well as
other delta towns. Reliable **Mai Linh**
runs to **Rach Gia**.

Phu Quoc
Island

well worth visiting for a few days' relaxation

★Phu Quoc is Vietnam's largest island with beautiful sandy beaches and crystal-clear waters along much of its coastline and forested hills and pepper plantations inland. The arrival of numerous new resorts and the opening of the new international airport has seen some of its virgin land disappear under concrete, but, for the moment, it remains a wonderful place and still extremely under-developed in comparison to the major Thai islands. *Colour map 4, B1.*

Sights

Duong Dong is the main town on the island and many of the hotels and resorts are near here on **Truong Beach**. Millions of fish can be seen laid out to dry on land and on tables – all destined for the pot. Before being bottled they are fermented. At the **Khai Hoan fish sauce factory** ① *free*, huge barrels act as vats, each containing fish and salt. If the sauce is made in concrete vats, the taste is lost and so the sauce is cheaper.

Coi Nguon Museum ① *149 Tran Hung Dao St, T77-398 0206, www.coinguon phuquoc.com, daily 0700-1700, 1 English-speaking guide*, displays a huge amount of island creatures, fishing paraphernalia, old currency and Chinese ceramics from shipwrecked boats.

The island is also a centre for South Sea pearls, with 10,000 collected offshore each year. At the gloriously kitch **Phu Quoc Pearl Gallery** ① *10 km south of Duong Dong, www.treasuresfromthedeep.com, daily 0800-1800*, a video demonstrates the farming operation, the tasting of pearl meat and pearl-making is illustrated in the gallery. Some 100 m south of the pearl farm on the coastal road there are two whale dedication temples, **Lang Ca Ong**. In front of one is a crude whale/dolphin statue.

Ganh Dau, at the northwest tip, is 35 km from Duong Dong. The townsfolk speak Khmer because refugees escaping the Khmer Rouge came here and settled with the locals. The Cambodian coast is 4-5 km away and can be seen, as can the last island of Vietnam. (The Cambodians actually claim Phu Quoc as their own.)

Essential Phu Quoc Island

Getting around

While some of the island's roads are surfaced many are still dirt tracks and so the best way to get around the entire island is by motorbike. There are plenty of motorbike taxis and motorbikes are easily available and cheap to hire. The only problem that visitors are likely to encounter is the very limited signposting, which can make some places pretty hard to find without some form of local assistance. Cars with drivers at fairly reasonable costs are available. Ask at hotels.

When to go

The best time to visit is December to May; during the monsoon seas on the east coast can be very rough.

Time required

Popular weekend destination, but take a few more days to fully explore the interior and take boat trips to outlying islands.

Best beaches

Ganh Dau, page 330
Bai Dai, page 331
Sao, page 331

Where to stay

During peak periods, such as Christmas and Tet, it is advisable to book accommodation well in advance. Most of the resorts lie along the west coast to the south of Duong Dong and are within a few kilometres of the airport. Others are on On Lang Beach.

The beach has a few palms and rocks to clamber on and there is a restaurant.

Bai Dai Beach, south of Ganh Danh, is a strip of white sand backed by casuarinas overlooking Turtle Island. Inland from here the area is heavily forested but the wood is protected by law. In this part of the island fish are laid out to dry on large trestle-tables or on the ground for use as fertilizer. South of Dai Beach is **Ong Lang Beach** where there are a couple of resorts, see Where to stay.

The dazzling white sands of **Sao Beach** on the southeast coast are stunning and worth visiting by motorbike. There are a couple of restaurants at the back of the beach.

The inland streams and waterfalls (Da Ban and Chanh streams) are not very dramatic in the dry season but still provide a relaxing place to swim and walk in the forests.

One of the biggest draws are the boat trips around the **An Thoi islands**, scattered islands, like chips off a block, off the southern coast, which offer opportunities for swimming, snorkelling, diving and fishing. It is also possible to stop off to visit an interesting fishing village at Thom Island.

Listings Phu Quoc Island *map p332*

$$$$ Chen Sea Resort & Spa
Ong Lang Beach, T077-399 5895, www.centarahotelsresorts.com/cpv.
A very inviting resort with lovely villas set back from the yellow sand beach with sunken bathtubs on generous verandas and outdoor rain showers. The narrow strip of golden sand is dotted with paprika-coloured umbrellas, and there's an infinity pool, spa, water sports and

atmospheric restaurant. Excellent buffet breakfast – don't miss the addictive smoothies. Highly recommended.

$$$$ La Veranda
Tran Hung Dao St, Long Beach, T077-398 2988, www.laverandaresort.com.
A beautiful luxury resort with rooms and villas set in luscious gardens leading on to the main beach on the island. All rooms are beautifully furnished and come with TV, DVD player and Wi-Fi. De luxe rooms and villas come with gorgeous 4-poster beds and drapes. There's a spa, pool and the delicious food of the Pepper Tree Restaurant. The welcome and service is exceptional.

Phu Quoc Island

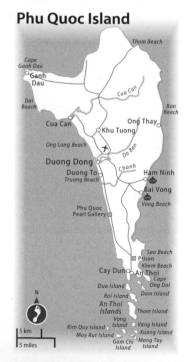

$$$$-$$$ Mai House Resort
Long Beach, T077-384 7003, maihouseresort@yahoo.com.
This is a beautiful resort run by the lovely Tuyet Mai and her husband. The architecture and design is all Mai's work – tasteful with plenty of attention to detail. Set in large flourishing gardens in front of a delicious slice of beach dotted with palms. The 20 a/c bungalows feature 4-poster beds, beamed roofs, pretty tiled bathrooms and balconies with carved balustrades. Sea-view rooms are bigger. Adjoining bungalows available for families. The open fronted small restaurant (with Wi-Fi access and places to lounge) overlooks the beach. One of the best places to eat on the island.

$$$$-$$$ Mango Bay Resort
Ong Lang Beach, T077-3981693 or T9-6968 1820 (mob), www.mangobayphuquoc.com.
A small and environmentally friendly resort located on the beach close to pepper farms. Some bungalows are made from rammed earth and are kitted out with bamboo furniture and tiled floors. There's information on birds and fish, and the restaurant provides a mixture of Vietnamese and Western food at very reasonable prices.

$$$ Bo Resort
Ong Lang Beach, T077-986142/3, www.boresort.com.
This feels like a great escape with 18 stilted bungalows set on a hillside amid flourishing gardens. Rooms come with large rustic bathrooms and alfresco showers. There's no road access to the wild stretch of beach where there are pines, hammocks, kayaks and a beach bar. There's Wi-Fi in the restaurant/bar

and candlelight at night. The owners are warm and friendly.

$$$-$$ Freedomland
Ong Lang Beach, 10-12 mins' walk from beach, T01-226 586802, www.freedomlandphuquoc.com.
This laid-back resort creates a community vibe as all guests eat together at the large dinner table and around campfires. The food is excellent. Wooden stilt bungalows with thatched roofs are scattered around the grounds. Very friendly and highly recommended.

$$ Beach Club
Long Beach, T077-398 0998, www.beachclubvietnam.com.
Luscious golden sands and thatched beach umbrellas at this fantastic, highly rated small resort. The ochre-coloured rooms and 4 bungalows are all close to the sea. It's good value and so always booked up. Reserve well in advance.

$$ Lang Toi
Sao Beach, T09 82337477, langtoi_restaurant@yahoo.com.vn.
With just 4 beautiful rooms complete with deep bathtubs, large balconies and tasteful wooden furnishings, this house is the best of the 2 options on the stunning Sao Beach. Beachfront restaurant serves all manner of seafood and simpler rice and noodle dishes. Recommened.

Restaurants

The food on Phu Quoc is generally very good, especially the fish and seafood. On the street in Duong Dong try the delicious *gio cuong* (fresh spring rolls). Along the river road a few restaurants also serve good Vietnamese dishes and seafood and are very popular with locals and Vietnamese tourists –

Truong Duong at 30/4 Thanh Tu (T09-146 1419) is one of the best.

Most of the resorts mentioned have beachfront restaurants. The night market is a fantastic place to try lots of different local food in a buzzing atmosphere.

$$$-$$ Itaca Lounge
125 Tran Hung Dao, T0773-992022, www.itacalounge.com.
Chilled out open air place with heavy Greek influences on the menu. Spanish chef Mateu Batista has 25 years of experience and creates a range of creative dished that make this one of the island's must-visit options.

$$$-$$ The Pepper Tree
La Veranda Resort (see Where to stay).
Fine dining in a refined seafront setting with perfect service. The ideal place for a special romantic meal. The pork with local pepper sauce is a treat.

$$$-$$ The Spice House, Cassia Cottage
Ba Keo Beach, T0773-848395, www.cassiacottage.com.
In a lovely garden setting, this fine restaurant has gained a solid reputation for its excellent barbecued seafood and good curries.

$ Buddy's
26 Nguyen Trai St, T77-399 4181.
This is a traveller crowd favourite serving Kiwi ice creams, great shakes and big burgers. Also brews good *Lavazza*.

$ La Cafe
11 Tran Hung Dao St, T90-820 1102.
A tiny streetside cafe serving yoghurts, shakes and breakfasts on cute black-lacquered furniture under beige umbrellas.

Bars and clubs

The Dog Bar
88 Tran Hung Dao St, near the Thien Hai Son Resort, T90-381 4688.
Well-located beer den with cold drinks, pool and sports TV.

Rory's (formerly Amigos)
Next to Veranda, 118/10 Tran Hung Dao, T091-707 0456.
Run by an affable Aussie couple, this beachfront bar and restaurant has a huge deck for great sun set views. Pizzas and burgers, grilled seafood and a large range of cocktails. Good promos and dancing later till the small hours.

Shopping

If you have Vietnamese friends or family and return home without a bottle of the fish sauce you will be in trouble. However, you cannot take the sauce on a **Vietnam Airlines** flight. The Duong Dong market and also the night market are the best places to head for gifts.

Coi Nguon, *149 Tran Hung Dao, T0773-980206, www.coinguonphuquoc.com.* A well-stocked shop selling a wide variety of wares using pearls, conch shells and driftwood, **Coi Nguon** is also home to a good museum.
Treasures from the Deep, *www.treasuresfromthedeep.com.* New Zealand jeweller, which is the best place to buy the pearls the island is famed for.

What to do

Most of the resorts are very happy to arrange tours and they are a good source of up-to-date information. Water sports, cycling tours, boat tours and walking can all be arranged.

Diving

Rainbow Divers, *Tran Hung Dao St, close to the market, T91-723 9433 (mob), www.divevietnam.com.* Long-standing operation with a very good reputation.

Tour operators

John's Tours, *New Star Café, 143 Tran Hung Dao St, T091-910 7086, www.johnsislandtours.com.* Run by the super helpful and friendly John Tran out of the **New Star Caféa** office (next to the alley to La Veranda) and various kiosks on the beach as well as hotel desks. John can organize anything for any budget and knows the island like the back of his hand. Snorkelling, squid fishing, island tours and car hire can all be arranged. Car hire and motorbikes with drivers also arranged.
Tony Travel, *100 Tran Hung Dao St or based at the Rainbow Divers office on Tran Hung Dao St opposite the market, T0913-197334, phuquoctonytourravelpq@yahoo.com.vn.* Kiosks on the beach too. Tony knows Phu Quoc extremely well and speaks fluent English. He would be able to organize almost anything. In his stable are island tours, snorkelling to the south and north islands, deep-sea fishing excursions, car and motorbike rental and hotel and transport reservations. He also runs **Rainbow Divers**.

Transport

You can get to Phu Quoc by boat from Rach Gia or Ha Tien or by plane from Rach Gia and Ho Chi Minh City. Most hotels will provide a free pick-up service from the airport if accommodation is booked in advance. *Xe om* drivers and taxis meet the ferries.

Air
There are daily flights to **HCMC** and **Rach Gia**.

Airline offices Vietnam Airlines, 122 Nguyen Trung Truc St, Duong Dong, T77-399667.

Boat
Most ferries leave from Vong and Nam Ninh ports near the beaches of the same names. John of **John's Tours** (see page 334) can sell all tickets and can advise on schedules. An Thoi port in the south.

Hong Tam, at **John's Tours**, ferries to **Ha Tien** daily at 0830, 1½ hrs. **Superdong**, 1 Tran Hung Dao St, Duong Dong, T077-348 6180. Ferries to **Rach Gia** from Vong Beach at 0800 and 1300, 2½ hrs 1300 arriving 1535. Ferries for **Ha Tien** leave a 0800, 1½ hrs. **Savana**, 21 Nguyen Trai St, Duong Dong, T0773-992999, 1 ferry per day to **Rach Gia**, 1240, 2½ hrs.

Duong Dong Express leaves for **Rach Gia** at 1245 arriving 1515, www. duongdongexpress.com.vn.

Vinashin, 21 Nguyen Trai St, T077-260 0155, leaves 0810.

Cawaco from Ham Ninh to **Ha Tien** at 0830 arriving 1000. Also departs Bai Vong 1400 arriving 1520.

Car, bicycle and motorbike
Cars, motorbikes and bicycles can be rented from resorts.

Taxi
Mai Linh, No 10 30 Thang 4 St, Duong Dong, T77-397 9797. **Sasco**, 379 Nguyen Trung Truc St, T77-399 5599.

Con Dao

★Con Dao is an archipelago of 14 islands and one of Vietnam's last relatively untouched wilderness areas with great possibilities for wildlife viewing and the country's best diving. The biggest and only permanently settled island is Con Son with a population of approximately 6000 people.

Sights → *Colour map 4, C3.*

The combination of mountains and islands, as well as its biodiversity, make Con Dao extremely special. It is also one of Vietnam's last relatively pristine areas. There are just a few main roads around Con Son and an unbelievable lack of traffic. The main hotels face out onto Con Son Bay behind the coastal road. The colourful fishing boats that used to bob and work the sea here have largely been moved to Ben Dam port although a few remain.

The prison system

The prison system operated between 1862 and 1975, first by the French and then by the Americans. **Prison Phu Hai**, which backs on to parts of the Saigon Con Dao Resort, was built in 1862 and is the largest prison on the islands with 10 detention rooms and 20 punishment cells. Inside, the chapel was built by the Americans in 1963. Next door is **Phu Son Prison** built in 1916. The third prison, **Phu Tho**, plus **Camp Phu Tuong** and **Camp Phu Phong** (built in 1962) contained the infamous 'tiger cages' where prisoners were chained and tortured; the enclosures still stand. Metal bars were placed across the roofs of the cells and guards would throw excrement and lime onto the prisoners. In addition, many prisoners were outside in areas known as 'sun-bathing compartments'. Not content on limiting torture methods, a cow manure enclosure was used to dunk prisoners in sewage up to 3 m deep. American-style tiger enclosures were built in 1971 at **Camp Phu Binh**. In total there were 504 tiger cages. Beyond the prisons, inland, is the **Hang Duong cemetery** where many of the victims of the prison are buried. The grave of Le Hong Phong, the very first General Secretary of the Communist Party in Vietnam (1935-1936) and Vo Thi Sau (1933-1952) can be seen among them.

A tour of the prisons and cemetery costs can be arranged through the museum, see below. There is an excellent and well-curated museum just outside the main

Essential Con Dao

Getting around

The main hotels offer a shuttle to the airport, but the best way to get around the island is by hiring a motorbike or a bicycle for shorter trips.

When to go

Between June and September is sea turtle nesting season (records show that the 1st and 15th of the month are best) although good weather is not guaranteed. February to April can be incredibly windy. The wet season lasts from May to November.

Time required

It's possible to see a lot of the island in two days, but three or four will allow you to truly enjoy it.

town, which offers a fascinating if disturbing insight into the island's past. A visit here is highly recommended.

There is a small museum and explanatory displays at the **National Park office headquarters** ① *see below, Mon-Fri 0700-1130, 1330-1700, Sat 0730-1100, 1400-1630.*

Con Dao National Park

29 Vo Thi Sau St, T64-383 0650, www. condaopark.com.vn.

There are a number of activities that can be organized in the national park, from snorkelling and swimming, to forest walks and birdwatching. Diving is available to see some of Con Dao's underwater features, such as its caves, as well as the coral reefs. In 1984 the forests on all 14 islands of the Con Dao archipelago were given official protection, and in 1993, 80% of the land area was designated a national park. In 1998 the park boundaries were expanded to include the surrounding sea.

In 1995, with support from the World Wildlife Fund, the park began a sea-turtle conservation project. Con Dao is the most important sea-turtle nesting site in Vietnam, with several hundred female green turtles (*Chelonia mydas*) coming ashore to lay their eggs every year. Occasionally the hawksbill turtle visits too. Park staff attach a tag to every turtle in order to identify returning turtles, and move the turtles' eggs if they are in danger of being flooded at high tide. The rest of the year the turtles migrate long distances. Recently, a turtle tagged in Con Dao was found in a fishing village in Cambodia – unfortunately the tag was insufficient protection to prevent it being eaten. Also in 1995, park staff identified the presence of dugongs (sea cows), which are mammals that feed on seagrass and can live to more than 70 years. Unfortunately, before the park was established dugongs were caught for meat so now the population in Con Dao is small and endangered.

The coral reefs surrounding the islands are among the most diverse in the country. Scientists have identified more than 200 species of coral and coral fish. In November 1997, typhoon Linda struck the islands and many of Con Dao's coral reefs were damaged.

In the forests scientists have identified more than 1000 plant species, of which several are unique to Con Dao and include many valuable medicinal and timber species. Bird life is also significant with rare species such as the pied imperial pigeon (*Ducula bicolor*) – Con Dao is the only place in Vietnam where you can see this bird –

BACKGROUND
Prisons to paradise

The Portuguese arrived on Con Dao in 1516 but it wasn't until 1702 that a trading post was set up here by the East India Trading Company. Because of the millions of sea birds that inhabited it, it was then called Bird Island. In 1773, it became the home of Nguyen Anh and many mandarin families who fled there after being defeated by the armies of the Tay Son. In 1832, the Con Dao archipelago was handed over to the French by Emperor Tu Duc. Prisons were built in 1862 by Admiral Bonard in which the French incarcerated their more obstinate political prisoners. Up to 12,000 people could be held in the completed prisons. The Con Dao prisons were later used by the government of South Vietnam to hold political prisoners. In 113 years of prison existence 200,000 people were incarcerated here and one tenth of those people died in prison. Remarkably, 153 prisoners volunteered to stay on in Con Son to live after 1975.

Despite grand plans to develop the island, it remains mercifully free of large-scale resorts. Six Senses Con Dao has taken up one of the very best stretches of sand while a Russian hotel is being built on the lighthouse road, but other than that the island has changed little over the last few years.

the red-billed tropicbird (*Phaethon aethereus*) – found on only a few islands in the world – and the brown booby (*Sula leucogaster*) – a rare sea bird that inhabits the park's most remote island, Hon Trung (Egg Island). Egg Island, a speedboat ride northeast of Con Son, is a rugged outcrop hosting thousands of seabirds including sooty and crested terns, white-bellied sea eagles, and the rare, in Vietnam, masked booby. Most of the threats to the islands' natural resources come from development in the form of new roads, houses and the new fishing port built in Ben Dam Bay – an area of once-beautiful coral reef and mangrove forest.

Beaches and bays

Ong Dung Beach can be reached by walking across Con Son Island downhill on a track through the jungle. Plenty of birds can be seen if you trek at the right time of day. You can snorkel around 300 m offshore. There is a forest protection centre at the bay where you can buy food and drink and hire snorkelling gear and a boat. See also Where to stay, below.

Bai Nhat Beach, just before Ben Dam Bay, is a beautiful wild stretch of sand where good swimming is possible.

North of Con Son is **Tre Lon Island**, said to be one of the best places in the archipelago to see coral reefs and reef fish; this was also used as an isolated French prison. Le Duan, former General Secretary of the Communist Party, was imprisoned here from 1931-1936.

Close to the airport is one of the island's best and most wild beaches at **Dam Trau**. Golden sands in a tight curved bay backed by casuarinas can be found here

Vo Thi Sau

Vo Thi Sau was born Ba Ria in 1933 and was executed in Con Dao in 1952. At the age of 14 this Vietnamese revolutionary heroine developed an interest in politics and a passionate hatred for the French.

In 1949 she obtained three hand-grenades and, with one, killed a French soldier and injured 20 others. She became a messenger and supplied food and ammunition to the Viet Minh.

In 1950 she tried to assassinate a village headman working for the French but the hand-grenade failed to go off. She was caught, tortured and sentenced to death. She was executed on 23 January 1952 at the age of 18.

but there are no island views. Signposted 'Mieu Cau' on the left just before the airport, it is a 15-minute walk, passing a pagoda flanked by two white horses.

Bay Canh Island is a major sea turtle nesting site; there is also a functioning French-built lighthouse dating from 1883. If you are interested in seeing the turtles arrange to stay overnight through the national park.

Cau Island, east of Bay Canh Island is the only other island in the archipelago with fresh water. It harbours the swifts that make the nests and turtles that come to lay their eggs. It was also an isolated French prison at one time. Pham Van Dong, a former prime minster of both North Vietnam and the reunited Vietnam (1955-1987), was incarcerated here for seven years, from 1929 to 1936.

For swimming, **Lo Voi Beach**, east of the hotels, is good for swimming as is **An Hai Beach** at the other end of the bay. Birdwatching is also possible around the freshwater lake – **Quang Trung** – swamps and tree-covered sand dunes near the park headquarters. Spotters could see the Brahminy kite (*Haliastur Indus*), white-bellied sea eagle, Javan pond heron and cinnamon bittern. On the way to Ong Dung you can see the white-rumped shama, greater racket-tailed drongo, the rare pied imperial pigeon and the even rarer red-billed tropicbird.

At **Dat Doc**, east of Con Son, is a very attractive and pristine bay backed by a sheer cliff face. The **Evason Hideaway & Six Senses Spa** company has built here.

Where to stay

$$$$ Six Senses Con Dao
Dat Doc Beach, www.sixsenses.com.
One of the most fabulous resort in all of
Southeast Asia, this is pure unadulterated
luxury. The duplex villas stretch along
a gorgeous stretch of sand which
is bookended by a grand green hill.
Each villa has its own private pool and
personal butler service. The restaurant
is absolutely first rate serving superb
international and local flavours. The
breakfast takes the 5-star experience to
another level with delicious a la carte
options (the Turkish poached eggs are
amazing) as well as a buffet complete
with a walk-in cold room. Highly
expensive but highly recommended.

$$$ Con Dao Resort
*8 Nguyen Duc Thuan St, T64-383 0939,
www.condaoresort.com.vn.*
Until **Six Senses** arrived on the scene,
this was the best resort on the island.
There are 41 rooms including some in
villas on the beach. The rooms feature
a/c bathtubs, TV and balconies. There's
a pool and a tennis court. There's also a
restaurant which is rather average. Staff
can arrange walking and motorbike tours
of the area.

$$$ Saigon Con Dao
*18 Ton Duc Thang St, T64-383 0336,
www.saigoncondao.com.*
These buildings on the seafront may
remind you of a Cornish seaside hotel
from the 1980s, but they are clean
and comfortable. The restaurant is
not particularly good and the buffet
breakfast caters to Vietnamese tastes.

$$-$ Con Dao Camping
Nguyen Duc Thuan St.
By the old pier, these simple A-frame
huts offer beachfront digs for those
on a budget. Rather dated, they are
nonetheless clean and offer sea views
at very cheap prices.

Restaurants

Until recently there was very little to
choose from on Con Dao, but there are
now a handful of good places in the
main town. There are also plenty of
places to grab a cheap bowl of noodles
around the market and the night food
street nearby features some noodle
stands as well as some seafood. On the
road to Con Dao Camping there are a
number of Vietnamese seafood places
catering to large groups.

$ Bar 200
Pham Van Dong, T064-363 0334.
This new addition to the town also
houses **Senses Diving** school. It's run by
2 Brits and a South African who opened
it up in part to satisfy their own food
cravings. You can therefore find great
Western options including salads and
pizzas as well as good espresso. A great
source of local information and very,
very friendly. A good spot to meet fellow
divers and travellers.

$ Infiniti
Pham Van Dong, T64-383 0083.
This is a very funky cafe which seems
rather out of place in Con Dao's main
town. Run by two friendly brothers, it
serves pizza, excellent chicken burgers,
sublime shakes, beers and cocktails. Also
does a barbecue party on weekends
and regular specials. A great find.

$ Six Senses Con Dao
See Where to stay.
The restaurant here is first-rate, with superb grilled seafood and wide range of local and international flavours. Also has an exceptional wine list. Highly recommended for a treat.

What to do

Boat tours
The National Park organizes boat tours depending on the number of people and the weather. These include trips to Hon Tre Lon, Hon Tre No, Hon Bay Canh and Hon Cau as well as points around Con Son Island.

Diving
This is the premier place to dive in Vietnam. Courses are offered by **Senses Diving** based at **Bar 200**

> **Tip...**
> To see the turtles hatching on Con Dao's beaches, visit May-October.

(see Restaurants). This is a very professional outfit run by highly experienced diver masters.

Transport

Air
Con Dao Airport, T64-383 1973. There are regular flights to and from **Ho Chi Minh City**. Weekly schedules vary throughout the year.

Boat
It is possible to reach Con Dao by boat, but the journey is a nightmare by all accounts and not recommended at all.

Phan Thiet
& Mui Ne

Sahara-like dunes, kitesurfing beaches and fishing villages

Phan Thiet is a fishing town at the mouth of the Ca Ty River. For the traveller the real attraction lies east of town in the form of the 20-km sweep of golden sand of Mui Ne. Here some of Vietnam's finest coastal resorts can be found with some excellent water sports and two of the country's most attractive golf courses. The town has become hugely popular with both kitesurfers and Russians, with plenty of businesses catering to both markets.

Phan Thiet → *Colour map 4, B5.*

Despite its modest appearance, Phan Thiet is the administrative capital of Binh Thuan Province. Its main attraction is the 18-hole golf course, designed by Nick Faldo. It is regarded as one of the best in Vietnam, and golfers come from all around the region to play it.

The most distinctive landmark in town is the municipal **water tower** completed in 1934. It is an elegant structure with a pagoda-like roof; built by the infamous 'Red Prince' and first president of Laos. The tower icon features in the logos of many local businesses and agencies. There are a few Ho Chi Minh relics, including a museum on Nguyen Truong To Street and the Duc Thanh school next door, where Ho Chi Minh taught in 1911, but otherwise nothing of interest at the museum.

Van Thuy Thu Temple ① *20A Ngu Ong St, 0730-1130 and 1400-1700*, is the oldest whale temple (built in 1762) in Vietnam. The temple houses more than 100 whale skeletons, including one specimen more than 22 m in length. Like all whale temples, it was originally built by the sea but, as sea levels have receded, this temple is now stranded in the middle of the neighbourhood.

★Mui Ne → *Colour map 4, B5.*

Mui Ne is the name of the famous sandy cape and the small fishing village that lies at its end. Mui Ne's claims to fame are its *nuoc mam* (fish sauce) and its beaches where it is possible to do a host of water sports including kiteboarding, for which it is justly famous. Body boarding and surfing are better December to January when there are more waves. The wind dies down at the end of April, and May has virtually no wind. The cape is dominated by some impressive sand dunes; some are golden but in other parts quite red, a reflection of the underlying geology.

Around the village visitors may notice a strong smell of rotting fish. This is the unfortunate but inevitable by-product of fish sauce fermenting in wooden barrels. The *nuoc mam* of Phan Thiet is made from anchovies, as *ca com* on the label testifies. The process takes a year but to Vietnamese palates it is worth every day. *Nuoc mam* from Phan Thiet is regarded highly but not as reverentially as that from the southern island of Phu Quoc.

There are still significant numbers of Cham (50,000) and Ra-glai (30,000) minorities who, until a century ago, were the dominant groups in the region. There are many relics of the Champa kingdom here in Binh Thuan Province, the best and easiest to find being **Po Shanu**, two Cham towers dating from the late eighth century on a hill on the Mui Ne road. They are now somewhat broken down but the road leading up to them makes a nice evening ride; you can watch the sun set and from this vantage point you'll see the physical make-up of the coastal plain and estuaries to the south and the central highlands to the north. Driving up the long climb towards Mui Ne the towers are on the right-hand side of the road and quite unmissable. Like Cham towers elsewhere in this part of the country they were constructed of brick bound together with resin of the day tree. Once the tower was completed timber was piled around it and ignited; the heat from the flames melted the resin, which solidified on cooling.

Essential Phan Thiet and Mui Ne

Getting around

Both motorbike taxis and Mai Linh car taxis abound in the town and along the Mui Ne strip.

When to go

The weather in Phan Thiet always seems nice. It is, of course, better in the dry season, December through April. Phan Thiet is most popular with overseas visitors (and the growing number of package tour operators) in the Christmas to Easter period when prices at the some of the better hotels rise by 20% or more. From December to March, Mui Ne loses portions of its beach to the sea.

Time required

Kitesurfers can linger for weeks here, but for the rest two to four days will be ample.

Best excursions from Mui Ne

The red dunes, page 346
The white dunes, page 346
Fairy Stream, page 346

Hon Rom and around

Hon Rom, about 15 km by motorbike or bicycle from Mui Ne, is the name of the undeveloped bay north of Mui Ne and is accessible only from Mui Ne. North of Hon Rom are **Suoi Nuoc**, **Binh Thien Village** and **Turtle Island**. The Full Moon Beach Resort runs the Full Moon Villas and Jibe's II at Suoi Nuoc.

Tourist information

Binh Thuan Tourist
82 Trung Trac St, T62-381 6821,
www.binhthuan-tourist.com.
Arranges tours and car rentals.

Where to stay

Phan Thiet

$$$$ DuParc Phan Thiet Ocean Dunes & Golf Resort
1 Ton Duc Thang St, T62-382 2393,
www.vietnamgolfresorts.com.
On the beach just outside Phan Thiet, this is set behind lovely gardens. 123 comfortable rooms (although some of these are showing their age) in a bland building and new well-appointed villas with beach views. Good facilities, 2 pools, 2 restaurants with tasty food, bar, tennis courts and gym. Guests enjoy a 30% discount on green fees at the adjacent 18-hole champion golf course, the **Ocean Dunes Golf Club**.

Mui Ne

Weekends tend to be busier as Mui Ne is a popular escape for expats from HCMC. There has been a great construction boom and there are now many places to stay at a range of prices. Fortunately supply has kept up with demand so Mui Ne offers good value. Advisable to book ahead as the popular places fill up fast particularly around Christmas and Tet and Vietnamese public holidays.

$$$$ Anantara Mui Ne Resort and Spa
Nguyen Dinh Chieu, T062-374 1888,
www.anantara.com.
A fantastic 5-star resort with impeccable service, good restaurant, sea-view rooms and a great slice of beach. The wine cellar is very well stocked and there is also an excellent gym.

$$$$ Mia Mui Ne
T62-384 7440, www.miamuine.com.
This is a gorgeous resort. Designed in the most charming style its bungalows and rooms are simple and cool and surrounded by dense and glorious vegetation. For inspiration and good taste it ranks among the best in Vietnam. Its pool has been extended and the bathrooms for the superior rooms enlarged. It has an excellent restaurantand bar. A good buffet breakfast is included.

$$$$ Victoria Phan Thiet Beach Resort & Spa
T62-381 3000, www.victoriahotels-asia.com.
Part of the **Victoria Group**, the resort has 59 upgraded thatched bungalows withoutdoor rain showers and 3 villas, built in country-house style in an attractive landscaped setting. It is well equipped with restaurants, bar, 2 pools, sports facilities, a children's club and a spa. A great place to bring kids who love the donkey that's available for rides in the grounds. Very friendly staff and a good buffet breakfast.

$$$$-$$$ Coco Beach (Hai Duong)
T62-384 7111-3, www.cocobeach.net.
The European owners live here and the place is well run. Not luxurious but friendly and impeccably kept. 28 wooden bungalows and 3 wooden, 2-bedroom 'villas' facing the beach. Beautiful setting, lovely pool and relaxing. Excellent restaurant and a beachclub. **Coco Beach** was the first

resort on Mui Ne and it is pleasing how it remains easily among the best.

$$$ Full Moon Beach
T62-384 7008, www.windsurf-vietnam.com.
Visitors are assured of a friendly reception by the French and Vietnamese couple who own and run the place. Accommodation is in a variety of types: some rooms are spacious, others a little cramped, some brick, some bamboo. The most attractive rooms have a sea view and constant breeze. There is a good restaurant. They also run the **Full Moon Village** along the coast in Suoi Nuoc which is a very tranquil spot away from all the other resorts.

$$$-$$ Saigon Mui Ne
T62-384 7303, www.saigonmuine resort.com.
This is a Saigon tourist resort, perfectly professional but lacking flair and imagination. Bungalows, pool, jacuzzi, restaurant, spa, fitness centre and kiteboarding classes.

$$-$ Hiep Hoa
T62-384 7262, T090-812 4149 (mob), hiephoatourism@yahoo.com.
This is an attractive place. Now with 15 a/c rooms. It's quiet, clean and with its own stretch of beach. Popular and should be booked in advance. Its rates are excellent value for Mui Ne; they go down in the low season.

$$-$ Mui Ne Backpackers Resort
88 Nguyen Dinh Chieu, T062-384 7047, www.muinebackpackers.com.
One of the best options for those on a budget and one of the longest standing in the area. There is a small swimming pool and a variety of different room options to choose from. Located right on the beach, the sea view.

Mui Ne
Of the hotel restaurants the **Mia** and **Victoria** stand out. Many hotels do good barbecues at the weekend. There are many local seafood joints along the main road either side of the resort strip where the catch of the day is grilled – it's best to wander along and pick the busiest place.

$$ El Latino
Nguyen Dinh Chieu, T62-3743 5950.
A very welcoming little spot serving up some quality Mexican fare including great tacos and burritos, although the servings are on the small side. Has some coaches for laid-back dining in a funky open-air space.

$$ Forest Restaurant
7 Nguyen Dinh Chieu St, T62-384 7589.
Local dishes and lots of seafood, this garden-jungle setting puts on live music throughout the evening. Popular with the town's expats recommend this place for the good food, despite the touristy vibe.

$$-$ Jibe's Beach Club
T62 384 7405. Open 0700-late.
Popular chill-out bar serving burgers, salads and food with a French bent thanks to the owner, Pascal. In the daytime there is a kitesurf school cafe vibe, but in the evenings white linens come out and there is a more sophisticated ambiance. Recommended.

$$-$ Shree Ganesh
57 Nguyen Dinh Chieu, T62-374 1330.
This popular Omar's franchise serves North Indian and Tandoori cuisine. One of the best in Mui Ne with consistently high reviews for many years.

Bars and cafés

Mui Ne

Jibe's Beach Club
See Restaurants.
A laid back bar with quieter tunes, some good wine and a beachfront setting.

Joe's Cafe
139 Nguyen Dinh Chieu St, T62-374 3447, joescafemuine.com.
Ever popular and always busy spot with live music every night in a garden setting.

Pogo
www.thepogobar.com.
Just down from **Sinh Tourist** with cocktails, and local and international food. Keeps going later than most thanks to the roaring bonfires.

Wax
68 Nguyen Dinh Chieu St, T62-384 7001.
Located beside the beach at Windchamp Resort, **Wax** is dance-part central, especially during holidays.

Shopping

Mui Ne
There is now a large selection of shops in Mui Ne spanning the west end of the beach. Almost anything can be found, from beachwear, water sports equipment, pearls and jewellery to lacquerware and crocodile leather.

What to do

Phan Thiet
Golf
Ocean Dunes Golf Club, *1 Ton Duc Thang St, T62-382 3366, www. oceandunesgolf.vn.* This Nick Faldo-designed 18-hole, 6147-m course is highly regarded. It has a fully equipped club house with bar and restaurant, pro-shop and locker rooms.

Tennis
Du Parc Ocean Dunes & Golf Resort, *see Where to stay.*

Mui Ne
The dunes and Fairy Stream
Tours to the red and white sand dunes and the Fairy Stream are top of most people's list when they visit Mui Ne and with very good reason. It's possible to hire a motorbike and venture out solo. The red dunes are very close to town and the white dunes are about an hour further on. Every motorbike hire place will be able to provide a map. The dunes are spectacular and best visited in the late afternoon. Kids hiring out plastic boards for sliding down the steep sand banks can be rather persistent. If you travel to the white dunes in the heat of the day, be sure to take enough fuel for the return leg and plenty of water for the dunes themselves. All tour operators offer trips to these dunes, some including jeep transport and rides on quad bikes.

Golf
Sea Links Golf & Country Club, *T62-374 1666, www.sealinksvietnam.com.* This 18-hole course has breathtaking 270-degree views of Mui Ne's coast. The property has been expanded to include a luxury hotel, villas, and has plans to develop a private beach, luxury hotel and shopping centre.

Therapies
The Village, *Victoria Phan Thiet Beach Resort & Spa, see Where to stay, above.*
The hotel's own on-site centre offers the best massage in town by the most experienced therapists.

Water sports

Mui Ne is the water sports capital of Vietnam. The waters can be crowded with windsurfers and kiteboarders. The combination of powerful wind and waves attract huge numbers of kitesurfers. Equipment and training is offered by numerous centres. **Jibe's Beach Club**, *T62-384 7405, T091-316 2005 (mob), www.windsurf-vietnam. com*. There are plenty of places offering lessons in town, but this is the original centre, which is part of and close to Full Moon Beach Resort. **Jibe's** is the importer of sea kayaks, windsurfers, surfboards, sailboats, SUP (stand-up paddle) and kitesurf equipment. Equipment is available for purchase or for hire by the hour, day or week. Hourly windsurf lessons, multi-day kite-surf lessons and boogie board and kayak hire.

Tour operators

Sinh Tourist, *144 Nguyen Dinh Chieu St, T62-384 7542, muinc@thcsinhtourist.vn.* A branch of the tour operator good for **Open Tour Bus** tickets and local tours to the sand dunes, fishing village and Phan Thiet city tour. Transport rented.

Victor Tours & Coco Cafe, *121A Nguyen Dinh Chieu, across from Full Moon Resort, T98-959 1599*. **Victor Tours** offers a full range of tour to all the local sites and books bus transport throughout Vietnam. Customs tours and unique outings are also available.

Transport

Bicycles and motorbikes

Xe oms are abundant in Phan Thiet town, as are reputable taxis. Bikes and motorbikes can be rented from hotels or tour operators, see **Victor Tours**, tour operators, above, and are the best way to explore the vicinity.

Bus and Open Tour Bus

The bus station is on the east side of town. Connections with all neighbouring towns. A local bus plies the nearby **Phan Thiet Coop** supermarket to Mui Ne route, as do taxis. Phuong Trang and Sinh Tourist Open Tour Buses drop off and pick up from all resorts on Mui Ne. The **Sinh Tourist** bus departs from its resort and Phuong Trang from its central office. To **Nha Trang** and **HCMC** twice a day at 1300 and 2345 (also 0800 to HCMC) 5½ hrs, both journeys. To **Dalat**, 7 hrs.

Phuong Trang, 97 Nguyen Dinh Chieu St, T62-374 3113, www.phuongtrang dalat.com. This Dalat-based company has emerged as the leader in Vietnam, with the most reliable, trustworthy and comfortable services anywhere south of Hué.

Car

Victor Tours can arrange car hire, as can most hotels.

Taxi

Taxis are plentiful and run on meters.

Train

The Phan Thiet train station connects with the old station at Muong Man, 12 km to the west, on its way to HCMC. Trains leave Phan Thiet daily at in the early afternoon. From Muong Man there are also slow trains north to **Hanoi**. The trip from Phan Thiet to **HCMC** is a comfortable and scenic route.

Background
Vietnam

History 349
Modern Vietnam 379
Culture 388
Religion 407
Land and environment 413
Books 420
Films 423

History

Vietnam prehistory

The earliest record of humans in Vietnam is from an archaeological site on Do Mountain, in the northern Thanh Hoa Province. The remains discovered here have been dated to the Lower Palaeolithic (early Stone Age). So far, all early human remains have been unearthed in North Vietnam, invariably in association with limestone cliff dwellings. Unusually, tools are made of basalt rather than flint, the more common material found at similar sites in other parts of the world.

Archaeological excavations have shown that between 5000 BC and 3000 BC, two important Mesolithic cultures occupied North Vietnam: these are referred to as the **Hoa Binh** and **Bac Son** cultures after the principal excavation sites in Tonkin. Refined stone implements and distinctive hand axes with polished edges (known as Bacsonian axes) are characteristic of the two cultures. These early inhabitants of Vietnam were probably small, dark-skinned and of Melanesian or Austronesian stock.

There are 2000 years of recorded Vietnamese history and another 2000 years of legend. The Vietnamese people trace their origins back to 15 tribal groups known as the **Lac Viet** who settled in what is now North Vietnam at the beginning of the Bronze Age. Here they established an agrarian kingdom known as Van-lang that seems to have vanished during the third century BC.

A problem with early **French archaeological studies** in Vietnam was that most of the scholars were either Sinologists or Indologists. In consequence, they looked to Vietnam as a receptacle of Chinese or Indian cultural influences and spent little time uncovering those aspects of culture, art and life that were indigenous in origin and inspiration.

Pre-colonial history

The beginning of Vietnamese recorded history coincides with the start of **Chinese cultural hegemony** over the north, in the second century BC. The Chinese dominated Vietnam for more than 1000 years until the 10th century AD and the cultural legacy is still very much in evidence, making Vietnam distinctive in Southeast Asia. Even after the 10th century, and despite breaking away from Chinese political domination, Vietnam was still overshadowed and greatly influenced by its illustrious neighbour to the north. Nonetheless, the fact that Vietnam could shrug off 1000 years of Chinese subjugation and emerge with a distinct cultural heritage and language says a lot for Vietnam's strength of national identity.

Ly Dynasty

The Ly Dynasty (1009-1225) was the first independent Vietnamese dynasty. Its capital, Thang Long, was at the site of present day Hanoi and the dynasty based its system of government and social relations closely upon the Chinese Confucianist model (see page 409).

The first Ly emperor, and one of Vietnam's great kings, was Ly Cong Uan who was born in AD 974. He is usually known by his posthumous title, **Ly Thai To**, and reigned for 19 years from 1009-1028. Ly Cong Uan was raised and educated by monks and acceded to the throne when, as the commander of the palace guard in Hoa Lu (the capital of Vietnam before Thang Long or Hanoi) and with the support of his great patron, the monk Van Hanh, he managed to gain the support of the Buddhist establishment and many local lords. During his reign, he enjoyed a reputation not just as a great soldier, but also as a devout man who paid attention to the interests and wellbeing of his people. He tried to re-establish the harmony between ruler and ruled which had suffered during the previous years and he even sent his son to live outside the walls of the palace so that he could gain a taste of ordinary life and an understanding of ordinary people.

Ly Cong Uan was succeeded by his son, Ly Phat Ma, who is better known as **Ly Thai Tong** (reigned 1028-1054). Ly Phat Ma had been prepared for kingship since birth and he proved to be an excellent ruler during his long reign. It is hard to generalize about this period in Vietnamese history because Ly Phat Ma adapted his pattern of rule no less than six times during his reign. Early on he challenged the establishment, contending for example that good governance was not merely a consequence of following best practice but depended upon good kingship. Later he was more of an establishment figure. Perhaps his greatest military success was the mounting of a campaign to defeat the Cham in 1044 from which he returned with shiploads of plunder. His greatest artistic legacy was the construction of the One Pillar Pagoda or Chua Mot Cot in Hanoi (see page 46).

Ly Phat Ma was succeeded by his son, Ly Nhat Ton, posthumously known as **Ly Thanh Tong** (reigned 1054-1072). History is not as kind about Ly Thanh Tong as it is about his two forebears. Nonetheless he did challenge the might of the Chinese along Vietnam's northern borders – largely successfully – and like his father also mounted a campaign against Champa (see page 353) in 1069. Records indicate that he spent a great deal of time trying to father a son and worked his way through numerous concubines and at last, a son was born to a concubine of common blood in 1066 and named Ly Can Duc.

Ly Can Duc was proclaimed emperor in 1072 when he was only six years old and, surprisingly, remained king until he died in 1127. His death marks the end of the Ly Dynasty for he left no heir and the crown passed to the maternal clan of his nephew. There followed a period of instability and it was not until 1225 that a new dynasty – the Tran Dynasty – managed to subdue the various competing cliques and bring a semblance of order to the country.

Tran Dynasty

Scholars do not know a great deal about the four generations of kings of the Tran Dynasty. It seems that they established the habit of marrying within the clan, and each king took queens who were either their cousins or, in one case, a half-sister. Such a long period of intermarriage, one imagines, would have had some far-reaching genetic consequences, although ironically the collapse of the dynasty seems to have been brought about after one foolish king decided to marry outside the Tran clan. The great achievement of the Tran Dynasty was to resist the expansionist tendencies of the Mongol forces, who conquered China in the 1250s and then set their sights on Vietnam. In 1284 a huge Mongol-Yuan force, consisting of no fewer than four armies, massed on the border to crush the Vietnamese. Fortunately the Tran were blessed with a group of brave and resourceful princes (the most notable of whom was Tran Quoc Tuan, better known – and now immortalized in street names in just about every Vietnamese town – as Tran Hung Dao), and in the end the forces of the Tran Dynasty were victorious.

Le Dynasty and the emergence of Vietnam

Le Loi

Despite 1000 years of Chinese domination and centuries of internal dynastic squabbles the Viet retained a strong sense of national identity and were quick to respond to charismatic leadership. As so often in Vietnam's history one man was able to harness nationalistic sentiment and mould the country's discontent into a powerful fighting force: in 1426 it was Le Loi. Together with the brilliant tactician **Nguyen Trai** (see box, page 352), Le Loi led a campaign to remove the Chinese from Vietnamese soil. Combining surprise, guerrilla tactics and Nguyen Trai's innovative and famous propaganda, designed to convince defending Ming of the futility of their position, the Viet won a resounding victory which led to the enlightened and artistically distinguished Le period. Le Loi's legendary victory lives on in popular form and is celebrated in the tale of the restored sword in water puppet performances across the country. Following his victory against the Ming he claimed the throne in 1428 and reigned until his death five years later.

Le Thanh Ton

With Le Loi's death the Le Dynasty worked its way through a succession of young kings who seemed to hold the throne barely long enough to warm the cushions before they were murdered. It was not until 1460 that a king of substance was to accede: Le Thanh Ton (reigned 1460-1497). His reign was a period of great scholarship and artistic accomplishment. He established the system of rule that was to guide successive Vietnamese emperors for 500 years. He also mounted a series of military campaigns, some as far as Laos to the west.

Le expansion

The expansion of the Vietnamese state, under the Le, south from its heartland in the Tonkin Delta, followed the decline of the Cham Kingdom at the end of the 15th century. By the early 18th century the Cham were extinct as an identifiable political and military force and the Vietnamese advanced still further south into the Khmer-controlled territories of the Mekong Delta. This geographical over-extension and the sheer logistical impracticability of ruling from distant Hanoi, disseminating edicts and collecting taxes, led to the disintegration of

Our country, Dai Viet, has long been, A land of ancient culture, With its own rivers and mountains, ways and customs, Different from those of the North.
  (Opening lines of *Proclamation of Victory Over the Invaders*.)

Nguyen Trai, mandarin, poet and nationalist, rose to prominence as an adviser to Le Loi during the 10-year campaign to eject the Ming from Dai Viet. His famous counsel "better to win hearts than citadels" (which mirrors similar advice during a war over 500 years later) was heeded by Le Loi who aroused patriotic fervour in his compatriots to achieve victory on the battlefield. It was on Nguyen Trai's suggestion that 100,000 defeated Ming troops were given food and boats to make their way home. After the war, Nguyen Trai accepted and later resigned a court post. He was a prolific composer of verse, which is considered some of the finest in the national annals.

On an overnight visit to Nguyen Trai, Emperor Le Thai Tong (Le Loi's son and heir) died unexpectedly. Scheming courtiers were able to fix the blame on Nguyen Trai who in 1442, along with three generations of his family, were executed, a punishment known as *tru di tam tôc*.

the – ever tenuous – imperial rule. Noble families, locally dominant, challenged the emperor's authority and the Le Dynasty gradually dissolved into internecine strife and regional fiefdoms, namely Trinh in the north and Nguyen in the south, a pattern that was to reassert itself some 300 years later. But although on paper the Vietnamese – now consisting of two dynastic houses, Trinh and Nguyen – appeared powerful, the people were mired in poverty.

There were numerous peasant rebellions in this period, of which the most serious was the **Tay Son rebellion** of 1771 (see box, page 241). One of the three Tay Son brothers, Nguyen Hue, proclaimed himself **Emperor Quang Trung** in 1788, only to die four years later. His death paved the way for the establishment of the **Nguyen Dynasty** – the last Vietnamese dynasty – in 1802. Despite the fact that this period heralded the arrival of the French – leading to their eventual domination of Vietnam – it is regarded as a golden period in Vietnamese history. During the Nguyen Dynasty, Vietnam was unified as a single state and Hué emerged as the heart of the kingdom.

History of the non-Viet civilizations

Any history of Vietnam must include the non-Vietnamese peoples and civilizations. The central and southern parts of Vietnam have only relatively recently been dominated by the Viets. Before that, these lands were in the hands of people of Indian or Khmer origins.

Funan (AD 100-600)

According to Chinese sources, Funan was a Hindu kingdom founded in the first century AD with its capital, Vyadhapura, close to the Mekong River near the border with Cambodia. A local legend records that Kaundinya, a great Indian Brahmin, acting on a dream, sailed to the coast of Vietnam carrying with him a bow and arrow. When he arrived, Kaundinya shot the arrow and where it landed he established the capital of Funan. Following this act, Kaundinya married the princess Soma, daughter of the local King of the Nagas (giant water serpents). The legend symbolizes the union between Indian and local cultural traditions – the naga representing indigenous fertility rites and customs, and the arrow, the potency of the Hindu religion.

Oc-Eo

Funan built its wealth and power on its strategic location on the sea route between China and the islands to the south. Maritime technology at the time forced seafarers travelling between China and island Southeast Asia and India to stop and wait for the winds to change before they could continue on their way. This sometimes meant a stay of up to five months. The large port city of Oc-Eo (see page 327) offered a safe harbour for merchant vessels and the revenues generated enabled the kings of the empire to expand rice cultivation, dominate a host of surrounding vassal states as far away as the Malay coast and South Burma, and build a series of impressive temples, cities and irrigation works.

Funan reached the peak of its powers in the fourth century and went into decline during the fifth century AD when improving maritime technology made Oc-Eo redundant as a haven for sailing vessels. By the mid-sixth century, Funan, having suffered from a drawn-out leadership crisis, was severely weakened. The Cham ultimately conquered. What is interesting about Funan is the degree to which it provided a model for future states in Southeast Asia. Funan's wealth was built on its links with the sea, and with its ability to exploit maritime trade. The later rulers of Champa, Langkasuka (Malaya), Srivijaya (Sumatra), and Malacca (Malaya) repeated this formula.

Champa (AD 200–1720)

In South Vietnam, where the dynastic lords achieved hegemony only in the 18th century, the kingdom of Champa – or Lin-yi as the Chinese called it – was the most significant power. The kingdom evolved in the second century AD and was focused on the narrow ribbon of lowland that runs north–south down the Annamite coast with its various capitals near the present-day city of Danang. Chinese sources record that in AD 192 a local official, Kiu-lien, rejected Chinese authority and established an independent kingdom. From then on, Champa's history was one of conflict with its neighbour; when Imperial China was powerful, Champa was subservient and sent ambassadors and tributes in homage to the Chinese court; when it was weak, the rulers of Champa extended their own influence and ignored the Chinese.

The difficulty for scholars is to decide whether Champa had a single identity or whether it consisted of numerous mini-powers with no dominant centre. The

ON THE ROAD

A Spanish account of Champa circa 1595

This account of Champa is taken from an anonymous manuscript compiled in Manila about 1590-1595, possibly as part of the documentation assembled by Don Luis Perez das Marinas in justification of his scheme for the conquest of Indochina.

"It is a land fertile in foodstuffs and cows and oxen and very healthy in itself. It is not thickly populated and the people are swarthy and heathens. In this kingdom there is no money nor silver with which to sell anything; and in order to buy what they need, they exchange foodstuffs for cotton blankets and other things that they make for the purpose of buying and selling with each other. Nobody is allowed to go shod, save only the king, and nobody can be married with more than two wives.

Food and drink

These people do not eat anything properly cooked, but only in raw or putrid condition; and in order to digest these foods, they are great drinkers of very strong spirits, which they drink little by little and very frequently, thinking it no disgrace to fall down from drinking too much.

Seasons

They divide the year into six festivals, during the first of which the vast majority of his vassals pay tribute to the king. The king goes to a field, and there they assemble all these tributes, out of which they make alms to the souls of the dead and perform great obsequies and funeral rites in their memory.

The second festival also lasts two months and they spend the whole of this time singing to the exclusion of everything else, except when they are actually eating their meals. During these festivals the women, of whatsoever condition they be, have liberty to do what they like for the space of three days, during which they are not asked to account for their behaviour.

During the third festival they go to the seaside, where they stay fishing for another two months. They make merry, catching enough fish to last them for the year, pickling it in their jars, with just a little salt, and they eat it putrid in this manner. And they thrive very strong and lusty on this food.

When the king returns to the city, they display lights by night and day, putting on plays and races in public, in which the king participates. This is the fourth of their festivals.

The fifth is when the king goes hunting elephants, of which there are many in this land, taking with him the nobility and their female elephants; and the females go into the place where the wild elephants are, which follow the former into a little space which they have stockaded off for this purpose, and there they keep them for some days until they are tamed.

The last festival which they celebrate Is a tiger-hunt. The tigers come to eat the buffaloes that are tied to a tree in certain places. They place sentinels over them, so that when the tigers approach, the king is informed. And as soon as this news arrives the king gets ready with a great number of Indians and nets, and they do with the tigers what they do with the elephants, surrounding them at once and killing them there and then. It is the custom with these Indians that at the time when they are occupied with this hunt, the king and his wife send out 100 or more Indians along the roads, with express order that they should not return without filling two gold basins which they give them, full of human gall, which must be from people of their own nation and not foreigners; and these emissaries do as they are told, not sparing anyone they meet, whether of high or low degree. As soon as they can catch a person on the road, they tie him at once to a tree, and there they cut out the gall … When all this is over the king and his wife bathe and wash with this human gall; and they say that in this way they cleanse themselves of their sins and their faults.

Justice

The justice of this people is peculiar, for they have no fixed criminal code, but only their personal opinions, and when the case is a serious one, they investigate it with two witnesses. Their oaths are made with fire and boiling oil, and those condemned to death are executed with extreme barbarity. Some are sentenced to be trampled to death by elephants; others are flogged to death; others are tortured for two or three days, during which time bits and pieces are cut out of their bodies with pincers until they die. And for very trifling and common offences, they cut off their feet, hands, arms and ears.

Death

They have another custom invented by the Devil himself, which is that when any leading personage dies, they cremate the body, after it has been kept for eight or 10 days until they have made the necessary preparations in accordance with the quality of the deceased, when they burn it in the field. When such a person dies, they seize all the household servants and keep them until the same day on which they burn the body of their master, and then they throw them alive into the flames, so that they can serve them therewith in the other … Another custom which they have, which is a very harsh one for women, is that when the husband dies, they burn the wife with him. They say that this law was made to prevent wives from giving poisonous herbs to their husbands, for there are very great witchcrafts and knaveries in these lands. They say that if the wife realizes that her husband will not live any longer than her, she will take good care of his life and ease, and will not dare to kill him with poison.

accepted wisdom at the moment is that Champa was more diffuse than previously thought and that only rarely during its history is it possible to talk of Champa in singular terms. The endless shifting of the capital of Champa is taken to reflect the shifting centres of power that characterized this 'kingdom'.

Like Funan, Champa built its power on its position on the maritime trading route through Southeast Asia. During the fourth century, as Champa expanded into formerly Funan-controlled lands, they came under the influence of the Indian cultural traditions of the Funanese. These were enthusiastically embraced by Champa's rulers who tacked the suffix '-varman' onto their names (for example, Bhadravarman) and adopted the Hindu-Buddhist cosmology. Though a powerful trading kingdom, Champa was geographically poorly endowed. The coastal strip between the Annamite highlands to the west, and the sea to the east, is narrow and the potential for extensive rice cultivation limited. This may explain why the Champa Empire was never more than a moderate power: it was unable to produce the agricultural surplus necessary to support an extensive court and army, and therefore could not compete with either the Khmers to the south nor with the Viets to the north. But the Cham were able to carve out a niche for themselves between the two, and to many art historians, their art and architecture represent the finest that Vietnam has ever produced (see page 396).

For over 1000 years the Cham resisted the Chinese and the Vietnamese. But by the time Marco Polo wrote of the Cham, in 1285, their power and prestige were much reduced. Champa saw a late flowering under King Binasuos who led numerous successful campaigns against the Viet, culminating in the sack of Hanoi in 1371. Subsequently, the treachery of a low-ranking officer led to Binasuos' death in 1390 and the military eclipse of the Cham by the Vietnamese. The demographic and economic superiority of the Viet coupled with their gradual drift south contributed most to the waning of the Cham Kingdom, but finally, in 1471 the Cham suffered a terrible defeat at the hands of the Vietnamese. Some 60,000 of their soldiers were killed and another 36,000 captured and carried into captivity, including the King and 50 members of the royal family. The kingdom shrank to a small territory in the vicinity of Nha Trang that survived until 1720 when surviving members of the royal family and many subjects fled to Cambodia to escape from the advancing Vietnamese.

The colonial period

One of the key motivating factors that encouraged the **French** to undermine the authority of the Vietnamese emperors was their treatment of Roman Catholics. Emperor Minh Mang issued an imperial edict outlawing the dissemination of Christianity as a heterodox creed in 1825. The first European priest to be executed was François Isidore Gagelin who was strangled by six soldiers as he knelt on a scaffold in Hué in 1833. In 1840 Minh Mang actually read the Old Testament in Chinese translation, declaring it to be 'absurd'.

Yet, Christianity continued to spread as Buddhism declined and there was a continual stream of priests willing to risk their lives proselytizing. In addition, the economy was in disarray and natural disasters common. Poor Vietnamese saw Christianity as a way to break the shackles of their feudal existence. Fearing a peasants' revolt, the Emperor ordered the execution of 25 European priests, 300 Vietnamese priests, and 30,000 Vietnamese Catholics between 1848 and 1860. Provoked by these killings, the French attacked and took Saigon in 1859. In 1862 **Emperor Tu Duc** signed a treaty ceding the three southern provinces to the French, thereby creating the colony of **Cochin China**. This treaty of 1862 effectively paved the way for the eventual seizure by the French of the whole kingdom.

In 1883 and 1884, the French forced the Emperor to sign treaties making Vietnam a French protectorate. The Emperor called on China for assistance and demanded that provinces resist French rule; but the imperial bidding proved ineffective, and in 1885 the **Treaty of Tientsin** recognized the French protectorates of Tonkin (North Vietnam) and Annam (Central Vietnam), to add to that of Cochin China (South Vietnam).

Resistance to the French: the prelude to revolution

Like other European powers in Southeast Asia, the French managed to achieve military victory with ease, but they failed to stifle Vietnamese nationalism. After 1900, as Chinese translations of the works of Rousseau, Voltaire and social Darwinists such as Herbert Spence began to find their way into the hands of the Vietnamese intelligentsia, so resistance grew. Foremost among these early nationalists were Phan Boi Chau (1867-1940) and Phan Chau Trinh (1871-1926) who wrote tracts calling for the expulsion of the French. But these men and others such as Prince Cuong De (1882-1951) were traditional nationalists, their beliefs rooted in Confucianism rather than revolutionary Marxism. Their efforts and perspectives were essentially in the tradition of the nationalists who had resisted Chinese domination over previous centuries.

Quoc Dan Dang (VNQDD), founded at the end of 1927, was the first nationalist party, while the first significant communist group was the **Indochina Communist Party (ICP)** established by **Ho Chi Minh** in 1930. Both the VNQDD and the ICP organized resistance to the French and there were numerous strikes and uprisings, particularly during the harsh years of the Great Depression. The Japanese 'occupation' from August 1940 (Vichy France permitted the Japanese full access to military facilities in exchange for allowing continued French administrative control) saw the creation of the **Viet Minh** to fight for the liberation of Vietnam from Japanese and French control.

The Vietnam wars

The First Indochina War (1945-1954)

The war started in September 1945 in the south of the country and in 1946 in the north. These years marked the onset of fighting **between the Viet Minh and the French** and the period is usually referred to as the First Indochina War. The communists, who had organized against the Japanese, proclaimed the creation of the **Democratic Republic of Vietnam (DRV)** on 2 September 1945 when Ho Chi Minh read out the Vietnamese **Declaration of Independence** in Hanoi's Ba Dinh Square. Ironically, this document was modelled closely on the American

Ho Chi Minh: 'He who enlightens'

Ho Chi Minh, one of a number of pseudonyms Ho adopted during his life, was born Nguyen Sinh Cung, or possibly Nguyen Van Thanh (Ho did not keep a diary during much of his life, so parts of his life are still a mystery), in Nghe An Province near Vinh on the 19 May 1890, and came from a poor scholar-gentry family. In the village, the family was aristocratic; beyond it they were little more than peasants. His father, though not a revolutionary, was a dissenter and rather than go to Hué to serve the French, he chose to work as a village school teacher. Ho must have been influenced by his father's implacable animosity towards the French, although Ho's early years are obscure. He went to Quoc Hoc College in Hué and then worked for a while as a teacher in Phan Thiet, a fishing village in South Annam.

In 1911, under the name Nguyen Tat Thanh, he travelled to Saigon and left the country as a messboy on the French ship *Amiral Latouche-Tréville*. He is said to have used the name 'Ba' so that he would not shame his family by accepting such lowly work. This marked the beginning of three years of travel during which he visited France, England, America (where the skyscrapers of Manhattan both amazed and appalled him) and North Africa. Seeing the colonialists on their own turf and reading such revolutionary literature as the French Communist Party newspaper *L'Humanité*, he was converted to communism. In Paris he mixed with leftists, wrote pamphlets and attended meetings of the French Socialist Party. He also took odd jobs: for a while he worked at the **Carlton Hotel** in London and became an assistant pastry chef under the legendary French chef Georges Escoffier.

An even more unlikely story emerges from Gavin Young's *A Wavering Grace* In the book he recounts an interview he conducted with Mae West in 1968 shortly after he had returned from reporting the Tet offensive. On hearing of Vietnam, Mae West innocently said that she "used to know someone *very*, very important there ... His name was Ho ... Ho ... Ho something". At the time she was staying at the Carlton while starring in a London show, *Sex*. She confided to Young: "There was this waiter, cook, I don't know what he was. I know he had the slinkiest eyes though. We met in the corridor. We – well ..." Young writes that "Her voice trailed off in a husky sigh..."

Gradually Ho became an even more committed communist, contributing articles to radical newspapers and working his way into the web of communist

Declaration of Independence. Indeed, the US was favourably disposed towards the Viet Minh and Ho Chi Minh. Operatives of the OSS (the wartime precursor to the CIA) met Ho Chi Minh and supported his efforts during the war and afterwards Roosevelt's inclination was to prevent France claiming their colony back. Only Winston Churchill's persuasion changed his mind.

The French, although they had always insisted that Vietnam be returned to French rule, were in no position to force the issue. Instead, in the south, it was and leftist groups. At the same time he remained, curiously, a French cultural chauvinist, complaining for example about the intrusion of English words like *le manager* and *le challenger* (referring to boxing contests) into the French language. He even urged the French prime minister to ban foreign words from the French press. In 1923 he left France for Moscow and was trained as a communist activist – effectively a spy. From there, Ho travelled to Canton where he was instrumental in forming the Vietnamese communist movement. This culminated in the creation of the Indochina Communist Party in 1930. His movements during these years are scantily documented: he became a Buddhist monk in Siam (Thailand), was arrested in Hong Kong for subversive activities and received a six month sentence, travelled to China several times, and in 1940 even returned to Vietnam for a short period – his first visit for nearly 30 years. Despite his absence from the country, the French had already recognized the threat that he posed and sentenced him to death in absentia in 1930. He did not adopt the pseudonym by which he is now best known – Ho Chi Minh – until the early 1940s.

Ho was a consummate politician and, despite his revolutionary fervour, a great realist. He was also a charming man, and during his stay in France between June and October 1946 he made a great number of friends. Robert Shaplen in his book *The Lost Revolution* (1965) talks of his "wit, his oriental courtesy, his savoir-faire… above all his seeming sincerity and simplicity". He talked with farmers and fishermen and debated with priests; he impressed people wherever he travelled. He died in Hanoi at his house in the former governor's residence in 1969.

Since the demise of communism in the former Soviet Union, the Vietnamese leadership have been concerned that secrets about Ho's life might be gleaned from old comintern files in Moscow by nosy journalists. To thwart such an eventuality, they have, reportedly, sent a senior historian to scour the archives. To date, Ho's image remains largely untarnished – making him an exception amongst the tawdry league of former communist leaders. But a Moscow-based reporter has unearthed evidence implying Ho was married, challenging the official hagiography that paints Ho as a celibate who committed his entire life to the revolution. It takes a brave Vietnamese to challenge established 'fact'. In 1991, when the popular Vietnamese *Youth* or *Tuoi Tre* newspaper dared to suggest that Ho had married Tang Tuyet Minh in China in 1926, the editor was summarily dismissed from her post.

British troops (mainly Gurkhas) who helped the small force of French against the Viet Minh. Incredibly, the British also ordered the Japanese, who had only just capitulated, to help fight the Vietnamese. When 35,000 French reinforcements arrived, the issue in the south – at least superficially – was all but settled, with Ca Mau at the southern extremity of the country falling on 21 October. From that point, the war in the south became an underground battle of attrition, with the north providing support to their southern comrades.

In the north, the Viet Minh had to deal with 180,000 rampaging Nationalist Chinese troops, while preparing for the imminent arrival of a French force. Unable to confront both at the same time, and deciding that the French were probably the lesser of two evils, Ho Chi Minh decided to negotiate. To make the DRV government more acceptable to the French, Ho Chi Minh proceeded cautiously, only nationalizing a few strategic industries, bringing moderates into the government, and actually dissolving the Indochina Communist Party (at least on paper) in November 1945. But in the same month, he also said: "The French colonialists should know that the Vietnamese people do not wish to spill blood, that it loves peace. But if it must sacrifice millions of combatants, lead a resistance for long years to defend the independence of the country, and preserve its children from slavery, it will do so. It is certain the resistance will win."

Chinese withdrawal In February 1946, the French and Chinese signed a treaty leading to the withdrawal of Chinese forces and shortly afterwards Ho Chi Minh concluded a treaty with French President de Gaulle's special emissary to Vietnam, Jean Sainteny, in which Vietnam was acknowledged as a 'free' (the Vietnamese word *doc lap* being translated as free, but not yet independent) state that was within the French Union and the Indochinese Federation.

It is interesting to note that in negotiating with the French, Ho Chi Minh was going against most of his supporters who argued for confrontation. But Ho Chi Minh, ever a pragmatist, believed at this stage that the Viet Minh were ill-trained and poorly armed and he appreciated the need for time to consolidate their position. The episode that is usually highlighted as the flashpoint that led to the resumption of hostilities was the French government's decision to open a customs house in Haiphong at the end of 1946. The Viet Minh forces resisted and the rest, as they say, is history. It seems that during the course of 1946 Ho Chi Minh changed his view of the best path to independence. Initially he asked: "Why should we sacrifice 50 or 100,000 men when we can achieve independence within five years through negotiation?" although he later came to the conclusion that it was necessary to fight for independence. The customs house episode might, therefore, be viewed as merely an excuse. The French claimed that 5000 Vietnamese were killed in the ensuing bombardment, versus five Frenchmen; the Vietnamese put the toll at 20,000.

In a pattern that was to become characteristic of the entire 25-year conflict, while the French controlled the cities, the Viet Minh were dominant in the countryside. By the end of 1949, with the success of the Chinese Revolution and the establishment of the Democratic People's Republic of Korea (North Korea) in 1948, the US began to offer support to the French in an attempt to stem the 'Red Tide' that seemed to be sweeping across Asia. At this early stage, the odds appeared stacked against the Viet Minh, but Ho Chi Minh was confident that time was on their side. As he remarked to Sainteny "If we have to fight, we will fight. You can kill 10 of my men for every one I kill of yours but even at those odds, I will win and you will lose". It also became increasingly clear that the French were not committed to negotiating a route to independence.

Dien Bien Phu (1954) and the Geneva Agreement The decisive battle of the First Indochina War was at Dien Bien Phu in the hills of the northwest, close to the border with Laos. At the end of 1953 the French, with American support, parachuted 16,000 men into the area in an attempt to protect Laos from Viet Minh incursions and to tempt them into open battle. The French in fact found themselves trapped, surrounded by Viet Minh and overlooked by artillery. There was some suggestion that the US might become involved, and even use tactical nuclear weapons, but this was not to be. In May 1954 the French surrendered – the most humiliating of French colonial defeats – effectively marking the end of the French presence in Indochina (for a fuller account, see box, page 86). In July 1954, in Geneva, the French and Vietnamese agreed to divide the country along the 17th parallel, so creating twostates – the communists occupying the north and the non-communists occupying the south. The border was kept open for 300 days and over that period about 900,000 – mostly Roman Catholic – Vietnamese travelled south. At the same time nearly 90,000 Viet Minh troops along with 43,000 civilians went north, although many Viet Minh remained in the south to continue the fight there.

The Second Indochina War (1954-1975)
The Vietnam War, but particularly the American part of that war, is probably the most minutely studied, reported, analysed and recorded in history. Yet, as with all wars, there are still large grey areas and continuing disagreement over important episodes.

Ngo Dinh Diem
At the time of the partition of Vietnam along the 17th parallel, the government in the south was chaotic and the communists could be fairly confident that in a short time their sympathizers would be victorious. This situation was to change with the rise of Ngo Dinh Diem. Born in Hué in 1901 to a Roman Catholic Confucian family, Diem wished to become a priest. He graduated at the top of his class from the French School of Administration and at the age of 32 was appointed to the post of minister of the interior at the court of Emperor Bao Dai. Here, according to the political scientist William Turley, "he worked with uncommon industry and integrity" only to resign in exasperation at court intrigues and French interference. He withdrew from political activity during the First Indochina War and in 1946 Ho Chi Minh offered him a post in the DRV government – an offer he declined.

Turley describes him as a man who was a creature of the past: "For Diem, the mandarin, political leadership meant rule by example, precept and paternalism. His Catholic upbringing reinforced rather than replaced the Confucian tendency to base authority on doctrine, morality and hierarchy. Utterly alien to him were the concepts of power-sharing and popular participation. He was the heir to a dying tradition, member of an elite that had been superbly prepared by birth, training, and experience to lead a Vietnam that no longer existed."

In July 1954 Diem returned from his self-imposed exile at the Maryknoll Seminary in New Jersey to become Premier of South Vietnam. It is usually alleged that the US administration was behind his rise to power, although this has yet to be proved. He held two rigged elections (in October 1955, 450,000 registered voters cast 605,025 votes) that gave some legitimacy to his administration in American eyes. He proceeded to suppress all opposition in the country. His brutal brother, Ngo Dinh Nhu, was appointed to head the security forces and terrorized much of Vietnamese society.

During the period of Diem's premiership, opposition to his rule, particularly in the countryside, increased. This was because the military's campaign against the Viet Minh targeted – both directly and indirectly – many innocent peasants. At the same time, the nepotism and corruption that was endemic within the administration also turned many people into Viet Minh sympathizers. That said, Diem's campaign was successful in undermining the strength of the Communist Party in the south. While there were perhaps 50,000-60,000 party members in 1954, this figure had declined through widespread arrests and intimidation to only 5000 by 1959.

The erosion of the Party in the south gradually led, from 1959, to the north changing its strategy towards one of more overt military confrontation. The same year also saw the establishment of Group 559, which was charged with the task of setting up what was to become the Ho Chi Minh Trail, along which supplies and troops were moved from the north to the south. But, even at this stage, the Party's forces in the south were kept from open confrontation and many of its leaders were hoping for victory without having to resort to open warfare. There was no call for a 'People's War' and armed resistance was left largely to guerrillas belonging to the Cao Dai (see page 412) and Hoa Hao (Buddhist millenarian) sects. The establishment of the National Liberation Front of Vietnam in 1960 was an important political and organizational development towards creating a credible alternative to Diem – although it did not hold its first congress until 1962.

The escalation of the armed conflict (1959-1963)

Viet Cong

The armed conflict began to intensify from the beginning of 1961 when all the armed forces under the communists' control were unified under the banner of the **People's Liberation Armed Forces (PLAF)**. By this time the Americans were already using the term Viet Cong (or VC) to refer to communist troops. They reasoned that the victory at Dien Bien Phu had conferred almost heroic status on the name Viet Minh. American psychological warfare specialists therefore invented the term Viet Cong, an abbreviation of *Viet-nam Cong-san* (or Vietnamese Communists) and persuaded the media in Saigon to begin substituting it for Viet Minh from 1956.

The election of **John F Kennedy** to the White House in January 1961 coincided with the communists' decision to widen the war in the south. In the same year Kennedy dispatched 400 special forces troops and 100 special military advisers to Vietnam, in flagrant contravention of the Geneva Agreement. With the cold war getting colder, and Soviet Premier Nikita Khrushchev confirming his support for wars of 'national liberation', Kennedy could not back down and by the end of 1962 there were 11,000 US personnel in South Vietnam. At the same time the NLF had around 23,000 troops at its disposal. Kennedy was still saying that: "In the final analysis, it's their war and they're the ones who have to win or lose it". But just months after the Bay of Pigs debacle in Cuba, Washington set out on the path that was ultimately to lead to America's first large-scale military defeat.

The bungling and incompetence of the forces of the south, the interference that US advisers and troops had to face, the misreading of the situation by US military commanders, and the skill – both military and political – of the communists, are most vividly recounted in Neil Sheehan's massive book, *A Bright Shining Lie* (see page 422). The conflict quickly escalated from 1959. The north infiltrated about 44,000 men and women into the south between then and 1964, while the number recruited in the south was between 60,000 and 100,000. In August 1959, the first consignment of arms was carried down the **Ho Chi Minh Trail** into South Vietnam. Meanwhile, Kennedy began supporting, arming and training the Army of the Republic of Vietnam (ARVN). The US however, shied away from any large-scale, direct confrontation between its forces and the Viet Cong.

An important element in Diem's military strategy at this time was the establishment of **strategic hamlet**s, better known simply as 'hamleting'. This strategy was modelled on British anti-guerrilla warfare during Malaya's communist insurgency, and aimed to deny the communists any bases of support in the countryside while at the same time making it more difficult for communists to infiltrate the villages and 'propagandize' there. The villages which were ringed by barbed wire were labelled 'concentration camps' by the communists, and the often brutal, forced relocation that peasants had to endure probably turned even more of them into communist sympathizers. Of the 7000-8000 villages sealed in this way, only a fifth could ever have been considered watertight.

In January 1963 at **Ap Bac**, not far from the town of My Tho, the communists scored their first significant victory in the south. Facing 2000 well-armed ARVN troops, a force of just 300-400 PLAF inflicted heavy casualties and downed five helicopters. After this defeat, many American advisers drew the conclusion that if the communists were to be defeated, it could not be left to the ARVN alone – US troops would have to become directly involved. As Lieutenant Colonel John Vann, a US Army officer, remarked after the debacle to the American media (as cited in Neil Sheehan's *A Bright Shining Lie*): "A miserable damn performance. These people won't listen. They make the same goddam mistakes over and over again in the same way."

In mid-1963 a Buddhist monk from Hué committed suicide by dousing his body with petrol and setting it alight. This was the first of a number of **self-immolations**, suggesting that even in the early days the Diem regime was not only losing the military war but also the 'hearts and minds' war. He responded with characteristic heavy handedness by ransacking suspect pagodas. On 2 December 1963, Diem and his brother Nhu were both assassinated during an army coup.

The US decision to enter the war has been the subject of considerable disagreement. Until recently, the received wisdom was that the US administration had already taken the decision, and manufactured events to justify their later actions. However, the publication of numerous State Department, Presidential, CIA, Defence Department and National Security Council files – all dating from 1964 – has shed new light on events leading up to American intervention.

In Roger Warner's *Back Fire* (1995), which deals largely with the CIA's secret war in Laos, he recounts a story of a war game commissioned by the Pentagon and played by the Rand Corporation in 1962. They were asked to play a week-long game simulating a 10-year conflict in Vietnam. At the end of the week, having committed 500,000 men, the US forces were bogged down, there was student unrest and the American population had lost confidence in their leaders and in the conduct of the war. When the game was played a year later but, on the insistence of the US Airforce, with much heavier aerial bombing, the conclusions were much the same. If only, if only …

By all accounts, **Lyndon Johnson** was a reluctant warrior. In the 1964 presidential campaign he repeatedly said: "We don't want our American boys to do the fighting for Asian boys". This was not just for public consumption. The files show that LBJ always doubted the wisdom of intervention. But he also believed that John F Kennedy had made a solemn pledge to help the South Vietnamese people, a pledge that he was morally obliged to keep.

It has usually been argued that the executive manufactured the **Gulf of Tonkin Incident** to force Congress and the public to approve an escalation of America's role in the conflict. It was reported that two American destroyers, the *USS Maddox* and *USS C Turner Joy*, were attacked without provocation in international waters on the 2 August 1964 by North Vietnamese patrol craft. The US responded by bombing shore installations while presenting the Gulf of Tonkin Resolution to an outraged Congress for approval. Only two Congressmen voted against the resolution and President Johnson's poll rating jumped from 42% to 72%. In reality, the *USS Maddox* had been involved in electronic intelligence gathering while supporting clandestine raids by South Vietnamese mercenaries – well inside North Vietnamese territorial waters. This deception only became apparent in 1971 when the **Pentagon papers**, documenting the circumstances behind the incident, were leaked to the *New York Times* (the Pentagon papers were commissioned by Defense Secretary McNamara in June 1967 and written by 36 Indochina experts).

But these events are not sufficient to argue that the incident was manufactured to allow LBJ to start an undeclared war against North Vietnam. On 4 August, Secretary of State Dean Rusk told the American representative at the United Nations that: "In no sense is this destroyer a pretext to make a big thing out of a little thing". Even as late as the end of 1964, the President was unconvinced by arguments that the US should become more deeply involved. On 31 August, McGeorge Bundy wrote in a memorandum to Johnson: "A still more drastic possibility which no one is discussing is the use of substantial US armed forces in operation against the Viet Cong. I myself believe that before we let this country go we should have a hard look at this grim alternative, and I do not at all think that it is a repetition of Korea."

But events overtook President Johnson, and by 1965 the US was firmly embarked on the road to defeat. In March 1965, he ordered the beginning of the air war against the north perhaps acting on Air Force General Curtis Le May's observation that "we are swatting flies when we should be going after the manure pile". **Operation Rolling Thunder**, the most intense bombing campaign any country had yet experienced, began in March 1965 and ran through to October 1968. In 3½ years, twice the tonnage of bombs was dropped on Vietnam (and Laos) as during the entire Second World War. During its peak in 1967, 12,000 sorties were being flown each month – a total of 108,000 were flown throughout 1967. North Vietnam claimed that 4000 out of its 5788 villages were hit. Most terrifying were the B-52s that dropped their bombs from such an altitude (17,000 m) that the attack could not even be heard until the bombs hit their targets. Each aircraft carried 20 tonnes of bombs. By the end of the American war in 1973, 14 million tonnes of all types of munitions had been used in Indochina, an explosive force representing 700 times that of the atomic bomb dropped on Hiroshima. As General Curtis Le May explained on 25 November 1965 – "We should bomb them back into the Stone Age". In the same month that Rolling Thunder commenced, marines landed at Danang to defend its airbase, and by June 1965 there were 74,000 US troops in Vietnam. Despite President Johnson's reluctance to commit the US to the conflict, events forced his hand. He realized that the undisciplined South Vietnamese could not prevent a communist victory. Adhering to the domino theory, and with his own and the US's reputation at stake, he had no choice. As Johnson is said to have remarked to his press secretary Bill Moyers: "I feel like a hitchhiker caught in a hail storm on a Texas highway. I can't win. I can't hide. And I can't make it stop."

Dispersal of the north's industry

In response to the bombing campaign, industry in the north was decentralized and dispersed to rural areas. Each province was envisaged as a self-sufficient production unit. The economic effect of this strategy was felt at the time in a considerable loss of productivity; a cost judged to be worth paying to protect the north's industrial base. In order to protect the population in the north, they too were relocated to the countryside. By the end of 1967 Hanoi's population was a mere 250,000 essential citizens – about a quarter of the pre-war figure. The same was true of other urban centres. What the primary US objective was in mounting the air war remains unclear. In part, it was designed to destroy the north's industrial base and its ability to wage war; to dampen the people's will to fight; to sow seeds of discontent; to force the leadership in the north to the negotiating table; and perhaps to punish those in the north for supporting their government. By October 1968 the US realized the bombing was having little effect and they called a halt. The legacy of Operation Rolling Thunder, however, would live on. Turley wrote: "... the bombing had destroyed virtually all industrial, transportation and communications facilities built since 1954, blotted out 10 to 15 years' potential

A war glossary

Agent Orange	herbicide used to defoliate forests
APC	armoured personnel carrier
ARVN	Army of the Republic of Vietnam; the army of the South
Body Count	the number of dead on a field of battle
BUFF	nickname for the B-52 bomber; stands for Big Ugly Fat Fellow or, more usually, Big Ugly Fat Fucker
COIN	counter-insurgency
DMZ	demilitarized zone; the border between North and South Vietnam at the 17th parallel
Dust-off	medical evacuation helicopter
DZ	parachute drop zone
FAC	forward air controller, an airborne spotter who directed bombers onto the target
Fire base	defence fortification for artillery, from which to support infantry
Fragging	to kill or attempt to kill with a fragmentation grenade; better known as the killing of US officers and NCOs by their own men. In 1970 one study reported 209 fraggings
Gook	slang, derogatory term for all Vietnamese
Grunt	slang for a US infantryman; the word comes from the 'grunt' emitted when shouldering a heavy pack
Huey	most commonly used helicopter, UH1
LZ	helicopter landing zone
Napalm	jellified fuel, the name derives from two of its constituents, naphthenic and palmitic acids. To be burnt by napalm after an

economic growth, flattened three major cities and 12 of 29 province capitals, and triggered a decline in per capita agricultural output".

However, it was not just the bombing campaign that was undermining the north's industrial and agricultural base. Socialist policies in the countryside were labelling small land owners as 'landlords' – in effect, traitors to the revolutionary cause – thus alienating many farmers. In the cities, industrial policies were no less short-sighted. Although Ho Chi Minh's policies in the battlefield were driven by hard-headed pragmatism, in the field of economic development they were informed – tragically – by revolutionary fervour.

William Westmoreland, the general appointed to command the American effort, aimed to use the superior firepower and mobility of the US to 'search and destroy' PAVN forces. North Vietnamese bases in the south were to be identified using modern technology, jungle hideouts revealed by dumping chemical defoliants and then attacked with shells, bombs and by helicopter-borne troops. In 'free-fire zones' the army and air force were permitted to use whatever level

	attack was terrible and one of the most famous photo images of the war (taken by Nick Ut) showed a naked local girl (Kim Phuc) running along a road at Trang Bang, northwest of Saigon after being burnt; the girl survived the attack by South Vietnamese aircraft and now lives in Canada
NLF	National Liberation Front
NVA	North Vietnamese Army
PAVN	People's Army of Vietnam
Phoenix	counter-insurgency programme established by the US after the Tet Offensive of 1968 (see page 369)
PLAF	People's Liberation Armed Forces; the army of the communist north
POW/MIA	prisoner of war/missing in action
Pungi stakes	sharpened bamboo stakes concealed in VC pits: accounted for 2% of US combat wounds
Purple Heart	medal awarded to US troops wounded in action
R&R	Rest & Recreation; leave
ROE	rules of engagement
Rome Plow	20 tonne bulldozer designed to clear forest. Equipped with a curved blade and sharp protruding spike it could split the largest trees
Tunnel Rats	US army volunteers who fought VC in the Cu Chi tunnels
VC, Charlie	Viet Cong (see page 362); US term for Vietnamese Communist; often shortened to Charlie from the phonetic alphabet, Victor Charlie
Viet Minh	Communist troops – later changed to Viet Cong (see above and page 362)
WP, Willy Pete	White phosphorous rocket used to mark a target

of firepower they felt necessary to dislodge the enemy. 'Body counts' became the measure of success and collateral damage – or civilian casualties – was a cost that just had to be borne. As one field commander famously explained: "We had to destroy the town to save it." By 1968 the US had more than 500,000 troops in Vietnam, while **South Korean, Australian, New Zealand, Filipino** and **Thai** forces contributed another 90,000. The ARVN officially had 1.5 million men under arms (100,000 or more of these were 'flower' or phantom soldiers, the pay for whom was pocketed by officers in an increasingly corrupt ARVN). Ranged against this vastly superior force were perhaps 400,000 PAVN and National Liberation Front forces.

1964-1968: who was winning?
The leadership in the north tried to allay serious anxieties about their ability to defeat the American-backed south by emphasizing human over physical and material resources. **Desertions** from the ARVN were very high – there were 113,000 from the army in 1965 alone (200,000 in 1975) – and the PAVN did record a number of significant

The Anzacs in Vietnam

In April 1964, President Johnson called for "more flags" to help defend South Vietnam. Among the countries that responded to his call were Australia and New Zealand. Australia had military advisers in Vietnam from 1962, but in April 1965 sent the First Battalion Royal Australian Regiment. Until 1972 there were about 7000 Australian combat troops in Vietnam, based in the coastal province of Phuoc Tuy, not far from Saigon. There, operating as a self-contained unit in a Viet Cong-controlled zone, and with the support of two batteries of 105 mm artillery (one from New Zealand), the Australians fought one of the most effective campaigns of the entire war.

As US Army Chief of Staff, General Westmoreland said: "Aggressiveness, quick reaction, the good use of firepower, and old-fashioned Australian courage have produced outstanding results."

Of the battles fought by the Australians in Phuoc Tuy, one of the most significant was **Long Tan**, on 18 August 1966. Although caught out by the advance of 4000 Viet Cong, the Australians successfully responded to inflict heavy casualties: 17 dead against about 250 VC. Following this they managed to expand control over large areas of the province, and then win the support of the local people. Unlike the Americans who adopted a policy of 'search and destroy', the Australians were more intent on a 'hearts and minds' strategy (COIN, or counter insurgency). Through various health, education and other civic action programmes, the Australians gained the confidence of many villagers, making it much harder for the VC to infiltrate rural areas of Phuoc Tuy.

This policy of gaining support of the local population was complemented by the highly effective use of small **Special Air Service** (SAS) teams who worked closely with the US Special Forces. Many of these men were transferred after fighting in the jungles of Borneo during the *Konfrontasi* between Malaysia and Indonesia. They came well trained in the art of jungle warfare and ended the war with the highest kill ratio of any similar unit: at least 500 VC dead, against none of their own to hostile fire. The Australians left Phuoc Tuy in late 1971, having lost 423 men. The ARVN were unable to fill the vacuum, and the Viet Cong quickly regained control of the area.

victories. The communists also had to deal with large numbers of desertions – 28,000 men in 1969. By 1967 world opinion, and even American public opinion, appeared to be swinging against the war. Within the US, **anti-war demonstrations** and 'teach-ins' were spreading, officials were losing confidence in the ability of the US to win the war, and the president's approval rating was sinking fast. As the US Secretary of Defense, Robert McNamara is quoted as saying in the *Pentagon Papers*: "... the picture of the world's greatest superpower killing or seriously injuring 1000 non-combatants a week, while trying to pound a tiny, backward nation into submission on an issue whose merits are hotly disputed, is not a pretty one."

But although the communists may have been winning the psychological and public opinion wars, they were increasingly hard-pressed to maintain this advantage on the ground. Continual American strikes against their bases, and the social and economic dislocations in the countryside, were making it more difficult for the communists to recruit supporters. At the same time, the fight against a vastly better equipped enemy was also taking its toll in sheer exhaustion. Despite what is now widely regarded as a generally misguided US military strategy in Vietnam, there were notable US successes (for example, the Phoenix Programme, see page 370). American GIs were always sceptical about the 'pacification' programmes that aimed to win the 'hearts and minds' war. GIs were fond of saying, 'If you've got them by the balls, their hearts and minds will follow.' At times, the US military and politicians appeared to view the average Vietnamese as inferior to the average American. This latent racism was reflected in General Westmoreland's remark that Vietnamese "don't think about death the way we do" and in the use by most US servicemen of the derogatory name 'gook' to refer to Vietnamese.

At the same time as the Americans were trying to win 'hearts and minds', the Vietnamese were also busy indoctrinating their men and women, and the population in the 'occupied' south. In Bao Ninh's moving *The Sorrow of War* (1994), the main character, Kien, who fights with a scout unit describes the indoctrination that accompanied the soldiers from their barracks to the field: "Politics continuously. Politics in the morning, politics in the afternoon, politics again in the evening. 'We won, the enemy lost. The enemy will surely lose. The north had a good harvest, a bumper harvest. The people will rise up and welcome you. Those who don't just lack awareness. The world is divided into three camps.' More politics."

By 1967, the war had entered a period of military (but not political) stalemate. As Robert McNamara writes in his book *In Retrospect: the Tragedy and Lessons of Vietnam*, it was at this stage that he came to believe that Vietnam was "a problem with no solution". In retrospect, he argues that the US should have withdrawn in late 1963, and certainly by late 1967. Massive quantities of US arms and money were preventing the communists from making much headway in urban areas, while American and ARVN forces were ineffective in the countryside – although incessant bombing and ground assaults wreaked massive destruction. A black market of epic proportions developed in Saigon, as millions of dollars of assistance went astray. American journalist Stanley Karnow once remarked to a US official that "we could probably buy off the Vietcong at US$500 a head". The official replied that they had already calculated the costs, but came to "US$2500 a head".

The Tet Offensive, 1968: the beginning of the end

By mid-1967, the communist leadership in the north felt it was time for a further escalation of the war in the south to regain the initiative. They began to lay the groundwork for what was to become known as the Tet (or New Year) Offensive – perhaps the single most important series of battles during the American War in Vietnam. During the early morning of 1 February 1968, shortly after noisy celebrations had welcomed in the New Year, 84,000 communist troops – almost all Viet Cong – simultaneously attacked targets in 105 urban centres. Utterly surprising the US and South Vietnamese, the Tet Offensive had begun.

Preparations for the offensive had been laid over many months. Arms, ammunition and guerrillas were smuggled and infiltrated into urban areas and detailed planning was undertaken. Central to the strategy was a 'sideshow' at Khe Sanh. By mounting an attack on the marine outpost at **Khe Sanh**, the communists successfully convinced the American and Vietnamese commanders that another Dien Bien Phu was underway. General Westmoreland moved 50,000 US troops away from the cities and suburbs to prevent any such humiliating repetition of the French defeat. But Khe Sanh was just a diversion, a feint designed to draw attention away from the cities. In this the communists were successful; for days after the Tet offensive, Westmoreland and the South Vietnamese President Thieu thought Khe Sanh to be the real objective and the attacks in the cities the decoy.

The most interesting aspect of the Tet Offensive was that although it was a strategic victory for the communists, it was also a considerable tactical defeat. They may have occupied the US embassy in Saigon for a few hours but, except in Hué, communist forces were quickly repulsed by US and ARVN troops. The government in the South did not collapse nor did the ARVN. Cripplingly high casualties were inflicted on the communists – cadres at all echelons were killed – morale was undermined and it became clear that the cities would not rise up spontaneously to support the communists. Tet, in effect, put paid to the VC as an effective fighting force. The fight was now increasingly taken up by the North Vietnamese Army (NVA). This was to have profound effects on the government of South Vietnam after reunification in 1975; southern communists and what remained of the political wing of the VC – the government in waiting – were entirely overlooked as northern communists were given all the positions of political power, a process that continues. This caused intense bitterness at the time and also explains the continued mistrust of many southerners for Hanoi. Walt Rostow wrote in 1995 that "Tet was an utter military and political defeat for the communists in Vietnam", but adding "yet a political disaster in the United States". But this was not to matter; Westmoreland's request for more troops was turned down and US public support for the war slumped still further as they heard reported that the US embassy itself had been 'over-run'. Those who for years had been claiming it was only a matter of time before the communists were defeated seemed to be contradicted by the scale and intensity of the offensive. Even President Johnson was stunned by the VC's successes for he too had believed the US propaganda. As it turned out the VC incursion was by a 20-man unit from Sapper Battalion C-10 who were all killed in the action. Their mission was not to take the embassy but to 'make a psychological gesture'. In that regard at least, the mission must have exceeded the leadership's wildest expectations.

The **Phoenix Programme**, established in the wake of the Tet Offensive, aimed to destroy the communists' political infrastructure in the Mekong Delta. Named after the Vietnamese mythical bird the Phung Hoang, which could fly anywhere, the programme sent CIA-recruited and trained Counter Terror Teams – in effect assassination units – into the countryside. The teams were ordered to try and capture communist cadres; invariably they fired first and asked questions later. By 1971, it was estimated that the programme had led to the capture of 28,000 members of the VCI (Viet Cong Infrastructure), the death of 20,000 and the defection of a further 17,000. By the early 1970s the countryside in the Mekong Delta was more peaceful than it had been for years; towns that were previously strongholds of the Viet Cong had reverted to the control of the local authorities. Critics have questioned what proportion of those killed, captured and sometimes tortured were communist cadres, but even communist documents admit that it seriously undermined their support network in the area. In these terms, the Phoenix Programme was a great success.

The costs

The Tet Offensive concentrated American minds. The costs of the war by that time had been vast. The US budget deficit had risen to 3% of Gross National Product by 1968, inflation was accelerating, and thousands of young men had been killed for a cause that, to many, was becoming less clear by the month. Before the end of the year President Johnson had ended the bombing campaign. Negotiations began in Paris in 1969 to try and secure an honourable settlement for the US. Although the last American combat troops were not to leave until March 1973, the Tet Offensive marked the beginning of the end. It was from that date the Johnson administration began to search seriously for a way out of the conflict. The illegal bombing of Cambodia in 1969 and the resumption of the bombing of the north in 1972 (the most intensive of the entire conflict) were only flurries of action on the way to an inevitable US withdrawal.

The Paris Agreement (1972)

US Secretary of State **Henry Kissinger** records the afternoon of 8 October 1972, a Sunday, as the moment when he realized that the communists were willing to agree a peace treaty. There was a great deal to discuss, particularly whether the treaty would offer the prospect of peaceful reunification, or the continued existence of two states: a communist north, and non-communist south. Both sides tried to force the issue: the US mounted further attacks and at the same time strengthened and expanded the ARVN. They also tried to play the 'Madman Nixon' card, arguing that **President Richard Nixon** was such a vehement anti-communist that he might well resort to the ultimate deterrent, the nuclear bomb. It is true that the PAVN was losing men through desertion and had failed to recover its losses in the Tet Offensive. Bao Ninh in his book *The Sorrow of War* about Kinh, a scout with the PAVN, wrote: "The life of the B3 Infantrymen after the Paris Agreement was a series of long suffering days, followed by months of retreating and months of counter-attacking, withdrawal, then counter-attack. The path of war seemed endless, desperate, and leading nowhere."

But the communist leadership knew well that the Americans were committed to withdrawal – the only question was when, so they felt that time was on their side. By 1972, US troops in the south had declined to 95,000, the bulk of whom were support troops. The north gambled on a massive attack to defeat the ARVN

ON THE ROAD
A nation at sea: the boat people

One of the most potent images of Vietnam during the 1970s and 80s was of foundering, overloaded vessels carrying 'boat people' to Hong Kong, Thailand, Malaysia and the Philippines. Beginning in 1976, but becoming a torrent from the late 1970s, these boat people initially fled political persecution. Later, most were economic migrants in search of a better life. Now the tragedy of the boat people is almost at an end and fast becoming a footnote in history as the last refugees are sent 'home' or onward to what they hope will be a better life.

Escaping the country was not easy. Many prospective boat people were caught by the authorities (often after having already paid the estimated US$500-3000 to secure a place on a boat), and sent to prison or to a re-education camp. Of those who embarked, it has been estimated that at least a third died at sea, from drowning or dehydration, and at the hands of pirates. The boats were usually small and poorly maintained, hardly seaworthy for a voyage across the East Sea. Captains rarely had charts (some did not even have an experienced sailor on board) and most had never ventured further afield than the coastal waters with which they were familiar.

By 1977, the exodus was so great that some freighters began to stop heaving-to to pick up refugees – a habit which, until then, had been sacrosanct among sailors. Malaysia instructed their coastal patrol vessels to force boats back out to sea – and in the first six months of 1979 they did just that to 267 vessels carrying an estimated 40,000 refugees. One boat drifted for days off Malaysia, with the passengers drinking their own urine, until they were picked up – but not before two children had died of dehydration. The Singapore and Malaysian governments adopted a policy of allowing boats to replenish their supplies, but not to land – forcing some vessels to sail all the way to Australia before they were assured of a welcome (over 8000 km). Cannibalism is also reported to have taken place; one boy who had only just survived being killed himself told a journalist: "After the body [of a boy] had been discovered, the boat master pulled it up out of the hold. Then he cut up the body. Everyone was issued a piece of meat about two fingers wide."

As numbers rose, so did the incidence of piracy – an age-old problem in the East Sea. Pirates, mostly Thai, realizing that the boats often carried families with all their possessions (usefully converted into portable gold) began to target the refugee boats. Some commentators have estimated that by the late 1970s, 30% of boats were being boarded, and the United Nations High Commissioner for Refugees (UNHCR) in 1981 reported that 81% of women had been raped. Sometimes the boats were boarded and plundered, the women raped, all the passengers murdered, and the boats sunk. Despite all these risks, Vietnamese continued to leave in huge numbers: by 1980 there were 350,000 awaiting resettlement in refugee camps in the countries of Southeast Asia and Hong Kong.

Most of these 'illegals' left from the south of Vietnam; identified with the former regime, they were systematically persecuted – particularly if they also happened to be ethnic Chinese or *Hoa* (the Chinese 'invasion' of 1979 did not help matters). But as conditions worsened in the north, large numbers also began to sail from Ha Long Bay and Haiphong. Soon the process became semi-official, as local and regional authorities realized that fortunes could be made providing boats and escorts. Large freighters began to carry refugees; the *Hai Hong* (1600 tonnes), which finally docked in Malaysia, was carrying 2500 passengers who claimed they had left with the cognizance of the authorities.

The peak period of the crisis spanned the years 1976-1979, with 270,882 leaving the country in 1979 alone. The flow of refugees slowed during 1980 and 1981 to about 50,000 and until 1988 averaged about 10,000 each year. But in the late 1980s the numbers picked up once again, with most sailing for Hong Kong and leaving from the north. It seems that whereas the majority of those sailing in the first phase (1976-1981) were political refugees, the second phase of the exodus was driven by economic pressures. Daily wage rates in Vietnam at that time were only 3000 dong (US$0.25), so it is easy to see the attraction of leaving for healthier economic climes. With more than 40,000 refugees in camps in Hong Kong, the Hong Kong authorities began to forcibly repatriate (euphemistically termed 'orderly return') those screened as economic migrants at the end of 1989 when 51 were flown to Hanoi. Such was the international outcry as critics highlighted fears of persecution that the programme was suspended. In May 1992, an agreement was reached between the British and Vietnamese governments to repatriate the 55,700 boat people living in camps in Hong Kong and the orderly return programme was quietly restarted. As part of their deal with China, the British government agreed to empty the camps before the handover date in 1997 (a target they failed to meet).

Ironically, the evidence is that those repatriated are doing well – better than those who never left the shores of Vietnam – and there is no real evidence of systematic persecution, despite the fears of such groups as Amnesty International. With the European Community and the UN offering assistance to returnees, they have set up businesses, enrolled on training courses and become embroiled in Vietnam's thrust for economic growth.

In early 1996, around 37,000 boat people were still living in camps in Hong Kong (mostly), Indonesia, Thailand, the Philippines and Japan. The difficulty is that those who are left are the least attractive to receiving countries. As Jahanshah Assadi of the UNHCR put it at the end of 1994, "Our Nobel Prize winners left a long time ago for the West", adding "What we have now is the bottom of the barrel." Even Vietnam is not enamoured with the idea of receiving ex-citizens who clearly do not wish to return. For the refugees themselves, they have been wasted years. As the UNHCR's Jean-Noel Wetterwald said in 1996: "Leaving Vietnam was the project of their lives." Now they're going back with nothing to show for the years and the tears.

and moved 200,000 men towards the demilitarized zone that marked the border between north and south. On 30 March the PAVN crossed into the south and quickly overran large sections of Quang Tri province. Simultaneous attacks were mounted in the west highlands, at Tay Ninh and in the Mekong Delta. For a while it looked as if the south would fall altogether. The US responded by mounting a succession of intense bombing raids that eventually forced the PAVN to retreat. The spring offensive may have failed, but like Tet, it was strategically important, for it demonstrated that without US support the ARVN was unlikely to be able to withstand a communist attack.

Both sides, by late 1972, were ready to compromise. Against the wishes of South Vietnam's President Nguyen Van Thieu, the US signed a treaty on 27 January 1973, the ceasefire going into effect on the same day. Before the signing, Nixon ordered the bombing of the north – the so-called Christmas Campaign. It lasted 11 days from 18 December (Christmas Day was a holiday) and was the most intensive of the war. With the ceasefire and President Thieu, however shaky, both in place, the US was finally able to back out of its nightmare and the last combat troops left in March 1973. As J William Fulbright, a highly influential member of the Senate and a strong critic of the US role in Vietnam, observed: "We [the US] have the power to do any damn fool thing we want, and we always seem to do it."

The Final Phase 1973-1975
The Paris Accord settled nothing; it simply provided a means by which the Americans could withdraw from Vietnam. It was never going to resolve the deep-seated differences between the two regimes and with only a brief lull, the war continued, this time without US troops. Thieu's government was probably in terminal decline even before the peace treaty was signed. Though ARVN forces were at their largest ever and, on paper, considerably stronger than the PAVN, many men were weakly committed to the cause of the south. Corruption was endemic, business was in recession, and political dissent was on the increase. The North's Central Committee formally decided to abandon the Paris Accord in October 1973; by the beginning of 1975 they were ready for the final offensive. It took only until April for the communists to achieve total victory. ARVN troops deserted in their thousands, and the only serious resistance was offered at Xuan Loc, less than 100 km from Saigon. President Thieu resigned on 27 April. ARVN generals, along with their men, were attempting to flee as the PAVN advanced on Saigon. The end was quick: at 1045 on 30 April a T-54 tank (number 843) crashed its way through the gates of the Presidential Palace, symbolizing the end of the Second Indochina War. For the US, the aftermath of the war would lead to years of soul searching; for Vietnam, to stagnation and isolation. A senior State Department figure, George Ball, reflected afterwards that the war was "probably the greatest single error made by America in its history".

Legacy of the Vietnam War

The Vietnam War (or 'American War' to the Vietnamese) is such an enduring feature of the West's experience of the country that many visitors look out for legacies of the conflict. There is no shortage of physically disabled Vietnamese. Many men were badly injured during the war, but large numbers also received their injuries while serving in Cambodia (1979-1989). It is tempting to associate deformed children with the enduring effects of the pesticide **Agent Orange** (1.7 million tonnes had been used by 1973), although this has yet to be proven scientifically; American studies claim that there is no significant difference in congenital malformation. One thing is certain: Agent Orange is detectable today only in tiny isolated spots, often near former military bases where chemicals were dumped. No scientific survey has found lingering widespread effects.

Bomb damage
Bomb damage is most obvious from the air: well over five million tonnes of bombs were dropped on the country (north and south) and there are said to be 20 million bomb craters – the sort of statistic people like to recount, but no one can legitimately verify. Many craters have yet to be filled in and paddy fields are still pockmarked. Some farmers have used these holes in the ground to farm fish and to use as small reservoirs to irrigate vegetable plots. War scrap was one of the country's most valuable exports. The cities in the north are surprisingly devoid of obvious signs of the bombing campaigns; Hanoi remains remarkably intact. In Hué the Citadel and the Forbidden Palace were extensively damaged during the Tet offensive in 1968 although much has now been rebuilt.

Psychological effect of the war
Even harder to measure is the effect of the war on the Vietnamese psyche. The Vietnamese Communist Party leadership still seem to be preoccupied by the conflict and school children are routinely shown war museums and Ho Chi Minh memorials. But despite the continuing propaganda offensive, people harbour surprisingly little animosity towards America or the West. Indeed, of all Westerners, it is often Americans who are most warmly welcomed, particularly in the south.

But it must be remembered that about 60% of Vietnam's population has been born since the US left in 1973, so have no memory of the American occupation. Probably the least visible but most lasting of all the effects of the war is in the number of elderly widowed women and the number of middle aged women who never married.

The deeper source of antagonism is the continuing divide between the north and south. It was to be expected that the forces of the north would exact their revenge on their foes in the south and many were relieved that the predicted bloodbath didn't materialize. But few would have thought that this revenge would be so long lasting. The 250,000 southern dead are not mourned or honoured, or even acknowledged. Former soldiers are denied jobs and the government doesn't recognize the need for national reconciliation.

This is the multiple legacy of the War on Vietnam and the Vietnamese. The legacy on the US and Americans is more widely appreciated. The key question that still occupies the minds of many, though, is, was it worth it? Economic historian Walt Rostow, ex-Singaporean prime minister Lee Kuan Yew and others would probably answer 'yes'. If the US had not intervened, communism would have spread farther in Southeast Asia; more dominoes, in their view, would have fallen. In 1973, when the US withdrawal was agreed, Lee Kuan Yew observed that the countries of Southeast Asia were much more resilient and resistant to communism than they had been, say, at the time of the Tet offensive in 1968. The US presence in Vietnam allowed them to reach this state of affairs. Yet Robert McNamara in his book *In Retrospect: the Tragedy and Lessons of Vietnam*, and one of the architects of US policy, wrote:

"Although we sought to do the right thing – and believed we were doing the right thing – in my judgment, hindsight proves us wrong. We both overestimated the effects of South Vietnam's loss on the security of the West and failed to adhere to the fundamental principle that, in the final analysis, if the South Vietnamese were to be saved, they had to win the war themselves."

After the war

The Socialist Republic of Vietnam (SRV) was born from the ashes of the Vietnam War on 2 July 1976 when former North and South Vietnam were reunified. Hanoi was proclaimed as the capital of the new country. But few Vietnamese would have guessed that their emergent country would be cast by the US in the mould of a pariah state for almost 18 years. First President George Bush I, and then his successor Bill Clinton, eased the US trade embargo bit by bit in a dance of appeasement and procrastination, as they tried to comfort American business clamouring for a slice of the Vietnamese pie, while also trying to stay on the right side of the vociferous lobby in the US demanding more action on the MIA (missing in action) issue. Appropriately, the embargo, which was first imposed on the former North in May 1964, and then nationwide in 1975, was finally lifted a few days before the celebrations of Tet, Vietnamese New Year, on 4 February 1994.

On the morning of 30 April 1975, just before 1100, a T-54 tank crashed through the gates of the Presidential Palace in Saigon, symbolically marking the end of the Vietnam War. Twenty years later, the same tank – number 843 – became a symbol of the past as parades and celebrations, and a good deal of soul searching, marked the anniversary of the end of the War. To many Vietnamese, in retrospect, 1975 was more a beginning than an end: it was the beginning of a collective struggle to come to terms with the war, to build a nation, to reinvigorate the economy and to excise the ghosts of the past.

Re-education camps

The newly formed Vietnam government ordered thousands of people to report for re-education camps in 1975. Those intended were ARVN members, ex-South Vietnam government members and those that had collaborated with the south regime including priests, artists, teachers and doctors. It was seen as a means of revenge and a way of indoctrinating the 'unbelievers' with communist propaganda. It was reported in the Indochina Newsletter in 1982 that some 80 camps existed with an estimated 100,000 still languishing in them seven years after the war ended. Detainees were initially told that they would be detained for between three days and one month. Those that were sent to the camp were forced to undertake physical labour and survived on very little food and without basic medical facilities.

The boat people
Many Vietnamese also fled, first illegally and then legally through the Orderly Departure Programme. See box, page 372.

Invasion of Cambodia
In April 1975, the Khmer Rouge took power in Cambodia. Border clashes with Vietnam erupted just a month after the Phnom Penh regime change but matters came to a head in 1977 when the Khmer Rouge accused Vietnam of seeking to incorporate Kampuchea into an Indochinese Federation. Hanoi's determination to oust Pol Pot only really became apparent on Christmas Day 1978, when 120,000 Vietnamese troops invaded. By 7 January they had installed a puppet government that proclaimed the foundation of the People's Republic of Kampuchea (PRK): Heng Samrin, a former member of the Khmer Rouge, was appointed president. The Vietnamese compared their invasion to the liberation of Uganda from Idi Amin – but for the rest of the world it was an unwelcome Christmas present. The new government was accorded scant recognition abroad, while the toppled government of Democratic Kampuchea retained the country's seat at the United Nations.

But the country's 'liberation' by Vietnam did not end the misery; in 1979 nearly half of Cambodia's population was in transit, either searching for their former homes or fleeing across the Thai border into refugee camps. The country reverted to a state of outright war again, for the Vietnamese were not greatly loved in Cambodia – especially by the Khmer Rouge. American political scientist Wayne Bert wrote: "The Vietnamese had long seen a special role for themselves in uniting and leading a greater Indochina Communist movement and the Cambodian Communists had seen with clarity that such a role for the Vietnamese could only be at the expense of their independence and prestige."

Under the Lon Nol and Khmer Rouge regimes, Vietnamese living in Cambodia were expelled or exterminated. Resentment had built up over the years Hanoi – exacerbated by the apparent ingratitude of the Khmer Rouge for Vietnamese assistance in fighting Lon Nol's US-supported Khmer Republic in the early 1970s. As relations between the Khmer Rouge and the Vietnamese deteriorated, the communist superpowers, China and the Soviet Union, polarised too – the former siding with Khmer Rouge and the latter with Hanoi.

The Vietnamese invasion had the full backing of Moscow, while the Chinese and Americans began their support for the anti-Vietnamese rebels.

Following the Vietnamese invasion, three main anti-Hanoi factions were formed. In June 1982 they banded together in an unholy alliance of convenience to fight the PRK and called themselves the Coalition Government of Democratic Kampuchea (CGDK), which was immediately recognised by the UN. The three factions of the CGDK were: The Communist Khmer Rouge whose field forces had recovered to at least 18,000 by the late 1980s. Supplied with weapons by China, they were concentrated in the Cardamom Mountains in the southwest and were also in control of some of the refugee camps along the Thai border. The National United Front for an Independent Neutral Peaceful and Co-operative Cambodia (Funcinpec) – known by most people as the Armée National Sihanoukiste (ANS). It was headed by Prince Sihanouk – although he spent most of his time exiled in Beijing; the group had fewer than 15,000 well-equipped troops – most of whom took orders from Khmer Rouge commanders. The anti-Communist Khmer People's National Liberation Front (KPNLF), headed by Son Sann, a former prime minister under Sihanouk. Its 5000 troops were reportedly ill-disciplined in comparison with the Khmer Rouge and the ANS.

The three CGDK factions were ranged against the 70,000 troops loyal to the government of President Heng Samrin and Prime Minister Hun Sen (previously a Khmer Rouge cadre.) they were backed by Vietnamese forces until September 1989.

In the late 1980s the Association of Southeast Asian Nations (ASEAN) – for which the Cambodian conflict had almost become its raison d'être – began steps to bring the warring factions together over the negotiating table. ASEAN countries were united in wanting the Vietnamese out of Cambodia. After Mikhail Gorbachev had come to power in the Soviet Union, Moscow's support for the Vietnamese presence in Cambodia gradually evaporated. Gorbachev began leaning on Vietnam as early as 1987, to withdraw its troops. Despite saying their presence in Cambodia was 'irreversible', Vietnam completed its withdrawal in September 1989, ending nearly 11 years of Hanoi's direct military involvement. The withdrawal led to an immediate upsurge in political and military activity, as forces of the exiled CGDK put increased pressure on the now weakened Phnom Penh regime to begin a round of power- sharing negotiations.

Border incursions with China

In February 1979 the Chinese marched into the far north of northern Vietnam justifying the invasion because of Vietnam's invasion of Cambodia, its treatment of Chinese in Vietnam, the ownership of the Paracel and Spratley Islands in the East Sea also claimed by China and a stand against Soviet expansion into Asia (Hanoi was strongly allied with the then USSR). They withdrew a month later following heavy casualties although both sides have claimed to be victorious. Vietnamese military hardware was far superior to the Chinese and their casualties were estimated to be between 20,000 and 60,000; Vietnamese casualties were around 15,000. In 1987 fighting again erupted on the Sino-Vietnamese border resulting in high casualties.

Modern Vietnam

Politics

The **Vietnamese Communist Party** (**VCP**) was established in Hong Kong in 1930 by Ho Chi Minh and arguably has been more successful than any other such party in Asia in mobilizing and maintaining support. While others have fallen, the VCP has managed to stay firmly in control. To enable them to get their message to a wider audience, the Communist Party of Vietnam have their own website, www.cpv.org.vn.

Vietnam is a one party state. In addition to the Communist Party the posts of president and prime minister were created when the constitution was revised in 1992. The president is head of state and the prime minister is head of the cabinet of ministries (including three deputies and 26 ministries), all nominated by the National Assembly. The current president is Truong Tan Sang and the current prime minister is Nguyen Tan Dung. Although the National Assembly is the highest instrument of state, it can still be directed by the Communist Party. The vast majority of National Assembly members are also party members. Elections for the National Assembly are held every five years. The Communist Party is run by a politburo of 15 members. The head is the general secretary, currently Nguyen Phu Trong. The politburo meets every five years and sets policy directions of the Party and the government. There is a Central Committee made up of 161 members, who are also elected at the Party Congress.

In 1986, at the Sixth Party Congress, the VCP launched its economic reform programme known as *doi moi*, which was a momentous step in ideological terms (see page 385). However, although the programme has done much to free up the economy, the party has ensured that it retains ultimate political power. Marxism-Leninism and Ho Chi Minh thought are still taught to Vietnamese school children and even so-called 'reformers' in the leadership are not permitted to diverge from the party line. In this sense, while economic reforms have made considerable progress (but see below) – particularly in the south – there is a very definite sense that the limits of political reform have been reached, at least for the time being.

From the late 1990s to the first years of the new millennium there have been a number of arrests and trials of dissidents charged with what might appear to be fairly innocuous crimes (see The future of communism in Vietnam, page 382) and, although the economic reforms enacted since the mid-1980s are still in place, the party resolutely rejects any moves towards greater political pluralism.

Despite the reforms, the leadership is still divided over the road ahead. But the fact that debate is continuing, sometimes openly, suggests that there is disagreement over the necessity for political reform and the degree of economic reform that should be encouraged.

In the country as a whole there is virtually no political debate at all, certainly not in the open. There are two reasons for this apparently curious state of affairs. First there is a genuine fear of discussing something that is absolutely taboo. Second, and more importantly, is the booming economy. Since the 1990s, **economic growth** in Vietnam has been unprecedented. In 2006 the growth rate was 8.2% but this dropped to 5.3% in 2009. As every politician knows, the one thing that keeps people happy is rising income. Hence with not much to complain about most Vietnamese people are content with their political status quo.

That said, in 2006, Bloc 8406, a pro-democracy group named after its founding date of 8 April 2006, was set up. Catholic priest Father Nguyen Van Ly, editor of the underground online magazine *Free Speech* and a founding member of Bloc 8406, was sentenced to eight years in jail for **anti-government activity**. Four others were also sentenced with him. In March 2007 Nguyen Van Dai and Le Thi Cong Nhan, two human rights lawyers, were arrested on the grounds of distributing material "dangerous to the State" and were sentenced to four and five years in prison respectively. As well as Bloc 8406, other pro-democracy movements include the US-based Viet Tan Party, www.viettan.org, with offices also in Australia, France, Japan, and the People's Democratic Party, among others.

International relations

In terms of international relations, Vietnam's relationship with the countries of the **Association of Southeast Asian Nations (ASEAN)** have warmed markedly since the dark days of the early and mid-1980s and in mid-1995 Vietnam became the association's seventh – and first communist – member. The delicious irony of Vietnam joining ASEAN was that it was becoming part of an organization established to counteract the threat of communist Vietnam itself – although everyone was too polite to point this out. No longer is there a deep schism between the capitalist and communist countries of the region, either in terms of ideology or management. The main potential flashpoint concerns Vietnam's long-term historical enemy – China. The enmity and suspicion that underlies the relationship between the world's last two real communist powers stretches back over 2000 years. Indeed, one of the great attractions to Vietnam of joining ASEAN was the bulwark that it created against a potentially aggressive and actually economically ascendant China.

China and Vietnam, along with Malaysia, Taiwan, Brunei and the Philippines, all claim part (or all) of the East Sea **Hoang Sa** (formerly **Spratly Islands**). These tiny islands, many no more than coral atolls, would have caused scarcely an international relations ripple were it not for the fact that they are thought to sit above huge oil reserves. Whoever can prove rights to the islands lays claim to this undersea wealth. China has been using its developing blue water navy to project its power southwards. This has led to skirmishes between Vietnamese and Chinese forces, and to diplomatic confrontation between China and just about all the other claimants. Although the parties are committed to settling the dispute without resort to force, most experts see the Spratly Islands as the key potential flashpoint in Southeast Asia – and one in which Vietnam is seen to be a central player. **Truong Sa** (formerly **Paracel Islands**) further north are similarly disputed by Vietnam and China.

Rapprochement with the US

One of the keys to a lasting economic recovery was a normalization of relations with the US. From 1975 until early 1994 the US made it largely illegal for any American or American company to have business relations with Vietnam. The US, with the support of Japan and other Western nations, also blackballed attempts by Vietnam to gain membership to the IMF, World Bank and Asian Development Bank, thus cutting off access to the largest source of cheap credit. In the past, it has been the former Soviet Union and the countries of the Eastern Bloc that have filled the gap, providing billions of dollars of aid (US$6 billion 1986-1990), training and technical expertise. But in 1990 the Soviet Union halved its assistance to Vietnam, making it imperative that the government improve relations with the West and particularly the US.

In April 1991 the US opened an official office in Hanoi to assist in the search for Missing in Action (MIAs), the first such move since the end of the war, and in December 1992 allowed US companies to sign contracts to be implemented after the US trade embargo had been lifted. In 1992, both Australia and Japan lifted their embargoes on aid to Vietnam and the US also eased restrictions on humanitarian assistance. Support for a **full normalization of relations** was provided by French President Mitterand during his visit in February 1993, the first by a Western leader since the end of the war. He said that the US veto on IMF and World Bank assistance had "no reason for being there", and applauded Vietnam's economic reforms. He also pointed out to his hosts that respect for human rights was now a universal obligation, which did not go down quite so well. Nonetheless he saw his visit as marking the end of one chapter and the beginning of another.

This inexorable process towards normalization continued with the full lifting of the trade embargo on 4 February 1994 when President Bill Clinton announced the normalization of trade relations. Finally, on 11 July 1995 Bill Clinton declared the full normalization of relations between the two countries and a month later Secretary of State Warren Christopher opened the new American embassy in Hanoi. On 9 May 1997 Douglas 'Pete' Peterson, the first 'post-war' American ambassador to Vietnam and a former POW who spent six years of the war in the infamous 'Hanoi Hilton', took up his post in the capital.

The progress towards normalization was so slow because many Americans still harbour painful memories of the war. With large numbers of ordinary people continuing to believe that servicemen shot down and captured during the war and listed as MIAs were still languishing in jungle jails, presidents Bush and Clinton had to tread exceedingly carefully.

The normalization of trade relations between the two countries was agreed in a meeting between Vietnamese and US officials in July 1999 and marked the culmination of three years' discussions. But conservatives in the politburo prevented the agreement being signed into law worried, apparently, about the social and economic side effects of such reform. This did not happen until 28 November 2001 when Vietnam's National Assembly finally ratified the treaty. It has led to a substantial increase in bilateral trade. In 2003 the USA imported US$4.5 billion worth of Vietnamese goods, roughly four times more than it exported to Vietnam. And not only goods: by 2004 the US Consulate General in

Ho Chi Minh City handled more applications for American visas than any other US mission in the world.

Recent progress

More good news came for Vietnam when it became the 150th member of the World Trade Organization in January 2007. The immediate effect was the lifting of import quotas from foreign countries thereby favouring Vietnamese exporters. Full benefits are expected to be realised when Vietnam hope to gains full market economy status in 2020. In June 2007 President Nguyen Minh Triet became the first president of Vietnam to visit the US. He met with George W Bush in Washington to discuss relations between the two countries; trade between the two former enemies now racks up US$9 billion a year. And, in October 2007, Vietnam was elected to the UN Security Council from 1 January 2008 as a non-permanent member for two years. In 2009, the International Bank for Reconstruction and Development loaned the country US$500 million.

The future of communism in Vietnam

In his book *Vietnam at the Crossroads*, BBC World Service commentator Michael Williams asks the question: "Does communism have a future in Vietnam?" He answers that "the short answer must be no, if one means by communism the classical Leninist doctrines and central planning". Instead some bastard form of communism has been in the process of evolving.

There is certainly **political opposition** and disenchantment in Vietnam. At present this is unfocused and dispersed. Poor people in the countryside, especially in the north, resent the economic gains in the cities, particularly those of the south. But this rump of latent discontent has little in common with those intellectual and middle class Vietnamese itching for more political freedom or those motivated entrepreneurs pressing for accelerated economic reforms or those Buddhist monks and Christians demanding freedom of worship and respect for human rights. Unless and until this loose broth of opposition groups coalesces, it is hard to see a coherent opposition movement evolving.

Nonetheless, each year a small number of brave, foolhardy or committed individuals challenge the authorities. Most are then arrested, tried, and imprisoned for various loosely defined crimes including anti-government activity.

The tensions between reform and control are constantly evident. A **press law** which came into effect in mid-1993 prohibits the publication of works "hostile to the socialist homeland, divulging state or [communist] party secrets, falsifying history or denying the gains of the revolution". Ly Quy Chung, a newspaper editor in Ho Chi Minh City, described the Vietnamese responding to the economic reforms "like animals being let out of their cage". But, he added, alluding to the tight control the VCP maintains over political debate, "Now we are free to graze around, but only inside the fences." The Party's attempts to control debate and the flow of information have extended to the internet. In 1997 a National Internet Control Board was established and all internet and email usage is strictly monitored. The authorities attempt to firewall topics relating to Vietnam in a hopeless attempt to censor incoming information. By 2004 a number of 'cyber-activists' were held on charges of disseminating information deemed injurious to national interests, see and www. hrw.org/en/news/2010/05/26/vietnam-stop-cyber-attacks-against-online-critics. The government continues to crack down on blogs and websites it sees critical of the government, according to Human Rights Watch. Facebook has also been periodically blocked and access to the BBC is limited in many places. The Vietnamese cyber police clearly credit the information highway with greater influence than any surfer.

Economy

Partition and socialist reconstruction 1955-1975
When the French left North Vietnam in 1954 they abandoned a country with scarcely any industry. The north remained predominantly an agrarian society and just 1.5% of 'material output' (the Socialist equivalent of GDP) was accounted for by modern industries. These employed a few thousand workers out of a population of about 13 million. The French added to the pitiful state of the industrial sector by dismantling many of the (mostly textile) factories that did exist, shipping the machinery back to France.

With **independence**, the government in the north embraced a socialist strategy of reconstruction and development. In the countryside, agricultural production was collectivized. Adopting Maoist policies, land reform proceeded apace. Revolutionary cadres were trained to spot 'greedy, cruel and imperialist landlords', farmers of above average wealth who might themselves have owned tiny plots. Leaders of land reform brigades applied Chinese-inspired rules through people's tribunals and summary justice. An estimated 10,000 people died; Ho Chi Minh was opposed to the worst excesses and, although he failed to curb the zealots, land reform in Vietnam was a much less bloody affair than it was in China.

In industry, likewise, the means of production were nationalized, co-operatives were formed, and planning was directed from the centre. Although evidence is hard to come by, it seems that even as early as the mid-1960s both the agricultural and industrial sectors were experiencing shortages of key inputs and were suffering from poor planning and mismanagement. The various sectors of the economy were inadequately linked, and the need for consumer goods was largely met by imports from China. But it was just at this time that the US bombing campaign 'Rolling Thunder' began in earnest (see page 365), and this served to obscure these economic difficulties. It was not until the late 1970s that the desperate need to introduce reforms became apparent. The bombing campaign also led to massive destruction and caused the government in the north to decentralize activity to the countryside in order to protect what little industry there was from the American attacks.

Reunification and a stab at socialist reconstruction (1975-1979)
With the reunification of Vietnam in 1975, it seems that most leaders in the north thought that the re-integration of the two economies, as well as their re-invigoration, would be a fairly straightforward affair. As one of the Party leadership

tellingly said during the Sixth Plenum at the end of 1979: "In the euphoria of victory which came so unexpectedly, we ... somewhat lost sight of realities; everything seemed possible to achieve, and quickly." This is understandable when it is considered that the north had just defeated the most powerful nation on earth. But the war disguised two economies that were both chronically inefficient and poorly managed, albeit for different reasons and in different ways. The tragedy was that just as this fact was becoming clear, the Vietnamese government embarked on another military adventure; this time the invasion and subsequent occupation of Cambodia in December 1978. Shortly afterwards, Hanoi had to deploy troops again to counter the Chinese 'invasion' in 1979. As a result, the authorities never had the opportunity of diverting resources from the military to the civilian sectors.

Conditions in the south were no better than in the north. The US had been supporting levels of consumption far above those which domestic production could match, the shortfall being met through massive injections of aid. Following the communists' victory, this support was ended – overnight. The Americans left behind an economy and society scarred by the war: three million unemployed, 500,000 prostitutes, 100,000 drug addicts, 400,000 amputees and 800,000 orphans. Nor did many in the south welcome their 'liberation'. The programme of socialist transition that began after 1975 was strongly resisted by large sections of the population and never achieved its aims. As resistance grew, the government became more repressive, thus leading to the exodus of hundreds of thousands of Vietnamese, who became known as the boat people (see page 372). Even as late as 1978, with the economy close to crisis, sections of the leadership were still maintaining that the problems were due to poor implementation, not to the fact that the policies were flawed. The key problem was bureaucratic centralism: if a factory wished to transport umbrellas from Tay Ninh to Ho Chi Minh city, less than 100 km apart, it was required to go through 17 agencies, obtain 15 seals, sign five contracts and pay numerous taxes.

The roots of economic reform (1979-1986)

In a bid to re-invigorate the economy, the Vietnamese government – like others throughout the communist and former communist world – has been introducing economic reforms. These date back to 1979 when a process of administrative decentralization was set in train. Farmers signed contracts with their collectives to deliver produce in return for access to land and inputs like fertilizers and pesticides, thereby returning many aspects of decision making to the farm level. Surplus production could be sold privately. Factories were made self-accounting, and workers' pay was linked to productivity. The reforms of 1979 also accepted a greater role for the private sector in marketing, agriculture and small-scale industry.

Unfortunately these reforms were generally unsuccessful in stimulating Vietnam's moribund economy. Agriculture performed reasonably, but industry continued to decline. Cadres at the regional and local levels often ignored directives from the centre and critical inputs needed to fuel growth were usually unavailable. Both national income and per capita incomes continued to shrink. The reform process is referred to as *doi moi* (renovation), the Vietnamese equivalent of Soviet perestroika, and implementation has not been easy.

Some commentators have argued that the economic reforms of 1979 showed that the Vietnamese government was forward-looking and prescient. However there is also considerable evidence to show that the pressure for reform was coming as much from the bottom as from the top. Farm households and agricultural cooperatives, it seems, were engaged in what became known as 'fence-breaking', bypassing the state planning system. The communist party, to some degree, was forced to follow where peasants had already gone. This raises the questions of how far Vietnam's command economy was truly commanding. Peasants devoted enormous efforts in time and energy to the cultivation of their small private plots and tried to bypass the collective system through what became known as *khóan chui* (sneaky contracts).

Doi moi: the end of central planning

Recognizing that the limited reforms of 1979 were failing to have the desired effect, the VCP leadership embraced a further raft of changes following the **Sixth Congress in 1986**. At the time, the Party daily, *Nhan Dan* wrote that never had "morale been so eroded, confidence been so low or justice been so abused". Subsidies on consumer goods were reduced and wages increased partially to compensate. There was also limited monetary reform although prices were still centrally controlled. In late 1987 the central planning system was reformed. The net effect of these changes was to fuel inflation.

Again, appreciating that the reforms were not having the desired effect, and with the advice of the IMF, a third series of changes were introduced in 1988 and 1989. The market mechanism was to be fully employed to determine wages, output and prices for the great majority of goods. The domestic currency, the dong, was further devalued to bring it into line with the black market rate and foreign investment actively encouraged.

But, with each series of reform measures, disquiet in some sections of the Party grew. For example, in 1993 government salary differentials were widened to better reflect responsibilities. Whereas under the old system the differential between the highest and lowest paid workers was only 3.5 to one, the gap under the new system is 13 to one. This may make good sense to World Bank economists, but it is hard to swallow for a party and leadership who have been raised on ideals of equality.

Until the Asian crisis was heralded with the collapse of the Thai baht at the end of the last century, the Vietnamese economy had done well to ride some pretty serious external shocks. With the collapse of communism in Eastern Europe, around 200,000 migrant workers returned to the country and had to be reintegrated. The decline in aid and assistance from the former Soviet Union (which was only partially compensated by aid from Russia) and the corresponding precipitous decline in trade from US$1.8 billion in 1990 to US$85 million in 1991 illustrates the extent to which Vietnam had to re-orientate its economy in the face of global political and economic change. No longer able to rely on the Soviet Union to bail it out (although even before then the Vietnamese would lament that the Soviets were 'Americans without dollars'), the Vietnamese government took the drastic step of banning the import of all luxury consumer goods in October 1991 in an attempt to save valuable foreign exchange.

Economic challenges

Let's start with the good news: Vietnam's economy is resilient and growing fast, the population is comparatively well educated and it has good access to world markets. Vietnam currently enjoys the highest rate of growth in one of the most economically dynamic regions in the world. This happy state of affairs is the product of a hard-working, underpaid labour force generating massive profits and of the switch from an agrarian economy to an industrial economy. In other words, 200 years after Britain, Vietnam is now undergoing its industrial revolution. Indeed industry and construction now account for 41% of Vietnam's economy with services accounting for an additional 38% and this figure is rising fast. One of the driving forces behind this growth has been the export of textiles – chiefly to the USA.

Not that it has always been this good. Not only did the Asian crisis put talk of Tiger economies on the back burner, but even before the crisis there were voices of caution. The gloss of the immediate post-*doi moi* years has dulled and people now accept that reforms will need to be both deeper and wider. For a start, many of the reforms apparently in place are not being implemented in the expected manner. Foreign investors, who initially piled into the country thinking there was money to be made, then started shying away, daunted by the red tape, bureaucratic inertia and corruption and since 2001 investment has rapidly increased. The greatest beneficiaries have been Ho Chi Minh City followed by Hanoi, Dong Nai and Binh Duong. By sector it is the service industry proving the overall winner with offices and apartments being the most heavily invested sector followed by hotels and tourism.

But Vietnam's problems do not begin and end with the reform programme. There are also many more rather more familiar challenges.

The population is growing rapidly in a country where there are 900 people for every square kilometre of agricultural land. As the World Bank has pointed out, this means "the country will have to develop on the basis of human resources rather than natural resources". But the human resources themselves need substantial 'upgrading'; despite rapid progress in poverty elimination, poverty in the countryside over large areas of the north and interior uplands remains the norm rather than the exception. Education and health facilities also require massive investment, not to mention the physical infrastructure including roads and power.

The country's export base is also still comparatively narrow: coffee, coal, oil, textiles, rice, footwear and marine products are the country's key exports. But this list grows all the time.

Economic growth has brought its own problems in the same way that has occurred in China. Inequalities, both spatial and personal, are widening. Growth in agriculture is down, while industry is expanding. So, while the economies of Hanoi and Ho Chi Minh City have been growing annually, the countryside is lagging far behind. Over recent years rural incomes have fallen as rice prices and other agricultural commodities have remained depressed. This is drawing people in from the countryside, creating urban problems both socially (for instance, unemployed people living in poor conditions with a lack of educational facilities) and economically (such as strains on the physical infrastructure). These inequalities will widen further in the short to medium term as the process of industrialization continues apace.

As with industry, the leadership is reluctant to allow rural people to run their own businesses and lives, continually interfering and fine-tuning and without addressing the key shortages which are of credit, training, skills and management. As Bui Quang Toan, senior researcher at the National Institute of Agricultural Planning and Projection, explained to a journalist from the Far Eastern Economic Review: "Cooperatives should be free of politics, free of administrative control … the government must give up the idea that they can use cooperatives as a tool to manage the people." Nevertheless Vietnam has made dramatic strides at reducing poverty, including rural poverty.

Culture

People

Vietnam is home to a total of 54 ethnic groups including the Vietnamese (or Kinh) themselves. Life has been hard for many of the minorities who have had to fight not only the French and Vietnamese but often each other in order to retain their territory and cultural identity. Traditions and customs have been eroded by outside influences such as Roman Catholicism and Communism although some of the less alien ideas have been successfully accommodated.

Highland people: the Montagnards of Vietnam

The highland areas of Vietnam are among the most linguistically and culturally diverse in the world. In total, the highland peoples number around seven million. As elsewhere in Southeast Asia, a broad distinction can be drawn in Vietnam between the peoples of the lowlands and valleys and the peoples of the uplands. The former tend to be settled, cultivate wet rice and are fairly closely integrated into the wider Vietnamese state; in most instances they are Viet. The latter are often migratory, cultivate upland crops often using systems of shifting cultivation and are comparatively isolated from the state. The generic term for these diverse peoples of the highlands is Montagnard (from the French, Mountain People), in Vietnamese *nguoi thuong* (highland citizen) or, rather less politely, *moi* (savage or slave). As far as the highland peoples themselves are concerned, they identify with their village and tribal group and not as part of a wider grouping, as highland inhabitants.

Relations between the minorities and the Vietnamese have not always been as good as they are officially portrayed. Recognizing and exploiting this mutual distrust and animosity, both the French and American armies recruited from among the minorities. In 1961 US Special Forces began organizing Montagnards into defence groups to prevent communist infiltration into the Central Highlands from the north. In recent years the government has come to regard the minorities as useful for tourism.

Potentially tourism is a more serious and insidious threat to the minorities' way of life than any they have yet had to face. A great deal has been written about cultural erosion by tourism and any visitor to a minority village should be aware of the extent to which he or she contributes to this process. Traditional means of livelihood are quickly abandoned when a higher living standard for less effort can be obtained from the tourist dollar. Long-standing societal and kinship ties are weakened by the intrusion of outsiders. Young people may question their society's values and traditions that may seem archaic, anachronistic and risible by comparison with those of the modern tourist. And dress and music lose all cultural significance and symbolism if they are allowed to become mere tourist attractions.

Nevertheless, this is an unavoidable consequence of Vietnam's decision to admit tourists to the highland areas. Perhaps fortunately, however, for the time being at least, many of the minorities are pretty inaccessible to the average traveller. Visitors

ON THE ROAD
Visiting minorities: house rules

Etiquette and customs vary between the minorities. However, the following are general rules of good behaviour that should be adhered to whenever possible.

1. Dress modestly without displaying too much flesh.
2. Ask permission before photographing anyone (old people, pregnant women and mothers with babies can object).
3. Only enter a house if invited.
4. Do not touch or photograph village shrines.
5. Do not smoke opium.
6. Avoid sitting or stepping on door sills.
7. Avoid displays of wealth and be sensitive when giving gifts (for children, pens are better than sweets).
8. Avoid introducing Western medicines.
9. Do not sit with the soles of your feet pointing at others (sit cross-legged).
10. If offered a cup of rice wine it is polite to down the first cup in one (what the Vietnamese call *tram phan tram* – 100%).

can minimize their impact by acting in a sensitive way. In addition, you can report to provincial tourism authorities on arrival to check the latest on areas where travel is permitted. But the minority areas of Vietnam are fascinating places and the immense variety of colours and styles of dress add greatly to the visitor's enjoyment.

Bahnar (Ba-na)
This is a Mon Khmer speaking minority group concentrated in the central highland provinces of Gia Lai-Kon Tum, numbering about 174,000. Locally powerful from the 15th to 18th centuries, they were virtually annihilated by neighbouring groups during the 19th century. Roman Catholic missionaries influenced the Bahnar greatly and they came to identify closely with the French. Some conversions to Roman Catholicism were made but Christianity, where it remains, is usually just an adjunct to Bahnar animism. Bahnar houses are built on stilts and in each village there is a communal house, or *rông*, which is the focus of social life. When a baby reaches his or her first full month he or she has their ears pierced in a village ceremony equivalent to the Vietnamese *day thang* (see box, page 31), only then is a child considered a full member of the community. Their society gives men and women relatively equal status. Male and female heirs inherit wealth and the families of either husband or wife can arrange marriage. Bahnar practise both settled and shifting cultivation.

Coho (Co-ho, also Kohor, K'Ho, Xre, Chil and Nop)
These are primarily found on the Lam Dong Plateau in Lam Dong Province (Dalat) with a population of about 100,000. Extended family groups live in longhouses or buon, sometimes up to 30 m long. Unusually, society is matrilineal and newly married men live with their wives' families. The children take their mother's name; if

Rite of passage: from baby to infant

In a poor country like Vietnam, staying alive for long enough to see one's own first birthday has not always been easy. Fortunately, infant mortality levels have fallen drastically, (from 156 in 1000 in 1960 to 33 in 1000 in 1996 and 19 in 1000 in 2005) but remain high by Western standards. Perhaps not surprisingly therefore, Vietnamese families celebrate two important milestones in the early lives of their children.

Day thang, or full month, is celebrated exactly one month after birth. Traditionally, the mother remained in bed with her heavily swaddled baby for the first month keeping him or her away from sun, rain and demon spirits. At one month the child is beyond the hazardous neo-natal stage and the mother would leave her bed and go out of the house to introduce her baby to the village. Today, the parents hold a small party for friends and neighbours.

Thoi noi is celebrated at the end of the first year; it marks the time the baby stops sleeping in the cot and, having reached a full year, it is also a thanksgiving that the child has reached the end of the most dangerous year of life. At the party the baby is presented with a tray on which are various items such as a pen, a mirror, scissors, some soil and food; whichever the baby takes first indicates its character and likely job: scissors for a tailor, pen for a teacher, soil for a farmer and so on. Babies are normally weaned at about this time: Some Vietnamese mothers use remarkably unsubtle but effective means for turning the baby from the breast, smearing the nipple with charcoal dust or Tiger Balm!

the wife dies young her smaller sister will take her place. Women wear tight-fitting blouses and skirts. Traditional shifting cultivation is giving way to settled agriculture.

Yao (Dao, also Mán)

The Yao live in northern Vietnam in the provinces bordering China, particularly in Lao Cai and Ha Giang. They number 6210,000 and include several sub-groupings, notably the Dao Quan Chet (Tight Trouser Dao), the Dao Tien (Money Dao) and the Dao Ao Dai (Long Dress Dao). As these names suggest, Yao people wear highly distinctive clothing although sometimes only on their wedding day. The **Dao Tien** or Money Dao of Hoa Binh and Son La provinces are unique among the Yao in that the women wear black skirts and leggings rather than trousers. A black jacket with red embroidered collar and cuffs, decorated at the back with coins (hence the name) together with a black red-tasselled turban and silver jewellery are also worn. By contrast men look rather plain in black jacket and trousers. Headgear tends to be elaborate and includes a range of shapes (from square to conical), fabrics (waxed hair to dried pumpkin fibres) and colours.

The women of many branches of Yao shave off their eyebrows and shave back their hair to the top of their head before putting on the turban; a hairless face and high forehead are traditionally regarded as attributes of feminine beauty.

Yao wedding customs are as complex as Yao clothing and vary with each group. Apart from parental consent, intending marriage partners must have compatible birthdays and the groom has to provide the bride's family with gifts worthy of their daughter. If he is unable to do this, a temporary marriage can take place but the outstanding presents must be produced and a permanent wedding celebrated before *their* daughter can marry.

The Yao live chiefly by farming: those in higher altitudes are swidden cultivators growing maize, cassava and rye. In the middle zone, shifting methods are again used to produce rice and maize, and on the valley floors sedentary farmers grow irrigated rice and rear livestock.

Spiritually the Yao have also opted for diversity; they worship *Ban Vuong*, their mythical progenitor, as well as their more immediate and real ancestors. The Yao also find room for elements of Taoism, and in some cases Buddhism and Confucianism, in their elaborate metaphysical lives. Never enter a Yao house unless invited; if tree branches are suspended above the gate to a village, guests are not welcome – reasons might include a post-natal but pre-naming period, sickness, death or special ceremony. Since the Yao worship the kitchen god, guests should not sit or stand immediately in front of the stove.

Ede (Ê-dê, also Rhadê)
Primarily concentrated in the Central Highlands province of Dac Lac and numbering nearly 270,000, they came into early contact with the French and are regarded as one of the more 'progressive' groups, adapting to modern life with relative ease. Traditionally the Ede live in longhouses on stilts; accommodated under one roof is the matrilineal extended family or commune. The commune falls under the authority of an elderly, respected woman known as the *khoa sang* who is responsible for communal property, especially the gongs and jars, which feature in important festivals.

Ede society is matrilocal in that after the girl's family selects a husband, he then comes to live with her. As part of the wedding festivities the two families solemnly agree that if one of the partners should break the wedding vow they will forfeit a minimum of one buffalo, a maximum of a set of gongs. Wealth and property are inherited solely by daughters.

Shifting cultivation is the traditional subsistence system, although this has given way in most areas to settled wet rice agriculture. Spiritually the Ede are polytheist: they number animism (recognizing the spirits of rice, soil, fire and water especially) and Christianity among their beliefs.

Giarai (Gia-rai, also Chó Ray)
Primarily found in Gia Lai and Kon Tum provinces (especially near Play Ku) and numbering 317,557, these are the largest group in the Central Highlands. They are settled cultivators and live in houses on stilts in villages called *ploi* or *bon*. The Giarai are animist and recognize the spiritual dimension of nature; ever since the seventh century they have had a flesh and blood King of Fire and King of Water whose spirit is invoked in rain ceremonies.

Hmong (Hmông, also Mèo and Mi(u)

These are widely spread across the highland areas of the country, but particularly near the Chinese border down to the 18th parallel. The Hmong number about 787,600 (over 1% of Vietnam's population) and live at higher altitudes, above 1500 m, than all other hill people. Comparatively recent migrants to Vietnam, the Hmong began to settle in the country during the 19th century after moving south from China. The Hmong language in its various dialects remained oral until the 1930s when a French priest attempted to Romanize it with a view to translating the Bible. A more successful attempt to create a written Hmong language was made in 1961 but has since fallen into disuse. Nevertheless – or perhaps because of this failure – the Hmong still preserve an extraordinarily rich oral tradition of legends, stories and histories. Hmong people are renowned for their beautiful folk songs. Each branch of the Hmong people preserves its own corpus of songs about love, work and festivals that are sung unaccompanied or with the accompaniment of the *khène*, a small bamboo pipe organ, a two-stringed violin, flutes, drums, gongs and jew's harps. Numerous Hmong dances also exist to celebrate various dates in the social calendar and to propitiate animist spirits.

They have played an important role in resisting both the French and the Vietnamese. Living at such high altitudes they tend to be one of the most isolated of all the hill people. Their way of life does not normally bring them into contact with the outside world that suits them well – the Hmong traders at Sapa are an exception.

High in the hills, flooding is not a problem so their houses are built on the ground, not raised up on stilts. Hmong villages are now increasingly found along the river valleys and roads as the government resettlement schemes aim to introduce them to a more sedentary form of agriculture. The Hmong practice slash-and-burn cultivation growing maize and dry rice. Traditionally opium has been a valuable cash crop. Although fields are often cleared on very steep and rocky slopes, the land is not terraced.

There are a number of different groups among the Hmong including the White, Black, Red and Flower Hmong that are distinguishable by the colour of the women's clothes. Black Hmong wear almost entirely black clothing with remarkable pointed black turbans. White Hmong women wear white skirts and the Red Hmong tie their heads in a red scarf while the Flower Hmong wrap their hair (with hair extensions) around their head like a broad-brimmed hat. However, such numerous regional variations occur that even experts on ethnic minority cultures sometimes have problems trying to identify which branch of Hmong they have encountered.

Serious social problems have occurred among the Hmong owing to opium addiction; with over 30% of the male population of some Hmong villages addicted, the drug has rendered many incapable of work, causing misery and malnutrition for their families and with the drug finding its way on to the streets of Vietnam's cities, the authorities have resolved to clamp down hard on opium production. This has had tragic consequences when the Hmong have tried to protect their livelihoods.

Muong (Mường)

Numbering more than one million the Muong are the fourth largest ethnic minority in Vietnam. They live in the area between northern Thanh Hoa Province and Yen Bai but mainly in Hoa Binh Province. It is thought that the Muong are descended from the same stock as the Viets: their languages are similar and there are also close similarities in culture and religion. But whereas the Vietnamese came under strong Chinese cultural influence from the early centuries of the Christian era, the Muong did not. The Muong belong to the Viet-Muong language group; their language is closest to Vietnamese of all the ethnic minority languages.

Muong practise wet and dry rice cultivation where possible, supplementing their income with cash crops such as manioc, tobacco and cotton. Weaving is still practised; items produced include pillowcases and blankets. Culturally the Muong are akin to the Thai Vietnamese ethnic minority and they live in stilt houses in small villages called *quel*; groupings of from three to 30 quel form a unit called a *muong*. Muong society is feudal in nature with each *muong* coming under the protection of a noble family (*lang*). The common people are not deemed worthy of family names so are all called Bui. Each year the members of a *muong* are required to labour for one day in fields belonging to the lang.

Marriages are arranged: girls, in particular, have no choice of spouse. Muong cultural life is rich, literature has been translated into Vietnamese and their legends, poems and songs are considered particularly fine.

Mnong (Mnông)

The Mnong number some 92,000 people and predominantly live in Dak Lak, Binh Phuoc and Binh Duong province with a smaller group living in Lam Dong province. The Mnong are hunter-gatherers and grow rice. The Mnong village is characterised by a longhouse on stilts although some groups live in normal sized stilt houses. Families are matrilineal and tradition sees the women bare topped and with distended earlobes. It is the Mnong who are the elephant catchers at Ban Don, see page 222.

Nung (Nùng)

Concentrated in Cao Bang and Lang Son provinces, adjacent to the Chinese border, the Nung number approximately 860,000 people. They are strongly influenced by the Chinese and most are Buddhist, but like both Vietnamese and Chinese the Nung practise ancestor worship too. In Nung houses a Buddhist altar is placed above the ancestor altar and, in deference to Buddhist teaching, they refrain from eating most types of meat. The Nung are settled agriculturalists and, where conditions permit, produce wet rice; all houses have their own garden in which fruit and vegetables are grown.

Tay (Tày, also Tho)

The Tay are the most populous ethnic minority in Vietnam; they number about 1.5 million and are found in the provinces of northwest Vietnam stretching from Quang Ninh east to Lao Cai. Tay society was traditionally feudal with powerful lords able to extract from the free and semi-free serfs' obligations such as droit de seigneur. Today Tay society is male dominated with important decisions being taken by men and eldest sons inheriting the bulk of the family's wealth.

Economically the Tay survive by farming and are highly regarded as wet rice cultivators, they are also noted for the production of fruits (pears, peaches, apricots and tangerines), herbs and spices. Diet is supplemented by animal and fish rearing and cash is raised by the production of handicrafts. The Tay live in houses on stilts, located in the river valleys. Tay architecture is quite similar in design to that of the Black Thai, but important differences may be identified, most notably the larger size of the Tay house, the deeper overhang of the thatched or (among more affluent Tay communities) tiled roof and the extent of the railed balcony that often encircles the entire house.

Like the Thai, Tay ancestors migrated south from southern China along with those of the Thai and they follow the three main religions of Buddhism, Confucianism and Taoism in addition to ancestor worship and animist beliefs. While Tay people have lived in close proximity to the Viet majority over a period of many centuries, their own language continues to be their primary means of communication. They hail from the Austro-Asian language family and specifically the Thai-Kadai language group. Tay literature has a long and distinguished history and much has been translated into Vietnamese. During the French colonial period missionaries Romanized Tay script.

Thai (Thái, also Tày D]m)

Numbering more than one million this is the second largest ethnic minority in Vietnam and ethnically distinct from the Thais of modern-day Thailand. There are two main sub-groups, the Black (Thai Den), who are settled mainly in Son La, Lai Chan, Lao Cai and Yen Bai provinces and the White Thái, who are found predominantly in Hoa Binh, Son La, Thanh Hoa and Vinh Phu provinces, as well as many others, including the Red Thai (Thai Do). The use of these colour-based classifications has usually been linked to the colour of their clothes, particularly the colour of women's shirts. However, there has been some confusion over the origins of the terms and there is every reason to believe that it has nothing to do with the colour of their attire and is possibly linked to the distribution of the sub-groups near the Red and Black rivers. The confusion of names becomes even more perplexing when the Vietnamese names for the sub-groups of Thai people are translated into Thai. Some scholars have taken Thai Den (Black Thai) to be Thai Daeng – *daeng* being the Thai word for red, thereby muddling up the two groups. With the notable exception of the White Thai communities of Hoa Binh, traditional costume for the women of both the Black and White Thai generally features a coloured blouse with a row of silver buttons down the front, a long black skirt, a coloured waist sash and a black headscarf embroidered with intricate, predominantly red and yellow designs.

The traditional costume of the White Thai women of Hoa Binh comprises a long black skirt with fitted waistband embroidered with either a dragon or chicken motif together with a plain pastel coloured blouse and gold and maroon sash.

The Thai cover a large part of northwest Vietnam, in particular the valleys of the Red River and the Da and the Ma rivers, spilling over into Laos and Thailand. They arrived in Vietnam between the fourth and 11th centuries from southern China and linguistically they are part of the wider Thai-Kadai linguistic grouping. Residents of Lac village in Mai Chau claim to have communicated with visitors from Thailand by means of this shared heritage.

The Thai tend to occupy lowland areas and they compete directly with the Kinh (ethnic Vietnamese) for good quality farmland that can be irrigated. They are masters of wet rice cultivation producing high yields and often two harvests each year. Their irrigation works are ingenious and incorporate numerous labour-saving devices including river-powered water wheels that can raise water several metres. Thai villages (ban) consist of 40 to 50 houses on stilts; they are architecturally attractive, shaded by fruit trees and surrounded by verdant paddy fields. Commonly located by rivers, one of the highlights of a Thai village is its suspension footbridge. The Thai are excellent custodians of the land and their landscapes and villages are invariably very scenic.

Owing to their geographical proximity and agricultural similarities with the Kinh it is not surprising to see cultural assimilation – sometimes via marriage – and most Thai speak Vietnamese. It's also interesting to note the extent to which the Thai retain a distinctive cultural identity, most visibly in their dress.

When a Thai woman marries, her parents-in-law give her a hair extension (can song) and a silver hair pin (khat pom) that she is expected to wear (even in bed) for the duration of the marriage. There are two wedding ceremonies, the first at the bride's house where the couple live for one to three years, followed by a second when they move to the husband's house.

Sedang (Xó-d]ng)
Concentrated in Gia Lai and Kon Tum provinces and numbering about 127,000, the Sedang live in extended family longhouses and society is patriarchal. The Sedang practise both shifting agriculture and the cultivation of wet rice. A highly war-like people, they almost wiped out the Bahnar in the 19th century. Sedang thought nothing of kidnapping neighbouring tribesmen to sacrifice to the spirits; indeed the practice of kidnapping was subsequently put to commercial use and formed the basis of a slave trade with Siam (Thailand). Sedang villages, or ploi, are usually well defended (presumably for fear of reprisal) and are surrounded by thorn hedges supplemented with spears and stakes. Complex rules designed to prevent in breeding limit the number of available marriage partners that sometimes results in late marriages.

Other groups
These are Hre (Hrê), in Quang Ngai and Binh Dinh provinces, numbering 113,000 and Stieng/Xtieng (Xtiêng) in Song Be province, with 66,788.

Viet (Kinh)
The 1999 census revealed that 86.2% of the population were ethnic Vietnamese. But with a well-run family planning campaign beginning to take effect in urban

areas and higher fertility rates among the ethnic minorities it is likely that this figure will fall. The history of the Kinh is marked by a steady southwards progression from the Red River basin to the southern plains and Mekong Delta. Today the Kinh are concentrated into the two great river deltas, the coastal plains and the main cities. Only in the central and northern highland regions are they outnumbered by ethnic minorities. Kinh social cohesion and mastery of intensive wet rice cultivation has led to their numerical, and subsequently political and economic, dominance of the country. Ethnic Vietnamese are also in Cambodia where some have been settled for generations; recent Khmer Rouge attacks on Vietnamese villages have, however, caused many to flee to Vietnam.

Cham

With the over-running of Champa in 1471 (see page 353) Cham cultural and ethnic identity was diluted by the more numerous ethnic Vietnamese. The Cham were dispossessed of the more productive lands and found themselves in increasingly marginal territory. Economically eclipsed and strangers in their own land, Cham artistic creativity atrophied, their sculptural and architectural skills, once the glory of Vietnam, faded and decayed like so many Cham temples and towers. It is estimated that there are, today, 132,873 Cham people in Vietnam, chiefly in central and southern Vietnam in the coastal provinces extending south from Quy Nhon. Small communities are to be found in Ho Chi Minh City and in the Mekong Delta around Chau Doc. They are artistically the poor relations of their forebears but skills in weaving and music live on.

The Cham of the south are typically engaged in fishing, weaving and other small scale commercial activities; urban Cham are poor and live in slum neighbourhoods. Further north the Cham are wet or dry rice farmers according to local topography; they are noted for their skill in wet rice farming and small-scale hydraulic engineering.

In southern Vietnam the majority of Cham are Muslim, a comparatively newly acquired religion although familiar from earlier centuries when many became acquainted with Islamic tenets through traders from India and the Indonesian isles. In central Vietnam most Cham are Brahminist and the cult of the linga remains an important feature of spiritual life.

Hoa: ethnic Chinese

There are nearly one million ethnic Chinese or Hoa in Vietnam, 80% living in the south of the country. Before reunification in 1975 there were even more; hundreds of thousands left due to persecution by the authorities and a lack of economic opportunities since the process of socialist transformation was initiated. There are now large Vietnamese communities abroad, particularly in Australia, on the west coast of the US and in France. It has been estimated that the total Viet-kieu population numbers some two million. With the reforms of the 1980s, the authorities' view of the Chinese has changed; they now appreciate the crucial role they played, and could continue to play, in the economy. Before 1975, the Hoa controlled 80% of industry in the south and 50% of banking and finance. Today, ethnic Chinese in Vietnam can own and operate businesses and are once again allowed to join the communist party, the army and to enter university. The dark days of the mid-to late 1970s seem to be over.

Viet Kieu: overseas Vietnamese

The largest community of overseas Vietnamese, about 1.1 million, live in the US. The next largest populations are resident in France (250,000) and Australia (160,000), with much smaller numbers in a host of other countries. In 1990, 40,000 returned to visit; in 2003, 340,000 returned 'home'.

Many Viet Kieu are former boat people (see box, page 372), while others left the country as part of the UN-administered Orderly Departure Programme that began in earnest in the late 1980s. A smaller number (and one wonders whether they are strictly classed as Viet Kieu) left Vietnam for one of the former COMECON countries at some point between the 1950s and 1980s either to study or to work. The largest number appear to have gone to East Germany from where many have returned to take up important political positions. Those fortunate enough to find themselves in dour East Germany at the time of reunification suddenly found themselves privileged to be citizens of one of the world's richest countries.

As the Viet Kieu have discovered some measure of prosperity in the West, the Vietnamese government is anxious to welcome them back – or rather, welcome their money. So far, however, flows of investment for productive purposes have been rather disappointing and largely concentrated in the service sector, particularly in hotels and restaurants. Far more is thought to have been invested in land and property as overseas Vietnamese have, since 2000, been able to purchase property in their own name. (This, incidentally, has contributed to property speculation and a dizzy spiral of price increases that have made land prices in Ho Chi Minh City and Hanoi some of the most expensive in Asia.) Part of the problem is that many Viet Kieu were escaping from persecution in Vietnam and of all people continue to harbour doubts about a government that is, in essence, the same as the one they fled. On the government's side, they worry that the Viet Kieu may be a destabilizing influence, perhaps even a Fifth Column intent on undermining the supremacy of the Communist Party. Again the leadership have cause for concern as the most vocal opponents of the US policy of rapprochement have been Viet Kieu.

Art and architecture

Dongson culture

The first flourishing of Vietnamese art occurred with the emergence of the Dongson culture (named after a small town near Thanh Hoa where early excavations were focused) on the coast of Annam and Tonkin between 500 and 200 BC. The inspiration for the magnificent bronzes produced by the artists of Dongson originated from China: the decorative motifs have clear affinities with earlier Chinese bronzes. At the same time, the exceptional skill of production and decoration argues that these pieces represent among the first, and finest, of

Southeast Asian works of art. This is most evident in the huge and glorious **bronze drums** that can be seen in museums in both Hanoi and Ho Chi Minh City.

Cham art

If there was ever a golden period in Vietnamese art and architecture, it was that of the former central Vietnamese **kingdom of Champa**, centred on the Annamite coast, which flowered in the 10th and 11th centuries. Tragically, however, many of the 250 sites recorded in historical records have been pillaged or damaged and only 20 have survived the intervening centuries in a reasonable state of repair. Most famous are the sites of My Son and Dong Duong, south of Danang. Many of the finest works have been spirited out of the country to private collections and foreign museums, while others were destroyed by bombing and artillery fire during the Vietnam War. Nonetheless, the world's finest collection – with some breathtakingly beautiful work – is to be found in Danang's **Museum of Champa Sculpture**.

The earliest Cham art belongs to the My Son E1 period (early eighth century). It shows stylistic similarities with Indian Sanchi and Gupta works, although even at this early stage in its development Cham art incorporated distinctive indigenous elements, most clearly seen in the naturalistic interpretation of human form. By the Dong Duong period (late ninth century), the Cham had developed a unique style of their own. Archaeologists recognize six periods of Cham art: My Son E1 (early eighth century), Hoa Lai (early ninth century), Dong Duong (late ninth century), Late Tra Kieu (late 10th century), Thap Mam (12th-13th century) and Po Klong Garai (13th-16th century).

The Cham Kingdom was ethnically and linguistically distinct, but was overrun by the Vietnamese in the 15th century. It might be argued, then, that their monuments and sculptures have little to do with Vietnam per se, but with a preceding dynasty.

Hué architecture

More characteristic of Vietnamese art and architecture are the pagodas and palaces at Hué and in and around Hanoi (see box, page 39). But even this art and architecture is not really 'Vietnamese', as it is highly derivative, drawing heavily on Chinese prototypes. Certainly there are some features that are peculiarly Vietnamese, but unlike the other countries of mainland Southeast Asia, the Vietnamese artistic tradition is far less distinct. Vietnamese artistic endeavour was directed more towards literature than the plastic arts.

Contemporary Vietnamese art

The beginnings of contemporary or modern Vietnamese art can be traced back to the creation of the **École de Beaux Arts Indochine** in Hanoi in 1925. By this time there was an emerging westernized intelligentsia in Vietnam who had been schooled in French ways and taught to identify, at least in part, with French culture. Much of the early painting produced by students taught at the École de Beaux Arts Indochine was romantic, portraying an idyllic picture of Vietnamese life

ON THE ROAD
Brilliance in bronze: rain drums of Dongson

Of the artefacts associated with the Dongson culture, none is more technologically or artistically impressive than the huge bronze kettledrums that have been unearthed. Understandably, Vietnamese archaeologists have been keen to stress the 'Vietnamese-ness' of these objects, rejecting many of the suggestions made by Western scholars that they are of Chinese or Indian inspiration. As Professor Pham Huy Thong of the Academy of Sciences writes, Western studies are "marked by insufficient source material, prejudices and mere deductions", and that their "achievements [in understanding the drums] remain insignificant". He supports the view that these magnificent objects were products of the forebears of the Viet people. The jury on the issue remains out.

The squat, waisted, bronze Dongson drums show their makers to have been master casters of the first order. They can measure over 1 m in height and width and consist of a decorated tympanum, a convex upper section, waisted middle, and expanding lower section. Decoration is both geometric and naturalistic, most notably on the finely incised drumhead. An area of continuing debate concerns the function of the drums. They have usually been found associated with human remains and other precious objects, leading archaeologists to argue that they symbolized power and prestige and were treasured objects in the community. Also known as rain drums, they are sometimes surmounted with bronze figures of frogs (or toads). It is thought that the drums were used as magical instruments to summon rain, frogs being associated with rain. Other decorative motifs include dancers (again, possibly part of rain-making rites) and boats with feather-crowned passengers (perhaps taking the deceased to the Kingdom of the Dead). Other Dongson drums have been found as far east as the island of Alor in Nusa Tenggara, Indonesia, indicating possible trade links between northern Vietnam and the archipelago.

As if to stress the nationalist symbolism of the drum, an image of an ornate tympanum is used as an icon by Vietnamese television, and Vietnam Airlines prints the motif on their tickets.

and landscape. It was also weak. However, by the 1930s a Vietnamese nationalist tone began to be expressed both in terms of subject matter and technique. For example, paintings on silk and lacquer became popular around this time.

In 1945, with the Declaration of Independence, the École de Beaux Arts Indochine closed, and art for art's sake came to an end. From this point, artists were strongly encouraged to join in the revolutionary project and, for example, paint posters of heroic workers, stoic peasants and brave soldiers. Painting landscapes or pictures of rural life was no longer on the agenda.

In 1950 a new **School of Fine Art** was established in Viet Bac with the sole remit of training revolutionary artists. Central control of art and artists became even more stringent after 1954 when many artists were sent away to re-education camps.

Established artists such as Bui Xuan Phai, for example, were no longer permitted either to exhibit or to teach so lacking were they in revolutionary credentials.

In 1957 a new premier art school was created in the capital: the **Hanoi School of Fine Arts**. Students were schooled in the methods and meanings of socialist-realism and Western art became, by definition, capitalist and decadent. But while the state saw to it that artists kept to the revolutionary line, fine art in North Vietnam never became so harsh and uncompromising as in China or the Soviet Union; there was always a romantic streak. In addition, the first director of the Hanoi School of Fine Arts, Nguyen Do Cung, encouraged his students to search for inspiration in traditional Vietnamese arts and crafts, in simple village designs and in archaeological artefacts. Old woodblock prints, for example, strongly influenced the artists of this period.

With *doi moi* – economic reform – has come a greater degree of artistic freedom. The first exhibition of abstract art in Vietnam was held in 1992. Today there are numerous art galleries in Hanoi and Ho Chi Minh City and while artists still paint within limits set by the Communist Party, these have been considerably relaxed.

Crafts

Lacquerware (son mai)

The art of making lacquerware is said to have been introduced into Vietnam after Emperor Le Thanh Ton (1443-1459) sent an emissary to the Chinese court to investigate the process. Lacquer is a resin from the son tree (*Rhus succedanea or R vernicifera*) that is then applied in numerous coats (usually 11) to wood (traditionally teak), leather, metal or porcelain. Prior to lacquering, the article must be sanded and coated with a fixative. The final coat is highly polished with coal powder. The piece may then be decorated with an incised design, painted, or inset with mother-of-pearl. If mother-of-pearl is to be used, appropriately shaped pieces of lacquer are chiselled out and the mother-of-pearl inset. This method is similar to that used in China, but different from Thailand and Burma. The designs in the north show Japanese influences, apparently because Japanese artists were employed as teachers at the École des Beaux Arts in Hanoi in the 1930s.

Non Lá conical hat

This cone-shaped hat is one of the most common and evocative sights in Vietnam's countryside. Worn by women (and occasionally men), it is usually woven from latania leaves. The poem hats of Hué are particularly well known (see Shopping, page 162). Although all peasants in Southeast Asia wear straw hats only the Vietnamese version is perfectly conical and as such instantly identifies the wearer. As well as providing protection from the weather it serves other functions such as fan and rice holder and can even be used for carrying water. It also makes an original lampshade, often to be seen hanging over a pool table in bars in Saigon. It is probably less versatile than its Cambodian equivalent, the *kramar* (cotton scarf), which acts as a sarong, towel, curtain, sheet and baby sling, among its other uses.

Ao dai

This garment exhibits more conspicuously what it was intended to hide. It is the national women's costume of Vietnam, literally, but prosaically it means 'long dress'. Ao dai consists of a long flowing tunic of diaphanous fabric worn over a pair of loose-fitting white pants; the front and rear sections of the tunic are split from the waist down. The modern design was created by a literary group called the *Tu Luc Van Doan* in 1932, based on ancient court costumes and Chinese dresses such as the chong san. In traditional society, decoration and complexity of design indicated the status of the wearer (for example, gold brocade and dragons were for the sole use of the emperor; purple for higher-ranked mandarins). The popularity of the *ao dai* is now worldwide and the annual Miss Ao Dai pageant at Long Beach attracts entrants from all over the US. Today *ao dai* is uniform for hotel receptionists and many office workers, particularly in Ho Chi Minh City but less so in cooler Hanoi.

Montagnard crafts

There are more than 50 ethnic minorities and their crafts are highly diverse. Textiles, jewellery and basketwork are the most widely available. The finely worked clothing of the Muong (with Dongson-derived motifs) and indigo-dyed cloth of the Bahnar are two examples of Montagnard crafts.

Drama and dance

Classical Vietnamese theatre, known as *hat boi* (*hat* = to sing; boi = gesture, pose), shows close links with the classical theatre of China. Emperor Tu Duc had a troupe of 150 female artists and employed stars from China via a series of extravagant productions. Since the partition of the country in 1954, there has developed what might be termed 'revolutionary realist' theatre and classical Vietnamese theatre is today almost defunct. However, the most original theatrical art form in Vietnam is *mua roi nuoc* or **water puppet theatre**. This seems to have originated in northern Vietnam during the early years of this millennium when it was associated with the harvest festival (at one time scholars thought water puppet theatre originated in China before being adopted in Vietnam). An inscription in Nam Ha province mentions a show put on in honour of King Ly Nhan Ton in 1121. By the time the French began to colonize Vietnam in the late 19th century it had spread to all of the major towns of the country.

As the name suggests, this form of theatre uses the surface of the water as the stage. Puppeteers, concealed behind a bamboo screen symbolizing an ancient village communal house, manipulate the characters while standing in a metre of water. The puppets – some over half a metre tall – are carved from water resistant *sung* wood that is also very lightweight and then painted in bright colours. Most need one puppeteer to manipulate them, but some require three or four. Plays are based on historical and religious themes: the origins of the Viet nation, legends, village life, and acts of heroism. Some include the use of fireworks – especially during battle scenes – while all performances are accompanied by folk opera singers and traditional instruments. Performances usually begin with the clown, Teu, taking the stage and he acts as a linking character between the various scenes.

The most famous and active troupe is based in Hanoi (see page 66), although in total there are about a dozen groups. Since the 1980s Vietnamese writers have turned their attention from revolutionary heroes to commentary on political and social issues of the day. Consequently, many plays have failed to see the light of day and those that have are often been badly mauled by the censoring committee's scissors; references to corrupt officials and policemen seldom make the transition from page to stage.

Language

The Vietnamese language has a reputation for being fiendishly difficult to master. Its origins are still the subject of dispute; at one time thought to be a Sino-Tibetan language (because it is tonal), it is now believed to be Austro-Asiatic and related to Mon-Khmer. Sometime after the ninth century, when Vietnam was under Chinese domination, Chinese ideograms were adapted for use with the Vietnamese language. This script – *chu nho* (scholar's script) – was used in all official correspondence and in literature right through to the early 20th century. Whether this replaced an earlier writing system is not known. As early Vietnamese nationalists tried to break away from Chinese cultural hegemony in the late 13th century, they devised their own script, based on Chinese ideograms but adapted to meet Vietnamese language needs. This became known as *chu nom* (vulgar script). So, while Chinese words formed the learned vocabulary of the intelligentsia (largely inaccessible to the man on the street or in the paddy field), non-Chinese words made up a parallel popular vocabulary.

Finally, in the 17th century, European missionaries under the tutelage of Father Alexandre-de-Rhodes created a system of Romanized writing: *quoc ngu* (national language). It is said that Rhodes initially thought Vietnamese sounded like the 'twittering of birds' (a view interestingly echoed by Graham Greene in *The Quiet American*: "To take an Annamite to bed with you is like taking a bird: they twitter and sing on your pillow") but had mastered the language in six months. The first *quoc ngu* dictionary (Vietnamese-Portuguese-Latin), *Dictionarium Annamiticum Lusitanum et Latinum*, was published in 1651. *Quoc ngu* uses marks – so-called diacritical marks – to indicate tonal differences. Initially it was ignored by the educated unless they were Roman Catholic and it was not until the early 20th century that its use became a mark of modernity among a broad spectrum of Vietnamese. Even then, engravings in the mausoleums and palaces of the royal family continued to use Chinese characters. It seems that the move from *chu nom* to *quoc ngu*, despite the fact that it was imposed by an occupying country, occurred as people realized how much easier it was to master. The first *quoc ngu* newspaper, *Gia Dinh Bao* (Gia Dinh Gazette), was published in 1865 and *quoc ngu* was adopted as the national script in 1920.

Standard Vietnamese is based on the language spoken by an educated person living in the vicinity of Hanoi. This has become, so to speak, Vietnam's equivalent of BBC English. There are also important regional dialects in the centre and south of the country and these differ from Standard Vietnamese in terms of tone and vocabulary, but use the same system of grammar.

Literature

In ancient Vietnam, texts were reproduced laboriously, by scribes, on paper made from the bark of the mulberry tree (*giay ban*). Examples exist in Ho Chi Minh City, Paris, Hanoi and Hué. Printing technology was introduced in the late 13th century, but due to the hot and humid climate no early examples exist.

Vietnam has a rich folk literature of fables, legends, proverbs and songs, most of which were transmitted by word of mouth. In the 17th and 18th centuries, satirical poems and, importantly, verse novels (*truyen*) appeared. These were memorized and recited by itinerant storytellers as they travelled from village to village.

Like much Vietnamese art, Vietnamese literature also owes a debt to China. Chinese characters and literary styles were duplicated and although a tradition of *nom* literature did evolve (*nom* being a hybrid script developed in the 13th century), Vietnamese efforts remained largely derivative. One exception was the scholarly **Nguyen Trai** (see box, page 352) who bridged the gap; he excelled in classical Chinese *chu nho* as well as producing some of the earliest surviving, and very fine, poetry and prose in the new *chu nom* script. An important distinction is between the literature of the intelligentsia (essentially Chinese) and that of the people (more individualistic). These latter *nom* works, dating from the 15th century onwards, were simpler and concerned with immediate problems and grievances. They can be viewed as the most Vietnamese of literary works and include *Chinh Phu Ngam* (Lament of a Soldier's Wife), an anti-war poem by Phan Huy Ich (1750-1822). The greatest Vietnamese literature was produced during the social and political upheavals of the 19th century: *Truyen Kieu* (The Tale of Kieu) written by Nguyen Du (1765-1820) is a classic of the period. This 3254-line story is regarded by most Vietnamese as their cultural statement par excellence (see the next section for a taster). Nguyen Du was one of the most skilled and learned mandarins of his time and was posted to China as Vietnam's Ambassador to the Middle Kingdom. On his return, Nguyen Du wrote the *Truyen Kieu* (or *Kim Van Kieu*), a celebration of Vietnamese culture, in the lines of which can be traced the essence of Vietnamese-ness.

French influence, and the spread of the Romanized Vietnamese script, led to the end of the Chinese literary tradition by the 1930s and its replacement by a far starker, freer, Western-derived style. Poetry of this period is known as *Tho Moi* (New Poetry). The communist period has seen restrictions on literary freedom and in recent years there have been numerous cases of authors and poets, together with journalists, being imprisoned owing to the critical nature of their work. Much of Vietnam's literature is allegorical (which people readily understand); this reflects a centuries-old intolerance of criticism by the mandarin and royal family. Although the Communist Party might be expected to approve of anti-royal sentiment in literature it seldom does, fearing that the Party itself is the true object of the writer's scorn.

Kieu: oriental Juliet or prototype Miss Saigon?

The tale of Kieu is a true story of pure love corrupted by greed and power. It also offers a fascinating glimpse into the Vietnamese mind and Vietnamese sexual mores. Kieu is in love with the young scholar Kim and early on in the story she displays her physical and moral qualities:

"A fragrant rose, she sparkled in full bloom, bemused his eyes, and kindled his desire. When waves of lust had seemed to sweep him off, his wooing turned to wanton liberties. She said: 'Treat not our love as just a game – please stay away from me and let me speak. What is a mere peach blossom that one should fence off the garden, thwart the bluebird's quest? But you've named me your bride – to serve her man, she must place chastity above all else.'"

But the overriding theme of the story is the ill-treatment of an innocent girl by a duplicitous and wicked world unopposed by Heaven. Unmoved by Kieu's sale into prostitution the fates actively oppose her wishes by keeping her alive when she attempts to kill herself.

Any respite in her tale of woe proves short-lived and joy turns quickly to pain. The story illustrates the hopelessness of women in a Confucianist, male-dominated world; Kieu likens herself to a raindrop with no control over where she will land. Early on in the story when Kim is away attending to family matters Kieu has to choose between Kim, to whom she has pledged herself, and her family. Such is the strength of family ties that she offers herself to be sold in marriage to raise money for her kith and kin:

"By what means could she save her flesh and blood? When evil strikes you bow to circumstance. As you must weigh and choose between your love and filial duty, which will turn the scale? She put aside all vows of love and troth – a child first pays the debts of birth and care."

Kieu gets married off to an elderly 'scholar' called Ma who is in fact a brothel keeper; but before removing her from her family he deflowers her. Kieu is now commercially less valuable but Ma believes he can remedy this:

"One smile of hers is worth pure gold – it's true. When she gets there, to pluck the maiden bud, princes and gentlefolk will push and shove. She'll bring at least three hundred liang, about what I have paid – net profit after that. A morsel dangles at my mouth – what God serves up I crave, yet money hate to lose. A heavenly peach within a mortal's grasp: I'll bend the branch, pick it, and quench my thirst. How many flower-fanciers on Earth can really tell one flower from the next? Juice from pomegranite skin and cockscomb blood will heal it up and lend the virgin look. In dim half-light some yokel will be fooled: she'll fetch that much, and not one penny less."

Kieu's sorrows deepen; she becomes a concubine of a married brothel patron, Thuc. After a year of happiness together with Thuc his spurned wife, Hoan, decides to spoil the fun. Kieu ends up as a slave serving Thuc and Hoan. She laments her fate knowing full well the reason for it:

"I've had an ample share of life's foul dust, and now this swamp of mud proves twice as vile. Will fortune never let its victims go but in its snares and toils hold fast a rose? I sinned in some past life and have to pay: I'll pay as flowers must fade and jade must break."

She later commits her only earthly crime stealing a golden bell and silver gong from the shrine she is charged with keeping, and flees to seek sanctuary in a Buddhist temple. But when her crime comes to light she is sent to live with the Bac family that, again on the pretext of marriage, sells her to another brothel. This time she meets a free-spirited warlord Tu Hai:

"A towering hero, he outfought all foes with club or fist and knew all arts of war. Between the earth and heaven he lived free...."

who rescues her from the brothel. They become soul- and bed-mates until, after six months, Tu Hai's wanderlust and urge to fight take him away from her. He returns a year later victorious in battle. At this stage the story reaches a happy (and false) ending; Tu Hai sends his Captains out to round up all those who have crossed Kieu's path.

"Awesome is Heaven's law of recompense – one haul and all were caught, brought back to camp. Under a tent erected in the midst, Lord Tu and his fair lady took their seats. No sooner had the drumroll died away than guards checked names, led captives to the gate. 'Whether they have used you well or ill,' he said, 'pronounce yourself upon their just deserts.' "

Those who have shown Kieu kindness are rewarded while those who have harmed her are tortured. The exception is Hoan who, cruel though she was, Kieu releases (after torture) in a show of mercy following Hoan's plea "I have a woman's mind, a petty soul, and jealousy's a trait all humans share" – Kieu had been living with Hoan's husband for a year.

All is well for five years until another warlord, Lord Ho, flatters Kieu encouraging her to persuade Tu to put down his sword and make peace with the emperor. Guileless Kieu does so and "Lord Tu lets flags hang loose, watch-drums go dead. He slackened all defence – imperial spies/observed his camp and learned of its true state." All is lost: Tu is killed, Kieu has betrayed her hero and she is married off to a tribal chief. She throws herself into a river but yet again fails to die. Eventually Kieu is reunited with Kim and her family:

"She glanced and saw her folks – they all were here: Father looked quite strong, and Mother spry; both sister Van and brother Quan grown up; and over there was Kim her love of yore."

Kieu and Kim hold a wedding feast and share a house but not a bed; Kim has sons by Van, Kieu's sister, and they all settle down to an untroubled life overseen by a more benevolent Heaven.

Huynh Sang Thong's translation (see page 422) is considered the finest and is accompanied by excellent notes which explain the Vietnamese phrasing of the original and which set the story in context. Translation and commentary will bring Truyen Kieu to a wider and, one hopes, appreciative audience and help shed some light on what many Vietnamese regard as their most important cultural statement.

A Vietnamese account of the 'American' War

Most visitors to Vietnam, if they were not involved in the war themselves, gain their views from literature and films made by Westerners, for Westerners. It is rare for people to have access to Vietnamese literary perspectives on the war, partly because most that do exist are not translated and because, in comparison to the torrent of especially American accounts, there have been comparatively few written by Vietnamese. One of these few is Bao Ninh's moving and poetic *The Sorrow of War* that was first published in Vietnamese in 1991 under the title *Thân Phân Cua Tinh Yêu*. In Vietnam it was a huge success, no doubt prompting its translation into English by Frank Palmos. The English edition was published in 1994 and it is now available in paperback, see page 422. This is not a romantic vision of war, a macho account relishing the fight, nor once revelling in victory, but a deeply sad and melancholic book. Perhaps this is because Bao Ninh is recounting his story from the position of one who was there. He served with the Glorious 27th Youth Brigade, joining-up in 1969 at the age of 17. Of the 500 who went to war with the Glorious 27th, he was one of just 10 to survive the conflict. For those who want an alternative perspective, the book is recommended.

Religion

Vietnam supports followers of all the major world religions, as well as those religions that are peculiarly Vietnamese: Theravada and Mahayana Buddhism, Protestant and Roman Catholic Christianity, Taoism, Confucianism, Islam, Cao Daism, Hoa Hao and Hinduism. In addition, spirit and ancestor worship (*To Tien*) are also practised. Confucianism, although not a formal religion, is probably the most pervasive doctrine of all. Nominal Christians and Buddhists will still pay attention to the moral and philosophic principles of Confucianism and it continues to play a central role in Vietnamese life.

Following the communist victory in 1975, the authorities moved quickly to curtail the influence of the various religions. Schools, hospitals and other institutions run by religious organizations were taken over by the state and many clergy either imprisoned and/or sent to re-education camps. The religious hierarchies were institutionalized, and proselytizing severely curtailed.

During the late 1980s and into the early 1990s some analysts identified an easing of the government's previously highly restrictive policies towards religious organizations. At the beginning of 1993, former General Secretary of the Vietnamese Communist Party, Do Muoi, even went so far as to make official visits to a Buddhist monastery and a Roman Catholic church. However it is clear the communist hierarchy is highly suspicious of priests and monks. They are well aware of the prominent role they played in South Vietnamese political dissension and are quick to crack down on any religious leader or organization that becomes involved in politics.

There is no question that more people today are attending Buddhist pagodas, Christian churches and Cao Dai temples. However, whether this rise in attendance at temples and churches actually means some sort of religious rebirth is questionable. Dang Nghiem Van, head of Hanoi's Institute of Religious Studies, poured scorn on the notion that young people are finding religion. They "are not religious", he said, "just superstitious. This isn't religion. It's decadence".

Mahayana Buddhism

Although there are both Theravada (also known as Hinayana) and Mahayana Buddhists in Vietnam, the latter are by far the more numerous. Buddhism was introduced into Vietnam in the second century AD: Indian pilgrims came by boat and brought the teachings of Theravada Buddhism, while Chinese monks came by land and introduced Mahayana Buddhism. In particular, the Chinese monk Mau Tu is credited with being the first person to introduce Mahayana Buddhism in AD 194-195.

Initially, Buddhism was very much the religion of the elite and did not impinge upon the common Vietnamese man or woman. It was not until the reign of Emperor Ly Anh Tong (1138-1175) that Buddhism was promoted as the state religion, nearly 1000 years after Mau Tu had arrived from China to spread the teachings of the Buddha. By that time it had begun to filter down to the village level, but as it did so

ON THE ROAD

In Siddhartha's footsteps: a short history of Buddhism

Buddhism was founded by Siddhartha Gautama, a prince of the Sakya tribe of Nepal, who probably lived from 563 to 483 BC. He achieved enlightenment and the word buddha means 'fully enlightened one', or 'one who has woken up'. Siddhartha Gautama is known by a number of names. In the West, he is usually referred to as The Buddha, ie the historic Buddha (but not just Buddha); more common in Southeast Asia is Sakyamuni, or Sage of the Sakyas (referring to his tribal origins).

Over the centuries, the life of the Buddha has become part legend and the Jataka tales that recount his various lives are colourful and convoluted. But central to Buddhist belief is that he was born under a sal tree, that he achieved enlightenment under a bodhi tree in the Bodh Gaya Gardens, that he preached the First Sermon at Sarnath, and that he died at Kusinagara (all in India or Nepal).

The Buddha was born at Lumbini (in present-day Nepal) as Queen Maya was on her way to her parents' home. She had an auspicious dream before the child's birth of being impregnated by an elephant, whereupon a sage prophesied Siddhartha would become either a great king or a great spiritual leader. His father, being keen that the first option of the prophesy be fulfilled, brought him up in all the princely skills – at which Siddhartha excelled – and ensured that he only saw beautiful things, not the harsher elements of life.

Despite his father's efforts Siddhartha saw four things while travelling between palaces: a helpless old man, a very sick man, a corpse being carried by lamenting relatives, and an ascetic, calm and serene as he begged for food. The young prince renounced his princely origins and left home to study under a series of spiritual teachers. He finally discovered the path to enlightenment

it became increasingly syncretic; Buddhism became enmeshed with Confucianism, Taoism, spirituality, mysticism and animism. In the 15th century it also began to lose its position to Confucianism as the dominant religion of the court.

There has been a resurgence of Buddhism since the 1920s. It was the self-immolation of Buddhist monks in the 1960s which provided a focus of discontent against the government in the south (see box, page 265), and since the communist victory in 1975, monks have remained an important focus of dissent, hence the persecution of Buddhists during the early years following reunification. Mahayana Buddhists are concentrated in the centre and north of the country and the dominant sect is the Thien (Zen) meditation sect. Of the relatively small numbers of Theravada Buddhists, the majority are of Cambodian stock and are concentrated in the Mekong Delta. In Vietnam, Buddhism is intertwined with Confucianism and Taoism. See also box, above.

at the Bodh Gaya Gardens in India. He then proclaimed his thoughts to a small group of disciples at Sarnath, near Benares, and continued to preach and attract followers until he died at the age of 81 at Kusinagara.

In the First Sermon at the deer park in Sarnath, the Buddha preached the Four Truths, still seen as the root of Buddhist belief and experience: suffering exists; there is a cause of suffering; suffering can be ended; and to end suffering it is necessary to follow the 'Noble Eightfold Path' – right speech, livelihood, action, effort, mindfulness, concentration, opinion and intention. Soon after the Buddha began preaching, a monastic order – the Sangha – was established. As the monkhood evolved in India, it also began to fragment into different sects. An important change was the belief that the Buddha was transcendent: he had never been born, nor had he died; he had always existed and his life on earth had been mere illusion. The emergence of these new concepts helped to turn what up until then was an ethical code of conduct, into a religion. It eventually led to a new Buddhist movement, Mahayana Buddhism, which split from the more traditional Theravada 'sect'.

Despite the division of Buddhism into two sects, the central tenets are common to both. Specifically, the principles pertaining to the Four Noble Truths, the Noble Eightfold Path, the Dependent Origination, the Law of Karma, and nirvana. In addition, the principles of non-violence and tolerance are also embraced by both sects. The differences between the two are of emphasis and interpretation. Theravada Buddhism is strictly based on the original Pali Canon, while the Mahayana tradition stems from later Sanskrit texts. Mahayana Buddhism also allows a broader interpretation of the doctrine. Other major differences are that while the Theravada tradition is more 'intellectual' and self-obsessed, stressing the attainment of wisdom and insight for oneself, Mahayana Buddhism emphasizes devotion and compassion.

Confucianism

Although Confucianism is not strictly a religion, the teachings of the Chinese sage and philosopher Confucius (551-479 BC) form the basis on which Vietnamese life and government were based for much of the historic period. Even today, Confucianist perspectives are, possibly, more strongly in evidence than communist ones. Confucianism was introduced from China during the Bac Thuoc Period (111 BC-AD 938) when the Chinese dominated the country. The 'religion' enshrined the concept of imperial rule by the mandate of heaven, constraining social and political change.

In essence, Confucianism stresses the importance of family and lineage and the worship of ancestors. Men and women in positions of authority were required to provide role models for the 'ignorant', while the state, epitomized in the emperor, was likewise required to set an example and to provide conditions of stability and fairness for his people. Crucially, children had to observe filial piety. This set of norms, which were drawn from the experience of the human encounter at the practical level, were enshrined in the Forty-seven Rules for Teaching and Changing first issued in 1663. A key element of Confucianist thought is the Three Bonds (tam cuong) – the loyalty of ministers to the emperor, obedience of children to their parents and submission of wives to their husbands. Added to these are mutual reciprocity among friends and benevolence towards strangers. Not surprisingly the communists are antipathetic to such a hierarchical view of society although ironically Confucianism, which inculcates respect for the elderly and authority, unwittingly lends support to a politburo occupied by old men. In an essay entitled 'Confucianism and Marxism', Vietnamese scholar Nguyen Khac Vien explains why Marxism proved an acceptable doctrine to those accustomed to Confucian values: "Marxism was not baffling to Confucians in that it concentrated man's thoughts on political and social problems. By defining man as the total of his social relationships, Marxism hardly came as a shock to the Confucian scholar who had always considered the highest aim of man to be the fulfilment of his social obligations... Bourgeois individualism, which puts personal interests ahead of those of society and petty bourgeois anarchism, which allows no social discipline whatsoever, are alien to both Confucianism and Marxism."

Taoism

Taoism was introduced from China into Vietnam at about the same time as Confucianism. It is based on the works of the Chinese philosophers Lao Tzu (circa sixth-fifth centuries BC) and Chuang Tzu (fourth century BC). Although not strictly a formal religion, it has had a significant influence on Buddhism (as it is practised in Vietnam) and on Confucianism. In reality, Taoism and Confucianism are two sides of the same coin: the Taoist side is poetry and spirituality; the Confucianist side, social ethics and the order of the world. Together they form a unity. Like Confucianism, it is not possible to give a figure to the number of followers of Taoism in Vietnam. It functions in conjunction with Confucianism and Buddhism and also often with Christianity, Cao Daism and Hoa Hao. Of all the world's religions, Taoism is perhaps the hardest to pin down. It has no formal code, no teachings and no creed. It is a cosmic religion. Even the word Tao is usually left untranslated or merely translated as 'The Way'. The inscrutability of it all is summed up in the writings of the Chinese poet Po Chu-i: "Those who speak know nothing, Those who know keep silence. These words, as I am told, were spoken by Lao Tzu. But if we are to believe that Lao Tzu was himself one who knew, how comes it that he wrote a book of five thousand words?"

Or to quote Chuang Tzu even more inscrutably: "Tao is beyond material existence ... it may be transmitted, but it cannot be received [possessed]. It may be attained, but cannot be seen. It exists prior to Heaven and Earth, and, indeed, for all eternity ... it is above the Zenith, but is not high; it is beneath the Nadir, but it is not low. It is prior to Heaven and Earth, but it is not ancient. It is older than the most ancient, but it is not old."

Central to Taoist belief is a world view based upon yin and yang, two primordial forces on which the creation and functioning of the world are based. The yin-yang is not specifically Taoist or Confucianist, but predates both and is associated with the first recorded Chinese ruler, Fu-hsi (2852-2738 BC). The well-known yin-yang symbol symbolizes the balance and equality between the great dualistic forces in the universe: dark and light, negative and positive, male and female. JC Cooper explains in *Taoism: the Way of the Mystic*, the symbolism of the black and white dots: "There is a point, or embryo, of black in the white and white in the black. This is essential to the symbolism since there is no being which does not contain within itself the germ of its opposite. There is no male without feminine characteristics and no female without its masculine attributes." Thus the dualism of the yin-yang is not absolute, but permeable.

To maintain balance and harmony in life it is necessary that a proper balance be maintained between yin (female) and yang (male). This is believed to be true both at the scale of the world and the nation, and also for an individual, for the human body is the world in microcosm. The root cause of illness is imbalance between the forces of yin and yang. Even foods have characters: 'hot' foods are yang and 'cold', yin. Implicit in this is the belief that there is a natural law underpinning all of life, a law upon which harmony ultimately rests. Taoism attempts to maintain this balance and thereby harmony. In this way, Taoism is a force promoting inertia, maintaining the status quo. Traditional relationships between fathers and sons, between siblings, within villages, and between the rulers and the ruled, are all rationalized in terms of maintaining balance and harmony. Forces for change – like communism and democracy – are resisted on the basis that they upset this balance.

Christianity

Christianity was first introduced into Vietnam in the 16th century by Roman Catholic missionaries from Portugal, Spain and France. The first Bishop of Vietnam was appointed in 1659 and by 1685 there were estimated to be 800,000 Roman Catholics in the country. For several centuries Christianity was discouraged, and at times, outlawed. Many Christians were executed and one of the reasons the French gave for annexing the country in the late 19th century was religious persecution. Today, 8-10% of the population are thought to be Roman Catholic; less than 1% are Protestant. This Christian population is served by around 2000 priests. Following reunification in 1975, many Roman Catholics in the former south were sent to re-education camps. They were perceived to be both staunchly pro-American and anti-communist and it was not until 1988 that many were returned to normal life.

Today, Roman Catholics are still viewed with suspicion by the state and priests felt to be drifting from purely religious concerns into any criticism of the state (seen as anti-government activity) are detained, such as Father Nguyen Van Ly, see page 380. And this is the key point: the Vietnamese remain tolerant and open in matters of religion and spirituality. It is the political overtones that come with any established religion that the authorities find impossible to accept. While memories of the role of the Roman Catholic church in the downfall of Polish communism linger relations between Hanoi and the Vatican are not warm and often strained and Rome finds it difficult to appoint bishops. However, in 2007 the prime minister became the first head of government to be received at the Vatican to discuss relations. More generally, the authorities have been slow to permit Vietnamese men to become ordained, and they have limited the production and flow of religious literature. Nevertheless centuries of existence in what for the Roman Catholic church has been the hostile environment of Vietnam has enabled it to reach an accommodation and degree of acceptance. Doubtless the brighter of the communist leaders realise the Roman Catholic church will be around long after their Party has disappeared.

Protestant sects have a much tougher time. This is partly due to the evangelical nature of much Protestantism that makes the authorities distinctly uneasy. Evangelical protestants have faced the brunt of the crackdowns in the last couple of years.

Islam and Hinduism

The only centres of Islam and Hinduism are among the Cham of the central coastal plain and Chau Doc. The Cham were converted to Islam by Muslim traders. There are several mosques in Ho Chi Minh City and Cholon, some of them built by Indians from Kerala.

Cao Daism

Cao Dai took root in southern Vietnam during the 1920s after Ngo Van Chieu, a civil servant, was visited by 'Cao Dai' or the 'Supreme Being' and was given the tenets of a new religion. Ngo received this spiritual visitation in 1919 on Phu Quoc Island. The Cao Dai later told Ngo in a seance that he was to be symbolized by a giant eye. The religion quickly gained the support of a large following of dispossessed peasants. It was both a religion and a nationalist movement. In terms of the former, it claimed to be a synthesis of Buddhism, Christianity, Taoism, Confucianism and Islam. Cao Dai 'saints' include Joan of Arc, the French writer Victor Hugo, Sir Winston Churchill, Sun Yat Sen, Moses and Brahma. Debates over doctrine are mediated through the spirits who are contacted on a regular basis through a strange wooden contraption called a *corbeille-à-bec* or planchette. The five Cao Dai commandments are: do not kill any living creature; do not covet; do not practise high living; do not be tempted; and do not slander by word. But, as well as being a religion, the movement also claimed that it would restore traditional Vietnamese attitudes and was anti-colonial and modestly subversive. Opportunist to a fault, Cao Dai followers sought the aid of the Japanese against the French, the Americans against the Viet Minh and the Viet Minh against the south. Following reunification in 1975, all Cao Dai lands were confiscated and their leadership emasculated. The centre of Cao Daism remains the Mekong Delta where – and despite the efforts of the communists – there are thought to be perhaps two million adherents and perhaps 1000 Cao Dai temples. The Cao Dai Great Temple is in the town of Tay Ninh, 100 km from Ho Chi Minh City (see page 274).

Hoa Hao

Hoa Hao is another Vietnamese religion that emerged in the Mekong Delta. It was founded by Huynh Phu So in 1939, a resident of Hoa Hao village in the province of Chau Doc. Effectively a schism of Buddhism, the sect discourages temple building and worship, maintaining that simplicity of worship is the key to better contact with God. There are thought to be perhaps 1-1.5 million adherents of Hoa Hao, predominantly in the Chau Doc area.

Land &
environment

The regions of Vietnam

The name Vietnam is derived from that adopted in 1802 by Emperor Gia Long: Nam Viet. This means, literally, the Viet (the largest ethnic group) of the south (Nam), and substituted for the country's previous name, Annam. The country is S-shaped, covers a land area of 329,600 sq km and has a coastline of 3000 km. The most important economic zones, containing the main concentrations of population, are focused on two large deltaic areas. In the north, there are the ancient rice fields and settlements of the Red River, and in the south, the fertile alluvial plain of the Mekong. In between, the country narrows to less than 50 km wide, with only a thin ribbon of fertile lowland suited to intensive agriculture. Much of the interior, away from the coastal belt and the deltas, is mountainous. Here ethnic minorities (Montagnards), along with some lowland Vietnamese resettled in so-called New Economic Zones since 1975, eke out a living on thin and unproductive soils. The rugged terrain means that only 25% of the land is actually cultivated. Of the rest, 20-25% is forested and some of this is heavily degraded.

The French subdivided Vietnam into three regions, administering each separately: Tonkin or Bac Ky (the north region), Annam or Trung Ky (the central region) and Cochin China or Nam Ky (the south region). Although these administrative divisions have been abolished, the Vietnamese still recognize their country as consisting of three regions, distinct in terms of geography, history and culture. Their new names are Bac Bo (north), Trung Bo (centre) and Nam Bo (south).

Northern Highlands

Vietnam consists of five major geographical zones. In the far north are the northern highlands, which ring the Red River Delta and form a natural barrier with China. The rugged mountains on the west border of this region – the Hoang Lien Son – exceed 3000 m in places. The tributaries of the Red River have cut deep, steep-sided gorges through the Hoang Lien Son, which are navigable by small boats. The eastern portion of this region, bordering the Gulf of Tonkin, is far less imposing; the mountain peaks of the west have diminished into foothills, allowing easy access to China. It was across these hills that the Chinese mounted their successive invasions of Vietnam, the last of which occurred as recently as 1979, see page 378.

Red River Delta

The second region lies in the embrace of the hills of the north. This, the Red River Delta, can legitimately claim to be the cultural and historical heart of the Viet nation. Hanoi lies at its core and it was here the first truly independent Vietnamese polity was established in AD 939 by Ngo Quyen. The delta covers almost 15,000 sq km and extends 240 km inland from the coast. Rice has been grown on the alluvial soils of the Red River for thousands of years. Yet despite the intricate web of canals, dykes and embankments, the Vietnamese have never been able to completely tame the river, and the delta is the victim of frequent and sometimes devastating floods. The area is very low-lying, rarely more than 3 m above sea level and often less than 1 m. The highwater mark is nearly 8 m above land level in some places. During the monsoon season, the tributaries of the Red River quickly become torrents rushing through the narrow gorges of the Hoang Lien Son, before emptying into the main channel that then bursts its banks. Although the region supports one of the highest agricultural population densities in the world, the inhabitants have frequently had to endure famines, most recently in 1989.

South of the Red River Delta
South of the Red River Delta region lie the central lowlands and the mountains of the Annamite Chain. The **Annam Highlands**, now known as **Truong Son Mountain Range**, form an important cultural divide between the Indianized nations of the west and the Sinicized cultures of the east. Its northern rugged extremity is in Thanh Hoa Province. From here the Truong Son stetches over 1200 km south, to peter out 80 km north of Ho Chi Minh City.

The highest peak is Ngoc Linh Mountain in Kon Tum Province at 2598 m. The Central Highlands form an upland plateau on which the hill resorts of **Buon Ma Thuot** and **Dalat** are situated. On the plateau, plantation agriculture and hill farms are interspersed with stands of bamboo and tropical forests. Once rich in wildlife, the plateau was a popular hunting ground during the colonial period.

Central coastal strip
To the east, the Annamite Chain falls off steeply, leaving only a narrow and fragmented band of lowland suitable for settlement: the central coastal strip. In places the mountains advance all the way to the coast, plunging into the sea as rock faces and making north–south communication difficult. At no point does the region extend more than 64 km inland, and it covers 6750 sq km. The soils are often rocky or saline, and irrigation is seldom possible. Nonetheless, the inhabitants have a history of sophisticated rice culture and it was here that the Champa Kingdom was established in the early centuries of the Christian era. These lowlands have also formed a conduit along which people have moved. Even today, the main north–south road and rail routes cut through the coastal lowlands.

Mekong Delta
Unlike the Red River Delta this region is not so prone to flooding and consequently rice production is more stable. The reason why flooding is less severe lies in the regulating effect of the Great Lake of Cambodia, the Tonlé Sap. During the rainy season, when the water flowing into the Mekong becomes too great for even this mighty river to absorb, rather than overflowing its banks, the water backs up into

ON THE ROAD

The Mekong: mother river of Southeast Asia

The Mekong River is one of the 12 great rivers of the world. It stretches 4500 km from its source on the Tibet Plateau in China to its mouth (or mouths) in the Mekong Delta of Vietnam. (On 11 April 1995 a Franco–British expedition announced that they had discovered the source of the Mekong – 5000 m high, at the head of the Rup-Sa Pass, and miles from anywhere. Each year, the river empties 475 billion cu m of water into the East Sea. Along its course it flows through Burma, Laos, Thailand, Cambodia and Vietnam – all countries constituting mainland Southeast Asia – as well as China. In both a symbolic and a physical sense it links the region. Bringing fertile silt to the land along its banks, but particularly to the Mekong Delta, the river contributes to Southeast Asia's agricultural wealth. In former times, a tributary of the Mekong that drains the Tonlé Sap (the Great Lake of Cambodia), provided the rice surplus on which the fabulous Angkor empire was founded. The Tonlé Sap acts like a great regulator, storing water in time of flood and then releasing it when levels recede.

The first European to explore the river was French naval officer Francis Garnier. His Mekong expedition (1866-68) followed the great river upstream from its delta in Cochin China (southern Vietnam). Of the 9960 km that the trip covered, 506 km were 'discovered' for the first time. The motivation for the trip was to find a southern route into the Heavenly Kingdom – China. But they failed. The river is navigable only as far as the Lao-Cambodian border where the Khone rapids make it impassable. Nonetheless, the expedition report is one of the finest of its genre. Today the Mekong itself is perceived as a source of potential economic wealth, not just as a path to riches. The Mekong Secretariat was established in 1957 to harness the waters of the river for irrigation and hydropower. The Secretariat devised a grandiose plan with a succession of seven huge dams that would store 142 billion cubic metres of water, irrigate 4.3 million ha of riceland and generate 24,200MW of power. But the Vietnam War disrupted construction. Only Laos' Nam Ngum Dam on a tributary of the Mekong was ever built and even though this generates just 150MW of power, electricity exports to Thailand are one of Laos' largest export earners. Now that the countries of mainland Southeast Asia are on friendly terms once more, the Secretariat and its scheme have been given a new lease of life. But in the intervening years, fears about the environmental consequences of big dams have raised new questions. The Mekong Secretariat has moderated its plans and is now looking at less ambitious and less contentious ways to harness the Mekong River. See also box, page 302, on hydrology of the delta.

the Tonlé Sap, which quadruples in area. The Mekong Delta covers 67,000 sq km and is drained by five branches of the Mekong, which divides as it flows towards the sea. The vast delta is one of the great rice bowls of Asia producing nearly half of the country's rice and over the years has been cut into a patchwork by the canals that have been dug to expand irrigation and rice cultivation. Largely forested until the late 19th century, the French supported the settlement of the area by Vietnamese peasants, recognizing that it could become enormously productive. The deposition of silt by the rivers that cut through the delta, means that the shoreline is continually advancing, by up to 80 m each year in some places. To the north of the delta lies Ho Chi Minh City. See also boxes, pages 302 and 415.

Flora and fauna

Together with overseas conservation agencies such as the Worldwide Fund for Nature (WWF), Vietnamese scientists have, in recent years, been enumerating and protecting their fauna and flora. The establishment of nature reserves began in 1962 with the gazetting of the Cuc Phuong National Park. Today there are a total of 87 reserves covering 3.3% of Vietnam's land area. However, some of them are too small to sustain sufficiently large breeding populations of endangered species and many parks are quite heavily populated. For instance 80,000 people live, farm and hunt within the 22,000 ha Bach Ma National Park. Vietnamese scientists with support from outside agencies, in particular the WWF, have begun the important task of cataloguing and protecting Vietnam's wildlife.

The **Javan rhinoceros** is one of the rarest large mammals in the world and until recently was thought only to survive in the Ujung Kulon National Park in West Java, Indonesia. However in November 1988 it was reported that a Stieng tribesman had shot a female Javan rhino near the Dong Nai River around 130 km northeast of Ho Chi Minh City. When he tried to sell the horn and hide he was arrested and this set in train a search to discover if there were any more of the animals in the area. Researchers discovered that Viet Cong soldiers operating in the area during the war saw – and killed – a number of animals. One former revolutionary, Tran Ngoc Khanh, reported that he once saw a herd of 20 animals and that between 1952 and 1976 some 17 animals were shot by the soldiers. With the Viet Cong shooting the animals whenever they chanced upon them, and the Americans spraying tonnes of defoliant on the area, it is a wonder than any survived through to the end of the war. However, a study by George Schaller and three Vietnamese colleagues in 1989 found tracks, also near the Dong Nai River, and estimated that a population of 10-15 animals probably still survived in a 750 sq km area of bamboo and dipterocarp forest close to and including Nam Cat Tien National Park.

This remarkable find was followed by, if anything, an even more astonishing discovery: of two completely new species of mammal. In 1992 British scientist Dr John MacKinnon discovered the skeleton of an animal now known as the **Vu Quang ox** (*Pseudoryx nghetinhensis*) but known to locals as *sao la*. The Vu Quang ox was the first new large mammal species to be found in 50 years; scientists were amazed that a large mammal could exist on this crowded planet without their knowledge. In June 1994 the first live specimen (a young calf) was captured and shortly afterwards a second one was caught and taken to the Forestry Institute in Hanoi. Sadly, both died in captivity but in early 1995 a third was brought in alive. The animals look anything but ox-like, and have the appearance, grace and manner

ON THE ROAD

Animals Asia

Vietnam is an enormously bio-diverse country with a host of magnificent native species such as the Tonkin snub-nosed monkey and Cat Ba languor, as well as Asiatic black bears and Malayan sun bears. However, Vietnam's wildlife is under tremendous pressure from the country's rapid economic growth with poaching and territory encroachment both major threats.

Many of Vietnam's indigenous species are exploited by the wildlife trade, with snake meat, 'weasel' coffee, bear bile medicines and exotic liquors containing endangered species often being offered to unwitting tourists.

A huge part of Animals Asia's work is education. Both Vietnamese and tourists need to know that the consumption of these often readily available products is destroying Vietnam's natural heritage as well as contributing to animal cruelty and the illegal wildlife trade. Every visitor to Vietnam can make an impact by refusing to condone animal cruelty and reporting any instances they come across.

Animals Asia's main objective is to stop the illegal bear bile trade, which persists in Vietnam despite being made illegal in 1992. Bears are kept in tiny cages often for decades, in order to have the bile painfully extracted from their gall bladder for use in traditional medicine. While the bodily fluid does have slight medicinal properties, these can be easily recreated using synthesized alternatives while the Vietnam Traditional Medicine Association, in collaboration with Animals Asia, has published a book of 32 herbal alternatives – none of which of course, require the horrific cruelty of bear farming.

Just over an hour's drive north of Hanoi, at the foot of Tam Dao Mountain, is Animals Asia's Vietnam Bear Rescue Centre. Here 110 bears are housed, often physically and emotionally scarred, rescued from bear farms around the country, or confiscated from poachers. While the sanctuary is not open to the public, visitors are very welcome at Open Day guided tours available twice a month on every second Saturday. See animalsasia.org for full details of Open Days and how to book.

(Tuan Bendixsen, Animals Asia's Vietnam Director)

of a small deer. The government responded to the discovery by extending the Vu Quang Nature Reserve and banning hunting of *sao la*. Local ethnic minorities, who have long regarded *sao la* as a tasty and not uncommon animal, have therefore lost a valued source of food and no longer have a vested interest in the animal's survival. In 1993 a new species of deer that has been named the **giant muntjac** was also found in the Vu Quang Nature Reserve. The scientists have yet to see it alive but villagers prize its meat and are reported to trap it in quite large numbers.

Large rare mammals are confined to isolated pockets where the government does its best to protect them from hunters. On Cat Ba Island, the national park is home to the world's last wild troops of white-headed langur. In North Vietnam tigers have been hunted close to extinction and further south territorial battles rage between elephants and farmers. Rampaging elephants sometimes cause loss of life and are in turn decimated by enraged villagers.

Among the **larger mammals**, there are small numbers of tiger (around 200), leopard, clouded leopard, Indian elephant, Malayan sun bear, Himalayan black bear, sambar deer, gibbon and gaur (wild buffalo). These are rarely seen, except in zoos. There are frequent news reports of farmers maiming or killing elephants after their crops have been trampled or their huts flattened. The larger reptiles include two species of crocodile, the estuarine (*Crocodilus porosus*) and Siamese (*Crocodilus siamensis*). The former grows to a length of 5 m and has been reported to have killed and eaten humans. Among the larger snakes are the reticulated python (*Python reticulatus*) and the smaller Indian python (*Python molurus*), both non-venomous constrictors. Venomous snakes include two species of cobra (the king cobra and common cobra), two species of krait and six species of pit viper.

Given the difficulty of getting to Vietnam's more remote areas, the country is hardly a haven for amateur naturalists. Professional photographers and naturalists have been escorted to the country's wild areas but this is not an option for the average visitor. Getting there requires time and contacts. A wander around the markets of Vietnam reveals the variety and number of animals that end up in the cooking pot, including deer, bear, snakes, monkeys and turtles. The Chinese penchant for exotic foods (such gastronomic wonders as tigers' testicles and bear's foot) has also become a predilection of the Vietnamese and most animals are fair game.

Birds

Birds have, in general, suffered rather less than mammals from over-hunting and the effects of the war. There have been some casualties however: the eastern sarus crane of the Mekong Delta – a symbol of fidelity, longevity and good luck – disappeared entirely during the war. However, in 1985 a farmer reported seeing a single bird, and by 1990 there were over 500 pairs breeding on the now pacified former battlefields. A sarus crane reserve has been established in Dong Thap Province. For more on birdwatching holidays, see page 20. The best time of year for birding is November to May.

Among the more unusual birds are the snake bird (named after its habit of swimming with its body submerged and only its snake-like neck and head above the surface), the argus pheasant, which the Japanese believe to be the mythical phoenix, the little bastard quail of which the male hatches and rears the young. But what may come as the real surprise to many visitors to Vietnam is that it has the highest number of endemic bird species of any country in mainland Southeast Asia. There are currently 12 endemic species of bird that can only be seen in Vietnam which is one reason it is becoming a popular destination for overseas birdwatchers. In addition to these 12 endemics there are many more near endemics, bird species restricted to Vietnam and a few neighbouring countries, and other distinct subspecies that may well be considered endemic species in the future.

An incredible diversity of birds live in the forest and wetland habitats of **Nam Cat Tien National Park**, see page 216 including an estimated 230 species of birds.

Endangered birds that can be found here include Germain's peacock pheasant, green peafowl and the highly elusive orange-necked partridge. You can hire a jeep at the park headquarters to visit areas further afield such as Bird Lake to look for visiting waders or Crocodile Lake where grey-headed fish eagle, lesser adjutant and Asian golden weaver may be seen, as well as the reintroduced Siamese crocodiles. During the walk through the forest to Crocodile Lake look out for bar-bellied and blue-rumped pitta, red-and-black and banded broadbill and orange-breasted trogon. Other interesting species at Cat Tien include scaly breasted partridge, Siamese fireback, woolly necked stork and grey-faced tit-babbler and white-bellied, great slaty, pale-headed and heart-spotted woodpecker. On the trails or the headquarters road, green-eared, blue-eared, lineated and – if you're lucky – red-vented barbet can often be seen perched high up in the roadside trees.

Twenty minutes by road from Dalat at **Langbian Mountain** the evergreen forests are home to many interesting birds including several endemic species. Key species to be found here include the silver pheasant, Indochinese cuckooshrike, Eurasian jay, mugimaki flycatcher, yellow-billed nuthatch and red crossbill. This is also the place to see three of Vietnam's most sought-after endemics: collared laughingthrush, Vietnamese cutia and Vietnamese greenfinch. Mount Langbian is best avoided at weekends and holidays when it is a popular destination for local tourists.

Tuyen Lam Lake, only 3 km from the centre of Dalat, is another hotspot for birders. Take a boat to far side of the lake where a track leads through the pines to areas of remnant tropical evergreen forest. With luck, the rare and endemic grey-crowned crocias, rediscovered in 1994 after not being seen for nearly 60 years, can be found. Other interesting species here include slender-billed oriole, maroon oriole, rufous-backed sibia, black-crowned parrotbill and orange-breasted, black-hooded and white-cheeked laughingthrush.

Ta Nung Valley, around 10 km from Dalat, holds pockets of remnant evergreen forest where many of the Dalat specialities can still be found including orange-breasted, black-hooded and white-cheeked laughing thrush, blue-winged minla, grey crowned crocias, black-crowned parrotbill and black-throated sunbird.

At **Bach Ma National Park**, see page 176, more than 330 species of bird have been recorded. Species include the annam partridge, crested argus, Blyth's kingfisher, coral-billed ground cuckoo, ratchet-tailed treepie, sultan tit and Indochinese wren-babbler. Others include red-collared woodpecker, bar-bellied and blue-rumped pitta and white-winged magpie.

There are several good trails in the forested hills above the tourist resort of **Tam Dao**, which is 1½ hours by road from Hanoi. Specialities of Tam Dao include chestnut bulbul, grey laughingthrush, rufous-headed and short-tailed parrotbill and fork-tailed sunbird. In the winter months look out for red-flanked bluetail, black-breasted and Japanese thrush and Fujian niltava.

In **Cuc Phuong National Park**, see page 137, an area of limestone hills covered with large tracts of primary forest, key bird species include silver pheasant, red-collared woodpecker, pied falconet, white-winged magpie, limestone wren-babbler and bar-bellied, blue-rumped and eared pitta.

Books

Books on the region

Fenton, James *All the Wrong Places: Adrift in the Politics of Asia (Penguin: London, 1988).* British journalist James Fenton skilfully and entertainingly recounts his experiences in Vietnam, Cambodia and the Philippines.

King, Ben F and Dickinson EC *A Field Guide to the Birds of South-East Asia (Collins: London, 1975).* Best regional guide to the birds of the region.

Osborne, Milton *Southeast Asia: An Introductory History (Allen & Unwin: Sydney, 2010).* Good history, clearly written, published in a portable paperback edition.

Reid, Anthony *Southeast Asia in the Age of Commerce 1450-1680: the Lands Below the Winds (Yale University Press: New Haven, 1988).* Perhaps the best history of everyday life in Southeast Asia, looking at such themes as physical well being, material culture and social organization.

Reid, Anthony *Southeast Asia in the Age of Commerce 1450-1680: Expansion and Crisis (Yale University Press: New Haven, 1993).* Volume 2 in this excellent history of the region.

Books on Vietnam

Biography and autobiography

Fenn, Charles *Ho Chi Minh: A Biographical Introduction (Studio Vista: London, 1973).*

Greene, Graham *Ways of Escape (1980).* Autobiographical.

Ho Chi Minh *Prison Diary (Hanoi: Foreign Languages Publishing House).*

A collection of poems by Ho while he was incarcerated in China in 1942. They record his prison experiences and his yearning for home.

Page, Tim *Derailed in Uncle Ho's Victory Garden (Touchstone Books, 1995).* War photojournalist Tim Page makes a return visit to Vietnam, amusing in places.

Economics, politics and development

Hayton, Bill *Vietnam - Rising Dragon (Yale University Press: 2010).* A new, well-researched insightful account into Vietnam today that seeks to enlighten readers about the current economic and political structures and issues in this rapidly growing country. Hayton spent time as a BBC reporter in Hanoi.

Scott, James C *The Moral Economy of the Peasant: Rebellion and Subsistence in Southeast Asia (New Haven: Yale University Press, 1976).* The classic historical study of the 'moral' economy of the peasant. Available as a portable paperback.

Templer, Robert *Shadows and Wind: A View of Life in Modern Vietnam (London: Little Brown, 1998).* Templer was an Agence France Presse correspondent and this is his account of modern Vietnam and where it is headed. It is a downbeat picture of the country, one where bureaucratic inertia and political heavy handedness constrain progress, but is a fascinating read.

Young, Marilyn *The Vietnam Wars 1945-1990 (Harper Collins: New York, 1990).* Good account of the origins, development and aftermath of the Vietnam wars.

History

Elliott, Mai *Sacred Willow: Four Generations in the Life of a Vietnamese Family (OUP: Oxford, 1999)*. Recounts the history of Vietnam through the life of the Duong family from the 19th century to the tragedy of Boat People. A story of Vietnam through Vietnamese eyes.

Marriott, Edward *Claude and Madeline: A True Story of War, Espionage and Passion (Picador 2005)*. This is an unputdownable tale of madness and bravado set in Vietnam and France.

Osborne, Roger *The Deprat Affair: Ambition, Revenge and Deceit in French Indochina (Jonathan Cape, 1999)*. An account of the extraordinary pickle into which Jacques Deprat, a brilliant young geologist, got himself. Whether he was guilty of professional deceit or not the book gives a useful insight into colonial society and mores in the first 2 decades of the 20th century.

Novels

Duras, Marguerite *The Lover (London: Flamingo, 1984)*. Now a film starring Jane March; this is the story of the illicit relationship between an expat French girl and a Chinese from Cholon set in the 1930s.

Greene, Graham *The Quiet American (Heinemann: London, 1954)*. What is remarkable about this novel is the way that it predicts America's experience in Vietnam. The two key figures are Alden Pyle, an idealistic young American, and Thomas Fowler, a hard-bitten and cynical British journalist. It is set in and around Saigon as the war between the French and the Viet Minh intensifies.

Grey, Anthony *Saigon (Pan: London, 1983)*. An entertaining novel.

Graphic novels

Tran, GB *Vietnamerica. The story of a young 2nd-generation Viet Kieu taken back to Vietnam*

Hanshaw, Julian *The Art of Pho. A surreal travelogue/dream of Little Blue and his mobile pho stall in Saigon.*

Travel and geography

Garstin, Crosbie *The Voyage from London to Indochina (Heinemann, 1928)*. Hilarious and rather irreverent account of a journey through Vietnam.

Lewis, Norman *A Dragon Apparent: Travels in Cambodia, Laos and Vietnam (1951)*. One of the finest of all travel books.

Stewart, Lucretia *Tiger Balm: Travels in Laos, Cambodia and Vietnam (London: Chatto & Windus, 1998)*.

Theroux, Paul *The Great Railway Bazaar (Penguin: London, 1977)*. Theroux describes a graphic account of one American's attempt to travel by rail between Saigon and Hué.

The Vietnamese wars

Cawthorne, Nigel *The Bamboo Cage (Leo Cooper, 1992)*. The story of MIAs and POWs.

Doyle, Jeff with Grey, Jeffrey and Pierce, Peter *Australia's Vietnam War, (A&M University Press, 2002)*. Australia's role in the Vietnam War is little known and this book examines Australia's motives for joining and contribution to America's war effort.

Fall, Bernard B *Hell in a Very Small Place: The Siege of Dien Bien Phu (Pall Mall Press, 1967)*.

Fitzgerald, Francis *Fire in the Lake (Vintage Books: New York, 1972)*. Pulitzer prize winner; a well-researched and readable account of the US involvement.

Harrison, James P *The Endless War: Fifty Years of Struggle in Vietnam (Free Press: New York, 1982).*

Herr, Michael *Dispatches (Knopf: New York, 1977).* An acclaimed account of the war written by a correspondent who experienced the conflict first hand.

Kaiser, David *American Tragedy: Kennedy, Johnson and the Origins of the Vietnam War, (Harvard University Press, 1999).* This account is based on newly opened archives and provides a penetrating insight into America's involvement in Vietnam.

Karnow, Stanley *Vietnam: A History (Viking Press: New York, 1983 and 1991).* A comprehensive and readable history; the best there is.

Kissinger, Henry *The White House Years (Little, Brown, 1979).* Part one of the memoirs of America's best known diplomat. This covers the first Nixon term and ends with the Paris Peace Accord of 1973. Also, *Years of Upheaval* (Little, Brown, 1982). This covers the turbulent months from his visit to Hanoi in February 1973 to Nixon's resignation in August 1974. And, *Years of Renewal* (Simon and Schuster, 1999). The third and concluding volume of the memoirs covers the end of the Vietnam war and collapse of the South.

McNamara, Robert S and Mark, Brian Van de *In Retrospect: The Tragedy and Lessons of Vietnam (Times/Random House: New York, 1995).* McNamara was Secretary for Defense from 1961 to 1968 and this is his cathartic account of the war. Informed from the inside, he concludes that the war was a big mistake.

Ninh, Bao *The Sorrow of War (Secker & Warburg, London, 1993).* Wartime novel by a North Vietnamese soldier, a wonderful account of emotions during and after the war.

Sheehan, Neil *A Bright Shining Lie (Jonathan Cape: London, 1989).* A meticulously researched 850-page account of the Vietnam War, based around the life of John Paul Vann. Recommended.

Sheehan, Neil *Two Cities: Hanoi and Saigon (in US After the War was Over)* (Jonathan Cape: London, 1992). A short but fascinating book that tries to link the past with the present in a part autobiography, part travelogue, part contemporary commentary.

Swain, Jon *River of Time (Heinemann, 1996).* A gripping account of this war correspondent's time throughout the Vietnam War. He expounds the interesting hypothesis that the reason the American generals were willing to sacrifice so many men was that they saw it as a rehearsal for a future war in Europe against the Red Army.

Young, Gavin *A Wavering Grace: A Vietnamese Family in War and Peace (London: Viking, 1997).* An account of the war – Young was a reporter – told through the lives of a Vietnamese family.

Vietnamese literature in English

Nguyen Du *The Tale of Kieu (also known as Truyen Kieu)* (Yale University Press: New Haven, 1983), translated by Huynh Sanh Thong. This is an early 19th-century Vietnamese classic and, for many, the masterpiece of Vietnamese poetry. It is also published in Vietnam (in English) by the Foreign Languages Publishing House. It tells the story of a beautiful girl and her doomed love affair with a soldier. See also page 403 for a detailed description of the work.

Films

Few countries have provided so much material for celluloid tales as Vietnam. The US movie houses cranked up for action in the post-Vietnam War era to provide some of the most harrowing, soul-searching and cinematically exciting films of the 20th century that focused on the US involvement in the war.

The better-known films on Vietnam are American as US filmakers have attempted to explain or come to terms with their country's disastrous involvement in Vietnam. Francis Ford Coppola's *Apocalypse Now* won two Oscars in 1979. Coppola substitutes Vietnam for the Africa of Joseph Conrad's *Heart of Darkness*; it remains the best known and most outstanding of all Vietnam films. *The Deer Hunter*, which stars Robert de Niro, won five Oscars in 1978. It charts the horrors into which three tough steelworkers were plunged in Vietnam. Stanley Kubrick's *Full Metal Jacket* (1987), followed GIs from Boot Camp to the Tet Offensive and was acclaimed as a "riveting condemnation of the Vietnam War". *Good Morning Vietnam* (1987) starred Robin Williams as an irreverent DJ working for the armed services radio. The comedy of the film is hilarious without trivializing the seriousness of the situation. Oliver Stone's trilogy of *Platoon* (1986), *Born on the Fourth of July* (1989) and *Heaven and Earth* (1993), is quite a contrast. The first two deal with the war from the perspective of the American soldier; *Platoon* examines the soldiers' experience in Vietnam; and *Born on the Fourth of July* explores adjusting to life after the war. *Heaven and Earth* looks at the war from the 1960s onwards from the perspective of a Vietnamese woman, Le Ly Hayslip, and the aftermath of war.

The film version of Graham Greene's novel of love, war, murder and betrayal, *The Quiet American*, was set in 1950s Saigon and was filmed in Vietnam in 2001. It was the first Hollywood blockbuster to be filmed in the country since the end of the war. It stars Sir Michael Caine as *Times* journalist Thomas Fowler, Brendan Fraser as American aid worker Alden Pyle and Do Thi Hai Yen as Phuong. The Hotel Continental, the social pivot of the time, is actually replicated on screen in the facing Hotel Caravelle across Lam Son Square (Place Garnier). The La Fontaine milk bar on Dong Khoi Street (Rue Catinat), frequented by Fowler's lover Phuong, is in present-day Ho Chi Minh City's Givral café and patisserie. The infamous double bomb scene in the Place Garnier in front of the Opera House and La Fontaine, a moment of epiphany for the jaded London hack, used hundreds of Vietnamese extras including mutilated Vietnam War victims. Hoi An doubled as the setting for the restaurant date between Pyle and Fowler – an engagement that Pyle would never make.

Three French films have captured the atmosphere of Vietnam at peace although with a frisson of tension never too far away: *Indochine* (directed by Régis Wargnier) won acclaim for its beautiful sets and scenery as well as an Oscar for Best Foreign Film in 1993. It is set in the 1930s and focuses on a mother (Catherine Deneuve), who runs a rubber plantation, and her adopted daughter, who both fall in love with the same man. It captures the vices and flaws of French colonial Vietnam before its demise. *L'Amant* (*The Lover*, 1992), directed by Jean-Jacques Annaud, charts the relationship of a young French girl (Jane March) with an older, Chinese businessman, in the colonial era; it was adapted from Margeurite Duras' book. The little-known but delightful *Scent of Green Papaya* (1993) by Tran Anh Hung is an account of family relationships and the secret love of the family's young servant. Set in Saigon in the 1950s, it was filmed entirely in a Paris studio.

Vietnamese-made films, however, have suffered arrested development. After the Second World War, Ho Chi Minh began making propaganda documentaries. In 1959 the first film was released – *On the Same River* – about a couple who were divided when the border along the 17th parallel was created in 1954.

Post-1975, when the country was reunified, all Vietnamese films were censored at the script stage and those that made it past the censor were state-funded. The tight grip of the Ministry of Culture suffocated any enterprising or criticial movie production. In 2002, the ministry reversed its policy on censorship of scripts and encouraged private film studios to open up. The turnaround, it said, was to encourage competition and investment to re-energize the industry. Since then, Vietnam has been undergoing a cinematic revolution.

However, judging from the persecutory response to Vietnamese actor Don Duong's role in the US movie *We Were Soldiers*, the day that Vietnamese film directors will be able to criticize the Vietnamese regime through the medium of film is a long way off. Don Duong angered national censors in 2002 by appearing in what the Vietnamese government saw as a movie with a pro-US stance. *We Were Soldiers* (directed by Randall Wallace) depicts the Battle of La Drang in the Central Highlands in 1965. Some 400 US troops, led by Lieutenant-Colonel Harold Moore (Mel Gibson), were completely swamped by 2000 North Vietnamese soldiers commandeered by Nguyen Huu An (Duong). The authorities said the film of the first major battle between the two enemies, which saw severe casualties on both sides and bloody hand-to-hand combat, distorted history. Vietnam's National Film Censorship Council moved to ban the actor from appearing in productions and to fine him. Other officials branded him a traitor. Duong, 50, eventually emigrated to the US in 2003.

Director Le Hoang's *Gai Nhay* (*Bar Girls*), about sex, drugs and HIV, has rocked cinema audiences since it was released in 2003. HIV and drugs are serious social problems in Vietnam. Produced by Ho Chi Minh's Liberation Studios, run by the army, the film about these contemporary social taboos suited the government as it documented the social evils of prostitution and drug addiction. It disturbingly portrays the grim lives of two working girls, Hoa (My Duyen) and Hanh (Minh Thu) and depicts gang rape and murder. It cost US$78,000 to make but raked in more than US$1 million at the box office and is Vietnam's biggest grossing movie.

It may have been pipped to the post, however, by the release of *The Rebel*, a US$1.5 million film made by Vietnamese-born Americans in Vietnam and released in 2006. Set in 1920s Vietnam, it tells of Vietnamese hired by their French colonial masters to hunt down rebels and uses some great martial arts action.

Luoi Troi (*Heaven's Net*), directed by Phi Tien Son, winner of a Vietnam Cinema Association Award and released in 2003, also marked a change in mood that heralds the end of propaganda-only films and a willingness to expose national problems, like the drug abuse and HIV in *Gai Nhay* and corruption in *Luoi Troi*. The latter film features the life of infamous mafia criminal Nam Cam who was blamed for a 15-year killing spree in Ho Chi Minh City. Other films of note include *Bi Dung So* (*Bi, Don't Be Afraid* – 2010) and *Cyclo* (1995).

Practicalities
Vietnam

Getting there 427
Getting around 429
Local customs and conduct . 432
Essentials A-Z 433
Index...................... 441
Advertisers' index.......... 447
Acknowledgements........ 446
Credits 448

Getting there

Air

Flights from Europe
In Western Europe, there are direct flights to Vietnam from London, Paris and Frankfurt with **Vietnam Airlines/Air France**. These code-shared flights last 12 hours. There are also direct **Vietnam Airlines** flights from Moscow.

Flights from other European hubs go via Bangkok, Singapore, Kuala Lumpur, Hong Kong or UAE states. Airlines include **Air France**, **Cathay Pacific**, **Emirates**, **Thai Airways**, **Singapore Airlines**, **Malaysia Airlines**, **Lufthansa** and **Qatar**. It is possible to fly into Hanoi and depart from Ho Chi Minh City although this does seem to rack up the return fare. Check details with flight agents and tour operators.

Flights from the USA and Canada
By far the best option is to fly via **Bangkok**, **Taipei**, **Tokyo** or **Hong Kong** and from there to Vietnam. The approximate flight time from Los Angeles to **Bangkok** is 21 hours. **United** flies from LA and Chicago via Tokyo and from San Francisco via Seoul to Vietnam. **Thai Airways**, **Delta**, **United** and **Air Canada** fly to Bangkok from a number of US and Canadian cities.

Flights from Australia and New Zealand
There are direct flights from Adelaide, Melbourne, Sydney, Perth, Auckland and Wellington with **Cathay Pacific**, **Malaysia Airlines**, **Singapore Airlines** and **Thai Airways**. **Qantas** flies from Sydney, Adelaide and Melbourne to Ho Chi Minh City. **Air Asia** has cheap flights via KL.

From Sydney the flights to Vietnam are eight hours 45 minutes direct.

Flights from Asia
Hanoi and HCMC are very well connected to cities all over East Asia, and Danang is also now welcoming a growing number of **international** flights.

Airport information
There are two main International airports in Vietnam: **Tan Son Nhat Airport** (SGN) in Ho Chi Minh City, see page 289, and **Noi Bai Airport** (HAN) in Hanoi, see page 71. **Danang** (DAD), see page 185, has some international flights.

Road

From Cambodia

There is a road crossing at Moc Bai on Highway 1 connecting Phnom Penh in Cambodia with Ho Chi Minh City via Tay Ninh Province, see page 275. Further south, there is a second crossing to Phnom Penh via Chau Doc at Vinh Xuong in the Mekong Delta by boat. Further south still there is another road crossing into Cambodia at Tinh Bien, approximately 22 km south of Chau Doc. And, right at the very south of the country, you can cross at Xà Xía. For crossings at Chau Doc, Tinh Bien and Xà Xía, see page 324.

From China

There are three land crossings between China and Vietnam: at Lao Cai, Dong Dang and Mong Cai. There is no train across the border at Lao Cai at the moment, see page 100. The train from Hanoi does cross at Dong Dang, page 117. The Mong Cai crossing is by road, see page 132.

From Laos

There is a popular road crossing open at Lao Bao, north of Hué, which enables travel through to Savannakhet in Laos, see page 148. In the north there is a crossing at Tay Trang near Dien Bien Phu, see page 90. Closer to Hanoi are the crossings at Nam Can (Nghe An Province) and Cau Treo (Ha Tinh Province) accessible from Vinh, see page 144. You can also cross close to Kontum at Bo-Y (Kontum Province), see page 229.

Sea

There are no normal sea crossings into Vietnam although an increasing number of cruise liners sail into Vietnamese waters. The only other international connection by boat is the Mekong River crossing from Phnom Penh to Chau Doc.

Train

Vietnam's only international rail connection is with China. There are connections with Beijing via Nanning to Hanoi crossing at Lang Son. The lines are slow and distances are great.

Getting around

If time is limited, by far the best option is to get an open-jaw flight where you fly into one city, say Hanoi, and out of Ho Chi Minh City (HCMC), although generally it is cheaper overall to fly into HCMC return and get an internal flight back to HCMC.

Remember that distances are huge and one or two internal flights may be needed. Vietnam Airlines has an excellent domestic network and services are good.

Hiring a self-drive car in Vietnam is not possible and trains (although a great way to travel) and public buses are very slow. Alternatives to the domestic air network include the tourist Open Tour Bus transport, taxis and tour operators for tours and transfers.

Air

Vietnam Airlines is the national carrier and flies to multiple domestic destinations. VietJetAir is the low-cost alternative and offers a good service. Remember that during holiday periods flights get extremely busy.

Road

Open Tour Buses, see below, are very useful and cheap for bridging important towns. Many travellers opt to take a tour to reach remote areas because of the lack of self-drive car hire and the dangers and slow speed of public transport.

Bus

Roads in Vietnam are notoriously dangerous. As American humourist PJ O'Rourke wrote: "In Japan people drive on the left. In China people drive on the right. In Vietnam it doesn't matter." Since Highway 1 is so dangerous and public transport buses are poor and slow, most travellers opt for the cheap and regular Open Tour Bus (private minibus or coach) that covers the length of the country. Almost every Vietnamese tour operator/travellers' café listed in this guide will have an agent. The buses run daily from their own offices and include the following stops: Ho Chi Minh City, Mui Ne, Nha Trang, Dalat, Hoi An, Hué, Ninh Binh and Hanoi. They will also stop off at tourist destinations along the way such as Lang Co, Hai Van Pass, Marble Mountains and Po Klong Garai for quick visits. You may join at any leg of the journey, paying for one trip or several as you go.

If you do opt for public buses note that most bus stations are on the outskirts of town; in bigger centres there may be several stations. Long-distance buses invariably leave very early in the morning (0400-0500). Buses are the cheapest form of transport, although sometimes foreigners find they are being asked for two to three times the correct price. Prices are normally prominently displayed at bus stations. Less comfortable but quicker are the minibus services, which ply the more popular routes.

Car hire

Self-drive car hire is not available in Vietnam. It is, however, possible to hire cars with drivers and this is a good way of getting to more remote areas with a group of people. Car hire prices increase by 50% or more during Tet.

Motorbike and bicycle hire

Most towns are small enough to get around by bicycle, and this can also be a pleasant way to explore the surrounding countryside. However, if covering large areas (touring around the Central Highlands, for example) then a motorbike will mean you can see more and get further off the beaten track.

Motorbikes and bicycles can be hired by the day in the cities, often from hotels and travellers' cafés. You do not need a driver's licence or proof of motorbike training to hire a motorbike in Vietnam, however, it is compulsory to wear a helmet. Also, lack of a license will no doubt invalidate your travel insurance.

Motorbike taxi and cyclo

Motorcycle taxis, known as *xe om* (*ôm* means to cuddle) are ubiquitous and cheap. You will find them on most street corners, outside hotels or in the street. If they see you before you see them, they will whistle to get your attention.

Cyclos are bicycle trishaws. Cyclo drivers charge double or more that of a *xe om*. A number of streets in the centres of Ho Chi Minh City and Hanoi are one-way or out of bounds to cyclos, necessitating lengthy detours which add to the time and cost. It is a wonderful way to get around the Old Quarter of Hanoi.

Taxi

Taxis ply the streets of Hanoi and Ho Chi Minh City and other large towns and cities. They are cheap, around 12,000d per kilometre. Always use the better-known taxi companies to avoid any issues. Mai Linh is one of the most widely found reliable firms.

River

The **Victoria** hotel chain (www.victoriahotels-asia.com) runs a Mekong Delta service for its guests. Ferries operate between Ho Chi Minh City and Vung Tau; Rach Gia and Phu Quoc; Ha Tien and Phu Quoc; Haiphong and Cat Ba Island; and Halong City and Cat Ba and Mong Cai.

Train

Train travel is exciting and overnight journeys are a good way of covering long distances. The Vietnamese rail network extends from Hanoi to Ho Chi Minh City. **Vietnam Railways** (www.vr.com.vn) runs the 2600-km rail network down the coast. With overnight stays at hotels along the way to see the sights, a rail sightseeing tour from Hanoi to Ho Chi Minh City should take a minimum of 10 days but you would need to buy tickets for each separate section of the journey.

The difference in price between first and second class is small and it is worth paying the extra. There are three seating classes and four sleeping classes including hard and soft seats and hard and soft sleepers; some are air-conditioned, others are not. The prices vary according to the class of cabin and the berth chosen; the bottom berth is more expensive than the top berth. All sleepers should be booked three days in advance. The kitchen on the Hanoi to Ho Chi Minh City service serves soups and simple, but adequate, rice dishes (it is a good idea to take additional food and drink on long journeys). The express trains (*Reunification Express*) take between an advertised 29½ to 34 hours.

Most ticket offices have some staff who speak English. Queues can be long and some offices keep unusual hours. If you are short of time and short on patience it may well pay to get a tour operator to book your ticket for a small commission or visit the Ho Chi Minh City railway office in Pham Ngu Lao or the Hanoi agency in the Old Quarter.

There are also rail routes from Hanoi to Haiphong, to Lang Son and to Lao Cai. The **Victoria** hotel chain runs a luxury carriage on the latter route.

Local customs and conduct

Vietnam is remarkably relaxed and easy going with regard to conventions. The people, especially in small towns and rural areas, can be pretty old-fashioned, but it is difficult to cause offence unwittingly.

Appearance

The main complaint Vietnamese have of foreigners is their fondness for dirty and torn clothing. Backpackers come in for particularly severe criticism and the term *tay ba lo* (literally 'Western backpacker') is a contemptuous one reflecting the low priority many budget travellers seem to allocate to personal hygiene and the antiquity and inadequacy of their shorts and vests.

Shoes should be removed before entering temples and before going into people's houses. Modesty should be preserved and excessive displays of bare flesh are not considered good form, particularly in temples and private houses. (Not that the Vietnamese are unduly prudish, they just like things to be kept in their proper place.) Shorts are fine for the beach and travellers' cafés but not for smart restaurants.

Conduct

Kissing and canoodling in public are likely to draw attention, not much of it favourable. But walking hand in hand is now accepted as a Western habit. Hand shaking among men is a standard greeting and although Vietnamese women will consent to the process, it is often clear that they would prefer not to.

Terms of address

Vietnamese names are written with the surname first, followed by the first name. Thus Nguyen Minh is not called Nguyen as we would presume in the West but Minh. The conventions around how to address people according to age are quite complicated and visitors will not be expected to master them.

Religion

The Vietnamese are open to religious experiences of all kinds. Vietnam is predominantly a Buddhist country. Following Chinese tradition, ancestor worship is widely practiced and animism (the belief in and worship of spirits of inanimate objects such as venerable trees, the land, mountains and so on) is widespread. The government is hostile to proselytizing, particularly by Christians. However, foreigners are perfectly free to attend services. In Ho Chi Minh City one or two services in the Notre Dame Cathedral are in French and in English. Protestant churches are found throughout the country to a lesser degree then the Roman Catholic Church but all services are in Vietnamese.

Essentials A-Z

Accident and emergency

Contact the relevant emergency service and your embassy. Make sure you obtain police/medical records in order to file insurance claims. If you need to report a crime, visit your local police station and take a local with you who speaks English. If you have a medical emergency, ask your hotel which nearby hospital is recommended. **Ambulance** T115, **Fire** T114, **Police** T113.

Children

Vietnamese love children and there are activities that will appeal to both adults and children alike. Some attractions in Vietnam offer children's concessions. In terms of discounts, the train travel is free to children under 5 and charges 50% of the adult fare for those aged 5-10. Baby products are found in major supermarkets in the main cities. In remoter regions, such as the north and the Central Highlands, and smaller towns, take everything with you.

Customs and duty free

Duty-free allowance is 400 cigarettes, 50 cigars or 100 g of tobacco, 1.5 litres of spirits, plus items for personal use. Export of wood products or antiques is banned. You cannot import pornography, anti-government literature, photos or movies nor culturally unsuitable children's toys.

Disabled travellers

Considering the proportion of the country's population that is seriously disabled, foreigners might expect better facilities and allowances for the immobile. But there are very few. However, some of the more upmarket hotels do have a few designated rooms for the disabled. For those with walking difficulties many of the better hotels do have lifts. Wheelchair access is improving with more shopping centres, hotels and restaurants providing ramps for easy access. People sensitive to noise will find Vietnam, at times, almost intolerable.

Drugs

In the south you may be offered weed, but rarely anything else, although ecstasy is becoming more popular among the younger generation. Attitudes to traffickers are harsh, although the death penalty (now by lethal injection and not firing squad) is usually reserved for Vietnamese and other Asians whose governments are less likely to kick up a fuss.

Electricity

Voltage 110-240. Sockets are round 2-pin. Sometimes they are 2 flat pin. A number of top hotels now use UK 3 square-pin sockets.

Embassies and consulates

For a list of Vietnamese embassies abroad, see http://embassy.goabroad.com.

Gay and lesbian

The Vietnamese are broadly tolerant of homosexuality although legal marriage unions remain impossible. There are no legal restraints for 2 people of the same sex co-habitating in the same room whether they Vietnamese or non-Vietnamese. There are several gay/gay friendly bars in central HCMC and Hanoi.

Health

See your doctor or travel clinic at least 6 weeks before your departure for general advice on travel risks, malaria and vaccinations (see also below). Make sure you have travel insurance, get a dental check-up (especially if you are going to be away for more than a month), know your own blood group and if you suffer a long-term condition such as diabetes or epilepsy make sure someone knows or that you have a **Medic Alert** bracelet/necklace with this information on it (www.medicalert.co.uk).

Health risks

Malaria exists in rural areas in Vietnam. However, there is no risk in the Red River Delta and the coastal plains north of Nha Trang. Neither is there a risk in Hanoi, HCMC, Danang and Nha Trang. The choice of malaria prophylaxis will need to be something other than chloroquine for most people, since there is such a high level of resistance to it. Always check with your doctor or travel clinic for the most up-to-date advice.

Malaria can cause death within 24 hrs. It can start as something just resembling an attack of flu. You may feel tired, lethargic, headachy, feverish; or more seriously, develop fits, followed by coma and then death. Have a low index of suspicion because it is very easy to write off vague symptoms, which may actually be malaria. If you have a temperature, go to a doctor as soon as you can and ask for a malaria test. On your return home if you suffer any of these symptoms, get tested as soon as possible, even if any previous test proved negative; the test could save your life.

The most serious viral disease is **dengue fever**, which is hard to protect against as the mosquitos bite throughout the day as well as at night. Bacterial diseases include **tuberculosis** (TB) and some causes of the more common traveller's **diarrhoea**. Lung fluke (**para-gonimiasis**) occurs in Vietnam. A fluke is a sort of flattened worm. In the Sin Ho district the locals like to eat undercooked or raw crabs, but our advice is to leave them to it. The crabs contain a fluke which, when eaten, travels to the lungs. The lung fluke may cause a cough, coughing 'blood', fever, chest pain and changes on your X-ray which will puzzle a British radiologist. The cure is the same drug that cures schistosomiasis (another fluke which can be acquired in some parts of the Mekong Delta).

Consult the WHO website, www.who.int, for further information and heed local advice on the ground. There are high rates of **HIV** in the region, especially among sex workers.

Medical services

Western hospitals staffed by foreign and Vietnamese medics exist in Hanoi and HCMC. See under medical services in each area for listings.

Useful websites

www.btha.org British Travel Health Association (UK). This is the official website of an organization of travel health professionals.

www.cdc.gov US government site that gives excellent advice on travel health and details of disease outbreaks.

www.fitfortravel.scot.nhs.uk A-Z of vaccine/health advice for each country.

www.who.int The WHO Blue Book lists the diseases of the world.

Vaccinations

The following vaccinations are advised: BCG, Hepatitis A, Japanese Encephalitis, Polio, Rabies, Tetanus, Typhoid and Yellow Fever.

Insurance

Always take out travel insurance before you set off and read the small print carefully. Check that the policy covers the activities you intend or may end up doing. Also check exactly what your medical cover includes, such as ambulance, helicopter rescue or emergency flights back home. Also check the payment protocol. You may have to pay up first before the insurance company reimburses you. Keep receipts for expensive personal effects, such as jewellery or cameras. Take photos of these items and note down all serial numbers. You are advised to shop around.

Internet

Although emailing is easy and Wi-Fi is widespread, access to the web is slightly restricted, for example BBC and Facebook are periodically blocked.

Language

You are likely to find some English spoken wherever there are tourist services but outside tourist centres communication can be a problem for those who have no knowledge of Vietnamese. Furthermore, the Vietnamese language is not easy to learn. For example, pronunciation presents enormous difficulties as it is tonal. On the plus side, Vietnamese is written in a Roman alphabet making life much easier; place and street names are instantly recognizable. French is still spoken and often very well by the more elderly and educated Vietnamese and older German speakers are common in the north too.

Media

The English-language daily *Viet Nam News* is widely available. Inside the back page is a 'What's on' section. The Word (www.wordhcmc.com and www.wordhanoi.com), a tourism and culture magazine, is available throughout the country. *The Guide*, a monthly magazine on leisure and tourism produced by the *Vietnam Economic Times*, can be found in tourist centres. *Asia Life*, Vietnam Traveller and *Time Out* all carry features. Online check out www.saigoneer.com for information on the south and www.hanoigrapevine.com for the north. There is news in English on VTV4 and a wide range of international channels is now widely available, especially at the better hotels.

Money

→ US$1 = 21,500d, €1 = 23,000d, £1 = 32,000d. Mar 2015.

The unit of currency is the Vietnam Dong. Under law, shops should only accept dong but in practice this is not enforced and dollars are accepted in some places. ATMs are plentiful in HCMC and Hanoi and are now pretty ubiquitous in all but the smallest of town, but it is a good idea to travel with US dollars cash as a back up. Try to avoid tatty notes.

Banks in the main centres will change other major currencies including UK sterling, Hong Kong dollars, Thai baht, Swiss francs, euros, Australian dollars, Singapore dollars and Canadian dollars. **Credit cards** are increasingly accepted, particularly Visa, MasterCard, Amex and JCB. Large hotels, expensive restaurants and medical centres invariably take them but beware of a surcharge of between 2.5% and 4.5%. Most hotels will not add a surcharge onto your bill if paying by credit card. Prepaid currency cards allow you to preload money from your bank account, fixed at the day's exchange rate, and are accepted anywhere that you can use debit or credit cards. They are issued by specialist money changing companies, such as Travelex, Caxton FX and the post office. You can top up and check your balance by phone, online and sometimes by text.

Cost of travelling

On a budget expect to pay around US$6-15 per night for accommodation and about US$6-12 for food. A good mid-range hotel will cost US$15-35. There are comfort and cost levels anywhere from here up to more than US$200 per night. For travelling, many use the Open Tour Buses as they are inexpensive and, by Vietnamese standards, 'safe'. Slightly more expensive are trains followed by planes.

Opening hours

Banks Mon-Fri 0800-1600. Many close 1100-1300 or 1130-1330.
Offices Mon-Fri 0730-1130, 1330-1630.
Restaurants, cafés, bars Daily from 0700 or 0800 although some open earlier. Bars are generally closed by midnight, but some stay open much later, particularly in HCMC.
Shops Daily 0800-2000. Some stay open longer, especially in tourist centres.

Police and the law

If you are robbed in Vietnam, report the incident to the police (for your insurance claim). If you are arrested, ask for consular assistance and English-speaking staff.

Involvement in politics, possession of political material, business activities that have not been licensed by appropriate authorities, or non-sanctioned religious activities (including proselytizing) can result in detention. Sponsors of small, informal religious gatherings such as bible-study groups in hotel rooms, as well as distributors of religious materials, have been detained, fined and expelled (source: US State Department). The army are extremely sensitive about all their military buildings and become exceptionally irate if you take a photo. Indeed there are signs to this effect outside all military installations.

Post

Postal services are pretty good. Post offices open daily 0700-2100; smaller ones close for lunch. Outgoing packages are opened and checked by the censor.

Safety

Travel advisories

The US State Department's travel advisory: **Travel Warnings & Consular Information Sheets**, www.travel.state.gov, and the **UK Foreign and Commonwealth Office**'s travel warning section, www.fco.gov.uk, are useful.

Do not take any valuables on to the streets of HCMC as bag and jewellery snatching is a problem. The situation in other cities is not so bad but take care in Nha Trang and Hanoi, as you would in any city. Always use major taxi firms and avoid those with blacked-out windows.

Lone women travellers generally have fewer problems than in many other Asian countries. The most common form of harassment usually consists of comic and harmless displays of macho behaviour.

Unexploded ordnance is still a threat in some areas. It is best not to stray too far from the beaten track especially in Central Vietnam.

In HCMC around Pham Ngu Lau Western men may be targeted by prostitutes on street corners, in tourist bars and those cruising on motorbikes.

Student travellers

Discount travel is provided to those under 22 and over 60. Anyone in full-time education is entitled to an **International Student Identity Card** (www.isic.org). These are issued by student travel offices and travel agencies and offer special rates on all forms of transport and other concessions and services. They sometimes permit free admission to museums and sights, at other times a discount on the admission.

Telephone

Vietnam's IDD is 0084; directory enquiries: 1080; operator-assisted domestic long-distance calls 103; international directory enquiries 143; yellow pages 1081.

To make a domestic call dial 0 + area code + phone number. Note that all numbers in this guide include the area code. All post offices provide international telephone services. Pay-as-you-go SIM cards are available from a number of operators including **Mobiphone** and **Vinaphone**. These are cheap and so are calls and data.

Time

Vietnam is 7 hrs ahead of GMT.

Tipping

Vietnamese do not normally tip if eating in small restaurants but may tip in expensive bars. Big hotels and restaurants add 5-10% service charge and the government tax of 10% to the bill.

Tourist information

Contact details for tourist offices and other resources are given in the listings sections throughout the text.

The national tourist office is **Vietnam National Administration of Tourism** (www.vietnamtourism.com), whose role is to promote Vietnam as a tourist destination rather than to provide tourist information. Visitors to its offices can get some information and maps but they are more likely to be offered tours. Good tourist information is available from tour operators in the main tourist centres.

Tour operators

For countrywide tour operators, see the What to do sections throughout the guide. For details of specialist tours and activities, see pages 20-23.

In the UK

Audley Travel, New Mill, New Mill Lane, Witney, Oxfordshire OX29 9SX, T01993-838000, www.audleytravel.com.
Buffalo Tours UK, The Old Church, 89B Quicks Rd, Wimbledon, London SW19 1EX, T020-8545 2830, www.buffalotours.com.
See Asia Differently, T020-8150 5150, SeeAsiaDifferently.com. A UK/Asian-based tour company specializing in customized Southeast Asian tours.

In North America

Adventure Center, 1311 63rd St, Suite 200, Emeryville, CA, T+1-800 228 8747, www.adventurecenter.com.
Global Spectrum, 3907 Laro Court, Fairfax, VA 22031, T+1-800 419 4446, www.globalspectrumtravel.com.
Hidden Treasure Tours, 509 Lincoln Boulevard, Long Beach, NY 11561, T877-761 7276 (USA toll free), www.hiddentreasuretours.com.

Journeys, 107 April Drive, Suite 3, Ann Arbor, MI 48103-1903, T734-665 4407, www.journeys.travel/.
Myths & Mountains, 976 Tree Court, Incline Village, Nevada 89451, T+1-800 670-MYTH, www.mythsandmountains.com.

In Australia and New Zealand

Buffalo Tours, L9/69 Reservoir St, Surry Hills, Sydney, Australia 2010, T61-2-8218 2198, www.buffalotours.com.
Intrepid Travel, 360 Bourke St, Melbourne, Victoria 3000, T+61-03-8602 0500, www.intrepidtravel.com.au.
Travel Indochina, Level 10, HCF House, 403 George St, Sydney, NSW 2000, T1300-138755 (toll free), www.travelindochina.com.au.

In Vietnam

Asia Pacific Travel, 87 Hoang Quoc Viet St, Cau Giay District, T4-3756 8868, www.asiapacifictravel.vn.
Buffalo Tours, 70 Ba Trieu, Hanoi, T+84 4 3828 0702. www.buffalotours.com.
Exotissimo, 80-82 Phan Xich Long St, Phu Nhuan District, Ho Chi Minh City, T+84 8-3995 9898, www.exotissimo.com.
Indochina Travelland, 10 Hang Mam, T+84 984 999 386, www.indochinatravelland.com.

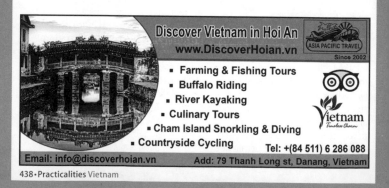

Visas and immigration

UK visitors have 2 options for visas. The first is to apply for a visa in the UK from the Vietnam embassy. The price for this changes regularly so it is best to contact the embassy direct. You must send the application form, fee and photos together with your passport. The 2nd option avoids this hassle – instead apply for an invitation letter (for example from Indochina Travelland – see above) and then pay for your visa on arrival at the airport. Those travelling in the region can obtain visas at Vietnamese consulates.

Immigration offices in Vietnam
Dalat
Lao Consulate, 12 Tran Quy Cap St, T511-382 1208, ketkeomanivong@yahoo.com, 0800-1130, 1330-1630.

Danang
12 Tran Quy Cap St, T511-382 1208, ketkeomanivong@yahoo.com, 0800-1130, 1330-1630.

Hanoi
Immigration office, 40A Hang Bai St, T4-3826 6200.

Ho Chi Minh City
Immigration office, 254 Nguyen Trai St, T08-3832 2300. Changes visa to specify overland exit via Moc Bai if travelling to Cambodia, or for overland travel to Laos or China. Also for visa extensions.

Working in Vietnam

Officially, anyone working in Vietnam should have a business visa and a work permit. Expats coming to work in Vietnam will, presumably, have all this

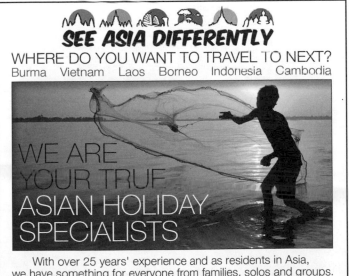

taken care of by their firm. In practice there appears to be a relaxed attitude on the part of the authorities to foreigners working in Vietnam for short periods. Those with specific skills, notably IT and English-language teaching, will not find it hard to get work. In Hanoi and HCMC there are hundreds of language schools keen to engage native speakers and the best ones pay quite well.

If you are planning on coming to work in Vietnam, contact your embassy or business group in Vietnam and they will be able to provide the most up-to-date information.

Voluntary work is available but best organized in advance through volunteer agencies such as **Voluntary Service Overseas** (www.vso.org.uk) and the **Australian Volunteers International** (www.osb.org.au). There are few NGOs in Vietnam compared with Thailand and Cambodia. In general, however, people with specific skills (speech therapists for instance) or with management expertise and those willing to make a commitment for 4 months or more will be of the greatest use. Another good resource is the **NGO Resource Centre** www.ngocentre.org.vn.

Index → *Entries in **bold** refer to maps*

A

accidents 433
accommodation 24
  price codes 24
activities 20
air travel 427, 429
ambulance 433
An Bang Beach 200
Annam 413
Annam Highlands, 414
anti-war demonstrations 368
architecture 397
Army of the Republic of Vietnam (ARVN) 363
art 397
  · Contemporary Vietnamese 398
avian flu 435

B

Ba Be National Park 111
Bac Can 110
Bac Ha 102
Bach Ma National Park and Hill Station 176
Bac Lieu 316
Bac My An Beach 186
Bac Son 117
Bahnar 389
Bai Dai Beach 211
Bai Tu Long 132
Ba-na villages 228
banks 436
Ba Vi National Park 56
beer 29
Ben Hai River 173
Ben Tre 299
betel nut 281

Bich Dong 135
bicycle hire 430
Binh Tay Market 269
birds 418
birdwatching 20
Black Lady Mountain (Nui Ba Den) 275
boat travel 428, 430
books 403, 420
border crossings 428
Bo-Y 229
Buon Jun 222
Buon Ma Thuot 218
Buon Tur 222
bus travel 429

C

Cam Ranh Bay 244
Ca Na 249
Can Tho 311, **313**
Cao Bang 112
Cao Binh Church 113
Cao Dai Great Temple 274
Cao Daism 412
Cao Dai Temple 182
Cao Lanh 309
Cao Mau 318
Car hire 430
Cat Ba Island 127, **128**
Cat Ba National Park 129
Cat Cat village 99
Cau Da 243
Cau Treo 144
Cham 396
Cham art 398
Cham kingdom 231
Champa 353
Cham Ponagar temple complex 231
Cham villages 324

Chau Doc 320
Chieng Yen 81
children 433
China Beach 186
Cholon (Chinatown) 267
Christianity 411
Chu Pao Pass 228
climate 17
climbing 21
Cochin China 357, 413
Co Loa Citadel 54
Con Dao National Park 337
Confucianism 409
conical hat 400
consulates 433
cookery classes 20
  Hoi an 199
crafts 400
Cua Dai Beach 200
Cua Lo 144
Cu Chi Tunnels 272
Cuc Phuong National Park 137
cuisine 26
customs 433
cycling 21
cyclos 430

D

Dalat 204, **206**
Danang 179, **180**
Danang Museum of Cham Sculpture 179
Demilitarized Zone (DMZ) 173
Democratic Republic of Vietnam (DRV) 357
dengue fever 434
de Rhodes, Father Alexandre 402

diarrhoea 434
Diem 363
Dien Bien Phu 86, **88**, 361
disabled travellers 433
diving 21
  Nha Trang 238
DMZ 173
Doc Lech 240
doi moi 384
dong 436
Dong Dang 117
Dong Duong 203
Dong Ha and the border
  with Laos 148
Dong Hoi 146
Dongson culture 397
Dongson drums 399
Dong Van 107
Dragon Island 299
drama 401
drink 26, 29
drugs 433
duty free 433
dynasties
  Le 351
  Ly 349
  Nguyen 352
  Tran 350

E

economy 383
  books 420
ecotourism 21
Ede 391
electricity 433
elephant rides, Pleiku 226
embassies 433
emergency 433
Emperor Tu Duc 357
ethnic Chinese 396
Ethnic groups 81
ethnic minority homestays
  Kontum 230

F

fauna 416
festivals 18
films 423
fire brigade 433
First Indochina War
  (1945-1954) 357
flora 416
food 26
French surrender, 1954 361
Funan 353

G

gay travellers 434
geography 413
Giac Lam Pagoda 270
Giac Vien Pagoda 270
Giarai 391
golf 22
Grottoes 80
Gulf of Tonkin Incident 364

H

Ha Giang 103
Haiphong 121
Hai Van Pass 176, 177
Halong Bay 125, **128**
Halong City 125
Handicraft villages 56
Hanoi 33, **36**, **41**
  36 Streets 35
  Ambassadors' Pagoda
    44
  Ba Dinh Square 46
  Citadel, The 52
  Den Hai Ba Trung 54
  Fine Arts Museum 51
  history 39
  Hoa Lo Prison 44
  Ho Chi Minh Museum 48
  Ho Chi Minh's house 46
  Ho Chi Minh's
    Mausoleum 45
  Ho Tay 52
  Ho Truc Bach 52
  listings 57
  Ly Quoc Su Pagoda 40
  Museum of Ethnology
    and B-52 memorials 53
  Museum of the
    Vietnamese Revolution
    42
  Museum of Vietnamese
    History 42
  Old Quarter 35
  One Pillar Pagoda 46
  Opera House 40
  Paul Doumer Bridge 52
  Presidential Palace 46
  Quan Thanh Pagoda 52
  Saint Joseph's Cathedral
    40
  Sofitel Metropole 42
  Stone Lady Pagoda 40
  street food 61
  street names 45
  Tay Ho Pagoda 53
  Temple of Literature
    48, 50
  Tran Quoc Pagoda 52
  urban renewal 43
  Vietnamese Women's
    Museum 52
  Vietnam Military History
    Museum and Citadel
    51
Ha Tien 327
health 434
Hien Luong Bridge 146, 174
Highland people 388
hill tribes 388
Hinduism 412
history 349
  ancient 349
  books 421
  colonial 356
  Pre-colonial 349

resistance to the French 357
HIV 434
Hmong 392
Hmong Kings 108
Hoa 396
Hoa Binh 79
Hoa Hao 412
Hoa Lu 134
Hoan Kiem Lake 33
Ho Chi Minh 144, 357, 379, 383
Ho Chi Minh City 253, **256**, **259**, **261**, **266**
  Archbishop's Palace 260
  Ben Thanh Market 264
  Botanical Gardens and Zoo 262
  Continental Hotel 255
  Fine Arts Museum 265
  General Post Office 257
  Ho Chi Minh City Museum 264
  Hotel Caravelle 255
  Independence Palace 258
  Lam Son Square 253
  Le Duan Street 262
  listings 276
  Mariamman Hindu Temple 264
  Museum of Vietnamese History 263
  Nguyen Hue Boulevard 255
  Notre Dame Cathedral 256
  Opera House 253
  Phung Son Tu Pagoda 266
  War Remnants Museum 260
  Xa Loi Pagoda 262
Ho Chi Minh Trail 173
Hoi, Assembly Halls 191
Hoi An 189, **192**
  Merchants' houses 193
homosexuality 434
Hon Chong 240
honda ôm 430
Hon Mun 239
Hon Rom 343
hospitals 434
hostels 25
hotels 24
  price codes 24
Hre 395
Hué 152, **157**, **159**
  Amphitheatre and Elephant Temple 172
  city centre 157
  sights 152
  Thien Mu Pagoda 166
  Tomb of Dong Khanh 171
  Tomb of Duc Duc 170
  Tomb of Emperor Gia Long 166
  Tomb of Emperor Minh Mang 168
  Tomb of Khai Dinh 171
  Tomb of Thieu Tri 169
  Tomb of Tu Duc 169
Hué architecture 398
Hung Kings' Temples 54
Huong Giang 152

I

immigration 439
Imperial City
  Hué 152
Indochina Communist Party (ICP) 357
Indochina Wars 357, 361
insurance 435
internet 435
Invasion of Cambodia 377
Islam 412

J

Japanese Covered Bridge 189
Japanese 'occupation' 357
Johnson, Lyndon 364

K

kayaking 22
  Kontum 230
Kenh Ga 138
Kennedy, John F 362
Khe Sanh 173, 370
Kim Lien village 144
Kinh 395
Kissinger, Henry 371
kitesurfing 22
Kontum 226
Ky Sam Temple 112

L

Lacquerware 400
Lac (White Thai village) 80
Lai Chau 91
Lak Lake 222
Lang Co 177
Lang Ga (Chicken Village) 210
Lang Son 116
language 402, 435
Lao Bao 148
Lao Cai 100
Lat village 210
Lau Chai village 98
laundries 25
law 436
Le Dynasty 351
Le Loi 351
lesbian travellers 434
Le Thanh Ton 351
Le Van Duyet 272
literature 403
  novels 421
Lung Cu 107
Ly Dynasty 349

M

Mac Kings' Temple 113
Mahayana Buddhism 407
Mai Chau 79
malaria 434
Marble Mountains
  (Nui Non Nuoc) 187
Marco Polo 356
markets 28
media 435
medical services 434
Mekong Delta
  geography 414
  hydrology 302
Mieu Island 239
Ming Dynasty Assembly
  Hall 268
Minh Danh 244
minibuses 429
M'nong villages 222
Mnong 393
Moc Chau 81
money 436
Mong Cai 132
Montagnards 388
motorbike hire 430
motorbike taxi 430
mountain biking 21
  Buon Ma Thuot 220
Mount Fan Si Pan 98
Mui Ca Mau National Park
  318
Mui Ne 342
Muong 393
Muong Lay 90
Museum of Vietnamese
  Traditional Medicine 272
My Khe Beach 186
My Son 201
My Tho 296, **297**

N

Nam Can 144
Nam Cat Tien National
  Park 216
Nam Dinh 134
Nam Khan 144
Nam O 178
Nam Phao 144
National Liberation Front
  of Vietnam 362
newspapers 435
Ngang Pass 145
Nghia An Assembly Hall
  267
Ngoan Muc Pass 249
Ngoc Son Temple and
  bridge 33
Ngo Dinh Diem 361
Nguyen Dynasty 352
Nguyen Trail 352
Nha Trang 231, **233**
Ninh Binh 133
Ninh Chu Beach 248
Ninh Van Bay 240
Nixon, President Richard
  371
Non Lá 400
Non Nuoc Beach 187
Northeast frontier 116
Nui Sam (Sam Mountain)
  323
Nung 393

O

Oc-Eo 327, 353
opening hours 436
open tour bus 429

P

Pac Bo 114
Paracel Islands 380
Paris Agreement (1972)
  371
people 388
People's Liberation Armed
  Forces (PLAF 362
Perfume Pagoda 56
Perfume River 152, 165
Pham Ngu Lao 266, **266**
Phan Rang 247
Phan Thiet 342
Phat Diem Cathedral 136
pho 26
Pho Bang 106
Phoenix Island 299
Phoenix Programme 370
Phong Nha Cave 146
Phong Nha-Ke Bang
  National Park 146
Phung Son Pagoda 270
Phuoc Hai Tu (Emperor of
  Jade Pagoda) 271
Phu Quoc Island 330, **332**
Po Klong Garai 247
police 433, 436
politics 379
  books 420
Po Ro Me 247
Porte díAnnam 145
postal services 436
price codes 24
public holidays 17, 19
Pu Luong Nature Reserve
  80

Q

Quan Am 48
Quan Am Pagoda 269
Quang Ngai 242
Quan Lan Island 132
Quoc Dan Dang (VNQDD)
  357

R

Rach Gia 325
rail travel 428, 430
Red River Delta 413

religion 407, 432
  Christianity 411
  Confucianism 409
  Islam and Hinduism 412
  Mahayana Buddhism 407
  Taoism 410
restaurants 26
  children 28
  price codes 24
Rhodes, Father Alexandre 402
rice wine 29
river travel 430
road travel 428, 429
Rock Pile 174

S

Sa Dec 305
safety 437
Salangane islands 239
Sam Son 143
Sapa 92, **93**, **98**
Sa Phin 107
SARS 434
Second Indochina War (1954-1975) 361
Sedang 395
Sen 144
17th Parallel 173
Sin Chai village 99
Sin Ho 90
snake wines 29
snorkelling 21
Socialist Republic of Vietnam (SRV) 376
Son La 82
Son My (My Lai) 242
Son My (My Lai) Massacre 243
spas 22
Special Air Service (SAS) 368
sport 20

Spratly Islands 380
Stieng 395
strategic hamlets 363
student travellers 437
syndicated loans 47

T

Tam Coc 135
Tam Son Assembly Hall 267
Taoism 410
Ta Phin 97
Ta Van village 98
taxis 430
Tay 393
Tay Son Rebellion (1771-1788) 241, 353
telephone 437
television 435
Tet 18
Tet Offensive 369
Thai 394
Thai Nguyen 110
Thanh Hoa 143
Thap Ba Hot Springs 240
Thap Doi Cham towers 242
theatre 401
Thien Hau Temples 268
Thuan An Beach 175
time 437
tipping 437
Tomb and Temple of Marshal Le Van Duyet 272
Tonkin 413
tourist information 437
tour operators 438
Trai Mat 210
train travel 428, 430
Tra Kieu 203
Tran Dynasty 350
Tran Hung Dao Temple 271
transport 427-431
traveller's cheques 436
Tra Vinh 304

Treaty of Tientsin 357
trekking 22
  Kontum 230
Tri An Lake 217
Trung Nguyen 18
Trung sisters 55
Truong Son Mountain Range 414
Tuan Tu 248
tuberculosis 434

U

U Minh Forest 318
Unicorn Island 299

V

Van Long Nature Reserve 137
VC, see Viet Cong 362
Viet Cong 362
Viet Kieu 397
Viet Minh, creation of 357
Vietnamese Communist Party (VCP) 379
Vietnam wars 357
Vietnam War tours 23
Vinh and around 144
Vinh Long 300
Vinh Nghiem Pagoda 271
visas 439
voluntary work 440

W

waterparks, Nha Trang 238
water puppet theatre 401
weather 153, 215, 254
Westmoreland, General William 366, 370
windsurfing 22
wine, rice 29
work in Vietnam 439

X

xe ôm 430
Xtieng 395
Xuan Thieu Beach 178

Y

Yen Minh 106
Yen Tu Mountains 126
Yersin, Alexandre 205, 235

yin and yang 410
Yok Don National Park 223

Acknowledgements

For help on the road my thanks go to: Ashley Carruthers, Allan Goodman, Ben Mitchell, Caroline Mills, Cyril Boucher, Deb and Howard Limbert, Etienne Bossot, Kon Sa Nay Luet, Khiem Vu, Linh Phan, Luke H Ford, Nguyen Tuan Dung, Nguyen Thanh Truc, Binh, Bamboo and all the other guides at Oxalis, Ryan Deboodt, Sophie Hughes, Soeren Pinstrup, Tran Nhat Quang and Van Phan Trang. I am also indebted to Claire Boobbyer, previous author of this book. Lastly, huge thanks to my wife and best friend, Beck.

FOOTPRINT

Features

A gift for Phuc Khoat 322
Alexandre Yersin 235
A nation at sea: the boat people 372
Animals Asia 417
A Spanish account of Champa circa 1595 354
A war glossary 366
Battle at Khe Sanh (1968) 174
Battle of Dien Bien Phu 86
Betel nut 281
Bird's nest soup 27
Bishop Cuenot 227
Brilliance in bronze: rain drums of Dongson 399
Buddhist martyrs: self-immolation as protest 265
Buon Ma Thuot's strategic importance 219
By train from Hué to Danang 165
Danang past to present 181
Danang specialities 184
Death and burial of Emperor Gia Long (1820) 167
Eunuch power 156
Forward thinking 123
From cave to Congress 115
Guild street name meanings and their current trades 45
History of the city 263
Hmong Kings of Sa Phin 108
Ho Chi Minh: 'He who enlightens' 358
Ho Chi Minh Trail 175
Hydrology of the Mekong Delta 302

In Siddhartha's footsteps: a short history of Buddhism 408
Into the deep 147
Mekong homestays 301
Military might 328
Nguyen Trai 352
People of the north 81
Prisons to paradise 338
Resistance in Son La 83
Rice research 315
Rite of passage: from baby to infant 390
Silk worms 201
Son My (My Lai) massacre 243
Street food 61
Superior God of the Southern Sea 244
Syndicated loans keep the sharks away 47
Tay Son Rebellion (1771-1788) 241
The Anzacs in Vietnam 368
The changing face 258
The examination of 1875 50
The Frontier Campaign of 1947-1950 118
The funeral of Khai Dinh 170
The Mekong: mother river of Southeast Asia 415
The story of Quan Am 48
The Trung sisters 55
The White Hat Revolt 105
UNESCO support 158
Urban renewal 43
Visiting minorities: house rules 389
Vo Thi Sau 339

Advertisers' index

Credits

Footprint credits

Editor: Stephanie Rebello
Production and layout: Emma Bryers
Maps: Kevin Feeney
Colour section: Angus Dawson

Publisher: Patrick Dawson
Managing Editor: Felicity Laughton
Administration: Elizabeth Taylor
Advertising sales and marketing:
John Sadler, Kirsty Holmes

Photography credits

Front cover: Kelvin Tran/Shutterstock.com
Back cover: Top: Kenny Thai/Shutterstock.
Bottom: Photographic Art Viet Nam/
Shutterstock.com

Colour section

Inside front cover: David Lloyd: David
Lloyd; shutterstock: jethuynh. **Page 1**:
dreamstime: Pavalache Stelian/Dreamstime.
com. **Page 2**: superstock: Hemis.fr/Hemis.fr.
Page 4: superstock: Luis Davilla/age fotostock,
imageBROKER/imageBROKER, Philippe Body/
age fotostock. **Page 5**: David Lloyd: David
Lloyd; superstock: Pipop Boosarakumwadi/
Dreamstime.com; superstock: Tips Images/
Tips Images. **Page 6**: dreamstime:
Hoxuanhuong/Dreamstime.com; superstock:
Philippe Body/age fotostock, Photononstop/
Photononstop. **Page 7**: dreamstime: Luciano
Mortula/Dreamstime.com, Simon Hack/
Dreamstime.com; David Lloyd: David
Lloyd; superstock: Steve Vidler/Steve Vidler.
Page 10: dreamstime: Olga Khoroshunova/
Dreamstime.com. **Page 11**: superstock: JTB
Photo/JTB Photo. **Page 13**: dreamstime: Olga
Khoroshunova/Dreamstime.com; superstock:
JTB Photo/JTB Photo. **Page 14**: shutterstock:
TheLightPainter. **Page 15**: shutterstock: Tonkin
image; superstock: Stuart Pearce/age fotostock.
Page 16: superstock: Neil Emmerson/Robert
Harding Picture Library

Printed in Spain by GraphyCems

Publishing information

Footprint Vietnam
7th edition
© Footprint Handbooks Ltd
May 2015

ISBN: 978 1 910120 32 3
CIP DATA: A catalogue record for this
book is available from the British Library

® Footprint Handbooks and the
Footprint mark are a registered
trademark of Footprint Handbooks Ltd

Published by Footprint
6 Riverside Court
Lower Bristol Road
Bath BA2 3DZ, UK
T +44 (0)1225 469141
F +44 (0)1225 469461
footprinttravelguides.com

Distributed in the USA by
National Book Network, Inc.

Every effort has been made to ensure
that the facts in this guidebook are
accurate. However, travellers should still
obtain advice from consulates, airlines,
etc about travel and visa requirements
before travelling. The authors and
publishers cannot accept responsibility
for any loss, injury or inconvenience
however caused.

Footprint Mini Atlas
Vietnam

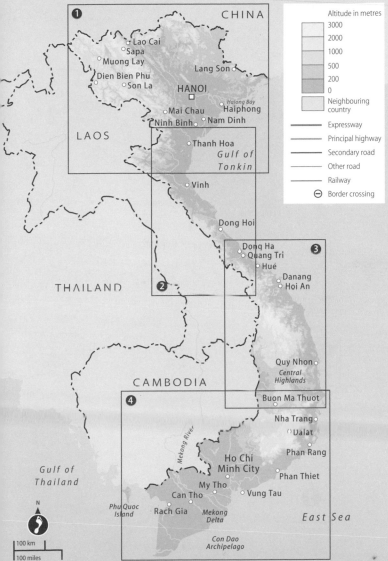

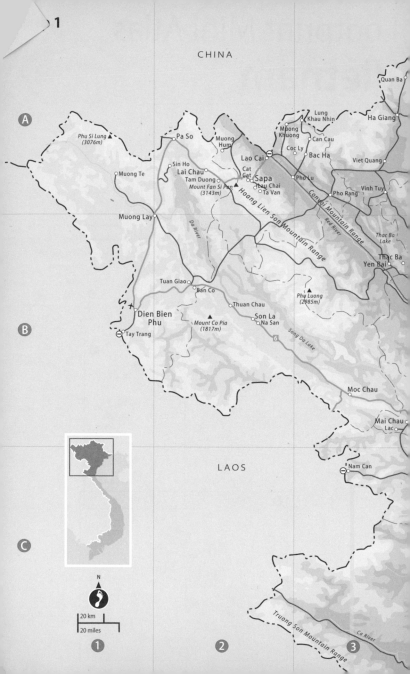

Map 2

Gulf of Tonkin

Ninh Binh
Bich Dong
Cuc Phuong National Park
Mo River

A

Thanh Hoa
Sam Son

1

Ca River

Truong Son Mountain Range

Cua Lo
Vinh

Ong Mountain (1587m)

8

Cau Treo

Ha Tinh

B

Ngang Pass

Highway 1

Phong Nha-Ke Bang National Park

Dong Hoi

Da Mao Mountain (665m)
Len Mu Mountain (918m)

Con Co Island

LAOS

17th Parallel
Truong Son Cemetery

Vinh Moc Tunnels

Voi Mep Mountain (1701m)

Ben Hai River

Dong Ha
Quang Tri

The Rock Pile

Highway 9

Khe Sanh (Huong Hoa)

Lao Bao

14

C

N

20 km
20 miles

1   **2**   **3**

Map 3

A

B

C

1

2

3

Dong Ha
9
Quang Tri
Thuan An
Beach
1
Hué
14
Cau Hai
Lagoon
Lang Co
Bach Ma
National Park
Hai Van
Pass
Danang
Bana
My Khe Beach
Kiem Lam
Nam Phuoc
My Son
Tra Kieu
Hoi An

Tam Ky
Chu Lai

My Lai

LAOS

Dak Glei
Ngoc Linh
(2598m)
Quang Ngai

Dak Nay

Bo-Y
Plei Kan
Dak To

Hoai Nhon

Yaly Power
Station
Kontum
Kontum
Plateau

CAMBODIA

Bien Ho
Lake

Ba Mountain
(892m)

Pleiku
Dekop
19
Kien My
Cha Dan
Quy Nhon

19
Le Thanh

14
Song Cau

N

Central
Highlands
Ba River

20 km
20 miles

Tuy Hoa
Da Rang River

4
Dac Lac Plateau

Dom Mon
Whale
Island

26
Yok Don
National Park
Ban Don
Doc Lech
Buon Ma Thuot
2
3
Ba Ho
Ninh Hoa
Dray Sap, Dray Nur &
Gia Long Waterfalls
Lak Lake

Map 4

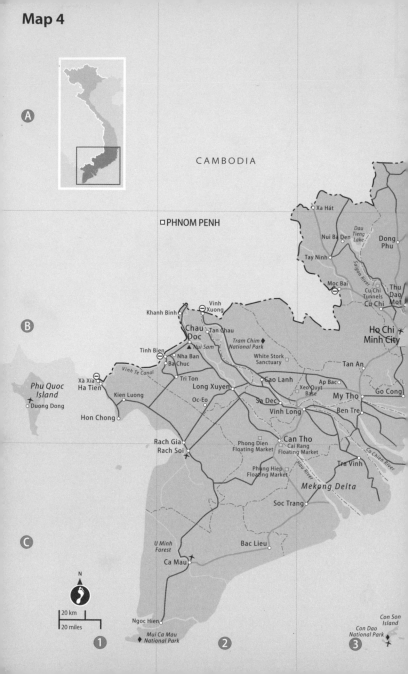

CAMBODIA

□PHNOM PENH

Xa Hát

Nui Ba Den

Dau Tieng Lake

Dong Phu

Tay Ninh

Saigon River

Moc Bai

Cu Chi Tunnels

Cu Chi

Thu Dao Mot

Ho Chi Minh City

Vinh Xuong

Khanh Binh

Chau Doc

Tan Chau

Tram Chim National Park

Tinh Bien

▲ Nui Sam

Nha Ban

White Stork Sanctuary

Tan An

Ba Chuc

Vinh Te Canal

Tri Ton

Cao Lanh

Ap Bac

Xa Xia Ha Tien

Xeo Quyt Base

My Tho

Go Cong

Phu Quoc Island

Long Xuyen

Duong Dong

Kien Luong

Oc-Eo

Sa Dec

Vinh Long

Ben Tre

Hon Chong

Can Tho

Phong Dien Floating Market

Cai Rang Floating Market

Rach Gia

Rach Soi

Hau River

Co Chien River

Phung Hiep Floating Market

Tra Vinh

Mekong Delta

Soc Trang

U Minh Forest

Bac Lieu

Ca Mau

Ngoc Hien

Mui Ca Mau National Park

Con Son Island

Con Dao National Park

N

20 km

20 miles

A   B   C

1   2   3

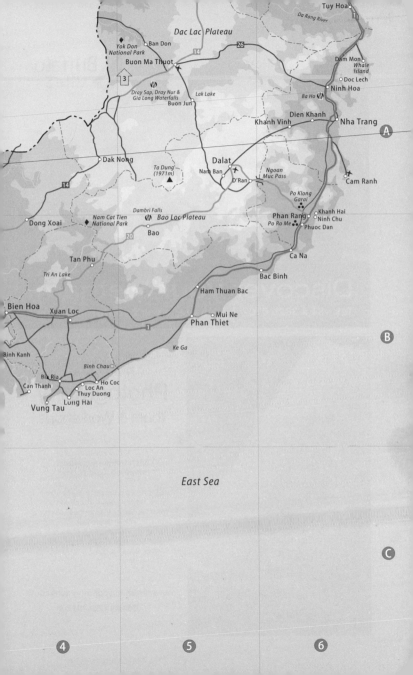